3RD EDITION

LONDON RAILWAY
ATLAS

JOE BROWN

Ian Allan
PUBLISHING

Preface to the Third edition

London, more than possibly any other city on Earth, owes its growth and continuing success to its intricate network of railways, which have been a part of the landscape for over 170 years and show no sign of losing their relevance or importance. Unlike much of the United Kingdom, London had lost relatively little of its passenger infrastructure during the 20th century and it could indeed be argued that with the recent additions of the Docklands Light Railway and Croydon Tramlink to the scene along with 'Heavy Rail' developments such as the Channel Tunnel Rail Link and East London Line Extension, London's passenger rail network is today at its zenith. Despite this, there are many long-forgotten branch lines and abandoned stations dotted around London; casualties of war, route duplication, trams, buses and the car. London's freight and industrial facilities did not fare anywhere near as well as the passenger facilities during the late 20th century; changes to the way that freight was carried and the abandonment of domestic coal in favour of central heating, combined with industrial decline, decimated the hundreds of goods and coal yards and rail-served industrial sites in London.

I commenced this project in 2004 after searching for a publication like this one to no avail: one that provided a diagrammatic representation of London's railway history. What began as a light-hearted hobby has since become a serious project, which has taken up hundreds of hours' work through map-drawing, indexing and research. Following on from publication of the First edition six years ago, publication of the Second edition three years later was a personal triumph, but within weeks I began work on this Third edition as London's railway geography continued to change apace. I have taken the opportunity to make more improvements to the format, the most significant being the conversion of all dates to DD/MM/YYYY format. In addition, I have re-drawn the entire work using satellite imagery and old Ordnance Survey maps as guides, resulting in far greater accuracy. I have also expanded coverage outwards to include previously omitted towns such as Slough, Tilbury, Gravesend, Orpington and Redhill. I feel the cartography and amount of information are greatly improved, and hope those of you who possess previous editions agree. A map of this scale can never be pin-point accurate, but I have attempted to achieve as close as possible to this goal while maintaining clarity. In some areas the railway infrastructure has changed repeatedly over time to the point that it is impossible to depict every historical permutation, so for some areas I have provided larger-scale maps giving the current layout alongside an historical snap-shot when pre-Beeching infrastructure was at its peak.

Despite many hours of research I am the first to acknowledge that there are quite probably some omissions (and dare I say it errors!), particularly regarding freight facilities on which available information is often scant. I have endeavoured to provide a hopefully near-complete history of London's passenger railways, although I have chosen to omit a handful of temporary, excursion and unadvertised stations which have had little bearing on London's railway history or for which I have been unable to find any significant information. Where dates were unobtainable, as a last resort I have used historical Ordnance survey maps to somewhat crudely infer an approximate date; I feel this is preferable to no date at all.

I very much regard this as a work in progress, and I would be delighted to hear from anyone who can provide me with further information. There are question marks against some dates in the index, and I would be very happy to receive locations and relevant dates for other goods, freight and industrial facilities that have been omitted, although I have had to be mindful in more complex areas not to overload the map with detail to the extent that it becomes a distraction. Regarding future developments, I have included those under construction such as 'Crossrail 1' and the East London Line Extension Phase 2, as well as proposed developments such as the 'Croxley Link' and Northern Line Battersea extension. As before, I have chosen to omit the Post Office Railway and London's first piece of railway infrastructure, the Surrey Iron Railway. I do not feel they have enough in common with railways in the modern sense, and moreover both would add a further layer of detail to already complex areas.

Please feel free to email me with any feedback or further information at: atlasupdate@blueyonder.co.uk

About the author:

I am a railway professional and near-lifelong London resident who since childhood had a keen interest in cartography as well as London's railway history. I joined London Underground as a Northern Line Guard in 1997 shortly after leaving school, and progressed to a 'Guard-Motorman' on that line in 1998 before transferring to be a District Line Train Operator at Parson's Green the following year. In 2001 I was promoted to Duty Manager Trains at Earl's Court, where I remained for six years before again being promoted to Train Operations Manager at Elephant & Castle (Bakerloo Line) in 2007. Since then I have gained experience managing station operations on the Marylebone Group of six Bakerloo Line stations, before returning to Trains management in 2011. I am currently Train Operations Manager at Wembley Park Depot on the Jubilee Line, with in excess of 200 drivers during a challenging yet exciting period preparing for the 2012 Olympic Games on the key Olympic line. I have produced the three editions of the London Railway Atlas around a busy work schedule on a home computer, self-taught on fairly basic software without any formal design training. Long-term I hope to continue updating this work every few years, perhaps with a view to tackling other cities or even the entire country in this same format, although the latter may be one for my retirement!

Thanks and dedications:

I would firstly like to thank Gary James for his never-ending patience and support during the eight years that it has taken for this third edition to be realised. Secondly a huge thank you to a multitude of people who offered feedback and information by email and post following publication of the first two editions; I cannot thank you all but special mention to James Tinkler, Brian Polley, Andy Cope, David Burnell, Simon Moore, Ken Weston, Phil Jones, John Sketcher, John Groves, Claude Hart, John Edser, Colin Hills, A. Porter, D. Roberts, Christopher Walker, David Bleicher, Gordon Wickham, Bob Allaway amd Dr Sunil Prasannan.

For my Nephews and Godsons Max and Felix Brown and Nephew and Niece Oscar and Jemima Thiagaraj.

In loving memory of Ruth Brown 1945-1989.

Joe Brown, London, April 2012

First published 2012
Reprinted 2013

ISBN 978 0 7110 3728 1

© Ian Allan Publishing 2012

Published by Ian Allan Publishing

an imprint of Ian Allan Publishing Ltd, Hersham, Surrey, KT12 4RG

Printed in England

Distributed in Canada and the United States of America by BookMasters Distribution Services

Visit the Ian Allan Publishing website at www.ianallanpublishing.com

Abbreviations

BAA	British Airports Authority	
BAK	Bakerloo Line	Abbreviated form of BSWR
BHR	Bexley Heath Railway	Absorbed by SECR 10.07.1900
BR	British Rail(ways)	Formed 01.01.1948 (Nationalisation)
BSWR	Baker Street & Waterloo Railway	Absorbed by UERL before opening, became Bakerloo Line
c.	circa	
CCEHR	Charing Cross, Euston & Hampstead Railway	Absorbed by UERL before opening, merged with CSLR to form Northern Line 13.09.1926
CE	Civil Engineers	
CEN	Central Line	Originally Central London Railway
Co.	Company	
CLR	Central London Railway	Absorbed by UERL 01.01.1913
CR	Caterham Railway	Absorbed by SER 1859
CSLR	City & South London Railway	Absorbed by UERL 01.01.1913, merged with CCEHR to form Northern Line 13.09.1926
CTL	Croydon Tramlink	Renamed 'London Tramlink Croydon' 01.01.2009
CVR	Chipstead Valley Railway	Absorbed by SECR 13.07.1899
C.W.	Carriage Wash	
DBS	Deutsche Bahn Schenker	Formerly EWS, acquired 28.06.2007 and renamed 01.01.2009
DIS	District Line	Originally Metropolitan District Railway, absorbed by UERL 09.04.1902
DLR	Docklands Light Railway	Controlled by TfL since 03.07.2000
DMU	Diesel Multiple Unit	
E	East	
EB	Eastbound	
ECR	Eastern Counties Railway	Absorbed by GER 01.07.1862
ECTJR	Eastern Counties & Thames Junction Railway	Absorbed by ECR 1847
EHLR	Edgware, Highgate & London Railway	Absorbed by GNR before opening, 07.1867
ELL	East London Line	Originally 'Metropolitan Line East London section', name came into use during 1980's
ELR	East London Railway	GER, LBSCR, SER, LCDR, MET & MDR joint (LNER / MET 01.01.1923), absorbed by SR 1925
EMU	Electric Multiple Unit	
EOR	Epping Ongar Railway	Preserved railway, commenced operation 10.10.2004
ES	Eurostar	
E.S.	Engine Shed	
EWIDBJR	East & West India Docks & Birmingham Junction Railway	Renamed NLR 01.01.1853
EWS	English, Welsh & Scottish Railway	Acquired by DBS 28.06.2007, renamed 01.01.2009
GCC	Gaslight & Coke Company	Leased to GER after 18.03.1874
GCR	Great Central Railway	Absorbed by LNER 01.01.1923
GER	Great Eastern Railway	Formed from ECR 01.07.1862, absorbed by LNER 01.01.1923
GNCR	Great Northern & City Railway	Absorbed by Metropolitan Railway 01.07.1913
GNPBR	Great Northern, Piccadilly & Brompton Railway	Absorbed by UERL before opening 09.04.1902, became Piccadilly Line
GNR	Great Northern Railway	Absorbed by LNER 01.01.1923
GRR	Gravesend & Rochester Railway	Absorbed by SER late 1845
GWR	Great Western Railway	Absorbed by BR 01.01.1948
HCL	Hammersmith & City Line	Formerly part of Metropolitan Line, given own name 30.07.1990
HCR	Hammersmith & City Railway	GWR & MET joint
HEX	Heathrow Express	Owned by BAA – British Airports Authority
HHR	Hundred of Hoo Railway	Absorbed by SER August 1880
HJR	Hampstead Junction Railway	Managed by NLR after 1864, absorbed by LNWR 1867
HS1	High Speed 1	High speed route between Channel Tunnel and St Pancras (LCOR)
HS2	High Speed 2	Proposed high speed route between London and Birmingham
Jcn.	Junction	
JUB	Jubilee Line	Formed 01.05.1979, partially from Bakerloo Line
km	Kilometres	
LBIR	London & Birmingham Railway	Absorbed by LNWR 16.07.1846
LBLR	London & Blackwall Railway	Leased to GER 18.03.1874, absorbed by LNER 01.01.1923
LBRR	London & Brighton Railway	Merged with LCRR to form LBSCR 27.02.1846
LBSCR	London, Brighton & South Coast Railway	Formed 27.02.1846 from LBRR and LCRR
LCC	London County Council	
LCDR	London, Chatham & Dover Railway	Merged with SER to form SECR 01.01.1899
LCOR	London & Continental Railway	Consortium that built Channel Tunnel Rail Link, leased to NR from outset
LCRR	London & Croydon Railway	Merged with LBRR to form LBSCR 27.02.1846
LGR	London & Greenwich Railway	Leased to SER 01.01.1845, absorbed by SR 01.01.1923
LMS	London, Midland & Scottish Railway	Formed 01.01.1923 from MID, LNWR & NLR
LNER	London & North Eastern Railway	Formed 01.01.1923 from GNR, GCR & GER
LNWR	London & North Western Railway	Formed 16.07.1846 from LBIR
LOROL	London Overground Rail Operations Ltd	Took over former 'Silverlink' franchise, commenced operation 11.11.2007
LPTB	London Passenger Transport Board	Formed 01.07.1933, became LTE (1st) 01.01.1948
LRT	London Regional Transport	Formed 19.06.1984, became LUL 01.04.1985
LSKD	London St Katherine's Dock Company	Later became part of PLA, operated by GER after 01.07.1896
LSWR	London & South Western Railway	Absorbed by SR 01.01.1923, 'London & Southampton Railway' until opening day
LTB	London Transport Board	Formed 01.01.1963, became LTE (2nd) 01.01.1970
LTC	London Tramlink Croydon	Formerly Croydon Tramlink
LTE (1st)	London Transport Executive (1st incarnation)	Formed 01.01.1948, became LTB 01.01.1963
LTE (2nd)	London Transport Executive (2nd incarnation)	Formed 01.01.1970, became LRT 19.06.1984
LTSR	London, Tilbury & Southend Railway	ECR / LBLR joint, leased to its builders 03.07.1854, absorbed by MID 07.08.1912
LUL	London Underground Ltd	Formed 01.04.1985
m	metres	
MDR	Metropolitan District Railway	Absorbed by UERL 09.04.1902
MER	Millwall Extension Railway	LBLR, East & West India Dock Co. and Millwall Dock Co. joint
MET	Metropolitan Railway	Absorbed by LPTB 01.07.1933
MHPR	Muswell Hill & Palace Railway	Operated by GNR from outset, absorbed 09.1911
MID	Midland Railway	Absorbed by LMS 01.01.1923
MKR	Mid Kent Railway	Absorbed by SER 29.07.1864
MPD	Motive Power Depot	
MPV	Multi-purpose Vehicle	Purpose built vehicles used on Network Rail for activities such as water-jetting and de-icing
N	North	
NB	Northbound	
NCL	Northern City Line	Abbreviated form of GNCR, transferred to BR 16.08.1976
NER	Northern & Eastern Railway	Leased to ECR 01.01.1844, absorbed by GER 1902
NLR	North London Railway	Operated by LNWR after 01.02.1909, absorbed by LMS 01.01.1923
NOR	Northern Line	Formed from CCEHR & CSLR 13.09.1926, 'Northern Line' name not used until 08.1937
NR	Network Rail	Formed 03.10.2002 when Railtrack renationalised

NSWJR	North & South Western Junction Railway	LNWR & LSWR joint (LNWR, NLR & MID joint after 1871, LMS after 01.01.1923)
OS	Ordnance Survey	
PIC	Piccadilly Line	Abbreviated form of GNPBR
PLA	Port of London Authority	
PRIV	Private	
RT	Railtrack	Formed from BR 01.04.1994 (privatisation)
Rwy.	Railway	
S	South	
S&T	Signal & Telegraph	
SB	Southbound	
Sdg.	Siding	
SECR	South Eastern & Chatham Railway	Formed from SER & LCDR 01.01.1899, absorbed by SR 01.01.1923
SER	South Eastern Railway	Absorbed by SECR 01.01.1899
SOR	Sevenoaks Railway	Later became Sevenoaks, Maidstone & Tunbridge Railway. Absorbed by LCDR 21.07.1879
Sq	Square	
SR	Southern Railway	Formed from LBSCR, LSWR & SECR 01.01.1923, absorbed by BR 01.01.1948
St	Saint or Street	
TFGR	Tottenham & Forest Gate Railway	MID & LTSR joint, LMS after 01.01.1923
TfL	Transport for London	Formed 03.07.2000, took control of LUL 15.07.2003, LOROL 11.11.2007
THJR	Tottenham & Hampstead Junction Railway	MID & GER joint, LMS & LNER joint after 01.01.1923
TMD	Traction maintenance depot	
TVR	Thames Valley Railway	Absorbed by LSWR 11.01.1867
UERL	Underground Electric Railways of London	Formed by merger of MDR, BSWR, GNPBR & CCEHR 1901-1902
VIC	Victoria Line	
VSPR	Victoria Station & Pimlico Railway	LBSCR, LCDR, GWR & LNWR joint
W	West	
WB	Westbound	
WBR	Whitechapel & Bow Railway	LTSR & MDR joint
WCIR	Waterloo & City Railway	Operated by LSWR from outset, Absorbed by 1906. Transferred to LUL 01.04.1994
WCL	Waterloo & City Line	
WCRR	Wimbledon & Croydon Railway	Absorbed by LBSCR 01.01.1866
WELCPR	West End of London & Crystal Palace Railway	Absorbed by LBSCR 1860
WLER	West London Extension Railway	LNWR, GWR, LBSCR & LSWR joint, LMS & SR joint after 01.01.1923
WLR	West London Railway	Leased to LBIR & GWR 1846, absorbed by LNWR & GWR 31.07.1854
WRR	Watford & Rickmansworth Railway	Absorbed by LNWR 1881
WW1	World War One	
WW2	World War Two	
XRAIL	Crossrail 1	Projected opening 2018

Glossary

Aggregate	Stone, gravel, sand etc used for construction
Bay platform	Dedicated platform for terminating trains at an otherwise through station
Bi-directional	Single track signalled for train movements in both directions; Single-line working
Bradshaw	George Bradshaw's 'Monthly Railway Guide'; the industry standard of timetables published from December 1841 onwards
Chain	Unit of measurement still used on NR routes, approximately 20 metres
Chord	Short section of line connecting two joining or crossing routes
Clipped	Method of securing a set of points rendering one route out of use
Covered way	Section of line artificially covered over, usually for development above (in essence a tunnel not necessitated by topography)
Curve	See 'chord'
Down	Direction of travel, generally away from London ('Up to London, down to the country')
End-on junction	The line of demarcation between two railway companies on plain track (e.g. Barrington Road Junction)
Flat junction	Junction without diveunders / flyovers
Flying junction	Junction arranged with diveunders / flyovers to minimise conflicting train movements (also 'Grade separated junction')
Halt	Unstaffed platform where trains stop by request only
Head shunt	Dead-end siding provided for trains to reverse and shunt back into a depot or goods yard
Hump	Hump marshalling yards used gravity to sort wagons after being propelled over a hump (e.g. Feltham, Temple Mills)
Level crossing	Two railway lines or a railway line and road intersecting on the same level
Logistics	The management of the flow of goods
Loop	See 'chord'. Also a simple siding connected to a main line at both ends, typically to allow fast trains to overtake slow, or can refer to a much longer section of railway connected to a main line at both ends (e.g. Hertford Loop)
Mothballed	Disused infrastructure maintained for possible future use (e.g. North Pole Depot)
Passing loop	Loop provided on single-track railway to allow 'up' and 'down' trains to pass each other
Run-around	Loop provided (usually at a terminus) to allow a locomotive to 'run around' its rake of coaches for the return journey
Single lead junction	Junction between two double track routes where one route merges to a single track before joining the other (e.g. Old Kew Junction)
Single-line working	See bi-directional
Stabling	'Parking' of rolling stock when not in use, e.g. overnight or between peak hours
Staggered	Where platforms on adjacent tracks are not parallel, usually either side of a level crossing (e.g. Mitcham Eastfields)
Terminal loop	A loop of track allowing trains to terminate without the need to reverse (e.g. Kennington, Heathrow Terminal 4)
Ticket platform	Platform, usually on approach to a terminus, where ticket inspectors would board to check tickets
Tramway	Railway line running along roadway
Turnback siding	Siding provided, usually between running lines, to allow terminating trains to reverse (e.g. Tooting Broadway, Archway)
Up	Direction of travel, generally towards London ('Up to London, down to the country')

EXPLANATION OF MAP SYMBOLS

Line symbols (each line depicts a single track):

— Open, or disused but remaining in situ

— Under construction

— Closed / dismantled

— Construction commenced but was abandoned

— Proposed

Junction (In use) · Junction (Under construction) · Junction (Dismantled) · Tunnel (Bored deep level) · Tunnel (Shallow level) · Turntable · Trainshed (e.g. depot building, goods shed) Note: station overall roofs omitted for clarity

Platform symbols:

▮ Open or under construction

▯ Closed

▯ Did not open

▯ Proposed

Text principles:

Black text	= Open / current
Red text	= Closed / previous
Blue text	= Future (Under construction / Proposed)

PLAIN TEXT = Passenger usage
ITALIC TEXT = Non-passenger usage

Naming principles:

All dates are in DD.MM.YYYY format and quoted as accurately as possible
Goods yards opened on same date as associated passenger station unless otherwise stated; the date quoted is that of closure

STATION (OPEN) — Current station name
Previous name (most recent) ⎤
Previous name (oldest) ⎦ — Previous station names in reverse chronological order
(01.01.1900)
Date of opening

STATION (CLOSED) — Station name at point of closure
Previous name (most recent) ⎤
Previous name (oldest) ⎦ — Previous station names in reverse chronological order
(01.01.1900 – 01.01.1950)
Date of opening   Date of closure

STATION (UNDER CONSTRUCTION / PROPOSED) — Proposed station name
(01.01.2020)
Estimated date of opening

NON-PASSENGER FACILITY (OPEN) — Current name
Previous name ⎤— Previous name
(01.01.1900)
Date of opening

NON-PASSENGER FACILITY (CLOSED) — Name at point of closure
Previous name ⎤— Previous name
(01.01.1900 – 01.01.1950)
Date of opening   Date of closure

Line chronology & parentage principles:

All lines currently open to passenger traffic are assumed to also be used for non-passenger purposes, e.g. stock movement, engineering, goods, etc
In some cases, the chronology / parentage of a stretch of line is too complex to be described as below, so an additional text box gives more detail on the map pages

Abbreviated name of company which opened line

MID	MID	MID	MID	LPTB 01.01.1950	NR
01.01.1900	01.01.1890 (01.01.1900)	01.01.1900	01.01.1900 (01.01.1900 – 01.01.1950)	ECR 01.01.1900 – 01.01.1970	01.01.2015
Line currently open to all traffic, date of opening	Date of opening to goods / Date of opening to passengers. Line currently open to all traffic, opened to non-passenger traffic before opening to passengers	Line currently open to non-passenger traffic which has never had regular passenger traffic, with date of opening	Date of opening to passengers / Date of closure to passengers. Line currently open to non-passenger traffic (with opening date) which has previously had passenger traffic, with dates of opening and closure to passenger traffic in red	Line currently open to all traffic which was built by a mainline railway company but subsequently transferred to present-day LUL, DLR or LTC. The black date / company refers to current use (e.g. in this case, LPTB services commenced 01.01.1950), the red date range refers to original use (e.g. opened by ECR 01.01.1900 and mainline services continued until 01.01.1970)	Line under construction or proposed, expected date of opening

MID	MID	MID	MID
01.01.1910 – 01.01.1930	01.01.1910 – 01.01.1930 (01.01.1950)	01.01.1910 (01.01.1920) – 01.01.1930 (01.01.1950)	01.01.1900
Date of opening to all traffic / Date of closure to all traffic. Closed line; date before hyphen denotes date of opening, date after hyphen denotes date of closure (if dates in italics, line never saw regular passenger services)	Line which closed to passenger traffic before closing to non-passenger traffic. Date before hyphen denotes date of opening to all traffic, dates after hyphen denote dates of closure in chronological order (passenger in plain text, non-passenger in italics)	Line which opened to non-passenger traffic before opening to passenger traffic, then closed to passenger traffic before closing to non-passenger traffic. The later opening / closure date is always quoted in brackets	Line where construction commenced but was abandoned, with company which abandoned line and date of abandonment (if known)

Line colour coding:

— Network Rail (formerly Railtrack, British Rail, and predecessors)	— LUL Hammersmith & City Line served by Circle Line
— Network Rail served by LUL District Line	— LUL Piccadilly Line
— Network Rail served by LUL Bakerloo Line	— LUL Victoria Line
— LUL District Line	— LUL Northern Line
— LUL District Line served by Piccadilly Line	— LUL Bakerloo Line
— LUL District Line served by Circle Line	— LUL Jubilee Line
— LUL District Line served by Hammersmith & City Line	— LUL Central Line
— LUL Metropolitan & East London Lines	— Docklands Light Railway (DLR)
— LUL Metropolitan Line served by Hammersmith & City and Circle Lines	— LUL Waterloo & City Line
— LUL Metropolitan Line served by mainline 'Chiltern' trains	— London Tramlink Croydon
— LUL Metropolitan Line served by Piccadilly Line	— Preserved & Miniature railways
— LUL Circle Line	
— LUL Hammersmith & City Line	

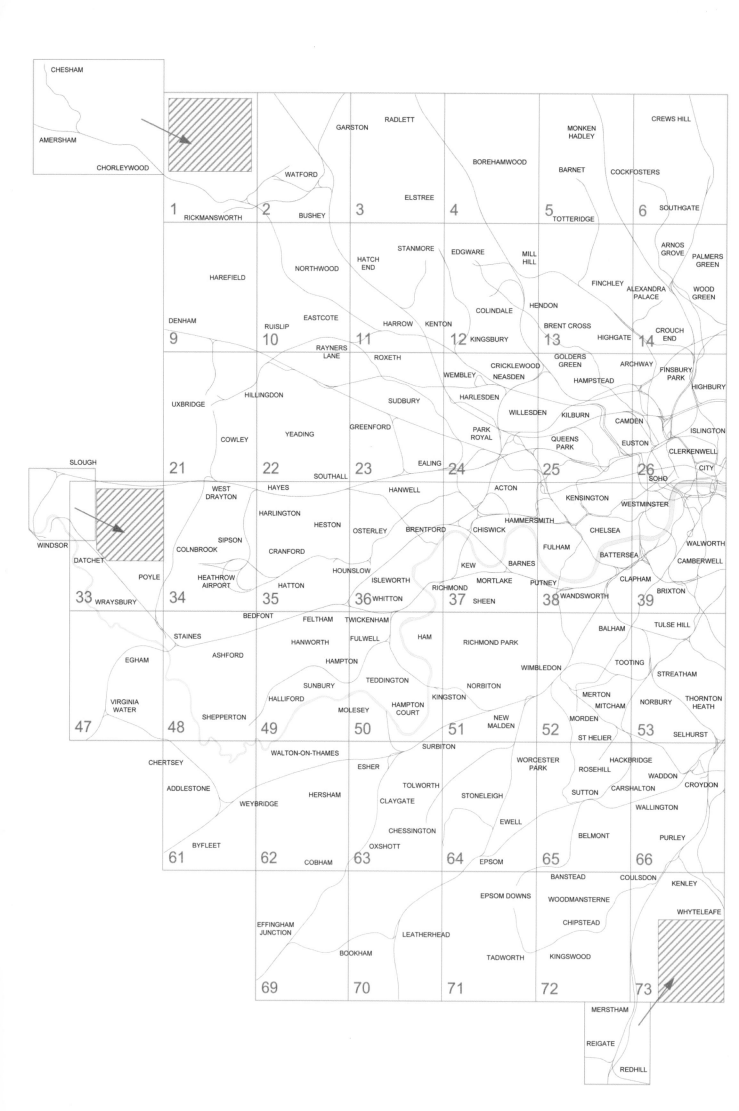

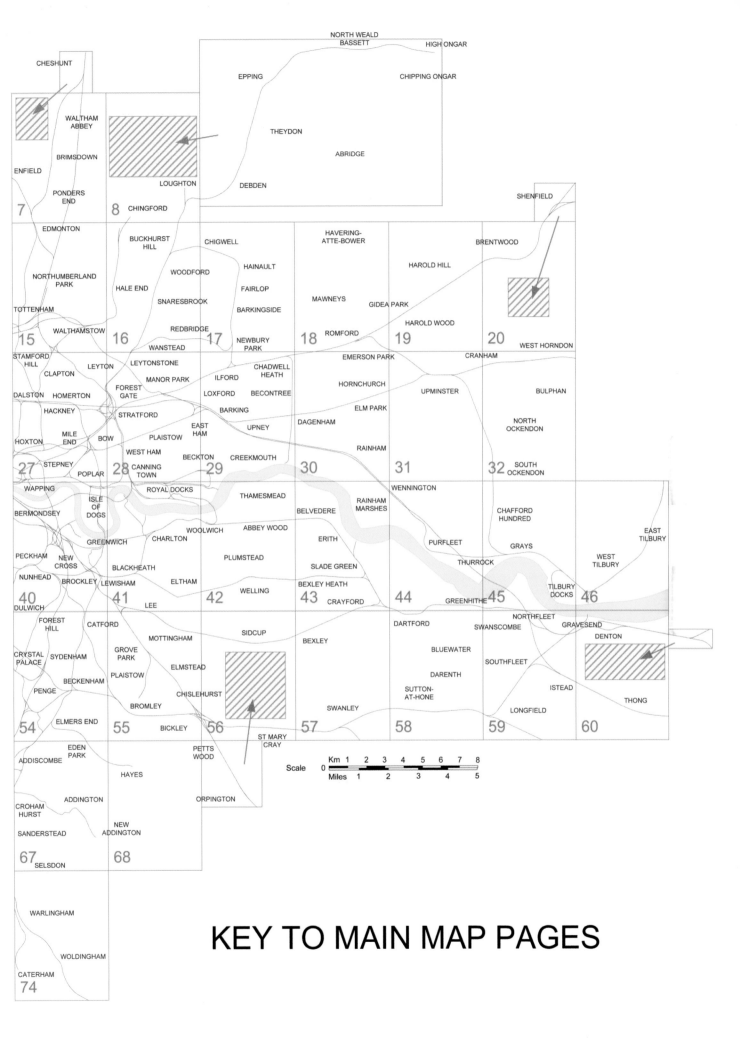

KEY TO MAIN MAP PAGES

Scale

Km 0 1 2 3 4 5 6 7 8

Miles 0 1 2 3 4 5

CHESHUNT

WALTHAM ABBEY

BRIMSDOWN

ENFIELD

PONDERS END

7

NORTH WEALD BASSETT

HIGH ONGAR

EPPING

CHIPPING ONGAR

THEYDON

ABRIDGE

DEBDEN

LOUGHTON

8 CHINGFORD

SHENFIELD

EDMONTON

BUCKHURST HILL

CHIGWELL

HAVERING-ATTE-BOWER

BRENTWOOD

NORTHUMBERLAND PARK

HALE END

WOODFORD

HAINAULT

HAROLD HILL

TOTTENHAM

SNARESBROOK

FAIRLOP

MAWNEYS

GIDEA PARK

WALTHAMSTOW

REDBRIDGE

BARKINGSIDE

HAROLD WOOD

15

16

WANSTEAD

17

NEWBURY PARK

18 ROMFORD

19

20 WEST HORNDON

STAMFORD HILL

LEYTONSTONE

CHADWELL HEATH

EMERSON PARK

CRANHAM

CLAPTON

LEYTON

MANOR PARK

ILFORD

HORNCHURCH

UPMINSTER

BULPHAN

DALSTON

HOMERTON

FOREST GATE

LOXFORD

BECONTREE

HACKNEY

STRATFORD

BARKING

ELM PARK

NORTH OCKENDON

HOXTON

MILE END

BOW

EAST HAM

UPNEY

DAGENHAM

WEST HAM

PLAISTOW

RAINHAM

STEPNEY

BECKTON

CREEKMOUTH

27

POPLAR

28 CANNING TOWN

29

30

31

32 SOUTH OCKENDON

WAPPING

ROYAL DOCKS

THAMESMEAD

WENNINGTON

BERMONDSEY

ISLE OF DOGS

RAINHAM MARSHES

CHAFFORD HUNDRED

EAST TILBURY

PECKHAM

GREENWICH

CHARLTON

WOOLWICH

BELVEDERE

PURFLEET

GRAYS

WEST TILBURY

NEW CROSS

ABBEY WOOD

ERITH

THURROCK

NUNHEAD

BLACKHEATH

PLUMSTEAD

SLADE GREEN

TILBURY DOCKS

BROCKLEY

LEWISHAM

ELTHAM

BEXLEY HEATH

40

41

LEE

42

WELLING

43 CRAYFORD

44

GREENHITHE

45

46

DULWICH

NORTHFLEET

FOREST HILL

CATFORD

SIDCUP

DARTFORD

SWANSCOMBE

GRAVESEND

DENTON

CRYSTAL PALACE

SYDENHAM

MOTTINGHAM

BEXLEY

BLUEWATER

SOUTHFLEET

PENGE

BECKENHAM

GROVE PARK

ELMSTEAD

DARENTH

ISTEAD

PLAISTOW

SUTTON-AT-HONE

THONG

ELMERS END

BROMLEY

CHISLEHURST

SWANLEY

LONGFIELD

54

55

BICKLEY

56

57

58

59

60

ADDISCOMBE

EDEN PARK

ST MARY CRAY

PETTS WOOD

HAYES

CROHAM HURST

ADDINGTON

ORPINGTON

SANDERSTEAD

NEW ADDINGTON

67 SELSDON

68

WARLINGHAM

WOLDINGHAM

CATERHAM

74

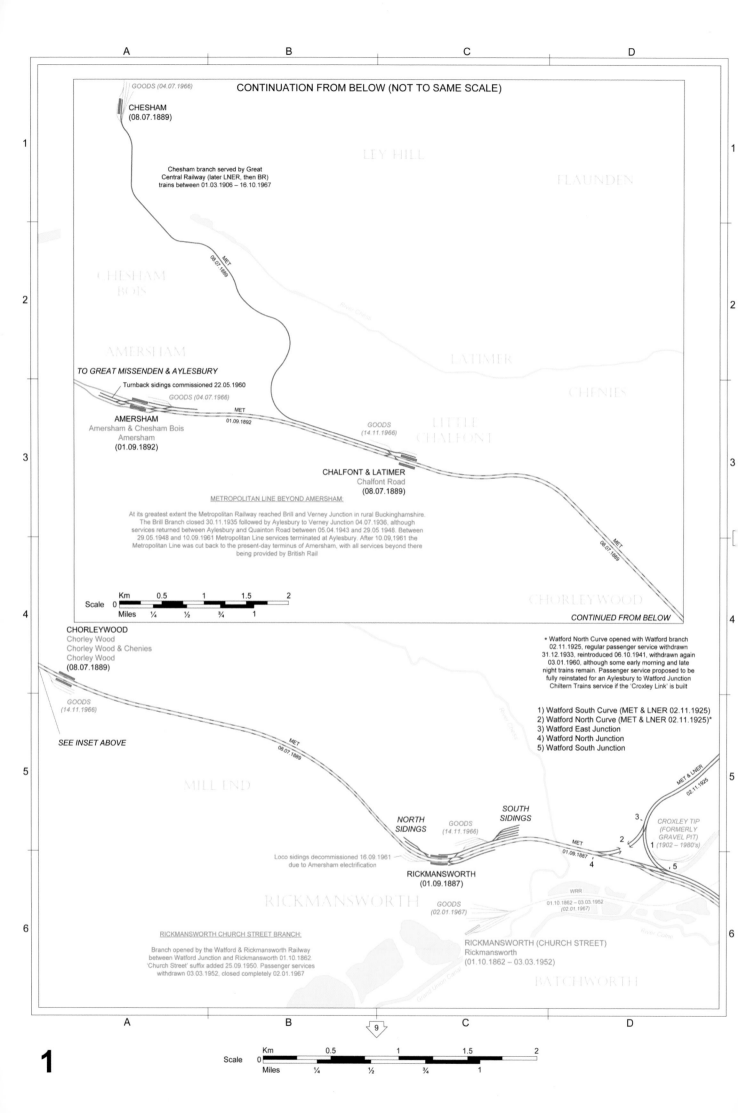

CONTINUATION FROM BELOW (NOT TO SAME SCALE)

GOODS (04.07.1966)

CHESHAM
(08.07.1889)

LEY HILL

FLAUNDEN

Chesham branch served by Great
Central Railway (later LNER, then BR)
trains between 01.03.1906 – 16.10.1967

CHESHAM
BOIS

MET
08.07.1889

AMERSHAM

LATIMER

CHENIES

TO GREAT MISSENDEN & AYLESBURY

Turnback sidings commissioned 22.05.1960

GOODS (04.07.1966)

MET
01.09.1892

LITTLE
CHALFONT

*GOODS
(14.11.1966)*

AMERSHAM
Amersham & Chesham Bois
Amersham
(01.09.1892)

CHALFONT & LATIMER
Chalfont Road
(08.07.1889)

MET
08.07.1889

METROPOLITAN LINE BEYOND AMERSHAM:

At its greatest extent the Metropolitan Railway reached Brill and Verney Junction in rural Buckinghamshire.
The Brill Branch closed 30.11.1935 followed by Aylesbury to Verney Junction 04.07.1936, although
services returned between Aylesbury and Quainton Road between 05.04.1943 and 29.05.1948. Between
29.05.1948 and 10.09.1961 Metropolitan Line services terminated at Aylesbury. After 10.09.1961 the
Metropolitan Line was cut back to the present-day terminus of Amersham, with all services beyond there
being provided by British Rail

Scale 0 | Km 0.5 | 1 | 1.5 | 2
Miles ¼ | ½ | ¾ | 1

CHORLEYWOOD

CONTINUED FROM BELOW

CHORLEYWOOD
Chorley Wood
Chorley Wood & Chenies
Chorley Wood
(08.07.1889)

* Watford North Curve opened with Watford branch
02.11.1925, regular passenger service withdrawn
31.12.1933, reintroduced 06.10.1941, withdrawn again
03.01.1960, although some early morning and late
night trains remain. Passenger service proposed to be
fully reinstated for an Aylesbury to Watford Junction
Chiltern Trains service if the 'Croxley Link' is built

*GOODS
(14.11.1966)*

1) Watford South Curve (MET & LNER 02.11.1925)
2) Watford North Curve (MET & LNER 02.11.1925)*
3) Watford East Junction
4) Watford North Junction
5) Watford South Junction

SEE INSET ABOVE

MET
08.07.1889

MILL END

MET & LNER
02.11.1925

*NORTH
SIDINGS*

*SOUTH
SIDINGS*

*GOODS
(14.11.1966)*

3

*CROXLEY TIP
(FORMERLY
GRAVEL PIT)
(1902 – 1980's)*

MET
01.09.1887

2

1

Loco sidings decommissioned 16.09.1961
due to Amersham electrification

4

5

RICKMANSWORTH
(01.09.1887)

RICKMANSWORTH

*GOODS
(02.01.1967)*

WRR
01.10.1862 – 03.03.1952
(02.01.1967)

RICKMANSWORTH CHURCH STREET BRANCH:

Branch opened by the Watford & Rickmansworth Railway
between Watford Junction and Rickmansworth 01.10.1862
'Church Street' suffix added 25.09.1950. Passenger services
withdrawn 03.03.1952, closed completely 02.01.1967

RICKMANSWORTH (CHURCH STREET)
Rickmansworth
(01.10.1862 – 03.03.1952)

BATCHWORTH

Scale 0 | Km 0.5 | 1 | 1.5 | 2
Miles ¼ | ½ | ¾ | 1

1

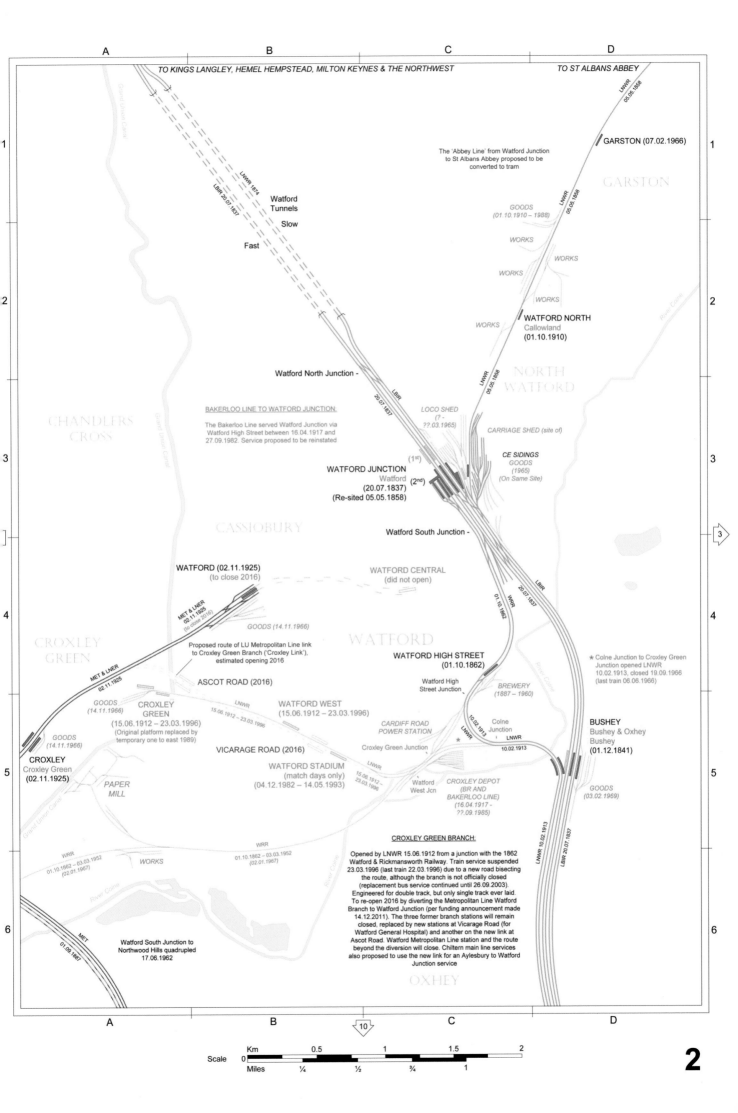

TO KINGS LANGLEY, HEMEL HEMPSTEAD, MILTON KEYNES & THE NORTHWEST

TO ST ALBANS ABBEY

GARSTON (07.02.1966)

The 'Abbey Line' from Watford Junction
to St Albans Abbey proposed to be
converted to tram

Watford Tunnels

Slow

Fast

GARSTON

GOODS
(01.10.1910 – 1988)

WORKS

WORKS

WORKS

WORKS

WORKS

Watford North Junction -

WATFORD NORTH
Callowland
(01.10.1910)

NORTH
WATFORD

CHANDLERS
CROSS

LOCO SHED
(? –
??.03.1965)

BAKERLOO LINE TO WATFORD JUNCTION:

The Bakerloo Line served Watford Junction via
Watford High Street between 16.04.1917 and
27.09.1982. Service proposed to be reinstated

CARRIAGE SHED (site of)

CE SIDINGS
GOODS
(1965)
(On Same Site)

WATFORD JUNCTION
Watford
(20.07.1837)
(Re-sited 05.05.1858)

(1st)

(2nd)

CASSIOBURY

Watford South Junction -

WATFORD (02.11.1925)
(to close 2016)

WATFORD CENTRAL
(did not open)

MET & LNER
02.11.1925
(to close 2016)

GOODS (14.11.1966)

WATFORD HIGH STREET
(01.10.1862)

★ Colne Junction to Croxley Green
Junction opened LNWR
10.02.1913, closed 19.09.1966
(last train 06.06.1966)

WATFORD

Proposed route of LU Metropolitan Line link
to Croxley Green Branch ('Croxley Link'),
estimated opening 2016

CROXLEY
GREEN

ASCOT ROAD (2016)

Watford High
Street Junction

BREWERY
(1887 – 1960)

MET & LNER
02.11.1925

GOODS
(14.11.1966)

CROXLEY
GREEN

LNWR
15.06.1912 – 23.03.1996

WATFORD WEST
(15.06.1912 – 23.03.1996)

CARDIFF ROAD
POWER STATION

Colne
Junction

LNWR

BUSHEY
Bushey & Oxhey
Bushey
(01.12.1841)

CROXLEY
GREEN
(15.06.1912 – 23.03.1996)
(Original platform replaced by
temporary one to east 1989)

VICARAGE ROAD (2016)

Croxley Green Junction

10.02.1913

GOODS
(03.02.1969)

GOODS
(14.11.1966)

WATFORD STADIUM
(match days only)
(04.12.1982 – 14.05.1993)

Watford
West Jcn

CROXLEY DEPOT
(BR AND
BAKERLOO LINE)
(16.04.1917 -
??.09.1985)

CROXLEY
Croxley Green
(02.11.1925)

PAPER
MILL

WRR
01.10.1862 – 03.03.1952
(02.01.1967)

LNWR 10.02.1913

LBIR 20.07.1837

CROXLEY GREEN BRANCH:

Opened by LNWR 15.06.1912 from a junction with the 1862
Watford & Rickmansworth Railway. Train service suspended
23.03.1996 (last train 22.03.1996) due to a new road bisecting
the route, although the branch is not officially closed
(replacement bus service continued until 26.09.2003).
Engineered for double track, but only single track ever laid.
To re-open 2016 by diverting the Metropolitan Line Watford
Branch to Watford Junction (per funding announcement made
14.12.2011). The three former branch stations will remain
closed, replaced by new stations at Vicarage Road (for
Watford General Hospital) and another on the new link at
Ascot Road. Watford Metropolitan Line station and the route
beyond the diversion will close. Chiltern main line services
also proposed to use the new link for an Aylesbury to Watford
Junction service

WORKS

WRR
01.10.1862 – 03.03.1952
(02.01.1967)

MET
01.06.1887

Watford South Junction to
Northwood Hills quadrupled
17.06.1962

OXHEY

Scale	Km 0		0.5		1		1.5		2

Miles		¼		½		¾		1

2

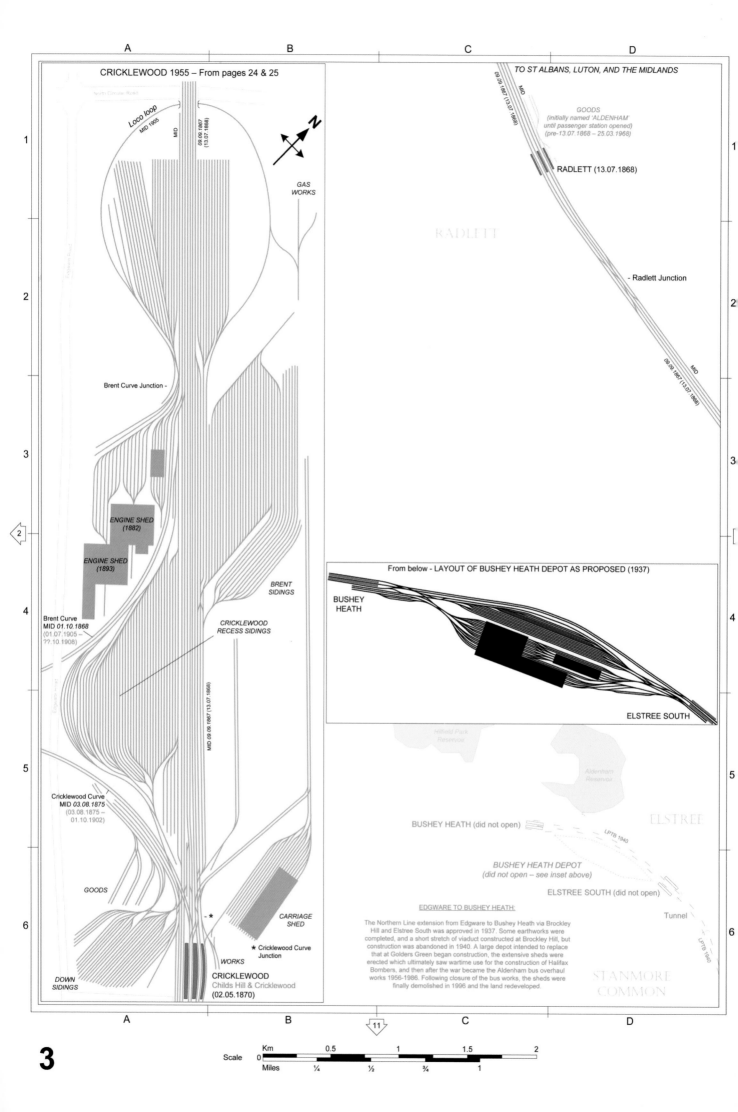

CRICKLEWOOD 1955 – From pages 24 & 25

Loco loop
MID 1905

MID

09.09.1867 (13.07.1868)

GAS WORKS

Brent Curve Junction -

ENGINE SHED (1882)

ENGINE SHED (1893)

Brent Curve
MID 01.10.1868
(01.07.1905 – ??.10.1908)

BRENT SIDINGS

CRICKLEWOOD RECESS SIDINGS

MID 09.09.1867 (13.07.1868)

Cricklewood Curve
MID 03.08.1875
(03.08.1875 – 01.10.1902)

GOODS

★

★ Cricklewood Curve Junction

- ★ Cricklewood Curve Junction

DOWN SIDINGS

WORKS

CARRIAGE SHED

CRICKLEWOOD
Childs Hill & Cricklewood
(02.05.1870)

TO ST ALBANS, LUTON, AND THE MIDLANDS

09.09.1867 (13.07.1868)   MID

GOODS
(initially named 'ALDENHAM'
until passenger station opened)
(pre-13.07.1868 – 25.03.1968)

RADLETT (13.07.1868)

RADLETT

- Radlett Junction

09.09.1867 (13.07.1868)   MID

From below - LAYOUT OF BUSHEY HEATH DEPOT AS PROPOSED (1937)

BUSHEY HEATH

ELSTREE SOUTH

Hilfield Park Reservoir

Aldenham Reservoir

ELSTREE

BUSHEY HEATH (did not open)

LPTB 1940

BUSHEY HEATH DEPOT
(did not open – see inset above)

ELSTREE SOUTH (did not open)

Tunnel

LPTB 1940

STANMORE COMMON

EDGWARE TO BUSHEY HEATH:

The Northern Line extension from Edgware to Bushey Heath via Brockley
Hill and Elstree South was approved in 1937. Some earthworks were
completed, and a short stretch of viaduct constructed at Brockley Hill, but
construction was abandoned in 1940. A large depot intended to replace
that at Golders Green began construction, the extensive sheds were
erected which ultimately saw wartime use for the construction of Halifax
Bombers, and then after the war became the Aldenham bus overhaul
works 1956-1986. Following closure of the bus works, the sheds were
finally demolished in 1996 and the land redeveloped.

3

Scale

Km
0   0.5   1   1.5   2

Miles
¼   ½   ¾   1

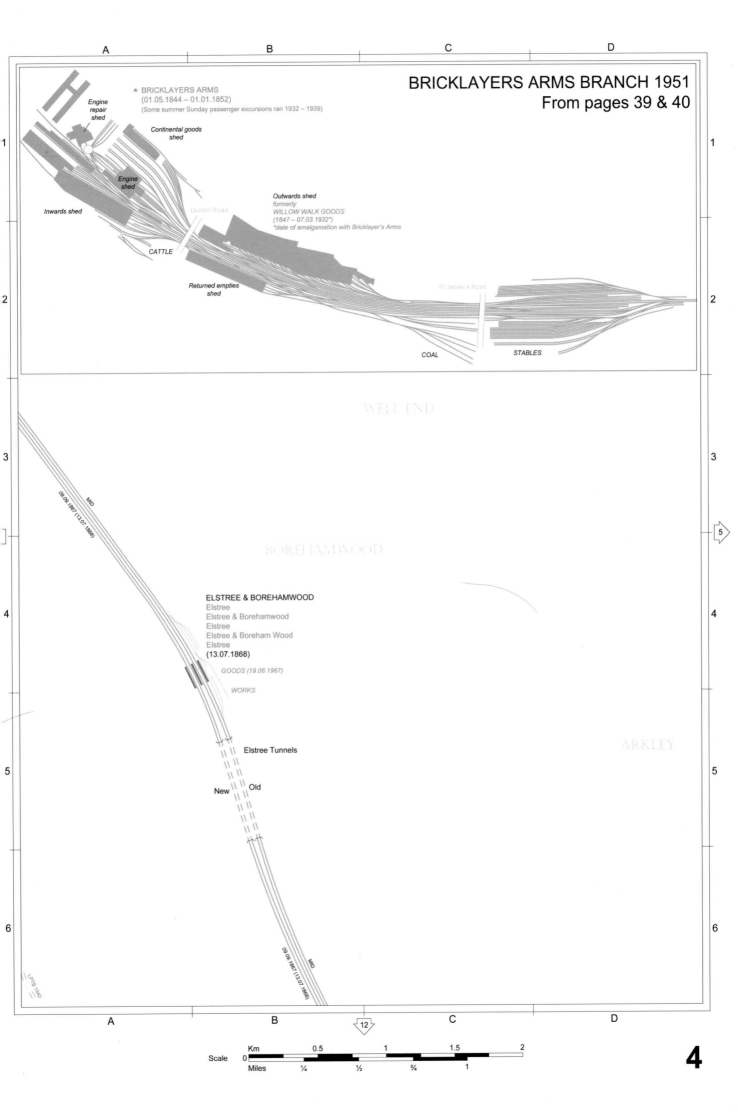

BRICKLAYERS ARMS BRANCH 1951
From pages 39 & 40

Engine
repair
shed

★ BRICKLAYERS ARMS
(01.05.1844 – 01.01.1852)
(Some summer Sunday passenger excursions ran 1932 – 1939)

Continental goods
shed

Engine
shed

Inwards shed

Dunton Road

Outwards shed
formerly
WILLOW WALK GOODS
(1847 – 07.03.1932*)
*date of amalgamation with Bricklayer's Arms

CATTLE

Returned empties
shed

St James's Road

COAL

STABLES

WELL END

MID

09.06.1867 (13.07.1868)

BOREHAMWOOD

5

ELSTREE & BOREHAMWOOD
Elstree
Elstree & Borehamwood
Elstree
Elstree & Boreham Wood
Elstree
(13.07.1868)

GOODS (19.06.1967)

WORKS

ARKLEY

Elstree Tunnels

New   Old

6

LPTB 1940

09.06.1867 (13.07.1868)

MID

12

Scale

| Km | 0 | | 0.5 | | 1 | | 1.5 | | 2 |

| Miles | | ¼ | | ½ | | ¾ | | 1 |

4

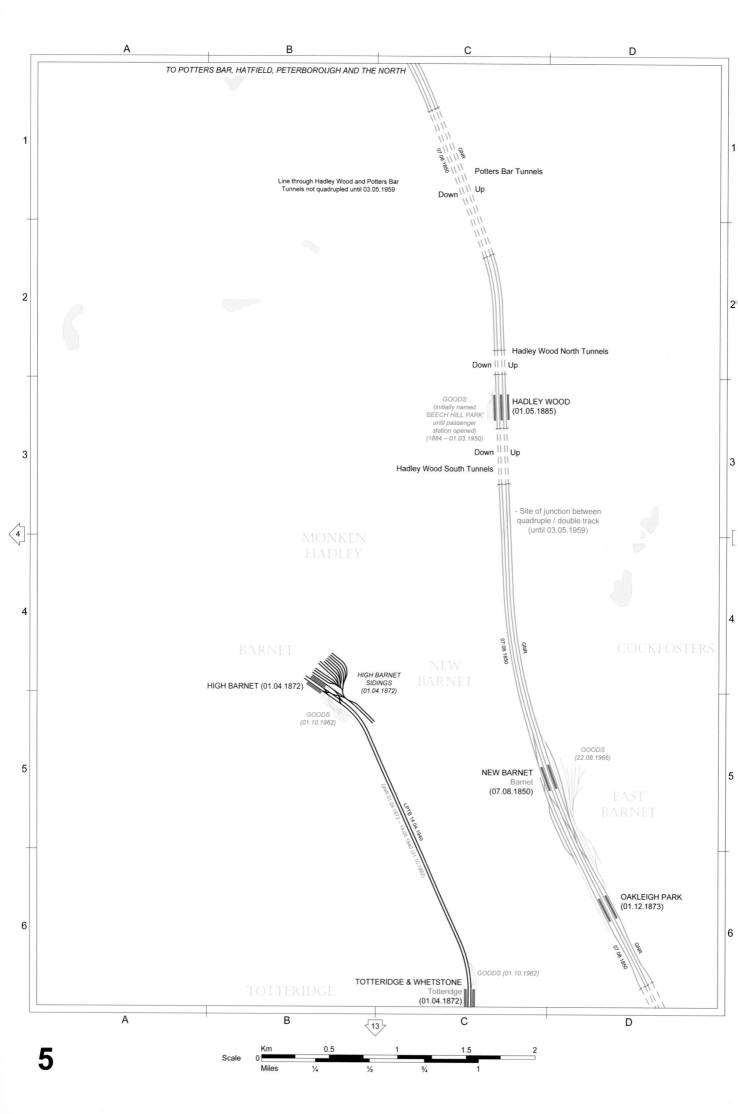

TO POTTERS BAR, HATFIELD, PETERBOROUGH AND THE NORTH

Line through Hadley Wood and Potters Bar
Tunnels not quadrupled until 03.05.1959

07.08.1850 GNR

Potters Bar Tunnels

Down   Up

Hadley Wood North Tunnels

Down   Up

GOODS
(initially named
'BEECH HILL PARK'
until passenger
station opened)
(1884 – 01.03.1950)

HADLEY WOOD
(01.05.1885)

Down   Up

Hadley Wood South Tunnels

- Site of junction between
quadruple / double track
(until 03.05.1959)

MONKEN
HADLEY

BARNET

07.08.1850   GNR

NEW
BARNET

COCKFOSTERS

HIGH BARNET (01.04.1872)

HIGH BARNET
SIDINGS
(01.04.1872)

GOODS
(01.10.1962)

GOODS
(22.08.1966)

NEW BARNET
Barnet
(07.08.1850)

EAST
BARNET

GNR 01.04.1872 - 14.04.1940   LPTB 14.04.1940 - 14.04.1940 (01.10.1962)

OAKLEIGH PARK
(01.12.1873)

GOODS (01.10.1962)

TOTTERIDGE & WHETSTONE
Totteridge
(01.04.1872)

07.08.1850   GNR

TOTTERIDGE

13

Scale
Km 0   0.5   1   1.5   2
Miles   ¼   ½   ¾   1

5

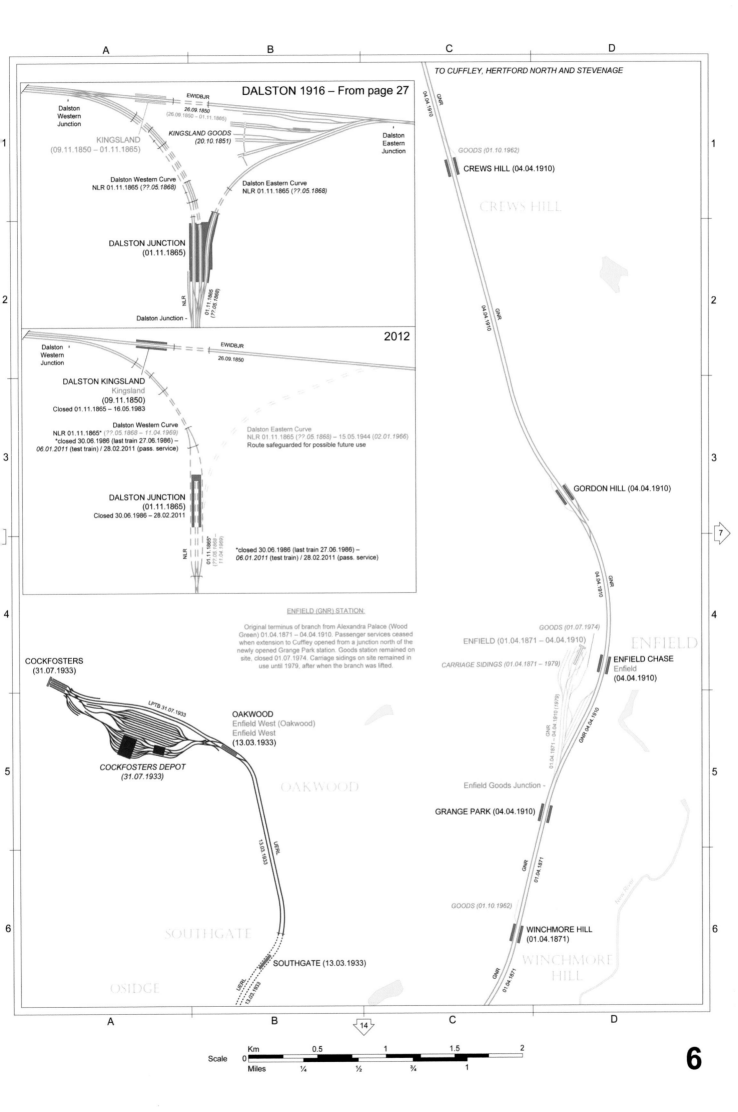

DALSTON 1916 – From page 27

Dalston
Western
Junction

KINGSLAND
(09.11.1850 – 01.11.1865)

EWIDBJR
26.09.1850
(26.09.1850 – 01.11.1865)

KINGSLAND GOODS
(20.10.1851)

Dalston
Eastern
Junction

Dalston Western Curve
NLR 01.11.1865 (??.05.1868)

Dalston Eastern Curve
NLR 01.11.1865 (??.05.1868)

DALSTON JUNCTION
(01.11.1865)

NLR

01.11.1865
(??.05.1868)

Dalston Junction -

2012

Dalston
Western
Junction

EWIDBJR
26.09.1850

DALSTON KINGSLAND
Kingsland
(09.11.1850)
Closed 01.11.1865 – 16.05.1983

Dalston Western Curve
NLR 01.11.1865* (??.05.1868 – 11.04.1969)
*closed 30.06.1986 (last train 27.06.1986) –
06.01.2011 (test train) / 28.02.2011 (pass. service)

Dalston Eastern Curve
NLR 01.11.1865 (??.05.1868) – 15.05.1944 (02.01.1966)
Route safeguarded for possible future use

DALSTON JUNCTION
(01.11.1865)
Closed 30.06.1986 – 28.02.2011

NLR

01.11.1865*
(??.05.1868 –
11.04.1969)

*closed 30.06.1986 (last train 27.06.1986) –
06.01.2011 (test train) / 28.02.2011 (pass. service)

TO CUFFLEY, HERTFORD NORTH AND STEVENAGE

04.04.1910

GNR

GOODS (01.10.1962)

CREWS HILL (04.04.1910)

CREWS HILL

04.04.1910

GNR

GORDON HILL (04.04.1910)

04.04.1910

GNR

ENFIELD (GNR) STATION:

Original terminus of branch from Alexandra Palace (Wood
Green) 01.04.1871 – 04.04.1910. Passenger services ceased
when extension to Cuffley opened from a junction north of the
newly opened Grange Park station. Goods station remained on
site, closed 01.07.1974. Carriage sidings on site remained in
use until 1979, after when the branch was lifted.

COCKFOSTERS
(31.07.1933)

LPTB 31.07.1933

COCKFOSTERS DEPOT
(31.07.1933)

OAKWOOD
Enfield West (Oakwood)
Enfield West
(13.03.1933)

OAKWOOD

SOUTHGATE

13.03.1933

UERL

OSIDGE

UERL
13.03.1933

SOUTHGATE (13.03.1933)

GOODS (01.07.1974)

ENFIELD (01.04.1871 – 04.04.1910)

ENFIELD

CARRIAGE SIDINGS (01.04.1871 – 1979)

ENFIELD CHASE
Enfield
(04.04.1910)

01.04.1871 – 04.04.1910 (1979)

GNR

GNR 04.04.1910

Enfield Goods Junction -

GRANGE PARK (04.04.1910)

GNR

01.04.1871

GOODS (01.10.1962)

WINCHMORE HILL
(01.04.1871)

WINCHMORE
HILL

GNR

01.04.1871

Km
Scale 0   0.5   1   1.5   2
Miles ¼   ½   ¾   1

6

7

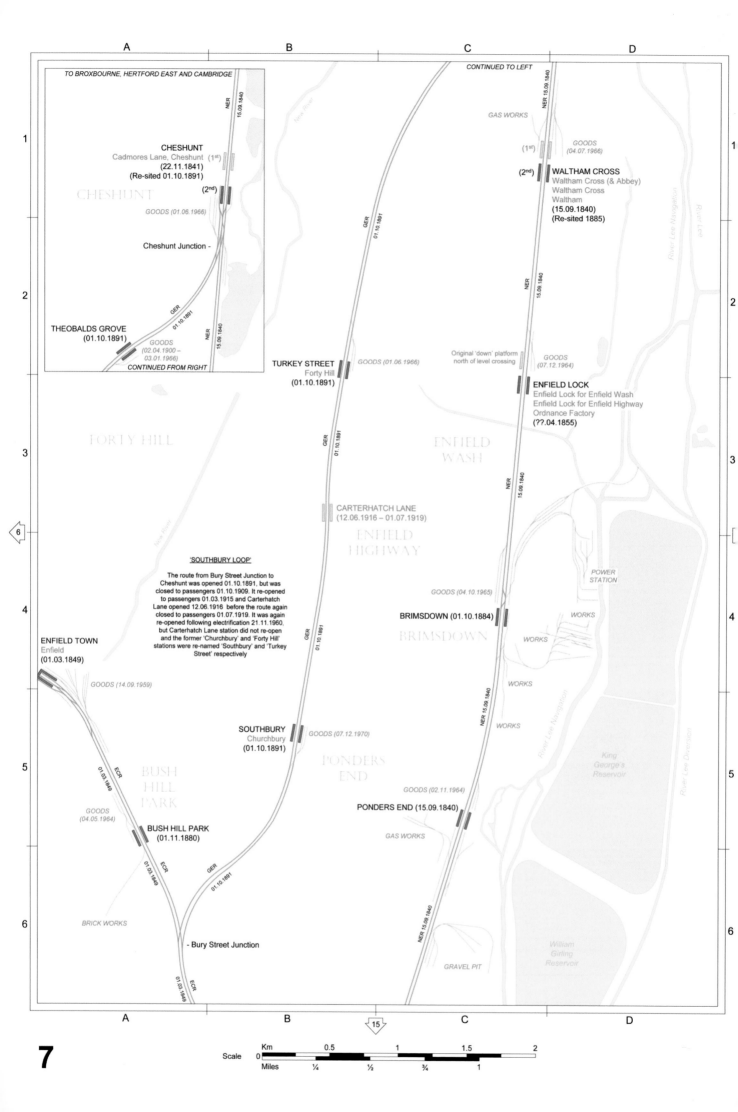

CHESHUNT
Cadmores Lane, Cheshunt (1st)
(22.11.1841)
(Re-sited 01.10.1891)

CHESHUNT

(2nd)

GOODS (01.06.1966)

Cheshunt Junction -

THEOBALDS GROVE
(01.10.1891)

GOODS (02.04.1900 – 03.01.1966)

CONTINUED FROM RIGHT

NER 15.09.1840

GER 01.10.1891

NER 15.09.1840

CONTINUED TO LEFT

GAS WORKS

(1st)

(2nd)

GOODS (04.07.1966)

WALTHAM CROSS
Waltham Cross (& Abbey)
Waltham Cross
Waltham
(15.09.1840)
(Re-sited 1885)

GER 01.10.1891

NER 15.09.1840

Original 'down' platform north of level crossing

GOODS (07.12.1964)

ENFIELD LOCK
Enfield Lock for Enfield Wash
Enfield Lock for Enfield Highway
Ordnance Factory
(??.04.1855)

TURKEY STREET
Forty Hill
(01.10.1891)

GOODS (01.06.1966)

GER 01.10.1891

FORTY HILL

New River

ENFIELD WASH

NER 15.09.1840

CARTERHATCH LANE
(12.06.1916 – 01.07.1919)

ENFIELD HIGHWAY

'SOUTHBURY LOOP'

The route from Bury Street Junction to Cheshunt was opened 01.10.1891, but was closed to passengers 01.10.1909. It re-opened to passengers 01.03.1915 and Carterhatch Lane opened 12.06.1916 before the route again closed to passengers 01.07.1919. It was again re-opened following electrification 21.11.1960, but Carterhatch Lane station did not re-open and the former 'Churchbury' and 'Forty Hill' stations were re-named 'Southbury' and 'Turkey Street' respectively

GOODS (04.10.1965)

BRIMSDOWN (01.10.1884)

BRIMSDOWN

POWER STATION

WORKS

WORKS

WORKS

WORKS

ENFIELD TOWN
Enfield
(01.03.1849)

GOODS (14.09.1959)

GER 01.10.1891

River Lee Navigation

King George's Reservoir

River Lee Diversion

SOUTHBURY
Churchbury
(01.10.1891)

GOODS (07.12.1970)

PONDERS END

GOODS (02.11.1964)

PONDERS END (15.09.1840)

ECR 01.03.1849

BUSH HILL PARK

GOODS (04.05.1964)

BUSH HILL PARK
(01.11.1880)

ECR 01.03.1849

GER 01.10.1891

NER 15.09.1840

GAS WORKS

BRICK WORKS

- Bury Street Junction

ECR 01.03.1849

GRAVEL PIT

William Girling Reservoir

NER 15.09.1840

7

Scale
Km   0   0.5   1   1.5   2
Miles   ¼   ½   ¾   1

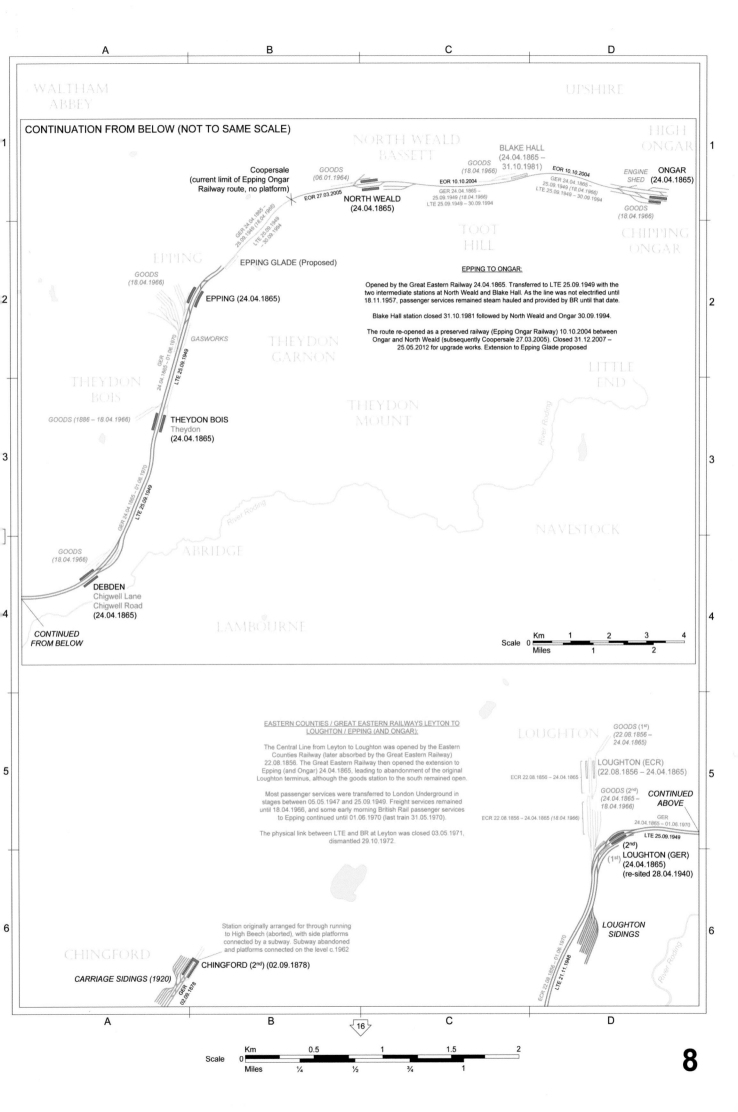

CONTINUATION FROM BELOW (NOT TO SAME SCALE)

WALTHAM
ABBEY

UPSHIRE

NORTH WEALD
BASSETT

HIGH
ONGAR

Coopersale
(current limit of Epping Ongar
Railway route, no platform)

GOODS
(06.01.1964)

BLAKE HALL
(24.04.1865 –
31.10.1981)

GOODS
(18.04.1966)

EOR 10.10.2004

ENGINE
SHED

ONGAR
(24.04.1865)

EOR 27.03.2005

EOR 10.10.2004

NORTH WEALD
(24.04.1865)

GER 24.04.1865 –
25.09.1949 (18.04.1966)
LTE 25.09.1949 – 30.09.1994

GER 24.04.1865 –
25.09.1949 (18.04.1966)
LTE 25.09.1949 – 30.09.1994

CHIPPING
ONGAR

GOODS
(18.04.1966)

EPPING GLADE (Proposed)

EPPING

TOOT
HILL

GOODS
(18.04.1966)

EPPING (24.04.1865)

EPPING TO ONGAR:

Opened by the Great Eastern Railway 24.04.1865. Transferred to LTE 25.09.1949 with the
two intermediate stations at North Weald and Blake Hall. As the line was not electrified until
18.11.1957, passenger services remained steam hauled and provided by BR until that date.

GASWORKS

THEYDON
GARNON

Blake Hall station closed 31.10.1981 followed by North Weald and Ongar 30.09.1994.

The route re-opened as a preserved railway (Epping Ongar Railway) 10.10.2004 between
Ongar and North Weald (subsequently Coopersale 27.03.2005). Closed 31.12.2007 –
25.05.2012 for upgrade works. Extension to Epping Glade proposed

LITTLE
END

THEYDON
BOIS

GOODS (1886 – 18.04.1966)

THEYDON BOIS
Theydon
(24.04.1865)

THEYDON
MOUNT

River Roding

NAVESTOCK

River Roding

GOODS
(18.04.1966)

ABRIDGE

DEBDEN
Chigwell Lane
Chigwell Road
(24.04.1865)

LAMBOURNE

CONTINUED
FROM BELOW

Scale 0 Km 1 2 3 4
Miles 1 2

EASTERN COUNTIES / GREAT EASTERN RAILWAYS LEYTON TO
LOUGHTON / EPPING (AND ONGAR):

The Central Line from Leyton to Loughton was opened by the Eastern
Counties Railway (later absorbed by the Great Eastern Railway)
22.08.1856. The Great Eastern Railway then opened the extension to
Epping (and Ongar) 24.04.1865, leading to abandonment of the original
Loughton terminus, although the goods station to the south remained open.

LOUGHTON

GOODS (1st)
(22.08.1856 –
24.04.1865)

LOUGHTON (ECR)
(22.08.1856 – 24.04.1865)

ECR 22.08.1856 – 24.04.1865

Most passenger services were transferred to London Underground in
stages between 05.05.1947 and 25.09.1949. Freight services remained
until 18.04.1966, and some early morning British Rail passenger services
to Epping continued until 01.06.1970 (last train 31.05.1970).

GOODS (2nd)
(24.04.1865 –
18.04.1966)

CONTINUED
ABOVE

ECR 22.08.1856 – 24.04.1865 (18.04.1966)

GER
24.04.1865 – 01.06.1970

The physical link between LTE and BR at Leyton was closed 03.05.1971,
dismantled 29.10.1972.

LTE 25.09.1949

(2nd)
(1st) LOUGHTON (GER)
(24.04.1865)
(re-sited 28.04.1940)

LOUGHTON
SIDINGS

Station originally arranged for through running
to High Beech (aborted), with side platforms
connected by a subway. Subway abandoned
and platforms connected on the level c.1962

CHINGFORD

CARRIAGE SIDINGS (1920)

CHINGFORD (2nd) (02.09.1878)

GER
02.09.1878

River Roding

16

Scale 0 Km 0.5 1 1.5 2
Miles ¼ ½ ¾ 1

8

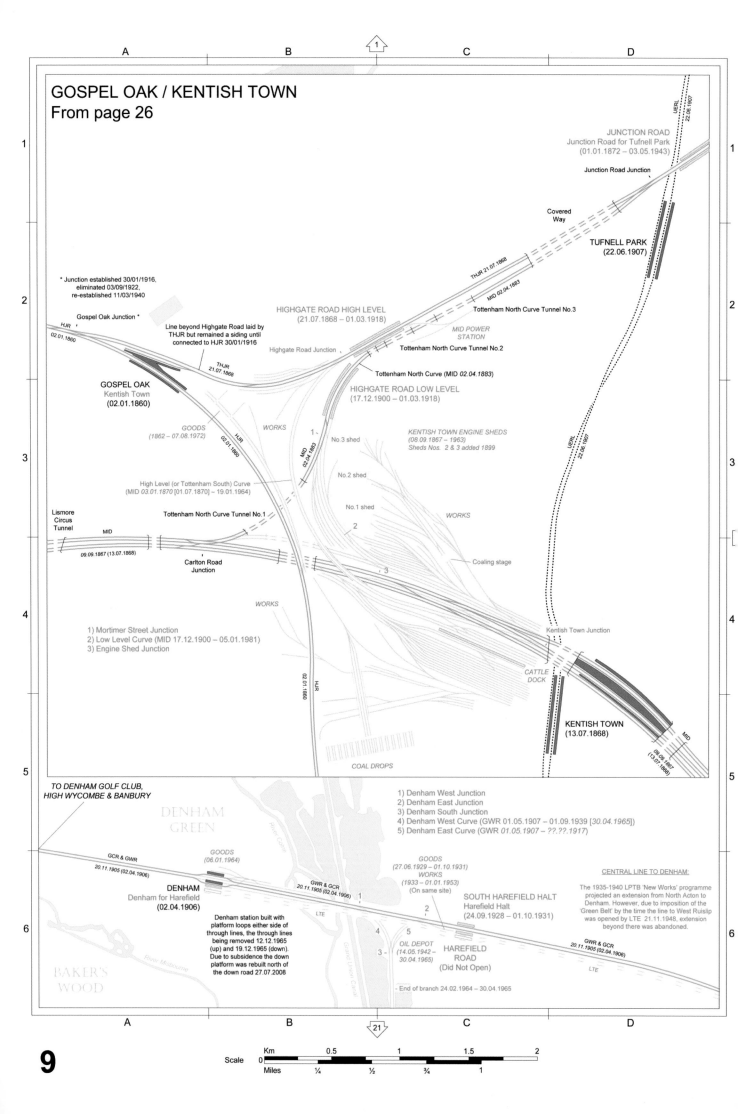

GOSPEL OAK / KENTISH TOWN
From page 26

JUNCTION ROAD
Junction Road for Tufnell Park
(01.01.1872 – 03.05.1943)

UERL 22.06.1907

Junction Road Junction

Covered Way

TUFNELL PARK
(22.06.1907)

THJR 21.07.1868

MID 02.04.1883

Tottenham North Curve Tunnel No.3

* Junction established 30/01/1916,
eliminated 03/09/1922,
re-established 11/03/1940

Gospel Oak Junction *

HJR 02.01.1860

Line beyond Highgate Road laid by
THJR but remained a siding until
connected to HJR 30/01/1916

HIGHGATE ROAD HIGH LEVEL
(21.07.1868 – 01.03.1918)

MID POWER STATION

Highgate Road Junction

Tottenham North Curve Tunnel No.2

THJR 21.07.1868

Tottenham North Curve (MID 02.04.1883)

GOSPEL OAK
Kentish Town
(02.01.1860)

GOODS
(1862 – 07.08.1972)

WORKS

HJR 02.01.1860

MID 02.04.1883

HIGHGATE ROAD LOW LEVEL
(17.12.1900 – 01.03.1918)

KENTISH TOWN ENGINE SHEDS
(08.09.1867 – 1963)
Sheds Nos. 2 & 3 added 1899

No.3 shed

No.2 shed

High Level (or Tottenham South) Curve
(MID 03.01.1870 [01.07.1870] – 19.01.1964)

No.1 shed

WORKS

UERL 22.06.1907

Lismore Circus Tunnel

Tottenham North Curve Tunnel No.1

MID
09.09.1867 (13.07.1868)

Carlton Road Junction

Coaling stage

Kentish Town Junction

1) Mortimer Street Junction
2) Low Level Curve (MID 17.12.1900 – 05.01.1981)
3) Engine Shed Junction

WORKS

02.01.1860 HJR

CATTLE DOCK

KENTISH TOWN
(13.07.1868)

MID
09.09.1867
(13.07.1868)

COAL DROPS

*TO DENHAM GOLF CLUB,
HIGH WYCOMBE & BANBURY*

1) Denham West Junction
2) Denham East Junction
3) Denham South Junction
4) Denham West Curve (GWR 01.05.1907 – 01.09.1939 [30.04.1965])
5) Denham East Curve (GWR 01.05.1907 – ??.??.1917)

DENHAM GREEN

River Colne

GCR & GWR
20.11.1905 (02.04.1906)

GOODS
(06.01.1964)

DENHAM
Denham for Harefield
(02.04.1906)

GWR & GCR
20.11.1905 (02.04.1906)

GOODS
(27.06.1929 – 01.10.1931)
WORKS
(1933 – 01.01.1953)
(On same site)

SOUTH HAREFIELD HALT
Harefield Halt
(24.09.1928 – 01.10.1931)

Denham station built with
platform loops either side of
through lines, the through lines
being removed 12.12.1965
(up) and 19.12.1965 (down).
Due to subsidence the down
platform was rebuilt north of
the down road 27.07.2008

LTE

Grand Union Canal

OIL DEPOT
(14.05.1942 – 30.04.1965)

HAREFIELD ROAD
(Did Not Open)

GWR & GCR
20.11.1905 (02.04.1906)

LTE

<u>CENTRAL LINE TO DENHAM:</u>

The 1935-1940 LPTB 'New Works' programme
projected an extension from North Acton to
Denham. However, due to imposition of the
'Green Belt' by the time the line to West Ruislip
was opened by LTE 21.11.1948, extension
beyond there was abandoned.

River Misbourne

BAKER'S WOOD

- End of branch 24.02.1964 – 30.04.1965

9

From page 26

Scale
Km 0 0.5 1 1.5 2
Miles ¼ ½ ¾ 1

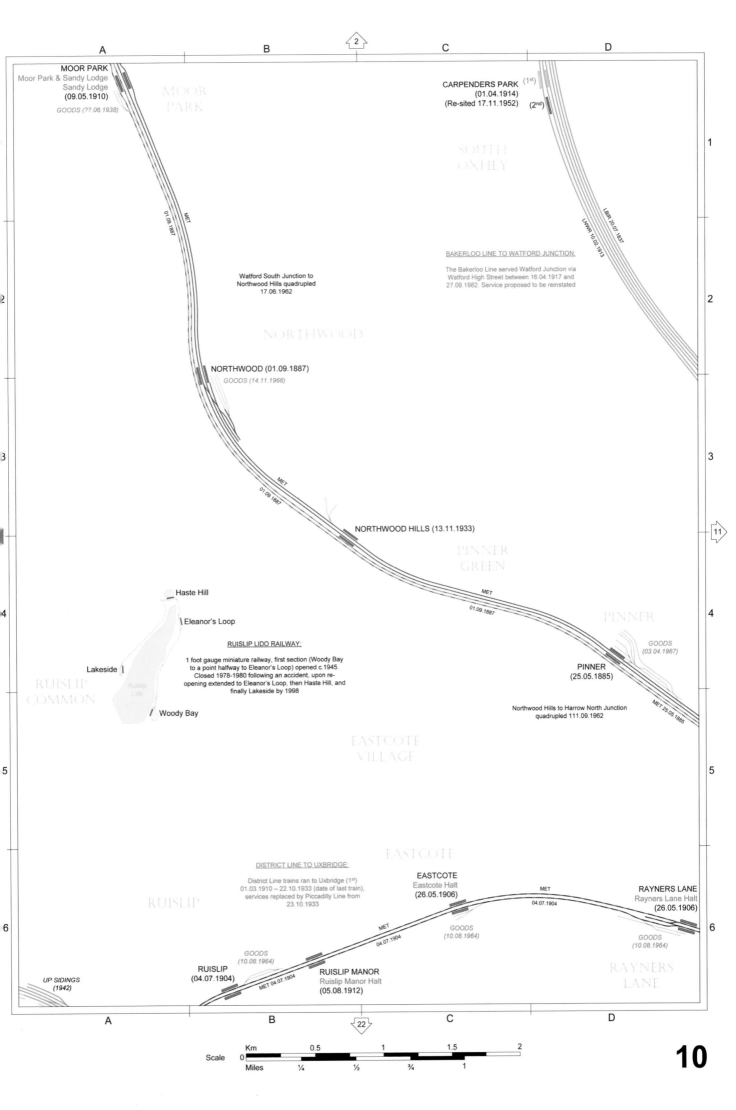

MOOR PARK
Moor Park & Sandy Lodge
Sandy Lodge
(09.05.1910)

GOODS (??.06.1938)

MOOR
PARK

CARPENDERS PARK (1st)
(01.04.1914)
(Re-sited 17.11.1952) (2nd)

SOUTH
OXHEY

01.09.1887

MET

LBR 20.07.1837

LNWR 10.02.1913

BAKERLOO LINE TO WATFORD JUNCTION:

The Bakerloo Line served Watford Junction via
Watford High Street between 16.04.1917 and
27.09.1982. Service proposed to be reinstated

Watford South Junction to
Northwood Hills quadrupled
17.06.1962

NORTHWOOD

NORTHWOOD (01.09.1887)

GOODS (14.11.1966)

MET
01.09.1887

NORTHWOOD HILLS (13.11.1933)

PINNER
GREEN

MET
01.09.1887

Haste Hill

Eleanor's Loop

RUISLIP LIDO RAILWAY:

1 foot gauge miniature railway, first section (Woody Bay
to a point halfway to Eleanor's Loop) opened c.1945.
Closed 1978-1980 following an accident, upon re-
opening extended to Eleanor's Loop, then Haste Hill, and
finally Lakeside by 1998

Lakeside

Ruislip
Lido

Woody Bay

RUISLIP
COMMON

PINNER

*GOODS
(03.04.1967)*

PINNER
(25.05.1885)

MET 25.05.1885

Northwood Hills to Harrow North Junction
quadrupled 111.09.1962

EASTCOTE
VILLAGE

EASTCOTE

DISTRICT LINE TO UXBRIDGE:

District Line trains ran to Uxbridge (1st)
01.03.1910 – 22.10.1933 (date of last train),
services replaced by Piccadilly Line from
23.10.1933

EASTCOTE
Eastcote Halt
(26.05.1906)

MET
04.07.1904

RAYNERS LANE
Rayners Lane Halt
(26.05.1906)

*GOODS
(10.08.1964)*

MET
04.07.1904

RAYNERS
LANE

RUISLIP

*GOODS
(10.08.1964)*

RUISLIP
(04.07.1904)

RUISLIP MANOR
Ruislip Manor Halt
(05.08.1912)

MET 04.07.1904

*GOODS
(10.08.1964)*

*UP SIDINGS
(1942)*

Scale
Km
0   0.5   1   1.5   2
Miles
¼   ½   ¾   1

10

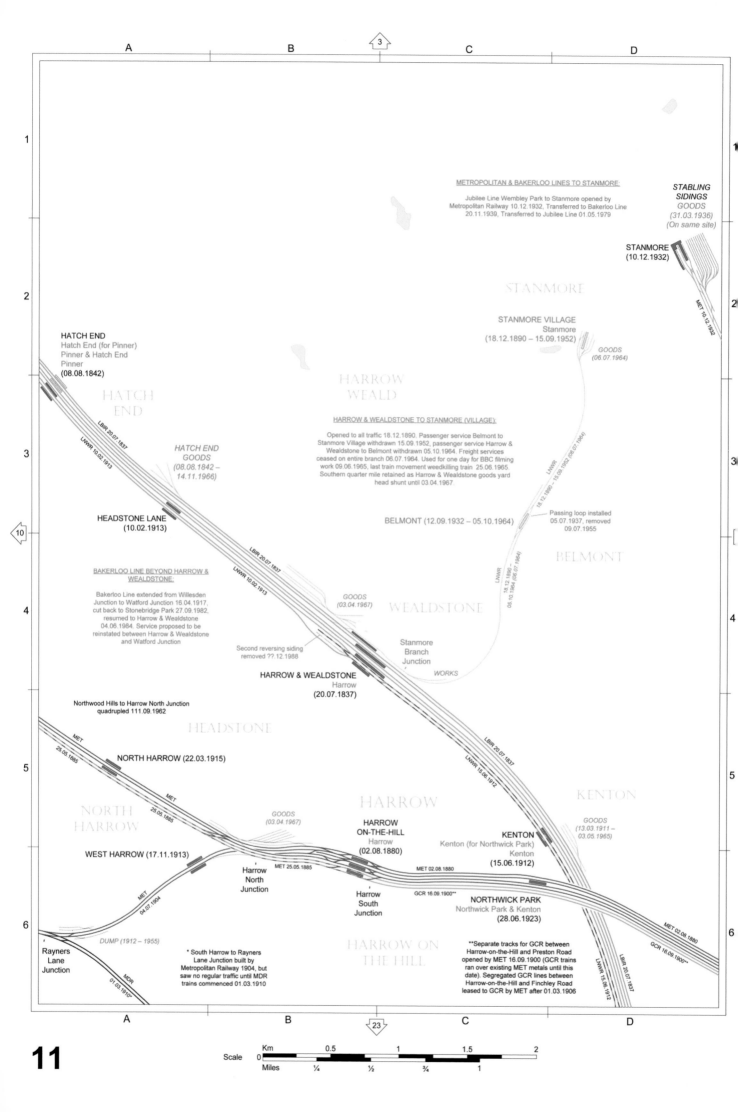

METROPOLITAN & BAKERLOO LINES TO STANMORE:

Jubilee Line Wembley Park to Stanmore opened by
Metropolitan Railway 10.12.1932, Transferred to Bakerloo Line
20.11.1939, Transferred to Jubilee Line 01.05.1979

*STABLING
SIDINGS
GOODS
(31.03.1936)
(On same site)*

STANMORE
(10.12.1932)

MET 10.12.1932

STANMORE

STANMORE VILLAGE
Stanmore
(18.12.1890 – 15.09.1952)

*GOODS
(06.07.1964)*

HATCH END
Hatch End (for Pinner)
Pinner & Hatch End
Pinner
(08.08.1842)

HARROW
WEALD

HARROW & WEALDSTONE TO STANMORE (VILLAGE):

Opened to all traffic 18.12.1890. Passenger service Belmont to
Stanmore Village withdrawn 15.09.1952, passenger service Harrow &
Wealdstone to Belmont withdrawn 05.10.1964. Freight services
ceased on entire branch 06.07.1964. Used for one day for BBC filming
work 09.06.1965, last train movement weedkilling train 25.06.1965.
Southern quarter mile retained as Harrow & Wealdstone goods yard
head shunt until 03.04.1967.

HATCH
END

LBIR 20.07.1837

LNWR 10.02.1913

*HATCH END
GOODS
(08.08.1842 –
14.11.1966)*

BELMONT (12.09.1932 – 05.10.1964)

LNWR 18.12.1890 – 15.09.1952 (06.07.1964)

Passing loop installed
05.07.1937, removed
09.07.1955

HEADSTONE LANE
(10.02.1913)

LBIR 20.07.1837

LNWR 10.02.1913

BELMONT

LNWR 18.12.1890 – 05.10.1964 (06.07.1964)

**BAKERLOO LINE BEYOND HARROW &
WEALDSTONE:**

Bakerloo Line extended from Willesden
Junction to Watford Junction 16.04.1917,
cut back to Stonebridge Park 27.09.1982,
resumed to Harrow & Wealdstone
04.06.1984. Service proposed to be
reinstated between Harrow & Wealdstone
and Watford Junction

*GOODS
(03.04.1967)*

WEALDSTONE

Stanmore
Branch
Junction

WORKS

Second reversing siding
removed ??.12.1988

HARROW & WEALDSTONE
Harrow
(20.07.1837)

Northwood Hills to Harrow North Junction
quadrupled 111.09.1962

HEADSTONE

LBIR 20.07.1837

LNWR 15.06.1912

KENTON

MET
25.05.1885

NORTH HARROW (22.03.1915)

MET
25.05.1885

HARROW

NORTH
HARROW

*GOODS
(03.04.1967)*

HARROW
ON-THE-HILL
Harrow
(02.08.1880)

KENTON
Kenton (for Northwick Park)
Kenton
(15.06.1912)

*GOODS
(13.03.1911 –
03.05.1965)*

WEST HARROW (17.11.1913)

MET 25.05.1885

Harrow
North
Junction

MET 02.08.1880

MET
04.07.1904

Harrow
South
Junction

GCR 16.09.1900**

NORTHWICK PARK
Northwick Park & Kenton
(28.06.1923)

MET 02.08.1880

GCR 16.09.1900**

Rayners
Lane
Junction

DUMP (1912 – 1955)

MDR
01.03.1910*

HARROW ON
THE HILL

* South Harrow to Rayners
Lane Junction built by
Metropolitan Railway 1904, but
saw no regular traffic until MDR
trains commenced 01.03.1910

**Separate tracks for GCR between
Harrow-on-the-Hill and Preston Road
opened by MET 16.09.1900 (GCR trains
ran over existing MET metals until this
date). Segregated GCR lines between
Harrow-on-the-Hill and Finchley Road
leased to GCR by MET after 01.03.1906

LNWR 15.06.1912

LBIR 20.07.1837

Scale

Km   0   0.5   1   1.5   2

Miles   ¼   ½   ¾   1

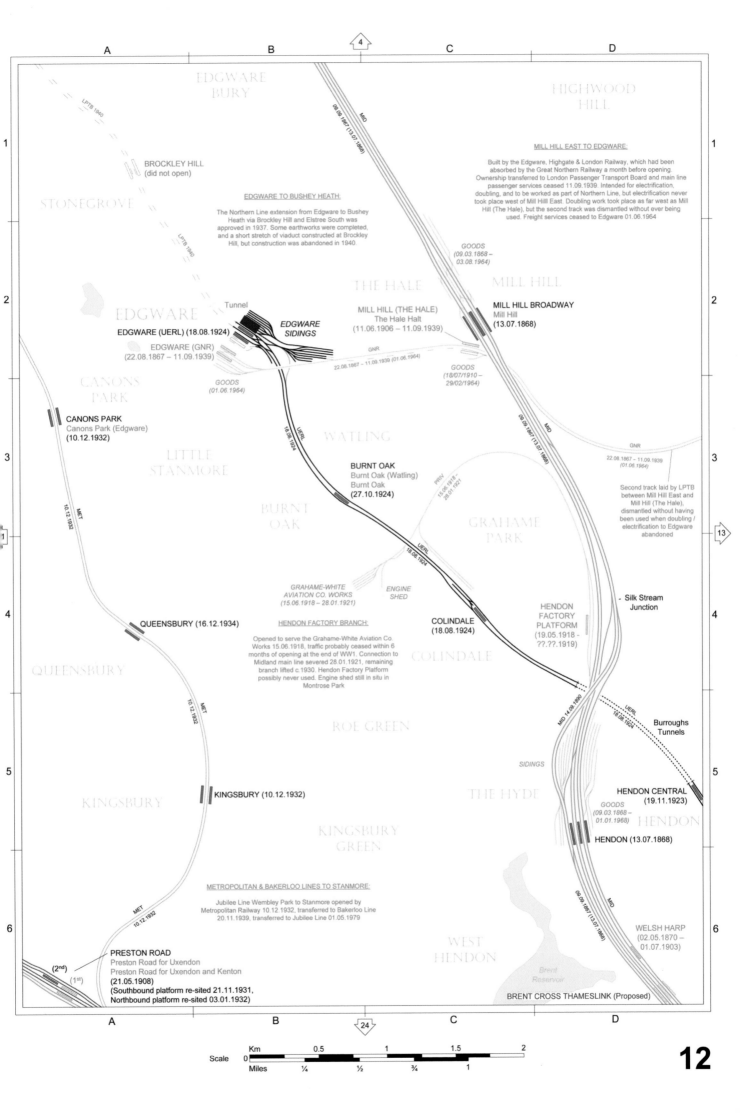

EDGWARE
BURY

HIGHWOOD
HILL

BROCKLEY HILL
(did not open)

STONEGROVE

MILL HILL EAST TO EDGWARE:

Built by the Edgware, Highgate & London Railway, which had been
absorbed by the Great Northern Railway a month before opening.
Ownership transferred to London Passenger Transport Board and main line
passenger services ceased 11.09.1939. Intended for electrification,
doubling, and to be worked as part of Northern Line, but electrification never
took place west of Mill Hill East. Doubling work took place as far west as Mill
Hill (The Hale), but the second track was dismantled without ever being
used. Freight services ceased to Edgware 01.06.1964

EDGWARE TO BUSHEY HEATH:

The Northern Line extension from Edgware to Bushey
Heath via Brockley Hill and Elstree South was
approved in 1937. Some earthworks were completed,
and a short stretch of viaduct constructed at Brockley
Hill, but construction was abandoned in 1940.

*GOODS
(09.03.1868 –
03.08.1964)*

THE HALE

MILL HILL

Tunnel

*EDGWARE
SIDINGS*

MILL HILL (THE HALE)
The Hale Halt
(11.06.1906 – 11.09.1939)

MILL HILL BROADWAY
Mill Hill
(13.07.1868)

EDGWARE
EDGWARE (UERL) (18.08.1924)
EDGWARE (GNR)
(22.08.1867 – 11.09.1939)

GNR
22.08.1867 – 11.09.1939 (01.06.1964)

*GOODS
(18/07/1910 –
29/02/1964)*

CANONS
PARK

*GOODS
(01.06.1964)*

GNR
22.08.1867 – 11.09.1939
(01.06.1964)

CANONS PARK
Canons Park (Edgware)
(10.12.1932)

WATLING

Second track laid by LPTB
between Mill Hill East and
Mill Hill (The Hale),
dismantled without having
been used when doubling /
electrification to Edgware
abandoned

LITTLE
STANMORE

BURNT OAK
Burnt Oak (Watling)
Burnt Oak
(27.10.1924)

BURNT
OAK

GRAHAME
PARK

PRIV
15.06.1918 –
28.01.1921

Silk Stream
Junction

*GRAHAME-WHITE
AVIATION CO. WORKS
(15.06.1918 – 28.01.1921)*

*ENGINE
SHED*

HENDON
FACTORY
PLATFORM
(19.05.1918 –
??.??.1919)

QUEENSBURY (16.12.1934)

HENDON FACTORY BRANCH:

COLINDALE
(18.08.1924)

COLINDALE

Opened to serve the Grahame-White Aviation Co.
Works 15.06.1918, traffic probably ceased within 6
months of opening at the end of WW1. Connection to
Midland main line severed 28.01.1921, remaining
branch lifted c.1930. Hendon Factory Platform
possibly never used. Engine shed still in situ in
Montrose Park

QUEENSBURY

ROE GREEN

Burroughs
Tunnels

SIDINGS

KINGSBURY

KINGSBURY (10.12.1932)

THE HYDE

HENDON CENTRAL
(19.11.1923)

*GOODS
(09.03.1868 –
01.01.1968)*

HENDON

KINGSBURY
GREEN

HENDON (13.07.1868)

METROPOLITAN & BAKERLOO LINES TO STANMORE:

Jubilee Line Wembley Park to Stanmore opened by
Metropolitan Railway 10.12.1932, transferred to Bakerloo Line
20.11.1939, transferred to Jubilee Line 01.05.1979

WEST
HENDON

WELSH HARP
(02.05.1870 –
01.07.1903)

*Brent
Reservoir*

PRESTON ROAD
Preston Road for Uxendon
Preston Road for Uxendon and Kenton
(21.05.1908)
(Southbound platform re-sited 21.11.1931,
Northbound platform re-sited 03.01.1932)

(2nd)
(1st)

BRENT CROSS THAMESLINK (Proposed)

Scale

Km   0   0.5   1   1.5   2
Miles   ¼   ½   ¾   1

12

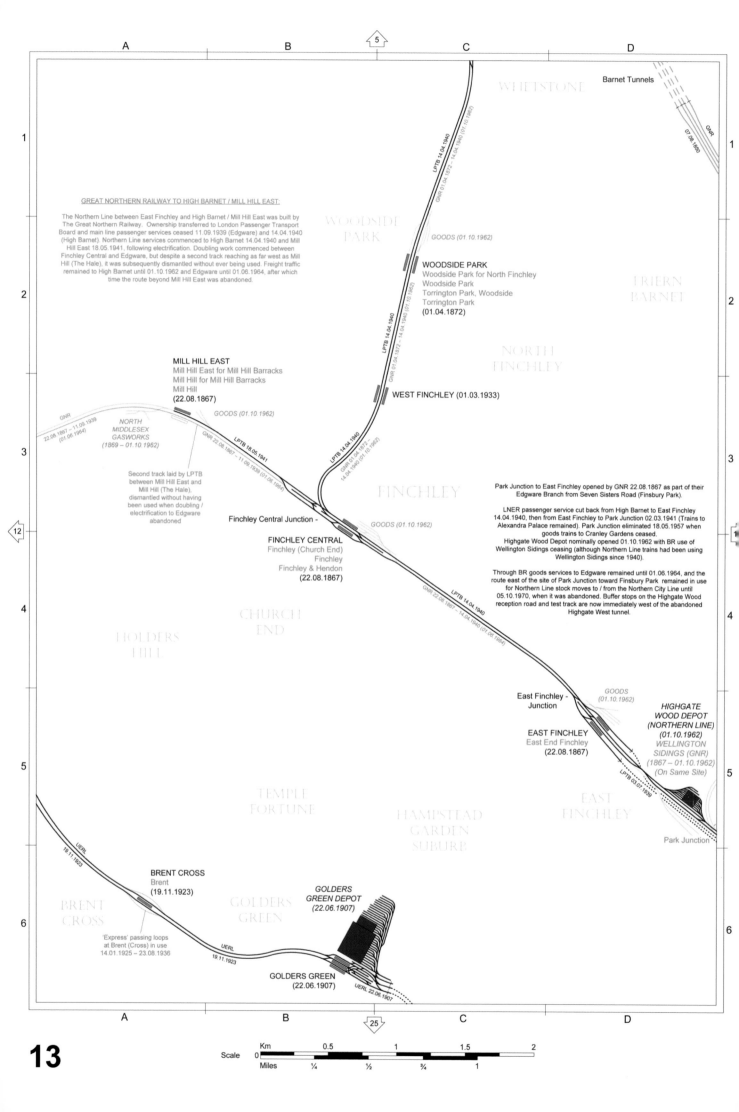

WHETSTONE

Barnet Tunnels

07.08.1850

GNR

LPTB 14.04.1940

GNR 01.04.1872 – 14.04.1940 (07.10.1962)

WOODSIDE PARK

FRIERN BARNET

GOODS (01.10.1962)

WOODSIDE PARK
Woodside Park for North Finchley
Woodside Park
Torrington Park, Woodside
Torrington Park
(01.04.1872)

LPTB 14.04.1940

GNR 01.04.1872 – 14.04.1940 (07.10.1962)

NORTH FINCHLEY

WEST FINCHLEY (01.03.1933)

GREAT NORTHERN RAILWAY TO HIGH BARNET / MILL HILL EAST:

The Northern Line between East Finchley and High Barnet / Mill Hill East was built by
The Great Northern Railway. Ownership transferred to London Passenger Transport
Board and main line passenger services ceased 11.09.1939 (Edgware) and 14.04.1940
(High Barnet). Northern Line services commenced to High Barnet 14.04.1940 and Mill
Hill East 18.05.1941, following electrification. Doubling work commenced between
Finchley Central and Edgware, but despite a second track reaching as far west as Mill
Hill (The Hale), it was subsequently dismantled without ever being used. Freight traffic
remained to High Barnet until 01.10.1962 and Edgware until 01.06.1964, after which
time the route beyond Mill Hill East was abandoned.

MILL HILL EAST
Mill Hill East for Mill Hill Barracks
Mill Hill for Mill Hill Barracks
Mill Hill
(22.08.1867)

GNR
22.08.1867 – 11.09.1939
(01.06.1964)

*NORTH
MIDDLESEX
GASWORKS
(1869 – 01.10.1962)*

GOODS (01.10.1962)

GNR 22.08.1867 – 11.09.1939 (07.06.1964)

LPTB 18.05.1941

LPTB 14.04.1940

GNR 01.04.1872 –
14.04.1940 (01.10.1962)

Second track laid by LPTB
between Mill Hill East and
Mill Hill (The Hale),
dismantled without having
been used when doubling /
electrification to Edgware
abandoned

FINCHLEY

Finchley Central Junction -

GOODS (01.10.1962)

FINCHLEY CENTRAL
Finchley (Church End)
Finchley
Finchley & Hendon
(22.08.1867)

12

CHURCH END

HOLDERS HILL

Park Junction to East Finchley opened by GNR 22.08.1867 as part of their
Edgware Branch from Seven Sisters Road (Finsbury Park).

LNER passenger service cut back from High Barnet to East Finchley
14.04.1940, then from East Finchley to Park Junction 02.03.1941 (Trains to
Alexandra Palace remained). Park Junction eliminated 18.05.1957 when
goods trains to Cranley Gardens ceased.
Highgate Wood Depot nominally opened 01.10.1962 with BR use of
Wellington Sidings ceasing (although Northern Line trains had been using
Wellington Sidings since 1940).

Through BR goods services to Edgware remained until 01.06.1964, and the
route east of the site of Park Junction toward Finsbury Park remained in use
for Northern Line stock moves to / from the Northern City Line until
05.10.1970, when it was abandoned. Buffer stops on the Highgate Wood
reception road and test track are now immediately west of the abandoned
Highgate West tunnel.

GNR 22.08.1867 – 14.04.1940 (07.06.1964)

LPTB 14.04.1940

East Finchley -
Junction

GOODS
(01.10.1962)

*HIGHGATE
WOOD DEPOT
(NORTHERN LINE)
(01.10.1962)*
*WELLINGTON
SIDINGS (GNR)
(1867 – 01.10.1962)
(On Same Site)*

EAST FINCHLEY
East End Finchley
(22.08.1867)

LPTB 03.07.1939

EAST FINCHLEY

Park Junction

TEMPLE FORTUNE

HAMPSTEAD GARDEN SUBURB

UERL
18.11.1923

BRENT CROSS
Brent
(19.11.1923)

BRENT CROSS

GOLDERS GREEN

*GOLDERS
GREEN DEPOT
(22.06.1907)*

'Express' passing loops
at Brent (Cross) in use
14.01.1925 – 23.08.1936

UERL
19.11.1923

GOLDERS GREEN
(22.06.1907)

UERL 22.06.1907

13

Scale

Km 0   0.5   1   1.5   2
Miles ¼   ½   ¾   1

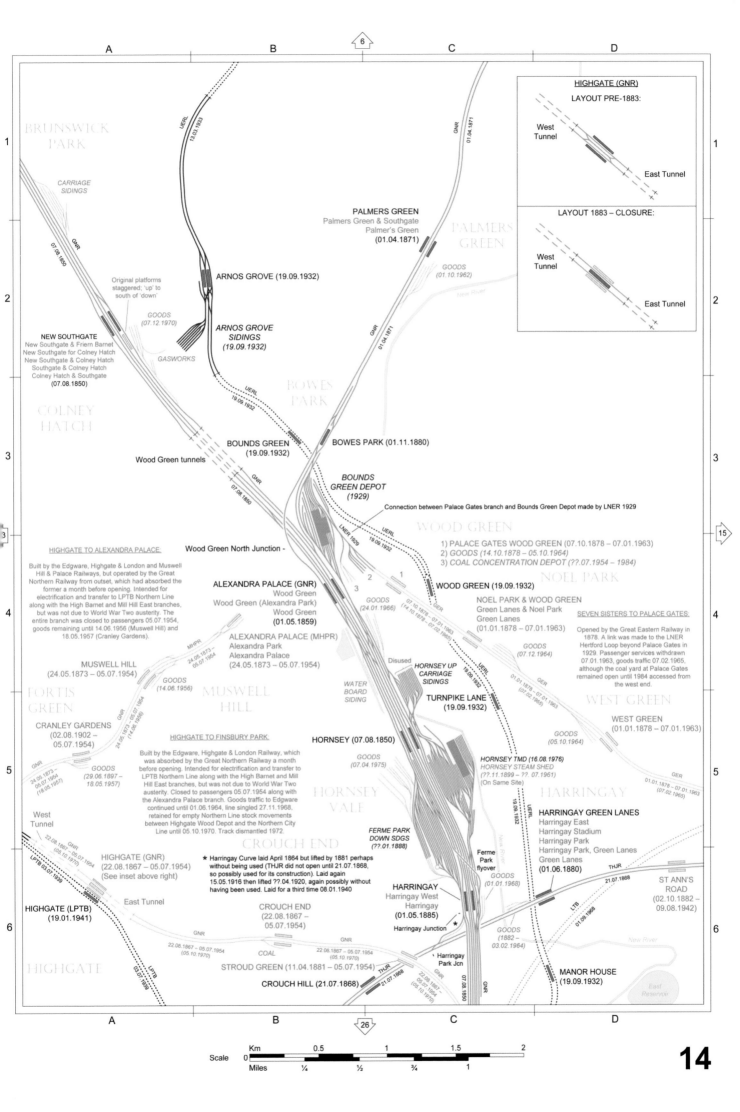

BRUNSWICK PARK

CARRIAGE SIDINGS

UERL 13.03.1933

GNR 07.08.1850

PALMERS GREEN
Palmers Green & Southgate
Palmer's Green
(01.04.1871)

GNR 01.04.1871

PALMERS GREEN

GOODS (01.10.1962)

New River

HIGHGATE (GNR)
LAYOUT PRE-1883:

West Tunnel

East Tunnel

LAYOUT 1883 – CLOSURE:

West Tunnel

East Tunnel

Original platforms staggered; 'up' to south of 'down'

ARNOS GROVE (19.09.1932)

ARNOS GROVE SIDINGS (19.09.1932)

GOODS (07.12.1970)

GASWORKS

GNR 01.04.1871

NEW SOUTHGATE
New Southgate & Friern Barnet
New Southgate for Colney Hatch
New Southgate & Colney Hatch
Southgate & Colney Hatch
Colney Hatch & Southgate
(07.08.1850)

COLNEY HATCH

UERL 19.09.1932

BOWES PARK

BOUNDS GREEN (19.09.1932)

BOWES PARK (01.11.1880)

Wood Green tunnels

GNR 07.08.1850

BOUNDS GREEN DEPOT (1929)

Connection between Palace Gates branch and Bounds Green Depot made by LNER 1929

WOOD GREEN

LNER 1929 UERL 19.09.1932

Wood Green North Junction -

HIGHGATE TO ALEXANDRA PALACE:

Built by the Edgware, Highgate & London and Muswell Hill & Palace Railways, but operated by the Great Northern Railway from outset, which had absorbed the former a month before opening. Intended for electrification and transfer to LPTB Northern Line along with the High Barnet and Mill Hill East branches, but was not due to World War Two austerity. The entire branch was closed to passengers 05.07.1954, goods remaining until 14.06.1956 (Muswell Hill) and 18.05.1957 (Cranley Gardens).

1) PALACE GATES WOOD GREEN (07.10.1878 – 07.01.1963)
2) GOODS (14.10.1878 – 05.10.1964)
3) COAL CONCENTRATION DEPOT (??.07.1954 – 1984)

NOEL PARK

ALEXANDRA PALACE (GNR)
Wood Green
Wood Green (Alexandra Park)
Wood Green
(01.05.1859)

3 2 1

GOODS (24.01.1966)

GER 07.10.1878 – 07.01.1963 (14.10.1878 – 07.02.1965)

WOOD GREEN (19.09.1932)

NOEL PARK & WOOD GREEN
Green Lanes & Noel Park
Green Lanes
(01.01.1878 – 07.01.1963)

SEVEN SISTERS TO PALACE GATES:

Opened by the Great Eastern Railway in 1878. A link was made to the LNER Hertford Loop beyond Palace Gates in 1929. Passenger services withdrawn 07.01.1963, although the coal yard at Palace Gates remained open until 1984 accessed from the west end.

ALEXANDRA PALACE (MHPR)
Alexandra Park
Alexandra Palace
(24.05.1873 – 05.07.1954)

MHPR 24.05.1873 – 05.07.1954

GOODS (07.12.1964)

GER 01.01.1878 – 07.01.1963 (07.02.1965)

MUSWELL HILL
(24.05.1873 – 05.07.1954)

Disused

HORNSEY UP CARRIAGE SIDINGS

WEST GREEN
(01.01.1878 – 07.01.1963)

FORTIS GREEN

GOODS (14.06.1956)

MUSWELL HILL

TURNPIKE LANE (19.09.1932)

WATER BOARD SIDING

CRANLEY GARDENS
(02.08.1902 – 05.07.1954)

GNR 24.05.1873 – 05.07.1954 (14.06.1956)

HORNSEY (07.08.1850)

GOODS (05.10.1964)

WEST GREEN

GNR 24.05.1873 – 05.07.1954 (18.05.1957)

GOODS (29.06.1897 – 18.05.1957)

GOODS (07.04.1975)

HIGHGATE TO FINSBURY PARK:

Built by the Edgware, Highgate & London Railway, which was absorbed by the Great Northern Railway a month before opening. Intended for electrification and transfer to LPTB Northern Line along with the High Barnet and Mill Hill East branches, but was not due to World War Two austerity. Closed to passengers 05.07.1954 along with the Alexandra Palace branch. Goods traffic to Edgware continued until 01.06.1964, line singled 27.11.1968, retained for empty Northern Line stock movements between Highgate Wood Depot and the Northern City Line until 05.10.1970. Track dismantled 1972.

HORNSEY VALE

HORNSEY TMD (16.08.1976)
HORNSEY STEAM SHED (??.11.1899 – ??.07.1961) (On Same Site)

UERL 19.09.1932

HARRINGAY

HARRINGAY GREEN LANES
Harringay East
Harringay Stadium
Harringay Park
Harringay Park, Green Lanes
Green Lanes
(01.06.1880)

West Tunnel

22.08.1867 – 05.07.1954 (05.10.1970)

GNR

FERME PARK DOWN SDGS (??.01.1888)

Ferme Park flyover

GOODS (01.01.1968)

LPTB 03.07.1939

HIGHGATE (GNR)
(22.08.1867 – 05.07.1954)
(See inset above right)

HIGHGATE (LPTB)
(19.01.1941)

East Tunnel

★ Harringay Curve laid April 1864 but lifted by 1881 perhaps without being used (THJR did not open until 21.07.1868, so possibly used for its construction). Laid again 15.05.1916 then lifted ??.04.1920, again possibly without having been used. Laid for a third time 08.01.1940

CROUCH END
(22.08.1867 – 05.07.1954)

HARRINGAY
Harringay West
Harringay
(01.05.1885)

THJR 21.07.1868

ST ANN'S ROAD
(02.10.1882 – 09.08.1942)

Harringay Junction ★

GOODS (1882 – 03.02.1964)

New River

GNR

GNR 22.08.1867 – 05.07.1954 (05.10.1970)

COAL

22.08.1867 – 05.07.1954 (05.10.1970)

Harringay Park Jcn

LTB 01.09.1968

LPTB 03.07.1939

STROUD GREEN (11.04.1881 – 05.07.1954)

THJR 21.07.1868

GNR 22.08.1867 – 05.07.1954 (05.10.1970)

GNR 07.08.1850

MANOR HOUSE (19.09.1932)

East Reservoir

HIGHGATE

CROUCH HILL (21.07.1868)

Scale
Km 0 0.5 1 1.5 2
Miles ¼ ½ ¾ 1

14

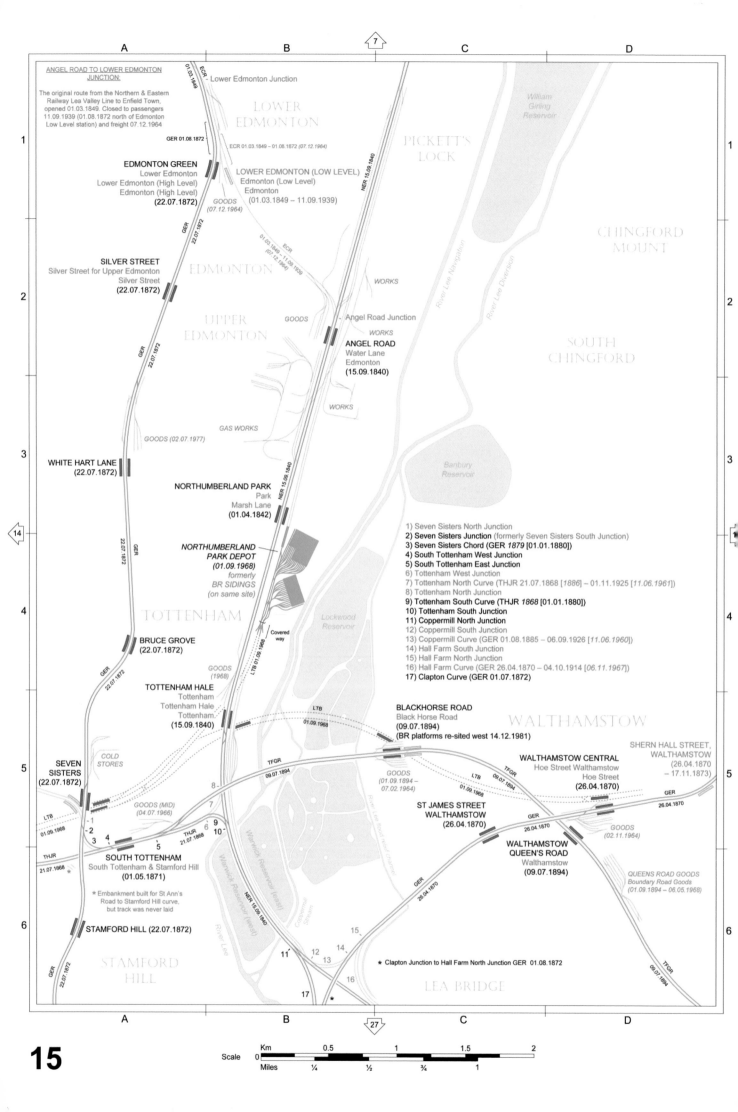

ANGEL ROAD TO LOWER EDMONTON
JUNCTION:

The original route from the Northern & Eastern
Railway Lea Valley Line to Enfield Town,
opened 01.03.1849. Closed to passengers
11.09.1939 (01.08.1872 north of Edmonton
Low Level station) and freight 07.12.1964

01.03.1849 — Lower Edmonton Junction

LOWER
EDMONTON

PICKETT'S
LOCK

*William
Girling
Reservoir*

GER 01.08.1872

ECR 01.03.1849 – 01.08.1872 (07.12.1964)

EDMONTON GREEN
Lower Edmonton
Lower Edmonton (High Level)
Edmonton (High Level)
(22.07.1872)

LOWER EDMONTON (LOW LEVEL)
Edmonton (Low Level)
Edmonton
(01.03.1849 – 11.09.1939)

CHINGFORD
MOUNT

*GOODS
(07.12.1964)*

SILVER STREET
Silver Street for Upper Edmonton
Silver Street
(22.07.1872)

EDMONTON

01.03.1849 ECR
(07.12.1964)
11.09.1939

SOUTH
CHINGFORD

UPPER
EDMONTON

GOODS

WORKS

Angel Road Junction

WORKS

ANGEL ROAD
Water Lane
Edmonton
(15.09.1840)

WORKS

WHITE HART LANE
(22.07.1872)

GOODS (02.07.1977)

GAS WORKS

*Banbury
Reservoir*

NORTHUMBERLAND PARK
Park
Marsh Lane
(01.04.1842)

*NORTHUMBERLAND
PARK DEPOT
(01.09.1968)
formerly
BR SIDINGS
(on same site)*

1) Seven Sisters North Junction
2) **Seven Sisters Junction** (formerly Seven Sisters South Junction)
3) Seven Sisters Chord (GER *1879* [01.01.1880])
4) South Tottenham West Junction
5) South Tottenham East Junction
6) Tottenham West Junction
7) Tottenham North Curve (THJR 21.07.1868 [*1886*] – 01.11.1925 [*11.06.1961*])
8) Tottenham North Junction
9) Tottenham South Curve (THJR *1868* [01.01.1880])
10) Tottenham South Junction
11) Coppermill North Junction
12) Coppermill South Junction
13) Coppermill Curve (GER 01.08.1885 – 06.09.1926 [*11.06.1960*])
14) Hall Farm South Junction
15) Hall Farm North Junction
16) Hall Farm Curve (GER 26.04.1870 – 04.10.1914 [*06.11.1967*])
17) **Clapton Curve** (GER 01.07.1872)

BRUCE GROVE
(22.07.1872)

*Covered
way*

*Lockwood
Reservoir*

TOTTENHAM

*GOODS
(1968)*

LTB 01.09.1968

TOTTENHAM HALE
Tottenham
Tottenham Hale
Tottenham
(15.09.1840)

LTB
01.09.1968

BLACKHORSE ROAD
Black Horse Road
(09.07.1894)
(BR platforms re-sited west 14.12.1981)

WALTHAMSTOW

SEVEN
SISTERS
(22.07.1872)

*COLD
STORES*

TFGR
09.07.1894

*GOODS
(01.09.1894 –
07.02.1964)*

LTB
01.09.1968

WALTHAMSTOW CENTRAL
Hoe Street Walthamstow
Hoe Street
(26.04.1870)

SHERN HALL STREET,
WALTHAMSTOW
(26.04.1870
– 17.11.1873)

TFGR
09.07.1894

GER
26.04.1870

LTB
01.09.1968

*GOODS (MID)
(04.07.1966)*

8

7

9
10

ST JAMES STREET
WALTHAMSTOW
(26.04.1870)

GER
26.04.1870

THJR
21.07.1868

-1
-2
3   4   5

WALTHAMSTOW
QUEEN'S ROAD
Walthamstow
(09.07.1894)

*GOODS
(02.11.1964)*

SOUTH TOTTENHAM
South Tottenham & Stamford Hill
(01.05.1871)

*QUEENS ROAD GOODS
Boundary Road Goods
(01.09.1894 – 06.05.1968)*

*Embankment built for St Ann's
Road to Stamford Hill curve,
but track was never laid

GER
26.04.1870

STAMFORD HILL **(22.07.1872)**

15 14

STAMFORD
HILL

11 12 13

16

* Clapton Junction to Hall Farm North Junction GER 01.08.1872

17

LEA BRIDGE

TFGR
09.07.1894

15

Scale

Km   0.5   1   1.5   2

Miles   ¼   ½   ¾   1

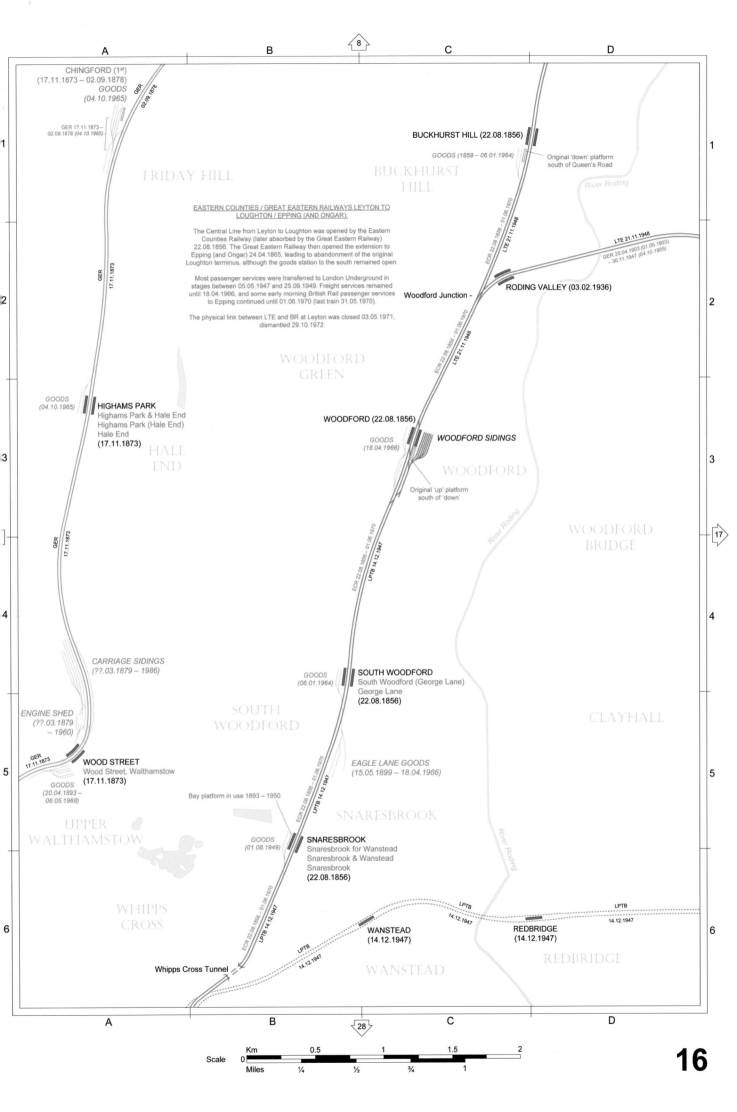

CHINGFORD (1st)
(17.11.1873 – 02.09.1878)
GOODS
(04.10.1965)

GER 17.11.1873 –
02.09.1878 *(04.10.1965)*

BUCKHURST HILL (22.08.1856)

GOODS (1859 – 06.01.1964)

Original 'down' platform
south of Queen's Road

FRIDAY HILL

BUCKHURST
HILL

River Roding

EASTERN COUNTIES / GREAT EASTERN RAILWAYS LEYTON TO
LOUGHTON / EPPING (AND ONGAR):

The Central Line from Leyton to Loughton was opened by the Eastern
Counties Railway (later absorbed by the Great Eastern Railway)
22.08.1856. The Great Eastern Railway then opened the extension to
Epping (and Ongar) 24.04.1865, leading to abandonment of the original
Loughton terminus, although the goods station to the south remained open.

Most passenger services were transferred to London Underground in
stages between 05.05.1947 and 25.09.1949. Freight services remained
until 18.04.1966, and some early morning British Rail passenger services
to Epping continued until 01.06.1970 (last train 31.05.1970).

The physical link between LTE and BR at Leyton was closed 03.05.1971,
dismantled 29.10.1972.

LTE 21.11.1948

GER 20.04.1903 (01.05.1903)
– 30.11.1947 (04.10.1965)

Woodford Junction

RODING VALLEY (03.02.1936)

WOODFORD
GREEN

GER 17.11.1873

GER

GOODS
(04.10.1965)

HIGHAMS PARK
Highams Park & Hale End
Highams Park (Hale End)
Hale End
(17.11.1873)

HALE
END

WOODFORD (22.08.1856)

GOODS
(18.04.1966)

WOODFORD SIDINGS

WOODFORD

Original 'up' platform
south of 'down'

River Roding

WOODFORD
BRIDGE

GER 17.11.1873

CARRIAGE SIDINGS
(??.03.1879 – 1986)

ENGINE SHED
(??.03.1879
– 1960)

GOODS
(06.01.1964)

SOUTH WOODFORD
South Woodford (George Lane)
George Lane
(22.08.1856)

EAGLE LANE GOODS
(15.05.1899 – 18.04.1966)

CLAYHALL

GER 17.11.1873

WOOD STREET
Wood Street, Walthamstow
(17.11.1873)

GOODS
(20.04.1893 –
06.05.1968)

SOUTH
WOODFORD

Bay platform in use 1893 – 1950

SNARESBROOK

River Roding

UPPER
WALTHAMSTOW

GOODS
(01.08.1949)

SNARESBROOK
Snaresbrook for Wanstead
Snaresbrook & Wanstead
Snaresbrook
(22.08.1856)

WHIPPS
CROSS

LPTB
14.12.1947

LPTB
14.12.1947

LPTB
14.12.1947

WANSTEAD
(14.12.1947)

REDBRIDGE
(14.12.1947)

REDBRIDGE

Whipps Cross Tunnel

LPTB
14.12.1947

WANSTEAD

Scale
Km   0   0.5   1   1.5   2
Miles   ¼   ½   ¾   1

16

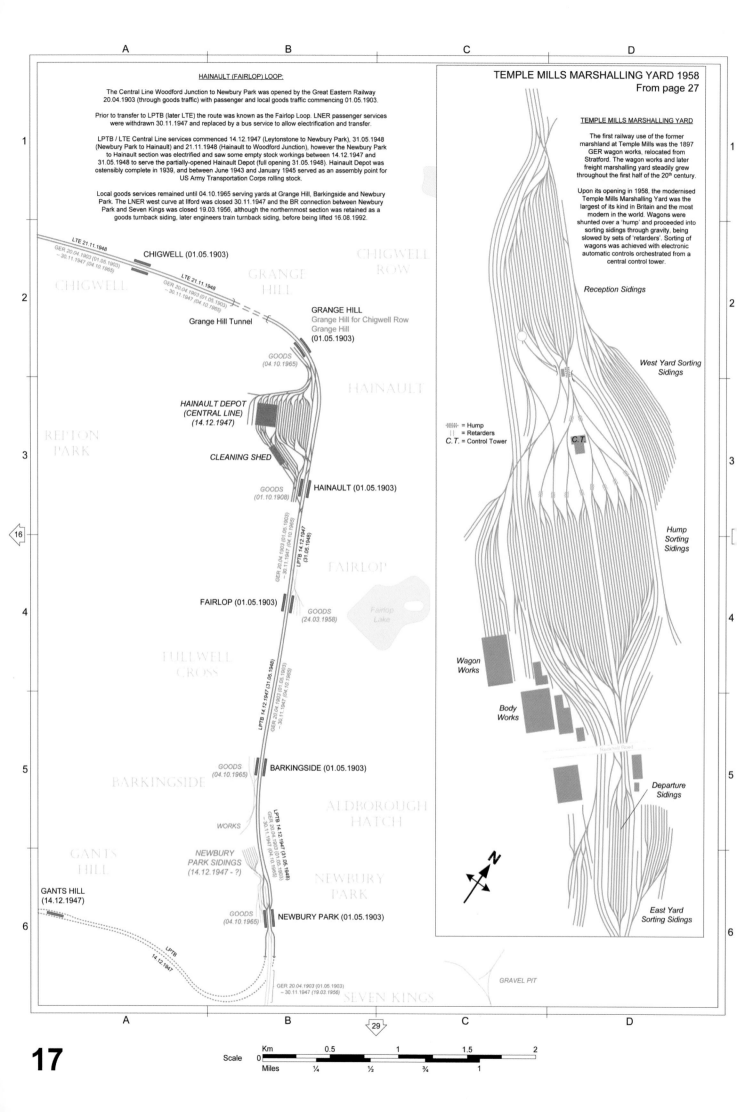

HAINAULT (FAIRLOP) LOOP:

The Central Line Woodford Junction to Newbury Park was opened by the Great Eastern Railway 20.04.1903 (through goods traffic) with passenger and local goods traffic commencing 01.05.1903.

Prior to transfer to LPTB (later LTE) the route was known as the Fairlop Loop. LNER passenger services were withdrawn 30.11.1947 and replaced by a bus service to allow electrification and transfer.

LPTB / LTE Central Line services commenced 14.12.1947 (Leytonstone to Newbury Park), 31.05.1948 (Newbury Park to Hainault) and 21.11.1948 (Hainault to Woodford Junction), however the Newbury Park to Hainault section was electrified and saw some empty stock workings between 14.12.1947 and 31.05.1948 to serve the partially-opened Hainault Depot (full opening 31.05.1948). Hainault Depot was ostensibly complete in 1939, and between June 1943 and January 1945 served as an assembly point for US Army Transportation Corps rolling stock.

Local goods services remained until 04.10.1965 serving yards at Grange Hill, Barkingside and Newbury Park. The LNER west curve at Ilford was closed 30.11.1947 and the BR connection between Newbury Park and Seven Kings was closed 19.03.1956, although the northernmost section was retained as a goods turnback siding, later engineers train turnback siding, before being lifted 16.08.1992.

TEMPLE MILLS MARSHALLING YARD 1958
From page 27

TEMPLE MILLS MARSHALLING YARD

The first railway use of the former marshland at Temple Mills was the 1897 GER wagon works, relocated from Stratford. The wagon works and later freight marshalling yard steadily grew throughout the first half of the 20th century.

Upon its opening in 1958, the modernised Temple Mills Marshalling Yard was the largest of its kind in Britain and the most modern in the world. Wagons were shunted over a 'hump' and proceeded into sorting sidings through gravity, being slowed by sets of 'retarders'. Sorting of wagons was achieved with electronic automatic controls orchestrated from a central control tower.

Reception Sidings

West Yard Sorting Sidings

= Hump
= Retarders
C.T. = Control Tower

C.T.

Hump Sorting Sidings

CHIGWELL (01.05.1903)

LTE 21.11.1948
GER 20.04.1903 (01.05.1903) ~ 30.11.1947 (04.10.1965)

LTE 21.11.1948
GER 20.04.1903 (01.05.1903) ~ 30.11.1947 (04.10.1965)

GRANGE HILL

Grange Hill Tunnel

GRANGE HILL
Grange Hill for Chigwell Row
Grange Hill
(01.05.1903)

GOODS
(04.10.1965)

HAINAULT DEPOT (CENTRAL LINE) (14.12.1947)

CLEANING SHED

GOODS
(01.10.1908)

HAINAULT (01.05.1903)

GER 20.04.1903 (01.05.1903) ~ 30.11.1947 (04.10.1965)

LPTB 14.12.1947 (31.05.1948)

FAIRLOP (01.05.1903)

GOODS
(24.03.1958)

Fairlop Lake

Wagon Works

Body Works

LPTB 14.12.1947 (31.05.1948)
GER 20.04.1903 (01.05.1903) ~ 30.11.1947 (04.10.1965)

GOODS
(04.10.1965)

BARKINGSIDE (01.05.1903)

WORKS

NEWBURY PARK SIDINGS (14.12.1947 - ?)

LPTB 14.12.1947 (31.05.1948)
GER 20.04.1903 (01.05.1903) ~ 30.11.1947 (04.10.1965)

Departure Sidings

GANTS HILL
(14.12.1947)

GOODS
(04.10.1965)

NEWBURY PARK (01.05.1903)

LPTB
14.12.1947

GER 20.04.1903 (01.05.1903) ~ 30.11.1947 (19.03.1956)

GRAVEL PIT

East Yard Sorting Sidings

N

17

Scale

Km 0   0.5   1   1.5   2

Miles ¼   ½   ¾   1

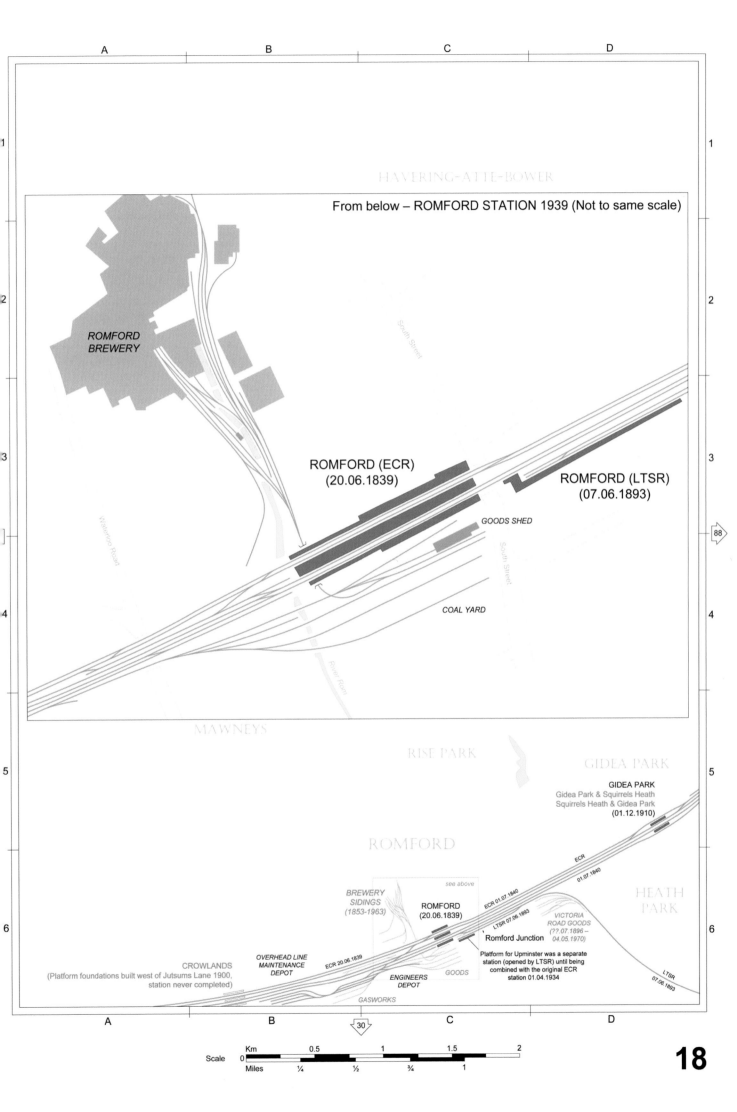

From below – ROMFORD STATION 1939 (Not to same scale)

ROMFORD
BREWERY

ROMFORD (ECR)
(20.06.1839)

ROMFORD (LTSR)
(07.06.1893)

GOODS SHED

COAL YARD

GIDEA PARK
Gidea Park & Squirrels Heath
Squirrels Heath & Gidea Park
(01.12.1910)

BREWERY
SIDINGS
(1853-1963)

ROMFORD
(20.06.1839)

see above

ECR 01.07.1840

ECR
01.07.1840

LTSR 07.06.1893

VICTORIA
ROAD GOODS
(??.07.1896 –
04.05.1970)

Romford Junction

Platform for Upminster was a separate
station (opened by LTSR) until being
combined with the original ECR
station 01.04.1934

CROWLANDS
(Platform foundations built west of Jutsums Lane 1900,
station never completed)

OVERHEAD LINE
MAINTENANCE
DEPOT

ECR 20.06.1839

ENGINEERS
DEPOT

GOODS

LTSR
07.06.1893

GASWORKS

Scale

Km   0   0.5   1   1.5   2

Miles   ¼   ½   ¾   1

18

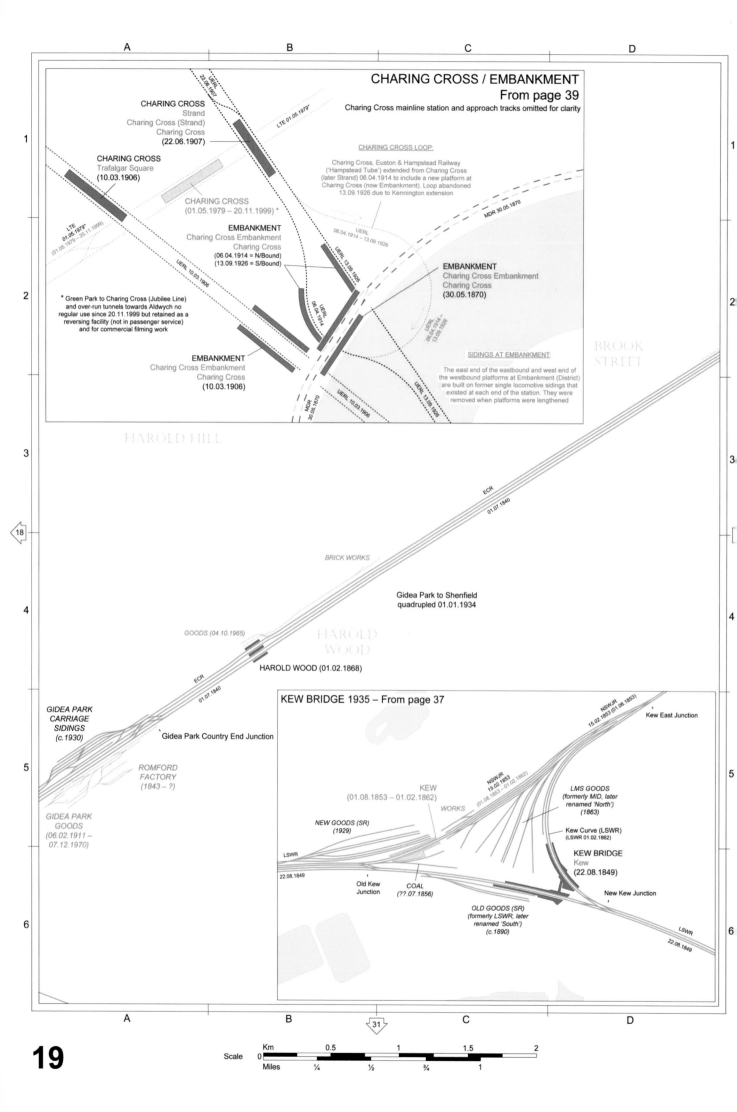

CHARING CROSS / EMBANKMENT
From page 39
Charing Cross mainline station and approach tracks omitted for clarity

CHARING CROSS
Strand
Charing Cross (Strand)
Charing Cross
(22.06.1907)

CHARING CROSS
Trafalgar Square
(10.03.1906)

CHARING CROSS
(01.05.1979 – 20.11.1999) *

LTE 01.05.1979*

22.06.1907

UERL

LTE
01.06.1979*
(01.05.1979 – 20.11.1999)

UERL 10.03.1906

MDR 30.05.1870

CHARING CROSS LOOP:

Charing Cross, Euston & Hampstead Railway
('Hampstead Tube') extended from Charing Cross
(later Strand) 06.04.1914 to include a new platform at
Charing Cross (now Embankment). Loop abandoned
13.09.1926 due to Kennington extension

UERL
06.04.1914 – 13.09.1926

EMBANKMENT
Charing Cross Embankment
Charing Cross
(06.04.1914 = N/Bound)
(13.09.1926 = S/Bound)

UERL 13.09.1926

UERL 06.04.1914

EMBANKMENT
Charing Cross Embankment
Charing Cross
(30.05.1870)

UERL
06.04.1914 –
13.09.1926

* Green Park to Charing Cross (Jubilee Line)
and over-run tunnels towards Aldwych no
regular use since 20.11.1999 but retained as a
reversing facility (not in passenger service)
and for commercial filming work

EMBANKMENT
Charing Cross Embankment
Charing Cross
(10.03.1906)

MDR
30.05.1870

UERL 13.09.1926

UERL 10.03.1906

SIDINGS AT EMBANKMENT:

The east end of the eastbound and west end of
the westbound platforms at Embankment (District)
are built on former single locomotive sidings that
existed at each end of the station. They were
removed when platforms were lengthened

BROOK
STREET

HAROLD HILL

ECR
01.07.1840

BRICK WORKS

Gidea Park to Shenfield
quadrupled 01.01.1934

GOODS (04.10.1965)

HAROLD
WOOD

HAROLD WOOD (01.02.1868)

ECR
01.07.1840

GIDEA PARK
CARRIAGE
SIDINGS
(c.1930)

Gidea Park Country End Junction

ROMFORD
FACTORY
(1843 – ?)

GIDEA PARK
GOODS
(06.02.1911 –
07.12.1970)

KEW BRIDGE 1935 – From page 37

NSWJR
15.02.1853 (01.08.1853)

Kew East Junction

KEW
(01.08.1853 – 01.02.1862)

NSWJR
15.02.1853
(01.08.1853 – 01.02.1862)

LMS GOODS
(formerly MID, later
renamed 'North')
(1863)

WORKS

Kew Curve (LSWR)
(LSWR 01.02.1862)

NEW GOODS (SR)
(1929)

KEW BRIDGE
Kew
(22.08.1849)

LSWR
22.08.1849

Old Kew
Junction

COAL
(??.07.1856)

New Kew Junction

OLD GOODS (SR)
(formerly LSWR, later
renamed 'South')
(c.1890)

LSWR
22.08.1849

18

31

Scale
Km
0   0.5   1   1.5   2
Miles
¼   ½   ¾   1

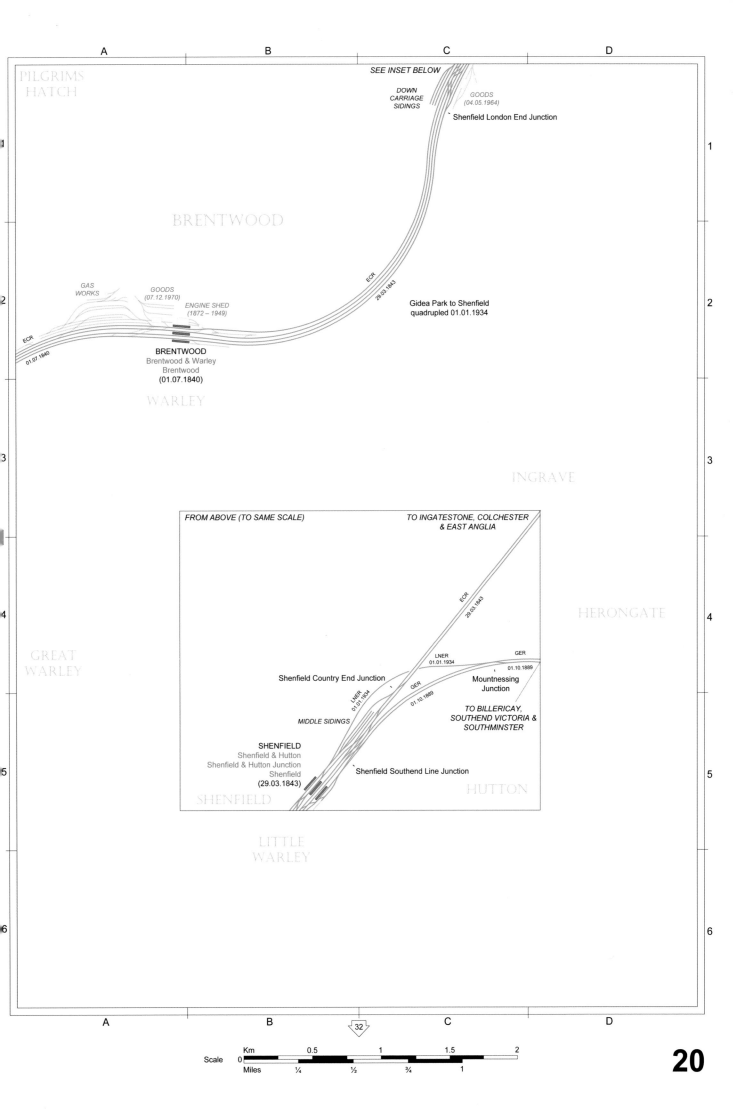

PILGRIMS
HATCH

BRENTWOOD

SEE INSET BELOW

*DOWN
CARRIAGE
SIDINGS*

*GOODS
(04.05.1964)*

Shenfield London End Junction

*GAS
WORKS*

*GOODS
(07.12.1970)*

*ENGINE SHED
(1872 – 1949)*

*ECR
29.03.1843*

Gidea Park to Shenfield
quadrupled 01.01.1934

*ECR
01.07.1840*

BRENTWOOD
Brentwood & Warley
Brentwood
(01.07.1840)

WARLEY

INGRAVE

FROM ABOVE (TO SAME SCALE)

*TO INGATESTONE, COLCHESTER
& EAST ANGLIA*

HERONGATE

*ECR
29.03.1843*

*LNER
01.01.1934*

GER

Shenfield Country End Junction

01.10.1889

Mountnessing
Junction

*LNER
01.01.1934*

*GER
01.10.1889*

*TO BILLERICAY,
SOUTHEND VICTORIA &
SOUTHMINSTER*

MIDDLE SIDINGS

SHENFIELD
Shenfield & Hutton
Shenfield & Hutton Junction
Shenfield
(29.03.1843)

Shenfield Southend Line Junction

SHENFIELD

HUTTON

GREAT
WARLEY

LITTLE
WARLEY

32

Scale

Km   0   0.5   1   1.5   2

Miles   ¼   ½   ¾   1

20

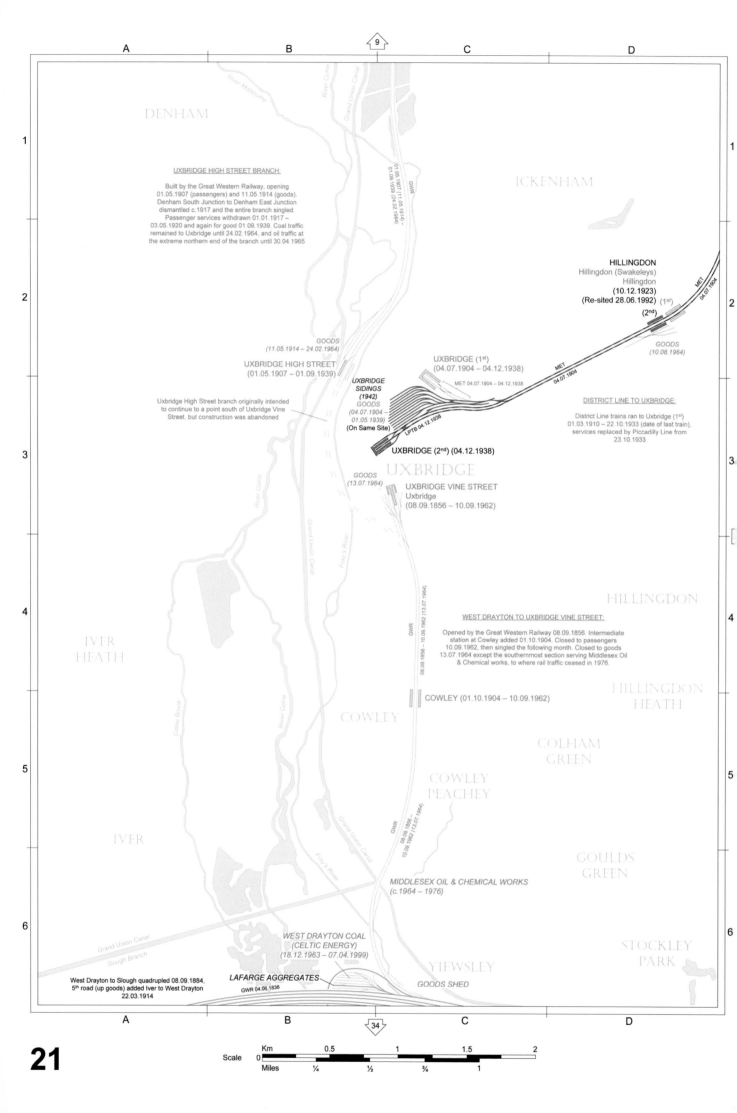

DENHAM

ICKENHAM

UXBRIDGE HIGH STREET BRANCH:

Built by the Great Western Railway, opening
01.05.1907 (passengers) and 11.05.1914 (goods).
Denham South Junction to Denham East Junction
dismantled c.1917 and the entire branch singled.
Passenger services withdrawn 01.01.1917 –
03.05.1920 and again for good 01.09.1939. Coal traffic
remained to Uxbridge until 24.02.1964, and oil traffic at
the extreme northern end of the branch until 30.04.1965

01.05.1907 (11.05.1914) –
01.09.1939 (24.02.1964)

GWR

HILLINGDON
Hillingdon (Swakeleys)
Hillingdon
(10.12.1923)
(Re-sited 28.06.1992) (1st)
(2nd)

MET
04.07.1904

GOODS
(11.05.1914 – 24.02.1964)

UXBRIDGE HIGH STREET
(01.05.1907 – 01.09.1939)

UXBRIDGE (1st)
(04.07.1904 – 04.12.1938)

GOODS
(10.08.1964)

MET 04.07.1904 – 04.12.1938

UXBRIDGE
SIDINGS
(1942)
GOODS
(04.07.1904 –
01.05.1939)
(On Same Site)

MET
04.07.1904

Uxbridge High Street branch originally intended
to continue to a point south of Uxbridge Vine
Street, but construction was abandoned

LPTB 04.12.1938

DISTRICT LINE TO UXBRIDGE:

District Line trains ran to Uxbridge (1st)
01.03.1910 – 22.10.1933 (date of last train),
services replaced by Piccadilly Line from
23.10.1933

UXBRIDGE (2nd) (04.12.1938)

GOODS
(13.07.1964)

UXBRIDGE

UXBRIDGE VINE STREET
Uxbridge
(08.09.1856 – 10.09.1962)

HILLINGDON

WEST DRAYTON TO UXBRIDGE VINE STREET:

Opened by the Great Western Railway 08.09.1856. Intermediate
station at Cowley added 01.10.1904. Closed to passengers
10.09.1962, then singled the following month. Closed to goods
13.07.1964 except the southernmost section serving Middlesex Oil
& Chemical works, to where rail traffic ceased in 1976.

IVER
HEATH

GWR
08.09.1856 – 10.09.1962 (13.07.1964)

HILLINGDON
HEATH

COWLEY (01.10.1904 – 10.09.1962)

COWLEY

COLHAM
GREEN

COWLEY
PEACHEY

GWR
08.09.1856 –
10.09.1962 (13.07.1964)

IVER

GOULDS
GREEN

MIDDLESEX OIL & CHEMICAL WORKS
(c.1964 – 1976)

WEST DRAYTON COAL
(CELTIC ENERGY)
(18.12.1963 – 07.04.1999)

YIEWSLEY

STOCKLEY
PARK

West Drayton to Slough quadrupled 08.09.1884,
5th road (up goods) added Iver to West Drayton
22.03.1914

LAFARGE AGGREGATES

GWR 04.06.1838

GOODS SHED

21

Scale
Km   0   0.5   1   1.5   2
Miles   ¼   ½   ¾   1

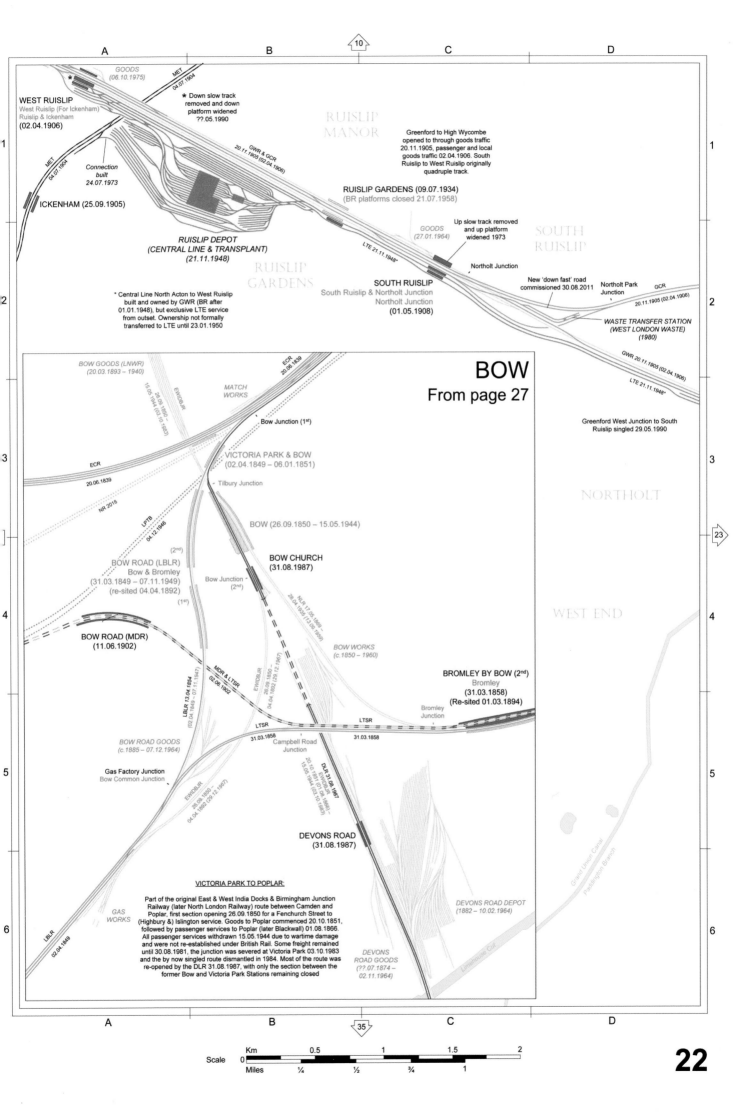

GOODS
(06.10.1975)

MET
04.07.1904

WEST RUISLIP
West Ruislip (For Ickenham)
Ruislip & Ickenham
(02.04.1906)

★ Down slow track
removed and down
platform widened
??.05.1990

RUISLIP
MANOR

Greenford to High Wycombe
opened to through goods traffic
20.11.1905, passenger and local
goods traffic 02.04.1906. South
Ruislip to West Ruislip originally
quadruple track.

MET
04.07.1904

Connection
built
24.07.1973

GWR & GCR
20.11.1905 (02.04.1906)

ICKENHAM (25.09.1905)

RUISLIP DEPOT
(CENTRAL LINE & TRANSPLANT)
(21.11.1948)

RUISLIP
GARDENS

RUISLIP GARDENS (09.07.1934)
(BR platforms closed 21.07.1958)

GOODS
(27.01.1964)

LTE 21.11.1948*

Up slow track removed
and up platform
widened 1973

SOUTH
RUISLIP

Northolt Junction

New 'down fast' road
commissioned 30.08.2011

Northolt Park
Junction

GCR
20.11.1905 (02.04.1906)

* Central Line North Acton to West Ruislip
built and owned by GWR (BR after
01.01.1948), but exclusive LTE service
from outset. Ownership not formally
transferred to LTE until 23.01.1950

SOUTH RUISLIP (01.05.1908)
South Ruislip & Northolt Junction
Northolt Junction
(01.05.1908)

WASTE TRANSFER STATION
(WEST LONDON WASTE)
(1980)

GWR 20.11.1905 (02.04.1906)

LTE 21.11.1948*

BOW
From page 27

Greenford West Junction to South
Ruislip singled 29.05.1990

BOW GOODS (LNWR)
(20.03.1893 – 1940)

EWJ&BJR
15.05.1944 (03.10.1983)
26.09.1850

MATCH
WORKS

ECR
20.06.1839

Bow Junction (1st)

VICTORIA PARK & BOW
(02.04.1849 – 06.01.1851)

ECR
20.06.1839

NR 2016

Tilbury Junction

BOW (26.09.1850 – 15.05.1944)

NORTHOLT

LPTB
04.12.1946

(2nd)

BOW ROAD (LBLR)
Bow & Bromley
(31.03.1849 – 07.11.1949)
(re-sited 04.04.1892)

BOW CHURCH
(31.08.1987)

Bow Junction
(2nd)

NLR 17.05.1869
28.04.1938 (13.06.1990)

WEST END

(1st)

BOW ROAD (MDR)
(11.06.1902)

BOW WORKS
(c.1850 – 1960)

BROMLEY BY BOW (2nd)
Bromley
(31.03.1858)
(Re-sited 01.03.1894)

MDR & LTSR
02.08.1902

EWJ&BJR
26.09.1850 (29.12.1967)

LBLR †3.04.1854
(02.04.1849 – 07.11.1947)

04.04.1892 (29.12.1967)

Bromley
Junction

LTSR
31.03.1858

LTSR
31.03.1858

Campbell Road
Junction

BOW ROAD GOODS
(c.1885 – 07.12.1964)

Gas Factory Junction
Bow Common Junction

EWJ&BJR
26.09.1850
04.04.1892 (29.12.1967)

DLR 31.08.1987
EWJ&BJR
20.10.1851 (01.08.1866)
15.05.1944 (03.10.1983)

DEVONS ROAD
(31.08.1987)

GAS
WORKS

VICTORIA PARK TO POPLAR:

Part of the original East & West India Docks & Birmingham Junction
Railway (later North London Railway) route between Camden and
Poplar, first section opening 26.09.1850 for a Fenchurch Street to
(Highbury &) Islington service. Goods to Poplar commenced 20.10.1851,
followed by passenger services to Poplar (later Blackwall) 01.08.1866.
All passenger services withdrawn 15.05.1944 due to wartime damage
and were not re-established under British Rail. Some freight remained
until 30.08.1981, the junction was severed at Victoria Park 03.10.1983
and the by now singled route dismantled in 1984. Most of the route was
re-opened by the DLR 31.08.1987, with only the section between the
former Bow and Victoria Park Stations remaining closed

DEVONS ROAD DEPOT
(1882 – 10.02.1964)

DEVONS
ROAD GOODS
(??.07.1874 –
02.11.1964)

Grand Union Canal
Paddington Branch

Limehouse Cut

LBLR
02.04.1849

Km
0   0.5   1   1.5   2
Scale
Miles
¼   ½   ¾   1

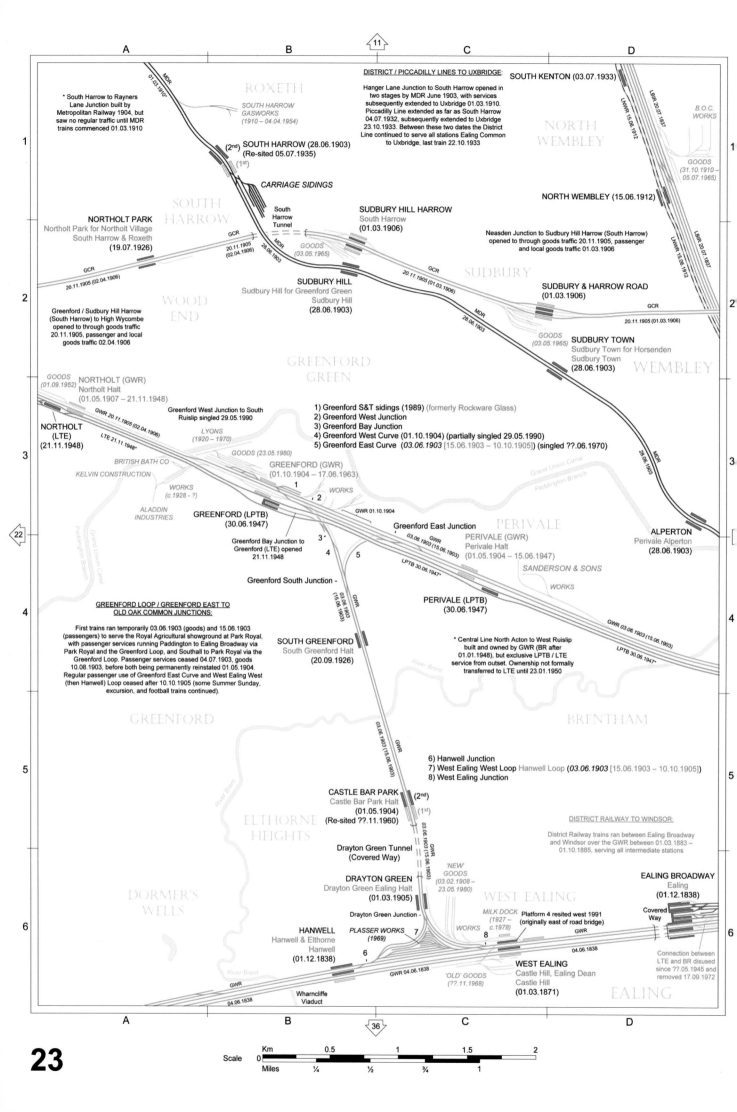

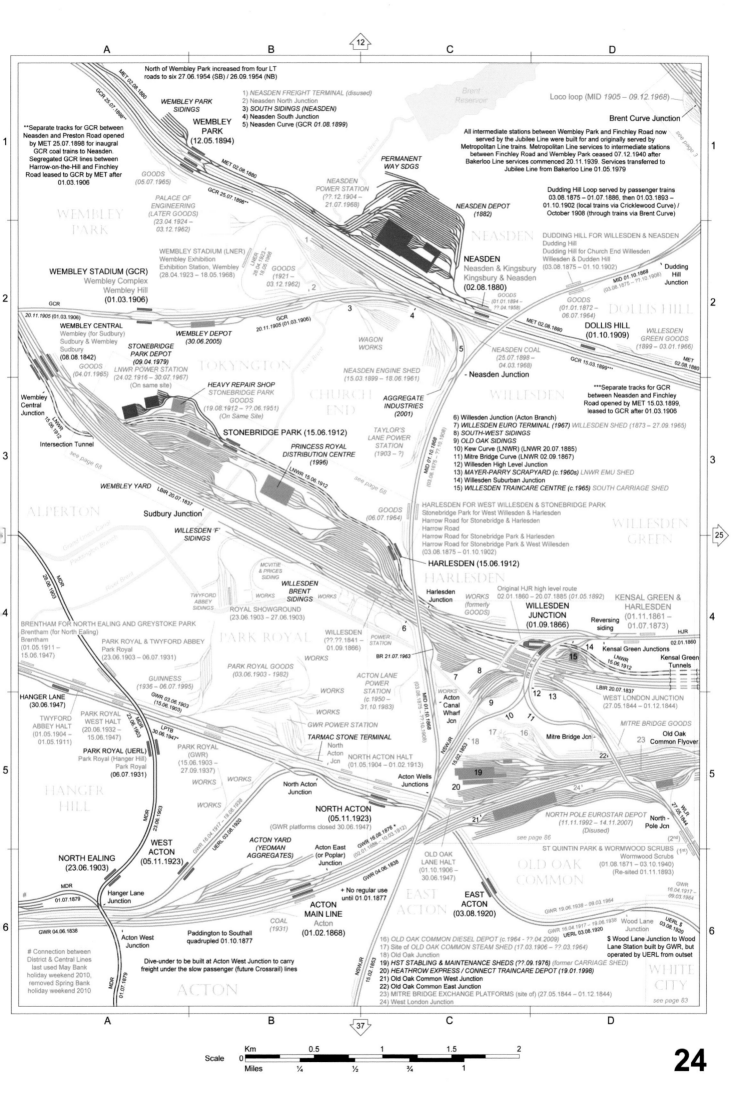

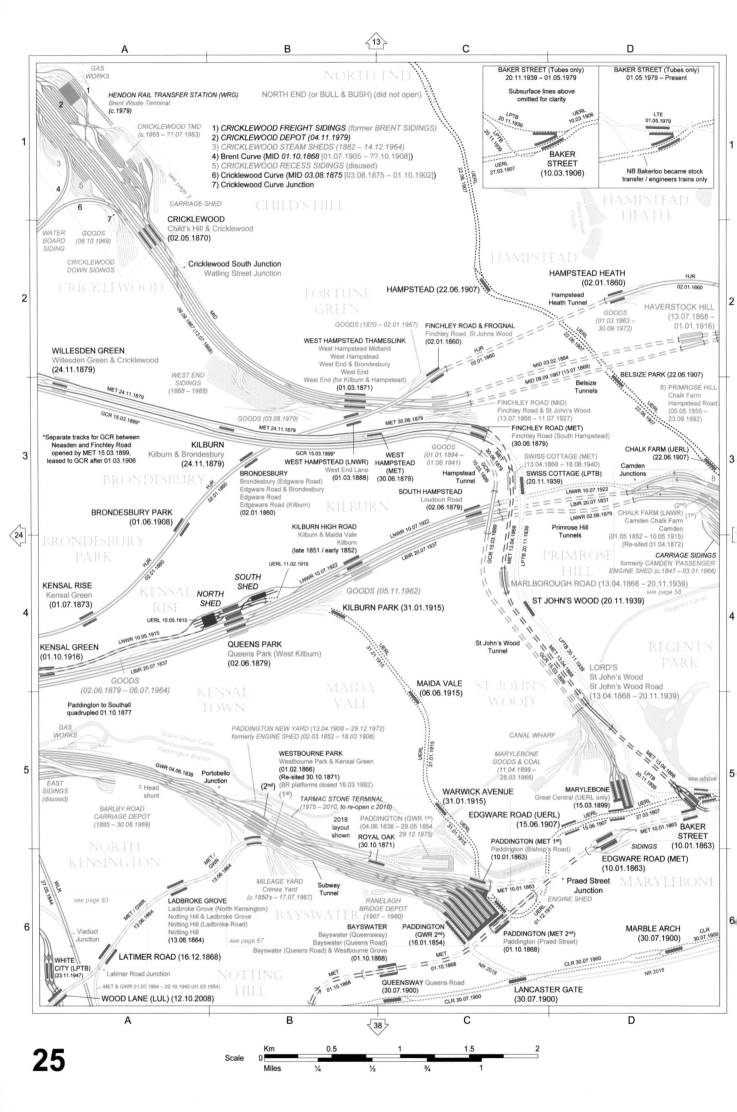

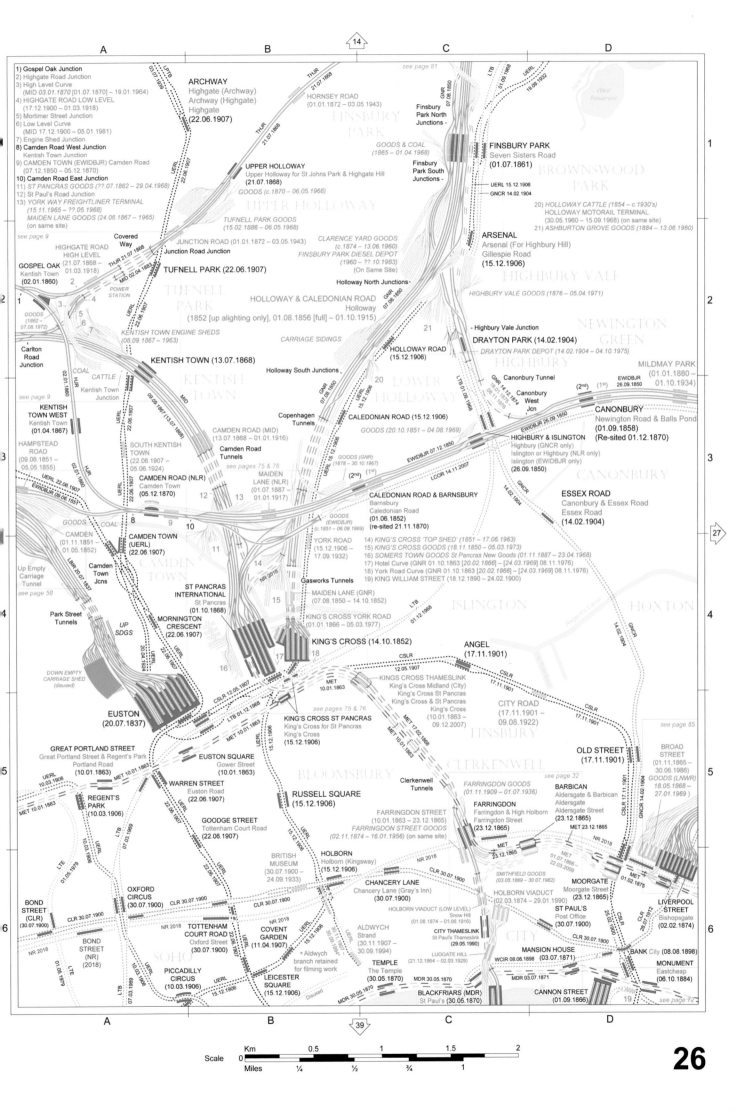

see page 81

ARCHWAY
Highgate (Archway)
Archway (Highgate)
Highgate
(22.06.1907)

HORNSEY ROAD
(01.01.1872 – 03.05.1943)

1) Gospel Oak Junction
2) Highgate Road Junction
3) High Level Curve
(MID 03.01.1870 [01.07.1870] – 19.01.1964)
4) HIGHGATE ROAD LOW LEVEL
(17.12.1900 – 01.03.1918)
5) Mortimer Street Junction
6) Low Level Curve
(MID 17.12.1900 – 05.01.1981)
7) Engine Shed Junction
8) Camden Road West Junction
Kentish Town Junction
9) CAMDEN TOWN (EWIDBJR) Camden Road
(07.12.1850 – 05.12.1870)
10) Camden Road East Junction
11) ST PANCRAS GOODS (??.07.1862 – 29.04.1968)
12) St Paul's Road Junction
13) YORK WAY FREIGHTLINER TERMINAL
(15.11.1965 – ??.05.1968)
MAIDEN LANE GOODS (24.06.1867 – 1965)
(on same site)

see page 9

GOODS & COAL
(1865 – 01.04.1968)

FINSBURY PARK
Seven Sisters Road
(01.07.1861)

UPPER HOLLOWAY
Upper Holloway for St Johns Park & Highgate Hill
(21.07.1868)
GOODS (c.1870 – 06.05.1968)

Finsbury Park North
Junctions -

Finsbury
Park South
Junctions -

UERL 15.12.1906
GNCR 14.02.1904

BROWNSWOOD PARK

HIGHGATE ROAD
HIGH LEVEL
GOSPEL OAK
Kentish Town
(02.01.1860)

TUFNELL PARK (22.06.1907)

JUNCTION ROAD (01.01.1872 – 03.05.1943)
Junction Road Junction

TUFNELL PARK GOODS
(15.02.1886 – 06.05.1968)

CLARENCE YARD GOODS
(c.1874 – 13.06.1960)
FINSBURY PARK DIESEL DEPOT
(1960 – ??.10.1983)
(On Same Site)

20) HOLLOWAY CATTLE (1854 – c.1930's)
HOLLOWAY MOTORAIL TERMINAL
(30.05.1960 – 15.09.1968) (on same site)
21) ASHBURTON GROVE GOODS (1884 – 13.06.1960)

ARSENAL
Arsenal (For Highbury Hill)
Gillespie Road
(15.12.1906)

HIGHBURY VALE

HIGHBURY VALE GOODS (1876 – 05.04.1971)

Covered
Way

Holloway North Junctions -

NEWINGTON GREEN

KENTISH TOWN ENGINE SHEDS
(08.09.1867 – 1963)

HOLLOWAY & CALEDONIAN ROAD
Holloway
(1852 [up alighting only], 01.08.1856 [full] – 01.10.1915)

CARRIAGE SIDINGS

- Highbury Vale Junction

DRAYTON PARK (14.02.1904)
DRAYTON PARK DEPOT (14.02.1904 – 04.10.1975)

POWER
STATION

GOODS
(1862 –
07.08.1972)

KENTISH TOWN (13.07.1868)

HOLLOWAY ROAD
(15.12.1906)

Holloway South Junctions -

HIGHBURY

MILDMAY PARK
(01.01.1880 –
01.10.1934)

Carlton
Road
Junction

COAL   CATTLE
Kentish Town
Junction

Copenhagen
Tunnels

Canonbury Tunnel
Canonbury
West
Jcn

(2nd)   (1st)

see page 9

KENTISH TOWN WEST
Kentish Town
(01.04.1867)

CALEDONIAN ROAD (15.12.1906)

GOODS (20.10.1851 – 04.08.1969)

HIGHBURY & ISLINGTON
Highbury (GNCR only)
Islington or Highbury (NLR only)
Islington (EWIDBJR only)
(26.09.1850)

CANONBURY
Newington Road & Balls Pond
(01.09.1858)
(Re-sited 01.12.1870)

HAMPSTEAD
ROAD
(09.06.1851 –
05.05.1855)

SOUTH KENTISH
TOWN
(22.06.1907 –
05.06.1924)

CAMDEN ROAD (MID)
(13.07.1868 – 01.01.1916)

Camden Road
Tunnels

see pages 75 & 76

CANONBURY

CAMDEN ROAD (NLR)
Camden Town
(05.12.1870)

MAIDEN
LANE (NLR)
(01.07.1887 –
01.01.1917)

(2nd)   (1st)

GOODS (GNR)
(1878 – 30.10.1967)

ESSEX ROAD
Canonbury & Essex Road
Essex Road
(14.02.1904)

GOODS
(1862 –

CAMDEN
(01.11.1851 –
01.05.1852)

**CAMDEN TOWN
(UERL)
(22.06.1907)**

GOODS
(EWIDBJR)
(c.1851 – 06.09.1969)

CALEDONIAN ROAD & BARNSBURY
Barnsbury
Caledonian Road
(01.06.1852)
(re-sited 21.11.1870)

Camden
Town Jcns

YORK ROAD
(15.12.1906 –
17.09.1932)

14) KING'S CROSS 'TOP SHED' (1851 – 17.06.1963)
15) KING'S CROSS GOODS (18.11.1850 – 05.03.1973)
16) SOMERS TOWN GOODS St Pancras New Goods (01.11.1887 – 23.04.1968)
17) Hotel Curve (GNR 01.10.1863 [20.02.1866] – [24.03.1969] 08.11.1976)
18) York Road Curve (GNR 01.10.1863 [20.02.1866] – [24.03.1969] 08.11.1976)
19) KING WILLIAM STREET (18.12.1890 – 24.02.1900)

Up Empty
Carriage
Tunnel

see page 58

Gasworks Tunnels

ISLINGTON

HOXTON

Park Street
Tunnels

UP
SDGS

**ST PANCRAS
INTERNATIONAL**
St Pancras
(01.10.1868)

MAIDEN LANE (GNR)
(07.08.1850 – 14.10.1852)

KING'S CROSS YORK ROAD
(01.01.1866 – 05.03.1977)

DOWN EMPTY
CARRIAGE SHED
(disused)

**MORNINGTON
CRESCENT
(22.06.1907)**

KING'S CROSS (14.10.1852)

ANGEL
(17.11.1901)

**EUSTON
(20.07.1837)**

KINGS CROSS THAMESLINK
King's Cross Midland (City)
King's Cross St Pancras
King's Cross & St Pancras
King's Cross
(10.01.1863 –
09.12.2007)

CITY ROAD
(17.11.1901 –
09.08.1922)

see page 85

KING'S CROSS ST PANCRAS
King's Cross for St Pancras
King's Cross
(15.12.1906)

BROAD
STREET
(01.11.1865 –
30.06.1986)
GOODS (LNWR)
18.05.1868 –
27.01.1969)

GREAT PORTLAND STREET
Great Portland Street & Regent's Park
Portland Road
(10.01.1863)

EUSTON SQUARE
Gower Street
(10.01.1863)

**OLD STREET
(17.11.1901)**

WARREN STREET
Euston Road
(22.06.1907)

**RUSSELL SQUARE
(15.12.1906)**

Clerkenwell
Tunnels

BARBICAN
Aldersgate & Barbican
Aldersgate
Aldersgate Street
(23.12.1865)

**REGENT'S
PARK
(10.03.1906)**

GOODGE STREET
Tottenham Court Road
(22.06.1907)

FARRINGDON GOODS
(01.11.1909 – 01.07.1936)

FARRINGDON
Farringdon & High Holborn
Farringdon Street
(23.12.1865)

BRITISH
MUSEUM
(30.07.1900 –
24.09.1933)

FARRINGDON STREET
(10.01.1863 – 23.12.1865)
FARRINGDON STREET GOODS
(02.11.1874 – 16.01.1956) (on same site)

HOLBORN
Holborn (Kingsway)
(15.12.1906)

SMITHFIELD GOODS
(03.05.1869 – 30.07.1962)

MOORGATE
Moorgate Street
(23.12.1865)

**BOND
STREET
(CLR)
(30.07.1900)**

**OXFORD
CIRCUS
(30.07.1900)**

CHANCERY LANE
Chancery Lane (Gray's Inn)
(30.07.1900)

HOLBORN VIADUCT
(02.03.1874 – 29.01.1990)

**LIVERPOOL
STREET**
Bishopsgate
(02.02.1874)

HOLBORN VIADUCT (LOW LEVEL)
Snow Hill
(01.08.1874 – 01.06.1916)

ST PAUL'S
Post Office
(30.07.1900)

CITY THAMESLINK
St Paul's Thameslink
(29.05.1990)

**BOND
STREET
(NR)
(2018)**

**TOTTENHAM
COURT ROAD**
Oxford Street
(30.07.1900)

**COVENT
GARDEN
(11.04.1907)**

ALDWYCH
Strand
(30.11.1907 –
30.09.1994)

* Aldwych
branch retained
for filming work

LUDGATE HILL
(21.12.1864 – 02.03.1929)

**MANSION HOUSE
(03.07.1871)**

BANK City (08.08.1898)

**PICCADILLY
CIRCUS
(10.03.1906)**

**LEICESTER
SQUARE
(15.12.1906)**

TEMPLE
The Temple
(30.05.1870)

MONUMENT
Eastcheap
(06.10.1884)

BLACKFRIARS (MDR)
St Paul's **(30.05.1870)**

**CANNON STREET
(01.09.1866)**

see page 72

Scale
Km   0   0.5   1   1.5   2
Miles   ¼   ½   ¾   1

26

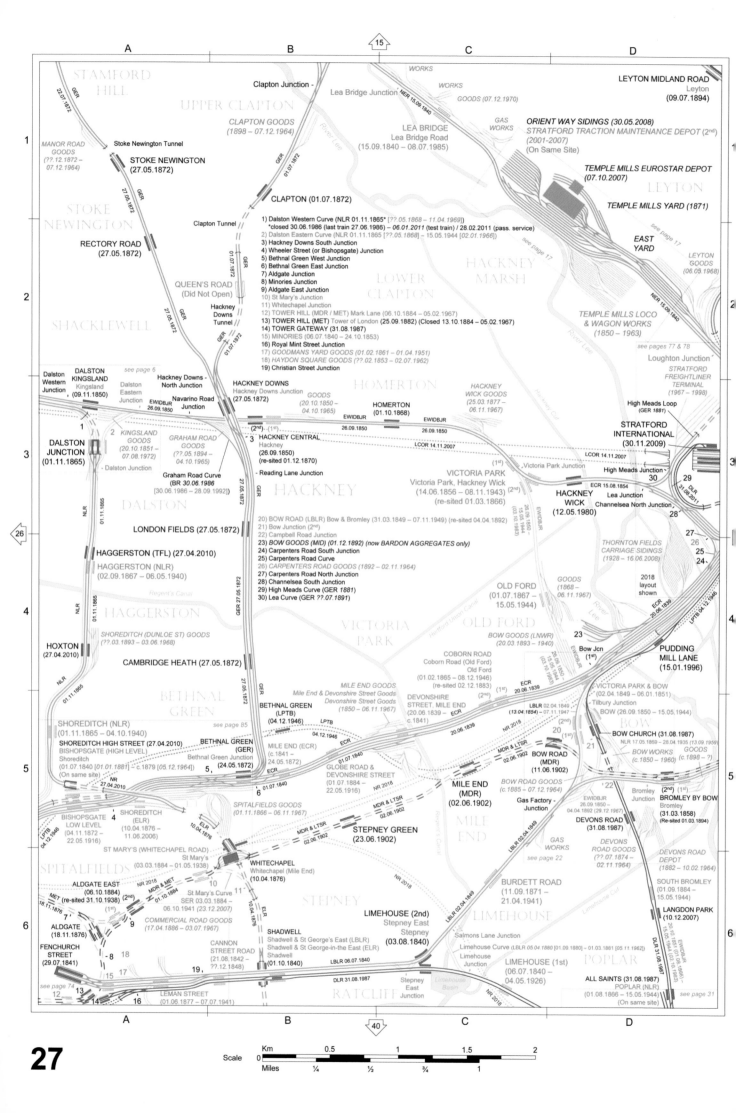

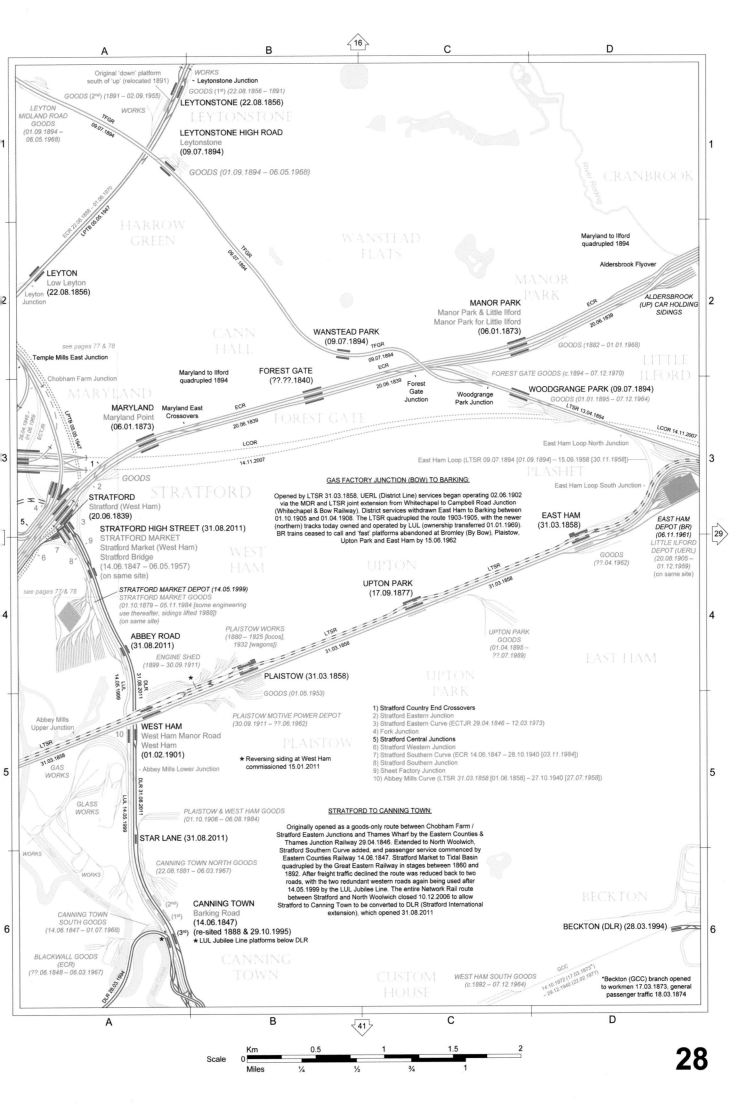

Original 'down' platform
south of 'up' (relocated 1891)

WORKS
~ Leytonstone Junction
GOODS (1ˢᵗ) (22.08.1856 – 1891)

LEYTONSTONE (22.08.1856)

GOODS (2ⁿᵈ) (1891 – 02.09.1955)

LEYTONSTONE HIGH ROAD
Leytonstone
(09.07.1894)

*LEYTON
MIDLAND ROAD
GOODS
(01.09.1894 –
06.05.1968)*

WORKS

LEYTONSTONE

GOODS (01.09.1894 – 06.05.1968)

CRANBROOK

*HARROW
GREEN*

LEYTON
Low Leyton
(22.08.1856)
Leyton
Junction

*Maryland to Ilford
quadrupled 1894*

Aldersbrook Flyover

*WANSTEAD
FLATS*

*MANOR
PARK*

ECR
20.06.1839

*ALDERSBROOK
(UP) CAR HOLDING
SIDINGS*

see pages 77 & 78

Temple Mills East Junction

~ Chobham Farm Junction

*CANN
HALL*

**WANSTEAD PARK
(09.07.1894)**

MANOR PARK
Manor Park & Little Ilford
Manor Park for Little Ilford
(06.01.1873)

*LITTLE
ILFORD*

MARYLAND

*Maryland to Ilford
quadrupled 1894*

**FOREST GATE
(??.??.1840)**

TFGR
09.07.1894

ECR
20.06.1839

Forest
Gate
Junction

GOODS (1882 – 01.01.1968)

FOREST GATE GOODS (c.1894 – 07.12.1970)

WOODGRANGE PARK (09.07.1894)

MARYLAND
Maryland Point
(06.01.1873)
Maryland East
Crossovers

ECR
20.06.1839

FOREST GATE

Woodgrange
Park Junction

GOODS (01.01.1895 – 07.12.1964)

LTSR 13.04.1854

LCOR 14.11.2007

*LCOR
14.11.2007*

East Ham Loop North Junction

GAS FACTORY JUNCTION (BOW) TO BARKING:

Opened by LTSR 31.03.1858, UERL (District Line) services began operating 02.06.1902
via the MDR and LTSR joint extension from Whitechapel to Campbell Road Junction
(Whitechapel & Bow Railway). District services withdrawn East Ham to Barking between
01.10.1905 and 01.04.1908. The LTSR quadrupled the route 1903-1905, with the newer
(northern) tracks today owned and operated by LUL (ownership transferred 01.01.1969).
BR trains ceased to call and 'fast' platforms abandoned at Bromley (By Bow), Plaistow,
Upton Park and East Ham by 15.06.1962.

East Ham Loop (LTSR 09.07.1894 [01.09.1894] – 15.09.1958 [30.11.1958])

PLASHET

East Ham Loop South Junction -

STRATFORD
Stratford (West Ham)
(20.06.1839)

STRATFORD HIGH STREET (31.08.2011)
STRATFORD MARKET
Stratford Market (West Ham)
Stratford Bridge
(14.06.1847 – 06.05.1957)
(on same site)

GOODS

STRATFORD

**EAST HAM
(31.03.1858)**

*EAST HAM
DEPOT (BR)
(06.11.1961)
LITTLE ILFORD
DEPOT (UERL)
(20.08.1905 –
01.12.1959)
(on same site)*

STRATFORD MARKET DEPOT (14.05.1999)
*STRATFORD MARKET GOODS
(01.10.1879 – 05.11.1984 [some engineering
use thereafter, sidings lifted 1988])
(on same site)*

*WEST
HAM*

**UPTON PARK
(17.09.1877)**

UPTON

*GOODS
(??.04.1962)*

see pages 77 & 78

**ABBEY ROAD
(31.08.2011)**

*PLAISTOW WORKS
(1880 – 1925 [locos],
1932 [wagons])*

*LTSR
31.03.1858*

*UPTON PARK
GOODS
(01.04.1895 –
??.07.1989)*

EAST HAM

*ENGINE SHED
(1899 – 30.09.1911)*

★

PLAISTOW (31.03.1858)

*LTSR
31.03.1858*

*UPTON
PARK*

*Abbey Mills
Upper Junction*

WEST HAM
West Ham Manor Road
West Ham
(01.02.1901)

GOODS (01.05.1953)

*PLAISTOW MOTIVE POWER DEPOT
(30.09.1911 – ??.06.1962)*

1) Stratford Country End Crossovers
2) Stratford Eastern Junction
3) Stratford Eastern Curve (ECTJR 29.04.1846 – 12.03.1973)
4) Fork Junction
5) Stratford Central Junctions
6) Stratford Western Junction
7) Stratford Southern Curve (ECR 14.06.1847 – 28.10.1940 [03.11.1984])
8) Stratford Southern Junction
9) Sheet Factory Junction
10) Abbey Mills Curve (LTSR 31.03.1858 [01.06.1858] – 27.10.1940 [27.07.1958])

PLAISTOW

- Abbey Mills Lower Junction

★ Reversing siding at West Ham
commissioned 15.01.2011

*LTSR
31.03.1858*

*GAS
WORKS*

*GLASS
WORKS*

STRATFORD TO CANNING TOWN:

Originally opened as a goods-only route between Chobham Farm /
Stratford Eastern Junctions and Thames Wharf by the Eastern Counties &
Thames Junction Railway 29.04.1846. Extended to North Woolwich,
Stratford Southern Curve added, and passenger service commenced by
Eastern Counties Railway 14.06.1847. Stratford Market to Tidal Basin
quadrupled by the Great Eastern Railway in stages between 1860 and
1892. After freight traffic declined the route was reduced back to two
roads, with the two redundant western roads again being used after
14.05.1999 by the LUL Jubilee Line. The entire Network Rail route
between Stratford and North Woolwich closed 10.12.2006 to allow
Stratford to Canning Town to be converted to DLR (Stratford International
extension), which opened 31.08.2011

*PLAISTOW & WEST HAM GOODS
(01.10.1906 – 06.08.1984)*

WORKS

STAR LANE (31.08.2011)

*CANNING TOWN NORTH GOODS
(22.08.1881 – 06.03.1967)*

WORKS

BECKTON

*CANNING TOWN
SOUTH GOODS
(14.06.1847 – 01.07.1968)*

(2ⁿᵈ)

CANNING TOWN
Barking Road
(14.06.1847)
(re-sited 1888 & 29.10.1995)
★ LUL Jubilee Line platforms below DLR

(1ˢᵗ)

(3ʳᵈ)

BECKTON (DLR) (28.03.1994)

*BLACKWALL GOODS
(ECR)
(??.06.1848 – 06.03.1967)*

★

*CANNING
TOWN*

*CUSTOM
HOUSE*

*WEST HAM SOUTH GOODS
(c.1892 – 07.12.1964)*

*GCC
14.10.1872 (17.03.1873*)
– 29.12.1940 (22.02.1971)*

*Beckton (GCC) branch opened
to workmen 17.03.1873, general
passenger traffic 18.03.1874

DLR 28.03.1994

Scale
Km
0   0.5   1   1.5   2
Miles
¼   ½   ¾   1

GER line from Newbury Park to Ilford / Seven Kings closed to passengers 30.11.1947 and freight 19.03.1956. Western curve closed to passenger and goods traffic 30.11.1947, eastern ('Seven Kings') curve never saw regular passenger traffic and was closed to goods 19.03.1956. Triangular junction formation obliterated by Ilford Depot 'New Shed' 1959

SEVEN KINGS

Ilford to Romford quadrupled 1899

CHADWELL HEATH
Chadwell Heath For Becontree
(11.01.1864)

ECR

ECR

20.06.1839

*GOODS
(1876 –
07.12.1970)*

GER 20.04.1903 (01.05.1903)
– 30.11.1947 (19.03.1956)

- Newbury Park Junction

**GOODMAYES
(08.02.1901)**

*ILFORD DEPOT
(c.1900 as Carriage sidings)*

*ILFORD CAR SHEDS
(??.03.1949)*

NEW SHED
(1959)

1

2

**SEVEN KINGS
(01.03.1899)**

ECR

20.06.1839

ECR

20.06.1839

1921 – 1934

LCC

*LEY STREET
YARD SIDINGS*

Ilford Depot Country End Junction
Seven Kings West Junction

*GOODS
(03.06.1901 –
31.07.1962)*

*GOODMAYES
MARSHALLING YARD
(1899 – 1962)*

**ILFORD
(20.06.1839)**

ECR

20.06.1839

Ilford Depot London
End Junction

*ILFORD GOODS
(06.05.1968)
(Milk dock remained open until c.1980)*

Ilford Carriage
Sidings Junction

1) Newbury Park Junction to Ilford Carriage Sidings Junction
(GER 20.04.1903 [01.05.1903] – 30.11.1947)
2) Seven Kings Curve (GER 20.04.1903 – 19.03.1956)

GOODMAYES

ILFORD

LOXFORD

Barking Station Junction

* Barking West Junction

BARKING – From below

Channel Tunnel Rail Link omitted for clarity
(bored below existing railway)

WORKS

Barking Tilbury
Line Junction West

BARKING (13.04.1854)

Connection between NR and LUL
installed for engineering train / stock
transfer purposes 14.09.2008

GOODS (1st)

Barking Tilbury
Line Junction East

Barking East Junction

BECONTREE ESTATE RAILWAY

A network of temporary railways built in
connection with construction of LCC
Becontree Estate, in operation 1921-1934.
The line ran from exchange sidings at
Chadwell Heath to a jetty on the Thames,
crossing above both LTSR lines. The
northern section ran along the centre of
present-day Valence Avenue

BECONTREE

River Roding

WORKS

WORKS

Barking Station Junction

BARKING

UPNEY

BECONTREE
Gale Street Halt
(28.06.1926)

LTSR

01.05.1885

Barking West
Junction

WORKS

Barking Tilbury
Line Junction West

**BARKING
(13.04.1854)**

GOODS (1st)

Barking Tilbury
Line Junction East

*BARKING SIDINGS (??.11.1958)
BARKING GOODS (2nd)
(c.1930's – 01.04.1957)
(on same site)*

**UPNEY
(12.09.1932)**

LTSR

01.05.1885

LTSR

01.05.1885

1921 – 1934

LCC

see above

WALLEND

LCOR 14.11.2007

LTSR 13.04.1854

*HOWARD TENENS
DISTRIBUTION DEPOT*

GORESBROOK

RIPPLE LANE YARD
*(opened c.1940, expanded to 'Hump'
yard 1961, closed 1968, replaced by
Freightliner terminal 1972)*

Main lines diverted
around expanded
Ripple Lane yard
27.05.1960

WEST YARD

LTSR 13.04.1854

*FREIGHTLINER
TERMINAL
(1972)*

Renwick
Road
Junction

THAMES VIEW

GORESBROOK (Proposed)

WORKS

DLR Dagenham Dock extension was planned for opening
c.2017, but funding for project was removed by TfL November
2008 pre-Public enquiry and remains on hold

DLR
20??

LCC
1921 – 1934

CREEKMOUTH

*Beckton (GCC) branch
opened to goods 14.10.1872,
workmen 17.03.1873, general
passenger traffic 18.03.1874

*BECKTON
GAS WORKS
(14.10.1872 –
22.02.1971)*

**BARKING RIVERSIDE
(Proposed)**

WORKS

JETTY

BECKTON (GCC)
(17.03.1873* –
29.12.1940)

DLR
20??

DLR
20??

Tunnel

CREEKMOUTH (Proposed)

*BARKING POWER STATIONS 'A', 'B' & 'C'
(1925 – 26.10.1981)*

Cross Ness

JETTY

Barking Creek

Barking Point

RIVER THAMES

DLR 28.03.1994

*WINSOR
PARK*

*BECKTON DEPOT
(28.03.1994)*

BECKTON RIVERSIDE (Proposed)

JETTY

Scale

Km
0   0.5   1   1.5   2

Miles
¼   ½   ¾   1

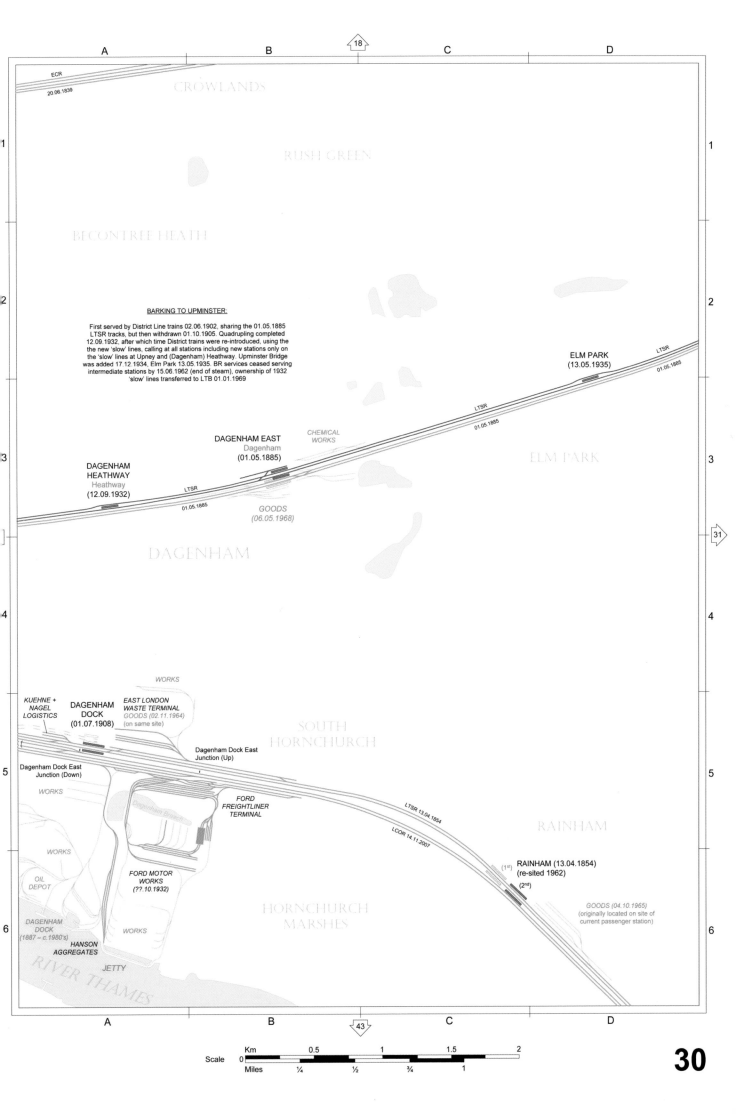

CROWLANDS

ECR
20.06.1839

RUSH GREEN

BECONTREE HEATH

BARKING TO UPMINSTER:

First served by District Line trains 02.06.1902, sharing the 01.05.1885
LTSR tracks, but then withdrawn 01.10.1905. Quadrupling completed
12.09.1932, after which time District trains were re-introduced, using the
the new 'slow' lines, calling at all stations including new stations only on
the 'slow' lines at Upney and (Dagenham) Heathway. Upminster Bridge
was added 17.12.1934, Elm Park 13.05.1935. BR services ceased serving
intermediate stations by 15.06.1962 (end of steam), ownership of 1932
'slow' lines transferred to LTB 01.01.1969

ELM PARK
(13.05.1935)

LTSR

LTSR
01.05.1885

DAGENHAM EAST
Dagenham
(01.05.1885)

CHEMICAL
WORKS

ELM PARK

LTSR
01.05.1885

DAGENHAM
HEATHWAY
Heathway
(12.09.1932)

LTSR

LTSR
01.05.1885

GOODS
(06.05.1968)

DAGENHAM

⟨31⟩

WORKS

KUEHNE +
NAGEL
LOGISTICS

DAGENHAM
DOCK
(01.07.1908)

EAST LONDON
WASTE TERMINAL
GOODS (02.11.1964)
(on same site)

SOUTH
HORNCHURCH

Dagenham Dock East
Junction (Up)

Dagenham Dock East
Junction (Down)

WORKS

FORD
FREIGHTLINER
TERMINAL

LTSR 13.04.1854

LCOR 14.11.2007

RAINHAM

WORKS

OIL
DEPOT

FORD MOTOR
WORKS
(??.10.1932)

(1st) RAINHAM (13.04.1854)
(re-sited 1962)

(2nd)

DAGENHAM
DOCK
(1887 – c.1980's)

HANSON
AGGREGATES

HORNCHURCH
MARSHES

WORKS

GOODS (04.10.1965)
(originally located on site of
current passenger station)

RIVER THAMES

JETTY

Scale

Km 0   0.5   1   1.5   2

Miles   ¼   ½   ¾   1

30

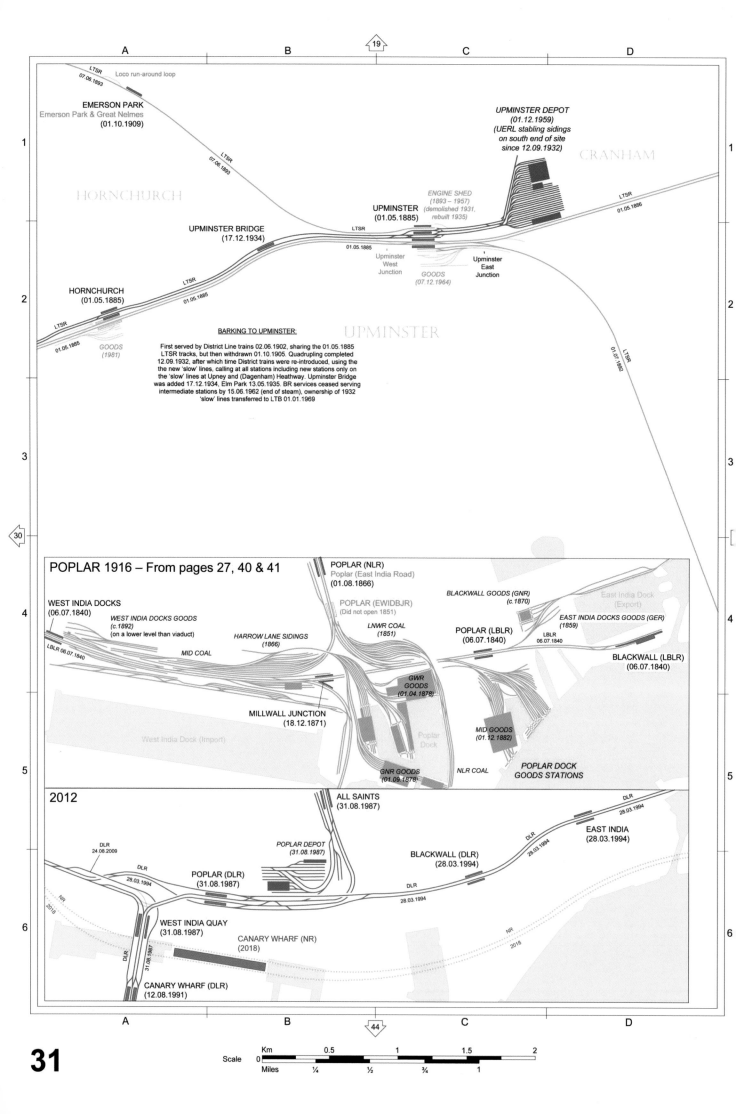

LTSR
07.06.1893

Loco run-around loop

EMERSON PARK
Emerson Park & Great Nelmes
(01.10.1909)

LTSR
07.06.1893

UPMINSTER DEPOT
(01.12.1959)
*(UERL stabling sidings
on south end of site
since 12.09.1932)*

CRANHAM

HORNCHURCH

*ENGINE SHED
(1893 – 1957)
(demolished 1931,
rebuilt 1935)*

UPMINSTER BRIDGE
(17.12.1934)

UPMINSTER
(01.05.1885)

LTSR
01.05.1886

LTSR

LTSR
01.05.1885

01.05.1885

Upminster
West
Junction

*GOODS
(07.12.1964)*

Upminster
East
Junction

LTSR

01.05.1885

HORNCHURCH
(01.05.1885)

LTSR

01.05.1885

*GOODS
(1981)*

UPMINSTER

LTSR
01.07.1892

BARKING TO UPMINSTER:

First served by District Line trains 02.06.1902, sharing the 01.05.1885
LTSR tracks, but then withdrawn 01.10.1905. Quadrupling completed
12.09.1932, after which time District trains were re-introduced, using the
new 'slow' lines, calling at all stations including new stations only on
the 'slow' lines at Upney and (Dagenham) Heathway. Upminster Bridge
was added 17.12.1934, Elm Park 13.05.1935. BR services ceased serving
intermediate stations by 15.06.1962 (end of steam), ownership of 1932
'slow' lines transferred to LTB 01.01.1969

⟨30⟩

POPLAR 1916 – From pages 27, 40 & 41

POPLAR (NLR)
Poplar (East India Road)
(01.08.1866)

*BLACKWALL GOODS (GNR)
(c.1870)*

East India Dock
(Export)

WEST INDIA DOCKS
(06.07.1840)

*WEST INDIA DOCKS GOODS
(c.1892)
(on a lower level than viaduct)*

POPLAR (EWIDBJR)
(Did not open 1851)

*LNWR COAL
(1851)*

*EAST INDIA DOCKS GOODS (GER)
(1859)*

POPLAR (LBLR)
(06.07.1840)

LBLR 06.07.1840

MID COAL

*HARROW LANE SIDINGS
(1866)*

LBLR
06.07.1840

BLACKWALL (LBLR)
(06.07.1840)

*GWR
GOODS
(01.04.1878)*

MILLWALL JUNCTION
(18.12.1871)

West India Dock (Import)

*MID GOODS
(01.12.1882)*

Poplar
Dock

*GNR GOODS
(01.09.1878)*

NLR COAL

*POPLAR DOCK
GOODS STATIONS*

2012

ALL SAINTS
(31.08.1987)

DLR
28.03.1994

DLR
24.08.2009

DLR

28.03.1994

POPLAR DEPOT
(31.08.1987)

BLACKWALL (DLR)
(28.03.1994)

DLR

28.03.1994

EAST INDIA
(28.03.1994)

NR

2018

POPLAR (DLR)
(31.08.1987)

DLR

28.03.1994

DLR
31.08.1987

WEST INDIA QUAY
(31.08.1987)

CANARY WHARF (NR)
(2018)

NR

2018

DLR

31.08.1987

CANARY WHARF (DLR)
(12.08.1991)

Scale

Km
0   0.5   1   1.5   2

Miles
¼   ½   ¾   1

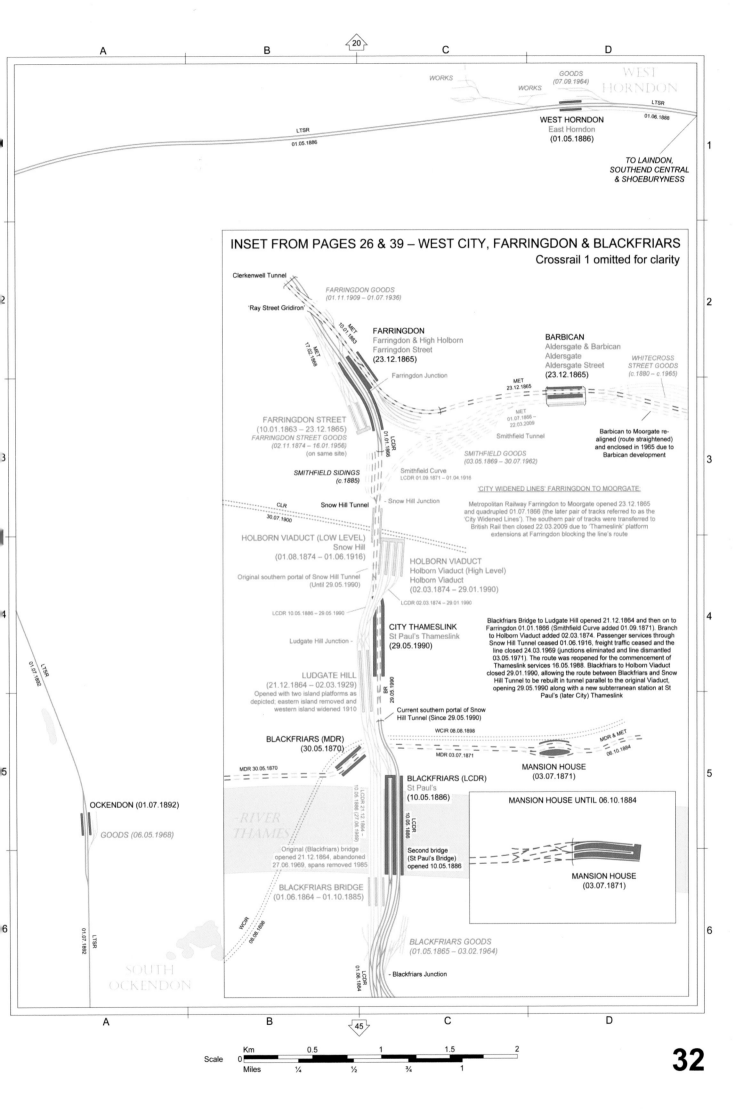

WORKS

WORKS

GOODS
(07.09.1964)

WEST
HORNDON

LTSR
01.06.1888

LTSR
01.05.1886

WEST HORNDON
East Horndon
(01.05.1886)

TO LAINDON,
SOUTHEND CENTRAL
& SHOEBURYNESS

INSET FROM PAGES 26 & 39 – WEST CITY, FARRINGDON & BLACKFRIARS
Crossrail 1 omitted for clarity

Clerkenwell Tunnel

FARRINGDON GOODS
(01.11.1909 – 01.07.1936)

'Ray Street Gridiron'

MET
10.01.1863

MET
17.02.1868

FARRINGDON
Farringdon & High Holborn
Farringdon Street
(23.12.1865)

Farringdon Junction

BARBICAN
Aldersgate & Barbican
Aldersgate
Aldersgate Street
(23.12.1865)

WHITECROSS
STREET GOODS
(c.1880 – c.1965)

MET
23.12.1865

MET
01.07.1866 –
22.03.2009

Smithfield Tunnel

Barbican to Moorgate re-
aligned (route straightened)
and enclosed in 1965 due to
Barbican development

FARRINGDON STREET
(10.01.1863 – 23.12.1865)
FARRINGDON STREET GOODS
(02.11.1874 – 16.01.1956)
(on same site)

LCDR
01.01.1866

SMITHFIELD GOODS
(03.05.1869 – 30.07.1962)

SMITHFIELD SIDINGS
(c.1885)

Smithfield Curve
LCDR 01.09.1871 – 01.04.1916

<u>'CITY WIDENED LINES' FARRINGDON TO MOORGATE:</u>

CLR
30.07.1900

Snow Hill Tunnel

- Snow Hill Junction

Metropolitan Railway Farringdon to Moorgate opened 23.12.1865
and quadrupled 01.07.1866 (the later pair of tracks referred to as the
'City Widened Lines'). The southern pair of tracks were transferred to
British Rail then closed 22.03.2009 due to 'Thameslink' platform
extensions at Farringdon blocking the line's route

HOLBORN VIADUCT (LOW LEVEL)
Snow Hill
(01.08.1874 – 01.06.1916)

HOLBORN VIADUCT
Holborn Viaduct (High Level)
Holborn Viaduct
(02.03.1874 – 29.01.1990)

Original southern portal of Snow Hill Tunnel
(Until 29.05.1990)

LCDR 02.03.1874 – 29.01.1990

LCDR 10.05.1886 – 29.05.1990

Blackfriars Bridge to Ludgate Hill opened 21.12.1864 and then on to
Farringdon 01.01.1866 (Smithfield Curve added 01.09.1871). Branch
to Holborn Viaduct added 02.03.1874. Passenger services through
Snow Hill Tunnel ceased 01.06.1916, freight traffic ceased and the
line closed 24.03.1969 (junctions eliminated and line dismantled
03.05.1971). The route was reopened for the commencement of
Thameslink services 16.05.1988. Blackfriars to Holborn Viaduct
closed 29.01.1990, allowing the route between Blackfriars and Snow
Hill Tunnel to be rebuilt in tunnel parallel to the original Viaduct,
opening 29.05.1990 along with a new subterranean station at St
Paul's (later City) Thameslink

CITY THAMESLINK
St Paul's Thameslink
(29.05.1990)

Ludgate Hill Junction -

BR
29.05.1990

LUDGATE HILL
(21.12.1864 – 02.03.1929)
Opened with two island platforms as
depicted; eastern island removed and
western island widened 1910

Current southern portal of Snow
Hill Tunnel (Since 29.05.1990)

WCIR 08.08.1898

MDR & MET
06.10.1884

BLACKFRIARS (MDR)
(30.05.1870)

MDR 03.07.1871

MDR 30.05.1870

BLACKFRIARS (LCDR)
St Paul's
(10.05.1886)

MANSION HOUSE
(03.07.1871)

MANSION HOUSE UNTIL 06.10.1884

OCKENDON (01.07.1892)

LTSR
01.07.1892

GOODS (06.05.1968)

-RIVER
THAMES

LCDR 21.12.1864 –
10.05.1886 (27.06.1969)

LCDR
10.05.1886

Original (Blackfriars) bridge
opened 21.12.1864, abandoned
27.06.1969, spans removed 1985

Second bridge
(St Paul's Bridge)
opened 10.05.1886

MANSION HOUSE
(03.07.1871)

BLACKFRIARS BRIDGE
(01.06.1864 – 01.10.1885)

WCIR
08.08.1898

SOUTH
OCKENDON

LTSR
01.07.1892

BLACKFRIARS GOODS
(01.05.1865 – 03.02.1964)

LCDR
01.06.1864

- Blackfriars Junction

LTSR
01.05.1886

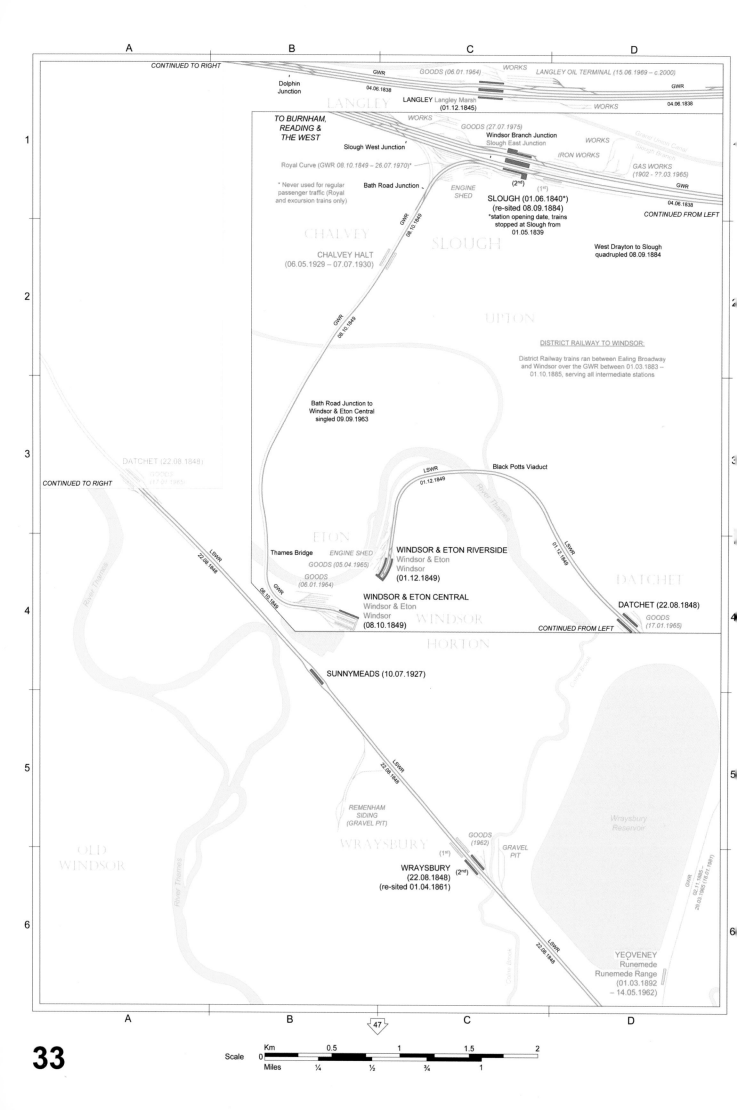

Dolphin
Junction

GWR
04.06.1838

GOODS (06.01.1964)   WORKS   LANGLEY OIL TERMINAL (15.06.1969 – c.2000)

GWR

LANGLEY   Langley Marsh
(01.12.1845)

WORKS

04.06.1838

LANGLEY

WORKS

GOODS (27.07.1975)

Windsor Branch Junction
Slough East Junction

WORKS

*Grand Union Canal
Slough Branch*

**TO BURNHAM,
READING &
THE WEST**

IRON WORKS

GAS WORKS
(1902 - ??.03.1965)

Slough West Junction

Royal Curve (GWR *08.10.1849 – 26.07.1970*)*

Bath Road Junction

ENGINE
SHED

(2nd)   (1st)

GWR

* Never used for regular
passenger traffic (Royal
and excursion trains only)

SLOUGH (01.06.1840*)
(re-sited 08.09.1884)
*station opening date, trains
stopped at Slough from
01.05.1839

04.06.1838

CONTINUED FROM LEFT

GWR
08.10.1849

CHALVEY

SLOUGH

West Drayton to Slough
quadrupled 08.09.1884

CHALVEY HALT
(06.05.1929 – 07.07.1930)

UPTON

GWR
08.10.1849

DISTRICT RAILWAY TO WINDSOR:

District Railway trains ran between Ealing Broadway
and Windsor over the GWR between 01.03.1883 –
01.10.1885, serving all intermediate stations

Bath Road Junction to
Windsor & Eton Central
singled 09.09.1963

GOODS
(17.01.1965)

LSWR
01.12.1849

Black Potts Viaduct

River Thames

LSWR
22.08.1848

ETON

Thames Bridge   ENGINE SHED

GOODS (05.04.1965)

GOODS
(06.01.1964)

GWR
08.10.1849

LSWR
01.12.1849

DATCHET

WINDSOR & ETON RIVERSIDE
Windsor & Eton
Windsor
(01.12.1849)

WINDSOR & ETON CENTRAL
Windsor & Eton
Windsor
(08.10.1849)

DATCHET (22.08.1848)

GOODS
(17.01.1965)

WINDSOR

HORTON

CONTINUED FROM LEFT

River Thames

Colne Brook

SUNNYMEADS (10.07.1927)

*OLD
WINDSOR*

LSWR
22.08.1848

REMENHAM
SIDING
(GRAVEL PIT)

WRAYSBURY

GOODS
(1962)

GRAVEL
PIT

*Wraysbury
Reservoir*

(1st)

(2nd)

WRAYSBURY
(22.08.1848)
(re-sited 01.04.1861)

Colne Brook

GWR
02.11.1885 –
29.03.1885 (16.01.1981)

LSWR
22.08.1848

YEOVENEY
Runemede
Runemede Range
(01.03.1892
– 14.05.1962)

Scale

Km   0   0.5   1   1.5   2

Miles   ¼   ½   ¾   1

33

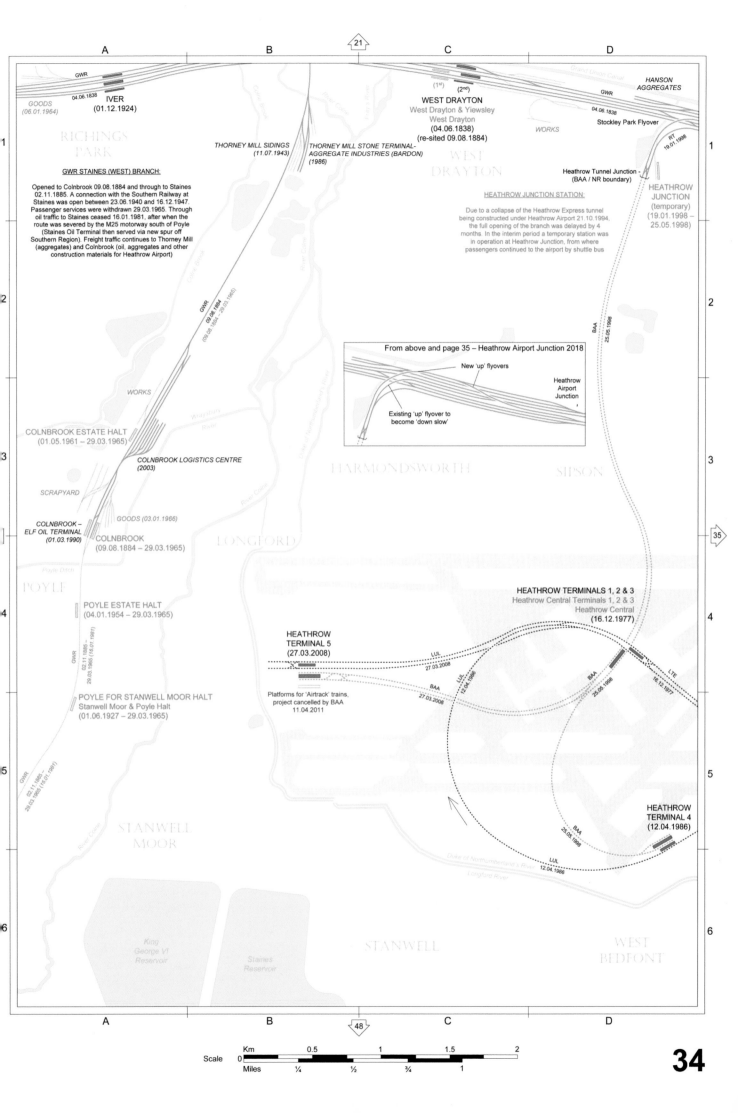

A   **B**   **C**   **D**

GWR

GOODS
(06.01.1964)

04.06.1838

IVER
(01.12.1924)

RICHINGS
PARK

THORNEY MILL SIDINGS
(11.07.1943)

THORNEY MILL STONE TERMINAL-
AGGREGATE INDUSTRIES (BARDON)
(1986)

(1st)   (2nd)

WEST DRAYTON
West Drayton & Yiewsley
West Drayton
(04.06.1838)
(re-sited 09.08.1884)

WEST
DRAYTON

HANSON
AGGREGATES

GWR

04.06.1838

Stockley Park Flyover

Brand Union Canal

WORKS

RT
19.01.1998

Heathrow Tunnel Junction -
(BAA / NR boundary)

HEATHROW
JUNCTION
(temporary)
(19.01.1998 –
25.05.1998)

GWR STAINES (WEST) BRANCH:

Opened to Colnbrook 09.08.1884 and through to Staines
02.11.1885. A connection with the Southern Railway at
Staines was open between 23.06.1940 and 16.12.1947.
Passenger services were withdrawn 29.03.1965. Through
oil traffic to Staines ceased 16.01.1981, after when the
route was severed by the M25 motorway south of Poyle
(Staines Oil Terminal then served via new spur off
Southern Region). Freight traffic continues to Thorney Mill
(aggregates) and Colnbrook (oil, aggregates and other
construction materials for Heathrow Airport)

HEATHROW JUNCTION STATION:

Due to a collapse of the Heathrow Express tunnel
being constructed under Heathrow Airport 21.10.1994,
the full opening of the branch was delayed by 4
months. In the interim period a temporary station was
in operation at Heathrow Junction, from where
passengers continued to the airport by shuttle bus

GWR
09.08.1884
(09.08.1884 – 29.03.1965)

BAA
25.05.1998

From above and page 35 – Heathrow Airport Junction 2018

New 'up' flyovers

Heathrow
Airport
Junction

Existing 'up' flyover to
become 'down slow'

COLNBROOK ESTATE HALT
(01.05.1961 – 29.03.1965)

COLNBROOK LOGISTICS CENTRE
(2003)

SCRAPYARD

HARMONDSWORTH

SIPSON

GOODS (03.01.1966)

COLNBROOK –
ELF OIL TERMINAL
(01.03.1990)

COLNBROOK
(09.08.1884 – 29.03.1965)

LONGFORD

Poyle Ditch

POYLE

POYLE ESTATE HALT
(04.01.1954 – 29.03.1965)

GWR
02.11.1885 –
29.03.1965 (16.01.1981)

HEATHROW TERMINALS 1, 2 & 3
Heathrow Central Terminals 1, 2 & 3
Heathrow Central
(16.12.1977)

HEATHROW
TERMINAL 5
(27.03.2008)

LUL
27.03.2008

LUL
12.04.1986

BAA
25.05.1998

LTE
16.12.1977

POYLE FOR STANWELL MOOR HALT
Stanwell Moor & Poyle Halt
(01.06.1927 – 29.03.1965)

Platforms for 'Airtrack' trains,
project cancelled by BAA
11.04.2011

BAA
27.03.2008

LUL
27.03.2008

BAA
25.05.1998

GWR
02.11.1885 –
29.03.1965 (16.01.1981)

STANWELL
MOOR

HEATHROW
TERMINAL 4
(12.04.1986)

BAA
25.05.1998

LUL
12.04.1986

King
George VI
Reservoir

Staines
Reservoir

STANWELL

WEST
BEDFONT

Duke of Northumberland's River
Longford River

River Colne

A   **B**   **C**   **D**

Scale

Km
0   0.5   1   1.5   2

Miles
¼   ½   ¾   1

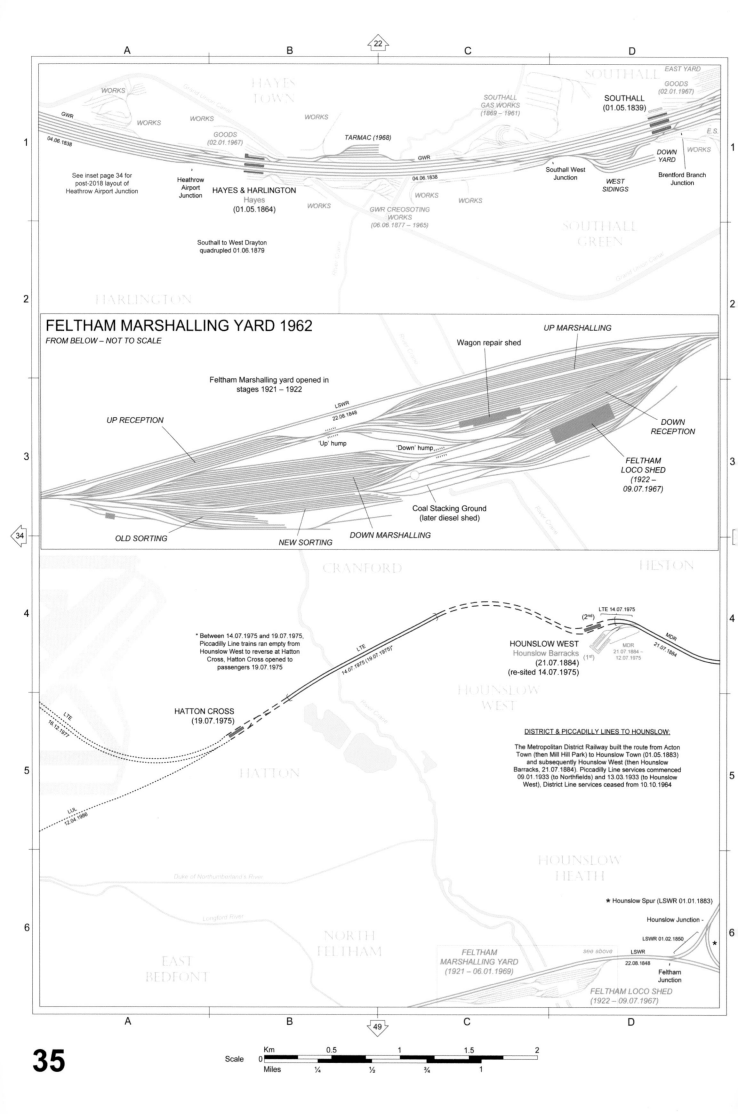

WORKS

HAYES
TOWN

SOUTHALL

EAST YARD

GOODS
(02.01.1967)

SOUTHALL
(01.05.1839)

WORKS

WORKS

WORKS

WORKS

GWR

04.06.1838

GOODS
(02.01.1967)

SOUTHALL
GAS WORKS
(1869 – 1961)

TARMAC (1968)

GWR

04.06.1838

E.S.

DOWN
YARD

WORKS

See inset page 34 for
post-2018 layout of
Heathrow Airport Junction

Heathrow
Airport
Junction

HAYES & HARLINGTON
Hayes
(01.05.1864)

Southall West
Junction

WEST
SIDINGS

Brentford Branch
Junction

WORKS

WORKS

WORKS

GWR CREOSOTING
WORKS
(06.06.1877 – 1965)

SOUTHALL
GREEN

HARLINGTON

Southall to West Drayton
quadrupled 01.06.1879

FELTHAM MARSHALLING YARD 1962

FROM BELOW – NOT TO SCALE

Feltham Marshalling yard opened in
stages 1921 – 1922

Wagon repair shed

UP MARSHALLING

UP RECEPTION

LSWR
22.06.1848

DOWN
RECEPTION

'Up' hump

'Down' hump

FELTHAM
LOCO SHED
(1922 –
09.07.1967)

Coal Stacking Ground
(later diesel shed)

OLD SORTING

NEW SORTING

DOWN MARSHALLING

CRANFORD

HESTON

LTE 14.07.1975

(2nd)

HOUNSLOW WEST
Hounslow Barracks
(21.07.1884)
(re-sited 14.07.1975)

MDR
21.07.1884

MDR
21.07.1884

* Between 14.07.1975 and 19.07.1975,
Piccadilly Line trains ran empty from
Hounslow West to reverse at Hatton
Cross, Hatton Cross opened to
passengers 19.07.1975

LTE
14.07.1975 (19.07.1975)*

(1st)

MDR
21.07.1884 –
12.07.1975

HOUNSLOW
WEST

LTE
16.12.1977

HATTON CROSS
(19.07.1975)

HATTON

DISTRICT & PICCADILLY LINES TO HOUNSLOW:

The Metropolitan District Railway built the route from Acton
Town (then Mill Hill Park) to Hounslow Town (01.05.1883)
and subsequently Hounslow West (then Hounslow
Barracks, 21.07.1884). Piccadilly Line services commenced
09.01.1933 (to Northfields) and 13.03.1933 (to Hounslow
West), District Line services ceased from 10.10.1964

LUL
12.04.1986

HOUNSLOW
HEATH

Duke of Northumberland's River

* Hounslow Spur (LSWR 01.01.1883)

Hounslow Junction -

Longford River

NORTH
FELTHAM

FELTHAM
MARSHALLING YARD
(1921 – 06.01.1969)

see above

LSWR 01.02.1850

LSWR
22.08.1848

*

EAST
BEDFONT

Feltham
Junction

FELTHAM LOCO SHED
(1922 – 09.07.1967)

Scale

Km   0   0.5   1   1.5   2

Miles   ¼   ½   ¾   1

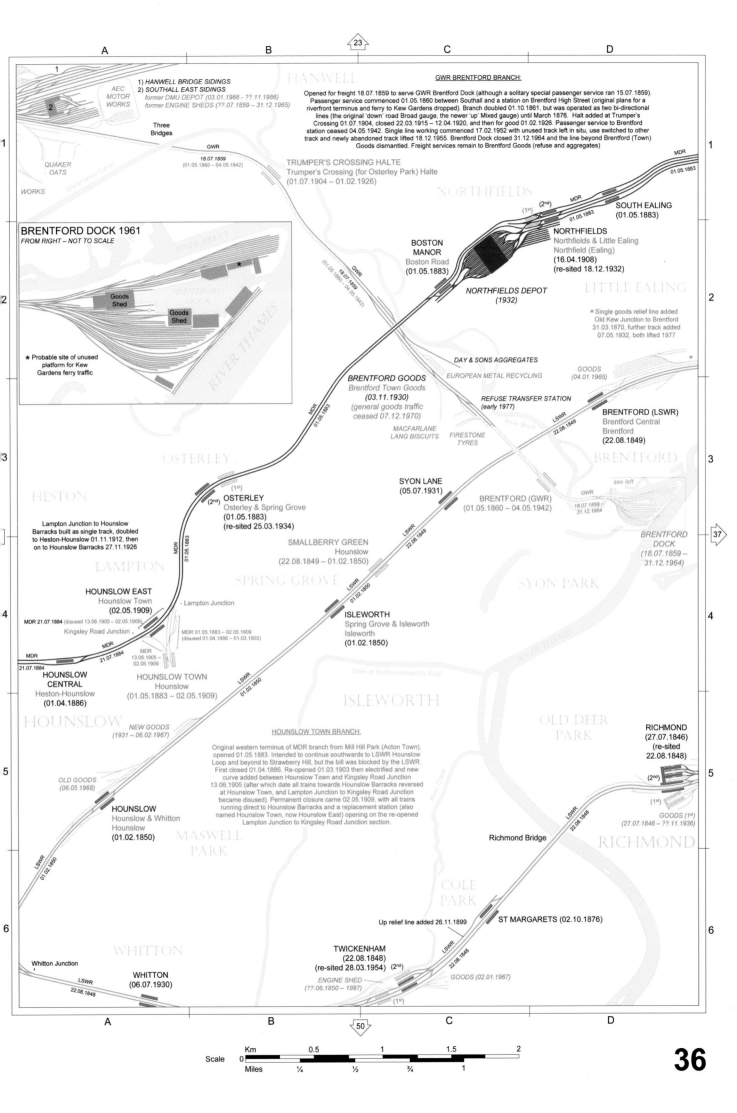

1) HANWELL BRIDGE SIDINGS
2) SOUTHALL EAST SIDINGS
former DMU DEPOT (03.01.1966 – ??.11.1986)
former ENGINE SHEDS (??.07.1859 – 31.12.1965)

AEC
MOTOR
WORKS

Three
Bridges

QUAKER
OATS

WORKS

GWR
18.07.1859
(01.05.1860 – 04.05.1942)

Grand Union Canal

GWR BRENTFORD BRANCH:

Opened for freight 18.07.1859 to serve GWR Brentford Dock (although a solitary special passenger service ran 15.07.1859). Passenger service commenced 01.05.1860 between Southall and a station on Brentford High Street (original plans for a riverfront terminus and ferry to Kew Gardens dropped). Branch doubled 01.10.1861, but was operated as two bi-directional lines (the original 'down' road Broad gauge, the newer 'up' Mixed gauge) until March 1876. Halt added at Trumper's Crossing 01.07.1904, closed 22.03.1915 – 12.04.1920, and then for good 01.02.1926. Passenger service to Brentford station ceased 04.05.1942. Single line working commenced 17.02.1952 with unused track left in situ, use switched to other track and newly abandoned track lifted 18.12.1955. Brentford Dock closed 31.12.1964 and the line beyond Brentford (Town) Goods dismantled. Freight services remain to Brentford Goods (refuse and aggregates)

HANWELL

BRENTFORD DOCK 1961
FROM RIGHT – NOT TO SCALE

RIVER BRENT

BRENTFORD DOCK

Goods
Shed

Goods
Shed

★ Probable site of unused
platform for Kew
Gardens ferry traffic

RIVER THAMES

GWR
(01.05.1860 – 04.05.1942)

TRUMPER'S CROSSING HALTE
Trumper's Crossing (for Osterley Park) Halte
(01.07.1904 – 01.02.1926)

NORTHFIELDS

MDR
01.05.1883

(1st) (2nd) MDR
01.05.1883

SOUTH EALING
(01.05.1883)

BOSTON
MANOR
Boston Road
(01.05.1883)

NORTHFIELDS
Northfields & Little Ealing
Northfield (Ealing)
(16.04.1908)
(re-sited 18.12.1932)

LITTLE EALING

NORTHFIELDS DEPOT
(1932)

★ Single goods relief line added
Old Kew Junction to Brentford
31.03.1870, further track added
07.05.1932, both lifted 1977

GOODS
(04.01.1965)

★

DAY & SONS AGGREGATES

EUROPEAN METAL RECYCLING

BRENTFORD GOODS
Brentford Town Goods
(03.11.1930)
*(general goods traffic
ceased 07.12.1970)*

REFUSE TRANSFER STATION
(early 1977)

MACFARLANE
LANG BISCUITS

FIRESTONE
TYRES

LSWR
22.08.1849

BRENTFORD (LSWR)
Brentford Central
Brentford
(22.08.1849)

BRENTFORD

MDR
01.05.1883

SYON LANE
(05.07.1931)

BRENTFORD (GWR)
(01.05.1860 – 04.05.1942)

GWR
18.07.1859 –
31.12.1964

see left

OSTERLEY

(1st)
(2nd) OSTERLEY
Osterley & Spring Grove
(01.05.1883)
(re-sited 25.03.1934)

HESTON

SMALLBERRY GREEN
Hounslow
(22.08.1849 – 01.02.1850)

LSWR
22.08.1849

SYON PARK

BRENTFORD
DOCK
(18.07.1859 –
31.12.1964)

37

Lampton Junction to Hounslow
Barracks built as single track, doubled
to Heston-Hounslow 01.11.1912, then
on to Hounslow Barracks 27.11.1926

LAMPTON

MDR
01.05.1883

SPRING GROVE

LSWR
01.02.1850

ISLEWORTH
Spring Grove & Isleworth
Isleworth
(01.02.1850)

RIVER THAMES

HOUNSLOW EAST
Hounslow Town
(02.05.1909)

- Lampton Junction

MDR 21.07.1884 (disused 13.06.1905 – 02.05.1909)

Kingsley Road Junction

MDR
21.07.1884

MDR 01.05.1883 – 02.05.1909
(disused 01.04.1886 – 01.03.1903)

MDR
13.06.1905 –
02.05.1909

MDR
21.07.1884

LSWR
01.02.1850

Duke of Northumberland's River

ISLEWORTH

OLD DEER
PARK

RICHMOND
(27.07.1846)
(re-sited
22.08.1848)

HOUNSLOW
CENTRAL
Heston-Hounslow
(01.04.1886)

HOUNSLOW TOWN
Hounslow
(01.05.1883 – 02.05.1909)

(2nd)

(1st)

GOODS (1st)
(27.07.1846 – ??.11.1936)

HOUNSLOW

NEW GOODS
(1931 – 06.02.1967)

HOUNSLOW TOWN BRANCH:

Original western terminus of MDR branch from Mill Hill Park (Acton Town), opened 01.05.1883. Intended to continue southwards to LSWR Hounslow Loop and beyond to Strawberry Hill, but the bill was blocked by the LSWR. First closed 01.04.1886. Re-opened 01.03.1903 then electrified and new curve added between Hounslow Town and Kingsley Road Junction 13.06.1905 (after which date all trains towards Hounslow Barracks reversed at Hounslow Town, and Lampton Junction to Kingsley Road Junction became disused). Permanent closure came 02.05.1909, with all trains running direct to Hounslow Barracks and a replacement station (also named Hounslow Town, now Hounslow East) opening on the re-opened Lampton Junction to Kingsley Road Junction section.

OLD GOODS
(06.05.1968)

HOUNSLOW
Hounslow & Whitton
Hounslow
(01.02.1850)

MASWELL
PARK

Richmond Bridge

RICHMOND

COLE
PARK

LSWR
22.08.1848

WHITTON

LSWR
01.02.1850

Up relief line added 26.11.1899

ST MARGARETS (02.10.1876)

Whitton Junction

LSWR
22.08.1848

WHITTON
(06.07.1930)

TWICKENHAM
(22.08.1848)
(re-sited 28.03.1954) (2nd)

ENGINE SHED
(??.06.1850 – 1897)

(1st)

LSWR
22.08.1848

GOODS (02.01.1967)

Scale
Km 0   0.5   1   1.5   2
Miles ¼   ½   ¾   1

36

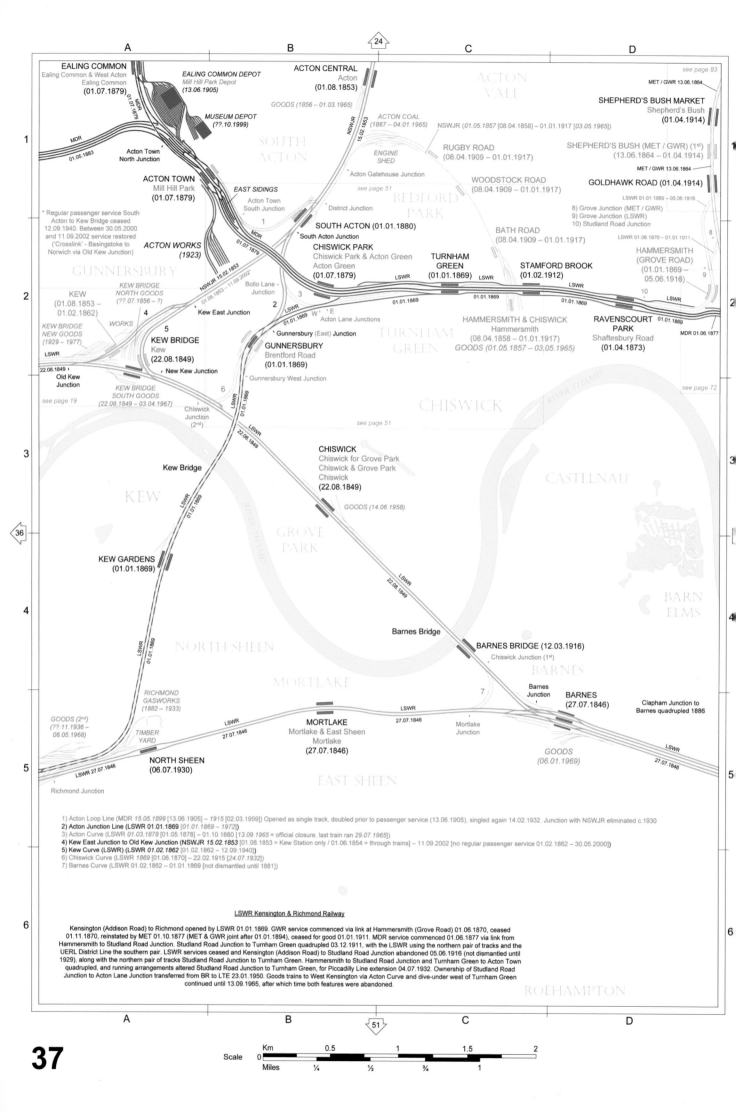

EALING COMMON
Ealing Common & West Acton
Ealing Common
(01.07.1879)

EALING COMMON DEPOT
Mill Hill Park Depot
(13.06.1905)

MUSEUM DEPOT
(??.10.1999)

ACTON CENTRAL
Acton
(01.08.1853)

GOODS (1856 – 01.03.1965)

ACTON
VALE

see page 83

MET / GWR 13.06.1864

SHEPHERD'S BUSH MARKET
Shepherd's Bush
(01.04.1914)

MDR

01.05.1883

Acton Town
North Junction

ACTON TOWN
Mill Hill Park
(01.07.1879)

EAST SIDINGS

Acton Town
South Junction

SOUTH
ACTON

ACTON COAL
1867 – 04.01.1965)

ENGINE
SHED

Acton Gatehouse Junction

see page 51

NSWJR *(01.05.1857 [08.04.1858] – 01.01.1917 [03.05.1965])*

RUGBY ROAD
(08.04.1909 – 01.01.1917)

BEDFORD
PARK

WOODSTOCK ROAD
(08.04.1909 – 01.01.1917)

SHEPHERD'S BUSH (MET / GWR) (1st)
(13.06.1864 – 01.04.1914)

MET / GWR 13.06.1864

GOLDHAWK ROAD (01.04.1914)

LSWR 01.01.1869 – 05.06.1916

8) Grove Junction (MET / GWR)
9) Grove Junction (LSWR)
10) Studland Road Junction

District Junction

SOUTH ACTON (01.01.1880)

South Acton Junction

BATH ROAD
(08.04.1909 – 01.01.1917)

LSWR 01.06.1870 – 01.01.1911

HAMMERSMITH
(GROVE ROAD)
(01.01.1869 –
05.06.1916)

* Regular passenger service South
Acton to Kew Bridge ceased
12.09.1940. Between 30.05.2000
and 11.09.2002 service restored
('Crosslink' - Basingstoke to
Norwich via Old Kew Junction)

ACTON WORKS
(1923)

CHISWICK PARK
Chiswick Park & Acton Green
Acton Green
(01.07.1879)

TURNHAM
GREEN
(01.01.1869)

STAMFORD BROOK
(01.02.1912)

GUNNERSBURY

KEW
(01.08.1853 –
01.02.1862)

KEW BRIDGE
NORTH GOODS
(??.07.1856 – ?)

Bollo Lane -
Junction

LSWR

01.01.1869

01.01.1869

LSWR

01.01.1869

8

9

10

LSWR

01.01.1869

NSWJR 15.02.1853

MDR

01.07.1879

4

2

3

Acton Lane Junctions

W

E

HAMMERSMITH & CHISWICK
Hammersmith
(08.04.1858 – 01.01.1917)
GOODS (01.05.1857 – 03.05.1965)

RAVENSCOURT
PARK
Shaftesbury Road
(01.04.1873)

01.01.1869 MDR 01.06.1877

Kew East Junction

01.06.1853 – 11.09.2002

LSWR

01.01.1869

KEW BRIDGE
NEW GOODS
(1929 – 1977)

WORKS

5

KEW BRIDGE
Kew
(22.08.1849)

Gunnersbury (East) Junction

GUNNERSBURY
Brentford Road
(01.01.1869)

LSWR

22.08.1849

New Kew Junction

Gunnersbury West Junction

TURNHAM

GREEN

Old Kew
Junction

KEW BRIDGE
SOUTH GOODS
(22.08.1849 – 03.04.1967)

see page 19

6

LSWR

01.01.1869

Chiswick
Junction
(2nd)

LSWR

22.08.1849

CHISWICK

see page 51

Kew Bridge

CHISWICK
Chiswick for Grove Park
Chiswick & Grove Park
Chiswick
(22.08.1849)

GOODS (14.06.1958)

CASTELNAU

RIVER THAMES

36

KEW

RIVER THAMES

GROVE
PARK

KEW GARDENS
(01.01.1869)

LSWR

01.01.1869

LSWR

22.08.1849

BARN
ELMS

Barnes Bridge

BARNES BRIDGE (12.03.1916)

Chiswick Junction (1st)

NORTH SHEEN

LSWR

01.01.1869

BARNES

RICHMOND
GASWORKS
(1882 – 1933)

MORTLAKE

Barnes
Junction

BARNES
(27.07.1846)

Clapham Junction to
Barnes quadrupled 1886

7

GOODS (2nd)
(??.11.1936 –
06.05.1968)

TIMBER
YARD

LSWR

27.07.1846

MORTLAKE
Mortlake & East Sheen
Mortlake
(27.07.1846)

LSWR

27.07.1846

Mortlake
Junction

GOODS
(06.01.1969)

LSWR

27.07.1846

NORTH SHEEN
(06.07.1930)

LSWR 27.07.1846

Richmond Junction

EAST SHEEN

1) Acton Loop Line (MDR *15.05.1899 [13.06.1905]* – *1915 [02.03.1959]*) Opened as single track, doubled prior to passenger service (13.06.1905), singled again 14.02.1932. Junction with NSWJR eliminated c.1930
2) Acton Junction Line (LSWR 01.01.1869 *[01.01.1869 – 1972]*)
3) Acton Curve (LSWR *01.03.1878 [01.05.1878]* – 01.10.1880 *[13.09.1965 = official closure, last train ran 29.07.1965]*)
4) Kew East Junction to Old Kew Junction (NSWJR *15.02.1853* [01.08.1853 = Kew Station only / 01.06.1854 = through trains] – 11.09.2002 [no regular passenger service 01.02.1862 – 30.05.2000])
5) Kew Curve (LSWR) (LSWR *01.02.1862* [01.02.1862 – 12.09.1940])
6) Chiswick Curve (LSWR *1869 [01.06.1870]* – 22.02.1915 [24.07.1932])
7) Barnes Curve (LSWR 01.02.1862 – 01.01.1869 [not dismantled until 1881])

LSWR Kensington & Richmond Railway

Kensington (Addison Road) to Richmond opened by LSWR 01.01.1869. GWR service commenced via link at Hammersmith (Grove Road) 01.06.1870, ceased
01.11.1870, reinstated by MET 01.10.1877 (MET & GWR joint after 01.01.1894), ceased for good 01.01.1911. MDR service commenced 01.06.1877 via link from
Hammersmith to Studland Road Junction. Studland Road Junction to Turnham Green quadrupled 03.12.1911, with the LSWR using the northern pair of tracks and the
UERL District Line the southern pair. LSWR services ceased and Kensington (Addison Road) to Studland Road Junction abandoned 05.06.1916 (not dismantled until
1929), along with the northern pair of tracks Studland Road Junction to Turnham Green. Hammersmith to Studland Road Junction and Turnham Green to Acton Town
quadrupled, and running arrangements altered Studland Road Junction to Turnham Green, for Piccadilly Line extension 04.07.1932. Ownership of Studland Road
Junction to Acton Lane Junction transferred from BR to LTE 23.01.1950. Goods trains to West Kensington via Acton Curve and dive-under west of Turnham Green
continued until 13.09.1965, after which time both features were abandoned.

ROEHAMPTON

37

Scale

Km
0   0.5   1   1.5   2

Miles
¼   ½   ¾   1

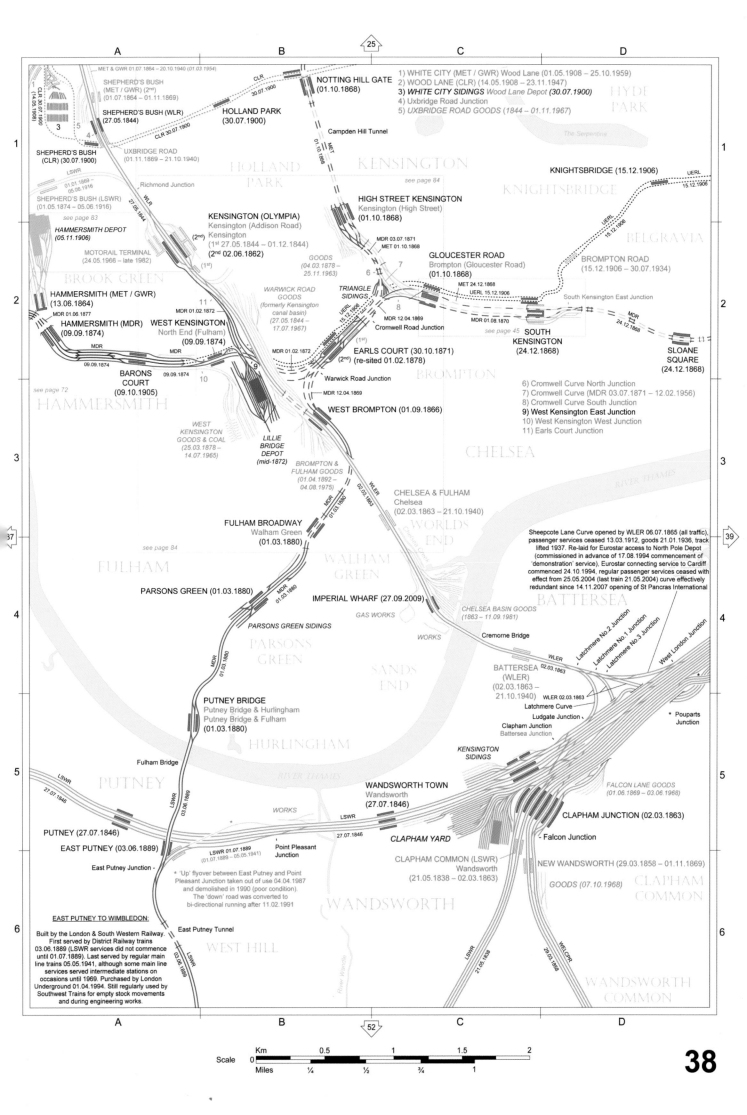

A B C D

MET & GWR 01.07.1864 – 20.10.1940 (01.03.1954)

SHEPHERD'S BUSH
(MET / GWR) (2nd)
(01.07.1864 – 01.11.1869)

SHEPHERD'S BUSH (WLR)
(27.05.1844)

CLR
30.07.1900

NOTTING HILL GATE
(01.10.1868)

HOLLAND PARK
(30.07.1900)

CLR 30.07.1900

1) WHITE CITY (MET / GWR) Wood Lane (01.05.1908 – 25.10.1959)
2) WOOD LANE (CLR) (14.05.1908 – 23.11.1947)
3) *WHITE CITY SIDINGS* Wood Lane Depot (30.07.1900)
4) Uxbridge Road Junction
5) *UXBRIDGE ROAD GOODS* (1844 – 01.11.1967)

HYDE
PARK

CLR 30.07.1900
(14.05.1908)
1 2
3 5
4

SHEPHERD'S BUSH
(CLR) (30.07.1900)

UXBRIDGE ROAD
(01.11.1869 – 21.10.1940)

LSWR

01.01.1869 –
05.06.1916

SHEPHERD'S BUSH (LSWR)
(01.05.1874 – 05.06.1916)

see page 83

HAMMERSMITH DEPOT
(05.11.1906)

MOTORAIL TERMINAL
(24.05.1966 – late 1982)

Campden Hill Tunnel

The Serpentine

KNIGHTSBRIDGE (15.12.1906)

UERL
15.12.1906

KNIGHTSBRIDGE

BELGRAVIA

MET
01.10.1868

HOLLAND
PARK

KENSINGTON

see page 84

HIGH STREET KENSINGTON
Kensington (High Street)
(01.10.1868)

BROMPTON ROAD
(15.12.1906 – 30.07.1934)

UERL
15.12.1906

Richmond Junction

WLR

27.05.1844

KENSINGTON (OLYMPIA)
Kensington (Addison Road)
Kensington
(1st 27.05.1844 – 01.12.1844)
(2nd 02.06.1862)

(2nd)

(1st)

MDR 03.07.1871
MET 01.10.1868

GOODS
(04.03.1878 –
25.11.1963)

7

6

GLOUCESTER ROAD
Brompton (Gloucester Road)
(01.10.1868)

MET 24.12.1868
UERL 15.12.1906

South Kensington East Junction

MDR
24.12.1868

BROOK GREEN

HAMMERSMITH (MET / GWR)
(13.06.1864)

MDR 01.06.1877

HAMMERSMITH (MDR)
(09.09.1874)

MDR

09.09.1874

WARWICK ROAD
SIDINGS

WARWICK ROAD
(formerly Kensington
canal basin)
(27.05.1844 –
17.07.1967)

11

WEST KENSINGTON
North End (Fulham)
(09.09.1874)

MDR 01.02.1872

TRIANGLE
SIDINGS

UERL
15.12.1906

(1st)

MDR 12.04.1869

Cromwell Road Junction

8

MDR 01.08.1870

see page 45

SOUTH
KENSINGTON
(24.12.1868)

SLOANE
SQUARE
(24.12.1868)

MDR
24.12.1868

09.09.1874

MDR

09.09.1874

BARONS
COURT
(09.10.1905)

see page 72

HAMMERSMITH

10

9

EARLS COURT (30.10.1871)
(2nd) (re-sited 01.02.1878)

Warwick Road Junction

MDR 12.04.1869

WEST
KENSINGTON
GOODS & COAL
(25.03.1878 –
14.07.1965)

LILLIE
BRIDGE
DEPOT
(mid-1872)

WEST BROMPTON (01.09.1866)

BROMPTON

CHELSEA

6) Cromwell Curve North Junction
7) Cromwell Curve (MDR 03.07.1871 – 12.02.1956)
8) Cromwell Curve South Junction
9) West Kensington East Junction
10) West Kensington West Junction
11) Earls Court Junction

BROMPTON &
FULHAM GOODS
(01.04.1892 –
04.08.1975)

RIVER THAMES

02.03.1863

WLER

MDR
01.03.1880

CHELSEA & FULHAM
Chelsea
(02.03.1863 – 21.10.1940)

FULHAM BROADWAY
Walham Green
(01.03.1880)

see page 84

FULHAM

WALHAM
GREEN

WORLDS
END

Sheepcote Lane Curve opened by WLER 06.07.1865 (all traffic),
passenger services ceased 13.03.1912, goods 21.01.1936, track
lifted 1937. Re-laid for Eurostar access to North Pole Depot
(commissioned in advance of 17.08.1994 commencement of
'demonstration' service), Eurostar connecting service to Cardiff
commenced 24.10.1994, regular passenger services ceased with
effect from 25.05.2004 (last train 21.05.2004) curve effectively
redundant since 14.11.2007 opening of St Pancras International

PARSONS GREEN (01.03.1880)

MDR
01.03.1880

IMPERIAL WHARF (27.09.2009)

GAS WORKS

WORKS

PARSONS
GREEN

PARSONS GREEN SIDINGS

CHELSEA BASIN GOODS
(1863 – 11.09.1981)

Cremorne Bridge

BATTERSEA

Latchmere No.2 Junction
Latchmere No.1 Junction
Latchmere No.3 Junction

West London Junction

PUTNEY BRIDGE
Putney Bridge & Hurlingham
Putney Bridge & Fulham
(01.03.1880)

SANDS
END

MDR

01.03.1880

WLER
02.03.1863

BATTERSEA
(WLER)
(02.03.1863 –
21.10.1940)

WLER 02.03.1863

Latchmere Curve

Ludgate Junction

* Pouparts
Junction

HURLINGHAM

Fulham Bridge

KENSINGTON
SIDINGS

Clapham Junction
Battersea Junction

LSWR

27.07.1846

PUTNEY

RIVER THAMES

WORKS

WANDSWORTH TOWN
Wandsworth
(27.07.1846)

LSWR

27.07.1846

FALCON LANE GOODS
(01.06.1869 – 03.06.1968)

CLAPHAM JUNCTION (02.03.1863)

LSWR

03.06.1889

LSWR

27.07.1846

CLAPHAM YARD

- Falcon Junction

PUTNEY (27.07.1846)

EAST PUTNEY (03.06.1889)

LSWR 01.07.1889
(01.07.1889 – 05.05.1941)

Point Pleasant
Junction

CLAPHAM COMMON (LSWR)
Wandsworth
(21.05.1838 – 02.03.1863)

NEW WANDSWORTH (29.03.1858 – 01.11.1869)

CLAPHAM
COMMON

East Putney Junction -

* 'Up' flyover between East Putney and Point
Pleasant Junction taken out of use 04.04.1987
and demolished in 1990 (poor condition).
The 'down' road was converted to
bi-directional running after 11.02.1991

GOODS (07.10.1968)

WANDSWORTH

EAST PUTNEY TO WIMBLEDON:

Built by the London & South Western Railway.
First served by District Railway trains
03.06.1889 (LSWR services did not commence
until 01.07.1889). Last served by regular main
line trains 05.05.1941, although some main
line services served intermediate stations on
occasions until 1969. Purchased by London
Underground 01.04.1994. Still regularly used by
Southwest Trains for empty stock movements
and during engineering works.

East Putney Tunnel

LSWR

03.06.1889

WEST HILL

LSWR

21.05.1838

WELCPR
29.03.1858

WANDSWORTH
COMMON

Km
Scale 0   0.5   1   1.5   2

Miles   ¼   ½   ¾   1

38

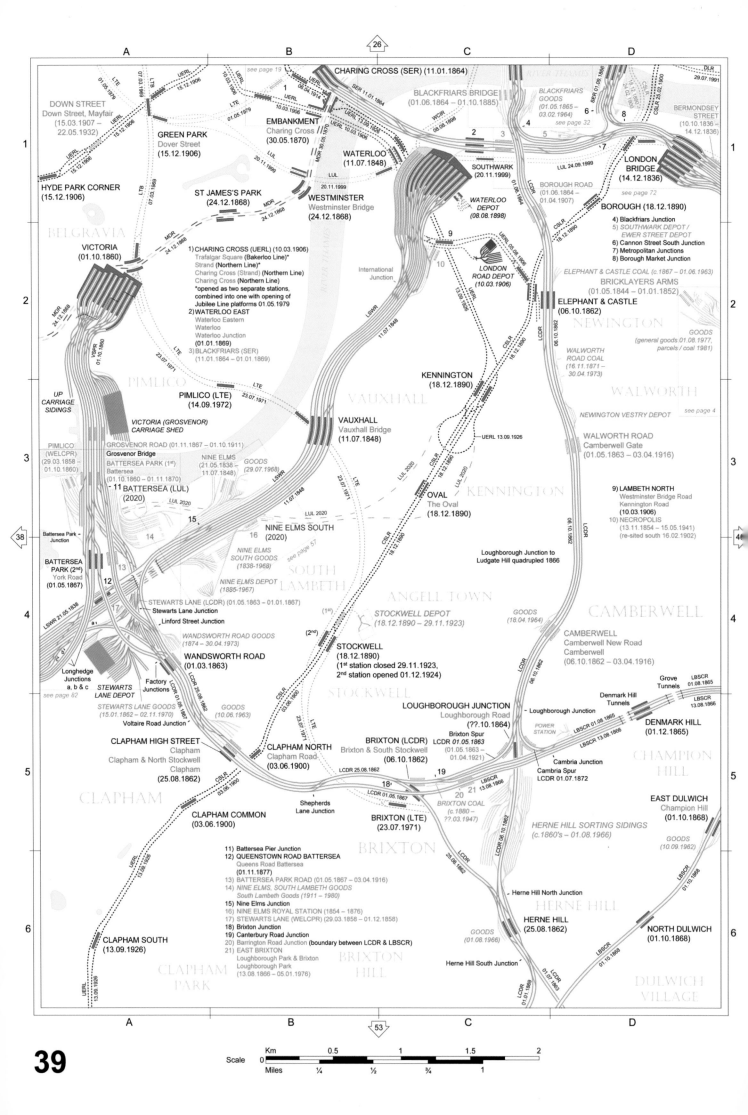

DOWN STREET
Down Street, Mayfair
(15.03.1907 –
22.05.1932)

GREEN PARK
Dover Street
(15.12.1906)

HYDE PARK CORNER
(15.12.1906)

ST JAMES'S PARK
(24.12.1868)

EMBANKMENT
Charing Cross
(30.05.1870)

WATERLOO
(11.07.1848)

WESTMINSTER
Westminster Bridge
(24.12.1868)

CHARING CROSS (SER) (11.01.1864)

BLACKFRIARS BRIDGE
(01.06.1864 – 01.10.1885)

BLACKFRIARS
GOODS
(01.05.1865 –
03.02.1964)
see page 32

BERMONDSEY ST
(10.10.1836 –
14.12.1836)

LONDON
BRIDGE
(14.12.1836)

SOUTHWARK
(20.11.1999)

WATERLOO
DEPOT
(08.08.1898)

LONDON
ROAD DEPOT
(10.03.1906)

International
Junction

BOROUGH (18.12.1890)

BOROUGH ROAD
(01.06.1864 –
01.04.1907)

see page 72

4) Blackfriars Junction
5) SOUTHWARK DEPOT /
   EWER STREET DEPOT
6) Cannon Street South Junction
7) Metropolitan Junctions
8) Borough Market Junction

VICTORIA
(01.10.1860)

1) CHARING CROSS (UERL) (10.03.1906)
   Trafalgar Square (Bakerloo Line)*
   Strand (Northern Line)*
   Charing Cross (Strand) (Northern Line)
   Charing Cross (Northern Line)
   *opened as two separate stations,
   combined into one with opening of
   Jubilee Line platforms 01.05.1979
2) WATERLOO EAST
   Waterloo Eastern
   Waterloo
   Waterloo Junction
   (01.01.1869)
3) BLACKFRIARS (SER)
   (11.01.1864 – 01.01.1869)

KENNINGTON
(18.12.1890)

ELEPHANT & CASTLE
(06.10.1862)

ELEPHANT & CASTLE COAL (01.1867 – 01.06.1963)

BRICKLAYERS ARMS
(01.05.1844 – 01.01.1852)

GOODS
(general goods 01.08.1977,
parcels / coal 1981)

WALWORTH
ROAD COAL
(16.11.1871 –
30.04.1973)

NEWINGTON VESTRY DEPOT

UP
CARRIAGE
SIDINGS

VICTORIA (GROSVENOR)
CARRIAGE SHED

PIMLICO (LTE)
(14.09.1972)

VAUXHALL
Vauxhall Bridge
(11.07.1848)

OVAL
The Oval
(18.12.1890)

UERL 13.09.1926

WALWORTH ROAD
Camberwell Gate
(01.05.1863 – 03.04.1916)

9) LAMBETH NORTH
   Westminster Bridge Road
   Kennington Road
   (10.03.1906)
10) NECROPOLIS
   (13.11.1854 – 15.05.1941)
   (re-sited south 16.02.1902)

PIMLICO
(WELCPR)
(29.03.1858 –
01.10.1860)

GROSVENOR ROAD (01.11.1867 – 01.10.1911)
Grosvenor Bridge

BATTERSEA PARK (1st)
Battersea
(01.10.1860 – 01.11.1870)

BATTERSEA (LUL)
(2020)

NINE ELMS
(21.05.1838 –
11.07.1848)

GOODS
(29.07.1968)

NINE ELMS SOUTH
(2020)

NINE ELMS
SOUTH GOODS
(1838-1968)

NINE ELMS DEPOT
(1885-1967)

Loughborough Junction to
Ludgate Hill quadrupled 1866

CAMBERWELL

GOODS
(18.04.1964)

Battersea Park –
Junction

BATTERSEA
PARK (2nd)
York Road
(01.05.1867)

STEWARTS LANE (LCDR) (01.05.1863 – 01.01.1867)
Stewarts Lane Junction
Linford Street Junction

WANDSWORTH ROAD GOODS
(1874 – 30.04.1973)

WANDSWORTH ROAD
(01.03.1863)

STOCKWELL DEPOT
(18.12.1890 – 29.11.1923)

STOCKWELL
(18.12.1890)
(1st station closed 29.11.1923,
2nd station opened 01.12.1924)

CAMBERWELL
Camberwell New Road
Camberwell
(06.10.1862 – 03.04.1916)

Grove
Tunnels

LBSCR
01.08.1865

Denmark Hill
Tunnels

LBSCR
13.08.1866

Longhedge
Junctions
a, b & c
see page 82

STEWARTS
LANE DEPOT

Factory
Junctions

STEWARTS LANE GOODS
(15.01.1862 – 02.11.1970)

Voltaire Road Junction

GOODS
(10.06.1963)

LOUGHBOROUGH JUNCTION
Loughborough Road
(??.10.1864)

Loughborough Junction

POWER
STATION

DENMARK HILL
(01.12.1865)

CHAMPION
HILL

CLAPHAM HIGH STREET
Clapham
Clapham & North Stockwell
Clapham
(25.08.1862)

CLAPHAM NORTH
Clapham Road
(03.06.1900)

BRIXTON (LCDR)
Brixton & South Stockwell
(06.10.1862)

Brixton Spur
LCDR 01.05.1863
(01.05.1863 –
01.04.1921)

Cambria Junction
Cambria Spur
LCDR 01.07.1872

EAST DULWICH
Champion Hill
(01.10.1868)

CLAPHAM
Shepherds
Lane Junction

CLAPHAM COMMON
(03.06.1900)

BRIXTON (LTE)
(23.07.1971)

BRIXTON COAL
(c.1880 –
??.03.1947)

HERNE HILL SORTING SIDINGS
(c.1860's – 01.08.1966)

GOODS
(10.09.1962)

BRIXTON

11) Battersea Pier Junction
12) QUEENSTOWN ROAD BATTERSEA
    Queens Road Battersea
    (01.11.1877)
13) BATTERSEA PARK ROAD (01.05.1867 – 03.04.1916)
14) NINE ELMS, SOUTH LAMBETH GOODS
    South Lambeth Goods (1911 – 1980)
15) Nine Elms Junction
16) NINE ELMS ROYAL STATION (1854 – 1876)
17) STEWARTS LANE (WELCPR) (29.03.1858 – 01.12.1858)
18) Brixton Junction
19) Canterbury Road Junction
20) Barrington Road Junction (boundary between LCDR & LBSCR)
21) EAST BRIXTON
    Loughborough Park & Brixton
    Loughborough Park
    (13.08.1866 – 05.01.1976)

Herne Hill North Junction

HERNE HILL
(25.08.1862)

GOODS
(01.08.1966)

NORTH DULWICH
(01.10.1868)

Herne Hill South Junction

CLAPHAM SOUTH
(13.09.1926)

Km
Scale
Miles

53

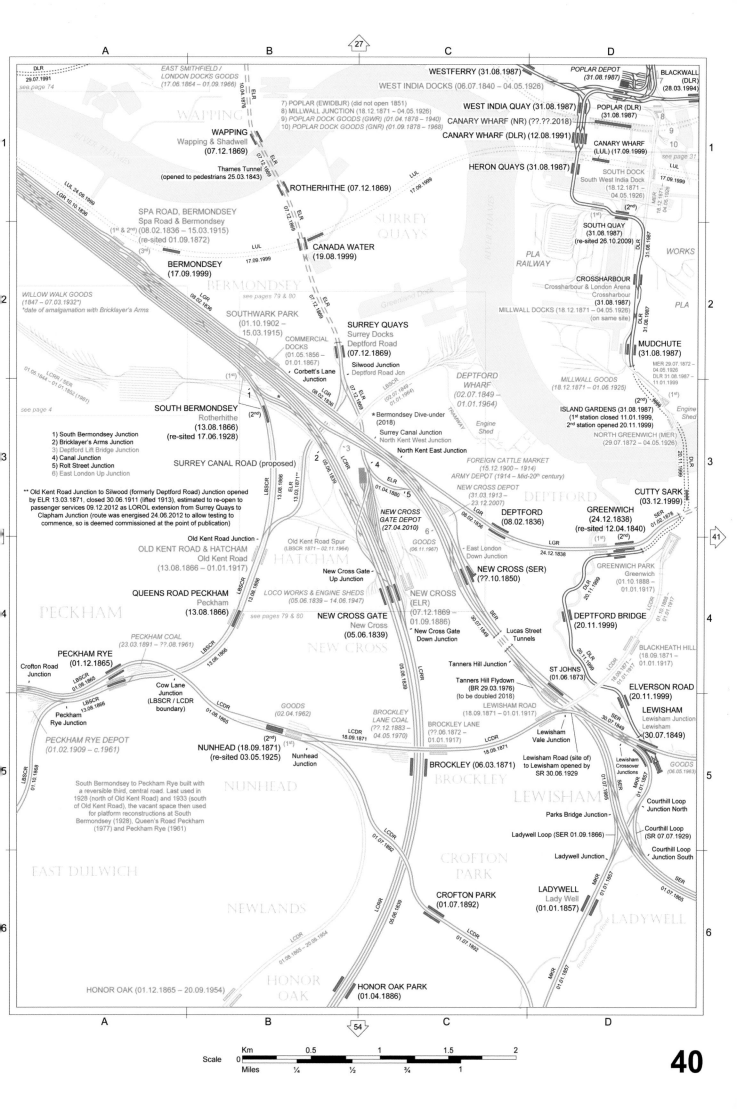

DLR
29.07.1991
see page 74

EAST SMITHFIELD /
LONDON DOCKS GOODS
(17.06.1864 – 01.09.1966)

WESTFERRY (31.08.1987)

WEST INDIA DOCKS (06.07.1840 – 04.05.1926)

POPLAR DEPOT
(31.08.1987)

BLACKWALL
(DLR)
(28.03.1994)

WAPPING

7) POPLAR (EWIDBJR) (did not open 1851)
8) MILLWALL JUNCTION (18.12.1871 – 04.05.1926)
9) POPLAR DOCK GOODS (GWR) (01.04.1878 – 1940)
10) POPLAR DOCK GOODS (GNR) (01.09.1878 – 1968)

WEST INDIA QUAY (31.08.1987)

CANARY WHARF (NR) (??.??.2018)

POPLAR (DLR)
(31.08.1987)

WAPPING
Wapping & Shadwell
(07.12.1869)

CANARY WHARF (DLR) (12.08.1991)

CANARY WHARF
(LUL) (17.09.1999)

see page 31

Thames Tunnel
(opened to pedestrians 25.03.1843)

ROTHERHITHE (07.12.1869)

HERON QUAYS (31.08.1987)

SOUTH DOCK
South West India Dock
(18.12.1871 –
04.05.1926)

SPA ROAD, BERMONDSEY
Spa Road & Bermondsey
(1st & 2nd) (08.02.1836 – 15.03.1915)
(re-sited 01.09.1872)

(3rd)

BERMONDSEY
(17.09.1999)

SURREY
QUAYS

CANADA WATER
(19.08.1999)

(1st)

(2nd)

SOUTH QUAY
(31.08.1987)
(re-sited 26.10.2009)

WILLOW WALK GOODS
(1847 – 07.03.1932*)
*date of amalgamation with Bricklayer's Arms

SOUTHWARK PARK
(01.10.1902 –
15.03.1915)

SURREY QUAYS
Surrey Docks
Deptford Road
(07.12.1869)

CROSSHARBOUR
Crossharbour & London Arena
Crossharbour
(31.08.1987)

MILLWALL DOCKS (18.12.1871 – 04.05.1926)
(on same site)

PLA
RAILWAY

WORKS

PLA

COMMERCIAL
DOCKS
(01.05.1856 –
01.01.1867)

Silwood Junction
Deptford Road Jcn

MUDCHUTE
(31.08.1987)

Corbett's Lane
Junction

LBSCR 1849
(02.07.1849 –
01.01.1964)

DEPTFORD
WHARF
(02.07.1849 –
01.01.1964)

MILLWALL GOODS
(18.12.1871 – 01.06.1925)

(1st)

(2nd)

ISLAND GARDENS (31.08.1987)
(1st station closed 11.01.1999,
2nd station opened 20.11.1999)

Engine
Shed

NORTH GREENWICH (MER)
(29.07.1872 – 04.05.1926)

SOUTH BERMONDSEY
Rotherhithe
(13.08.1866)
(re-sited 17.06.1928)

(1st)

(2nd)

* Bermondsey Dive-under
(2018)

Surrey Canal Junction
North Kent West Junction

North Kent East Junction

FOREIGN CATTLE MARKET
(15.12.1900 – 1914)
ARMY DEPOT (1914 – Mid-20th century)

CUTTY SARK
(03.12.1999)

1) South Bermondsey Junction
2) Bricklayer's Arms Junction
3) Deptford Lift Bridge Junction
4) Canal Junction
5) Rolt Street Junction
6) East London Up Junction

NEW CROSS DEPOT
(31.03.1913 –
23.12.2007)

SURREY CANAL ROAD (proposed)

NEW CROSS
GATE DEPOT
(27.04.2010)

DEPTFORD
(08.02.1836)

GREENWICH
(24.12.1838)
(re-sited 12.04.1840)

** Old Kent Road Junction to Silwood (formerly Deptford Road) Junction opened
by ELR 13.03.1871, closed 30.06.1911 (lifted 1913), estimated to re-open to
passenger services 09.12.2012 as LOROL extension from Surrey Quays to
Clapham Junction (route was energised 24.06.2012 to allow testing to
commence, so is deemed commissioned at the point of publication)

GOODS
(06.11.1967)

East London
Down Junction

(1st)

(2nd)

Old Kent Road Junction -
OLD KENT ROAD & HATCHAM
Old Kent Road
(13.08.1866 – 01.01.1917)

Old Kent Road Spur
(LBSCR 1871 – 02.11.1964)

HATCHAM

New Cross Gate -
Up Junction

NEW CROSS (SER)
(??.10.1850)

GREENWICH PARK
Greenwich
(01.10.1888 –
01.01.1917)

QUEENS ROAD PECKHAM
Peckham
(13.08.1866)

LOCO WORKS & ENGINE SHEDS
(05.06.1839 – 14.06.1947)

see pages 79 & 80

NEW CROSS
(ELR)
(07.12.1869 –
01.09.1886)

NEW CROSS GATE
New Cross
(05.06.1839)

New Cross Gate
Down Junction

DEPTFORD BRIDGE
(20.11.1999)

PECKHAM

NEW CROSS

BLACKHEATH HILL
(18.09.1871 –
01.01.1917)

PECKHAM RYE
(01.12.1865)

Crofton Road
Junction

Lucas Street
Tunnels

ELVERSON ROAD
(20.11.1999)

Cow Lane
Junction
(LBSCR / LCDR
boundary)

Tanners Hill Junction

ST JOHNS
(01.06.1873)

Peckham
Rye Junction

GOODS
(02.04.1962)

BROCKLEY
LANE COAL
(??.12.1883 –
04.05.1970)

Tanners Hill Flydown
(BR 29.03.1976)
(to be doubled 2018)

LEWISHAM ROAD
(18.09.1871 – 01.01.1917)

LEWISHAM
Lewisham Junction
Lewisham
(30.07.1849)

PECKHAM RYE DEPOT
(01.02.1909 – c.1961)

(2nd)

(1st)

Nunhead
Junction

BROCKLEY LANE
(??.06.1872 –
01.01.1917)

Lewisham Vale Junction

NUNHEAD (18.09.1871)
(re-sited 03.05.1925)

Lewisham Road (site of)
to Lewisham opened by
SR 30.06.1929

Lewisham
Crossover
Junctions

GOODS
(06.05.1962)

South Bermondsey to Peckham Rye built with
a reversible third, central road. Last used in
1928 (north of Old Kent Road) and 1933 (south
of Old Kent Road), the vacant space then used
for platform reconstructions at South
Bermondsey (1928), Queen's Road Peckham
(1977) and Peckham Rye (1961)

BROCKLEY (06.03.1871)

BROCKLEY

LEWISHAM

Courthill Loop
Junction North

Parks Bridge Junction

Courthill Loop
(SR 07.07.1929)

EAST DULWICH

Ladywell Loop (SER 01.09.1866)

Ladywell Junction

Courthill Loop
Junction South

NEWLANDS

CROFTON
PARK

CROFTON PARK
(01.07.1892)

LADYWELL
Lady Well
(01.01.1857)

LADYWELL

HONOR OAK (01.12.1865 – 20.09.1954)

HONOR
OAK

HONOR OAK PARK
(01.04.1886)

Scale
Km
0   0.5   1   1.5   2
Miles
¼   ½   ¾   1

40

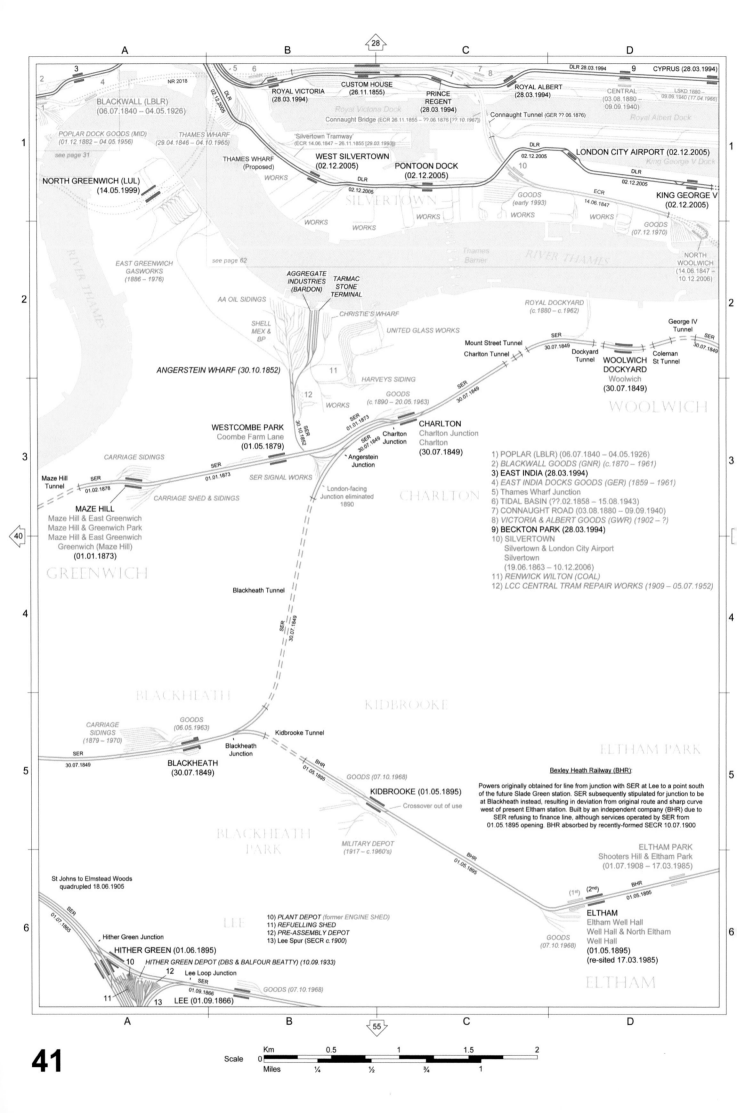

3
2
4
NR 2018
BLACKWALL (LBLR)
(06.07.1840 – 04.05.1926)
1

5   6
ROYAL VICTORIA
(28.03.1994)

CUSTOM HOUSE
(26.11.1855)

PRINCE
REGENT
(28.03.1994)

7   8
ROYAL ALBERT
(28.03.1994)

DLR 28.03.1994   9   CYPRUS (28.03.1994)

CENTRAL
(03.08.1880 –
09.09.1940)

LSKD 1880 –
09.09.1940 (17.04.1956)

POPLAR DOCK GOODS (MID)
(01.12.1882 – 04.05.1956)

THAMES WHARF
(29.04.1846 – 04.10.1965)

Royal Victoria Dock

Connaught Bridge (ECR 26.11.1855 – ??.06.1876 [??.10.1967])

Connaught Tunnel (GER ??.06.1876)

Royal Albert Dock

see page 31

THAMES WHARF
(Proposed)

'Silvertown Tramway'
(ECR 14.06.1847 – 26.11.1855 [29.03.1993])

WEST SILVERTOWN
(02.12.2005)

PONTOON DOCK
(02.12.2005)

DLR
02.12.2005

LONDON CITY AIRPORT (02.12.2005)

10   DLR
02.12.2005

King George V Dock

NORTH GREENWICH (LUL)
(14.05.1999)

WORKS

DLR
02.12.2005

ECR
14.06.1847

KING GEORGE V
(02.12.2005)

WORKS

WORKS

GOODS
(early 1993)

WORKS

WORKS

GOODS
(07.12.1970)

EAST GREENWICH
GASWORKS
(1886 – 1976)

see page 62

SILVERTOWN

Thames
Barrier

RIVER THAMES

NORTH
WOOLWICH
(14.06.1847 –
10.12.2006)

RIVER THAMES

AGGREGATE
INDUSTRIES
(BARDON)

TARMAC
STONE
TERMINAL

ROYAL DOCKYARD
(c.1880 – c.1962)

George IV
Tunnel

AA OIL SIDINGS

CHRISTIE'S WHARF

Mount Street Tunnel

SER

SER
30.07.1849

SHELL
MEX &
BP

UNITED GLASS WORKS

Charlton Tunnel

Dockyard
Tunnel

Coleman
St Tunnel

WOOLWICH

ANGERSTEIN WHARF (30.10.1852)

11

HARVEYS SIDING

SER
30.07.1849

SER
01.01.1873

Dockyard
Tunnel

WOOLWICH
DOCKYARD
Woolwich
(30.07.1849)

12

GOODS
(c.1890 – 20.05.1963)

Charlton
Junction

CHARLTON

CARRIAGE SIDINGS

WORKS

SER
01.01.1873

SER
30.07.1849

SER
30.10.1852

CHARLTON
Charlton Junction
Charlton
(30.07.1849)

WESTCOMBE PARK
Coombe Farm Lane
(01.05.1879)

SER

SER SIGNAL WORKS

Angerstein
Junction

1) POPLAR (LBLR) (06.07.1840 – 04.05.1926)
2) BLACKWALL GOODS (GNR) (c.1870 – 1961)
3) EAST INDIA (28.03.1994)
4) EAST INDIA DOCKS GOODS (GER) (1859 – 1961)
5) Thames Wharf Junction
6) TIDAL BASIN (??.02.1858 – 15.08.1943)
7) CONNAUGHT ROAD (03.08.1880 – 09.09.1940)
8) VICTORIA & ALBERT GOODS (GWR) (1902 – ?)
9) BECKTON PARK (28.03.1994)
10) SILVERTOWN
    Silvertown & London City Airport
    Silvertown
    (19.06.1863 – 10.12.2006)
11) RENWICK WILTON (COAL)
12) LCC CENTRAL TRAM REPAIR WORKS (1909 – 05.07.1952)

Maze Hill
Tunnel

SER
01.02.1878

CARRIAGE SHED & SIDINGS

SER
01.01.1873

London-facing
Junction eliminated
1890

MAZE HILL
Maze Hill & East Greenwich
Maze Hill & Greenwich Park
Maze Hill & East Greenwich
Greenwich (Maze Hill)
(01.01.1873)

GREENWICH

Blackheath Tunnel

SER
30.07.1849

BLACKHEATH

KIDBROOKE

ELTHAM PARK

CARRIAGE
SIDINGS
(1879 – 1970)

GOODS
(06.05.1963)

SER
30.07.1849

Blackheath
Junction

Kidbrooke Tunnel

BLACKHEATH
(30.07.1849)

BHR
01.05.1895

GOODS (07.10.1968)

Bexley Heath Railway (BHR):

Powers originally obtained for line from junction with SER at Lee to a point south
of the future Slade Green station. SER subsequently stipulated for junction to be
at Blackheath instead, resulting in deviation from original route and sharp curve
west of present Eltham station. Built by an independent company (BHR) due to
SER refusing to finance line, although services operated by SER from
01.05.1895 opening. BHR absorbed by recently-formed SECR 10.07.1900

KIDBROOKE (01.05.1895)

Crossover out of use

BLACKHEATH
PARK

MILITARY DEPOT
(1917 – c.1960's)

BHR
01.05.1895

ELTHAM PARK
Shooters Hill & Eltham Park
(01.07.1908 – 17.03.1985)

St Johns to Elmstead Woods
quadrupled 18.06.1905

(1st)   (2nd)   BHR
01.05.1895

SER
01.07.1895

LEE

10) PLANT DEPOT (former ENGINE SHED)
11) REFUELLING SHED
12) PRE-ASSEMBLY DEPOT
13) Lee Spur (SECR c.1900)

ELTHAM
Eltham Well Hall
Well Hall & North Eltham
Well Hall
(01.05.1895)
(re-sited 17.03.1985)

Hither Green Junction

HITHER GREEN (01.06.1895)

10   HITHER GREEN DEPOT (DBS & BALFOUR BEATTY) (10.09.1933)

12   Lee Loop Junction

GOODS
(07.10.1968)

ELTHAM

11

13   LEE (01.09.1866)

SER
01.09.1866

GOODS (07.10.1968)

Scale

Km
0   0.5   1   1.5   2

Miles
¼   ½   ¾   1

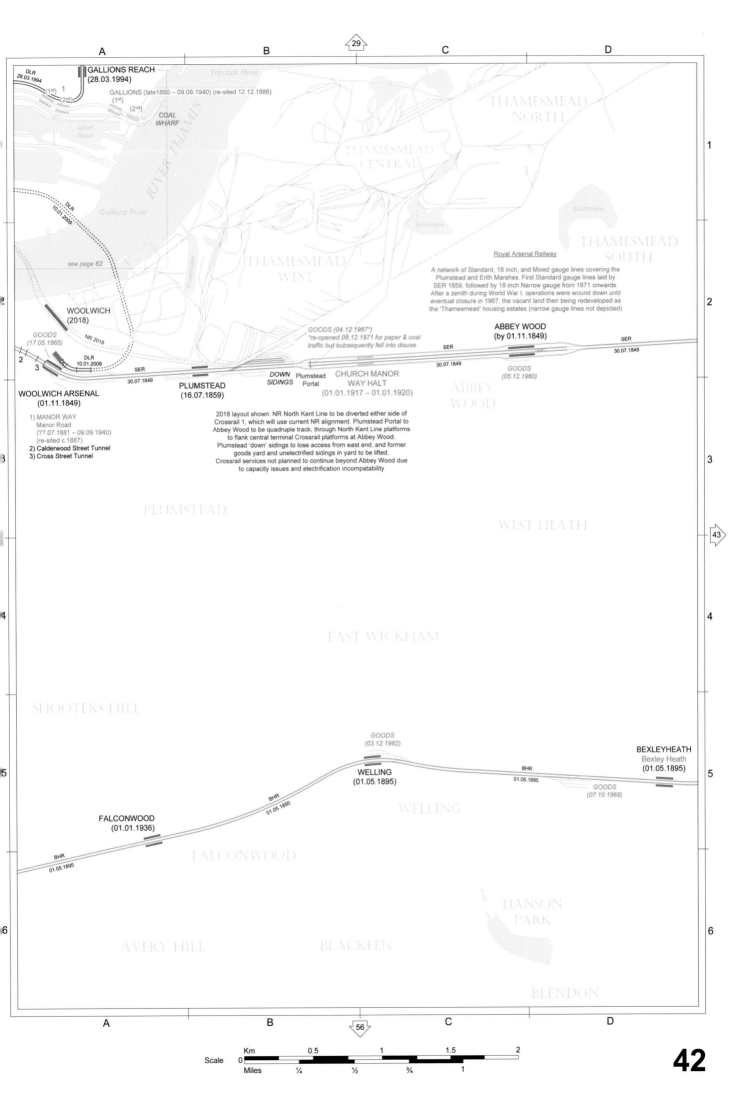

A   B   C   D

1

see page 62

DLR
28.03.1994

GALLIONS REACH
(28.03.1994)

GALLIONS (late1880 – 09.09.1940) (re-sited 12.12.1886)
(1st)   (2nd)

Tripcock Ness

COAL
WHARF

*Albert
Basin*

River Thames

DLR
10.01.2009

Gallions Point

THAMESMEAD
NORTH

THAMESMEAD
CENTRAL

THAMESMEAD
WEST

Southmere

THAMESMEAD
SOUTH

2

WOOLWICH
(2018)

NR 2018

*GOODS
(17.05.1965)*

2

3

DLR
10.01.2009

SER
30.07.1849

WOOLWICH ARSENAL
(01.11.1849)

1) MANOR WAY
Manor Road
(??.07.1881 – 09.09.1940)
(re-sited c.1887)
2) Calderwood Street Tunnel
3) Cross Street Tunnel

PLUMSTEAD
(16.07.1859)

*DOWN
SIDINGS*

Plumstead
Portal

**CHURCH MANOR
WAY HALT**
(01.01.1917 – 01.01.1920)

GOODS (04.12.1967)
*re-opened 08.12.1971 for paper & coal
traffic but subsequently fell into disuse*

SER
30.07.1849

SER

*GOODS
(05.12.1960)*

ABBEY WOOD
(by 01.11.1849)

SER
30.07.1849

ABBEY
WOOD

Royal Arsenal Railway

A network of Standard, 18 inch, and Mixed gauge lines covering the
Plumstead and Erith Marshes. First Standard gauge lines laid by
SER 1859, followed by 18 inch Narrow gauge from 1871 onwards.
After a zenith during World War I, operations were wound down until
eventual closure in 1967, the vacant land then being redeveloped as
the 'Thamesmead' housing estates (narrow gauge lines not depicted)

2018 layout shown: NR North Kent Line to be diverted either side of
Crossrail 1, which will use current NR alignment. Plumstead Portal to
Abbey Wood to be quadruple track, through North Kent Line platforms
to flank central terminal Crossrail platforms at Abbey Wood.
Plumstead 'down' sidings to lose access from east end, and former
goods yard and unelectrified sidings in yard to be lifted.
Crossrail services not planned to continue beyond Abbey Wood due
to capacity issues and electrification incompatability

3

PLUMSTEAD

WEST HEATH

43

4

EAST WICKHAM

5

SHOOTERS HILL

*GOODS
(03.12.1962)*

WELLING
(01.05.1895)

BHR
01.05.1895

WELLING

BHR
01.05.1895

*GOODS
(07.10.1968)*

BEXLEYHEATH
Bexley Heath
(01.05.1895)

5

FALCONWOOD
(01.01.1936)

BHR
01.05.1895

BHR
01.05.1895

FALCONWOOD

DANSON
PARK

6

AVERY HILL

BLACKFEN

BLENDON

A   B   C   D

Scale
Km   0   0.5   1   1.5   2
Miles   ¼   ½   ¾   1

42

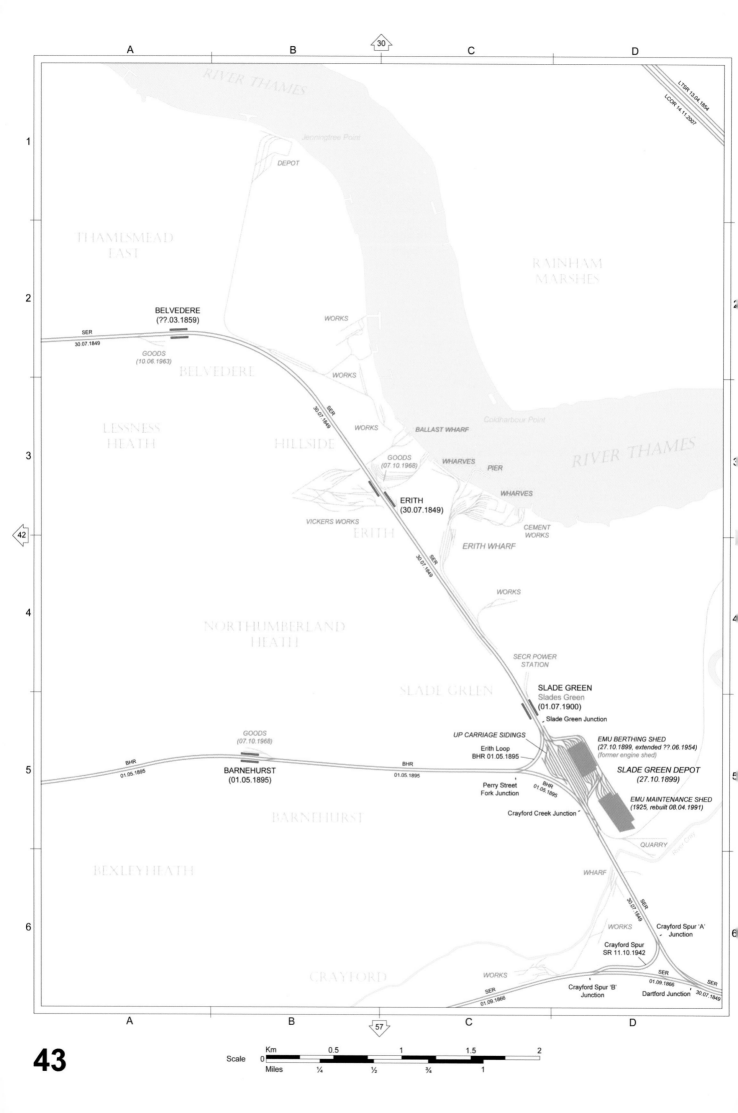

RIVER THAMES

Jenningtree Point

DEPOT

THAMESMEAD
EAST

RAINHAM
MARSHES

WORKS

BELVEDERE
(??.03.1859)

SER
30.07.1849

GOODS
(10.06.1963)

BELVEDERE

WORKS

LESSNESS
HEATH

SER
30.07.1849

HILLSIDE

WORKS

BALLAST WHARF

Coldharbour Point

RIVER THAMES

GOODS
(07.10.1968)

WHARVES

PIER

ERITH
(30.07.1849)

WHARVES

VICKERS WORKS

ERITH

CEMENT
WORKS

SER
30.07.1849

ERITH WHARF

42

WORKS

NORTHUMBERLAND
HEATH

SECR POWER
STATION

SLADE GREEN

SLADE GREEN
Slades Green
(01.07.1900)

Slade Green Junction

GOODS
(07.10.1968)

UP CARRIAGE SIDINGS

EMU BERTHING SHED
(27.10.1899, extended ??.06.1954)
(former engine shed)

BHR
01.05.1895

BARNEHURST
(01.05.1895)

BHR
01.05.1895

Erith Loop
BHR 01.05.1895

SLADE GREEN DEPOT
(27.10.1899)

Perry Street
Fork Junction

BHR
01.05.1895

EMU MAINTENANCE SHED
(1925, rebuilt 08.04.1991)

Crayford Creek Junction

BARNEHURST

QUARRY

River Cray

BEXLEYHEATH

WHARF

Crayford Spur 'A'
Junction

WORKS

SER
30.07.1849

Crayford Spur
SR 11.10.1942

CRAYFORD

WORKS

Crayford Spur 'B'
Junction

SER
01.09.1866

Dartford Junction

SER
01.09.1866

SER
30.07.1849

LTSR 13.04.1854

LCOR 14.11.2007

43

Scale

Km
0   0.5   1   1.5   2

Miles   ¼   ½   ¾   1

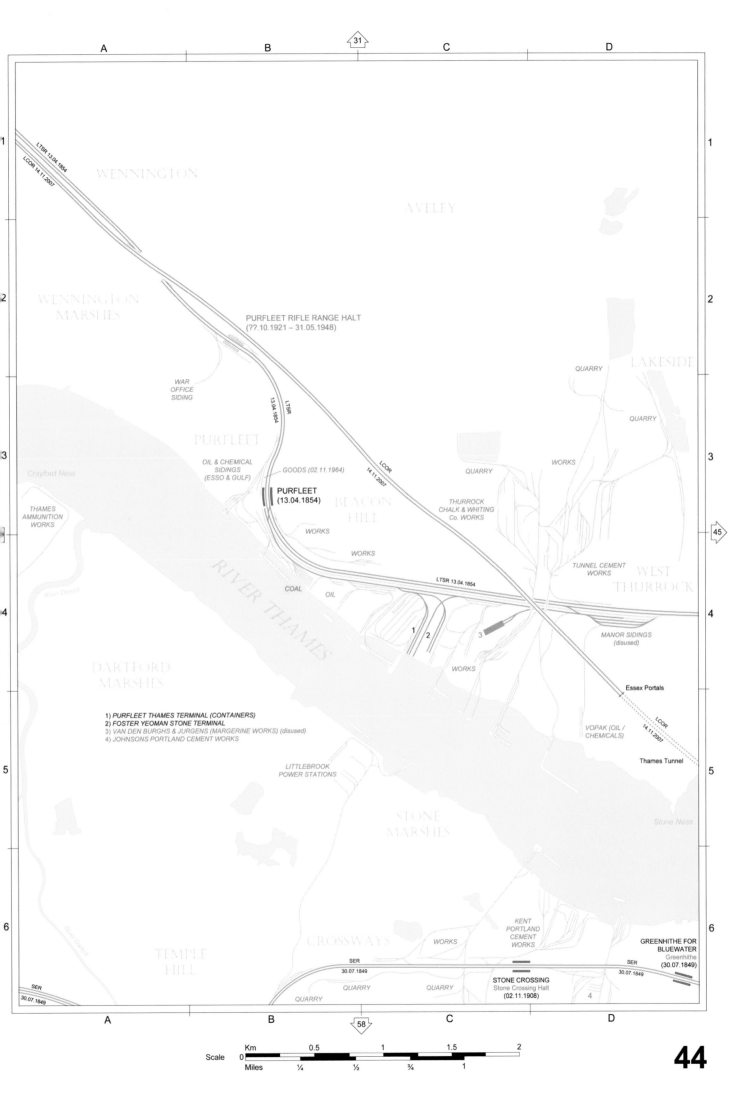

A   B   C   D

LTSR 13.04.1854

LCOR 14.11.2007

WENNINGTON

AVELEY

WENNINGTON MARSHES

LAKESIDE

PURFLEET RIFLE RANGE HALT
(??.10.1921 – 31.05.1948)

QUARRY

WAR OFFICE SIDING

QUARRY

13.04.1854 LTSR

PURFLEET

WORKS

QUARRY

OIL & CHEMICAL SIDINGS
(ESSO & GULF)

LCOR 14.11.2007

GOODS (02.11.1964)

QUARRY

Crayford Ness

PURFLEET
(13.04.1854)

BEACON HILL

THURROCK CHALK & WHITING Co. WORKS

THAMES AMMUNITION WORKS

WORKS

45

WORKS

TUNNEL CEMENT WORKS

WEST THURROCK

River Darent

COAL   OIL

RIVER THAMES

LTSR 13.04.1854

1   2

3

MANOR SIDINGS (disused)

DARTFORD MARSHES

WORKS

Essex Portals

1) PURFLEET THAMES TERMINAL (CONTAINERS)
2) FOSTER YEOMAN STONE TERMINAL
3) VAN DEN BURGHS & JURGENS (MARGERINE WORKS) (disused)
4) JOHNSONS PORTLAND CEMENT WORKS

VOPAK (OIL / CHEMICALS)

LCOR 14.11.2007

Thames Tunnel

LITTLEBROOK POWER STATIONS

STONE MARSHES

Stone Ness

CROSSWAYS

KENT PORTLAND CEMENT WORKS

WORKS

GREENHITHE FOR BLUEWATER
Greenhithe
(30.07.1849)

TEMPLE HILL

SER
30.07.1849

STONE CROSSING
Stone Crossing Halt
(02.11.1908)

SER
30.07.1849

SER
30.07.1849

QUARRY   QUARRY   QUARRY

4

A   B   C   D

Scale
Km   0   0.5   1   1.5   2
Miles   ¼   ½   ¾   1

44

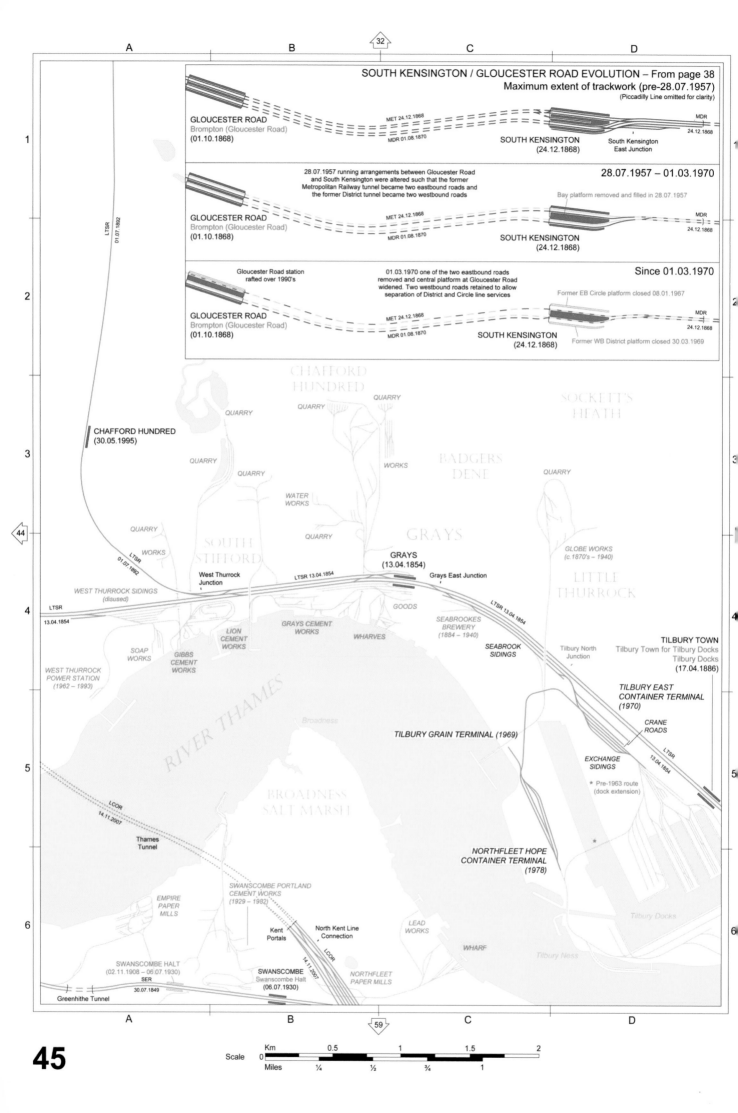

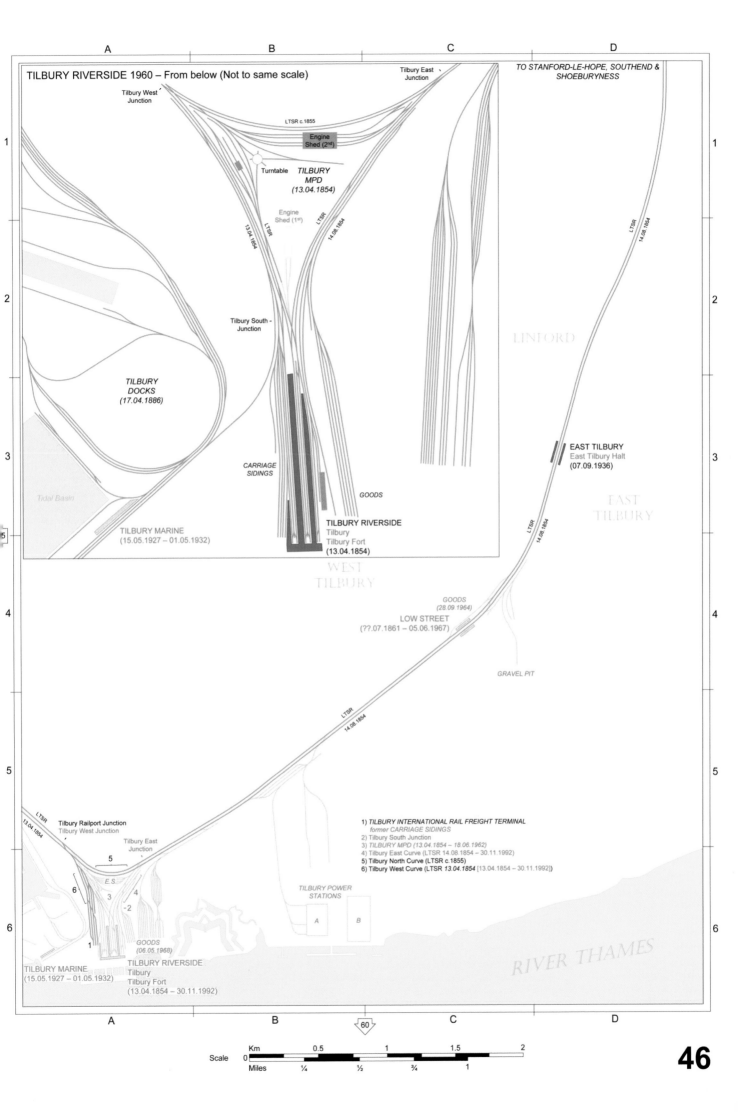

TILBURY RIVERSIDE 1960 – From below (Not to same scale)

Tilbury East Junction

Tilbury West Junction

TO STANFORD-LE-HOPE, SOUTHEND & SHOEBURYNESS

LTSR c.1855

Engine Shed (2nd)

Turntable

TILBURY MPD (13.04.1854)

Engine Shed (1st)

13.04.1854

LTSR

14.08.1854

Tilbury South - Junction

LTSR 14.08.1854

LINFORD

TILBURY DOCKS (17.04.1886)

EAST TILBURY
East Tilbury Halt
(07.09.1936)

EAST TILBURY

CARRIAGE SIDINGS

GOODS

Tidal Basin

TILBURY MARINE
(15.05.1927 – 01.05.1932)

TILBURY RIVERSIDE
Tilbury
Tilbury Fort
(13.04.1854)

WEST TILBURY

GOODS
(28.09.1964)

LTSR 14.08.1854

LOW STREET
(??.07.1861 – 05.06.1967)

GRAVEL PIT

LTSR 14.08.1854

LTSR 13.04.1854

Tilbury Railport Junction
Tilbury West Junction

Tilbury East Junction

5

E.S.

6
4

3

-2

1) *TILBURY INTERNATIONAL RAIL FREIGHT TERMINAL*
   former CARRIAGE SIDINGS
2) Tilbury South Junction
3) *TILBURY MPD (13.04.1854 – 18.06.1962)*
4) Tilbury East Curve (LTSR 14.08.1854 – 30.11.1992)
5) Tilbury North Curve (LTSR c.1855)
6) Tilbury West Curve (LTSR *13.04.1854* [13.04.1854 – 30.11.1992])

TILBURY POWER STATIONS

A   B

1

GOODS
(06.05.1968)

TILBURY MARINE
(15.05.1927 – 01.05.1932)

TILBURY RIVERSIDE
Tilbury
Tilbury Fort
(13.04.1854 – 30.11.1992)

RIVER THAMES

Scale
Km 0   0.5   1   1.5   2
Miles   ¼   ½   ¾   1

60

46

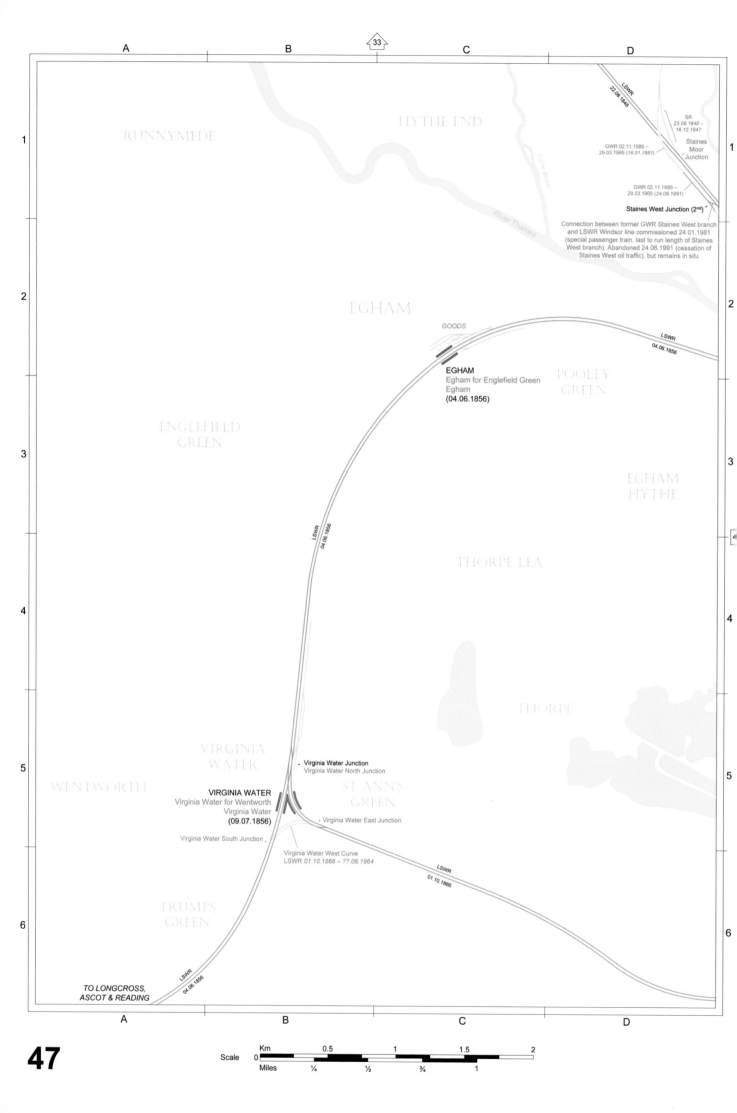

A   B   C   D

1

RUNNYMEDE

HYTHE END

Colne Brook

River Thames

LSWR 22.08.1848

SR
23.06.1940 –
16.12.1947

Staines
Moor
Junction

GWR 02.11.1885 –
29.03.1965 (16.01.1981)

GWR 02.11.1885 –
29.03.1965 (24.06.1991)

Staines West Junction (2nd)

Connection between former GWR Staines West branch
and LSWR Windsor line commissioned 24.01.1981
(special passenger train, last to run length of Staines
West branch). Abandoned 24.06.1991 (cessation of
Staines West oil traffic), but remains in situ

2

EGHAM

GOODS

LSWR
04.06.1856

POOLEY
GREEN

EGHAM
Egham for Englefield Green
Egham
(04.06.1856)

ENGLEFIELD
GREEN

3

EGHAM
HYTHE

LSWR
04.06.1856

THORPE LEA

4

THORPE

5

VIRGINIA
WATER

WENTWORTH

Virginia Water Junction
Virginia Water North Junction

ST ANN'S
GREEN

VIRGINIA WATER
Virginia Water for Wentworth
Virginia Water
(09.07.1856)

Virginia Water East Junction

Virginia Water South Junction

Virginia Water West Curve
LSWR 01.10.1866 – ??.06.1964

LSWR
01.10.1866

6

TRUMP'S
GREEN

LSWR
04.06.1856

*TO LONGCROSS,
ASCOT & READING*

A   B   C   D

47

Scale

Km   0   0.5   1   1.5   2

Miles   ¼   ½   ¾   1

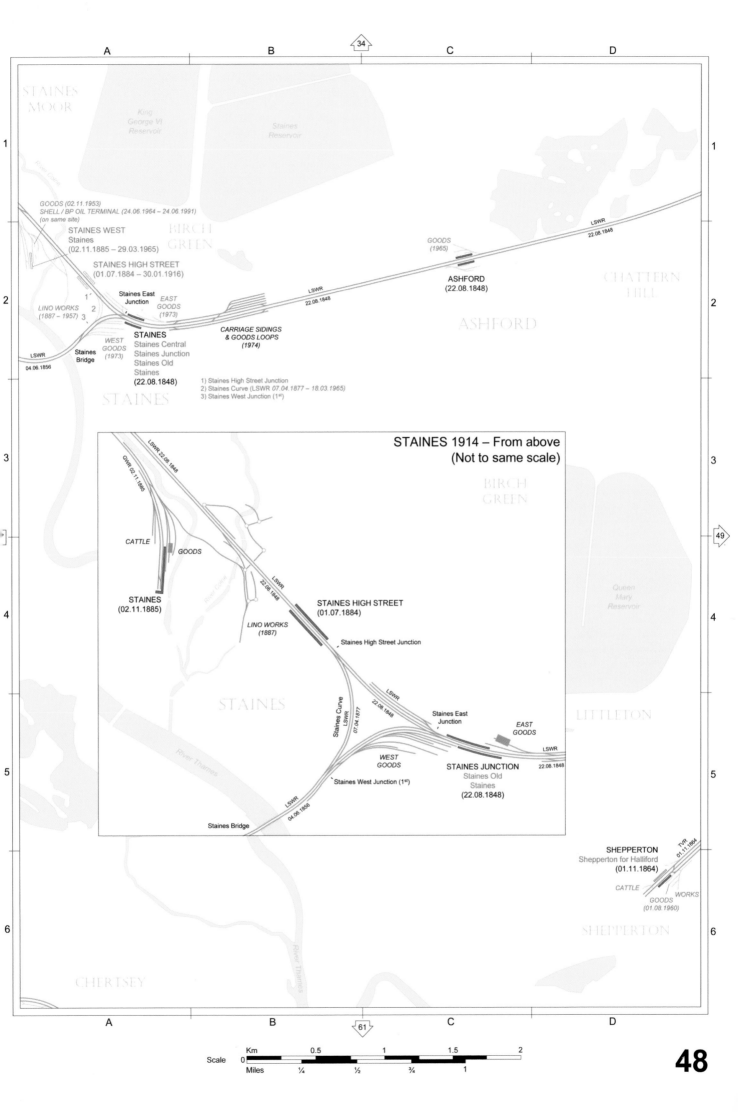

STAINES MOOR

King George VI Reservoir

Staines Reservoir

BIRCH GREEN

CHATTERN HILL

GOODS (02.11.1953)
SHELL / BP OIL TERMINAL (24.06.1964 – 24.06.1991)
(on same site)

STAINES WEST
Staines
(02.11.1885 – 29.03.1965)

STAINES HIGH STREET
(01.07.1884 – 30.01.1916)

Staines East
Junction

EAST
GOODS
(1973)

LINO WORKS
(1887 – 1957)

LSWR
22.08.1848

GOODS
(1965)

ASHFORD
(22.08.1848)

ASHFORD

LSWR
22.08.1848

WEST
GOODS
(1973)

Staines
Bridge

STAINES
Staines Central
Staines Junction
Staines Old
Staines
(22.08.1848)

CARRIAGE SIDINGS
& GOODS LOOPS
(1974)

1) Staines High Street Junction
2) Staines Curve (LSWR 07.04.1877 – 18.03.1965)
3) Staines West Junction (1st)

LSWR
04.06.1856

STAINES

STAINES 1914 – From above
(Not to same scale)

BIRCH GREEN

LSWR 22.08.1848

GWR 02.11.1885

CATTLE

GOODS

STAINES
(02.11.1885)

LINO WORKS
(1887)

River Colne

LSWR
22.08.1848

STAINES HIGH STREET
(01.07.1884)

Staines High Street Junction

Queen Mary Reservoir

STAINES

LITTLETON

Staines Curve

LSWR
07.04.1877

LSWR
22.08.1848

Staines East
Junction

EAST
GOODS

LSWR
22.08.1848

WEST
GOODS

River Thames

Staines West Junction (1st)

STAINES JUNCTION
Staines Old
Staines
(22.08.1848)

LSWR
04.06.1856

Staines Bridge

SHEPPERTON
Shepperton for Halliford
(01.11.1864)

TVR
01.11.1864

CATTLE

GOODS
(01.08.1960)

WORKS

SHEPPERTON

CHERTSEY

River Thames

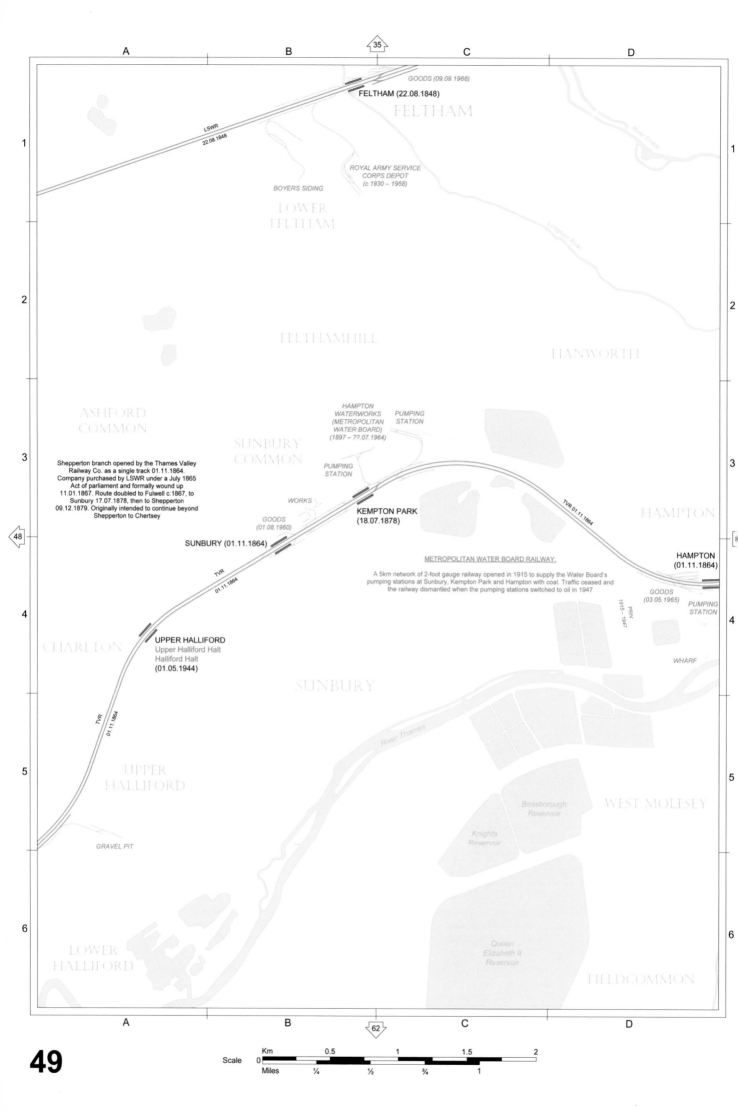

GOODS (09.09.1968)

FELTHAM (22.08.1848)

FELTHAM

LSWR
22.08.1848

ROYAL ARMY SERVICE
CORPS DEPOT
(c.1930 – 1958)

BOYERS SIDING

LOWER
FELTHAM

FELTHAMHILL

HANWORTH

ASHFORD
COMMON

HAMPTON
WATERWORKS
(METROPOLITAN
WATER BOARD)
(1897 – ??.07.1964)

PUMPING
STATION

SUNBURY
COMMON

PUMPING
STATION

Shepperton branch opened by the Thames Valley
Railway Co. as a single track 01.11.1864.
Company purchased by LSWR under a July 1865
Act of parliament and formally wound up
11.01.1867. Route doubled to Fulwell c.1867, to
Sunbury 17.07.1878, then to Shepperton
09.12.1879. Originally intended to continue beyond
Shepperton to Chertsey

WORKS

GOODS
(01.08.1960)

KEMPTON PARK
(18.07.1878)

TVR 01.11.1864

HAMPTON

SUNBURY (01.11.1864)

METROPOLITAN WATER BOARD RAILWAY:

HAMPTON
(01.11.1864)

TVR
01.11.1864

A 5km network of 2-foot gauge railway opened in 1915 to supply the Water Board's
pumping stations at Sunbury, Kempton Park and Hampton with coal. Traffic ceased and
the railway dismantled when the pumping stations switched to oil in 1947

GOODS
(03.05.1965)

PRV
1915 – 1947

PUMPING
STATION

CHARLTON

UPPER HALLIFORD
Upper Halliford Halt
Halliford Halt
(01.05.1944)

SUNBURY

WHARF

UPPER
HALLIFORD

TVR
01.11.1864

River Thames

WEST MOLESEY

Bessborough
Reservoir

GRAVEL PIT

Knights
Reservoir

LOWER
HALLIFORD

Queen
Elizabeth II
Reservoir

FIELDCOMMON

49

Scale

Km
0   0.5   1   1.5   2

Miles
¼   ½   ¾   1

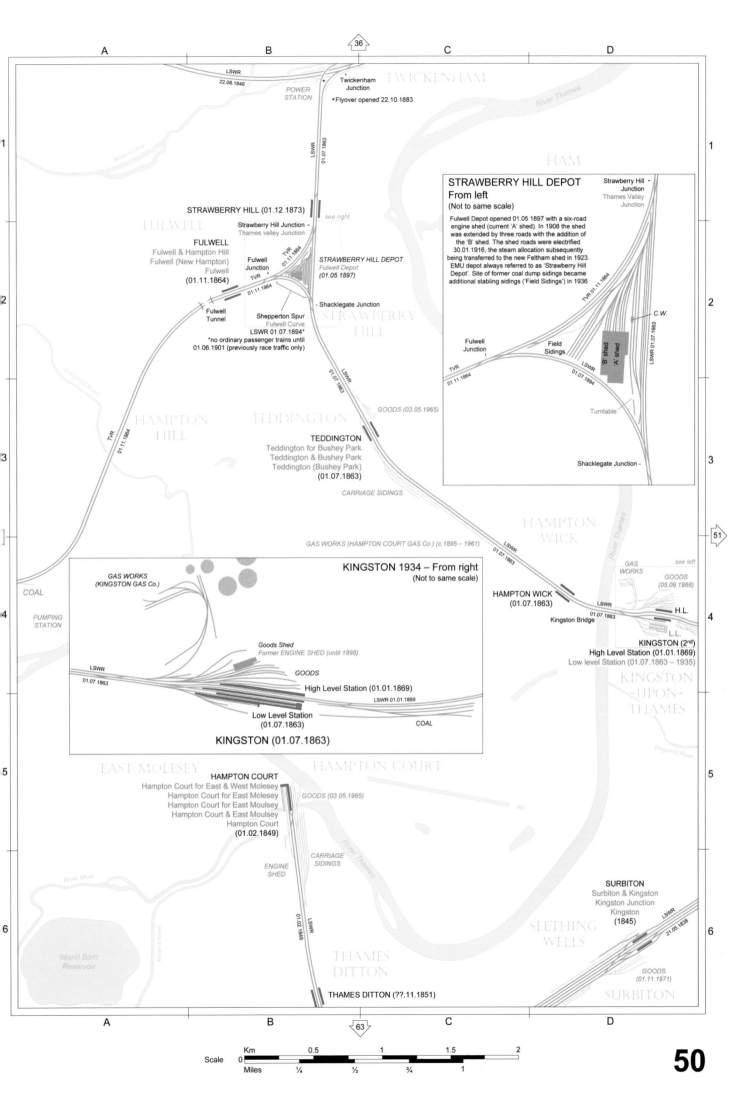

TWICKENHAM

LSWR
22.08.1848

POWER
STATION

*Twickenham
Junction
*Flyover opened 22.10.1883

River Thames

HAM

LSWR
01.07.1863

STRAWBERRY HILL (01.12.1873)

FULWELL

FULWELL
Fulwell & Hampton Hill
Fulwell (New Hampton)
Fulwell
(01.11.1864)

Strawberry Hill Junction -
Thames valley Junction

see right

TVR
01.11.1864

Fulwell
Junction

TVR

TVR
01.11.1864

STRAWBERRY HILL DEPOT
Fulwell Depot
(01.05.1897)

Fulwell Tunnel

Shepperton Spur
Fulwell Curve
LSWR 01.07.1894*
*no ordinary passenger trains until
01.06.1901 (previously race traffic only)

- Shacklegate Junction

STRAWBERRY
HILL

STRAWBERRY HILL DEPOT
From left
(Not to same scale)

Strawberry Hill -
Junction
Thames Valley
Junction

Fulwell Depot opened 01.05.1897 with a six-road
engine shed (current 'A' shed). In 1908 the shed
was extended by three roads with the addition of
the 'B' shed. The shed roads were electrified
30.01.1916, the steam allocation subsequently
being transferred to the new Feltham shed in 1923.
EMU depot always referred to as 'Strawberry Hill
Depot'. Site of former coal dump sidings became
additional stabling sidings ('Field Sidings') in 1936.

TVR 01.11.1864

C.W.

Fulwell
Junction

TVR
01.11.1864

Field
Sidings

LSWR
01.07.1894

'B' shed 'A' shed

LSWR 01.07.1863

Turntable

Shacklegate Junction -

LSWR
01.07.1863

HAMPTON
HILL

TEDDINGTON

TVR
01.11.1864

GOODS (03.05.1965)

TEDDINGTON
Teddington for Bushey Park
Teddington & Bushey Park
Teddington (Bushey Park)
(01.07.1863)

CARRIAGE SIDINGS

HAMPTON
WICK

GAS WORKS (HAMPTON COURT GAS Co.) (c.1895 – 1961)

LSWR
01.07.1863

GAS
WORKS

see left

GOODS
(05.09.1966)

COAL

PUMPING
STATION

GAS WORKS
(KINGSTON GAS Co.)

KINGSTON 1934 – From right
(Not to same scale)

Goods Shed
Former ENGINE SHED (until 1898)

LSWR
01.07.1863

GOODS

High Level Station (01.01.1869)

LSWR 01.01.1869

Low Level Station
(01.07.1863)

COAL

KINGSTON (01.07.1863)

HAMPTON WICK
(01.07.1863)

Kingston Bridge

LSWR
01.07.1863

H.L.

L.L.

KINGSTON (2nd)
High Level Station (01.01.1869)
Low level Station (01.07.1863 – 1935)

KINGSTON
-UPON-
THAMES

EAST MOLESEY

HAMPTON COURT

HAMPTON COURT
Hampton Court for East & West Molesey
Hampton Court for East Molesey
Hampton Court for East Moulsey
Hampton Court & East Moulsey
Hampton Court
(01.02.1849)

GOODS (03.05.1965)

CARRIAGE
SIDINGS

ENGINE
SHED

River Mole

River Ember

Island Barn
Reservoir

LSWR
01.02.1849

THAMES
DITTON

SEETHING
WELLS

SURBITON
Surbiton & Kingston
Kingston Junction
Kingston
(1845)

LSWR
21.05.1838

GOODS
(01.11.1971)

SURBITON

THAMES DITTON (??.11.1851)

Scale

Km
0   0.5   1   1.5   2

Miles
¼   ½   ¾   1

50

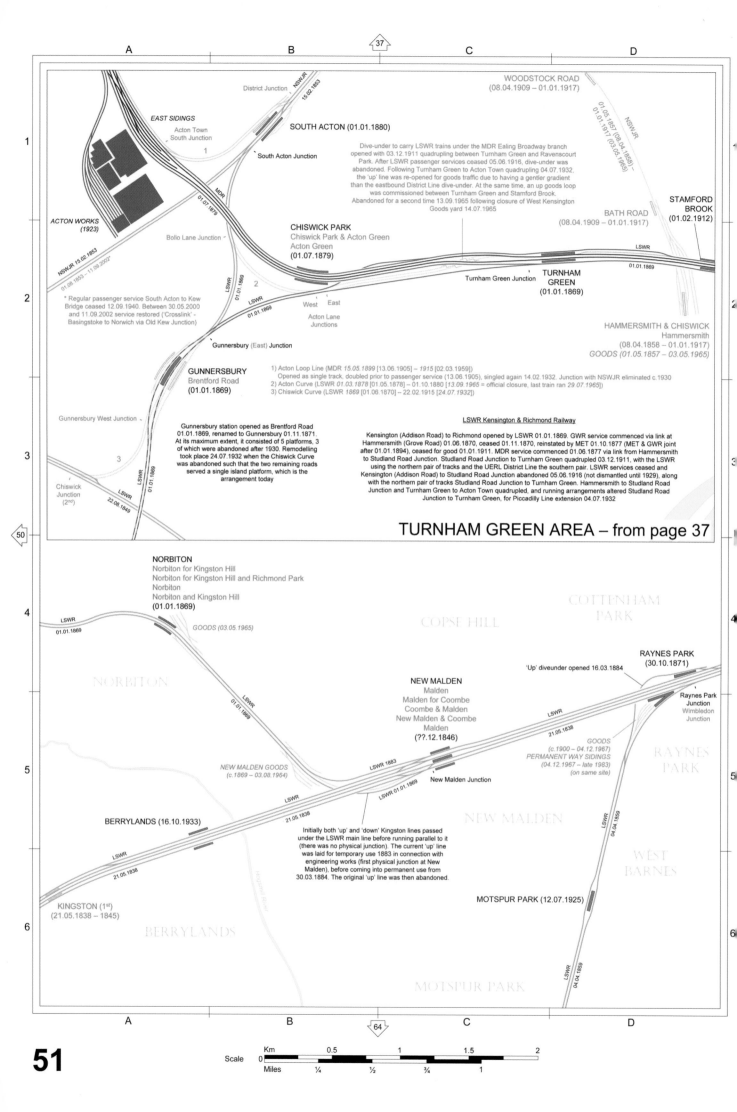

WOODSTOCK ROAD
(08.04.1909 – 01.01.1917)

EAST SIDINGS

District Junction

NSWJR
15.02.1853

Acton Town
South Junction

SOUTH ACTON (01.01.1880)

1

South Acton Junction

Dive-under to carry LSWR trains under the MDR Ealing Broadway branch
opened with 03.12.1911 quadrupling between Turnham Green and Ravenscourt
Park. After LSWR passenger services ceased 05.06.1916, dive-under was
abandoned. Following Turnham Green to Acton Town quadrupling 04.07.1932,
the 'up' line was re-opened for goods traffic due to having a gentler gradient
than the eastbound District Line dive-under. At the same time, an up goods loop
was commissioned between Turnham Green and Stamford Brook.
Abandoned for a second time 13.09.1965 following closure of West Kensington
Goods yard 14.07.1965

STAMFORD
BROOK
(01.02.1912)

MDR
01.07.1879

ACTON WORKS
(1923)

BATH ROAD
(08.04.1909 – 01.01.1917)

Bollo Lane Junction

CHISWICK PARK
Chiswick Park & Acton Green
Acton Green
(01.07.1879)

LSWR

01.01.1869

NSWJR 15.02.1853

01.08.1853 – 11.09.2002*

LSWR
01.01.1869

2

Turnham Green Junction

TURNHAM
GREEN
(01.01.1869)

* Regular passenger service South Acton to Kew
Bridge ceased 12.09.1940. Between 30.05.2000
and 11.09.2002 service restored ('Crosslink' -
Basingstoke to Norwich via Old Kew Junction)

LSWR
01.01.1869

West   East

Acton Lane
Junctions

HAMMERSMITH & CHISWICK
Hammersmith
(08.04.1858 – 01.01.1917)
GOODS (01.05.1857 – 03.05.1965)

Gunnersbury (East) Junction

GUNNERSBURY
Brentford Road
(01.01.1869)

1) Acton Loop Line (MDR 15.05.1899 [13.06.1905] – 1915 [02.03.1959])
   Opened as single track, doubled prior to passenger service (13.06.1905), singled again 14.02.1932. Junction with NSWJR eliminated c.1930
2) Acton Curve (LSWR 01.03.1878 [01.05.1878] – 01.10.1880 [13.09.1965 = official closure, last train ran 29.07.1965])
3) Chiswick Curve (LSWR 1869 [01.06.1870] – 22.02.1915 [24.07.1932])

Gunnersbury West Junction

3

LSWR
01.01.1869

LSWR Kensington & Richmond Railway

Gunnersbury station opened as Brentford Road
01.01.1869, renamed to Gunnersbury 01.11.1871.
At its maximum extent, it consisted of 5 platforms, 3
of which were abandoned after 1930. Remodelling
took place 24.07.1932 when the Chiswick Curve
was abandoned such that the two remaining roads
served a single island platform, which is the
arrangement today

Kensington (Addison Road) to Richmond opened by LSWR 01.01.1869. GWR service commenced via link at
Hammersmith (Grove Road) 01.06.1870, ceased 01.11.1870, reinstated by MET 01.10.1877 (MET & GWR joint
after 01.01.1894), ceased for good 01.01.1911. MDR service commenced 01.06.1877 via link from Hammersmith
to Studland Road Junction. Studland Road Junction to Turnham Green quadrupled 03.12.1911, with the LSWR
using the northern pair of tracks and the UERL District Line the southern pair. LSWR services ceased and
Kensington (Addison Road) to Studland Road Junction abandoned 05.06.1916 (not dismantled until 1929), along
with the northern pair of tracks Studland Road Junction to Turnham Green. Hammersmith to Studland Road
Junction and Turnham Green to Acton Town quadrupled, and running arrangements altered Studland Road
Junction to Turnham Green, for Piccadilly Line extension 04.07.1932

Chiswick
Junction
(2nd)

LSWR
01.01.1869

22.08.1849

TURNHAM GREEN AREA – from page 37

NORBITON
Norbiton for Kingston Hill
Norbiton for Kingston Hill and Richmond Park
Norbiton
Norbiton and Kingston Hill
(01.01.1869)

COTTENHAM
PARK

COPSE HILL

RAYNES PARK
(30.10.1871)

4

LSWR
01.01.1869

GOODS (03.05.1965)

NORBITON

'Up' diveunder opened 16.03.1884

Raynes Park
Junction
Wimbledon
Junction

NEW MALDEN
Malden
Malden for Coombe
Coombe & Malden
New Malden & Coombe
Malden
(??.12.1846)

LSWR
01.01.1869

LSWR

21.05.1838

GOODS
(c.1900 – 04.12.1967)
PERMANENT WAY SIDINGS
(04.12.1967 – late 1983)
(on same site)

RAYNES
PARK

5

NEW MALDEN GOODS
(c.1869 – 03.08.1964)

LSWR 1883

New Malden Junction

LSWR

LSWR 01.01.1869

NEW MALDEN

LSWR
04.04.1859

BERRYLANDS (16.10.1933)

21.05.1838

Initially both 'up' and 'down' Kingston lines passed
under the LSWR main line before running parallel to it
(there was no physical junction). The current 'up' line
was laid for temporary use 1883 in connection with
engineering works (first physical junction at New
Malden), before coming into permanent use from
30.03.1884. The original 'up' line was then abandoned.

WEST
BARNES

LSWR

21.05.1838

MOTSPUR PARK (12.07.1925)

LSWR
04.04.1859

KINGSTON (1st)
(21.05.1838 – 1845)

6

BERRYLANDS

MOTSPUR PARK

Scale

Km
0   0.5   1   1.5   2

Miles   ¼   ½   ¾   1

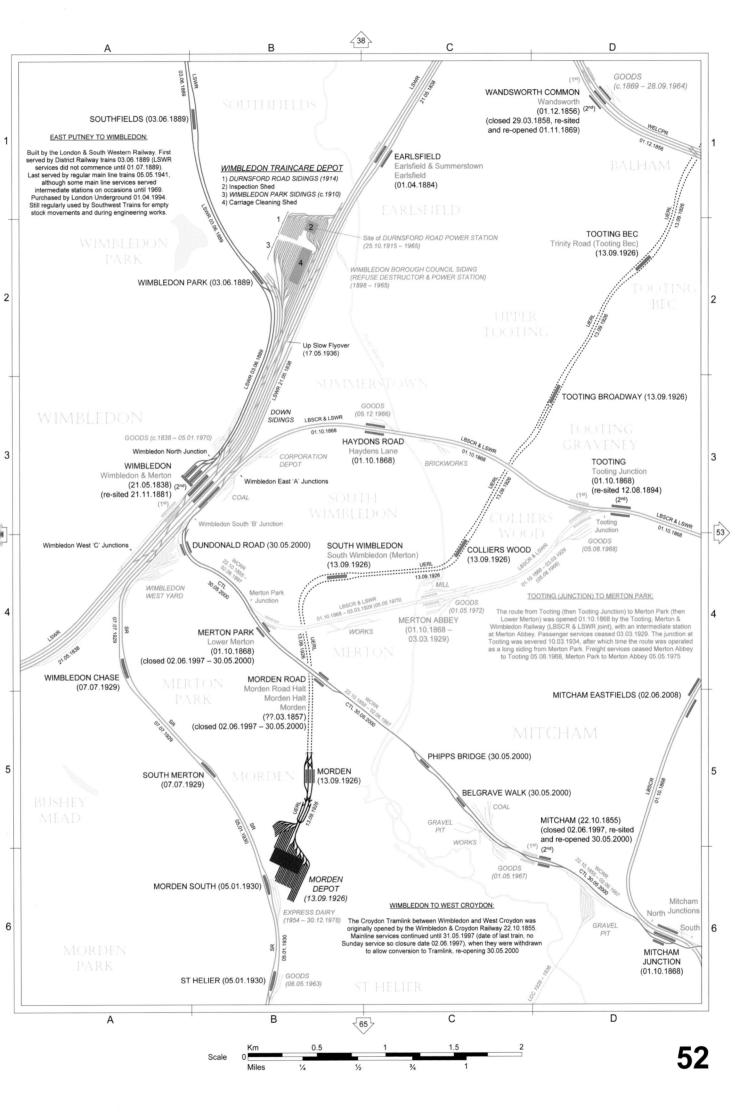

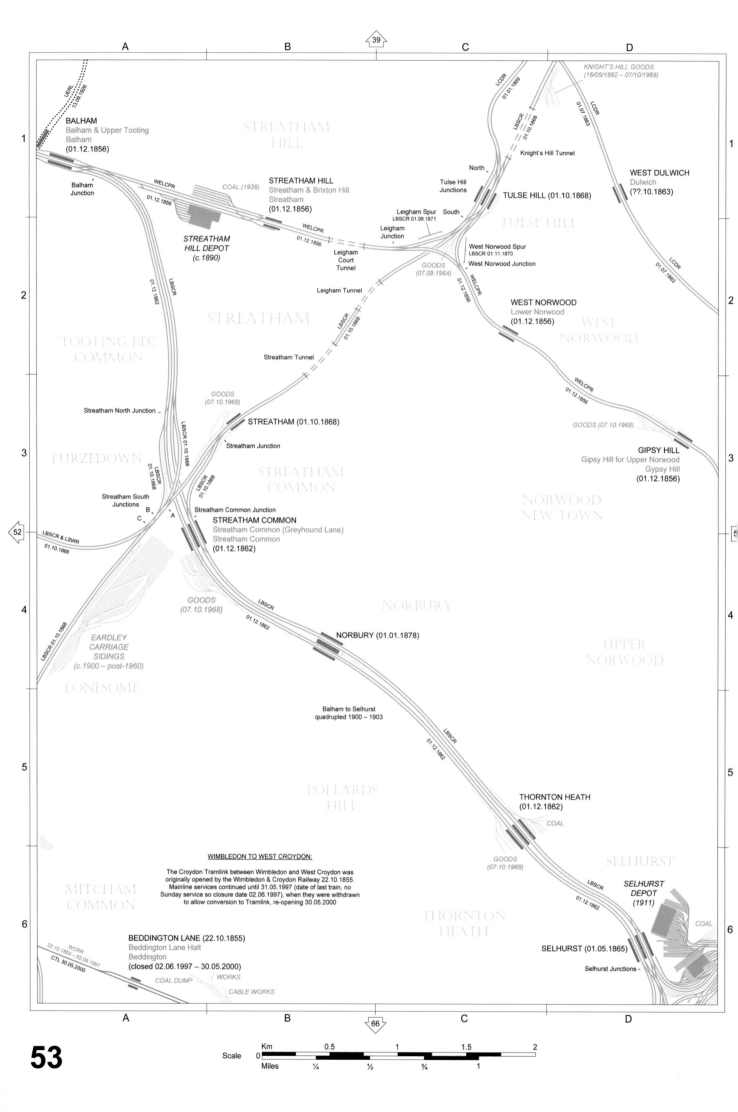

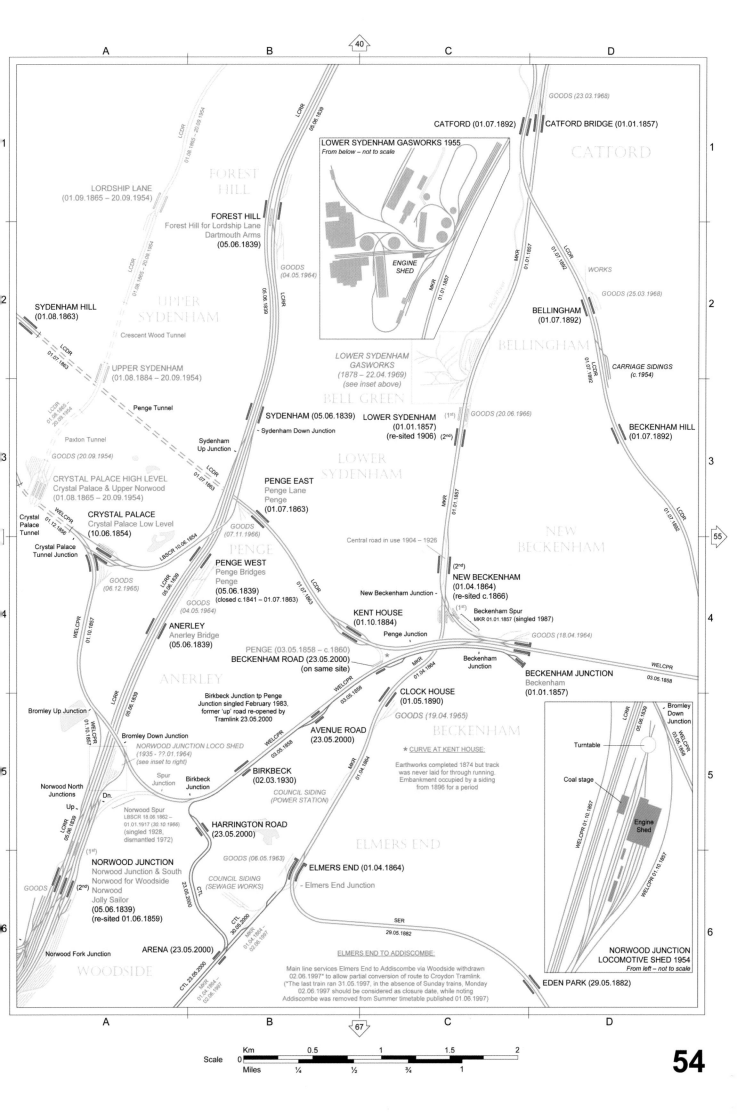

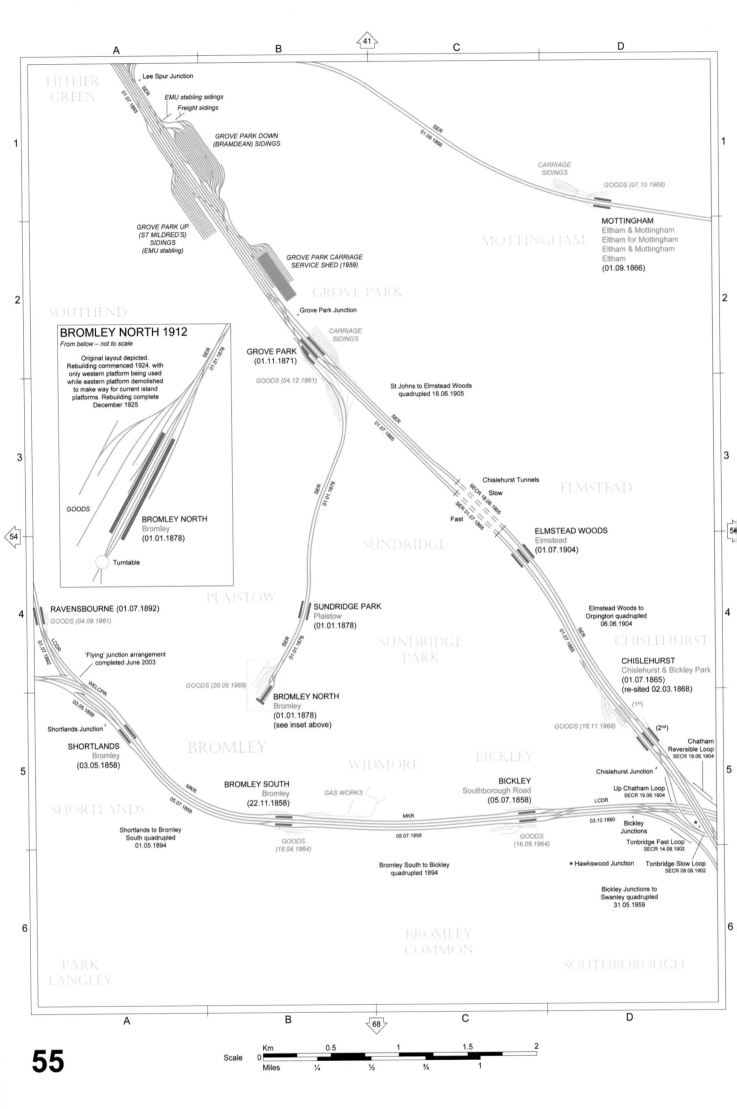

HITHER GREEN

Lee Spur Junction

SER

01.07.1865

EMU stabling sidings

Freight sidings

GROVE PARK DOWN
(BRAMDEAN) SIDINGS

SER
01.09.1866

CARRIAGE
SIDINGS

GOODS (07.10.1968)

MOTTINGHAM
Eltham & Mottingham
Eltham for Mottingham
Eltham & Mottingham
Eltham
(01.09.1866)

MOTTINGHAM

GROVE PARK UP
(ST MILDRED'S)
SIDINGS
(EMU stabling)

GROVE PARK CARRIAGE
SERVICE SHED (1959)

GROVE PARK

SOUTHEND

BROMLEY NORTH 1912

From below – not to scale

Original layout depicted.
Rebuilding commenced 1924, with
only western platform being used
while eastern platform demolished
to make way for current island
platforms. Rebuilding complete
December 1925

SER
01.01.1878

GOODS

BROMLEY NORTH
Bromley
(01.01.1878)

Turntable

Grove Park Junction

CARRIAGE
SIDINGS

GROVE PARK
(01.11.1871)

GOODS (04.12.1961)

St Johns to Elmstead Woods
quadrupled 18.06.1905

SER
01.07.1865

Chislehurst Tunnels

SECR 18.06.1905

Slow

SER 01.07.1865

Fast

ELMSTEAD

ELMSTEAD WOODS
Elmstead
(01.07.1904)

SER
01.01.1878

SUNDRIDGE

RAVENSBOURNE (01.07.1892)

GOODS (04.09.1961)

LCDR
01.07.1892

'Flying' junction arrangement
completed June 2003

WELCPR
03.05.1858

Shortlands Junction

SHORTLANDS
Bromley
(03.05.1858)

SHORTLANDS

PLAISTOW

SUNDRIDGE PARK
Plaistow
(01.01.1878)

SER
01.01.1878

SUNDRIDGE
PARK

GOODS (20.05.1968)

BROMLEY NORTH
Bromley
(01.01.1878)
(see inset above)

BROMLEY

WIDMORE

GAS WORKS

Elmstead Woods to
Orpington quadrupled
06.06.1904

SER
01.07.1865

CHISLEHURST

CHISLEHURST
Chislehurst & Bickley Park
(01.07.1865)
(re-sited 02.03.1868)

(1st)

GOODS (18.11.1968)

(2nd)

Chatham
Reversible Loop
SECR 19.06.1904

Chislehurst Junction

BICKLEY

BICKLEY
Southborough Road
(05.07.1858)

Up Chatham Loop
SECR 19.06.1904

LCDR
03.12.1860

MKR
05.07.1858

Shortlands to Bromley
South quadrupled
01.05.1894

BROMLEY SOUTH
Bromley
(22.11.1858)

GOODS
(18.04.1964)

MKR
05.07.1858

05.07.1858

GOODS
(16.05.1964)

Bickley
Junctions

Tonbridge Fast Loop
SECR 14.09.1902

* Hawkswood Junction

Tonbridge Slow Loop
SECR 08.09.1902

Bickley Junctions to
Swanley quadrupled
31.05.1959

Bromley South to Bickley
quadrupled 1894

SHORTLANDS

BROMLEY
COMMON

PARK
LANGLEY

SOUTHBOROUGH

Scale

Km 0   0.5   1   1.5   2

Miles ¼   ½   ¾   1

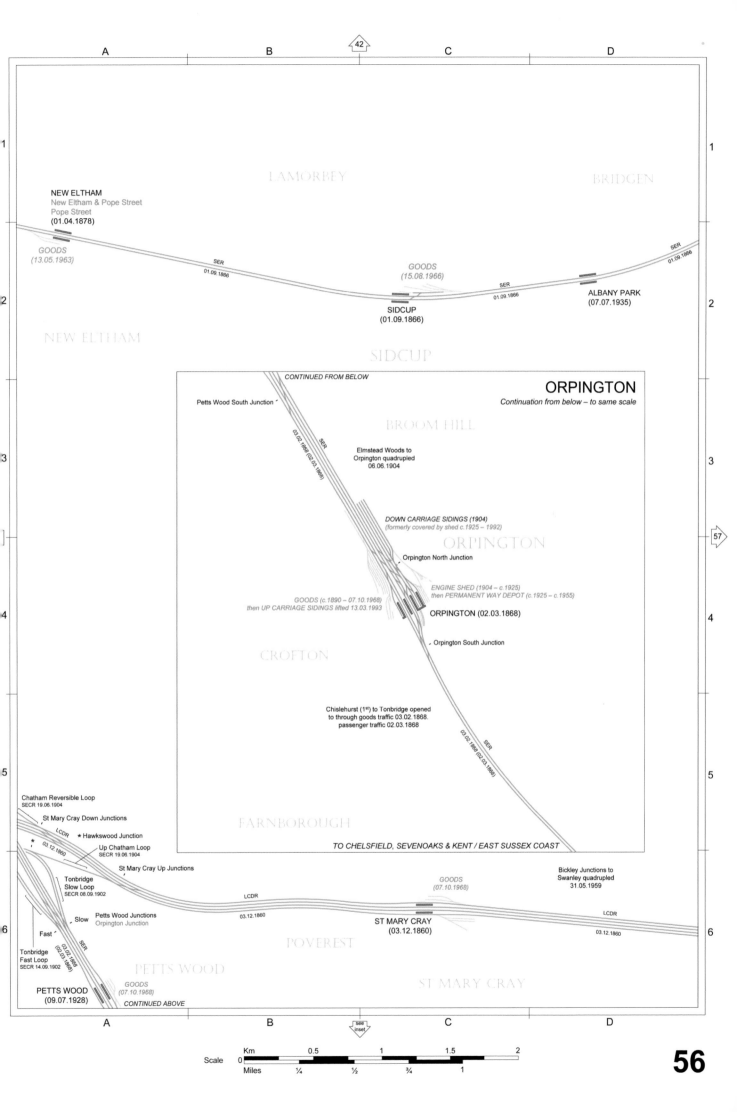

LAMORBEY

BRIDGEN

NEW ELTHAM
New Eltham & Pope Street
Pope Street
(01.04.1878)

GOODS
(13.05.1963)

SER
01.09.1866

SER
01.09.1866

NEW ELTHAM

GOODS
(15.08.1966)

SER
01.09.1866

ALBANY PARK
(07.07.1935)

SER
01.09.1866

SIDCUP
(01.09.1866)

SIDCUP

CONTINUED FROM BELOW

Petts Wood South Junction

ORPINGTON
Continuation from below – to same scale

BROOM HILL

03.02.1868 (02.03.1868)

SER

Elmstead Woods to
Orpington quadrupled
06.06.1904

DOWN CARRIAGE SIDINGS (1904)
(formerly covered by shed c.1925 – 1992)

ORPINGTON

Orpington North Junction

ENGINE SHED (1904 – c.1925)
then PERMANENT WAY DEPOT (c.1925 – c.1955)

GOODS (c.1890 – 07.10.1968)
then UP CARRIAGE SIDINGS lifted 13.03.1993

ORPINGTON (02.03.1868)

Orpington South Junction

CROFTON

Chislehurst (1st) to Tonbridge opened
to through goods traffic 03.02.1868.
passenger traffic 02.03.1868

03.02.1868 (02.03.1868)

SER

Chatham Reversible Loop
SECR 19.06.1904

St Mary Cray Down Junctions

LCDR   * Hawkswood Junction

*   Up Chatham Loop
03.12.1860   SECR 19.06.1904

St Mary Cray Up Junctions

Tonbridge
Slow Loop
SECR 08.09.1902

Slow   Petts Wood Junctions
Orpington Junction

Fast

Tonbridge
Fast Loop
SECR 14.09.1902

PETTS WOOD
(09.07.1928)

FARNBOROUGH

TO CHELSFIELD, SEVENOAKS & KENT / EAST SUSSEX COAST

GOODS
(07.10.1968)

Bickley Junctions to
Swanley quadrupled
31.05.1959

LCDR

03.12.1860

LCDR
03.12.1860

ST MARY CRAY
(03.12.1860)

LCDR
03.12.1860

POVEREST

ST MARY CRAY

03.02.1868
(02.03.1868)

SER

PETTS WOOD

GOODS
(07.10.1968)

CONTINUED ABOVE

Scale
Km   0   0.5   1   1.5   2
Miles   ¼   ½   ¾   1

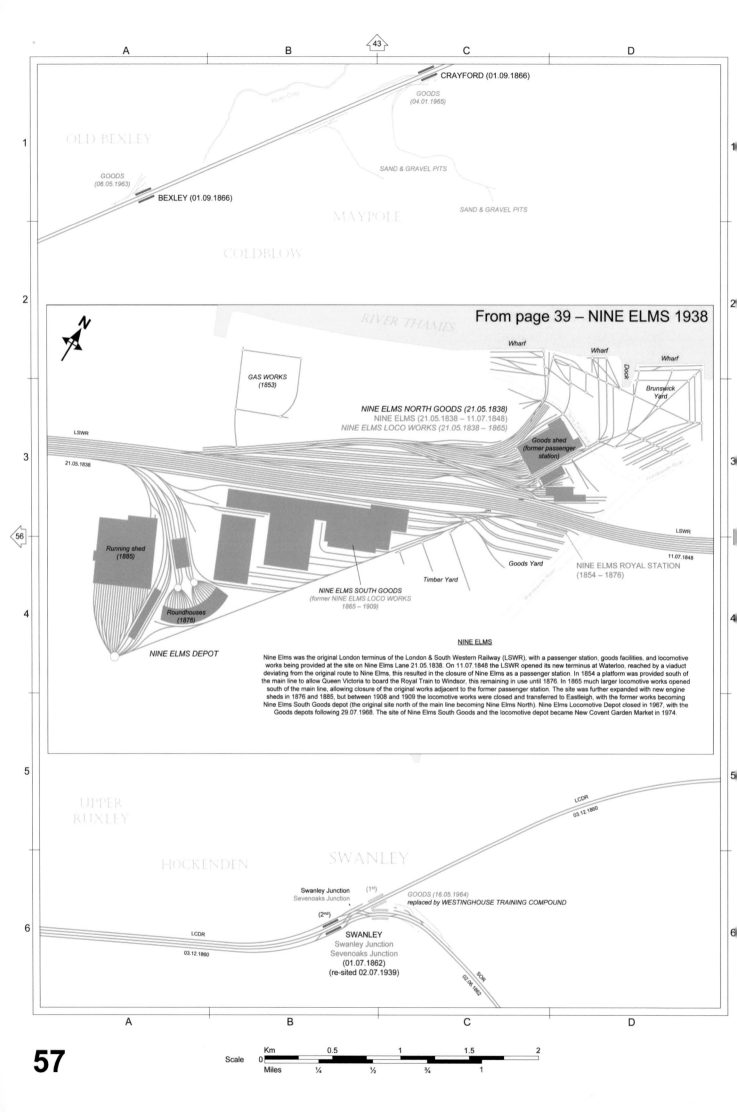

CRAYFORD (01.09.1866)

GOODS
(04.01.1965)

River Cray

OLD BEXLEY

SAND & GRAVEL PITS

GOODS
(06.05.1963)

BEXLEY (01.09.1866)

MAYPOLE

COLDBLOW

SAND & GRAVEL PITS

From page 39 – NINE ELMS 1938

RIVER THAMES

Wharf

Wharf

Wharf

Dock

Brunswick
Yard

GAS WORKS
(1853)

NINE ELMS NORTH GOODS (21.05.1838)
NINE ELMS (21.05.1838 – 11.07.1848)
NINE ELMS LOCO WORKS (21.05.1838 – 1865)

LSWR

21.05.1838

Goods shed
(former passenger
station)

LSWR

11.07.1848

Running shed
(1885)

Roundhouses
(1876)

NINE ELMS SOUTH GOODS
(former NINE ELMS LOCO WORKS
1865 – 1909)

Timber Yard

Goods Yard

NINE ELMS ROYAL STATION
(1854 – 1876)

NINE ELMS DEPOT

NINE ELMS

Nine Elms was the original London terminus of the London & South Western Railway (LSWR), with a passenger station, goods facilities, and locomotive works being provided at the site on Nine Elms Lane 21.05.1838. On 11.07.1848 the LSWR opened its new terminus at Waterloo, reached by a viaduct deviating from the original route to Nine Elms, this resulted in the closure of Nine Elms as a passenger station. In 1854 a platform was provided south of the main line to allow Queen Victoria to board the Royal Train to Windsor, this remaining in use until 1876. In 1865 much larger locomotive works opened south of the main line, allowing closure of the original works adjacent to the former passenger station. The site was further expanded with new engine sheds in 1876 and 1885, but between 1908 and 1909 the locomotive works were closed and transferred to Eastleigh, with the former works becoming Nine Elms South Goods depot (the original site north of the main line becoming Nine Elms North). Nine Elms Locomotive Depot closed in 1967, with the Goods depots following 29.07.1968. The site of Nine Elms South Goods and the locomotive depot became New Covent Garden Market in 1974.

UPPER
RUXLEY

LCDR

03.12.1860

HOCKENDEN

SWANLEY

Swanley Junction
Sevenoaks Junction

(1st)

GOODS (16.05.1964)
replaced by WESTINGHOUSE TRAINING COMPOUND

(2nd)

LCDR

03.12.1860

SWANLEY
Swanley Junction
Sevenoaks Junction
(01.07.1862)
(re-sited 02.07.1939)

SQR

02.06.1862

Scale

Km
0   0.5   1   1.5   2

Miles
¼   ½   ¾   1

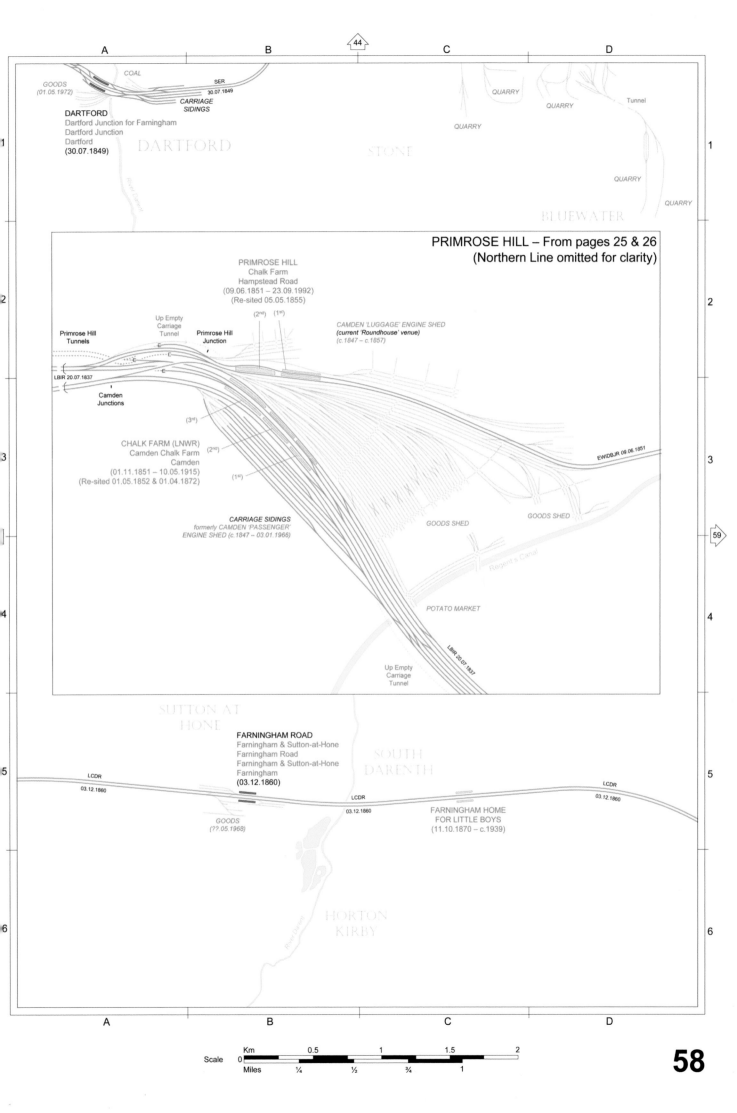

GOODS
(01.05.1972)

COAL

SER
30.07.1849

CARRIAGE
SIDINGS

DARTFORD
Dartford Junction for Farningham
Dartford Junction
Dartford
(30.07.1849)

DARTFORD

STONE

QUARRY

QUARRY

QUARRY

Tunnel

QUARRY

QUARRY

BLUEWATER

PRIMROSE HILL – From pages 25 & 26
(Northern Line omitted for clarity)

PRIMROSE HILL
Chalk Farm
Hampstead Road
(09.06.1851 – 23.09.1992)
(Re-sited 05.05.1855)

(2nd) (1st)

CAMDEN 'LUGGAGE' ENGINE SHED
(current 'Roundhouse' venue)
(c.1847 – c.1857)

Primrose Hill
Tunnels

Up Empty
Carriage
Tunnel

Primrose Hill
Junction

LBIR 20.07.1837

Camden
Junctions

(3rd)

CHALK FARM (LNWR)
Camden Chalk Farm
Camden
(01.11.1851 – 10.05.1915)
(Re-sited 01.05.1852 & 01.04.1872)

(2nd)

(1st)

EWIDBJR 09.06.1851

CARRIAGE SIDINGS
formerly CAMDEN 'PASSENGER'
ENGINE SHED (c.1847 – 03.01.1966)

GOODS SHED

GOODS SHED

59

Regent's Canal

POTATO MARKET

LBIR 20.07.1837

Up Empty
Carriage
Tunnel

SUTTON AT
HONE

FARNINGHAM ROAD
Farningham & Sutton-at-Hone
Farningham Road
Farningham & Sutton-at-Hone
Farningham
(03.12.1860)

SOUTH
DARENTH

LCDR
03.12.1860

LCDR
03.12.1860

LCDR
03.12.1860

LCDR
03.12.1860

GOODS
(??.05.1968)

FARNINGHAM HOME
FOR LITTLE BOYS
(11.10.1870 – c.1939)

HORTON
KIRBY

Scale

Km
0   0.5   1   1.5   2

Miles
¼   ½   ¾   1

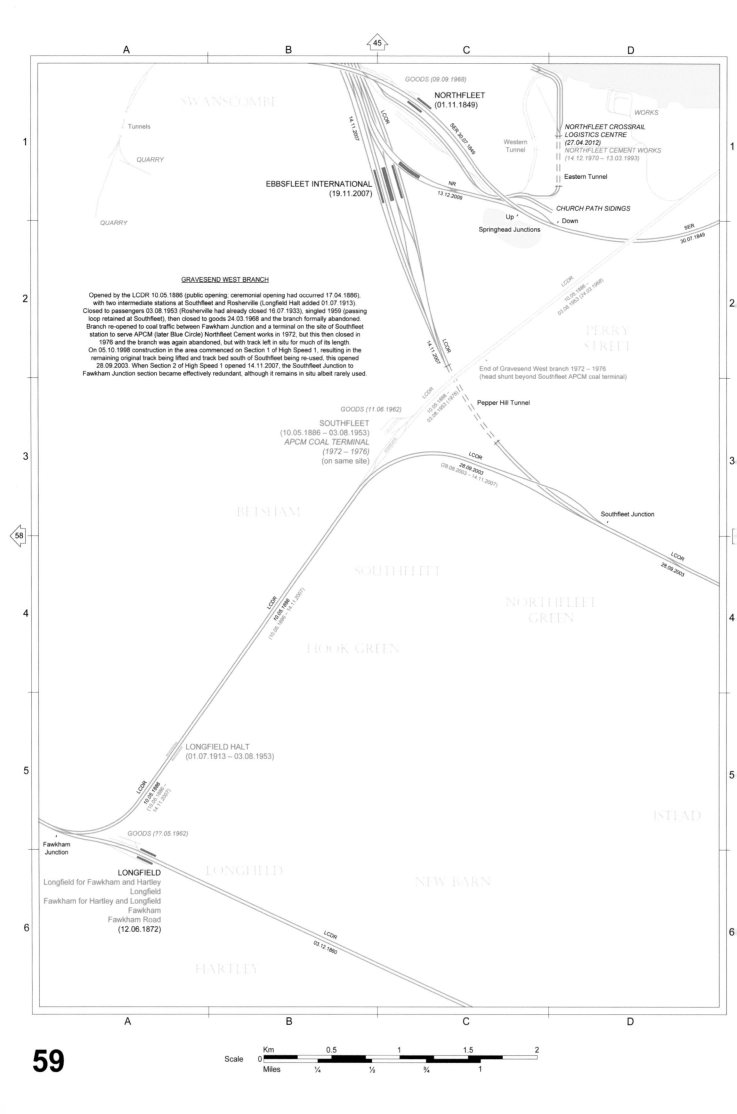

A   B   C   D

1

SWANSCOMBE

Tunnels

QUARRY

GOODS (09.09.1968)

NORTHFLEET
(01.11.1849)

14.11.2007

LCOR

SER 30.07.1849

Western
Tunnel

WORKS

NORTHFLEET CROSSRAIL
LOGISTICS CENTRE
(27.04.2012)
NORTHFLEET CEMENT WORKS
(14.12.1970 – 13.03.1993)

Eastern Tunnel

1

EBBSFLEET INTERNATIONAL
(19.11.2007)

NR
13.12.2009

CHURCH PATH SIDINGS

Up
Springhead Junctions

Down

SER
30.07.1849

QUARRY

2

GRAVESEND WEST BRANCH

Opened by the LCDR 10.05.1886 (public opening; ceremonial opening had occurred 17.04.1886),
with two intermediate stations at Southfleet and Rosherville (Longfield Halt added 01.07.1913).
Closed to passengers 03.08.1953 (Rosherville had already closed 16.07.1933), singled 1959 (passing
loop retained at Southfleet), then closed to goods 24.03.1968 and the branch formally abandoned.
Branch re-opened to coal traffic between Fawkham Junction and a terminal on the site of Southfleet
station to serve APCM (later Blue Circle) Northfleet Cement works in 1972, but this then closed in
1976 and the branch was again abandoned, but with track left in situ for much of its length.
On 05.10.1998 construction in the area commenced on Section 1 of High Speed 1, resulting in the
remaining original track being lifted and track bed south of Southfleet being re-used, this opened
28.09.2003. When Section 2 of High Speed 1 opened 14.11.2007, the Southfleet Junction to
Fawkham Junction section became effectively redundant, although it remains in situ albeit rarely used.

LCOR
10.05.1886 –
03.08.1953 (24.03.1968)

*PERRY
STREET*

2

14.11.2007

LCOR

LCOR
10.05.1886 –
03.08.1953 (1976)

End of Gravesend West branch 1972 – 1976
(head shunt beyond Southfleet APCM coal terminal)

Pepper Hill Tunnel

GOODS (11.06.1962)

SOUTHFLEET
(10.05.1886 – 03.08.1953)
APCM COAL TERMINAL
(1972 – 1976)
(on same site)

LCOR
28.09.2003
(28.09.2003 – 14.11.2007)

3

BETSHAM

Southfleet Junction

LCOR
28.09.2003

58

SOUTHFLEET

*NORTHFLEET
GREEN*

4

LCDR
10.05.1886
(10.05.1886 – 14.11.2007)

HOOK GREEN

4

LONGFIELD HALT
(01.07.1913 – 03.08.1953)

5

LCDR
10.05.1886 –
(10.05.1886 –
14.11.2007)

5

ISTEAD

Fawkham
Junction

GOODS (??.05.1962)

6

LONGFIELD
Longfield for Fawkham and Hartley
Longfield
Fawkham for Hartley and Longfield
Fawkham
Fawkham Road
(12.06.1872)

LONGFIELD

NEW BARN

LCDR
03.12.1860

6

HARTLEY

A   B   C   D

Scale
0
Km   0.5   1   1.5   2
Miles   ¼   ½   ¾   1

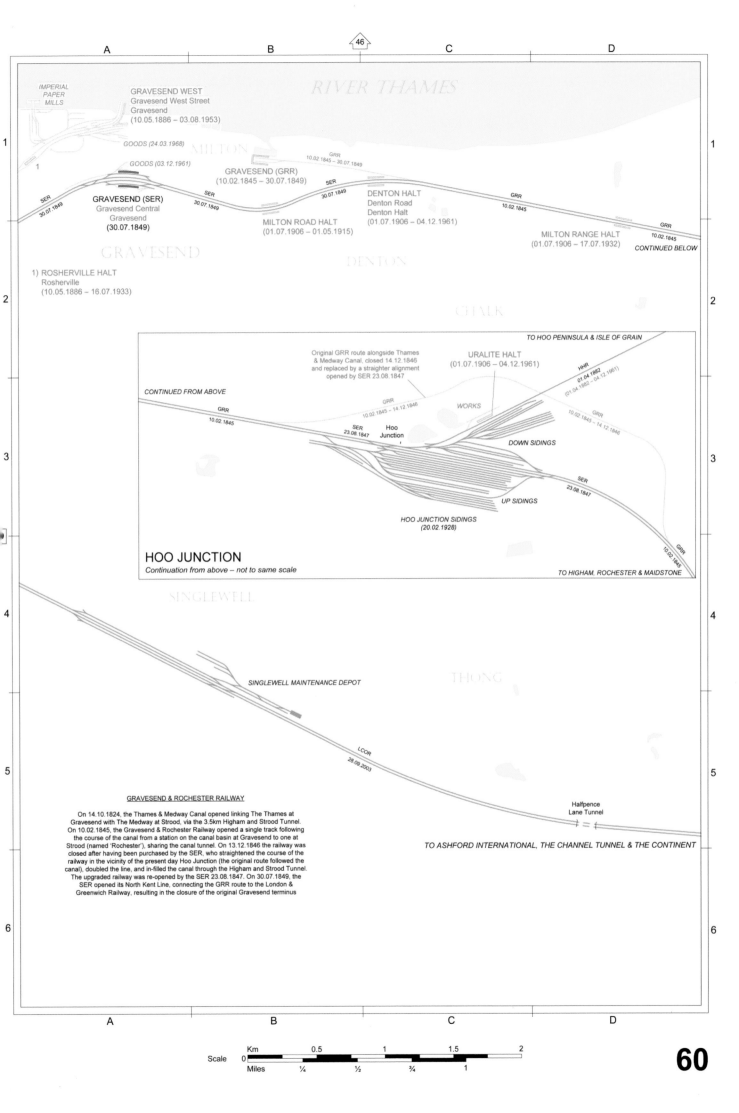

IMPERIAL
PAPER
MILLS

RIVER THAMES

GRAVESEND WEST
Gravesend West Street
Gravesend
(10.05.1886 – 03.08.1953)

GOODS (24.03.1968)

MILTON

GOODS (03.12.1961)

GRR
10.02.1845 – 30.07.1849

GRAVESEND (GRR)
(10.02.1845 – 30.07.1849)

SER
30.07.1849

1

SER
30.07.1849

GRAVESEND (SER)
Gravesend Central
Gravesend
(30.07.1849)

SER
30.07.1849

SER
30.07.1849

DENTON HALT
Denton Road
Denton Halt
(01.07.1906 – 04.12.1961)

GRR
10.02.1845

GRR
10.02.1845

MILTON ROAD HALT
(01.07.1906 – 01.05.1915)

GRAVESEND

DENTON

MILTON RANGE HALT
(01.07.1906 – 17.07.1932)

CONTINUED BELOW

CHALK

1) ROSHERVILLE HALT
Rosherville
(10.05.1886 – 16.07.1933)

TO HOO PENINSULA & ISLE OF GRAIN

Original GRR route alongside Thames
& Medway Canal, closed 14.12.1846
and replaced by a straighter alignment
opened by SER 23.08.1847

URALITE HALT
(01.07.1906 – 04.12.1961)

HHR
01.04.1882
(01.04.1852 – 04.12.1961)

CONTINUED FROM ABOVE

GRR
10.02.1845

GRR
10.02.1845 – 14.12.1846

WORKS

SER
23.08.1847

Hoo
Junction

GRR
10.02.1845 – 14.12.1846

DOWN SIDINGS

SER
23.08.1847

UP SIDINGS

HOO JUNCTION SIDINGS
(20.02.1928)

GRR
10.02.1845

HOO JUNCTION
Continuation from above – not to same scale

TO HIGHAM, ROCHESTER & MAIDSTONE

SINGLEWELL

THONG

SINGLEWELL MAINTENANCE DEPOT

LCOR
28.09.2003

Halfpence
Lane Tunnel

TO ASHFORD INTERNATIONAL, THE CHANNEL TUNNEL & THE CONTINENT

GRAVESEND & ROCHESTER RAILWAY

On 14.10.1824, the Thames & Medway Canal opened linking The Thames at
Gravesend with The Medway at Strood, via the 3.5km Higham and Strood Tunnel.
On 10.02.1845, the Gravesend & Rochester Railway opened a single track following
the course of the canal from a station on the canal basin at Gravesend to one at
Strood (named 'Rochester'), sharing the canal tunnel. On 13.12.1846 the railway was
closed after having been purchased by the SER, who straightened the course of the
railway in the vicinity of the present day Hoo Junction (the original route followed the
canal), doubled the line, and in-filled the canal through the Higham and Strood Tunnel.
The upgraded railway was re-opened by the SER 23.08.1847. On 30.07.1849, the
SER opened its North Kent Line, connecting the GRR route to the London &
Greenwich Railway, resulting in the closure of the original Gravesend terminus

---

Scale

Km 0   0.5   1   1.5   2

Miles   ¼   ½   ¾   1

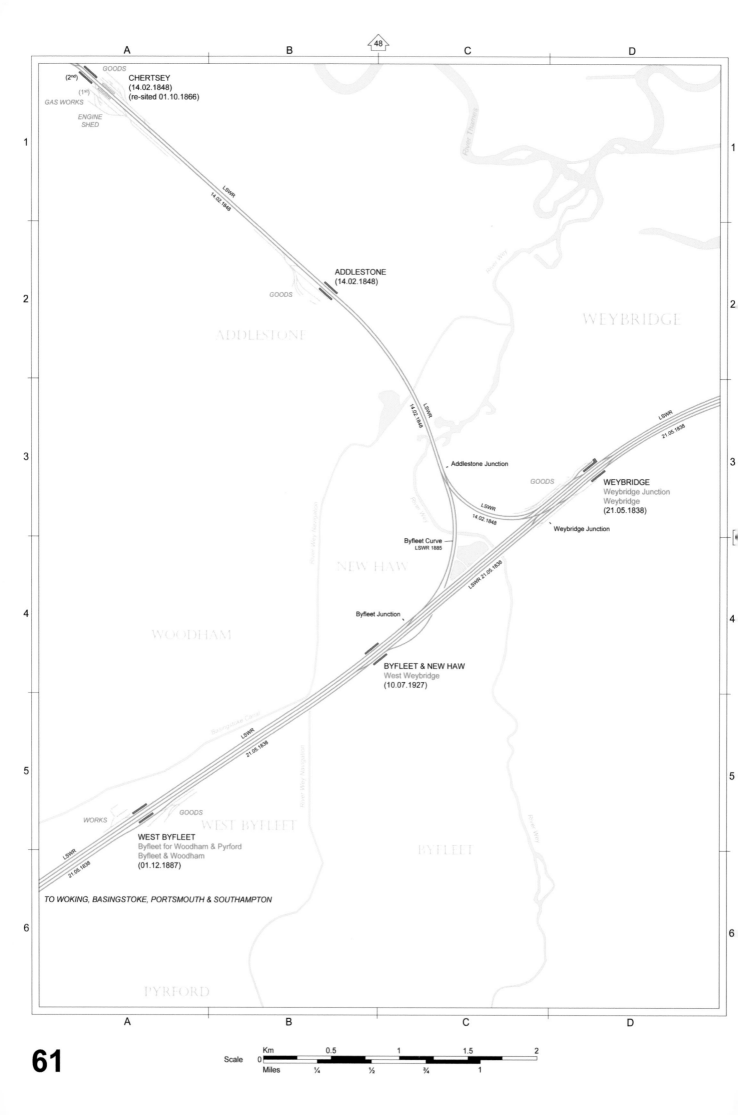

CHERTSEY
(14.02.1848)
(re-sited 01.10.1866)

(2nd)
GOODS
(1st)
GAS WORKS
ENGINE
SHED

LSWR
14.02.1848

ADDLESTONE
(14.02.1848)

GOODS

ADDLESTONE

WEYBRIDGE

LSWR
21.05.1838

LSWR
14.02.1848

Addlestone Junction

GOODS

WEYBRIDGE
Weybridge Junction
Weybridge
(21.05.1838)

River Wey

River Wey Navigation

Weybridge Junction

Byfleet Curve
LSWR 1885

NEW HAW

LSWR 21.05.1838

Byfleet Junction

WOODHAM

BYFLEET & NEW HAW
West Weybridge
(10.07.1927)

Basingstoke Canal

LSWR
21.05.1838

River Wey Navigation

WORKS
GOODS

WEST BYFLEET

BYFLEET

River Wey

LSWR
21.05.1838

WEST BYFLEET
Byfleet for Woodham & Pyrford
Byfleet & Woodham
(01.12.1887)

TO WOKING, BASINGSTOKE, PORTSMOUTH & SOUTHAMPTON

PYRFORD

61

Scale

Km
0   0.5   1   1.5   2

Miles
¼   ½   ¾   1

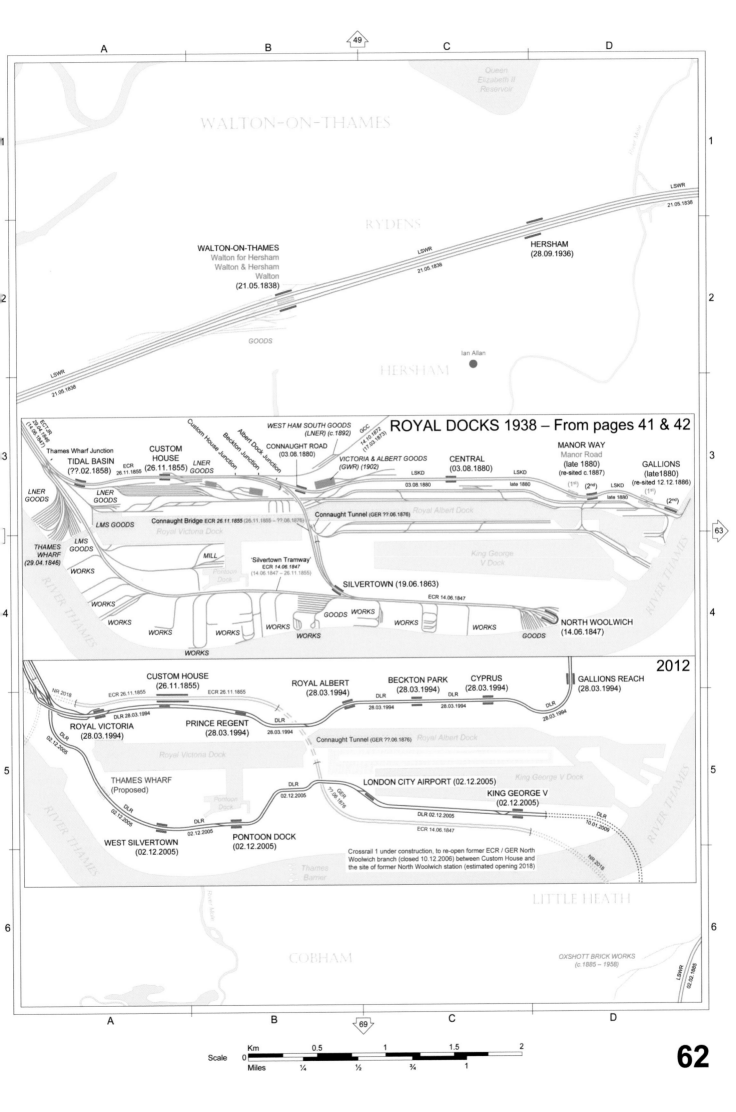

WALTON-ON-THAMES

RYDENS

LSWR
21.05.1838

WALTON-ON-THAMES
Walton for Hersham
Walton & Hersham
Walton
(21.05.1838)

LSWR
21.05.1838

HERSHAM
(28.09.1936)

GOODS

Ian Allan ●

HERSHAM

LSWR
21.05.1838

ROYAL DOCKS 1938 – From pages 41 & 42

ECTJR
29.04.1846
(14.06.1847)

Thames Wharf Junction

TIDAL BASIN
(??.02.1858)

ECR
26.11.1855

Custom House Junction

CUSTOM
HOUSE
(26.11.1855)

LNER
GOODS

Beckton Junction

Albert Dock Junction

WEST HAM SOUTH GOODS
(LNER) (c.1892)

GCC
14.10.1872
(17.03.1873)

CONNAUGHT ROAD
(03.08.1880)

VICTORIA & ALBERT GOODS
(GWR) (1902)

CENTRAL
(03.08.1880)

LSKD

03.08.1880

MANOR WAY
Manor Road
(late 1880)
(re-sited c.1887)

LSKD

late 1880

(1st) (2nd)

LSKD

late 1880

GALLIONS
(late1880)
(re-sited 12.12.1886)

(1st)

(2nd)

LNER
GOODS

LNER
GOODS

LMS GOODS

Connaught Bridge ECR 26.11.1855 (26.11.1855 – ??.06.1876)

Connaught Tunnel (GER ??.06.1876)

Royal Albert Dock

Royal Victoria Dock

THAMES
WHARF
(29.04.1846)

LMS
GOODS

MILL

'Silvertown Tramway'
ECR 14.06.1847
(14.06.1847 – 26.11.1855)

King George
V Dock

WORKS

Pontoon
Dock

SILVERTOWN (19.06.1863)

ECR 14.06.1847

WORKS

WORKS

WORKS

GOODS WORKS

WORKS

WORKS

WORKS

NORTH WOOLWICH
(14.06.1847)

WORKS

WORKS

GOODS

RIVER THAMES

RIVER THAMES

63

2012

NR 2018

CUSTOM HOUSE
(26.11.1855)

ECR 26.11.1855

ECR 26.11.1855

ROYAL ALBERT
(28.03.1994)

DLR

BECKTON PARK
(28.03.1994)

DLR
28.03.1994

CYPRUS
(28.03.1994)

DLR

GALLIONS REACH
(28.03.1994)

DLR
28.03.1994

DLR 28.03.1994

ROYAL VICTORIA
(28.03.1994)

DLR
02.12.2005

PRINCE REGENT
(28.03.1994)

DLR
28.03.1994

Connaught Tunnel (GER ??.06.1876)

Royal Albert Dock

Royal Victoria Dock

THAMES WHARF
(Proposed)

Pontoon
Dock

DLR
02.12.2005

DLR
02.12.2005

GER
??.06.1876

DLR
02.12.2005

LONDON CITY AIRPORT (02.12.2005)

King George V Dock

KING GEORGE V
(02.12.2005)

DLR 02.12.2005

ECR 14.06.1847

DLR
10.01.2009

NR 2018

WEST SILVERTOWN
(02.12.2005)

PONTOON DOCK
(02.12.2005)

Thames
Barrier

Crossrail 1 under construction, to re-open former ECR / GER North
Woolwich branch (closed 10.12.2006) between Custom House and
the site of former North Woolwich station (estimated opening 2018)

RIVER THAMES

LITTLE HEATH

COBHAM

OXSHOTT BRICK WORKS
(c.1885 – 1958)

LSWR
02.02.1885

Scale
Km
0   0.5   1   1.5   2
Miles
¼   ½   ¾   1

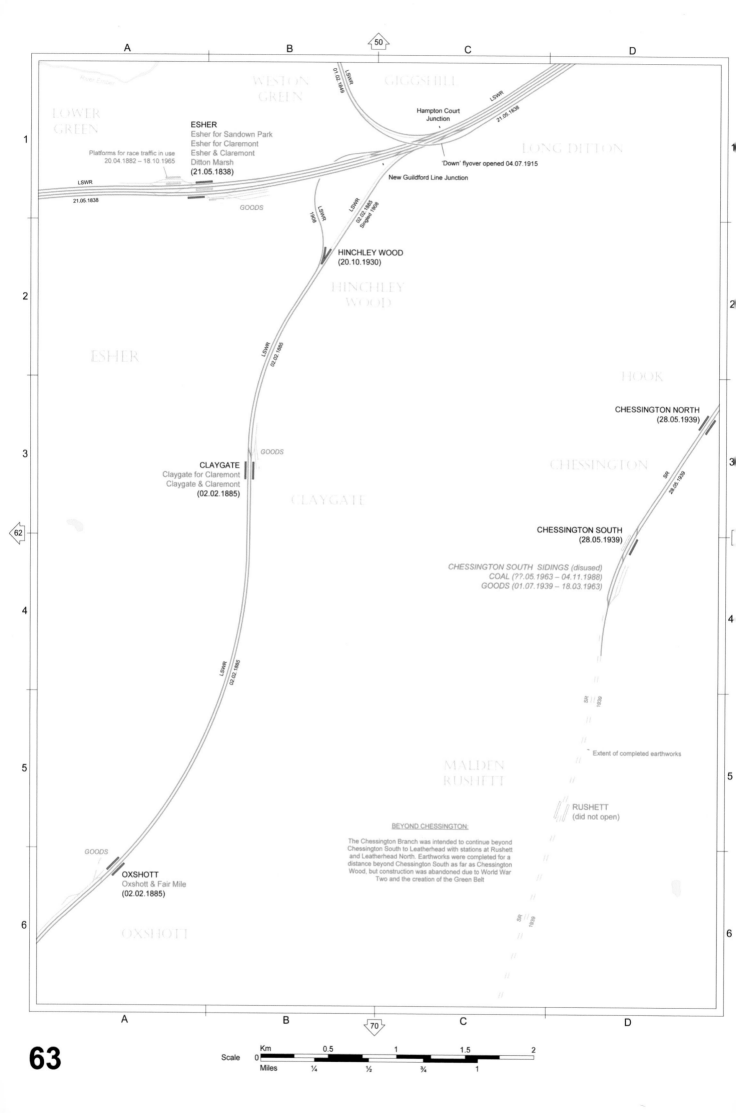

50

A   B   C   D

LOWER
GREEN

WESTON
GREEN

GIGGSHILL

1

ESHER
Esher for Sandown Park
Esher for Claremont
Esher & Claremont
Ditton Marsh
(21.05.1838)

Platforms for race traffic in use
20.04.1882 – 18.10.1965

Hampton Court
Junction

LONG DITTON

LSWR
01.02.1849

LSWR
21.05.1838

1

LSWR
21.05.1838

'Down' flyover opened 04.07.1915

New Guildford Line Junction

LSWR
21.05.1838

GOODS

LSWR
1908

LSWR
02.02.1885
Singled 1908

HINCHLEY WOOD
(20.10.1930)

2

ESHER

HINCHLEY
WOOD

2

HOOK

LSWR
02.02.1885

CHESSINGTON NORTH
(28.05.1939)

3

GOODS

CLAYGATE
Claygate for Claremont
Claygate & Claremont
(02.02.1885)

CLAYGATE

CHESSINGTON

SR
28.05.1939

3

62

CHESSINGTON SOUTH
(28.05.1939)

CHESSINGTON SOUTH SIDINGS (disused)
COAL (??.05.1963 – 04.11.1988)
GOODS (01.07.1939 – 18.03.1963)

4

LSWR
02.02.1885

4

SR
1939

Extent of completed earthworks

5

MALDEN
RUSHETT

5

RUSHETT
(did not open)

GOODS

BEYOND CHESSINGTON:

The Chessington Branch was intended to continue beyond
Chessington South to Leatherhead with stations at Rushett
and Leatherhead North. Earthworks were completed for a
distance beyond Chessington South as far as Chessington
Wood, but construction was abandoned due to World War
Two and the creation of the Green Belt

OXSHOTT
Oxshott & Fair Mile
(02.02.1885)

SR
1939

6

OXSHOTT

6

A   B   C   D

70

63

Scale
Km 0   0.5   1   1.5   2
Miles   ¼   ½   ¾   1

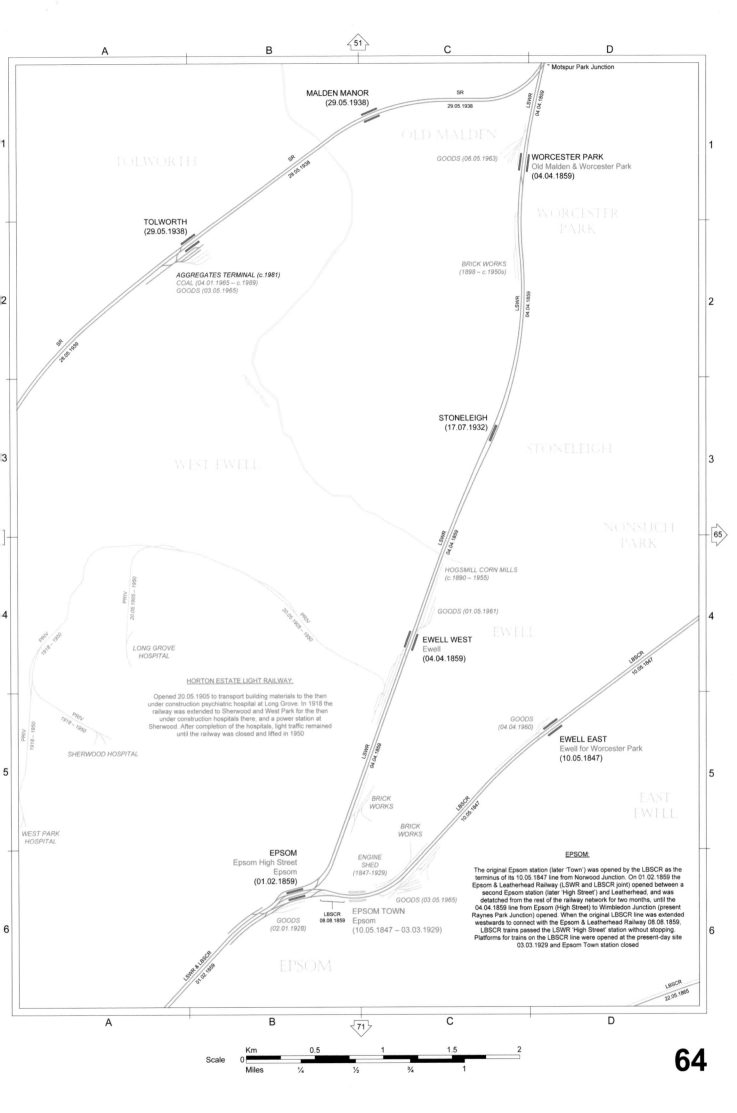

~ Motspur Park Junction

MALDEN MANOR
(29.05.1938)

SR
29.05.1938

OLD MALDEN

GOODS (06.05.1963)

WORCESTER PARK
Old Malden & Worcester Park
(04.04.1859)

LSWR
04.04.1859

SR
29.05.1938

TOLWORTH
(29.05.1938)

WORCESTER
PARK

AGGREGATES TERMINAL (c.1981)
COAL (04.01.1965 – c.1989)
GOODS (03.05.1965)

BRICK WORKS
(1898 – c.1950s)

LSWR
04.04.1859

SR
28.05.1939

Hogsmill River

STONELEIGH
(17.07.1932)

STONELEIGH

WEST EWELL

NONSUCH
PARK

65

PRIV
20.05.1905 – 1950

PRIV
20.05.1905 – 1950

LSWR
04.04.1859

HOGSMILL CORN MILLS
(c.1890 – 1955)

GOODS (01.05.1961)

PRIV
1918 – 1950

LONG GROVE
HOSPITAL

EWELL WEST
Ewell
(04.04.1859)

EWELL

LBSCR
10.05.1847

HORTON ESTATE LIGHT RAILWAY.

Opened 20.05.1905 to transport building materials to the then
under construction psychiatric hospital at Long Grove. In 1918 the
railway was extended to Sherwood and West Park for the then
under construction hospitals there, and a power station at
Sherwood. After completion of the hospitals, light traffic remained
until the railway was closed and lifted in 1950

PRIV
1918 – 1950

GOODS
(04.04.1960)

EWELL EAST
Ewell for Worcester Park
(10.05.1847)

PRIV
1918 – 1950

SHERWOOD HOSPITAL

LSWR
04.04.1859

BRICK
WORKS

EAST
EWELL

LBSCR
10.05.1847

WEST PARK
HOSPITAL

BRICK
WORKS

ENGINE
SHED
(1847-1929)

EPSOM:

The original Epsom station (later 'Town') was opened by the LBSCR as the
terminus of its 10.05.1847 line from Norwood Junction. On 01.02.1859 the
Epsom & Leatherhead Railway (LSWR and LBSCR joint) opened between a
second Epsom station (later 'High Street') and Leatherhead, and was
detatched from the rest of the railway network for two months, until the
04.04.1859 line from Epsom (High Street) to Wimbledon Junction (present
Raynes Park Junction) opened. When the original LBSCR line was extended
westwards to connect with the Epsom & Leatherhead Railway 08.08.1859,
LBSCR trains passed the LSWR 'High Street' station without stopping.
Platforms for trains on the LBSCR line were opened at the present-day site
03.03.1929 and Epsom Town station closed

EPSOM
Epsom High Street
Epsom
(01.02.1859)

GOODS (03.05.1965)

LBSCR
08.08.1859

EPSOM TOWN
Epsom
(10.05.1847 – 03.03.1929)

GOODS
(02.01.1928)

LSWR & LBSCR
01.02.1859

EPSOM

LBSCR
22.05.1865

Scale
Km 0 0.5 1 1.5 2
Miles ¼ ½ ¾ 1

64

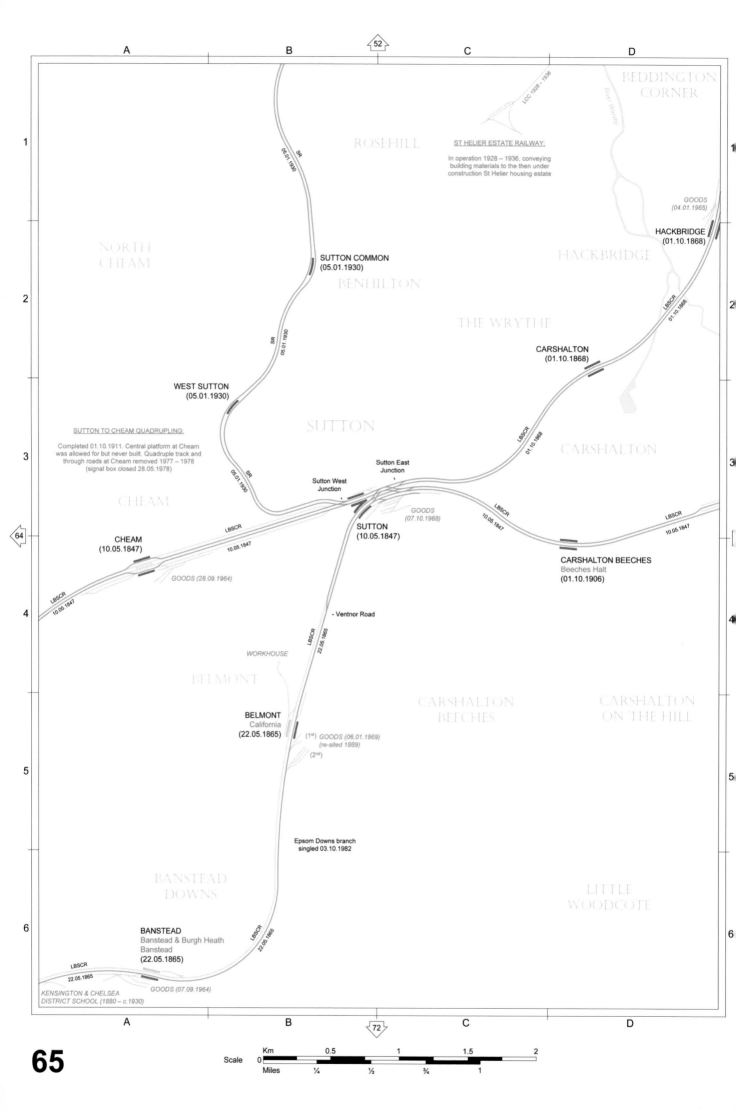

BEDDINGTON
CORNER

LCC 1928 – 1936

ST HELIER ESTATE RAILWAY:

In operation 1928 – 1936, conveying
building materials to the then under
construction St Helier housing estate

*GOODS
(04.01.1965)*

HACKBRIDGE
(01.10.1868)

ROSEHILL

05.01.1930

SR

SUTTON COMMON
(05.01.1930)

BENHILTON

HACKBRIDGE

05.01.1930

SR

THE WRYTHE

LBSCR
01.10.1868

WEST SUTTON
(05.01.1930)

CARSHALTON
(01.10.1868)

SUTTON

CARSHALTON

SUTTON TO CHEAM QUADRUPLING:

Completed 01.10.1911. Central platform at Cheam
was allowed for but never built. Quadruple track and
through roads at Cheam removed 1977 – 1978
(signal box closed 28.05.1978)

05.01.1930

SR

Sutton East
Junction

LBSCR
01.10.1868

CHEAM

Sutton West
Junction

CHEAM
(10.05.1847)

LBSCR
10.05.1847

*GOODS
(07.10.1968)*

SUTTON
(10.05.1847)

LBSCR
10.05.1847

LBSCR
10.05.1847

64

GOODS (28.09.1964)

CARSHALTON BEECHES
Beeches Halt
(01.10.1906)

LBSCR
10.05.1847

LBSCR
10.05.1847

- Ventnor Road

LBSCR
22.05.1865

WORKHOUSE

BELMONT

CARSHALTON
BEECHES

CARSHALTON
ON THE HILL

BELMONT
California
(22.05.1865)

(1st) *GOODS (06.01.1969)*
(re-sited 1889)

(2nd)

LITTLE
WOODCOTE

Epsom Downs branch
singled 03.10.1982

BANSTEAD
DOWNS

BANSTEAD
Banstead & Burgh Heath
Banstead
(22.05.1865)

LBSCR
22.05.1865

LBSCR
22.05.1865

GOODS (07.09.1964)

*KENSINGTON & CHELSEA
DISTRICT SCHOOL (1880 – c.1930)*

65

Scale
Km 0   0.5   1   1.5   2
Miles   ¼   ½   ¾   1

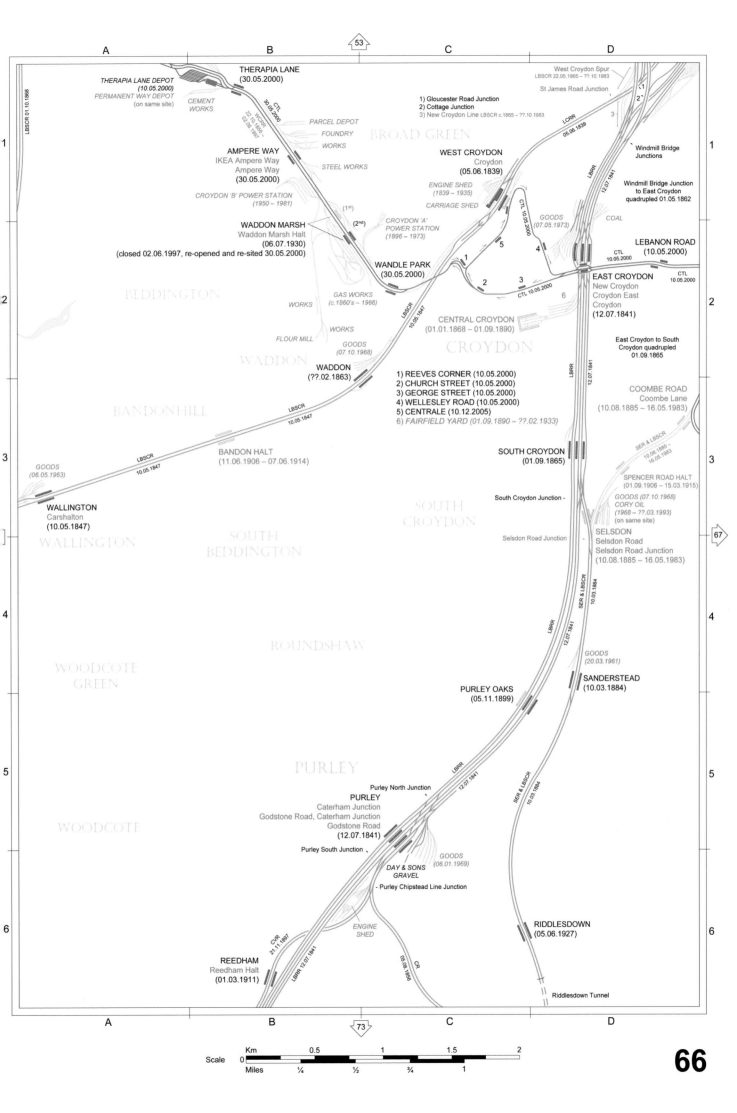

A   B   C   D

LBSCR 01.10.1868

THERAPIA LANE
(30.05.2000)

West Croydon Spur
LBSCR 22.05.1865 – ??.10.1983

St James Road Junction

THERAPIA LANE DEPOT
(10.05.2000)
PERMANENT WAY DEPOT
(on same site)

CEMENT
WORKS

CTL 30.05.2000

22.10.1865 – 02.06.1997

1) Gloucester Road Junction
2) Cottage Junction
3) New Croydon Line *LBSCR c.1865 – ??.10.1983*

LCRR 05.06.1839

Windmill Bridge
Junctions

AMPERE WAY
IKEA Ampere Way
Ampere Way
(30.05.2000)

PARCEL DEPOT
FOUNDRY
WORKS

BROAD GREEN

WEST CROYDON
Croydon
(05.06.1839)

LBRR 12.07.1841

Windmill Bridge Junction
to East Croydon
quadrupled 01.05.1862

STEEL WORKS

ENGINE SHED
(1839 – 1935)

CARRIAGE SHED

CTL 10.06.2000

GOODS
(07.05.1973)

COAL

LEBANON ROAD
(10.05.2000)

CROYDON 'B' POWER STATION
(1950 – 1981)

(1st)

(2nd)

CROYDON 'A'
POWER STATION
(1896 – 1973)

5

4

CTL 10.05.2000

WADDON MARSH
Waddon Marsh Halt
(06.07.1930)
(closed 02.06.1997, re-opened and re-sited 30.05.2000)

WANDLE PARK
(30.05.2000)

1

2

3

6

EAST CROYDON
New Croydon
Croydon East
Croydon
(12.07.1841)

CTL 10.05.2000

CTL 10.05.2000

BEDDINGTON

GAS WORKS
(c.1860's – 1966)

WORKS

LBSCR 10.05.1847

CENTRAL CROYDON
(01.01.1868 – 01.09.1890)

CROYDON

East Croydon to South
Croydon quadrupled
01.09.1865

WADDON

FLOUR MILL

WORKS

GOODS
(07.10.1968)

WADDON
(??.02.1863)

1) REEVES CORNER (10.05.2000)
2) CHURCH STREET (10.05.2000)
3) GEORGE STREET (10.05.2000)
4) WELLESLEY ROAD (10.05.2000)
5) CENTRALE (10.12.2005)
6) *FAIRFIELD YARD (01.09.1890 – ??.02.1933)*

LBRR 12.07.1841

COOMBE ROAD
Coombe Lane
(10.08.1885 – 16.05.1983)

BANDONHILL

LBSCR 10.05.1847

SER & LBSCR
10.08.1885 – 16.05.1983

SOUTH CROYDON
(01.09.1865)

SPENCER ROAD HALT
(01.09.1906 – 15.03.1915)

GOODS
(06.05.1963)

LBSCR 10.05.1847

BANDON HALT
(11.06.1906 – 07.06.1914)

South Croydon Junction -

GOODS (07.10.1968)
CORY OIL
(1968 – ??.03.1993)
(on same site)

WALLINGTON
Carshalton
(10.05.1847)

Selsdon Road Junction - -

SELSDON
Selsdon Road
Selsdon Road Junction
(10.08.1885 – 16.05.1983)

WALLINGTON

SOUTH
BEDDINGTON

SOUTH
CROYDON

ROUNDSHAW

SER & LBSCR 10.03.1884

LBRR 12.07.1841

GOODS
(20.03.1961)

WOODCOTE
GREEN

PURLEY OAKS
(05.11.1899)

SANDERSTEAD
(10.03.1884)

PURLEY

LBRR 12.07.1841

Purley North Junction

PURLEY
Caterham Junction
Godstone Road, Caterham Junction
Godstone Road
(12.07.1841)

SER & LBSCR 10.03.1884

WOODCOTE

Purley South Junction

GOODS
(06.01.1969)

DAY & SONS
GRAVEL

- Purley Chipstead Line Junction

RIDDLESDOWN
(05.06.1927)

CVR 21.11.1897

ENGINE
SHED

LBRR 12.07.1841

CR 05.08.1856

REEDHAM
Reedham Halt
(01.03.1911)

Riddlesdown Tunnel

A   B   C   D

Scale

Km
0   0.5   1   1.5   2

Miles
¼   ½   ¾   1

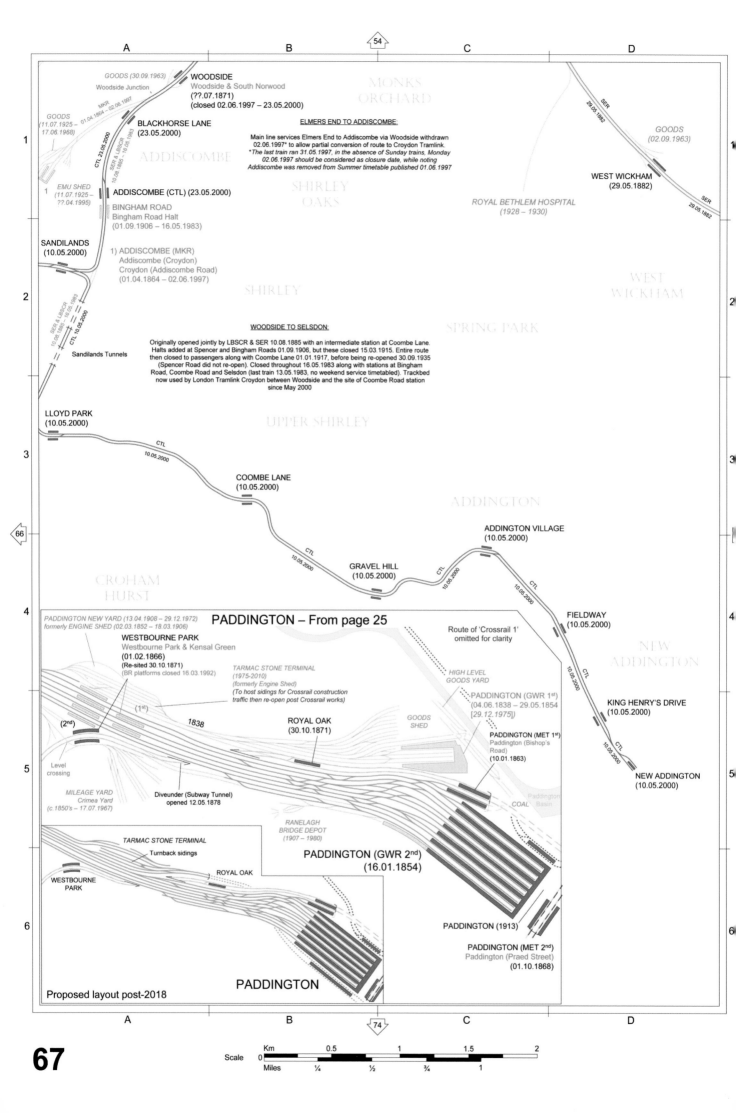

A B C D

GOODS (30.09.1963)
Woodside Junction

WOODSIDE
Woodside & South Norwood
(??.07.1871)
(closed 02.06.1997 – 23.05.2000)

MONKS
ORCHARD

GOODS
(11.07.1925 –
17.06.1968)

MKR
01.04.1864 – 02.06.1997

BLACKHORSE LANE
(23.05.2000)

ELMERS END TO ADDISCOMBE:

Main line services Elmers End to Addiscombe via Woodside withdrawn
02.06.1997* to allow partial conversion of route to Croydon Tramlink.
*The last train ran 31.05.1997, in the absence of Sunday trains, Monday
02.06.1997 should be considered as closure date, while noting
Addiscombe was removed from Summer timetable published 01.06.1997

SER
29.05.1882

GOODS
(02.09.1963)

ADDISCOMBE

EMU SHED
(11.07.1925 –
??.04.1995)

ADDISCOMBE (CTL) (23.05.2000)

SHIRLEY
OAKS

WEST WICKHAM
(29.05.1882)

SER
29.05.1882

BINGHAM ROAD
Bingham Road Halt
(01.09.1906 – 16.05.1983)

ROYAL BETHLEM HOSPITAL
(1928 – 1930)

SANDILANDS
(10.05.2000)

1) ADDISCOMBE (MKR)
Addiscombe (Croydon)
Croydon (Addiscombe Road)
(01.04.1864 – 02.06.1997)

SHIRLEY

WEST
WICKHAM

SER & LBSCR
10.08.1885 – 16.05.1983
CTL 10.05.2000

SPRING PARK

Sandilands Tunnels

WOODSIDE TO SELSDON:

Originally opened jointly by LBSCR & SER 10.08.1885 with an intermediate station at Coombe Lane.
Halts added at Spencer and Bingham Roads 01.09.1906, but these closed 15.03.1915. Entire route
then closed to passengers along with Coombe Lane 01.01.1917, before being re-opened 30.09.1935
(Spencer Road did not re-open). Closed throughout 16.05.1983 along with stations at Bingham
Road, Coombe Road and Selsdon (last train 13.05.1983, no weekend service timetabled). Trackbed
now used by London Tramlink Croydon between Woodside and the site of Coombe Road station
since May 2000

LLOYD PARK
(10.05.2000)

UPPER SHIRLEY

CTL
10.05.2000

COOMBE LANE
(10.05.2000)

ADDINGTON

ADDINGTON VILLAGE
(10.05.2000)

CROHAM
HURST

CTL
10.05.2000

GRAVEL HILL
(10.05.2000)

CTL
10.05.2000

CTL
10.05.2000

FIELDWAY
(10.05.2000)

NEW
ADDINGTON

PADDINGTON NEW YARD (13.04.1908 – 29.12.1972)
formerly ENGINE SHED (02.03.1852 – 18.03.1906)

PADDINGTON – From page 25

Route of 'Crossrail 1'
omitted for clarity

WESTBOURNE PARK
Westbourne Park & Kensal Green
(01.02.1866)
(Re-sited 30.10.1871)
(BR platforms closed 16.03.1992)

TARMAC STONE TERMINAL
(1975-2010)
(formerly Engine Shed)
(To host sidings for Crossrail construction
traffic then re-open post Crossrail works)

HIGH LEVEL
GOODS YARD

PADDINGTON (GWR 1st)
[04.06.1838 – 29.05.1854]
[29.12.1975]

CTL
10.05.2000

KING HENRY'S DRIVE
(10.05.2000)

(2nd)

(1st)

1838

GOODS
SHED

ROYAL OAK
(30.10.1871)

PADDINGTON (MET 1st)
Paddington (Bishop's
Road)
(10.01.1863)

CTL
10.05.2000

Level
crossing

MILEAGE YARD
Crimea Yard
(c.1850's – 17.07.1967)

Diveunder (Subway Tunnel)
opened 12.05.1878

NEW ADDINGTON
(10.05.2000)

Paddington
Basin

COAL

TARMAC STONE TERMINAL
Turnback sidings

RANELAGH
BRIDGE DEPOT
(1907 – 1980)

WESTBOURNE
PARK

ROYAL OAK

PADDINGTON (GWR 2nd)
(16.01.1854)

PADDINGTON (1913)

PADDINGTON (MET 2nd)
Paddington (Praed Street)
(01.10.1868)

PADDINGTON

Proposed layout post-2018

A B C D

Scale
Km
0 0.5 1 1.5 2
Miles
¼ ½ ¾ 1

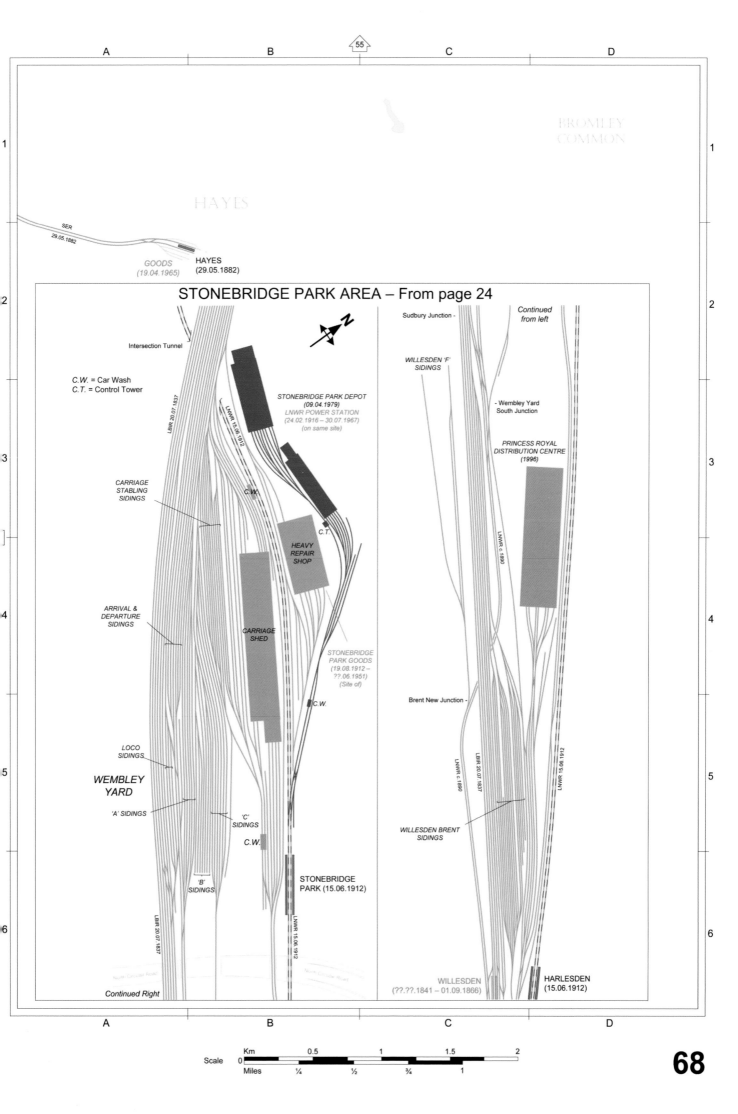

STONEBRIDGE PARK AREA – From page 24

SER
29.05.1882

GOODS
(19.04.1965)

HAYES
(29.05.1882)

HAYES

BROMLEY
COMMON

Intersection Tunnel

C.W. = Car Wash
C.T. = Control Tower

LBIR 20.07.1837

LNWR 15.06.1912

STONEBRIDGE PARK DEPOT
(09.04.1979)
LNWR POWER STATION
(24.02.1916 – 30.07.1967)
(on same site)

Sudbury Junction -

Continued
from left

WILLESDEN 'F'
SIDINGS

- Wembley Yard
South Junction

PRINCESS ROYAL
DISTRIBUTION CENTRE
(1996)

CARRIAGE
STABLING
SIDINGS

C.W.

C.T.

HEAVY
REPAIR
SHOP

ARRIVAL &
DEPARTURE
SIDINGS

CARRIAGE
SHED

STONEBRIDGE
PARK GOODS
(19.08.1912 –
??.06.1951)
(Site of)

LNWR c.1890

C.W.

Brent New Junction -

LOCO
SIDINGS

WEMBLEY
YARD

'A' SIDINGS

'C'
SIDINGS

C.W.

LNWR c.1890

LBIR 20.07.1837

LNWR 15.06.1912

WILLESDEN BRENT
SIDINGS

'B'
SIDINGS

STONEBRIDGE
PARK (15.06.1912)

LBIR 20.07.1837

LNWR 15.06.1912

WILLESDEN
(??.??.1841 – 01.09.1866)

HARLESDEN
(15.06.1912)

Continued Right

Scale

Km
0   0.5   1   1.5   2

Miles
¼   ½   ¾   1

68

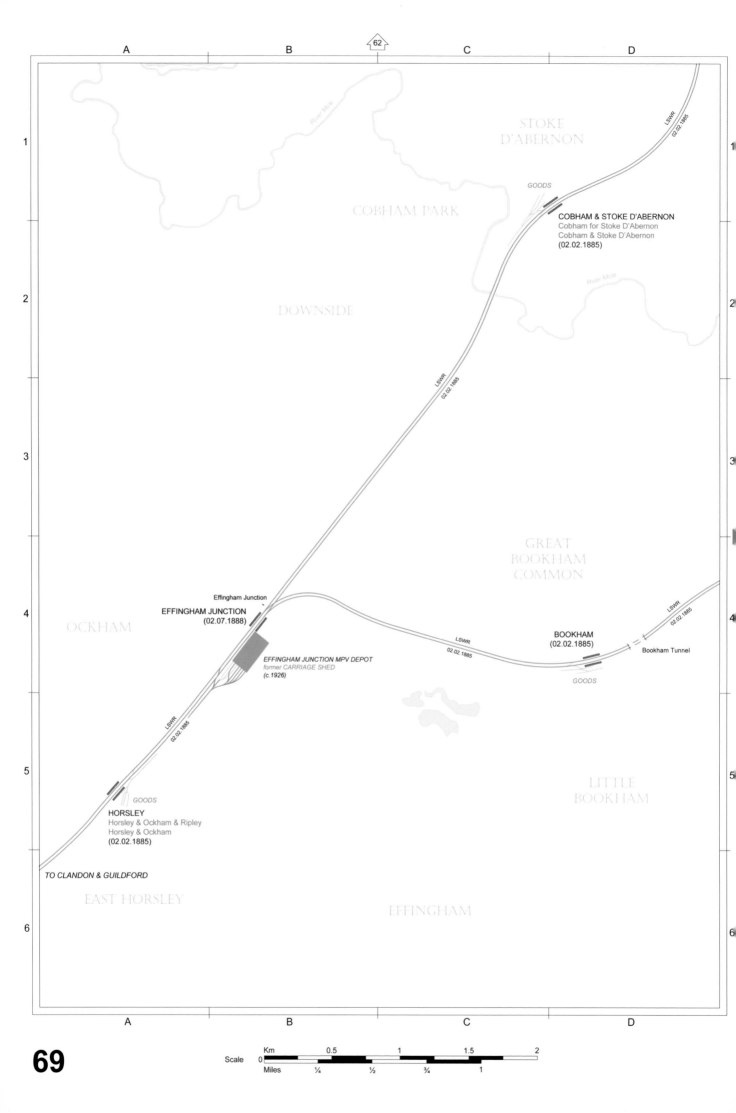

A B C D

1

STOKE
D'ABERNON

COBHAM PARK

GOODS

COBHAM & STOKE D'ABERNON
Cobham for Stoke D'Abernon
Cobham & Stoke D'Abernon
(02.02.1885)

LSWR
02.02.1885

River Mole

2

DOWNSIDE

River Mole

LSWR
02.02.1885

3

GREAT
BOOKHAM
COMMON

Effingham Junction

EFFINGHAM JUNCTION
(02.07.1888)

LSWR
02.02.1885

BOOKHAM
(02.02.1885)

LSWR
02.02.1885

4

OCKHAM

EFFINGHAM JUNCTION MPV DEPOT
former CARRIAGE SHED
(c.1926)

Bookham Tunnel

GOODS

LSWR
02.02.1885

LITTLE
BOOKHAM

5

GOODS

HORSLEY
Horsley & Ockham & Ripley
Horsley & Ockham
(02.02.1885)

TO CLANDON & GUILDFORD

EAST HORSLEY

EFFINGHAM

6

69

Scale

Km 0 0.5 1 1.5 2

Miles ¼ ½ ¾ 1

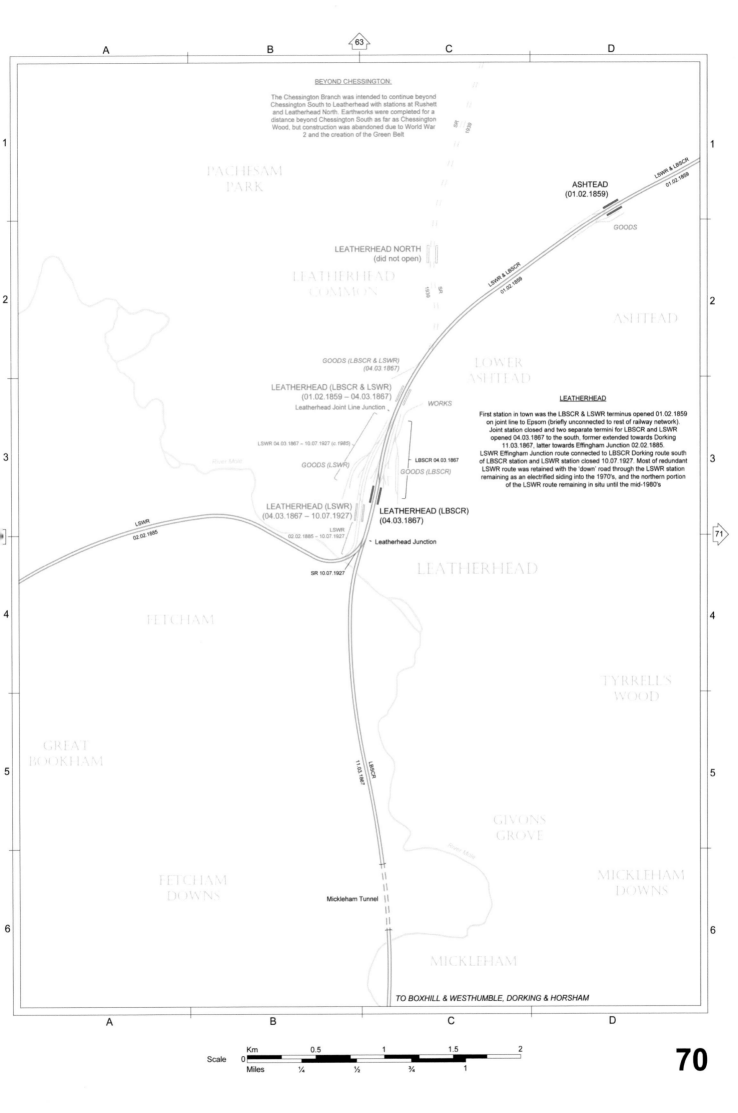

BEYOND CHESSINGTON:

The Chessington Branch was intended to continue beyond
Chessington South to Leatherhead with stations at Rushett
and Leatherhead North. Earthworks were completed for a
distance beyond Chessington South as far as Chessington
Wood, but construction was abandoned due to World War
2 and the creation of the Green Belt

PACHESAM
PARK

ASHTEAD
(01.02.1859)

LSWR & LBSCR
01.02.1859

GOODS

LEATHERHEAD NORTH
(did not open)

LEATHERHEAD
COMMON

LSWR & LBSCR
01.02.1859

ASHTEAD

LOWER
ASHTEAD

GOODS (LBSCR & LSWR)
(04.03.1867)

LEATHERHEAD (LBSCR & LSWR)
(01.02.1859 – 04.03.1867)

Leatherhead Joint Line Junction

WORKS

LEATHERHEAD

First station in town was the LBSCR & LSWR terminus opened 01.02.1859
on joint line to Epsom (briefly unconnected to rest of railway network).
Joint station closed and two separate termini for LBSCR and LSWR
opened 04.03.1867 to the south, former extended towards Dorking
11.03.1867, latter towards Effingham Junction 02.02.1885.
LSWR Effingham Junction route connected to LBSCR Dorking route south
of LBSCR station and LSWR station closed 10.07.1927. Most of redundant
LSWR route was retained with the 'down' road through the LSWR station
remaining as an electrified siding into the 1970's, and the northern portion
of the LSWR route remaining in situ until the mid-1980's

LSWR 04.03.1867 – 10.07.1927 (c.1985)

River Mole

GOODS (LSWR)

LBSCR 04.03.1867

GOODS (LBSCR)

LEATHERHEAD (LSWR)
(04.03.1867 – 10.07.1927)

LEATHERHEAD (LBSCR)
(04.03.1867)

LSWR
02.02.1885

LSWR
02.02.1885 – 10.07.1927

Leatherhead Junction

SR 10.07.1927

LEATHERHEAD

LSWR
02.02.1885

FETCHAM

TYRRELL'S
WOOD

GREAT
BOOKHAM

11.03.1867   LBSCR

GIVONS
GROVE

River Mole

FETCHAM
DOWNS

MICKLEHAM
DOWNS

Mickleham Tunnel

MICKLEHAM

TO BOXHILL & WESTHUMBLE, DORKING & HORSHAM

71

Scale

Km   0   0.5   1   1.5   2

Miles   ¼   ½   ¾   1

70

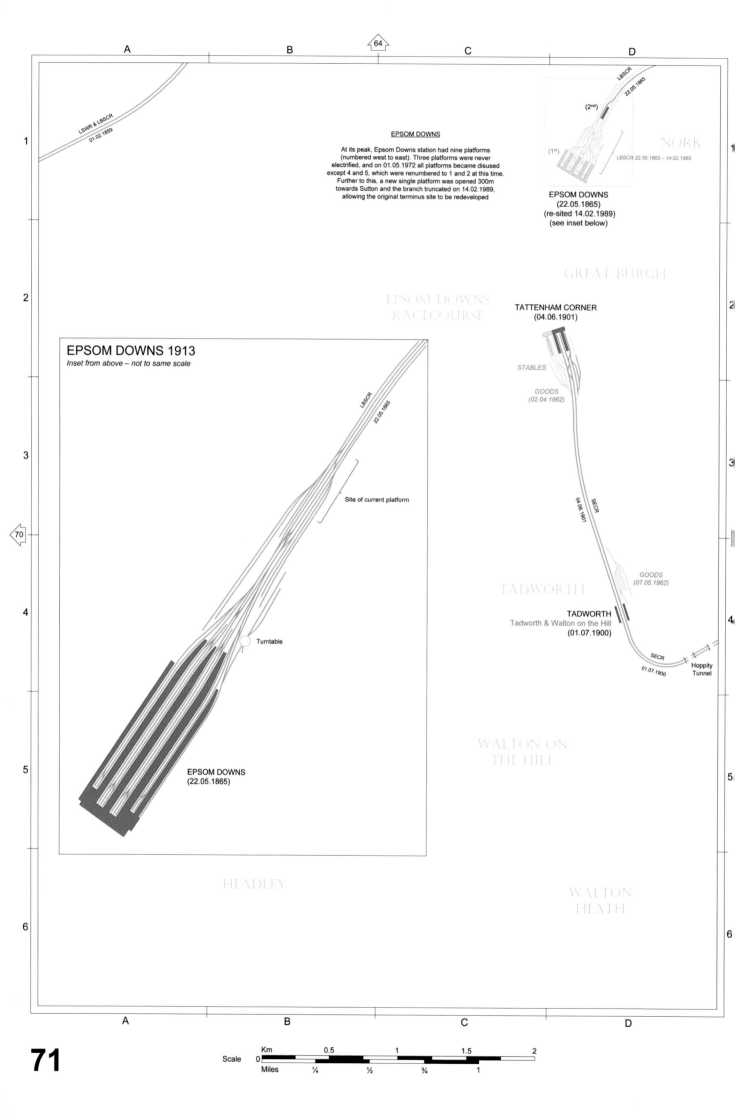

A   B   C   D

LSWR & LBSCR
01.02.1859

EPSOM DOWNS

At its peak, Epsom Downs station had nine platforms (numbered west to east). Three platforms were never electrified, and on 01.05.1972 all platforms became disused except 4 and 5, which were renumbered to 1 and 2 at this time. Further to this, a new single platform was opened 300m towards Sutton and the branch truncated on 14.02.1989, allowing the original terminus site to be redeveloped

(2nd)

(1st)

LBSCR 22.05.1865 – 14.02.1989

LBSCR
22.05.1865

NORK

EPSOM DOWNS
(22.05.1865)
(re-sited 14.02.1989)
(see inset below)

GREAT BURGH

EPSOM DOWNS
RACECOURSE

TATTENHAM CORNER
(04.06.1901)

EPSOM DOWNS 1913
Inset from above – not to same scale

LBSCR
22.05.1865

STABLES

GOODS
(02.04.1962)

Site of current platform

70

SECR
04.06.1901

GOODS
(07.05.1962)

TADWORTH

○ Turntable

TADWORTH
Tadworth & Walton on the Hill
(01.07.1900)

EPSOM DOWNS
(22.05.1865)

SECR
01.07.1900

Hoppity
Tunnel

WALTON ON
THE HILL

HEADLEY

WALTON
HEATH

Scale

Km   0   0.5   1   1.5   2

Miles   ¼   ½   ¾   1

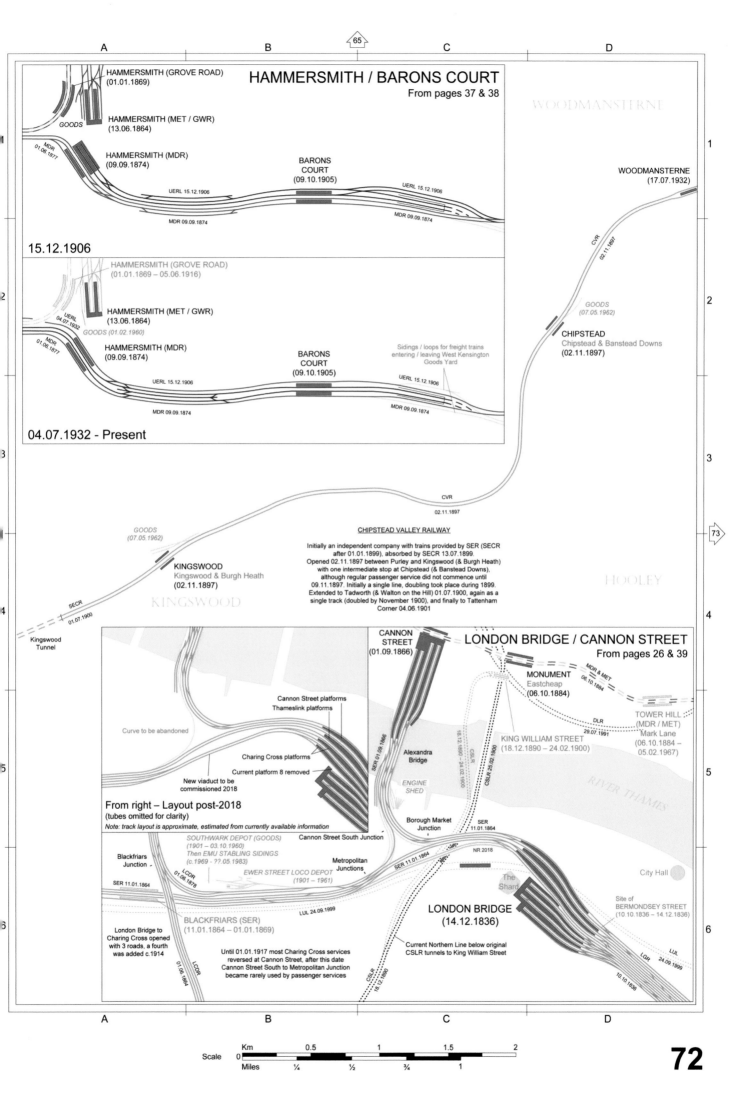

HAMMERSMITH / BARONS COURT
From pages 37 & 38

HAMMERSMITH (GROVE ROAD)
(01.01.1869)

GOODS

HAMMERSMITH (MET / GWR)
(13.06.1864)

MDR
01.06.1877

HAMMERSMITH (MDR)
(09.09.1874)

BARONS
COURT
(09.10.1905)

UERL 15.12.1906

MDR 09.09.1874

UERL 15.12.1906

MDR 09.09.1874

15.12.1906

HAMMERSMITH (GROVE ROAD)
(01.01.1869 – 05.06.1916)

UERL
04.07.1932

HAMMERSMITH (MET / GWR)
(13.06.1864)

GOODS (01.02.1960)

MDR
01.06.1877

HAMMERSMITH (MDR)
(09.09.1874)

BARONS
COURT
(09.10.1905)

UERL 15.12.1906

MDR 09.09.1874

Sidings / loops for freight trains
entering / leaving West Kensington
Goods Yard

UERL 15.12.1906

MDR 09.09.1874

04.07.1932 - Present

WOODMANSTERNE

WOODMANSTERNE
(17.07.1932)

CVR
02.11.1897

GOODS
(07.05.1962)

CHIPSTEAD
Chipstead & Banstead Downs
(02.11.1897)

CVR
02.11.1897

HOOLEY

CHIPSTEAD VALLEY RAILWAY

Initially an independent company with trains provided by SER (SECR
after 01.01.1899), absorbed by SECR 13.07.1899.
Opened 02.11.1897 between Purley and Kingswood (& Burgh Heath)
with one intermediate stop at Chipstead (& Banstead Downs),
although regular passenger service did not commence until
09.11.1897. Initially a single line, doubling took place during 1899.
Extended to Tadworth (& Walton on the Hill) 01.07.1900, again as a
single track (doubled by November 1900), and finally to Tattenham
Corner 04.06.1901

GOODS
(07.05.1962)

KINGSWOOD
Kingswood & Burgh Heath
(02.11.1897)

KINGSWOOD

SECR
01.07.1900

Kingswood
Tunnel

73

CANNON
STREET
(01.09.1866)

LONDON BRIDGE / CANNON STREET
From pages 26 & 39

MONUMENT
Eastcheap
(06.10.1884)

MDR & MET
06.10.1884

SER 01.09.1866

KING WILLIAM STREET
(18.12.1890 – 24.02.1900)

DLR
29.07.1991

TOWER HILL
(MDR / MET)
Mark Lane
(06.10.1884 –
05.02.1967)

Alexandra
Bridge

CSLR 18.12.1890 – 24.02.1900

CSLR 25.02.1900

RIVER THAMES

Cannon Street platforms

Thameslink platforms

Charing Cross platforms

Curve to be abandoned

Current platform 8 removed

New viaduct to be
commissioned 2018

From right – Layout post-2018
(tubes omitted for clarity)
Note: track layout is approximate, estimated from currently available information

*ENGINE
SHED*

Borough Market
Junction

SER
11.01.1864

SOUTHWARK DEPOT (GOODS)
(1901 – 03.10.1950)
Then EMU STABLING SIDINGS
(c.1969 - ??.05.1983)

Cannon Street South Junction

Metropolitan
Junctions

SER 11.01.1864

NR 2018

City Hall

Blackfriars
Junction

LCDR
01.06.1878

EWER STREET LOCO DEPOT
(1901 – 1961)

SER 11.01.1864

The
Shard

LUL 24.09.1999

LONDON BRIDGE
(14.12.1836)

Site of
BERMONDSEY STREET
(10.10.1836 – 14.12.1836)

SER 11.01.1864

BLACKFRIARS (SER)
(11.01.1864 – 01.01.1869)

London Bridge to
Charing Cross opened
with 3 roads, a fourth
was added c.1914

Until 01.01.1917 most Charing Cross services
reversed at Cannon Street, after this date
Cannon Street South to Metropolitan Junction
became rarely used by passenger services

Current Northern Line below original
CSLR tunnels to King William Street

CSLR
18.12.1890

LCDR
01.06.1864

LGR
10.10.1836

LUL
24.09.1999

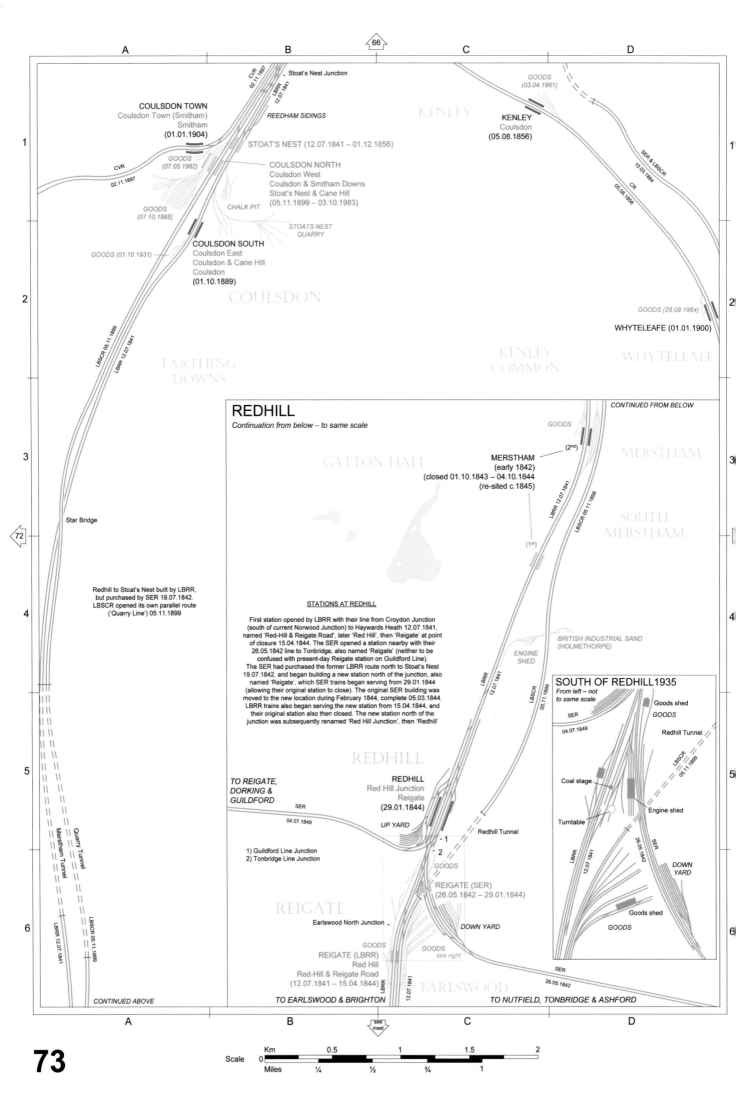

A B C D

1

COULSDON TOWN
Coulsdon Town (Smitham)
Smitham
(01.01.1904)

CVR
02.11.1897

Stoat's Nest Junction

CVR
02.11.1897

LBRR
12.07.1841

REEDHAM SIDINGS

GOODS
(07.05.1962)

GOODS
(03.04.1961)

KENLEY

KENLEY
Coulsdon
(05.08.1856)

STOAT'S NEST (12.07.1841 – 01.12.1856)

SER & LBSCR
10.03.1884

CR
05.08.1856

COULSDON NORTH
Coulsdon West
Coulsdon & Smitham Downs
Stoat's Nest & Cane Hill
(05.11.1899 – 03.10.1983)

GOODS
(07.10.1958)

CHALK PIT

STOATS NEST
QUARRY

COULSDON SOUTH
Coulsdon East
Coulsdon & Cane Hill
Coulsdon
(01.10.1889)

GOODS (01.10.1931)

COULSDON

GOODS (28.09.1964)

WHYTELEAFE (01.01.1900)

2

KENLEY
COMMON

WHYTELEAFE

FARTHING
DOWNS

LBSCR 05.11.1899
LBRR 12.07.1841

3

CONTINUED FROM BELOW

REDHILL
Continuation from below – to same scale

GOODS

MERSTHAM
(early 1842)
(closed 01.10.1843 – 04.10.1844)
(re-sited c.1845)

(2nd)

MERSTHAM

GATTON HALL

LBRR 12.07.1841

LBSCR 05.11.1899

SOUTH
MERSTHAM

Star Bridge

4

(1st)

Redhill to Stoat's Nest built by LBRR,
but purchased by SER 19.07.1842.
LBSCR opened its own parallel route
('Quarry Line') 05.11.1899

STATIONS AT REDHILL

First station opened by LBRR with their line from Croydon Junction
(south of current Norwood Junction) to Haywards Heath 12.07.1841,
named 'Red-Hill & Reigate Road', later 'Red Hill', then 'Reigate' at point
of closure 15.04.1844. The SER opened a station nearby with their
26.05.1842 line to Tonbridge, also named 'Reigate' (neither to be
confused with present-day Reigate station on Guildford Line).
The SER had purchased the former LBRR route north to Stoat's Nest
19.07.1842, and began building a new station north of the junction, also
named 'Reigate', which SER trains began serving from 29.01.1844
(allowing their original station to close). The original SER building was
moved to the new location during February 1844, complete 05.03.1844.
LBRR trains also began serving the new station from 15.04.1844, and
their original station also then closed. The new station north of the
junction was subsequently renamed 'Red Hill Junction', then 'Redhill'

BRITISH INDUSTRIAL SAND
(HOLMETHORPE)

ENGINE
SHED

LBRR
12.07.1841

LBSCR
05.11.1899

SOUTH OF REDHILL 1935
*From left – not
to same scale*

Goods shed
GOODS

Redhill Tunnel

LBSCR
05.11.1899

5

Merstham Tunnel

Quarry Line

Coal stage

Engine shed

SER
04.07.1849

Turntable

SER
26.05.1842

LBRR
12.07.1841

DOWN
YARD

TO REIGATE,
DORKING &
GUILDFORD

SER
04.07.1849

REDHILL
Red Hill Junction
Reigate
(29.01.1844)

UP YARD

Redhill Tunnel

1) Guildford Line Junction
2) Tonbridge Line Junction

1
2

GOODS

Goods shed

REDHILL

GOODS

REIGATE (SER)
(26.05.1842 – 29.01.1844)

6

REIGATE

Earlswood North Junction

DOWN YARD

GOODS
see right

GOODS

GOODS

REIGATE (LBRR)
Red Hill
Red-Hill & Reigate Road
(12.07.1841 – 15.04.1844)

LBRR
12.07.1841

SER
26.05.1842

EARLSWOOD

CONTINUED ABOVE

TO EARLSWOOD & BRIGHTON

TO NUTFIELD, TONBRIDGE & ASHFORD

A B C D

see
inset

73

Scale

Km
0   0.5   1   1.5   2

Miles   ¼   ½   ¾   1

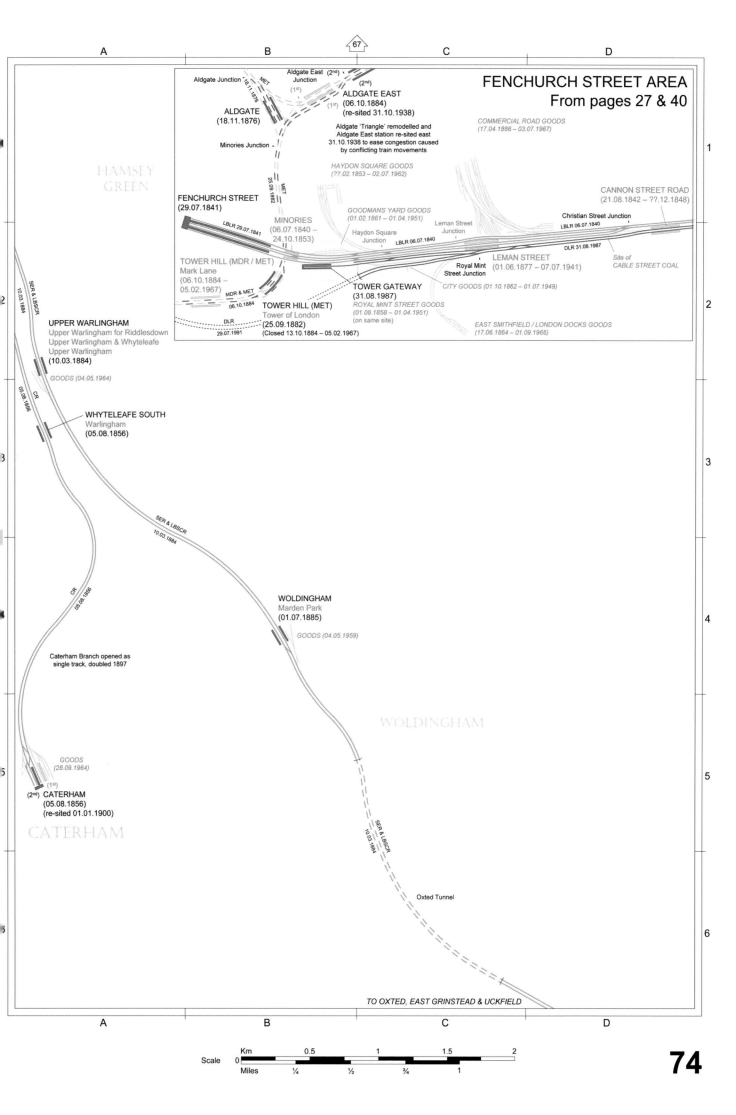

FENCHURCH STREET AREA
From pages 27 & 40

Aldgate East (2nd)
Aldgate Junction Junction
                    (1st)   (2nd)
MET
18.11.1876
ALDGATE EAST
(06.10.1884)
(1st)   (re-sited 31.10.1938)

ALDGATE
(18.11.1876)

Aldgate 'Triangle' remodelled and
Aldgate East station re-sited east
31.10.1938 to ease congestion caused
by conflicting train movements

Minories Junction

COMMERCIAL ROAD GOODS
(17.04.1886 – 03.07.1967)

HAMSEY
GREEN

HAYDON SQUARE GOODS
(??.02.1853 – 02.07.1962)

MET
25.09.1882

CANNON STREET ROAD
(21.08.1842 – ??.12.1848)

FENCHURCH STREET
(29.07.1841)

LBLR 29.07.1841

Christian Street Junction
LBLR 06.07.1840

MINORIES
(06.07.1840 –
24.10.1853)

GOODMANS YARD GOODS
(01.02.1861 – 01.04.1951)

Haydon Square
Junction

Leman Street
Junction

DLR 31.08.1987

TOWER HILL (MDR / MET)
Mark Lane
(06.10.1884 –
05.02.1967)

LBLR 06.07.1840

LEMAN STREET
(01.06.1877 – 07.07.1941)

Site of
CABLE STREET COAL

MDR & MET
06.10.1884

Royal Mint
Street Junction

TOWER GATEWAY
(31.08.1987)

CITY GOODS (01.10.1862 – 01.07.1949)

TOWER HILL (MET)
Tower of London
(25.09.1882)
(Closed 13.10.1884 – 05.02.1967)

DLR
29.07.1991

TOWER HILL (MET)
ROYAL MINT STREET GOODS
(01.08.1858 – 01.04.1951)
(on same site)

EAST SMITHFIELD / LONDON DOCKS GOODS
(17.06.1864 – 01.09.1966)

SER & LBSCR
10.03.1884

CR
05.08.1856

UPPER WARLINGHAM
Upper Warlingham for Riddlesdown
Upper Warlingham & Whyteleafe
Upper Warlingham
(10.03.1884)

GOODS (04.05.1964)

WHYTELEAFE SOUTH
Warlingham
(05.08.1856)

SER & LBSCR
10.03.1884

CR
05.08.1856

WOLDINGHAM
Marden Park
(01.07.1885)

GOODS (04.05.1959)

WOLDINGHAM

Caterham Branch opened as
single track, doubled 1897

GOODS
(28.09.1964)

(1st)

(2nd) **CATERHAM**
(05.08.1856)
(re-sited 01.01.1900)

CATERHAM

SER & LBSCR
10.03.1884

Oxted Tunnel

TO OXTED, EAST GRINSTEAD & UCKFIELD

Scale

Km
0   0.5   1   1.5   2

Miles
       ¼   ½   ¾   1

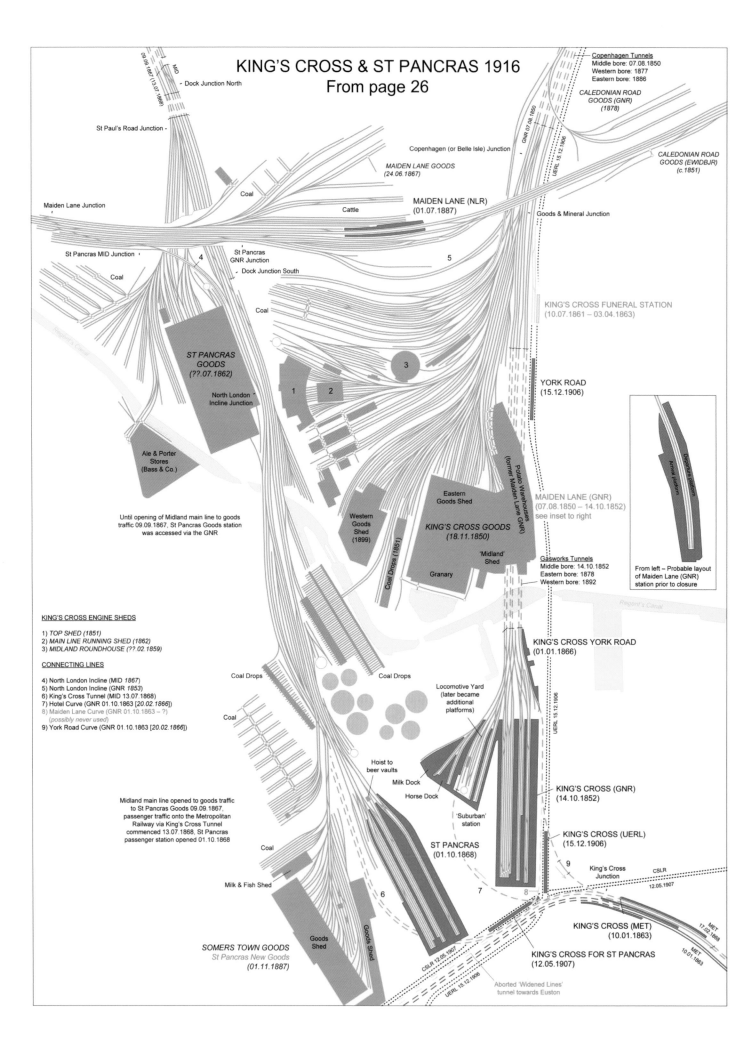

KING'S CROSS & ST PANCRAS 1916
From page 26

09.09.1867 (13.07.1868)

MID

Dock Junction North

St Paul's Road Junction

Copenhagen Tunnels
Middle bore: 07.08.1850
Western bore: 1877
Eastern bore: 1886

CALEDONIAN ROAD
GOODS (GNR)
(1878)

Copenhagen (or Belle Isle) Junction

GNR 07.08.1850

UERL 15.12.1906

CALEDONIAN ROAD
GOODS (EWIDBJR)
(c.1851)

MAIDEN LANE GOODS
(24.06.1867)

Maiden Lane Junction

Coal

Cattle

MAIDEN LANE (NLR)
(01.07.1887)

Goods & Mineral Junction

St Pancras MID Junction

4

St Pancras
GNR Junction

5

Coal

Dock Junction South

KING'S CROSS FUNERAL STATION
(10.07.1861 – 03.04.1863)

Coal

ST PANCRAS
GOODS
(??.07.1862)

3

YORK ROAD
(15.12.1906)

North London
Incline Junction

1

2

Ale & Porter
Stores
(Bass & Co.)

Eastern
Goods Shed

Potato Warehouses
(former Maiden Lane GNR)

MAIDEN LANE (GNR)
(07.08.1850 – 14.10.1852)
see inset to right

Departure platform
Arrival platform

Western
Goods
Shed
(1899)

KING'S CROSS GOODS
(18.11.1850)

'Midland'
Shed

Until opening of Midland main line to goods
traffic 09.09.1867, St Pancras Goods station
was accessed via the GNR

Coal Drops (1851)

Granary

Gasworks Tunnels
Middle bore: 14.10.1852
Eastern bore: 1878
Western bore: 1892

From left – Probable layout
of Maiden Lane (GNR)
station prior to closure

Regent's Canal

KING'S CROSS ENGINE SHEDS

1) TOP SHED (1851)
2) MAIN LINE RUNNING SHED (1862)
3) MIDLAND ROUNDHOUSE (??.02.1859)

CONNECTING LINES

4) North London Incline (MID 1867)
5) North London Incline (GNR 1853)
6) King's Cross Tunnel (MID 13.07.1868)
7) Hotel Curve (GNR 01.10.1863 [20.02.1866])
8) Maiden Lane Curve (GNR 01.10.1863 – ?)
   (possibly never used)
9) York Road Curve (GNR 01.10.1863 [20.02.1866])

KING'S CROSS YORK ROAD
(01.01.1866)

Coal Drops

Coal Drops

Coal

Locomotive Yard
(later became
additional
platforms)

KING'S CROSS (GNR)
(14.10.1852)

Midland main line opened to goods traffic
to St Pancras Goods 09.09.1867,
passenger traffic onto the Metropolitan
Railway via King's Cross Tunnel
commenced 13.07.1868, St Pancras
passenger station opened 01.10.1868

Hoist to
beer vaults

Milk Dock

Horse Dock

'Suburban'
station

KING'S CROSS (UERL)
(15.12.1906)

9

King's Cross
Junction

CSLR
12.05.1907

Coal

ST PANCRAS
(01.10.1868)

7

8

UERL 15.12.1906

Milk & Fish Shed

6

Goods Shed

KING'S CROSS (MET)
(10.01.1863)

MET
17.02.1868

MET
10.01.1863

SOMERS TOWN GOODS
St Pancras New Goods
(01.11.1887)

Goods
Shed

CSLR 12.05.1907

KING'S CROSS FOR ST PANCRAS
(12.05.1907)

UERL 15.12.1906

Aborted 'Widened Lines'
tunnel towards Euston

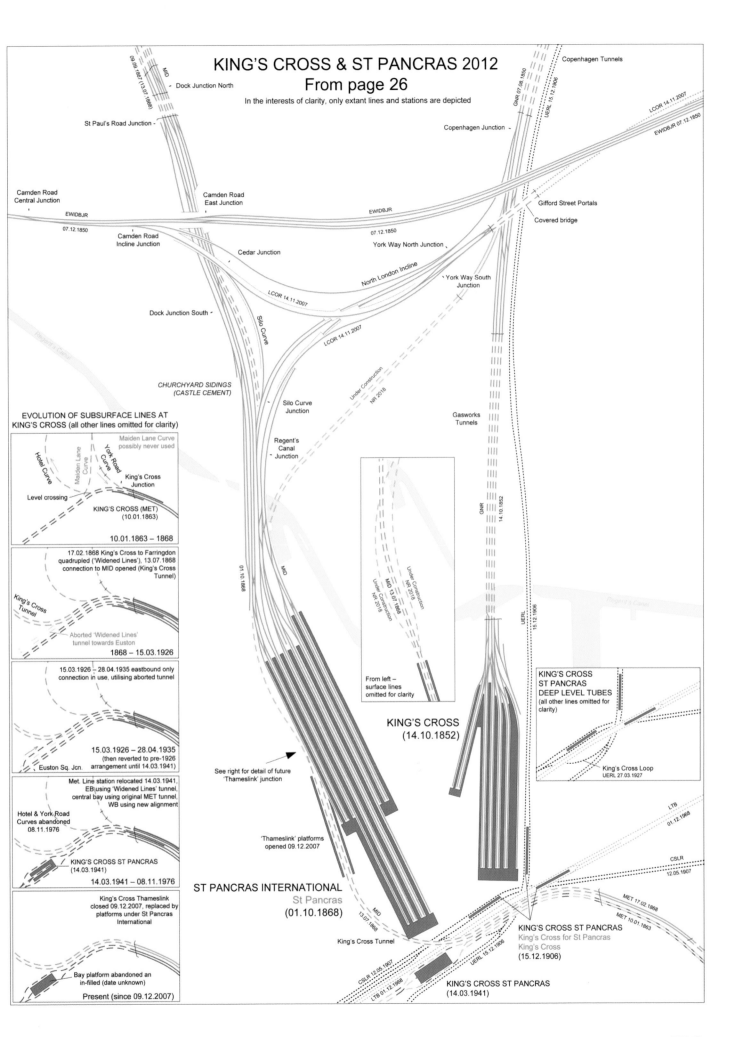

King's Cross Tunnel

KING'S CROSS & ST PANCRAS 2012
From page 26
In the interests of clarity, only extant lines and stations are depicted

Copenhagen Tunnels

GNR 07.08.1850

UERL 15.12.1906

LCOR 14.11.2007

EWIDBJR 07.12.1850

Copenhagen Junction

Dock Junction North

St Paul's Road Junction

Gifford Street Portals

Covered bridge

Camden Road
Central Junction

Camden Road
East Junction

EWIDBJR

EWIDBJR

07.12.1850

07.12.1850

Camden Road
Incline Junction

Cedar Junction

York Way North Junction

York Way South
Junction

North London Incline

LCOR 14.11.2007

Dock Junction South

Silo Curve

LCOR 14.11.2007

Under Construction
NR 2018

CHURCHYARD SIDINGS
(CASTLE CEMENT)

Silo Curve
Junction

Gasworks
Tunnels

Regent's
Canal
Junction

GNR

14.10.1852

EVOLUTION OF SUBSURFACE LINES AT
KING'S CROSS (all other lines omitted for clarity)

Maiden Lane Curve
possibly never used

Hotel Curve

Maiden Lane
Curve

York Road
Curve

King's Cross
Junction

Level crossing

KING'S CROSS (MET)
(10.01.1863)

10.01.1863 – 1868

17.02.1868 King's Cross to Farringdon
quadrupled ('Widened Lines'), 13.07.1868
connection to MID opened (King's Cross
Tunnel)

King's Cross
Tunnel

Aborted 'Widened Lines'
tunnel towards Euston

1868 – 15.03.1926

15.03.1926 – 28.04.1935 eastbound only
connection in use, utilising aborted tunnel

Euston Sq. Jcn.

15.03.1926 – 28.04.1935
(then reverted to pre-1926
arrangement until 14.03.1941)

Met. Line station relocated 14.03.1941,
EB using 'Widened Lines' tunnel,
central bay using original MET tunnel,
WB using new alignment

Hotel & York Road
Curves abandoned
08.11.1976

KING'S CROSS ST PANCRAS
(14.03.1941)

14.03.1941 – 08.11.1976

King's Cross Thameslink
closed 09.12.2007, replaced by
platforms under St Pancras
International

Bay platform abandoned an
in-filled (date unknown)

Present (since 09.12.2007)

From left –
surface lines
omitted for clarity

Under Construction
NR 2018

Under Construction
MID 13.07.1868
NR 2018

KING'S CROSS
(14.10.1852)

See right for detail of future
'Thameslink' junction

01.10.1868

MID

KING'S CROSS
ST PANCRAS
DEEP LEVEL TUBES
(all other lines omitted for
clarity)

King's Cross Loop
UERL 27.03.1927

UERL

15.12.1906

LTB

01.12.1968

CSLR

12.05.1907

MET 17.02.1868

MET 10.01.1863

'Thameslink' platforms
opened 09.12.2007

ST PANCRAS INTERNATIONAL
St Pancras
(01.10.1868)

MID

13.07.1868

King's Cross Tunnel

CSLR 12.05.1907

LTB 01.12.1968

UERL 15.12.1906

KING'S CROSS ST PANCRAS
(14.03.1941)

KING'S CROSS ST PANCRAS
King's Cross for St Pancras
King's Cross
(15.12.1906)

76

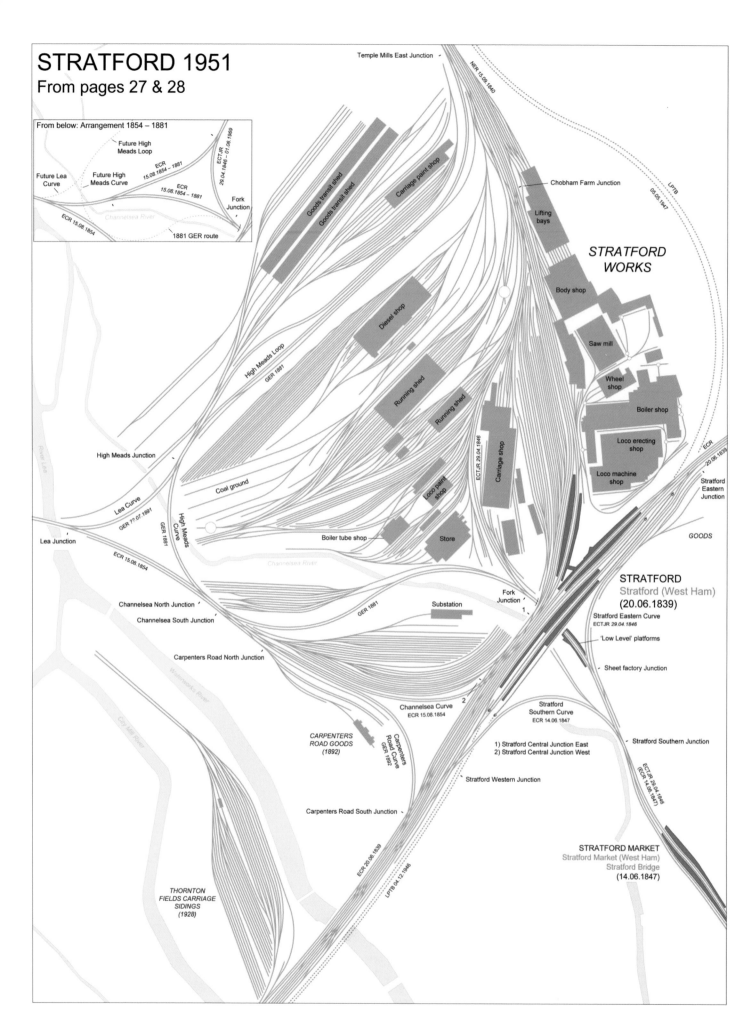

STRATFORD 1951
From pages 27 & 28

From below: Arrangement 1854 – 1881

Future High Meads Loop

Future Lea Curve

Future High Meads Curve

ECR 15.08.1854 – 1881

ECR 15.08.1854 – 1881

ECTJR 29.04.1846 – 01.06.1969

Fork Junction

ECR 15.08.1854

Channelsea River

1881 GER route

Temple Mills East Junction

NER 15.08.1840

LPTB 05.05.1947

Chobham Farm Junction

Lifting bays

STRATFORD WORKS

Goods transit shed

Goods transit shed

Carriage paint shop

Body shop

Saw mill

Wheel shop

Boiler shop

Diesel shop

Running shed

Running shed

Loco erecting shop

Loco machine shop

ECR 20.06.1839

Stratford Eastern Junction

High Meads Loop

GER 1881

ECTJR 29.04.1846

Carriage shop

High Meads Junction

Coal ground

Loco paint shop

Lea Curve

GER ??.07.1891

High Meads Curve

GER 1881

Boiler tube shop

Store

GOODS

Lea Junction

ECR 15.08.1854

STRATFORD
Stratford (West Ham)
(20.06.1839)

Stratford Eastern Curve
ECTJR 29.04.1846

'Low Level' platforms

Channelsea North Junction

Channelsea South Junction

Substation

GER 1881

Fork Junction

1

2

Sheet factory Junction

Carpenters Road North Junction

Channelsea Curve
ECR 15.08.1854

Stratford Southern Curve
ECR 14.06.1847

1) Stratford Central Junction East
2) Stratford Central Junction West

Stratford Southern Junction

ECTJR 29.04.1846
(ECR 14.06.1847)

CARPENTERS ROAD GOODS
(1892)

Carpenters Road Curve
GER 1892

Stratford Western Junction

Carpenters Road South Junction

ECR 20.06.1839

LPTB 04.12.1946

STRATFORD MARKET
Stratford Market (West Ham)
Stratford Bridge
(14.06.1847)

THORNTON FIELDS CARRIAGE SIDINGS
(1928)

River Lea

Channelsea River

Waterworks River

City Mill River

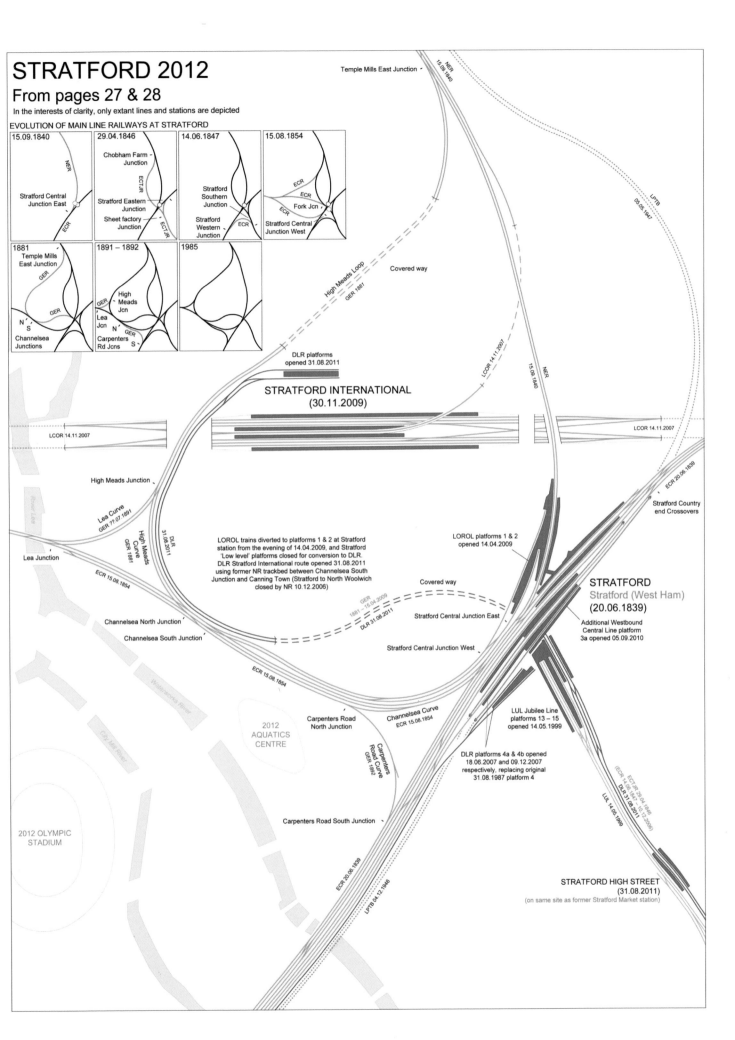

STRATFORD 2012

From pages 27 & 28

In the interests of clarity, only extant lines and stations are depicted

EVOLUTION OF MAIN LINE RAILWAYS AT STRATFORD

15.09.1840
NER
Stratford Central
Junction East
ECR

29.04.1846
Chobham Farm
Junction
ECTJR
Stratford Eastern
Junction
Sheet factory
Junction
ECTJR

14.06.1847
Stratford
Southern
Junction
Stratford
Western
Junction
ECR

15.08.1854
ECR
ECR
Fork Jcn
ECR
Stratford Central
Junction West

1881
Temple Mills
East Junction
GER
GER
N   S
Channelsea
Junctions

1891 – 1892
GER
High
Meads
Jcn
Lea
Jcn
N   GER
Carpenters   S
Rd Jcns

1985

Temple Mills East Junction

15.08.1840 NER

05.05.1947 LPTB

High Meads Loop
GER 1881

Covered way

LCOR 14.11.2007

15.08.1840 NER

DLR platforms
opened 31.08.2011

STRATFORD INTERNATIONAL
(30.11.2009)

LCOR 14.11.2007

LCOR 14.11.2007

ECR 20.06.1839

Stratford Country
end Crossovers

High Meads Junction

Lea Curve
GER 77.07.1891

High
Meads
Curve
GER 1881

DLR
31.08.2011

Lea Junction

ECR 15.08.1854

LOROL trains diverted to platforms 1 & 2 at Stratford
station from the evening of 14.04.2009, and Stratford
'Low level' platforms closed for conversion to DLR.
DLR Stratford International route opened 31.08.2011
using former NR trackbed between Channelsea South
Junction and Canning Town (Stratford to North Woolwich
closed by NR 10.12.2006)

LOROL platforms 1 & 2
opened 14.04.2009

Covered way

GER
1881 – 15.04.2009
DLR 31.08.2011

Stratford Central Junction East

Channelsea North Junction

Channelsea South Junction

Stratford Central Junction West

STRATFORD
Stratford (West Ham)
(20.06.1839)

Additional Westbound
Central Line platform
3a opened 05.09.2010

ECR 15.08.1854

Channelsea Curve
ECR 15.08.1854

Carpenters Road
North Junction

2012
AQUATICS
CENTRE

Carpenters
Road Curve
GER 1892

LUL Jubilee Line
platforms 13 – 15
opened 14.05.1999

DLR platforms 4a & 4b opened
18.06.2007 and 09.12.2007
respectively, replacing original
31.08.1987 platform 4

ECTJR 29.04.1846
(ECR FOR 1847 / 10.12.2006)

LUL 14.05.1999

Carpenters Road South Junction

2012 OLYMPIC
STADIUM

ECR 20.06.1839

LPTB 04.12.1846

STRATFORD HIGH STREET
(31.08.2011)
(on same site as former Stratford Market station)

River Lea

City Mill River

Waterworks River

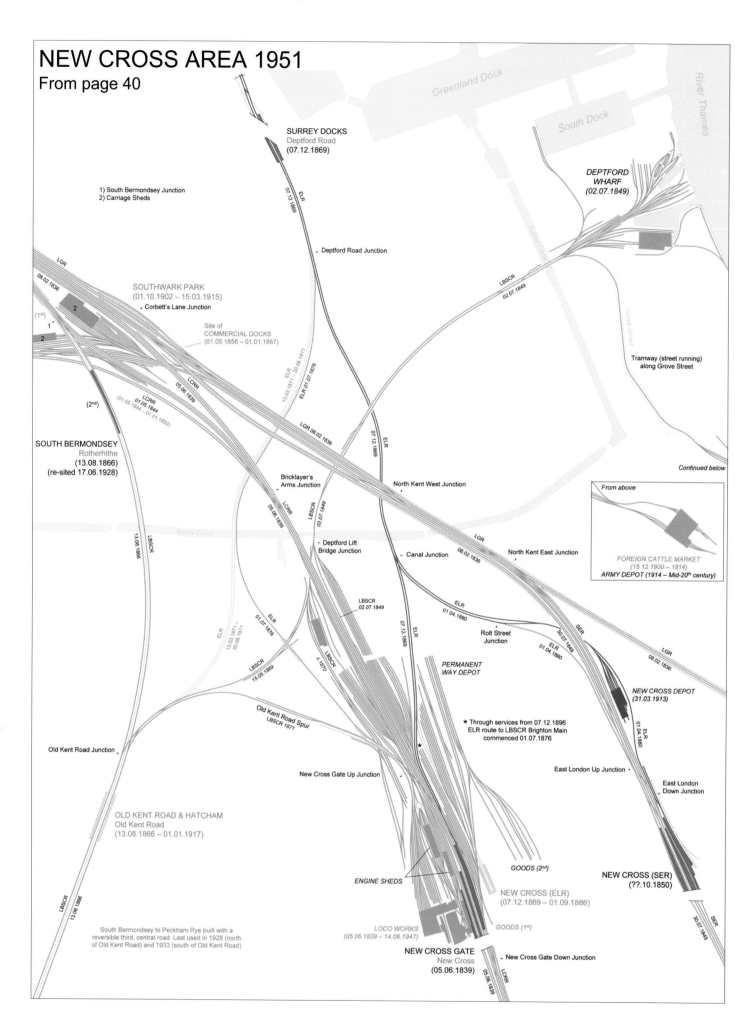

1) South Bermondsey Junction
2) Carriage Sheds

SURREY DOCKS
Deptford Road
(07.12.1869)

DEPTFORD
WHARF
(02.07.1849)

Deptford Road Junction

Tramway (street running)
along Grove Street

SOUTHWARK PARK
(01.10.1902 – 15.03.1915)
Corbett's Lane Junction

Site of
COMMERCIAL DOCKS
(01.05.1856 – 01.01.1867)

SOUTH BERMONDSEY
Rotherhithe
(13.08.1866)
(re-sited 17.06.1928)

Bricklayer's
Arms Junction

North Kent West Junction

Continued below

From above

Deptford Lift
Bridge Junction

Canal Junction

North Kent East Junction

FOREIGN CATTLE MARKET
(15.12.1900 – 1914)
ARMY DEPOT (1914 – Mid-20th century)

Rolt Street
Junction

PERMANENT
WAY DEPOT

NEW CROSS DEPOT
(31.03.1913)

Old Kent Road
Spur
LBSCR 1871

* Through services from 07.12.1896
ELR route to LBSCR Brighton Main
commenced 01.07.1876

East London Up Junction

East London
Down Junction

Old Kent Road Junction

New Cross Gate Up Junction

OLD KENT ROAD & HATCHAM
Old Kent Road
(13.08.1866 – 01.01.1917)

ENGINE SHEDS

GOODS (2nd)

NEW CROSS (SER)
(??.10.1850)

NEW CROSS (ELR)
(07.12.1869 – 01.09.1886)

South Bermondsey to Peckham Rye built with a
reversible third, central road. Last used in 1928 (north
of Old Kent Road) and 1933 (south of Old Kent Road)

LOCO WORKS
(05.06.1839 – 14.06.1947)

GOODS (1st)

NEW CROSS GATE
New Cross
(05.06.1839)

New Cross Gate Down Junction

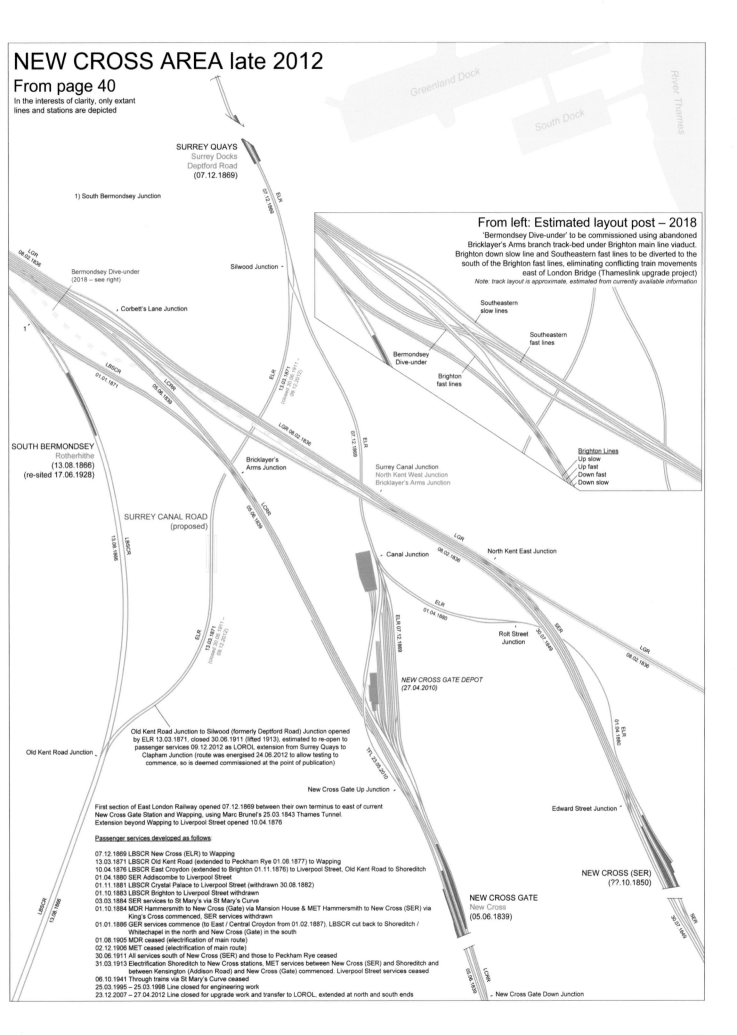

Greenland Dock

South Dock

River Thames

SURREY QUAYS
Surrey Docks
Deptford Road
(07.12.1869)

07.12.1869 ELR

1) South Bermondsey Junction

Silwood Junction

LGR 08.02.1836

Bermondsey Dive-under
(2018 – see right)

Corbett's Lane Junction

LBSCR 01.01.1871

LCRR 05.06.1839

13.03.1871 – (closed 30.06.1911 – 09.12.2012)

ELR

07.12.1869 ELR

LGR 08.02.1836

SOUTH BERMONDSEY
Rotherhithe
(13.08.1866)
(re-sited 17.06.1928)

1

Bricklayer's
Arms Junction

Surrey Canal Junction
North Kent West Junction
Bricklayer's Arms Junction

SURREY CANAL ROAD
(proposed)

LBSCR 13.08.1866

LCRR 05.06.1839

LCRR 05.06.1839

LGR 08.02.1836

North Kent East Junction

Canal Junction

ELR 01.04.1880

SER 30.07.1849

LGR 08.02.1836

ELR 13.03.1871 (closed 30.06.1911 – 09.12.2012)

ELR 07.12.1869

Rolt Street
Junction

ELR

Old Kent Road Junction

NEW CROSS GATE DEPOT
(27.04.2010)

ELR 01.04.1880

Old Kent Road Junction to Silwood (formerly Deptford Road) Junction opened
by ELR 13.03.1871, closed 30.06.1911 (lifted 1913), estimated to re-open to
passenger services 09.12.2012 as LOROL extension from Surrey Quays to
Clapham Junction (route was energised 24.06.2012 to allow testing to
commence, so is deemed commissioned at the point of publication)

TFL 23.05.2010

New Cross Gate Up Junction

Edward Street Junction

First section of East London Railway opened 07.12.1869 between their own terminus to east of current
New Cross Gate Station and Wapping, using Marc Brunel's 25.03.1843 Thames Tunnel.
Extension beyond Wapping to Liverpool Street opened 10.04.1876

Passenger services developed as follows:

07.12.1869 LBSCR New Cross (ELR) to Wapping
13.03.1871 LBSCR Old Kent Road (extended to Peckham Rye 01.08.1877) to Wapping
10.04.1876 LBSCR East Croydon (extended to Brighton 01.11.1876) to Liverpool Street, Old Kent Road to Shoreditch
01.04.1880 SER Addiscombe to Liverpool Street
01.11.1881 LBSCR Crystal Palace to Liverpool Street (withdrawn 30.08.1882)
01.10.1883 LBSCR Brighton to Liverpool Street withdrawn
03.03.1884 SER services to St Mary's via St Mary's Curve
01.10.1884 MDR Hammersmith to New Cross (Gate) via Mansion House & MET Hammersmith to New Cross (SER) via
            King's Cross commenced, SER services withdrawn
01.01.1886 GER services commence (to East / Central Croydon from 01.02.1887), LBSCR cut back to Shoreditch /
            Whitechapel in the north and New Cross (Gate) in the south
01.08.1905 MDR ceased (electrification of main route)
02.12.1906 MET ceased (electrification of main route)
30.06.1911 All services south of New Cross (SER) and those to Peckham Rye ceased
31.03.1913 Electrification Shoreditch to New Cross stations, MET services between New Cross (SER) and Shoreditch and
            between Kensington (Addison Road) and New Cross (Gate) commenced. Liverpool Street services ceased
06.10.1941 Through trains via St Mary's Curve ceased
25.03.1995 – 25.03.1998 Line closed for engineering work
23.12.2007 – 27.04.2012 Line closed for upgrade work and transfer to LOROL, extended at north and south ends

NEW CROSS (SER)
(??.10.1850)

NEW CROSS GATE
New Cross
(05.06.1839)

LBSCR 13.08.1866

LCRR 05.06.1839

SER 30.07.1849

New Cross Gate Down Junction

From left: Estimated layout post – 2018

'Bermondsey Dive-under' to be commissioned using abandoned
Bricklayer's Arms branch track-bed under Brighton main line viaduct.
Brighton down slow line and Southeastern fast lines to be diverted to the
south of the Brighton fast lines, eliminating conflicting train movements
east of London Bridge (Thameslink upgrade project)
Note: track layout is approximate, estimated from currently available information

Southeastern
slow lines

Southeastern
fast lines

Bermondsey
Dive-under

Brighton
fast lines

Brighton Lines
Up slow
Up fast
Down fast
Down slow

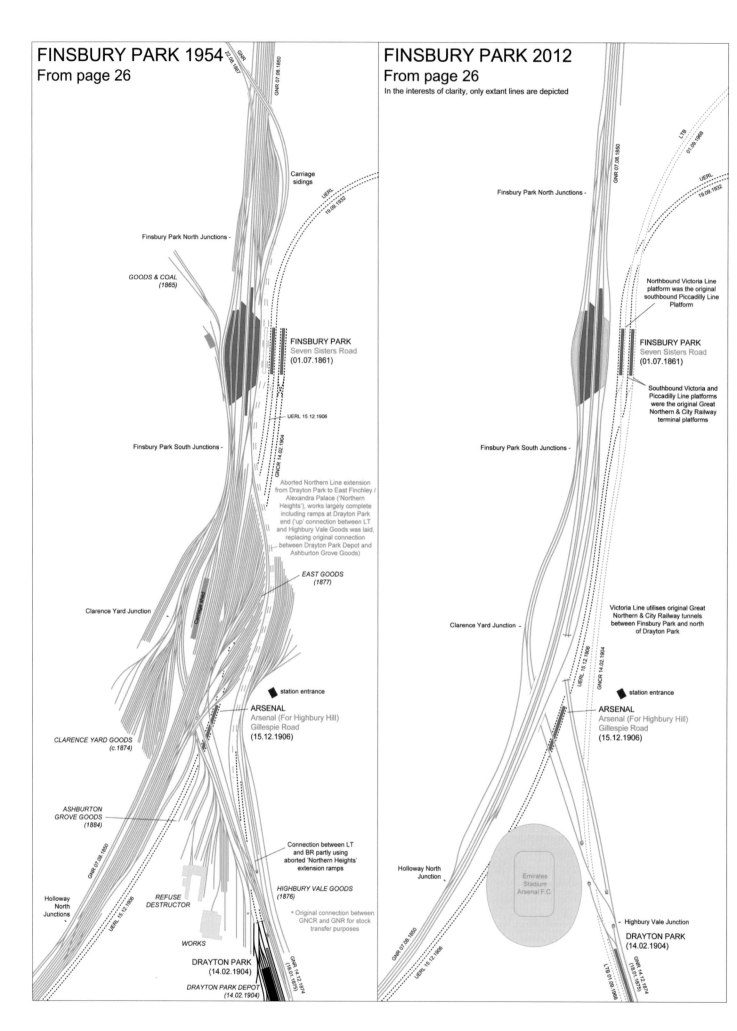

FINSBURY PARK 1954
From page 26

GNR 22.08.1867

GNR

GNR 07.08.1850

Carriage
sidings

UERL 19.09.1932

Finsbury Park North Junctions -

GOODS & COAL
(1865)

FINSBURY PARK
Seven Sisters Road
(01.07.1861)

UERL 15.12.1906

GNCR 14.02.1904

Finsbury Park South Junctions -

Aborted Northern Line extension
from Drayton Park to East Finchley /
Alexandra Palace ('Northern
Heights'), works largely complete
including ramps at Drayton Park
end ('up' connection between LT
and Highbury Vale Goods was laid,
replacing original connection
between Drayton Park Depot and
Ashburton Grove Goods)

EAST GOODS
(1877)

Clarence Yard Junction

Carriage shed

station entrance

ARSENAL
Arsenal (For Highbury Hill)
Gillespie Road
(15.12.1906)

CLARENCE YARD GOODS
(c.1874)

ASHBURTON
GROVE GOODS
(1884)

GNR 07.08.1850

Connection between LT
and BR partly using
aborted 'Northern Heights'
extension ramps

Holloway
North
Junctions

UERL 15.12.1906

REFUSE
DESTRUCTOR

HIGHBURY VALE GOODS
(1876)

* Original connection between
GNCR and GNR for stock
transfer purposes

WORKS

DRAYTON PARK
(14.02.1904)

DRAYTON PARK DEPOT
(14.02.1904)

GNR 14.12.1874
(01.01.1875)

FINSBURY PARK 2012
From page 26
In the interests of clarity, only extant lines are depicted

GNR 07.08.1850

LTB
01.09.1968

UERL
19.09.1932

Finsbury Park North Junctions -

Northbound Victoria Line
platform was the original
southbound Piccadilly Line
Platform

FINSBURY PARK
Seven Sisters Road
(01.07.1861)

Southbound Victoria and
Piccadilly Line platforms
were the original Great
Northern & City Railway
terminal platforms

Finsbury Park South Junctions -

Victoria Line utilises original Great
Northern & City Railway tunnels
between Finsbury Park and north
of Drayton Park

Clarence Yard Junction -

UERL 15.12.1906

GNCR 14.02.1904

station entrance

ARSENAL
Arsenal (For Highbury Hill)
Gillespie Road
(15.12.1906)

Holloway North
Junction

Emirates
Stadium
Arsenal F.C.

GNR 07.08.1850

UERL 15.12.1906

Highbury Vale Junction

DRAYTON PARK
(14.02.1904)

LTB 01.09.1968

GNR 14.12.1874
(01.01.1875)

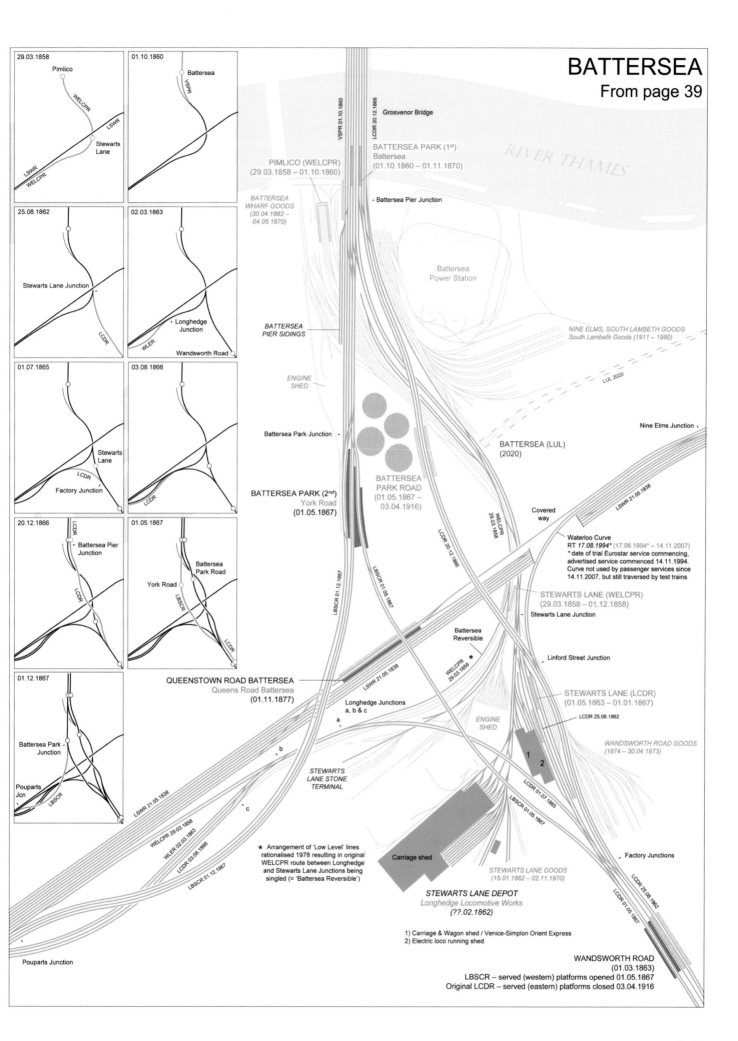

RIVER THAMES

29.03.1858
Pimlico
WELCPR
LSWR
Stewarts Lane
LSWR
WELCPR

01.10.1860
Battersea
VSPR

25.08.1862
Stewarts Lane Junction
LCDR

02.03.1863
Longhedge Junction
WLER
Wandsworth Road

01.07.1865
Stewarts Lane
LCDR
Factory Junction

03.08.1866
LCDR

20.12.1866
LCDR
Battersea Pier Junction
LCDR

01.05.1867
Battersea Park Road
York Road
LBSCR
LCDR

01.12.1867
Battersea Park Junction
Pouparts Jcn
LBSCR

VSPR 01.10.1860

LCDR 20.12.1866

Grosvenor Bridge

BATTERSEA PARK (1st)
Battersea
(01.10.1860 – 01.11.1870)

- Battersea Pier Junction

PIMLICO (WELCPR)
(29.03.1858 – 01.10.1860)

BATTERSEA WHARF GOODS
(30.04.1862 – 04.05.1970)

Battersea Power Station

BATTERSEA PIER SIDINGS

NINE ELMS, SOUTH LAMBETH GOODS
South Lambeth Goods (1911 – 1980)

LUL 2020

ENGINE SHED

Battersea Park Junction -

BATTERSEA (LUL)
(2020)

Nine Elms Junction

BATTERSEA PARK ROAD
(01.05.1867 – 03.04.1916)

BATTERSEA PARK (2nd)
York Road
(01.05.1867)

LSWR 21.05.1838

WELCPR 29.03.1858

Covered way

Waterloo Curve
RT 17.08.1994* (17.08.1994* – 14.11.2007)
* date of trial Eurostar service commencing,
advertised service commenced 14.11.1994.
Curve not used by passenger services since
14.11.2007, but still traversed by test trains

LCDR 20.12.1866

LBSCR 01.12.1867

LBSCR 01.05.1867

STEWARTS LANE (WELCPR)
(29.03.1858 – 01.12.1858)
- Stewarts Lane Junction

- Linford Street Junction

Battersea Reversible

WELCPR 29.03.1858 ★

STEWARTS LANE (LCDR)
(01.05.1863 – 01.01.1867)

LCDR 25.08.1862

WANDSWORTH ROAD GOODS
(1874 – 30.04.1973)

QUEENSTOWN ROAD BATTERSEA
Queens Road Battersea
(01.11.1877)

LSWR 21.05.1838

Longhedge Junctions
a, b & c
a

b

ENGINE SHED

1
2

STEWARTS LANE STONE TERMINAL

c

LSWR 21.05.1838

WELCPR 29.03.1858

WLER 02.03.1863

LCDR 03.08.1866

LBSCR 01.12.1867

★ Arrangement of 'Low Level' lines
rationalised 1978 resulting in original
WELCPR route between Longhedge
and Stewarts Lane Junctions being
singled (= 'Battersea Reversible')

Carriage shed

LBSCR 01.05.1867

LCDR 01.07.1865

Factory Junctions

LCDR 25.08.1862

STEWARTS LANE GOODS
(15.01.1862 – 02.11.1970)

LCDR 01.05.1867

STEWARTS LANE DEPOT
Longhedge Locomotive Works
(??.02.1862)

1) Carriage & Wagon shed / Venice-Simplon Orient Express
2) Electric loco running shed

Pouparts Junction

WANDSWORTH ROAD
(01.03.1863)
LBSCR – served (western) platforms opened 01.05.1867
Original LCDR – served (eastern) platforms closed 03.04.1916

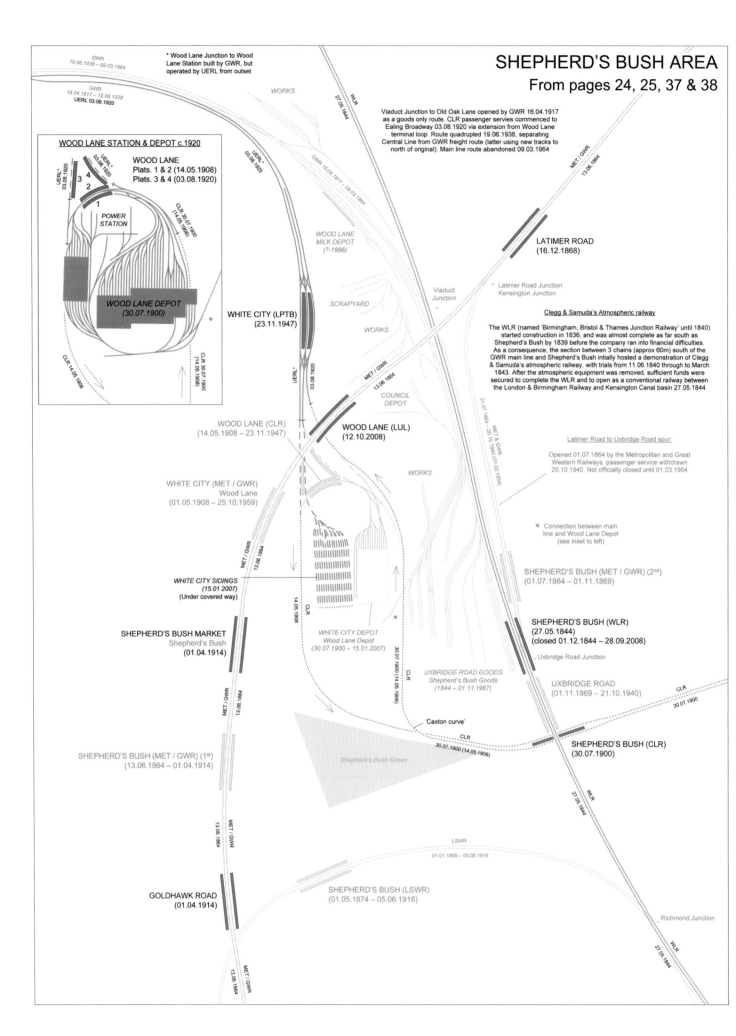

* Wood Lane Junction to Wood
Lane Station built by GWR, but
operated by UERL from outset

GWR
19.06.1938 – 09.03.1964

GWR
16.04.1917 – 19.06.1938
UERL 03.08.1920

WORKS

27.05.1844 WLR

UERL
03.08.1920

GWR 16.04.1917 – 09.03.1964

MET / GWR
13.06.1864

Viaduct Junction to Old Oak Lane opened by GWR 16.04.1917
as a goods only route. CLR passenger servies commenced to
Ealing Broadway 03.08.1920 via extension from Wood Lane
terminal loop. Route quadrupled 19.06.1938, separating
Central Line from GWR freight route (latter using new tracks to
north of original). Main line route abandoned 09.03.1964

WOOD LANE STATION & DEPOT c.1920

UERL*
03.08.1920

UERL*
03.08.1920

3 4 2
1

WOOD LANE
Plats. 1 & 2 (14.05.1908)
Plats. 3 & 4 (03.08.1920)

LATIMER ROAD
(16.12.1868)

POWER
STATION

CLR 30.07.1900
(14.05.1908)

Latimer Road Junction
Kensington Junction

WOOD LANE
MILK DEPOT
(?-1966)

Clegg & Samuda's Atmospheric railway

The WLR (named 'Birmingham, Bristol & Thames Junction Railway' until 1840)
started construction in 1836, and was almost complete as far south as
Shepherd's Bush by 1839 before the company ran into financial difficulties.
As a consequence, the section between 3 chains (approx 60m) south of the
GWR main line and Shepherd's Bush intially hosted a demonstration of Clegg
& Samuda's atmospheric railway, with trials from 11.06.1840 through to March
1843. After the atmospheric equipment was removed, sufficient funds were
secured to complete the WLR and to open as a conventional railway between
the London & Birmingham Railway and Kensington Canal basin 27.05.1844

WOOD LANE DEPOT
(30.07.1900)

SCRAPYARD

WORKS

WHITE CITY (LPTB)
(23.11.1947)

CLR 14.05.1908

Viaduct
Junction

MET / GWR
13.06.1864

01.07.1864 –
20.10.1940 (01.03.1954)
MET & GWR

UERL*
03.08.1920

CLR 30.07.1900
(14.05.1908)

COUNCIL
DEPOT

Latimer Road to Uxbridge Road spur:

Opened 01.07.1864 by the Metropolitan and Great
Western Railways, passenger service withdrawn
20.10.1940. Not officially closed until 01.03.1954

WOOD LANE (CLR)
(14.05.1908 – 23.11.1947)

WOOD LANE (LUL)
(12.10.2008)

WORKS

* Connection between main
line and Wood Lane Depot
(see inset to left)

WHITE CITY (MET / GWR)
Wood Lane
(01.05.1908 – 25.10.1959)

MET / GWR
13.06.1864

SHEPHERD'S BUSH (MET / GWR) (2nd)
(01.07.1864 – 01.11.1869)

WHITE CITY SIDINGS
(15.01.2007)
(Under covered way)

CLR
14.05.1908

30.07.1900 (14.05.1908)
CLR

SHEPHERD'S BUSH (WLR)
(27.05.1844)
(closed 01.12.1844 – 28.09.2008)

SHEPHERD'S BUSH MARKET
Shepherd's Bush
(01.04.1914)

WHITE CITY DEPOT
Wood Lane Depot
(30.07.1900 – 15.01.2007)

Uxbridge Road Junction

UXBRIDGE ROAD GOODS
Shepherd's Bush Goods
(1844 – 01.11.1967)

UXBRIDGE ROAD
(01.11.1869 – 21.10.1940)

CLR
30.07.1900

MET / GWR
13.06.1864

SHEPHERD'S BUSH (MET / GWR) (1st)
(13.06.1864 – 01.04.1914)

'Caxton curve'

CLR
30.07.1900 (14.05.1908)

SHEPHERD'S BUSH (CLR)
(30.07.1900)

Shepherd's Bush Green

WLR
27.05.1844

MET / GWR
13.06.1864

LSWR

01.01.1869 – 05.06.1916

GOLDHAWK ROAD
(01.04.1914)

SHEPHERD'S BUSH (LSWR)
(01.05.1874 – 05.06.1916)

Richmond Junction

MET / GWR
13.06.1864

WLR
27.05.1844

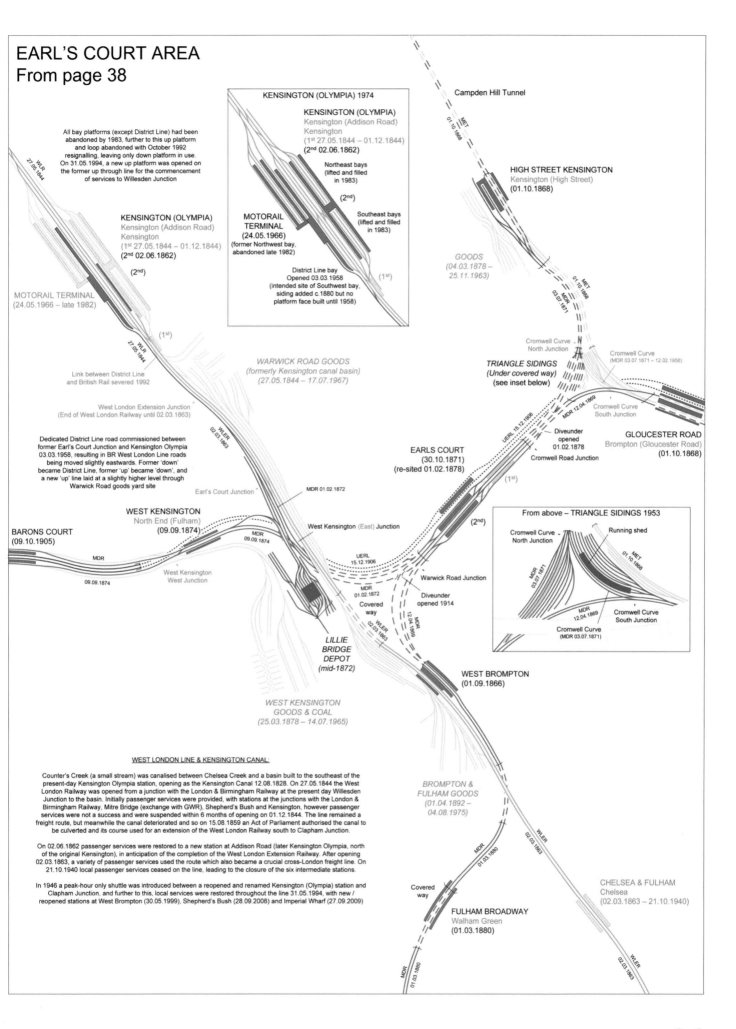

All bay platforms (except District Line) had been
abandoned by 1983, further to this up platform
and loop abandoned with October 1992
resignalling, leaving only down platform in use.
On 31.05.1994, a new up platform was opened on
the former up through line for the commencement
of services to Willesden Junction

KENSINGTON (OLYMPIA) 1974

KENSINGTON (OLYMPIA)
Kensington (Addison Road)
Kensington
(1st 27.05.1844 – 01.12.1844)
(2nd 02.06.1862)

Northeast bays
(lifted and filled
in 1983)

KENSINGTON (OLYMPIA)
Kensington (Addison Road)
Kensington
(1st 27.05.1844 – 01.12.1844)
(2nd 02.06.1862)

(2nd)

MOTORAIL
TERMINAL
(24.05.1966)
(former Northwest bay,
abandoned late 1982)

Southeast bays
(lifted and filled
in 1983)

MOTORAIL TERMINAL
(24.05.1966 – late 1982)

District Line bay
Opened 03.03.1958
(intended site of Southwest bay,
siding added c.1880 but no
platform face built until 1958)

(1st)

(1st)

WLR
27.05.1844

HIGH STREET KENSINGTON
Kensington (High Street)
(01.10.1868)

Campden Hill Tunnel

MET
01.10.1868

GOODS
(04.03.1878 –
25.11.1963)

MET
01.10.1868

MDR
03.07.1871

Cromwell Curve
North Junction

WARWICK ROAD GOODS
(formerly Kensington canal basin)
(27.05.1844 – 17.07.1967)

TRIANGLE SIDINGS
(Under covered way)
(see inset below)

Cromwell Curve
(MDR 03.07.1871 – 12.02.1956)

West London Extension Junction
(End of West London Railway until 02.03.1863)

WLER
02.03.1863

UERL 15.12.1906

MDR 12.04.1869

Diveunder
opened
01.02.1878

Cromwell Curve
South Junction

Dedicated District Line road commissioned between
former Earl's Court Junction and Kensington Olympia
03.03.1958, resulting in BR West London Line roads
being moved slightly eastwards. Former 'down'
became District Line, former 'up' became 'down', and
a new 'up' line laid at a slightly higher level through
Warwick Road goods yard site

EARLS COURT
(30.10.1871)
(re-sited 01.02.1878)

Cromwell Road Junction

GLOUCESTER ROAD
Brompton (Gloucester Road)
(01.10.1868)

Earl's Court Junction

MDR 01.02.1872

(1st)

(2nd)

From above – TRIANGLE SIDINGS 1953

WEST KENSINGTON
North End (Fulham)
(09.09.1874)

West Kensington (East) Junction

Cromwell Curve
North Junction

Running shed

BARONS COURT
(09.10.1905)

MDR
09.09.1874

West Kensington
West Junction

UERL
15.12.1906

Warwick Road Junction

MET
01.10.1868

MDR
03.07.1871

MDR

09.09.1874

MDR
01.02.1872

Covered
way

Diveunder
opened 1914

MDR
12.04.1869

MDR
12.04.1869

Cromwell Curve
South Junction

WLER
02.03.1863

Cromwell Curve
(MDR 03.07.1871)

LILLIE
BRIDGE
DEPOT
(mid-1872)

WEST BROMPTON
(01.09.1866)

WEST KENSINGTON
GOODS & COAL
(25.03.1878 – 14.07.1965)

BROMPTON &
FULHAM GOODS
(01.04.1892 –
04.08.1975)

WLER
02.03.1863

WEST LONDON LINE & KENSINGTON CANAL:

Counter's Creek (a small stream) was canalised between Chelsea Creek and a basin built to the southeast of the
present-day Kensington Olympia station, opening as the Kensington Canal 12.08.1828. On 27.05.1844 the West
London Railway was opened from a junction with the London & Birmingham Railway at the present day Willesden
Junction to the basin. Initially passenger services were provided, with stations at the junctions with the London &
Birmingham Railway, Mitre Bridge (exchange with GWR), Shepherd's Bush and Kensington, however passenger
services were not a success and were suspended within 6 months of opening on 01.12.1844. The line remained a
freight route, but meanwhile the canal deteriorated and so on 15.08.1859 an Act of Parliament authorised the canal to
be culverted and its course used for an extension of the West London Railway south to Clapham Junction.

On 02.06.1862 passenger services were restored to a new station at Addison Road (later Kensington Olympia, north
of the original Kensington), in anticipation of the completion of the West London Extension Railway. After opening
02.03.1863, a variety of passenger services used the route which also became a crucial cross-London freight line. On
21.10.1940 local passenger services ceased on the line, leading to the closure of the six intermediate stations.

In 1946 a peak-hour only shuttle was introduced between a reopened and renamed Kensington (Olympia) station and
Clapham Junction, and further to this, local services were restored throughout the line 31.05.1994, with new /
reopened stations at West Brompton (30.05.1999), Shepherd's Bush (28.09.2008) and Imperial Wharf (27.09.2009)

Link between District Line
and British Rail severed 1992

CHELSEA & FULHAM
Chelsea
(02.03.1863 – 21.10.1940)

Covered
way

MDR
01.03.1880

FULHAM BROADWAY
Walham Green
(01.03.1880)

WLER
02.03.1863

MDR
01.03.1880

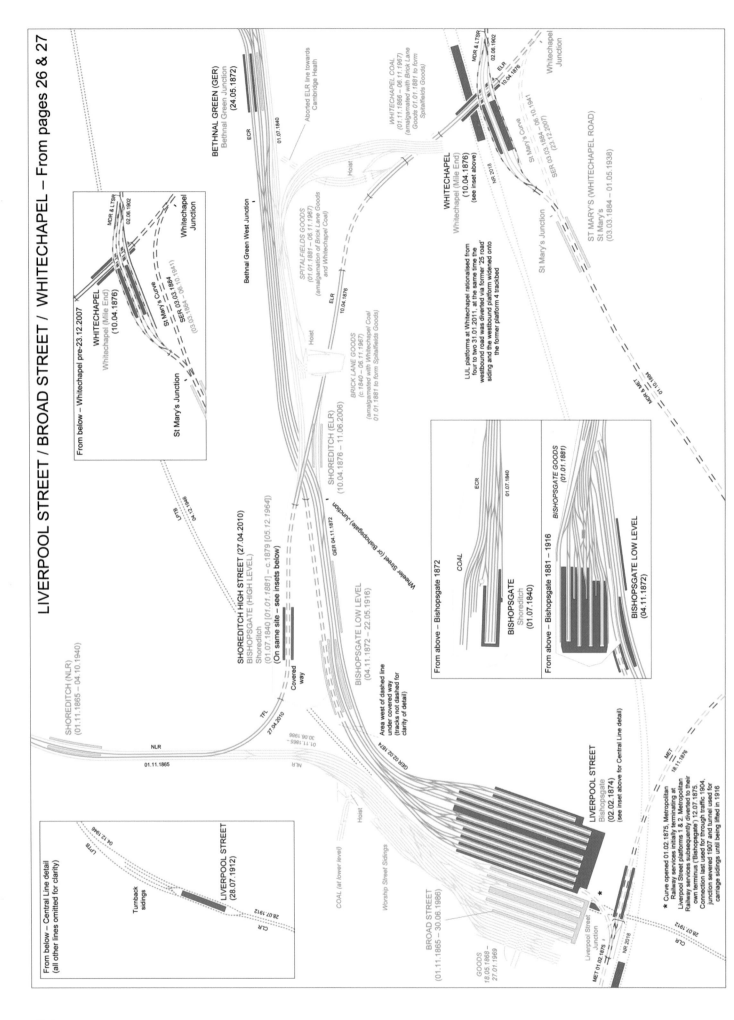

LIVERPOOL STREET / BROAD STREET / WHITECHAPEL – From pages 26 & 27

From below – Whitechapel pre-23.12.2007

WHITECHAPEL
Whitechapel (Mile End)
(10.04.1876)

MDR & LTSR
02.06.1902

St Mary's Curve
SER 03.03.1884
(03.03.1884 – 06.10.1941)

Whitechapel Junction

St Mary's Junction

BETHNAL GREEN (GER)
Bethnal Green Junction
(24.05.1872)

ECR
01.07.1840

Aborted ELR line towards
Cambridge Heath

Bethnal Green West Junction

SPITALFIELDS GOODS
(01.01.1881 – 06.11.1967)
(amalgamation of Brick Lane Goods
and Whitechapel Coal)

Hoist

Hoist

BRICK LANE GOODS
(c.1840 – 06.11.1967)
(amalgamated with Whitechapel Coal
01.01.1881 to form Spitalfields Goods)

ELR
10.04.1876

SHOREDITCH (ELR)
(10.04.1876 – 11.06.2006)

Wheeler Street (or Bishopsgate) Junction
GER 04.11.1872

WHITECHAPEL COAL
(01.11.1866 – 06.11.1967)
(amalgamated with Brick Lane
Goods 01.01.1881 to form
Spitalfields Goods)

WHITECHAPEL
Whitechapel (Mile End)
(10.04.1876)
(see inset above)

MDR & LTSR
02.06.1902

ELR
10.04.1876

NR 2018

St Mary's Curve
SER 03.03.1884
(23.12.2007)

St Mary's Junction

ST MARY'S (WHITECHAPEL ROAD)
St Mary's
(03.03.1884 – 01.05.1938)

Whitechapel Junction

MDR & MET
01.10.1884

LUL platforms at Whitechapel rationalised from
four to two 31.01.2011, at the same time the
westbound road was diverted via former '25 road'
siding and the westbound platform widened onto
the former platform 4 trackbed

SHOREDITCH (NLR)
(01.11.1865 – 04.10.1940)

SHOREDITCH HIGH STREET (27.04.2010)
BISHOPSGATE (HIGH LEVEL)
Shoreditch
(01.07.1840 [01.01.1881] – c.1879 [05.12.1964])
(On same site – see insets below)

NLR
01.11.1865

TFL
27.04.2010

Covered
way

BISHOPSGATE LOW LEVEL
(04.11.1872 – 22.05.1916)

Area west of dashed line
under covered way
(tracks not dashed for
clarity of detail)

GER 02.02.1874
NLR
01.11.1865 – 30.06.1986

From above – Bishopsgate 1872

ECR
01.07.1840

COAL

BISHOPSGATE
Shoreditch
(01.07.1840)

From above – Bishopsgate 1881 – 1916

BISHOPSGATE GOODS
(01.01.1881)

BISHOPSGATE LOW LEVEL
(04.11.1872)

From below – Central Line detail
(all other lines omitted for clarity)

LPTB
04.12.1946

Turnback
sidings

LIVERPOOL STREET
(28.07.1912)

CLR
28.07.1912

COAL (at lower level)

Hoist

Worship Street Sidings

LIVERPOOL STREET
Bishopsgate
(02.02.1874)
(see inset above for Central Line detail)

MET
18.11.1876

BROAD STREET
(01.11.1865 – 30.06.1986)

GOODS
18.05.1868 –
27.01.1969

Liverpool Street
Junction

MET 01.02.1875

NR 2018

CLR
28.07.1912

* Curve opened 01.02.1875, Metropolitan
Railway services initially terminating at
Liverpool Street platforms 1 & 2. Metropolitan
Railway services subsequently diverted to their
own terminus (Bishopsgate) 12.07.1875.
Connection last used for through traffic 1904,
junction severed 1907 and tunnel used for
carriage sidings until being lifted in 1916

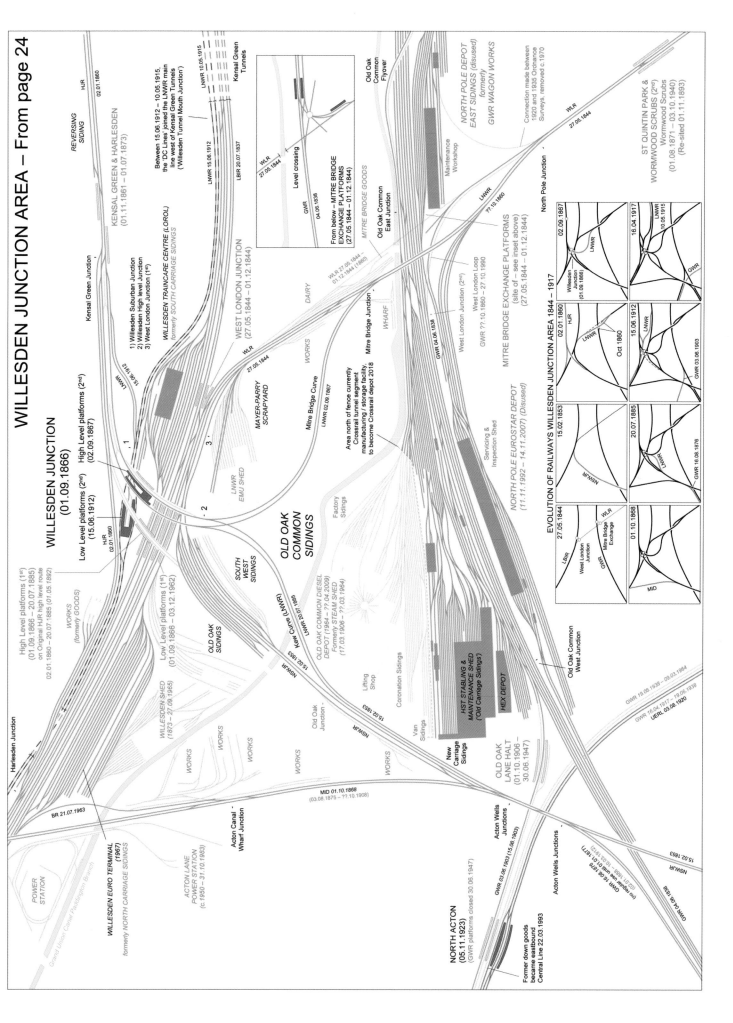

Index

Names quoted are the current names or the name at the point of closure. As many alternative names are quoted as possible with dates of name changes noted, but please note that at any given time names could vary between different timetables and station name boards, even between name boards on different platforms of the same station. If two stations shared the same name, they are differentiated through the addition of the abbreviated railway company name which opened that station in brackets. Where more than one station shared the same name and were built by the same railway company, they are differentiated chronologically through the suffix (1st), (2nd), etc.

Entries in black plain capital text denote open passenger stations, red closed, blue under construction or proposed (2012). Previous names are listed in reverse chronological order in red lower-case indented text below.
Entries in black italic capital text denote open non-passenger facilities, red closed, blue under construction or proposed (2012). Entries in black lower-case text denote in-use railway features, e.g. junctions, curves, or tunnels, red disused

Dates are given as accurately as possible. Italic dates refer to non-passenger usage. Goods yards are listed with the associated passenger station if applicable, unless the location of the goods yard was significantly remote from the passenger station. Where a station had a goods yard associated with it, dates of opening and closing are stated for both passenger and goods facilities, differentiated by 'P' and 'G'. The same principle applies to connecting curves / loops, although in this case 'G' relates to any non-passenger usage. In some cases approximate dates are quoted where no reliable source can be found, these are generally inferred from Ordnance Survey maps with the rationale stated in the notes.

In some cases research established conflicting information. Where sufficient doubt remains about which information is correct, all is stated with their respective sources noted.

Opening dates are the first full day of normal service unless otherwise indicated, closure dates are the first full traffic day without trains unless otherwise indicated. For example, if a station was only open Monday-Friday and was last served on a Friday, the following Monday's date is quoted as the closure date. Minor periods of closure (e.g. due to engineering works, terrorism, enemy action etc.) are generally omitted, although some of significant length or interest are recorded.

Some stations (e.g. Dalston Junction, Homerton, Shepherds Bush [WLR]) were closed for long periods of their existence, but as they were ultimately rebuilt on the same site, the original opening date is given with the period of closure recorded in the notes. Minor re-siting of stations are recorded in the notes under a single index entry.

A

NAME: (Previous names indented below)	Page / grid:		Date opened:	Date closed:	Opening company:	NOTES:
Abbey Mills Curve	28 / 5A	P	01/06/1858	27/10/1940	LTSR	Abbey Mills Curve open to passengers 01/06/1858 - 27/10/1940
		G	*31/03/1858*	*27/07/1958*		
Abbey Mills Lower Junction	28 / 5A		31/03/1858	27/07/1958	LTSR	Junction at south end of Abbey Mills Curve
Abbey Mills Upper Junction	28 / 5A		31/03/1858	27/07/1958	LTSR	Junction at north end of Abbey Mills Curve
ABBEY ROAD	28 / 4A		31/08/2011	N/A	DLR	
ABBEY WOOD	42 / 2C	P	??/??/1849	N/A	SER	Opening date unknown, either on or by 01/11/1849, does not appear to have opened with rest of line (30/07/1849)
		G	*??/??/1849*	*05/12/1960*		Goods yard closed 05/12/1960. To be rebuilt with four platforms as eastern terminus of Crossrail 1 2018
Acton Canal Wharf Junction	24 / 5C & 86		21/07/1963	N/A	BR	Date is that of opening of curve to WCML, access to various works alongside canal existed before this date
ACTON CENTRAL	37 / 1B	P	01/08/1853	N/A	NSWJR	Bay platform formerly on 'up' side. 'Central' suffix added 01/11/1925. Goods yard opened 1856, closed 01/03/1965
Acton		G	*??/??/1856*	*01/03/1965*		
ACTON COAL	37 / 1C		*??/??/1867*	*04/01/1965*	NSWJR	
Acton Curve	37 / 2B & 51 / 2B	P	01/05/1878	01/10/1880	LSWR	Briefly carried passenger traffic 01/05/1878 - 01/10/1880. Last used for access to West Kensington Goods & coal,
		G	*01/03/1878*	*13/09/1965*		last train 29/07/1965, 13/09/1965 is official closure date
Acton East (or Poplar) Junction	24 / 6B		16/08/1876	N/A	GWR	Curve to NSWJR opened 16/08/1876, but saw no regular use until 01/01/1877
Acton Gatehouse Junction	37 / 1B		01/05/1857	03/05/1965	NSWJR	Junction between NSWJR main line and their Hammersmith & Chiswick Branch
Acton Lane East Junction	37 / 2B & 51 / 2B		03/12/1911	13/09/1965	LSWR	LSWR dive-under opened due to quadrupling works Ravenscourt Park to Turnham Green, later goods use only
ACTON LANE POWER STATION	24 / 5C & 86		*c.1950*	*31/10/1983*	PRIV	
Acton Lane West Junction	37 / 2B & 51 / 2B		01/03/1878	13/09/1965	LSWR	Junction at east end of Acton Curve
Acton Loop Line	37 / 2B & 51 / 1A	P	13/06/1905	02/03/1959	MDR	First used for construction traffic for MDR extension to South Harrow. Doubled shortly before passenger services
		G	*15/05/1899*	*22/02/1915*		commenced 13/06/1905. Goods traffic ceased 22/02/1915 and connection at north end 'clipped' out of use (not
						physically removed until c.1930). Branch singled 14/02/1932. Service withdrawn and branch dismantled 02/03/1959
ACTON MAIN LINE	24 / 6B	P	01/02/1868	N/A	GWR	Coal yard closed 1931. 'Main Line' suffix added 01/11/1949
Acton		G	*01/02/1868*	*??/??/1931*		
ACTON TOWN	37 / 1B		01/07/1879	N/A	MDR	Rebuilt and renamed 01/03/1910, further rebuilt 1933. First served by Piccadilly Line 04/07/1932.
Mill Hill Park						South Acton Shuttle served bay platform 5 until 28/02/1959.
Acton Town North Junction	37 / 1A		01/05/1883	N/A	MDR	Extensively remodelled 1932 during Turnham Green to Northfields quadrupling
Acton Town South Junction	37 / 2B & 51 / 1A		15/05/1899	01/03/1959	MDR	First passenger use 13/06/1905, last freight use 1915
Acton Wells Junctions	24 / 5C & 86		01/10/1868	N/A	MID / NSWJR	Junction between MID Dudding Hill Loop and NSWJR. Junction with GWR curve to Acton added 01/01/1877
Acton West Junction	24 / 6A		c.1931	N/A	GWR	Seemingly established during the yard's 1931 expansion. To be reconstructed with a dive-under for 2018
ACTON WORKS (RAILWAY ENGINEERING WORKS)	37 / 2A & 51 / 1A		*??/??/1923*	N/A	UERL	Works for heavy overhaul of LUL rolling stock
ACTON YARD (YEOMAN AGGREGATES)	24 / 6B		*??/01/1877*	N/A	GWR	Yard established by GWR January 1877. Expanded 03/06/1901 and again 1931. Closed as a marshalling yard
						24/05/1984, remaining in use for stone traffic (Yeoman Aggregates)
ADDINGTON VILLAGE	67 / 4C		10/05/2000	N/A	CTL	
ADDISCOMBE (MKR)	67 / 1A	P	01/04/1864	02/06/1997	MKR	Opened as 'Croydon (Addiscombe Road)', renamed 'Croydon (Addiscombe)' 01/04/1925, 'Addiscombe (Croydon)'
Addiscombe (Croydon)		G	*11/07/1925*	*17/06/1968*		??/03/1926, 'Croydon' suffix dropped 13/06/1955. Goods yard did not open until 11/07/1925, closed 17/06/1968.
Croydon (Addiscombe)						Reduced to one operational platform (platform 2) March 1996 due to signal box being destroyed in an arson attack
Croydon (Addiscombe Road)						Elmers End to Addiscombe last train 31/05/1997, but as no Sunday service timetabled, Monday 02/06/1997 is
						given as closure date (although station removed from 1997 Summer timetable published 01/06/1997)
ADDISCOMBE (CTL)	67 / 1A		23/05/2000	N/A	CTL	
ADDISCOMBE EMU SHED	67 / 1A		*11/07/1925*	*??/04/1995*	SR	Shed commissioned on 11/07/1925 according to kentrail.org.uk, electrification of branch planned for 01/12/1925
						but was delayed until 28/02/1926, so presumably no regular use for EMU stabling before this date
						Closed as a traincrew depot 12/04/1993, although stabling of 4EPB units continued until withdrawal April 1995
						(shed was never cleared for stabling of 'Networker' EMUs)
ADDLESTONE	61 / 2B	P	14/02/1848	N/A	LSWR	
		G	*14/02/1848*	*c.1965*		
Addlestone Junction	61 / 3C		??/??/1885	N/A	LSWR	Junction at north end of Byfleet Curve
AEC MOTOR WORKS	36 / 1A		?	?	PRIV	
AGGREGATE INDUSTRIES LTD (NEASDEN)	24 / 3C		*??/??/2001*	N/A	PRIV	
ALBANY PARK	56 / 2D		07/07/1935	N/A	SR	
Albert Dock Junction	62 / 3B		03/08/1880	08/09/1940	LSKD / GER	Junction of Gallions branch
Aldersbrook Flyover	28 / 2D		06/10/1947	N/A	LNER	
ALDERSBROOK (UP) CAR HOLDING SIDINGS	28 / 2D		*c.1894*	N/A	GER	Appear on OS maps after 1895, may have been opened at same time as GER quadrupling work (c.1894)
ALDGATE	27 / 6A & 74 / 1B		18/11/1876	N/A	MET	
Aldgate Junction	27 / 6A & 74 / 1B		01/10/1884	N/A	MET	
ALDGATE EAST	27 / 6A & 74 / 1B		06/10/1884	N/A	MDR / MET	Relocated East 30/10/1938 (Junction remodelling to ease congestion around Aldgate Triangle)
Aldgate East Junction	27 / 6A & 74 / 1B		06/10/1884	N/A	MDR / MET	Relocated East 30/10/1938 (Junction remodelling to ease congestion around Aldgate Triangle)
ALDWYCH	26 / 6B		30/11/1907	30/09/1994	UERL (GNPBR)	Opened as 'Strand', renamed 'Aldwych' 09/05/1915. Closed 21/09/1940 - 01/07/1946 (World War II)
Strand						Aldwych Branch closed to passengers 30/09/1994, but track and a 1972 Mk1 Stock train retained for filming work
Alexandra Bridge	72 / 5C		01/09/1866	N/A	SER	
ALEXANDRA PALACE (GNR)	14 / 4B	P	01/05/1859	N/A	GNR	Opened as 'Wood Green', suffix '(Alexandra Park)' added 01/08/1864, dropped 18/03/1971.
Wood Green		G	*01/05/1859*	*24/01/1966*		Renamed 'Alexandra Palace' 17/05/1982. Goods yard closed 24/01/1966
Wood Green (Alexandra Park)						
Wood Green						
ALEXANDRA PALACE (MHPR)	14 / 4B		24/05/1873	05/07/1954	MHPR	Nominally opened by Muswell Hill & Palace Railway, but operated by GNR from opening. Closed and re-opened
Alexandra Park (1891-1892 only)						several times; closed 01/08/1873 - 01/05/1875 plus on several other occasions thereafter (mostly during Winter),
Alexandra Palace						known as Alexandra Park 1891-1892. Open without interruption 01/04/1898 to 29/10/1951, when closed again until
						07/01/1952. Finally permanently closed 05/07/1954. Had been intended for electrification and transfer to LT
						Northern Line, but works abandoned post-World War II.
ALL SAINTS	27 / 6D		31/08/1987	N/A	DLR	On Site of former NLR Poplar Station
ALPERTON	23 / 3D		28/06/1903	N/A	MDR	Renamed 'Alperton' 07/10/1910. First served Piccadilly Line 04/07/1932, last served District Line 23/10/1933
Perivale Alperton						
AMERSHAM	1 / 3A	P	01/09/1892	N/A	MET	'& Chesham Bois' 12/03/1922 - ??/??/1934. Metropolitan Line services beyond Amersham ceased 10/09/1961
Amersham & Chesham Bois		G	*01/09/1892*	*04/07/1966*		Goods yard closed 04/07/1966
Amersham						
AMPERE WAY	66 / 1B		10/05/2000	N/A	CTL	'IKEA' Prefix 18/10/2006 - ??/03/2008 (Sponsorship deal)
IKEA Ampere Way						
Ampere Way						
ANERLEY	54 / 4A		05/06/1839	N/A	LCRR	Suffix 'Bridge' dropped c.1840. According to Mitchell & Smith, initially spelt 'Annerley'. Rebuilt 1853-4 (quadrupling)
Anerley Bridge						
ANGEL	26 / 4C		17/11/1901	N/A	CSLR	Terminus from opening until 12/05/1907. Closed 09/08/1922 - 20/04/1924 (tunnel widening). Rebuilt with Northbound
						road routed via new tunnel 19/10/1992

NAME: (Previous names indented below)	Page / grid:		Date opened:	Date closed:	Opening company	NOTES:
ANGEL ROAD	15 / 2B	P	15/09/1840	N/A	NER	Opened as 'Edmonton', renamed 'Water Lane' 01/03/1849, 'Angel Road' 01/01/1864
Water Lane		G	15/09/1840	?		Goods yard opened with passenger station, but closure date unknown
Edmonton						
Angel Road Junction	15 / 2B		01/03/1849	07/12/1964	ECR	Originally 'Edmonton Junction'; junction of ECR Enfield (Town) branch with NER Lea Valley line. Angel Road Junction
Edmonton Junction						to Lower Edmonton Junction closed 07/12/1964
Angerstein Junction	41 / 3B		30/10/1852	N/A	SER / PRIV	Junction between Angerstein Wharf branch and SER North Kent Line. London-facing junction eliminated 1890
ANGERSTEIN WHARF	41 / 2B		30/10/1852	N/A	PRIV	Angerstein Wharf Branch privately built by John Angerstein, but leased to SER from outset. Purchased by SER 1898
						Several industrial sidings were present for various purposes: AA Oil Co. and BP / Shell Mex (Oil), Christie's
						(sleeper & telegraph pole works), United Glass works, Renwick Wilton (coal), as well as giving access to East
						Greenwich gasworks and the LCC Central Tram repair works. Today the wharf handles solely aggregates traffic
						(Bardon and Tarmac)
APCM COAL TERMINAL (SOUTHFLEET)	59 / 3C		??/??/1972	??/??/1976	PRIV	Established on site of former Southfleet station at end of branch from Fawkham Junction (former LCDR Gravesend
						West branch, closed 24/03/1968). Supplied coal to nearby Northfleet Cement works (APCM, later Blue Circle)
ARCHWAY	26 / 1A		22/06/1907	N/A	UERL (CCEHR)	Terminus 22/06/1907 - 03/07/1939, opened as 'Highgate'. 'Archway' prefix added 11/06/1939, reversed 19/01/1941,
Highgate (Archway)						'Highgate' prefix dropped ??/12/1947
Archway (Highgate)						
Highgate						
ARENA	54 / 6B		23/05/2000	N/A	CTL	Became a junction a week after opening (30/05/2000) with addition of branch to Elmers End
ARNOS GROVE	14 / 2B		19/09/1932	N/A	UERL (GNPBR)	Terminus of extension from Finsbury Park 19/09/1932 - 13/03/1933
ARNOS GROVE SIDINGS	14 / 2A		19/09/1932	N/A	UERL (GNPBR)	Stabling Sidings for Piccadilly Line
ARSENAL	26 / 2C & 81		15/12/1906	N/A	UERL (GNPBR)	Opened as 'Gillespie Road', renamed 'Arsenal (for Highbury Hill)' 31/10/1932, suffix gradually dropped
Arsenal (for Highbury Hill)						
Gillespie Road						
ASCOT ROAD	2 / 4A		??/??/2016	N/A	LUL (MET)	Proposed station on Metropolitan Line Watford Junction extension, estimated opening 2016
ASHBURTON GROVE GOODS	26 / 2C & 81		??/??/1884	13/06/1960	GNR	
ASHFORD	48 / 2C	P	22/08/1848	N/A	LSWR	Goods yard closed 1965
		G	22/08/1848	??/??/1965		
ASHTEAD	70 / 1D	P	01/02/1859	N/A	LBSCR / LSWR	
		G	01/02/1859	c.1965		
AVENUE ROAD	54 / 5B		23/05/2000	N/A	CTL	

B

NAME:	Page / grid:		Date opened:	Date closed:	Opening company	NOTES:
BAKER STREET	25 / 5D		10/01/1863	N/A	MET	Platforms to Swiss Cottage open 13/04/1868 (Now Metropolitan Line Platforms), BSWR platforms open 10/03/1906
						Bakerloo Line platforms to Stanmore opened 20/11/1939, Jubilee Line opened 01/05/1979
BALHAM	53 / 1A		01/12/1856	N/A	WELCPR	UERL (later Northern Line) station opened 06/12/1926. '& Upper Tooting' suffix added ??/03/1927,
Balham & Upper Tooting						dropped 06/10/1969 (applied to main line station only)
Balham						
Balham Junction	53 / 1A		01/12/1862	N/A	LBSCR	
BANDON HALT	66 / 3B		11/06/1906	07/06/1914	LBSCR	
BANK	26 / 6D		08/08/1898	N/A	WCIR	Opened by Waterloo & City Railway as 'City' 08/08/1898. CSLR and CLR platforms open 25/02/1900 and 30/07/1900
City (WCIR only)						respectively as 'Bank'. Waterloo & City platforms renamed from 'City' to 'Bank' 1940, DLR platforms open 29/07/1991
						Southbound Northern Line tunnel proposed to be re-bored to serve a new platform to alleviate overcrowding
						Transport and Works Act Order application late 2012, construction to start 2015, completion 2021
BANSTEAD	65 / 6A	P	22/05/1865	N/A	LBSCR	Suffix '& Burgh Heath' 01/06/1898 - ??/08/1928. Goods yard closed 07/09/1964 (note: Jackson refers to goods not
Banstead & Burgh Heath		G	22/05/1865	07/09/1964		being into use until 'about 1880', but Borley gives goods opening on same date as passenger, and goods yard is
Banstead						visible on 1871 OS). Former 'up' platform closed and branch singled 03/10/1982
BARBICAN	26 / 6D & 32 / 3D		23/12/1865	N/A	MET	Opened as 'Aldersgate Street', City Widened Lines platforms (later Network Rail) added 01/03/1866, 'Street' suffix
Aldersgate & Barbican						dropped 01/11/1910. '& Barbican' suffix added ??/??/1923, 'Aldersgate' prefix dropped 01/12/1968. Network Rail
Aldersgate						platforms closed 20/03/2009, although westbound NR services had ceased stopping at Barbican prior to this date
Aldersgate Street						
BARKING	29 / 4A	P	13/04/1854	N/A	LTSR	Served by District Railway since 02/06/1902 (no service 30/09/1905 - 01/04/1908), Served by Metropolitan Railway
		G	13/04/1854	01/04/1957		since 04/05/1936 ('Hammersmith & City Line' since 30/07/1990). Goods yard originally on 'up' side of station,
						relocated to east c.1930 to present site of Barking LUL Sidings, closed 01/04/1957. Station rebuilt 1959-1961
Barking East Junction	29 / 4B		11/05/1959	N/A	LTSR	All junctions in Barking area extensively remodelled 1959
BARKING POWER STATIONS 'A', 'B' & 'C'	29 / 6C		??/??/1925	26/10/1981	PRIV	Station 'A' opened 1925, extended via Station 'B', both closed 15/03/1976. Station 'C' built 1954, closed 26/10/1981
BARKING RIVERSIDE	29 / 5D		TBA	N/A	DLR	Gallions Reach to Dagenham Dock was proposed to open c.2017, but funding removed November 2008
BARKING SIDINGS	29 / 4B		??/11/1958	N/A	LTE (DIS)	Stabling sidings for District and Hammersmith & City Line trains, opened on site of Barking Goods (2nd)
Barking Station Junction	29 / 3A		11/05/1959	N/A	BR	All junctions in Barking area extensively remodelled and new flyovers commissioned 11/05/1959
Barking Tilbury Line Junction East	29 / 4A		01/06/1888	N/A	BR	All junctions in Barking area extensively remodelled 1959
Barking Tilbury Line Junction West	29 / 3A		11/05/1959	N/A	BR	All junctions in Barking area extensively remodelled and new flyovers commissioned 11/05/1959
Barking West Junction	29 / 3A		11/05/1959	N/A	BR	All junctions in Barking area extensively remodelled and new flyovers commissioned 11/05/1959
BARKINGSIDE	17 / 5B	P	01/05/1903	N/A	GER	Closed 22/05/1916 - 01/07/1919. LNER passenger trains ceased on Fairlop Loop 30/11/1947 to allow
		G	01/05/1903	04/10/1965		electrification and transfer to LTE. First served by LTE Central Line 31/05/1948. Goods yard closed 04/10/1965
BARLBY ROAD CARRIAGE DEPOT	25 / 5A		??/??/1885	30/06/1969	GWR	Site partially re-used for North Pole Depot (disused)
BARNEHURST	43 / 5B	P	01/05/1895	N/A	BHR	Goods yard closed 07/10/1968
		G	01/05/1895	07/10/1968		
BARNES	37 / 5D	P	27/07/1846	N/A	LSWR	Expanded to 4 platforms during quadrupling 1886. Goods yard closed 06/01/1969
		G	27/07/1846	06/01/1969		
BARNES BRIDGE	37 / 4C		12/03/1916	N/A	LSWR	Opening coincided with electrification of Hounslow Loop
Barnes Bridge	37 / 4C		22/08/1849	N/A	LSWR	Rebuilt 1894 - 1895 (strengthening)
Barnes Junction	37 / 5C		22/08/1849	N/A	LSWR	
Barnet Tunnels	13 / 1D		07/08/1850	N/A	GNR	
BARONS COURT	38 / 2A & 84 & 72		09/10/1905	N/A	UERL (MDR)	UERL (GNPBR) platforms opened 15/12/1906 to north of District platforms, reconfigured with Piccadilly Line between
						District Line platforms 04/07/1932
Barrington Road Junction	39 / 5C		01/08/1865	01/01/1923	LBSCR / LCDR	'End on' junction between LBSCR and LCDR west of East Brixton station, demarcation eliminated at Grouping
BATH ROAD	37 / 2C & 51 / 1D		08/04/1909	01/01/1917	NSWJR	
Bath Road Junction	33 / 1C		08/10/1849	N/A	GWR	Originally junction at southern end of Royal Curve (closed 26/07/1970), today point where Windsor Branch
						becomes single track (branch singled 09/09/1963)
BATTERSEA (LUL)	39 / 3A & 82		c.2020	N/A	LUL (NOR)	Proposed terminus of Northern Line extension from Kennington
BATTERSEA (WLER)	38 / 4C		02/03/1863	21/10/1940	WLER	Passenger service withdrawn Willesden Junction to Clapham Junction 21/10/1940
BATTERSEA PARK (1st)	39 / 3A & 82		01/10/1860	01/11/1870	LBSCR	Renamed 01/07/1862. Also referred to as 'Battersea Park & Steamboat Pier'
Battersea						
BATTERSEA PARK (2nd)	39 / 4A & 82		01/05/1867	N/A	LBSCR	Opened as 'York Road', renamed 'York Road & Battersea Park' 01/11/1870, 'Battersea Park & York Road' 01/01/1877,
Battersea Park & York Road						suffix dropped 01/06/1885
York Road & Battersea Park						
York Road						
Battersea Park Junction	39 / 3A & 82		01/12/1867	N/A	LBSCR	
BATTERSEA PARK ROAD	39 / 4A & 82		01/05/1867	03/04/1916	LCDR	Renamed 01/11/1877
Battersea Park (York Road)						
Battersea Pier Junction	39 / 3A & 82		01/12/1860	N/A	LCDR / VSPR	
BATTERSEA PIER SIDINGS	82		?	N/A	LBSCR	
BATTERSEA WHARF GOODS	82		30/04/1862	04/05/1970	LBSCR	
BAYSWATER	25 / 6C		01/10/1868	N/A	MET	Opened as 'Bayswater', renamed 'Bayswater (Queens Road) & Westbourne Grove' ??/??/1923,
Bayswater (Queensway)						suffix '& Westbourne Grove' dropped ??/??/1933, renamed 'Bayswater (Queensway)' 01/09/1946,
Bayswater (Queens Road)						suffix gradually dropped. First served by District Line to Edgware Road 01/11/1926, 'Circle Line' service provided
Bayswater (Queens Road) & Westbourne Grove						by a combination of Metropolitan and District Line trains and did not receive its own identity as a line until c.1949
Bayswater						Closed 23/07/2011 - 23/08/2011 (engineering work)
BECKENHAM HILL	54 / 3D		01/07/1892	N/A	LCDR	
BECKENHAM JUNCTION	54 / 4D	P	01/01/1857	N/A	MKR	Initially terminus of MKR from Lewisham, WELCPR from Bromley Junction to Shortlands added 03/05/1858
Beckenham		G	01/01/1857	18/04/1964		Suffix 'Junction' added 01/04/1864. Originally two goods yards, north and south of passenger station, south yard
						closed c.1928 (now Tramlink platforms). North yard closed 18/04/1964, but remained in use as a coal concentration
						depot until 1982. Croydon Tramlink terminus platforms opened 23/05/2000 on former south goods yard site
Beckenham Junction	54 / 4C		03/05/1858	N/A	WELCPR / MKR	
BECKENHAM ROAD	54 / 4C		23/05/2000	N/A	CTL	On site of former Penge station (WELCPR), closed c.1860
Beckenham Spur	54 / 4C	P	01/01/1857	N/A	MKR	Regular passenger traffic ceased after 15/10/1939. Singled 1987. Passenger services re-introduced 29/05/1995
		G	01/01/1857	N/A		

NAME: (Previous names indented below)	Page / grid:	Date opened:	Date closed:	Opening company:	NOTES:
BECKTON (GCC)	29 / 6A	17/03/1873	29/12/1940	GCC	Opened 17/03/1873 (workmen only), general passenger traffic commenced 18/03/1874. Passenger services withdrawn from Beckton and Gallions 29/12/1940
BECKTON (DLR)	28 / 6D	28/03/1994	N/A	DLR	
BECKTON DEPOT	29 / 6A	*28/03/1994*	N/A	DLR	DLR Depot
BECKTON GAS WORKS	29 / 6B	*14/10/1872*	*22/02/1971*	GCC	Last train from works departed 01/06/1970, 22/02/1971 is official date of closure. Track lifted by 1973
Beckton Junction	62 / 3B	03/08/1880	07/09/1940	LSKD	Divergence of Beckton and Gallions Branches
BECKTON PARK	41 / 1D & 62 / 5C	28/03/1994	N/A	DLR	
BECKTON RIVERSIDE	29 / 6A	TBA	N/A	DLR	Gallions Reach to Dagenham Dock was proposed to open c.2017, but funding removed November 2008
BECONTREE	29 / 3D	28/06/1926	N/A	LMS	Opened on existing LTSR Main Line (now 'fast' tracks). Renamed 18/07/1932. First served by District Line after
Gale Street Halt					quadrupling and addition of platforms on new 'slow' tracks 12/09/1932. Last served British Rail 15/06/1962 and 'fast' platforms abandoned. Transferred to LTB 01/01/1969.
BECONTREE ESTATE RAILWAY	29 / 2D	*??/??/1921*	*??/??/1934*	LCC	Transported building materials during construction of Becontree Estate. Extended to a wharf on The Thames
BEDDINGTON LANE	53 / 6A	22/10/1855	N/A	WCRR	Opened as 'Beddington', 'Lane' suffix added January 1887. 'Halt' suffix added 1919, dropped 06/05/1969
Beddington Lane Halt					Wimbledon to West Croydon closed by Railtrack 31/05/1997 (date of last train; official date of closure 02/06/1997)
Beddington					Re-opened as Tramlink stop also named 'Beddington Lane' towards the west of original site, opening 30/05/2000
BELGRAVE WALK	52 / 5C	30/05/2000	N/A	CTL	
BELLINGHAM	54 / 2D	P 01/07/1892	N/A	LCDR	Goods yard stated as opening with passenger station in Borley, but no evidence on 1897 OS (present by 1916)
		G *c.1900*	*25/03/1968*	SECR	Closed 25/03/1968, also accessed Robertson's jam factory. Carriage sidings south of station laid out c.1954 to replace stabling facilities closed at Crystal palace (High Level)
BELMONT (LMS)	11 / 3C	12/09/1932	05/10/1964	LMS	Passing loop in use 05/07/1937 - 09/07/1955 Became passenger terminus 15/09/1952. Belmont to Harrow & Wealdstone withdrawn 05/10/1964, branch previously closed to goods 06/07/1964
BELMONT (LBSCR)	65 / 5B	P 22/05/1865	N/A	LBSCR	Renamed 01/10/1875. Goods yard relocated south 1889, closed 06/01/1969 (note: Jackson refers to goods not
California		G *22/05/1865*	*06/01/1969*		being into use until 'about 1880', but Borley gives goods opening on same date as passenger, and goods yard is visible on 1866 OS). Former 'up' platform closed and branch singled 03/10/1982
BELSIZE PARK	25 / 3D	22/06/1907	N/A	UERL (CCEHR)	
Belsize Tunnels	25 / 3D	07/09/1867	N/A	MID	Midland Main line first goods train ran 07/09/1867, first passenger 13/07/1868 (to King's Cross MET) Second tunnel added 03/02/1884 (today's 'slow' tunnel, with original tunnel now 'fast')
BELVEDERE	43 / 2A	P ??/03/1859	N/A	SER	Exact opening date unknown: first appeared in timetables March 1859. Goods yard closed 10/06/1963
		G *??/03/1859*	*10/06/1963*		
BERMONDSEY	40 / 2A	17/09/1999	N/A	LUL (JUB)	Terminus of services from Stratford 17/07/1999 - 24/09/1999
Bermondsey Dive-under	40 / 3B & 80	??/??/2018	N/A	NR	New diver-under proposed to open in connection with 'Thameslink' upgrade 2018, using part of former Bricklayers Arms branch to remove conflicting train movements approaching London Bridge
BERMONDSEY STREET	39 / 1D & 72 / 6D	10/10/1836	14/12/1836	LGR	Temporary London terminus of London & Greenwich Railway
BERRYLANDS	51 / 5B	16/10/1933	N/A	SR	
BETHNAL GREEN (GER)	27 / 5B & 85	24/05/1872	N/A	GER	Referred to as '- Junction' at times until 1895. Platforms on Stratford lines closed 08/12/1946
Bethnal Green Junction					
BETHNAL GREEN (LPTB)	27 / 5B	04/12/1946	N/A	LPTB (CEN)	
Bethnal Green East Junction	27 / 5B	27/05/1872	N/A	GER	
Bethnal Green West Junction	27 / 5B & 85	04/11/1872	N/A	GER	Divergence of GER extension to Bishopsgate Low Level (later Liverpool Street) from original ECR route to Bishopsgate High Level (latter abandoned 05/12/1964). Junction remains as set of crossovers.
BEXLEY	57 / 1A	P 01/09/1866	N/A	SER	Goods yard closed 06/05/1963
		G *01/09/1866*	*06/05/1963*		
BEXLEYHEATH	42 / 5D	P 01/05/1895	N/A	BHR	Initially referred to as either 'Bexleyheath' or 'Bexley Heath'.
Bexley Heath		G *01/05/1895*	*07/10/1968*		Goods yard situated 400m West of passenger station, closed 07/10/1968
BICKLEY	55 / 5C	P 05/07/1858	N/A	MKR	Terminus of MKR extension from Shortlands. Renamed 01/10/1860. Line extended to Rochester Bridge 03/12/1860
Southborough Road		G *05/07/1858*	*16/05/1964*		Rebuilt 1893-4 (quadrupling). Goods yard closed 16/05/1964
Bickley Junctions	55 / 5D	08/09/1902	N/A	SECR	Junctions at north end of Tonbridge Loops, 'slow' junction opened 08/09/1902, 'fast' 14/09/1902
BINGHAM ROAD	67 / 1A	01/09/1906	16/05/1983	LBSCR / SER	Closed 15/03/1915 - 30/09/1935, permanently closed 16/05/1983, later replaced by CTL 'Addiscombe' station to north
BIRKBECK	54 / 5B	02/03/1930	N/A	SR	'Up' platform closed and route singled ??/02/1983. Croydon Tramlink opened 23/05/2000 using 'Up' alignment, with the former BR 'up' platform consequently rebuilt and re-opened
Birkbeck Junction	54 / 5B	??/02/1983	N/A	BR	Commencement of single NR track to Penge Junction (originally double track throughout)
BISHOPSGATE (HIGH LEVEL)	27 / 5A & 85	P 01/07/1840	c.1879	ECR	Passenger terminus for ECR 01/07/1840 - 01/11/1875 although occasional passenger services remained until c.1879.
Bishopsgate		G *01/01/1881*	*05/12/1964*		Renamed 'Bishopsgate' 27/07/1846. 'High level' suffix 04/11/1872. Goods traffic commenced 01/01/1881,
Shoreditch					lasting until 05/12/1964. LOROL station 'Shoreditch High Street' opened on same site 27/04/2010
BISHOPSGATE (LOW LEVEL)	27 / 5A & 85	04/11/1872	22/05/1916	GER	Functioned as an additional GER terminus to the 'High Level' station until Liverpool Street opened 02/02/1874
Black Potts Viaduct	33 / 3C	01/12/1849	N/A	LSWR	
BLACKFRIARS (MDR)	26 / 6C & 32 / 5B	30/05/1870	N/A	MDR	Main Line station opened by LCDR 10/05/1886 as 'St Paul's', renamed 'Blackfriars' 01/02/1937. LU platforms closed
St Paul's (LCDR only)					27/02/2009 - 20/02/2012 due to redevelopment works, NR platforms extensively rebuilt during same period and consequently closed 20/11/2010 - 16/01/2011. New entrance on South bank of The Thames opened 06/12/2011
BLACKFRIARS (SER)	39 / 1C & 72 / 6A	11/01/1864	01/01/1869	SER	Replaced by Waterloo Junction (= East) to west
Great Surrey Street					
BLACKFRIARS BRIDGE	39 / 1C & 32 / 6C	01/06/1864	01/10/1885	LCDR	Terminus until 21/12/1864. Replaced by St Paul's (= Blackfriars) on north bank of Thames (opened 10/05/1886)
Blackfriars Bridge	32 / 6C	21/12/1864	27/06/1969	LCDR	Spans removed 1985, piers remain. Easternmost piers re-used for Blackfriars station redevelopment
BLACKFRIARS GOODS	39 / 1C & 32 / 6C	*01/05/1865*	*03/02/1964*	LCDR	
Blackfriars Junction	39 / 1C & 32 & 72	01/06/1878	N/A	LCDR	Western end of curve between LCDR and SER
BLACKHEATH	41 / 5A	P 30/07/1849	N/A	SER	Opened with west-facing bay platforms on both 'up' and 'down' sides. Extensive carriage sidings laid out to west
		G *30/07/1849*	*06/05/1963*		1879, but were not electrified with main line 06/06/1926. Goods yard closed 06/05/1963, bays and sidings all decommissioned with rationalisation 15/03/1970 and signal boxes closed
BLACKHEATH HILL	40 / 4D	18/09/1871	01/01/1917	LCDR	Terminus 18/09/1871 - 01/10/1888. Passenger service withdrawn Nunhead to Greenwich Park 01/01/1917
Blackheath Junction	41 / 5B	01/05/1895	N/A	SER / BHR	Junction between SER North Kent Line and Bexleyheath Railway
Blackheath Tunnel	41 / 4B	30/07/1849	N/A	SER	
BLACKHORSE LANE	67 / 1A	23/05/2000	N/A	CTL	
BLACKHORSE ROAD	15 / 5C	P 09/07/1894	N/A	TFGR	Goods yard open 01/09/1894 - 07/12/1964. Victoria Line opened 01/09/1968. BR platforms resited west 14/12/1981
Black Horse Road		G *01/09/1894*	*07/12/1964*		to improve interchange. Main line platforms originally referred to as either 'Black Horse Road' or 'Blackhorse Road', usually the former, until the 14/12/1981 resiting when they became 'Blackhorse Road' permanently
BLACKWALL (DLR)	40 / 1D & 31 / 6C	28/03/1994	N/A	DLR	
BLACKWALL (LBLR)	41 / 1A & 31 / 4D	06/07/1840	04/05/1926	LBLR	Served by NLR 01/09/1870 - 01/07/1890. Passenger service Stepney East to Blackwall withdrawn 04/05/1926
BLACKWALL GOODS (ECR)	28 / 6A	*??/06/1848*	*06/03/1967*	ECR	Accessed by a branch off the ECR North Woolwich Branch and bridge across The River Lea
Blackwall Pepper Warehouses					Also referred to as 'Blackwall Pepper Warehouses'
BLACKWALL GOODS (GNR)	41 / 1A & 31 / 4C	*c.1870*	*c.1961*	GNR	Borley gives c.1870 (shipping traffic only) and 1900 (general goods) for opening, and c.1961 for closure Jackson gives years of opening / closing as 1860 / 1961
BLAKE HALL	8 / 1C	P 24/04/1865	31/10/1981	GER	Epping to Ongar transferred to LTE 25/09/1949, Electrified 18/11/1957. Goods yard closed 18/04/1966
		G *24/04/1865*	*18/04/1966*		Was not re-opened by the Epping-Ongar Railway on account of now being a private residence
Bollo Lane Junction	37 / 2B & 51 / 2B	01/03/1878	13/09/1965	LSWR	Junction at West end of Acton Curve
BOND STREET (CLR)	26 / 6A	24/09/1900	N/A	CLR	'Davies Street' until opening. Jubilee Line platforms opened 01/05/1979.
BOND STREET (NR)	26 / 6A	??/??/2018	N/A	NR (XRAIL)	Station on 'Crossrail 1', under construction for 2018 opening
BOOKHAM	69 / 4D	P 02/02/1885	N/A	LSWR	Referred to as 'Bookham Common' in opening notice, but had always been 'Bookham' in Bradshaw
		G *02/02/1885*	*c.1965*		
BOROUGH	39 / 1D	18/12/1890	N/A	CSLR	Named 'Great Dover Street' until opening. Closed 16/07/1922 - 23/02/1925 (tunnel widening), and 02/07/1999 - 05/09/1999 (tunnel works)
Borough Market Junction	39 / 1D & 72 / 5C	01/09/1866	N/A	SER	Junction for Cannon Street
BOROUGH ROAD	39 / 1C	01/06/1864	01/04/1907	LCDR	
BOSTON MANOR	36 / 2C	01/05/1883	N/A	MDR	Renamed 11/12/1911. First served by Piccadilly Line 13/03/1933. District Line service ceased 10/10/1964
Boston Road					
BOUNDS GREEN	14 / 3B	19/09/1932	N/A	UERL (GNPBR)	
BOUNDS GREEN DEPOT	14 / 3B	*??/??/1929*	N/A	LNER	
BOW	27 / 5D & 22	26/09/1850	15/05/1944	EWIDBJR	Platforms on line to Bromley (LTSR) added 17/05/1869, closed to regular traffic 01/01/1915 (Plaistow to Bow shuttle) Passenger service Dalston Junction to Poplar withdrawn 15/05/1944 (enemy action), official closure 23/04/1945
BOW CHURCH	27 / 5D & 22	31/08/1987	N/A	DLR	
BOW GOODS (MID)	27 / 4D	*01/12/1892*	N/A	MID	Opened by MID, transferred to BR Eastern c.1956. Currently serves Bardon Aggregates only
BOW GOODS (LNWR)	27 / 4D & 22	*20/03/1893*	*??/??/1940*	LNWR	
Bow Junction (1st)	27 / 4D & 22	02/04/1849	N/A	LBLR / ECR	Junction between ECR and LBLR (Blackwall Extension Railway)
Bow Junction (2nd)	27 / 5D & 22	20/10/1851	29/12/1967	EWIDBJR	Junction of EWIDBJR (later NLR) routes to Poplar and Fenchurch Street (via Gas Factory Junction)
BOW ROAD (LBLR)	27 / 5D & 22	02/04/1849	07/11/1949	LBLR	Opened with Blackwall Extension Railway (LBLR) 02/04/1849 as 'Bow & Bromley', closed 29/09/1850.
Bow & Bromley					Re-opened 10/10/1876 on same site as 'Bow Road', re-sited north of Bow Road 04/04/1892. Closed 21/04/1941 - 09/12/1946 & 06/01/1947 - 06/10/1947. Passenger services Fenchurch Street to Stratford withdrawn 07/11/1949
BOW ROAD (MDR)	27 / 5D & 22	11/06/1902	N/A	MDR / LTSR	Served by Metropolitan Line since 30/03/1936 ('Hammersmith & City Line' since 30/07/1990)

NAME: (Previous names indented below)	Page / grid:	Date opened:	Date closed:	Opening company:	NOTES:
BOW ROAD GOODS	27 / 5D & 22	??/??/1885	07/12/1964	GER	
BOW WORKS	27 / 5D & 22	c.1850	??/??/1960	NLR	North London Railway Loco Works, enlarged 1863 & 1882
BOYERS SIDING (FELTHAM)	49 / 1B	c.1900	c.1935	PRIV	Market garden. Sidings not present on 1895 OS, but had appeared by 1914. Housing built on site by WW2
BOWES PARK	14 / 3B	01/11/1880	N/A	GNR	Terminating siding added 1911, removed 1950, relaid 1974
BRENT CROSS	13 / 6A	19/11/1923	N/A	UERL (CCEHR)	Express passing loops commissioned 04/01/1925, abolished 23/08/1936, used by a handful of timetabled trains daily
Brent					Renamed 20/07/1976
BRENT CROSS THAMESLINK	12 / 6D	TBA	N/A	NR	Proposed new station in connection with regeneration project
Brent Curve	25 / 1A & 3 / 4A	P 01/07/1905	??/10/1908	MID	Opened to goods, along with rest of Dudding Hill Loop, 01/10/1868. Some through passenger services operated
		G 01/10/1868	N/A		between 01/07/1905 - October 1908
Brent Curve Junction	24 / 1D & 3 / 3A	01/10/1868	N/A	MID	Junction between Midland Main Line and Dudding Hill Loop. Saw passenger trains 01/07/1905 - ??/10/1908
Brent New Junction	68 / 5C	c.1940	N/A	LMS	Junction with Willesden 'F' sidings
BRENTFORD (GWR)	36 / 3D	01/05/1860	04/05/1942	GWR	Closed 22/03/1915 - 12/04/1920. Passenger service on GWR Brentford Branch withdrawn 04/05/1942
BRENTFORD (LSWR)	36 / 3D	P 22/08/1849	N/A	LSWR	'Brentford Central' 05/06/1950 - 12/05/1980. Goods yard closed 04/01/1965, parcels traffic ceased 07/09/1980
Brentford Central		G 22/08/1849	04/01/1965		
Brentford					
Brentford Branch Junction	35 / 1D	18/07/1859	N/A	GWR	
BRENTFORD DOCK	36 / 3D	18/07/1859	31/12/1964	GWR	Originally intended to have a passenger station to serve ferries to Kew Gardens, and platform may have been
					constructed for this purpose on north side of dock. Special passenger service ran on branch 15/07/1859,
					regular goods traffic commenced three days later
BRENTFORD GOODS	36 / 3C	03/11/1930	N/A	GWR	Opened as 'Brentford Town' goods as distinct from LSWR goods station, today known as 'Brentford Goods'
Brentford Town Goods					Closed to general goods traffic 07/12/1970, but stone (Day & sons) and domestic waste traffic remain
					The domestic waste terminal opened in early 1977
BRENTHAM FOR NORTH EALING AND GREYSTOKE PARK	24 / 4A	01/05/1911	15/06/1947	GWR	Replaced Twyford Abbey Halt. Closed 01/02/1915 - 29/03/1920. Suffix 'for North Ealing' added 1932, with further
Brentham (for North Ealing)					suffix 'and Greystoke Park' subsequently added, until closure
Brentham					
BRENTWOOD	20 / 2A	P 01/07/1840	N/A	ECR	Country terminus of ECR from opening until 29/03/1843. Name carried with '& Warley' 01/11/1882 - 20/02/1969.
Brentwood & Warley		G 01/07/1840	07/12/1970		Engine shed opened 1872, closed 1949. Rebuilt through quadrupling work 01/01/1934.
Brentwood					Goods yard closed 07/12/1970
BREWERY SIDINGS (ROMFORD)	18 / 6C	??/??/1853	??/??/1963	PRIV	Originally accessed via a wagon hoist and turntable, tunnel under and incline up to main line added in 1860's
BRICKLAYERS ARMS	39 / 2D & 4	P 01/05/1844	01/01/1852	SER / LCRR	Closed to passengers 01/01/1852, although some Summer Sunday excursion trains operated 1932-1939
		G 01/05/1844	??/??/1981		Amalgamated with Willow Walk Goods 07/03/1932. Remained in use for general goods until 01/08/1977,
					some parcels & coal traffic remained until 1981
Bricklayers Arms Junction	40 / 3B & 79 / 80	01/05/1844	N/A	LCRR	Originally junction between LCRR and LCRR / SER Bricklayers Arms branch (traffic ceased by 1981)
					Today junction where spur leaves former LCRR to join South London Line (opened 01/01/1871)
BRIMSDOWN	7 / 4C	P 01/10/1884	N/A	GER	Goods yard closed 04/10/1965
		G 01/10/1884	04/10/1965		
BRITISH INDUSTRIAL SAND (HOLMETHORPE)	73 / 4D	c.1870	c.1990's	PRIV	Rail-served brickworks had existed on site since at least 1871 (OS). Later became Standard Brick Co., then
					British Industrial Sand. Complex included exchange sidings with three shunters and engine shed, closure date
					unknown, extant in 1990 edition of Baker, disused and disconnected but in situ in 2002 edition of Quail
BRITISH MUSEUM	26 / 6B	30/07/1900	24/09/1933	CLR	Replaced by Central Line platforms at Holborn (Kingsway) (opened 25/09/1933)
BRIXTON (LCDR)	39 / 5C	06/10/1862	N/A	LCDR	Suffix '& South Stockwell' 01/05/1863 - 09/07/1934. Platforms on route to Denmark Hill closed 1929, demolished
Brixton & South Stockwell					during 1930
Brixton					
BRIXTON (LTE)	39 / 5C	23/07/1971	N/A	LTE (VIC)	Southern terminus of Victoria Line
BRIXTON COAL	39 / 5C	c.1880	??/03/1947	MID	
Brixton Junction	39 / 5C	01/05/1863	N/A	LCDR	Junction between 1862 LCDR route from Herne Hill to Stewarts Lane and 01/05/1863 line to Loughborough Junction
Brixton Spur	39 / 5C	P 01/05/1863	01/04/1921	LCDR	Previously closed to passengers 02/04/1916 - 04/10/1920, remains in use primarily for stock transfer
		G 01/05/1863	N/A		Also referred to as 'West Curve'
BROAD STREET	26 / 6D & 85	P 01/11/1865	30/06/1986	NLR	ex-Richmond trains diverted to North Woolwich 13/05/1985, remaining ex-Watford Junction services diverted to
		G 18/05/1868	27/01/1969	LNWR	temporary platform north of original station July 1985, allowing demolition to commence. Temporary platform closed
					due to diversion of remaining trains to Liverpool Street via Graham Road Curve 30/06/1986 (last train 27/06/1986)
BROCKLEY	40 / 5C	06/03/1871	N/A	LBSCR	
BROCKLEY HILL	12 / 1A	N/A	N/A	LPTB (NOR)	On Northern Line extension to Bushey Heath from Edgware. Construction abandoned 1940
BROCKLEY LANE	40 / 5C	??/06/1872	01/01/1917	LCDR	Exact opening date unknown (June 1872). Passenger service withdrawn Nunhead to Greenwich Park 01/01/1917
BROCKLEY LANE COAL	40 / 5C	??/12/1883	04/05/1970	GNR	'Martins Siding' on down side became LNWR Coal Yard 1885
BROMLEY-BY-BOW	27 / 5D & 22	P 31/03/1858	N/A	LTSR	Opened by LTSR as 'Bromley', damaged by fire 1892, rebuilt to West 01/03/1894. Goods yard opened c.1898
Bromley		G c.1898	?		First served by District Railway 02/06/1902, line quadrupled 1905, District trains then using 'Slow' lines. Served by
					Metropolitan Line since 30/03/1936 ('Hammersmith & City Line' since 30/07/1990). 'Fast' platforms abandoned
					15/06/1962. Renamed 18/05/1967. Ownership transferred to LTB 01/01/1969. Goods yard closure date unknown.
Bromley Down Junction	54 / 5A	03/05/1858	N/A	WELCPR	
Bromley Junction	27 / 5D & 22	17/05/1869	13/09/1959	NLR / LTSR	Resited to the West with Bromley Station 01/03/1894
BROMLEY NORTH	55 / 5B	P 01/01/1878	N/A	SER	Renamed 01/06/1899. Originally two side platforms astride three roads terminating in a turntable. In 1924 rebuilding
Bromley		G 01/01/1878	20/05/1968		commenced, with the western platform remaining in use while the eastern was demolished, replaced by current
					island platforms. Completed December 1925, remaining original platform abandoned. Goods yard closed 20/05/1968
BROMLEY SOUTH	55 / 5B	P 22/11/1858	N/A	MKR	Opening date given as 22/11/1858 in Borley but 05/07/1858 in Quick (latter is date line through station opened)
Bromley		G 22/11/1858	18/04/1964		Alternative original name of 'Bromley Common' given in Dewick, but not mentioned in any other publication
					Renamed 'Bromley South' 01/06/1899. Rebuilt 1893-1894 (quadrupling). Goods yard closed 18/04/1964
Bromley Up Junction	54 / 5A	03/05/1858	N/A	WELCPR	
BROMPTON & FULHAM GOODS	38 / 3B & 84	01/04/1892	04/08/1975	LNWR	
BROMPTON ROAD	38 / 2D	15/12/1906	30/07/1934	UERL (GNPBR)	
BRONDESBURY	25 / 3A	02/01/1860	N/A	HJR	Opened as 'Edgware Road (Kilburn)', '& Brondesbury' suffix added 01/01/1872, renamed 'Brondesbury
Brondesbury (Edgware Road)					(Edgware Road)' 01/01/1873, renamed 'Brondesbury' 01/01/1883. Closed 29/10/1995 - 29/09/1996
Edgware Road & Brondesbury					
Edgware Road					
Edgware Road (Kilburn)					
BRONDESBURY PARK	25 / 3A	01/06/1908	N/A	LNWR	Closed 29/10/1995 - 29/09/1996 (engineering works)
BRUCE GROVE	15 / 4A	22/07/1872	N/A	GER	
BUCKHURST HILL	16 / 1D	P 22/08/1856	N/A	ECR	'Down' platform originally south of Queen's Road. Majority of Passenger services transferred to LTE 21/11/1948
		G ??/??/1859	06/01/1964		First Trains in the morning remained British Rail services until 01/06/1970. Goods yard open 1859 - 06/01/1964
BURDETT ROAD	27 / 6C	11/09/1871	21/04/1941	LBLR	Closed 29/12/1940 (enemy action), closed again 10/04/1941 (enemy action) and did not re-open
					21/04/1941 is the 'official' closure date.
BURNT OAK	12 / 3B	27/10/1924	N/A	UERL (CCEHR)	'Watling' suffix introduced c.1928, gradually dropped
Burnt Oak (Watling)					
Burnt Oak					
Burroughs Tunnels	12 / 5D	18/08/1924	N/A	UERL (CCEHR)	
Bury Street Junction	7 / 6A	01/10/1891	N/A	GER	No passenger service Bury Street Junction to Cheshunt Junction 01/10/1909 - 01/03/1915 & 01/07/1919 - 21/11/1960
BUSHEY	2 / 5D	P 01/12/1841	N/A	LBIR	Served by London Underground Bakerloo Line Trains 16/04/1917 - 24/09/1982. '& Oxhey' dropped 06/05/1974
Bushey & Oxhey		G 01/12/1841	03/02/1969		Goods yard closed 03/02/1969
Bushey					
BUSHEY HEATH	3 / 5C	N/A	N/A	LPTB (NOR)	Intended terminus of Northern Line extension from Edgware. Construction abandoned 1940
BUSHEY HEATH DEPOT	3 / 6D	N/A	N/A	LPTB (NOR)	Was to replace Golders Green Depot. Sheds constructed but track never laid, sheds used for construction of
					Halifax Bombers during WW2, and then later became Aldenham bus overhaul works between 1956-1986
BUSH HILL PARK	7 / 5A	P 01/11/1880	N/A	GER	Goods yard closed 04/05/1964
		G 01/11/1880	04/05/1964		
BYFLEET & NEW HAW	61 / 4C	01/07/1927	N/A	SR	Opened as 'West Weybridge', renamed 12/06/1961
West Weybridge					
Byfleet Curve	61 / 4C	P ??/??/1885	N/A	LSWR	Lightly used by passenger services
		G ??/??/1885	N/A		
Byfleet Junction	61 / 4C	??/??/1885	N/A	LSWR	Junction at south end of Byfleet Curve

NAME: (Previous names indented below)	Page / grid	Date opened:	Date closed:	Opening company:	NOTES:
CABLE STREET COAL	74 / 2D	*c.1893*	*post-1954*	PRIV	On south side of LBLR viaduct between Grove St and Cannon St Rd. Not noted in Borley, but illustrated in Connor 'Fenchurch St to Barking', which notes wagon traversers supplied in 1893 and shows yard open in 1954
Calderwood Street Tunnel	42 / 2A	30/07/1849	N/A	SER	
CALEDONIAN ROAD	26 / 3B	15/12/1906	N/A	UERL (GNPBR)	
CALEDONIAN ROAD & BARNSBURY	26 / 3C	10/06/1852	N/A	EWIDBJR	Opened as 'Caledonian Road', renamed 'Barnsbury' 01/07/1870, Re-sited to west as 'Barnsbury' 21/11/1870
Barnsbury					Prefix 'Caledonian Road' added 22/05/1893. Closed 20/02/2010 - 01/06/2010, upon re-opening, platforms
Caledonian Road					reconfigured with new island platform 2 & 3 in between two pairs of tracks, and platform 1 to south abandoned
CALEDONIAN ROAD GOODS (GNR)	26 / 3B & 75	??/??/1878	30/10/1967	GNR	Adjacent to North London Railway but no physical connection to it
CALEDONIAN ROAD GOODS (EWIDBJR)	26 / 3B & 75	*c.1851*	06/09/1969	EWIDBJR	Originally on north side of line, relocated to south side 1869, transferred to LNWR 01/09/1871
CAMBERWELL	39 / 4D	P 06/10/1862	03/04/1916	LCDR	Opened as 'Camberwell', 'New Road' suffix added 01/05/1863, dropped 01/10/1908
Camberwell New Road		G 06/10/1862	18/04/1964		Passenger station closed 03/04/1916, goods & coal yard closed 18/04/1964
Camberwell					
Cambria Junction	39 / 5D	01/07/1872	N/A	LCDR / LBSCR	Junction at southern end of Cambria Spur. Sometimes referred to 'Cambria Road Junction'
Cambria Spur	39 / 5C	P 01/07/1872	N/A	LCDR	Also referred to as 'East Curve'
		G 01/07/1872	N/A		
CAMBRIDGE HEATH	27 / 4B	27/05/1872	N/A	GER	Closed 22/05/1916 - 05/05/1919, 27/07/1984 - September 1984 (fire), 17/02/1986 - 16/03/1986 (rebuilding)
CAMDEN	26 / 3A & 58	P 01/11/1851	01/05/1852	LNWR	Opened as a ticket platform c.1844, full opening 01/11/1851. Replaced by station of same name slightly to north
		G c.1839	?		01/05/1852 (see entry for 'Chalk Farm LNWR'). Borley states goods opened 'probably' 1839, gives no closure date
CAMDEN CARRIAGE SIDINGS	25 / 4D & 58	*c.1960's*	N/A	LNWR	Formerly Camden Engine shed
CAMDEN CHALK FARM	25 / 3D & 58	01/05/1852	01/04/1872	LNWR	Replaced Camden (1st) to south, replaced by Camden Chalk Farm (2nd) to north (later 'Chalk Farm')
Camden					
CAMDEN 'PASSENGER' ENGINE SHED	25 / 4D & 58	*c.1847*	03/01/1966	LNWR	Built at same time as Camden Roundhouse, both replacing earlier LBIR structure on Roundhouse site
					Extended 1932, closed to steam 09/09/1963 then diesel 03/01/1966. Demolished, became Camden carriage sidings
Camden Junctions	25 / 3D	09/06/1851	N/A	LNWR / EWIDBJR	Extensively remodelled with the addition of 'flying' junctions to the 'DC' lines 10/07/1922
CAMDEN 'LUGGAGE' ENGINE SHED	58	*c.1847*	*c.1857*	LNWR	Replaced earlier LBIR engine shed on same site, became obsolete within 10 years (too small for engines).
					Utilised as warehouse for approx. 100 years, became cultural / music venue 1964 (Camden Roundhouse)
CAMDEN ROAD (MID)	26 / 3B	13/07/1868	01/01/1916	MID	
CAMDEN ROAD (NLR)	26 / 3A	05/12/1870	N/A	NLR	Replaced first Camden Town station to east. Renamed 'Camden Road' 25/09/1950. Reduced from 4 tracks to 2
Camden Town					in 1984. Closed 20/02/2010 - 01/06/2010 (LOROL upgrade works)
Camden Road Central Junction	76	14/11/2007	N/A	LCOR / NR	
Camden Road East Junction	26 / 3A & 76	??/??/1984	N/A	BR	Junction formed when quadruple track through Camden Road reduced to double in 1984
Camden Road Incline Junction	76	14/11/2007	N/A	LCOR / NR	
Camden Road Tunnels	26 / 3B	07/09/1867	N/A	MID	Midland Main line first goods train ran 07/09/1867, first passenger 13/07/1868 (to King's Cross MET)
Camden Road West Junction	26 / 3A	03/01/1860	N/A	HJR / NLR	Junction renamed 26/03/1955
Kentish Town Junction					
CAMDEN TOWN (CCEHR)	26 / 4A	22/06/1907	N/A	UERL (CCEHR)	
CAMDEN TOWN (EWIDBJR)	26 / 3A	07/12/1850	05/12/1870	EWIDBJR	Original station on St Pancras Way, opened as 'Camden Town'. Renamed 'Camden Road' 1853, reverted to
Camden Road					'Camden Town' 01/07/1870. Replaced by Camden Town (NLR) Station to West 05/12/1870
Camden Town					
Camden Town Junctions	26 / 4A	22/06/1907	N/A	UERL (CCEHR)	Extensively remodelled 20/04/1924 due to extension of Bank Branch from Euston
Campbell Road Junction	27 / 5D & 22	02/06/1902	13/09/1959	LTSR / MDR	Junction between LTSR and MDR, physical connection removed 13/09/1959 (although name still in use)
Campden Hill Tunnel	38 / 1B & 84	01/10/1868	N/A	MET	
CANADA WATER	40 / 2B	19/08/1999	N/A	LUL (ELL)	Jubilee Line platforms opened 17/09/1999. East London Line platforms closed 22/12/2007, re-opened 27/04/2010
					as TfL (LOROL)
Canal Junction	40 / 3C & 79 / 80	01/04/1880	N/A	ELR	Junction formed when spur from ELR to New Cross (SER) opened
CANARY WHARF (DLR)	40 / 1D & 31 / 6A	12/08/1991	N/A	DLR	Opened to construction workers 02/04/1991, date given is public opening. Closed 09/02/1996 - 09/03/1996 (bomb)
CANARY WHARF (LUL)	40 / 1D	17/09/1999	N/A	LUL (JUB)	
CANARY WHARF (NR)	40 / 1D & 31 / 6B	??/??/2018	N/A	NR (XRAIL)	Proposed station on Crossrail 1 Abbey Wood branch, to open 2018
CANNING TOWN	28 / 6A	14/06/1847	N/A	ECTJR	Renamed 01/07/1873, originally on south side of Barking Road, relocated to north side 1888 in connection with
Barking Road					quadrupling works. Closed 29/05/1994 in connection with Jubilee Line extension works, re-opened 29/10/1995
					on a new site again south of Barking Road and to south of original 1847 site. DLR platforms opened 05/03/1998,
					LUL Jubilee Line platforms opened 14/05/1999. NR platforms closed 09/12/2006, re-opened as DLR 31/08/2011
CANNING TOWN NORTH GOODS	28 / 6A	22/08/1881	06/03/1967	LNWR	Renamed 'North' by BR 01/07/1950 to distinguish from 'South'
CANNING TOWN SOUTH GOODS	28 / 6A	14/06/1847	01/07/1968	GER	Renamed 'South' by BR 01/07/1950 to distinguish from 'North'
CANNON STREET	26 / 6D & 72 / 4C	01/09/1866	N/A	SER	Metropolitan & District Railways joint station opened 06/10/1884
CANNON STREET ROAD	27 / 6A & 74 / 2D	21/08/1842	??/12/1848	LBLR	
Cannon Street South Junction	39 / 1D & 72 / 5C	01/09/1866	N/A	SER	Proposed to be eliminated (Western curve to be abandoned due to Thameslink works at Metropolitan Junction)
CANONBURY	26 / 3D	01/09/1858	N/A	NLR	Opened as 'Newington Road & Balls Pond' 01/09/1858, re-sited west and renamed 'Canonbury' 01/12/1870
Newington Road & Balls Pond					Closed 20/02/2010 - 01/06/2010 (LOROL upgrade works), upon re-opening trains called at northern platforms
					3 & 4 (previously southern 1 & 2 used), all four platforms restored to use from 06/01/2011
Canonbury Tunnel	26 / 3C	P 18/01/1875	08/11/1976	GNR	Line through tunnel singled 1988 due to electrification (clearance for overhead wires)
		G 14/12/1874	N/A		
Canonbury West Junction	26 / 3D	14/12/1874	N/A	NLR / GNR	
CANONS PARK	12 / 3A	10/12/1932	N/A	MET	Opened by Metropolitan Railway. 'Edgware' Suffix dropped ??/09/1933
Canons Park (Edgware)					Transferred to Bakerloo Line 20/11/1939, Jubilee Line 01/05/1979
Canterbury Road Junction	39 / 5C	01/08/1865	N/A	LCDR	Junction between 01/05/1863 LCDR line between Brixton and Loughborough Junctions and 01/08/1865 line to
					Crystal Palace (High Level)
Carlton Road Junction	26 / 2A & 9	02/04/1883	N/A	MID	
CARPENDERS PARK	10 / 1D	01/04/1914	N/A	LNWR	Re-sited south 17/11/1952. Served by London Underground Bakerloo Line Trains 16/04/1917 - 24/09/1982
Carpenters Road Curve	27 / 4D & 77 / 78	P N/A	N/A	GER	No regular passenger traffic carried
		G ??/??/1892	N/A		
CARPENTERS ROAD GOODS	27 / 4D & 77	??/??/1892	02/11/1964	GER	
Carpenters Road North Junction	27 / 3D & 77 / 78	??/??/1892	N/A	GER	Junction at north end of Carpenters Road Curve
Carpenters Road South Junction	27 / 4D & 77 / 78	??/??/1892	N/A	GER	Junction at south end of Carpenters Road Curve
CARSHALTON	65 / 2D	01/10/1868	N/A	LBSCR	
CARSHALTON BEECHES	65 / 4D	01/10/1906	N/A	LBSCR	Renamed 01/04/1925
Beeches Halt					
CARTERHATCH LANE	7 / 3B	12/06/1916	01/07/1919	GER	
CASTLE BAR PARK	23 / 5C	01/05/1904	N/A	GWR	Original wooden platforms replaced by concrete structures to north ??/11/1960. 'Halt' suffix dropped 05/05/1969
Castle Bar Park Halt					
CATERHAM	74 / 5A	P 05/08/1856	N/A	CR	Rebuilt slightly to the west 01/01/1900. Goods yard closed 28/09/1964
		G 05/08/1856	28/09/1964		
CATFORD	54 / C1	01/07/1892	N/A	LCDR	
CATFORD BRIDGE	54 / D1	P 01/01/1857	N/A	MKR	Goods yard closed 23/03/1968
		G 01/01/1857	23/03/1968		
Cedar Junction	76	14/11/2007	N/A	LCOR / NR	
CENTRAL	41 / 1D & 62 / 3C	03/08/1880	09/09/1940	LSKD	Initially temporary terminus per Quick, Connor and Jackson ('for first few weeks' in latter), precise date of
					services to Gallions commencing unknown, but had appeared in Bradshaw by November 1880
					Gallions branch single until 14/11/1881. Operated by GER after 1896, ownership later transferred to PLA.
					Branch closed from 09/09/1940 due to 'Black Saturday' air raid 07/09/1940 (no Sunday service after 27/06/1915).
					Listed as 'Royal Albert Dock Central' in Borley, also referred to as such in 1914 GER timetable per Quick.
					Became a 'halt' 01/11/1933
CENTRAL CROYDON	66 / 2C	01/01/1868	01/09/1890	LBSCR	Closed 01/12/1871 - 01/06/1886. Between 1886 re-opening and 1890 final closure often also 'Croydon Central'
CENTRALE	66 / 2C	10/12/2005	N/A	CTL	
CHADWELL HEATH	29 / 1D	P 11/01/1864	N/A	GER	Suffix 'for Becontree' used between 1927 and 1955. Goods yard opened 1876, closed 07/12/1970
Chadwell Heath for Becontree		G ??/??/1876	07/12/1970		
Chadwell Heath					
CHAFFORD HUNDRED	45 / 3A	30/05/1995	N/A	RT	Ceremonial opening 29/05/1995
CHALFONT & LATIMER	1 / 3C	P 08/07/1889	N/A	MET	Renamed 01/11/1915. Goods yard closed 14/11/1966
Chalfont Road		G 08/07/1889	14/11/1966		
CHALK FARM (UERL)	25 / 3D	22/06/1907	N/A	UERL (CCEHR)	Named 'Adelaide Road' until opening
CHALK FARM (LNWR)	25 / 3D	01/05/1852	10/05/1915	LNWR	Replaced first 'Camden' to south. Suffix '(Chalk Farm)' added 1866. Re-sited north 01/04/1872 for better interchange
Camden (Chalk Farm)					with NLR. Renamed 'Chalk Farm' 1876
Camden					
CHALVEY HALT	33 / 2C	06/05/1929	07/07/1930	GWR	

NAME: (Previous names indented below)	Page / grid:		Date opened:	Date closed:	Opening company:	NOTES:
CHANCERY LANE	26 / 6C		30/07/1900	N/A	CLR	'Gray's Inn' suffix introduced 25/06/1934, gradually dropped
Chancery Lane (Gray's Inn)						
Chancery Lane						
Channelsea Curve	77	P	15/08/1854	N/A	GER	No regular passenger traffic 1881 - 30/05/2000 then 11/09/2002 - 14/04/2009. Quadrupled 14/04/2009
		G	*15/08/1854*	N/A		
Channelsea North Junction	27 / 3D & 77 / 78		??/??/1881	N/A	GER	Junction at south end of High Meads Loop
Channelsea South Junction	27 / 3D & 77 / 78		??/??/1881	N/A	GER	Re-arranged due to new Stratford platforms 1 & 2 opening from the evening of 14/04/2009
CHARING CROSS (SER)	39 / 1B		11/01/1864	N/A	SER	Closed 05/12/1905 - 19/03/1906 (roof collapse) & 24/07/1993 - 16/08/1993 (track remodelling)
CHARING CROSS (UERL)	39 / 1B & 19		10/06/1906	N/A	UERL (BSWR)	Bakerloo Line platforms opened 10/06/1906 as 'Trafalgar Square', retaining this name until 01/05/1979. Northern Line platforms opened as separate station 'Charing Cross' 22/06/1907, renamed 'Charing Cross (Strand)' 06/04/1914, then 'Strand' 01/05/1915. Northern Line platforms closed 16/06/1973 - 01/05/1979 in connection with Jubilee Line construction. Jubilee Line platforms opened, Northern Line platforms re-opened, and station combined as 'Charing Cross' 01/05/1979. Jubilee Line platforms closed when line diverted at Green Park to Westminster 20/11/1999, retained for emergency train turnback (out of service) and for filming work
Strand (Northern Line)						
Charing Cross (Strand) (Northern Line)						
Charing Cross (Northern Line)						
Trafalgar Square (Bakerloo Line)						
CHARLTON	41 / 3B	P	30/07/1849	N/A	SER	Goods yard does not appear to have opened with passenger station: Borley gives goods opening date of c.1904, but a coal yard is depicted on 1895 OS map (none apparent on the 1882 survey), so opening date c.1890 assumed. Suffix 'Junction' often added between 1877/8 and 1928/9, with this name appearing on station nameboards and OS maps. Bay platform on 'down' side added when branch to Greenwich (Maze Hill) opened 01/01/1873. At some point the bay road was incorporated into the goods yard and fenced off. Goods yard closed 20/05/1963
Charlton Junction		G	*c.1890*	*20/05/1963*		
Charlton						
Charlton Junction	41 / 3B		01/01/1873	N/A	SER	Junction between SER North Kent Line and branch to Greenwich (Maze Hill)
Charlton Tunnel	41 / 2C		30/07/1849	N/A	SER	
Chatham Loops	55 / 5D & 56 / 6A	P	19/06/1904	N/A	SECR	Originally 'up' and 'down', but former 'down' loop resignalled for bidirectional working 1983 (= 'Reversible')
		G	*19/06/1904*	N/A	SECR	Referred to as 'Chislehurst Loops' until 1959
CHEAM	65 / 4A	P	10/05/1847	N/A	LBSCR	Line through station quadrupled 01/10/1911, central island platform allowed for but never built. Through roads removed 1977-8 (signal box closed 28/05/1978). Goods yard closed 28/09/1964
		G	*10/05/1847*	*28/09/1964*		
CHELSEA & FULHAM	38 / 3C & 84		02/03/1863	14/09/1940	WLER	'& Fulham' after 01/01/1902. Passenger service withdrawn Willesden Junction to Clapham Junction 14/09/1940
Chelsea						
CHELSEA BASIN GOODS	38 / 4C		*??/??/1863*	*11/09/1981*	LNWR / GWR	
CHERTSEY	61 / 1A	P	14/02/1848	N/A	LSWR	Re-sited 01/10/1866 to opposite side of level crossing when line extended to Virginia Water
		G	*14/02/1848*	*c.1965*		
CHESHAM	1 / 1A	P	08/07/1889	N/A	MET	Served by GCR trains (later LNER, later BR) 01/03/1906 - 16/10/1967. Goods yard closed 04/07/1966
		G	*08/07/1889*	*04/07/1966*		
CHESHUNT	7 / 1B	P	22/11/1841	N/A	NER	Original station 150m north of present site. Opened as 'Cadmores Lane Cheshunt' by NER 22/11/1841, closed 1842
Cadmores Lane, Cheshunt		G	*22/11/1841*	*01/06/1966*		Re-opened 31/05/1846 as 'Cheshunt', re-sited to present site 01/10/1891. Goods yard closed 01/06/1966
Cheshunt Junction	7 / 2B		01/10/1891	N/A	GER	
CHESSINGTON NORTH	63 / 3D		28/05/1939	N/A	SR	
CHESSINGTON SOUTH	63 / 4D	P	28/05/1939	N/A	SR	Intended to be a through station en route to Leatherhead, but line never completed beyond goods yard and 'up' platform never used (footbridge not completed). Goods yard opened 01/07/1939 (per Jackson, Borley states goods yard opened with passenger station), closed 18/03/1963 (see Chessington South Sidings)
		G	*01/07/1939*	*18/03/1963*		
CHESSINGTON SOUTH SIDINGS (disused)	63 / 4D		*01/07/1939*	N/A	SR	Originally Chessington South goods yard, closed to general goods 18/03/1963. Re-opened as coal concentration depot May 1963, closed 04/11/1988. Some sidings remain in situ (continuation of branch), but are disused
CHIGWELL	17 / 2A		01/05/1903	N/A	GER	Fairlop Loop closed by LNER 30/11/1947 for electrification and transfer to LTE Central Line, re-opened 21/11/1948
CHINGFORD (1st)	16 / 1A	P	17/11/1873	02/09/1878	GER	Original terminus of extension from Walthamstow. Closed to passengers 02/09/1878, goods 04/10/1965
		G	*17/11/1873*	*04/10/1965*		Often referred to as 'Bull Lane'
CHINGFORD (2nd)	8 / 6B		02/09/1878	N/A	GER	New passenger terminus opened to north of original, which closed the same day. Arranged for through running on an aborted extension to High Beech; stub of extension blocked and platforms connected beyond buffers c.1962. Carriage sidings added 1920, and subsequently expanded.
CHIPSTEAD	72 / 2D	P	02/11/1897	N/A	CVR	02/11/1897 is given as opening date for Chipstead Valley Railway (Purley to Kingswood) in Borley, but it also states regular passenger service 'probably' commenced 09/11/1897, Quick states first train 09/11/1897, so 02/11/1897 may have been official / ceremonial opening. Suffix dropped 09/07/1923. Goods yard closed 07/05/1962
Chipstead & Banstead Downs		G	*02/11/1897*	*07/05/1962*		
CHISLEHURST	55 / 5D	P	01/07/1865	N/A	SER	Renamed 01/09/1866. Passenger station re-sited to the south 02/03/1868. Goods yard closed 18/11/1968
Chislehurst & Bickley Park		G	*01/07/1865*	*18/11/1968*		
Chislehurst Junction	55 / 5D		19/06/1904	N/A	SECR	Junctions at north end of Chatham Loops
Chislehurst Tunnels	55 / 3C		01/07/1865	N/A	SER	Fast tunnel opened 01/07/1865, Slow tunnel added by SECR 18/06/1905 (St Johns to Elmstead Woods quadrupling)
CHISWICK	37 / 3B	P	22/08/1849	N/A	LSWR	Suffix in use 01/11/1872 - 1955 ('for Grove Park' after c.1920). Goods yard closed 14/06/1958
Chiswick for Grove Park		G	*22/08/1849*	*14/06/1958*		
Chiswick & Grove Park						
Chiswick						
Chiswick Curve	37 / 3B & 51 / 3A	P	01/06/1870	22/02/1915	LSWR	Opened at same time as Kensington (Addison Road) to Richmond, passenger service 01/06/1870 - 22/02/1915
		G	*01/01/1869*	*24/07/1932*		
Chiswick Junction (1st)	37 / 4C		01/02/1862	01/01/1869	LSWR	Junction at north end of Barnes Curve. Barnes Curve disused since 01/01/1869 but not dismantled until 1881
Chiswick Junction (2nd)	37 / 3A & 51 / 3A		01/01/1869	24/07/1932	LSWR	Junction at south end of Chiswick Curve
CHISWICK PARK	37 / 2B & 51 / 2B		01/07/1879	N/A	MDR	Opened as 'Acton Green', renamed 'Chiswick Park & Acton Green' ??/03/1887, renamed 'Chiswick Park' 01/03/1910. Completely rebuilt 1932-33 due to quadrupling works
Chiswick Park & Acton Green						
Acton Green						
Chobham Farm Junction	28 / 3A & 77		29/04/1846	01/06/1969	ECTJR / NER	
CHORLEYWOOD	1 / 4A	P	08/07/1889	N/A	MET	Opened as 'Chorley Wood', '& Chenies' suffix in use 01/11/1915 - c.1934 (LPTB) and c.1950 (BR)
Chorley Wood		G	*08/07/1889*	*14/11/1966*		Became 'Chorleywood' c.1964 (LTB) and 1987 (BR). Goods yard closed 14/11/1966
Chorley Wood & Chenies						
Chorley Wood						
Christian Street Junction	27 / 6A & 74 / 2D		17/04/1886	N/A	LTSR	Originally Junction for Commercial Road Goods, Now point where 4 tracks become 2
CHURCH MANOR WAY HALT	42 / 2C		01/01/1917	01/01/1920	SECR	Provided for munitions workers
CHURCH PATH SIDINGS	59 / 1D		*14/11/2007*	N/A	LCOR	Stabling / turnback sidings built in connection with HS1
CHURCH STREET	66 / 2C		10/05/2000	N/A	CTL	
CHURCHYARD SIDINGS	76		*??/??/1868*	N/A	MID	Now Castle Cement terminal
CITY GOODS	74 / 2C		*01/10/1862*	*01/07/1949*	MID	Site subsequently used for DLR Bank extension tunnel portals. Hydraulic accumulator tower remains in situ (listed)
CITY ROAD	26 / 5C		17/11/1901	09/08/1922	CSLR	
CITY THAMESLINK	26 / 6C & 32 / 4C		29/05/1990	N/A	BR	Renamed 30/09/1991
St Paul's Thameslink						
CLAPHAM COMMON (LSWR)	38 / 5C		21/05/1838	02/03/1863	LSWR	Renamed ??/07/1846. Replaced by Clapham Junction Station to North
Wandsworth						
CLAPHAM COMMON (CSLR)	39 / 5A		03/06/1900	N/A	CSLR	Terminus of City & South London Railway 03/06/1900 - 13/09/1926. Closed 28/11/1923 - 01/12/1924
CLAPHAM HIGH STREET	39 / 5B	P	25/08/1862	N/A	LCDR	Suffix '& North Stockwell' in use between 01/05/1863 and 27/09/1937. LBSCR platforms opened 01/05/1867. LCDR platforms closed 03/04/1916. Station also referred to as 'Clapham Road' or 'Clapham Road & North Stockwell' LSWR timetable for trains serving here to / from Ludgate Hill referred to 'Clapham Town' (distinct from 'Junction'). Goods yard closed 10/06/1963. Renamed 'Clapham High Street' 15/05/1989.
Clapham		G	*25/08/1862*	*10/06/1963*		
Clapham & North Stockwell						
Clapham						
CLAPHAM JUNCTION	38 / 5D		02/03/1863	N/A	LSWR / LBSCR	Replaced Clapham Common (LSWR) station to south
Clapham Junction	38 / 5D		27/07/1846	N/A	LSWR	Junction between original LSWR line to Southampton and branch to Richmond
Battersea Junction						
CLAPHAM NORTH	39 / 5B		03/06/1900	N/A	CSLR	Closed 28/11/1923 - 01/12/1924, Renamed 13/09/1926
Clapham Road						
CLAPHAM SOUTH	39 / 6A		13/09/1926	N/A	UERL (NOR)	
CLAPHAM YARD	38 / 5C		*c.1850's*	N/A	LSWR	Sidings had appeared in angle between lines between 1850 and 1863
CLAPTON	27 / 1B		01/07/1872	N/A	GER	Goods yard remote to north (see separate entry)
Clapton Curve	15 / 6B	P	01/07/1872	N/A	GER	
		G	*01/07/1872*	N/A		
CLAPTON GOODS	27 / 1B		*??/??/1898*	*07/12/1964*	GER	Yard enlarged 02/07/1900
Clapton Junction	27 / 1B		01/08/1872	N/A	GER	
Clapton Tunnel	27 / 1B		01/07/1872	N/A	GER	
CLARENCE YARD GOODS	26 / 2C & 81		*c.1874*	*13/06/1960*	GNR	Yard enlarged 1881, upon closure replaced by Finsbury Park Diesel Depot
Clarence Yard Junction	81		c.1874	N/A	GNR	Formerly divergence of Clarence Yard goods, currently junction between Down goods and down line ex-Canonbury
CLAYGATE	63 / 3B	P	02/02/1885	N/A	LSWR	Named 'Claygate & Claremont' until 1913, then '- for Claremont' until 1955, when suffix dropped
Claygate for Claremont		G	*02/02/1885*	*c.1965*		
Claygate & Claremont						
Clerkenwell Tunnels	26 / 5C & 32 / 2B		10/01/1863	N/A	MET	Quadrupled 17/02/1868
CLOCK HOUSE	54 / 5C	P	01/05/1890	N/A	SER	Named 'Penge Road' until opening. Goods yard closed 19/04/1965
		G	*01/05/1890*	*19/04/1965*		

NAME: (Previous names indented below)	Page / grid:		Date opened:	Date closed:	Opening company:	NOTES:
COBHAM & STOKE D'ABERNON Cobham for Stoke D'Abernon Cobham & Stoke D'Abernon	69 / 1D	P G	02/02/1885 02/02/1885	N/A c.1965	LSWR	Opening notice referred to 'Stoke D'Abernon & Cobham', but never appeared as such in Bradshaw. 'for' was substituted for '&' 1913 - 09/09/1953
COBORN ROAD Coborn Road (Old Ford) Old Ford	27 / 5C		01/02/1865	08/12/1946	GER	Opened as 'Old Ford', renamed 'Coborn Road (Old Ford)' 01/03/1879, but suffix usually omitted. Re-sited west 02/12/1883. Closed 22/05/1916 - 05/05/1919, then for good 08/12/1946.
COCKFOSTERS	6 / 4A		31/07/1933	N/A	LPTB (PIC)	
COCKFOSTERS DEPOT	6 / 5A		31/07/1933	N/A	LPTB (PIC)	
Coleman Street Tunnel	41 / 2D		30/07/2011	N/A	SER	
COLINDALE	12 / 4C		18/08/1924	N/A	UERL (CCEHR)	
COLLIERS WOOD	52 / 4C		13/08/1926	N/A	UERL (NOR)	
COLNBROOK	34 / 3A	P G	09/08/1884 09/08/1884	29/03/1965 03/01/1966	GWR	Terminus of branch from West Drayton 09/08/1884 - 02/11/1885. Passing loop and 'up' platform opened 02/05/1904. Passenger service withdrawn between West Drayton and Staines West 29/03/1965 and Colnbrook station closed; goods yard remained open until 03/01/1966. Oil terminal opened on site 01/03/1990
COLNBROOK ESTATE HALT	34 / 3A		01/05/1961	29/03/1965	BR	
COLNBROOK LOGISTICS CENTRE	34 / 3A		c.2003	N/A	PRIV	Terminal for Heathrow Airport construction materials built for Terminal 5 construction
COLNBROOK OIL TERMINAL (ELF)	34 / 3A		01/03/1990	N/A	PRIV	Aviation Fuel terminal for Heathrow Airport
Colne Junction	2 / 5C		10/02/1913	19/09/1966	LNWR	Last train on Colne Junction to Croxley Green Junction spur 06/06/1966, date is that of official closure / removal
COMMERCIAL DOCKS	40 / 2B & 79		01/05/1856	01/01/1867	SER	
COMMERCIAL ROAD GOODS	27 / 6A & 74 / 1C		17/04/1886	03/07/1967	LTSR	
Connaught Bridge	41 / 1C & 62 / 3B	P G	26/11/1855 26/11/1855	??/06/1976 ??/10/1967	ECR	Crossing of channel between Victoria and Albert Docks, passenger traffic diverted via Connaught Tunnel from June 1876 but route retained for heavier goods trains (1/50 gradients associated with Connaught Tunnel). Passenger services restored 30/09/1935 - 28/03/1936 due to temporary Connaught Tunnel closure. Last goods movement October 1967, line dismantled soon afterwards
CONNAUGHT ROAD	41 / 1C & 62 / 3B		03/08/1880	08/09/1940	LSKD	Gallions branch single until 14/11/1881. Operated by GER after 1896, ownership later transferred to PLA. Branch closed from 09/09/1940 due to 'Black Saturday' air raid 07/09/1940 (no trains on Sundays since 27/06/1915) Listed as 'Royal Albert Dock, Connaught Road' in Borley
Connaught Tunnel	41 / 1C & 62	P G	??/06/1876 ??/06/1876	10/12/2006 29/03/1993	GER	North Woolwich Branch diverted underground due to construction of Royal Albert Dock. No service 30/09/1935 - 28/03/1936, 08/09/1940 - 01/01/1941 and 29/05/1994 - 29/10/1995. Passenger route singled 25/08/1969, the original 'up' road then becoming bi-directional and the original 'down' becoming a siding accessing the 'Silvertown Tramway' (taken out of use 29/03/1993). Stratford to North Woolwich closed by Network Rail 10/12/2006. Currently being refurbished to be re-used by Crossrail 1 Abbey Wood branch opening 2018
COOMBE LANE	67 / 3B		10/05/2000	N/A	CTL	
COOMBE ROAD Coombe Lane	66 / 3D		10/08/1885	16/05/1983	LBSCR / SER	Closed 01/01/1917 - 30/09/1935, Renamed upon re-opening, closed again 16/05/1983
Coopersale	8 / 1B		27/03/2005	N/A	EOR	Current limit of Epping Ongar Railway operation, no platform. Service from North Weald commenced Easter 2005 Service suspended 31/12/2007 - 25/05/2012 (engineering works)
Copenhagen Junction	75 / 76		??/??/1853	N/A	GNR / NLR	Also referred to as 'Belle Isle Junction'
Copenhagen Tunnels	26 / 3B & 75 / 76		07/08/1850	N/A	GNR	Middle bore first, West bore opened 1877, East bore 1886. East bore abandoned c.1977
Coppermill Curve	15 / 6B	P G	01/08/1885 01/08/1885	06/09/1926 11/06/1960	GER	Regular passenger service ceased 06/09/1926, freight use ceased and curve abandoned 11/06/1960
Coppermill North Junction	15 / 6B		01/07/1872	N/A	GER	Junction between Lea Valley Line and Clapton Curve
Coppermill South Junction	15 / 6B		01/08/1885	11/06/1960	GER	Junction between Lea Valley Line and Coppermill Curve (see notes for latter)
Corbett's lane Junction	40 / 3B & 79 / 80		05/06/1839	N/A	LGR / LCRR	Junction between LGR and LCRR
CORY OIL (SELSDON)	66 / 3D		c.1968	??/03/1993	PRIV	On site of Selsdon goods yard (closed 07/10/1968). Closed March 1993, track remains in situ
Cottage Junction	66 / 1D		??/10/1983	N/A	BR	Created through remodelling of Gloucester Road Triangle 1983
COULSDON NORTH Coulsdon West Coulsdon & Smitham Downs Stoat's Nest & Cane Hill	73 / 1B	P G	05/11/1899 05/11/1899	03/10/1983 07/10/1968	LBSCR	Renamed 'Coulsdon & Smitham Downs' 01/06/1911, renamed 'Coulsdon West' 09/07/1923 for 3 weeks, then finally renamed 'Coulsdon North' 01/08/1923. Goods yard closed 07/10/1968 Opened as two through and two terminal platforms (with goods yard beyond terminal platforms), weekend services ceased September 1965, then peak hours only from May 1970. Closed altogether 03/10/1983
COULSDON SOUTH Coulsdon East Coulsdon & Cane Hill Coulsdon	73 / 2A	P G	01/10/1889 01/10/1889	N/A 01/10/1931	SER	Suffix '& Cane Hill' added 1896. Renamed 'Coulsdon East' 09/07/1923 for 3 weeks then 'Coulsdon South' 01/08/1923 Goods yard closed 01/10/1931
COULSDON TOWN Coulsdon Town (Smitham) Smitham	73 / 1A	P G	01/01/1904 01/01/1904	N/A 07/05/1962	SECR	Closed 01/01/1917 - 01/01/1919. Goods yard closed 07/05/1962. Renamed 22/05/2011, initially 'Coulsdon Town (Smitham)' on TfL map and Southern timetable, while station nameboards displayed both 'Coulsdon Town' and 'Coulsdon Town (formerly Smitham)' after renaming. Winter timetable 11/12/2011 became simply 'Coulsdon Town'
Courthill Loop	40 / 5D	P G	07/07/1929 07/07/1929	N/A N/A	SR SR	
Courthill Loop North Junction	40 / 5D		07/07/1929	N/A	SR	Junction at north end of Courthill Loop
Courthill Loop South Junction	40 / 6D		07/07/1929	N/A	SR	Junction at south end of Courthill Loop
COVENT GARDEN	26 / 6B		11/04/1907	N/A	UERL (GNPBR)	
Cow Lane Junction	40 / 4A		01/08/1865	N/A	LCDR / LBSCR	Boundary between LCDR & LBSCR ('End-on' Junction)
COWLEY	21 / 5C		01/10/1904	10/09/1962	GWR	Passenger services withdrawn from Uxbridge Vine Street Branch 10/09/1962
CRANLEY GARDENS	14 / 5A	P G	02/08/1902 29/06/1897	05/07/1954 08/05/1957	GNR	Opened to goods first, passenger station opened 02/08/1902. Closed to passengers when Alexandra Palace to Finsbury Park service withdrawn 05/07/1954 after a previous closure period 29/10/1951 - 07/01/1952. Branch had been intended for electrification and transfer to LT Northern Line, but works abandoned post-WW2. Goods yard closed 08/05/1957 and route to Park Junction abandoned
CRAYFORD	57 / 1C	P G	01/09/1866 01/09/1866	N/A 04/01/1965	SER	Goods yard closed 04/01/1965
Crayford Creek Junction	43 / 5D		01/05/1895	N/A	BHR / SER	
Crayford Spur	43 / 6D	P G	11/10/1942 11/10/1942	N/A N/A	SR SR	Borley refers to spur opening in 1918 and closing to regular traffic c.1920, before re-opening 11/10/1942, however contemporary OS maps show no evidence of the line before WW2
Crayford Spur "A" Junction	43 / 6D		11/10/1942	N/A	SR	Junction at north end of Crayford Spur
Crayford Spur "B" Junction	43 / 6D		11/10/1942	N/A	SR	Junction at south end of Crayford Spur
CREEKMOUTH	29 / 6C		TBA	N/A	DLR	Gallions Reach to Dagenham Dock was proposed to open c.2017, but funding removed November 2008
Cremorne Bridge	38 / 4C		02/03/1863	N/A	WLER	
Crescent Wood Tunnel	54 / 2A		01/08/1865	20/09/1954	LCDR	Nunhead to Crystal Palace (High Level) closed 20/09/1954 (Passengers and Goods)
CREWS HILL	6 / 1C	P G	04/04/1910 04/04/1910	N/A 01/10/1962	GNR	Goods yard closed 01/10/1962
CRICKLEWOOD Childs Hill & Cricklewood	25 / 2A & 3 / 6A	P G	02/05/1870 02/05/1870	N/A 06/10/1969	MID	Renamed 01/05/1903. Goods yard closed 06/10/1969
Cricklewood Curve	25 / 1A & 3 / 5A	P G	03/08/1875 03/08/1875	01/10/1902 N/A	MID	Opened to passenger & goods traffic 03/08/1875. No passenger traffic between 01/07/1886 - 01/03/1893 Passenger traffic withdrawn for good 01/10/1902, freight traffic remains
Cricklewood Curve Junction	25 / 1A & 3 / 6A		03/08/1875	N/A	MID	
CRICKLEWOOD DEPOT	25 / 1A		04/11/1979	N/A	BR	Built for Midland main line electrification, completed Bedford - Moorgate May 1982 and into St Pancras Summer 1982. Depot and associated signal box commissioned 04/11/1979 but only used for storage of class 317 EMUs between delivery and their entry into passenger service October 1983 (delayed by trade union dispute). Following introduction of 'Thameslink' service 16/05/1988, maintenance moved to Selhurst Depot and Cricklewood Depot became largely disused and the EMU shed rented out. Some FCC EMU and Midland Mainline HST/DMU stabling remains on site.
CRICKLEWOOD DOWN SIDINGS	25 / 2A & 3 / 6A		c.1870's	c.1960's	MID	Had appeared by late 19th century, possibly laid in association with Cricklewood Curve. Lifted by 1970's.
CRICKLEWOOD ENGINE SHED	25 / 1A & 3 / 4A		??/??/1882	14/12/1964	MID	1st shed 1882, 2nd added 1893. After steam stabling ceased, sheds used for diesel stabling for a short while
CRICKLEWOOD FREIGHT SIDINGS *Cricklewood Brent Sidings*	25 / 1A & 3 / 4B		c.1870	N/A	MID	First sidings on 'up' side had appeared by early 1870's, greatly expanded in late 19th and early 20th centuries Most of goods sidings removed to allow construction of the TMD then EMU depot, some retained and remain
CRICKLEWOOD RECESS SIDINGS	25 / 1A & 3 / 5A		c.1870's	N/A	MID	Had appeared by late 19th century, possibly laid in association with Cricklewood Curve. Only 4 disused sidings remain, hosted Redland (now Lafarge) aggregate terminal until early 2000's
Cricklewood South Junction Watling Street Junction	25 / 2A		25/06/1899	N/A	MID	
CRICKLEWOOD TRACTION MAINTENANCE DEPOT (TMD)	25 / 1A		c.1965	??/07/1983	BR	Replaced Cricklewood Engine Shed, maintained diesel locos and DMUs for Midland main line
CROFTON PARK	40 / 6C		01/07/1892	N/A	LCDR	
Crofton Road Junction	40 / 4A		?	N/A	LCDR / LBSCR	
Cromwell Curve	38 / 2C & 84	P G	03/07/1871 03/07/1871	12/02/1956 12/02/1956	MDR	Opening coincided with MDR's platforms at High Street Kensington
Cromwell Curve North Junction	38 / 2C & 84		03/07/1871	12/02/1956	MDR	Junction at north end of Cromwell Curve
Cromwell Curve South Junction	38 / 2C & 84		03/07/1871	12/02/1956	MDR	Junction at south end of Cromwell Curve
Cromwell Road Junction	38 / 2B & 84		03/07/1871	N/A	MDR	Remodelled as 'flying' junction 01/02/1878

NAME: (Previous names indented below)	Page / grid:		Date opened:	Date closed:	Opening company:	NOTES:
CROSSHARBOUR	40 / 2D		31/08/1987	N/A	DLR	On site of former Millwall Docks station. '& London Arena' suffix added 14/08/1995, not dropped until 2007
Crossharbour & London Arena						despite The London Arena having been demolished in June 2006. Closed by IRA bomb at South Quay 09/02/1996 -
Crossharbour						15/04/1996. Southern terminus of DLR during Lewisham extension works 11/01/1999 - 20/11/1999
Cross Street Tunnel	42 / 2A		30/07/1849	N/A	SER	
CROUCH END	14 / 6B		22/08/1867	05/07/1954	GNR	Closed when Alexandra Palace to Finsbury Park service withdrawn 05/07/1954 after a previous closure period
						29/10/1951 - 07/01/1952. Branch had been intended for electrification and transfer to LPTB Northern Line,
						but works abandoned post-WW2
CROUCH HILL	14 / 6C		21/07/1868	N/A	THJR	Closed 31/01/1870 - 01/10/1870
CROWLANDS	18 / 6B		N/A	N/A	GER	Platform foundations built west of Jutsums Lane 1900, but station never completed
CROXLEY	2 / 5A	P	02/11/1925	N/A	MET / LNER	LNER services ceased 04/05/1926. 'Green' suffix dropped 23/05/1949. Goods yard closed 14/11/1966
Croxley Green		G	*02/11/1925*	*14/11/1966*		
CROXLEY DEPOT	2 / 5C		*16/04/1917*	*??/09/1985*	LNWR	Facilities shared by Bakerloo Line and mainline until 24/09/1982
CROXLEY GREEN	2 / 5A	P	15/06/1912	23/03/1996	LNWR	Goods yard closed 14/11/1966. Platform relocated east 1989 (temporary structure due to subsidence).
		G	*15/06/1912*	*14/11/1966*		Last train ran on Croxley Green Branch 22/03/1996, initially closed 'temporarily' for bridge work, replaced by bus
						service which ran until 26/09/2003.
Croxley Green Junction	2 / 5C		10/02/1913	19/09/1966	LNWR	Last train on Colne Junction to Croxley Green Junction spur 06/06/1966, date is that of official closure / removal
CROXLEY TIP	1 / 6D		*??/??/1902*	*1980's*	MET	LT refuse tip, former gravel pit. Regular use into 1980's per Horne 'Metropolitan Line - an illustrated history'
CROYDON 'A' POWER STATION	66 / 2C		*??/??/1896*	*??/??/1973*	PRIV	
CROYDON 'B' POWER STATION	66 / 1B		*??/??/1950*	*??/??/1981*	PRIV	
CRYSTAL PALACE	54 / 4A	P	10/06/1854	N/A	LBCSR	Suffix 'Low Level' 01/11/1898 - 13/06/1955 to distinguish from LCDR station. Goods yard closed 06/12/1965
Crystal Palace Low Level		G	*10/06/1854*	*06/12/1965*		Original (eastern) section of station remodelled to accommodate LOROL services, commenced 23/05/2010
Crystal Palace						
CRYSTAL PALACE HIGH LEVEL	54 / 3A	P	01/08/1865	20/09/1954	LCDR	Suffix '& Upper Norwood' added 01/11/1898 after which time 'High Level' was sometimes omitted.
Crystal Palace & Upper Norwood		G	*01/08/1865*	*20/09/1954*		Renamed 'Crystal Palace High Level' 09/07/1923. Closed 01/01/1917 - 01/03/1919 and 22/05/1944 - 04/03/1946.
Crystal Palace High Level & Upper Norwood						Nunhead to Crystal Palace (High Level) closed 20/09/1954 (Passengers and Goods)
Crystal Palace High Level						
Crystal Palace Tunnel	54 / 3A		01/12/1856	N/A	WELCPR	
Crystal Palace Tunnel Junction	54 / 4A		01/10/1857	N/A	LBSCR / WELCPR	
CUSTOM HOUSE	41 / 1B & 62		26/11/1855	N/A	ECR	Bay platform provided on 'down' side for terminating trains ex-Gallions. Station became temporary terminus from
Custom House Victoria Dock						08/09/1940 due to 'Black Saturday' air raid the previous day, North Woolwich service not restored until 01/01/1941
Victoria Dock, Custom House						and Gallions service was never restored. Also referred to as 'Victoria Dock, Custom House' and 'Custom House
Custom House						Victoria Dock'. DLR Platforms opened 28/03/1994. NR platforms closed 10/12/2006, to re-open 2018 (Crossrail 1)
Custom House Junction	62 / 3B		??/06/1876	??/10/1967	GER	Junction between routes via Connaught Bridge and Connaught Tunnel
CUTTY SARK	40 / 3D		03/12/1999	N/A	DLR	
CYPRUS	41 / 1D & 62 / 5C		28/03/1994	N/A	DLR	

D

NAME	Page / grid		Date opened	Date closed	Opening company	NOTES
DAGENHAM DOCK	30 / 5A	P	01/07/1908	N/A	LTSR	Goods yard closed 02/11/1964, site became East London Waste Terminal. Proposed terminus of DLR extension
		G	*01/07/1908*	*02/11/1964*		from Gallions Reach
DAGENHAM DOCK	30 / 6A		*??/??1887*	*c.1980's*	PRIV	Rail-served dock, sidings still apparent on OS maps until mid-1980's
Dagenham Dock East Junction (Down)	30 / 5A		14/11/2007	N/A	LCOR / NR	
Dagenham Dock East Junction (Up)	30 / 5B		14/11/2007	N/A	LCOR / NR	
DAGENHAM EAST	30 / 3B	P	01/05/1885	N/A	LTSR	Served by District Railway trains 02/06/1902 - 01/10/1905. Reintroduced 12/09/1932 when route quadrupled,
Dagenham		G	*01/05/1885*	*06/05/1968*		District Line trains utilising the new 'slow' platforms. 'East' suffix added 01/05/1949. British Rail services withdrawn
						by 15/06/1962 and 'fast' platforms abandoned. Goods yard closed 06/05/1968. Ownership of 'Slow' platforms
						transferred to LTB 01/01/1969.
DAGENHAM HEATHWAY	30 / 3A		12/09/1932	N/A	LMS	Barking to Upminster quadrupled and 2 new stations opened by LMS 12/09/1932, but LMS service never provided
Heathway						Served solely by District Line from opening. Renamed 01/05/1949, ownership transferred to LTB 01/01/1969
Dalston Eastern Curve	27 / 3A & 6	P	01/11/1865	15/05/1944	NLR	Opened to passengers 01/11/1865, goods May 1868. Passenger service suspended 15/05/1944 (enemy action),
		G	*??/05/1868*	*02/01/1966*		was never reinstated. Regular goods traffic ceased 01/03/1965, points removed 02/01/1966. Route safeguarded
						for possible future re-opening for LOROL services
Dalston Eastern Junction	27 / 3A & 6		01/11/1865	02/01/1966	NLR	Junction at north end of Dalston Eastern Curve
DALSTON JUNCTION	27 / 3A & 6		01/11/1865	N/A	NLR	Platforms 5 & 6 closed 15/05/1944, 3 & 4 closed 08/11/1976. Closed completely 30/06/1986 - 27/04/2010
Dalston Junction	27 / 3A & 6		01/11/1865	02/01/1966	NLR	Junction at south end of Dalston Western and Eastern Curves
DALSTON KINGSLAND	27 / 3A & 6		09/11/1850	N/A	BR	Opened as 'Kingsland' 09/11/1850, closed 01/11/1865 when Broad Street extension opened by NLR and platforms
Kingsland						subsequently demolished. Goods yard to east (see 'Kingsland Goods'). Re-opened as 'Dalston Kingsland' 16/05/1983
						Closed 20/02/2010 - 01/06/2010 (LOROL upgrade works)
Dalston Western Curve	27 / 3A & 6	P	01/11/1865	N/A	NLR	Carried goods traffic from May 1868 to 11/04/1969. Closed with Broad Street and Dalston Junction Stations
		G	*??/05/1868*	*11/04/1969*		30/06/1986 and dismantled, but subsequently reinstated (06/01/2011 test train, 28/02/2011 passenger service)
Dalston Western Junction	27 / 3A & 6		01/11/1865	N/A	NLR	Junction eliminated 30/06/1986 - 06/01/2011 (date of first test train), no physical connection at present
DARTFORD	58 / 1A	P	30/07/1849	N/A	SER	Suffix 'Junction' added 1870, 'for Farningham' added 1871, reverted to 'Dartford' 1879/80. Remodelled 1895
Dartford Junction for Farningham		G	*30/07/1849*	*01/05/1972*		to three through lines with the third road extending to Dartford Junction, carriage sidings expanded to current five
Dartford Junction						at this time (there were previously two). Goods yard closed 01/05/1972. Remodelled to four bidirectional through
Dartford						lines / four platform faces 05/08/1973
Dartford Junction	43 / 6D		01/09/1866	N/A	SER	
DATCHET	33 / 4D	P	22/08/1848	N/A	LSWR	Terminus of extension from Richmond until 01/12/1849. Goods yard closed 17/01/1965
		G	*22/08/1848*	*17/01/1965*		
DAY & SONS GRAVEL (PURLEY)	66 / 5C		?	N/A	PRIV	Established on site of Purley goods yard, closed 06/01/1969
DEBDEN	8 / 4A	P	24/04/1865	N/A	GER	Opened as 'Chigwell Road', renamed 'Lane' 01/12/1865. Closed 22/05/1916 - 03/02/1919
Chigwell Lane		G	*24/04/1865*	*18/04/1966*		Ownership and majority of passenger services transferred to LTE and station renamed 'Debden' 25/09/1949
Chigwell Road						First Trains in the morning remained British Rail services until 01/06/1970. Goods yard closed 18/04/1966
DENHAM	9 / 6B	P	02/04/1906	N/A	GCR / GWR	Suffix 'for Harefield' 01/10/1907 - 1955. Goods yard closed 06/01/1964. Through roads removed 12/12/1965 (up)
Denham for Harefield		G	*02/04/1906*	*06/01/1964*		& 19/12/1965 (down). Down platform relocated to north of track 27/07/2008 due to subsidence under original
Denham						Projected terminus of Central Line extension from West Ruislip, but works cancelled during WW2
Denham East Curve	9 / 6C	P	N/A	N/A	GWR	Denham East curve only saw occasional goods traffic and was lifted during WW1
		G	*01/05/1907*	*??/??/1917*		
Denham East Junction	9 / 6C		01/05/1907	??/??/1917	GWR	Junction between Denham East Curve and GWR / GCR main line
Denham South Junction	9 / 6C		01/05/1907	30/04/1965	GWR	Junction eliminated when East curve lifted c.1917, but reinstated 14/05/1942 - 30/04/1965 for access to oil depot
Denham West Curve	9 / 6C	P	01/05/1907	01/09/1939	GWR	Uxbridge High Street branch closed 01/09/1939 (passengers) & 24/02/1964 (goods), but northern portion
		G	*01/05/1907*	*30/04/1965*		remained open to serve an oil depot until 30/04/1965
Denham West Junction	9 / 6B		01/05/1907	30/04/1965	GWR	Junction between Uxbridge High Street branch and GWR / GCR main line
DENMARK HILL	39 / 5D		01/12/1865	N/A	LBSCR	Entire station owned by LBSCR, but the northern platforms used exclusively by LCDR opened first on 01/12/1865,
						line through station having opened 4 months earlier on 01/08/1865. Southern (LBSCR) platforms added 13/08/1866
Denmark Hill Tunnels	39 / 5D		01/08/1865	N/A	LBSCR	North bore opened 01/08/1865, south bore 13/08/1866
DENTON HALT	60 / 1C		01/07/1906	04/12/1961	SECR	Named 'Denton Road' 1914 - 1919, otherwise 'Denton Halt'
Denton Road						
Denton Halt						
DEPTFORD	40 / 3C		08/02/1836	N/A	LGR	Country terminus of LGR 08/02/1836 - 24/12/1838. 3-road engine shed provided on 'up' side, with an incline down
						to carriage storage under the viaduct arches (incline still in situ, and 'listed'). Shed closed 1904
						Station closed 15/03/1915 as a WW1 economy, did not re-open until 19/07/1926
DEPTFORD BRIDGE	40 / 4D		20/11/1999	N/A	DLR	
Deptford Lift Bridge Junction	40 / 3B & 79		15/05/1869	01/01/1964	LBSCR	Junction where Deptford Wharf branch split into lines to Old Kent Road (added 05/05/1869) and separate 'up' and
						'down' lines to New Cross (Gate). Separate 'up' line added 01/10/1884 (until this date Deptford Wharf branch joined
						LBSCR main line on 'down' side only). Entire branch and connection virtually closed 14/10/1963, officially 01/01/1964
DEPTFORD WHARF	40 / 2C & 79		*02/07/1849*	*01/01/1964*	LBSCR	Was virtually closed by 14/10/1963, 01/01/1964 is official date of closure
DEVONSHIRE STREET, MILE END	27 / 5C		20/06/1839	c.1841	ECR	London Terminus of ECR 20/06/1839 - 01/07/1840. Definitely remained open after line extended to Bishopsgate,
						but exact closure date unknown; late 1840 or early 1841 coinciding roughly with Mile End (ECR) opening to west
DEVONS ROAD	27 / 5D & 22		31/08/1987	N/A	DLR	
DEVONS ROAD DEPOT	27 / 5D & 22		*??/??/1882*	*10/02/1964*	NLR	Locomotive Depot, upon losing last steam allocation 25/08/1958, became Britain's first diesel-only depot
DEVONS ROAD GOODS	27 / 5D & 22		*??/07/1874*	*02/11/1964*	LNWR	Originally coal only, opened to general goods February 1891
District Junction (South Acton)	37 / 1B & 51 / 1B		15/05/1899	??/??/1915	MDR / NSWJR	Points 'clipped' out of use since 1915 (last traffic the year before), but not physically removed until c.1930
Dock Junction North	75 / 76		01/10/1868	N/A	MID	Junction between MID routes to St Pancras terminus and MET 'Widened Lines'
Dock Junction South	75 / 76		01/11/1887	N/A	MID	Formerly divergence of line to Somers Town goods, currently crossovers on Midland main line
Dockyard Tunnel	41 / 2D		30/07/1849	N/A	SER	
DOLLIS HILL	24 / 2D		01/10/1909	N/A	MET	Suffix '& Gladstone Park' in use 1931-1933. First served Bakerloo Line 20/11/1939. Last served Metropolitan Line
Dollis Hill & Gladstone Park						07/11/1940. Bakerloo Line service replaced by Jubilee Line 01/05/1979
Dollis Hill						

NAME: (Previous names indented below)	Page / grid:	Date opened:	Date closed:	Opening company	NOTES:
Dolphin Junction	33 / 1B	01/06/1879	N/A	GWR	Junctions between 'fast' and 'slow' lines between Langley and Slough
DOWN EMPTY CARRIAGE SHED (EUSTON)	26 / 4A	?	c.2007	LNWR	In situ but disused, last train movements thought to be early 2007 to remove stored vans
DOWN SIDINGS (PLUMSTEAD)	42 / 2B	c.1900	N/A	SER	No sidings apparent on 1896 OS, but had appeared by 1914. Three electrified stabling sidings & two unelectrified East end access and unelectrified sidings to be removed due to construction of Plumstead Portal (Crossrail 1)
DOWN SIDINGS (SHENFIELD)	20 / 1C	01/01/1934	N/A	LNER	Not in regular use
DOWN SIDINGS (WIMBLEDON)	52 / 3B	c.1895	N/A	LSWR	Berthing sidings, apparent on 1895 OS, one greatly extended 1898 to access Wimbledon Borough Council siding electrified c.1935, shortened 1984
DOWN STREET	39 / 1A	15/03/1907	22/05/1932	UERL (GNPBR)	Opened with 'Mayfair' suffix, subsequently dropped
Down Street, Mayfair					
DOWN YARD (REDHILL)	73 / 6C	c.1900	N/A	SECR	Not depicted on 1896 OS, but appeared on 1913 survey
DOWN YARD (SOUTHALL)	35 / 1D	01/05/1839	N/A	GWR	On site of first goods yard at Southall
DRAYTON GREEN	23 / 6C	01/03/1905	N/A	GWR	Renamed 'Drayton Green' 05/05/1969
Drayton Green Ealing Halt					
Drayton Green Junction	23 / 6C	03/06/1903	N/A	GWR	
Drayton Green Tunnel	23 / 6C	??/04/1974	N/A	BR	Covered Way erected over line in connection with housing development above, completed April 1974
DRAYTON PARK	26 / 2C & 81	14/02/1904	N/A	GNCR	Opened by GNCR, absorbed by Metropolitan Railway 01/07/1913, transferred to LPTB Edgware - Morden Line (later Northern Line) 01/07/1933. Became northern terminus of line from Moorgate 04/10/1964 (Victoria Line works). Closed by LTE 05/10/1975, re-opened by British Rail 16/08/1976
DRAYTON PARK DEPOT	26 / 2C & 81	14/02/1904	05/10/1975	GNCR	GNCR depot, closed when Northern City Line closed by LTE prior to transfer to BR. Was connected to GNR
DUDDING HILL FOR WILLESDEN & NEASDEN	24 / 2D	P 03/08/1875	01/10/1902	MID	Opened to goods traffic 01/01/1872, passenger station opened 03/08/1875 as 'Willesden & Dudden Hill'.
Dudding Hill		G 01/01/1872	06/07/1964		Renamed 'Dudding Hill for Church End Willesden' 01/02/1876, then 'Dudding Hill' 01/05/1878, then 'Dudding Hill for
Dudding Hill for Church End Willesden					Willesden & Neasden' 01/06/1880. Closed to passengers 02/07/1888 - 01/03/1893, then for good 01/10/1902.
Willesden & Dudden Hill					Goods yard closed 06/07/1964.
Dudding Hill Junction	24 / 2D	02/05/1870	N/A	MID	
DUNDONALD ROAD	52 / 4A	30/05/2000	N/A	CTL	
DURNSFORD ROAD POWER STATION	52 / 2B	25/10/1915	??/??/1965	LSWR	LSWR power station, opening date denotes first section of route to be supplied (Wimbledon - East Putney) After closure and demolition, Wimbledon Traincare Depot inspection shed erected on site 1976
DURNSFORD ROAD SIDINGS	52 / 2B	??/??/1914	N/A	LSWR	Originally 15-road shed built to stable LSWR's first fleet of electric multiple units, which entered service 25/10/1915 1914 shed demolished c.1974 and replaced by Wimbledon Traincare Depot inspection shed to south

E

EAGLE LANE GOODS	16 / 5B	15/05/1899	18/04/1966	GER	
EALING BROADWAY	23 / 6D	01/12/1838	N/A	GWR	Suffix 'Broadway' added 1875. Served by District Railway since 01/07/1879. Served by Central London Railway
Ealing					since 03/08/1920. Connection between LTE and BR east of station removed 17/09/1972 (disused since ??/05/1945) Connection between District / Central Lines last used 02/05/2010, removed by start of traffic 31/05/2010
EALING COMMON	37 / 1A	01/07/1879	N/A	MDR	Suffix '& West Acton' 1886 - 01/03/1910. Served by Piccadilly Line since 04/07/1932
Ealing Common & West Acton					
Ealing Common					
EALING COMMON DEPOT	37 / 1A	13/06/1905	N/A	MDR	District Line Depot built 1904-1905 for stabling electric trains, date quoted is that of the first section electrified.
Mill Hill Park Depot					Used also for Piccadilly Line stabling 04/07/1932 - 10/10/1964, but had carried out overhaul work for GNPBR trains since that line's opening (15/12/1906)
EARDLEY CARRIAGE SIDINGS	53 / 4A	c.1900	post-1960	LBSCR	Exact opening date unknown; do not appear on 1898 OS, but had appeared on 1909 version. Never electrified Regular use ceased c.1960, but sidings remained in situ and used occasionally for several more years
EARL'S COURT	38 / 2B & 84	30/10/1871	N/A	MDR	Resited to west side of Earl's Court Road 01/02/1878 after first structure destroyed by fire 30/12/1875 GNPBR platforms opened 15/12/1906. Closed 22/11/1997 - 06/04/1998 and 23/11/2001 - 05/03/2002 (Piccadilly Line only, escalator works)
Earl's Court Junction	38 / 2B & 84	01/02/1872	03/03/1958	MDR / WLER	Junction between MDR and WLER, removed when segregated District Line track provided to Kensington Olympia
EARLSFIELD	52 / 1C	01/04/1884	N/A	LSWR	Suffix '& Summerstown' 1884 - 01/06/1902. Originally two platforms, one on each side of four-track formation
Earlsfield & Summerstown					(before up slow flyover opened at Wimbledon 17/05/1936, slow lines were outside fast). Island platform constructed
Earlsfield					between former 'fast' lines for 17/05/1936 reconfiguration ('slow' south of 'fast'), original 'up' platform on 'up fast' line subsequently abandoned and further demolished. 'Down fast' platform remains, but is not regularly used
Earlswood North Junction	73 / 6C	05/11/1899	N/A	LBSCR / SER	
EAST ACTON	24 / 6C	03/08/1920	N/A	CLR	Viaduct Junction to North Acton opened by GWR 16/04/1917, but no passenger service until CLR
EAST BRIXTON	39 / 5C	13/08/1866	05/01/1976	LBSCR	Terminus of LBSCR extension from Corbett's Lane Junction until 01/05/1867 high level route to Shepherd's Lane
Loughborough Park & Brixton					Junction opened. Renamed 'Loughborough Park & Brixton' ??/01/1870, then 'East Brixton' 01/01/1894
Loughborough Park					Closed 19/05/1926 - 20/09/1926, then for good 05/01/1976 (lack of patronage)
EAST CROYDON	66 / 2D	P 12/07/1841	N/A	LBRR	Opened as 'Croydon', 'East' suffix added ??/02/1850, reversed to 'East Croydon' 01/05/1862. Adjoining station for
East Croydon Local / East Croydon Main		G 12/07/1841	07/05/1973		local traffic named 'New Croydon' opened 01/05/1862, renamed 'East Croydon Local' 01/06/1909, on which date
New Croydon / East Croydon					the adjoining original station was renamed 'East Croydon Main'. Two stations combined as 'East Croydon' ??/07/1924
Croydon East					Goods yard closed 07/05/1973. Croydon Tramlink opened 10/05/2000 at street level outside station entrance.
Croydon					
EAST DULWICH	39 / 5D	P 01/10/1868	N/A	LBSCR	Renamed 01/06/1888. Goods yard closed 10/09/1962
Champion Hill		G 01/10/1868	10/09/1962		
EAST FINCHLEY	13 / 5D	P 22/08/1867	N/A	GNR	Renamed 01/02/1887. First served by, and ownership transferred to, LPTB Northern Line 03/07/1939
East End Finchley		G 22/08/1867	01/10/1962		(terminus of LPTB Northern Line extension from Archway 03/07/1939 - 14/04/1940). Became terminus of LNER service from Finsbury Park 14/04/1940 when LPTB took over High Barnet service. All LNER passenger trains withdrawn 02/03/1941. Goods yard closed 01/10/1962
East Finchley Junction	13 / 5D	03/07/1939	N/A	LPTB / LNER	Junction of Northern Line with former LNER route to Finsbury Park (now depot access)
EAST GOODS YARD (FINSBURY PARK)	81	??/??/1877	13/06/1960	GNR	
EAST GREENWICH GAS WORKS	41 / 2A	??/??/1886	??/??/1976	PRIV	Constructed 1881-1886, initially internal railway network only but connection to SER Angerstein Wharf branch added c. early 20th century (between 1899 and 1916 per OS maps). Production ceased 1976
EAST HAM	28 / 4D	P 31/03/1858	N/A	LTSR	First served by District Railway 02/06/1902, line quadrupled 1905, District trains then using 'slow' platforms to north
		G 31/03/1858	??/04/1962		Served by Metropolitan Line since 30/03/1936 ('Hammersmith & City Line') since 30/07/1990) Bay platform ex-Kentish Town via TFGR and THJR abandoned 26/10/1958 (last train 15/09/1958) Main line services non-stopped since 15/06/1962, and 'Fast' platforms abandoned. Goods yard closed ??/04/1962
EAST HAM DEPOT	28 / 3D	06/11/1961	N/A	BR	Built for LTSR electrification on Site of former District Line Little Ilford Depot, date is that of first AC electric service
East Ham Loop	28 / 3D	P 09/07/1894	15/09/1958	LTSR	First goods use 01/09/1894, last passenger use 15/09/1958 (TFGR trains diverted to Barking)
		G 01/09/1894	30/11/1958		
East Ham Loop North Junction	28 / 3D	09/07/1894	30/11/1958	LTSR	Junction at north end of East Ham Loop
East Ham Loop South Junction	28 / 3D	09/07/1894	30/11/1958	LTSR	Junction at south end of East Ham Loop
EAST INDIA	41 / 1A & 31 / 5D	28/03/1994	N/A	DLR	
EAST INDIA DOCKS GOODS	41 / 1A & 31 / 4D	??/??/1859	??/??/1961	GER	
East London Down Junction	40 / 4C & 79	01/04/1880	16/04/1966	SER / ELR	SER service to Liverpool Street via ELR commenced 01/04/1880. Rolt Street Junction to New Cross (SER) became bi-directional (former 'down' only spur) 01/10/1884 when ELR bay platform opened at New Cross. 'Up' spur remained in use for goods / through traffic until 16/04/1966 when this and the connection on the 'down' side were both taken out of use (removed 1968)
East London Up Junction	40 / 3C & 79	01/04/1880	16/04/1966	SER / ELR	See notes for 'East London Down Junction' above
EAST LONDON WASTE TERMINAL	30 / 5A	?	N/A	PRIV	Shanks & McEwan, on site of former Dagenham Dock goods yard (closed 02/11/1964)
EAST PUTNEY	38 / 5A	03/06/1889	N/A	LSWR	Platforms to / from Putney Bridge opened first (built by LSWR but operated by MDR from outset). Platforms on curve
					to Wandsworth Town opened 01/07/1889, regular service withdrawn 05/05/1941, although some services called on occasions until 1969. Point Pleasant Junction to Wimbledon still used for empty stock working and diversions.
East Putney Junction	38 / 6A	01/07/1889	N/A	LSWR	First use of East Putney Junction to Point Pleasant Junction 01/07/1889
East Putney Tunnel	38 / 6A	03/06/1889	N/A	LSWR	Built by LSWR, but first use by MDR 03/06/1889. Ownership transferred to LU 01/04/1994
EAST SIDINGS (ACTON TOWN)	37 / 1B & 51 / 1A	04/07/1932	N/A	UERL	Current layout since 1932 quadrupling Turnham Green - Acton Town
EAST SMITHFIELD / LONDON DOCKS GOODS	40 / 1A & 74 / 2C	17/06/1864	01/09/1966	GER	
EAST TILBURY	46 / 3D	07/09/1936	N/A	LMS	Suffix 'Halt' dropped February 1949
East Tilbury Halt					
EASTCOTE	10 / 6C	P 26/05/1906	N/A	MET	Served by District Line Trains 01/03/1910 - 23/10/1933, Piccadilly Line thereafter. Suffix 'Halt' until 1934/5
Eastcote Halt		G 26/05/1906	10/08/1964		Goods yard closed 10/08/1964
EBBSFLEET INTERNATIONAL	59 / 1B	19/11/2007	N/A	LCOR	Opened five days after line. Two International and two Domestic platforms at low level, two Domestic platforms at high level. Latter did not receive regular train service until 13/12/2009 (Faversham to St Pancras)
EDEN PARK	54 / 6D	29/05/1882	N/A	SER	
EDGWARE (GNR)	12 / 2B	P 22/08/1867	11/09/1939	GNR	Closed to passengers 11/09/1939, goods 01/06/1964
		G 22/08/1867	01/06/1964		
EDGWARE (UERL)	12 / 2B	18/08/1924	N/A	UERL (CCEHR)	Built for through running to Bushey Heath, but extension abandoned c.1940
EDGWARE ROAD (MET)	25 / 6D	10/01/1863	N/A	MET	Rebuilt 01/11/1926

NAME: (Previous names indented below)	Page / grid:	Date opened:	Date closed:	Opening company:	NOTES:
EDGWARE ROAD (UERL)	25 / 6D	15/06/1907	N/A	UERL (BSWR)	Northern terminus of Bakerloo Line 15/06/1907 - 01/12/1913
EDGWARE SIDINGS	12 / 2B	*18/08/1924*	N/A	UERL (CCEHR)	Northern Line stabling sidings. Southern fan on site of aborted curve to GNR Edgware branch
EDMONTON GREEN	15 / 1B	22/07/1872	N/A	GER	Opened as 'Edmonton (High Level)' as distinct from the existing 01/03/1849 station (which became 'Low Level')
Lower Edmonton					Both stations renamed 'Lower Edmonton' ('High Level' and 'Low Level' respectively) 01/07/1883
Lower Edmonton (High Level)					Suffix 'High Level' dropped when 'Low Level' station closed to passengers 11/09/1939 (remained open for goods)
Edmonton (High Level)					Renamed 'Edmonton Green' 28/09/1992
Edward Street Junction	80	?	N/A	BR	
EFFINGHAM JUNCTION	69 / 4B	02/07/1888	N/A	LSWR	
Effingham Junction	69 / 4B	02/02/1885	N/A	LSWR	
EFFINGHAM JUNCTION MPV DEPOT	69 / 4B	*c.1926*	N/A	SR	Originally EMU stabling shed commissioned for electrification of route (1926), became disused c.mid-1990's
					Used by AMEC as a base for MPVs since late 2003, fully commissioned as an MPV maintenance depot 2005
EGHAM	47 / 2C	P 04/06/1856	N/A	LSWR	Suffix 'for Englefield Green' 17/07/1902 - 1955. Date of goods yard closure unknown
Egham for Englefield Green		G *04/06/1856*	*c.1960's*		
Egham					
ELEPHANT & CASTLE	39 / 2D	06/10/1862	N/A	LCDR	Initially temporary, replaced by permanent structure ??/02/1863. Terminus until 01/06/1864. CSLR station opened
					18/12/1890 (closed 29/11/1923 - 01/12/1924), BSWR station opened 05/08/1906 (closed 10/11/1996 - 14/07/1997)
					Original BSWR 'over-run' tunnels headed due east under New Kent Road, diverted to head due south under
					Newington Butts in 1940 as initial works for the aborted Camberwell extension
ELEPHANT & CASTLE COAL	39 / 2D	*??/??/1871*	*01/07/1963*	GNR	GNR coal depot accessed via LCDR
ELM PARK	30 / 2D	13/05/1935	N/A	LMS	Barking to Upminster quadrupled by LMS 12/09/1932, new station opened at Elm Park 13/05/1935, served by
					District Line exclusively from opening. Ownership transferred to LTB 01/01/1969
ELMERS END	54 / 6B	P 01/04/1864	N/A	MKR	Goods yard closed 06/05/1963. 'Down' bay secured out of use 1985. Branch to Addiscombe closed 02/06/1997
		G *01/04/1864*	*06/05/1963*		Croydon Tramlink opened 30/05/2000 using former bay platform on 'up' side
Elmers End Junction	54 / 6B	29/05/1882	02/06/1997	SER	Resited 50m south 1956 (platform extension). Elmers End to Addiscombe closed by RT 02/06/1997
ELMSTEAD WOODS	55 / 4C	01/07/1904	N/A	SECR	Renamed 01/10/1908
Elmstead					
ELSTREE & BOREHAMWOOD	4 / 4B	P 13/07/1868	N/A	MID	Opened as 'Elstree'. Suffix '& Boreham Wood' added 01/06/1869, dropped 01/04/1904, added again
Elstree		G *13/07/1868*	*19/06/1967*		as '& Borehamwood' 21/09/1953, dropped again 06/05/1974, restored again by mid 1988
Elstree & Borehamwood					Goods yard closed 19/06/1967.
Elstree					
Elstree & Boreham Wood					
Elstree					
ELSTREE SOUTH	3 / 6D	N/A	N/A	LPTB (NOR)	On Northern Line extension to Bushey Heath from Edgware. Construction abandoned 1940
Elstree Tunnels	4 / 5B	09/09/1867	N/A	MID	
ELTHAM	41 / 6D	P 01/05/1895	N/A	BHR	Opened as 'Well Hall', suffix '& North Eltham' added 01/10/1916. Renamed 'Eltham Well Hall' 26/09/1927.
Eltham Well Hall		G *01/05/1895*	*07/10/1968*	BHR	Goods yard expanded 1915, closed 07/10/1968. Relocated east and renamed 'Eltham' 17/03/1985 due to
Well Hall & North Eltham					construction of A2 Rochester Way Relief road through original station site, adjacent Eltham Park station closed on
Well Hall					same date due to proximity of new station
ELTHAM PARK	41 / 6D	01/07/1908	17/03/1985	SECR	Renamed 26/09/1927. Replaced by Eltham Station 17/03/1985 (see note above)
Shooters Hill & Eltham Park					
ELVERSON ROAD	40 / 5D	20/11/1999	N/A	DLR	
EMBANKMENT	39 / 1B & 19	30/05/1870	N/A	MDR	BSWR platforms added 10/03/1906 (closed 10/11/1996 - 14/07/1997). CCEHR Loop platform added 06/04/1914,
Charing Cross Embankment					southbound platform on Kennington extension opened 13/09/1926. Renamed 'Charing Cross Embankment'
Charing Cross					04/08/1974, shortened to 'Embankment' 12/09/1976.
EMERSON PARK	31 / 1A	01/10/1909	N/A	LTSR	Suffix '& Great Nelmes' only appeared on one station nameboard and was not published elsewhere
Emerson Park & Great Nelmes					Loco run-around loop installed for terminating trains 14/10/1909, subsequently removed
EMPIRE PAPER MILLS	45 / 6A	*??/??1908*	*c.1970*	PRIV	Connection to North Kent line appears to have been removed with 08/11/1970 resignalling of Greenhithe area, but
					internal railway network within works remained active for at least a decade longer
Engine Shed Junction	26 / 2A & 9	16/12/1900	05/01/1981	MID	Junction at south end of Low Level Curve, abandoned after diversion of Barking Trains to Gospel Oak
ENFIELD	6 / 4D	P 01/04/1871	04/04/1910	GNR	Original terminus of branch from Wood Green (Alexandra Palace). Passenger station closed 04/04/1910 when
		G *01/04/1871*	*01/07/1974*		extension from Grange Park to Cuffley opened (replaced by present day Enfield Chase).
					Goods yard closed 01/07/1974, carriage sidings remained in use on west side of former station until 1979
ENFIELD CHASE	6 / 4D	04/04/1910	N/A	GNR	Replaced original Enfield (GNR) station when line extended from Grange Park to Cuffley.
Enfield					Suffix 'Chase' added 01/07/1923
Enfield Goods Junction	6 / 5D	04/04/1910	??/??/1979	GNR	Junction formed when route opened from Grange Park to Cuffley, eliminated when carriage sidings at original
					Enfield (GNR) station abandoned 1979
ENFIELD LOCK	7 / 3C	P ??/04/1855	N/A	ECR	Exact opening date unknown. First reference to 'Ordnance Factory' in timetable April 1855. Renamed 'Enfield Lock
Enfield Lock for Enfield Wash		G *??/04/1855*	*07/12/1964*		for Enfield Highway' 01/04/1886. Suffix altered to 'for Enfield Wash' 01/11/1910, dropped 1955. 'Down' platform
Enfield Lock for Enfield Highway					originally sited north of level crossing, rebuilt to south c.1890/91. Goods yard closed 07/12/1964.
Ordnance Factory					
ENFIELD TOWN	7 / 4A	P 01/03/1849	N/A	ECR	Suffix 'Town' added 01/04/1886. Goods yard closed 14/09/1959
Enfield		G *01/03/1849*	*14/09/1959*		
EPPING	8 / 2B	P 24/04/1865	N/A	GER	Ownership and majority of passenger services transferred to LTE 25/09/1949. First Trains in the morning remained
		G *24/04/1865*	*18/04/1966*		British Rail services until 01/06/1970 (last train 31/05/1970). Goods yard closed 18/04/1966
EPPING GLADE	8 / 2B	N/A	N/A	EOR	Proposed western terminus of Epping-Ongar Railway
EPSOM	64 / 6B	P 01/02/1859	N/A	LSWR / LBSCR	Opened as temporary terminus of LSWR / LBSCR Epsom & Leatherhead Railway to Leatherhead, became a
Epsom High Street		G *01/02/1859*	*02/01/1928*		through station when line to LSWR main line at future site of Raynes Park opened 04/04/1859. When connection to
Epsom					LBSCR Epsom (Town) station opened 08/08/1859, LBSCR trains continued to call at Epsom (Town) and passed
					LSWR station without stopping. Sometimes referred to as 'Epsom High Street' 1874-1884 to distinguish from
					LBSCR's 'Town' and 'Downs' stations. Platforms opened on LBSCR line 03/03/1929, allowing Epsom Town station
					to close. Goods yard closed 02/01/1928, with goods traffic being transferred to Epson (Town)
EPSOM DOWNS	71 / 1D	22/05/1865	N/A	LBSCR	Station had 9 platform faces at its peak, from 01/05/1972 all but platforms 4 & 5 (re-numbered 1 & 2) abandoned.
					Resited 300 metres east 14/02/1989 as a single platform, site of original station sold for housing development
EPSOM TOWN	64 / 6C	P 10/05/1847	03/03/1929	LBSCR	Terminus 10/05/1847 - 01/02/1859. Suffix 'Town' used at times c.1870-1900 and again permanently after 09/07/1923.
Epsom		G *10/05/1847*	*03/05/1965*		Closed to passengers 03/03/1929 when platforms opened at Epsom (former LSWR). Goods yard closed 03/05/1965
ERITH	43 / 3C	P 30/07/1849	N/A	SER	Original layout was platforms staggered either side of a foot crossing, subsequent platform lengthenings have
		G *30/07/1849*	*07/10/1968*		resulted in slight overlap of facing platforms. Goods yard closed 07/10/1968
Erith Loop	43 / 5C	P 01/05/1895	N/A	BHR	Opened with rest of BHR
		G *01/05/1895*	N/A		
ERITH WHARF	43 / 3C	*c.1880*	*c.1970*	SER	Not on 1872 OS map, but had appeared by 1895. Depicted on OS into the 1970's, but date of abandonment unknown
ESHER	63 / 1A	P 21/05/1838	N/A	LSWR	Opened as 'Ditton Marsh' (per opening notice; also referred to as 'Esher & Hampton Court' in some timetables)
Esher for Sandown Park		G *21/05/1838*	*c.1965*		Renamed 'Esher & Claremont' 1844, 'Esher for Claremont' 1912/3, then 'Esher for Sandown Park' 1934, suffix
Esher for Claremont					dropped 13/06/1955. Additional pair of platforms on 'up' side added for returning race traffic from Sandown Park
Esher & Claremont					racecourse 20/04/1882, closed 18/10/1965
Ditton Marsh					
Essex Portals	44 / 5D	14/11/2007	N/A	LCOR	
ESSEX ROAD	26 / 3D	14/02/1904	N/A	GNCR	Opened by GNCR, absorbed by Metropolitan Railway 01/07/1913, transferred to LPTB Edgware - Morden Line (later
Canonbury & Essex Road					Northern Line) 01/07/1933. Closed by LTE 05/10/1975, re-opened by British Rail 16/08/1976. 'Canonbury &-' prefix
Essex Road					20/07/1922 - 11/07/1948
EUROPEAN METAL RECYCLING (BRENTFORD)	36 / 3C	?	?	PRIV	Formerly Perry Metals, sidings shown in situ in Quail, but have been removed
EUSTON	26 / 5A	20/07/1837	N/A	LBIR	London & Birmingham Railway terminus referred to as 'Euston Square' or simply 'London' at times in early history.
					CSLR platforms opened 12/05/1907 (closed 09/081922 - 20/04/1924), terminus until 20/04/1924.
					CCEHR platforms opened 22/06/1907, Victoria Line platforms opened 01/12/1968
EUSTON SQUARE	26 / 5B	10/01/1863	N/A	MET	Renamed 01/11/1909
Gower Street					
Euston Square Junction	76	15/03/1926	27/04/1935	MET	Link between Metropolitan and City Widened Lines using aborted 'Widened Lines' tunnel to Euston (eastbound only)
					Name given as 'Euston Square Junction' in Borley, Clives Underground Line Guides gives 'Chalton Street Junction'
EWELL EAST	64 / 5D	P 10/05/1847	N/A	LBSCR	Suffix 'for Worcester Park' in use after 1871. Renamed 'Ewell East' 09/07/1923. Goods yard closed 04/04/1960
Ewell for Worcester Park		G *10/05/1847*	*04/04/1960*		
Ewell					
EWELL WEST	64 / 4C	P 04/04/1859	N/A	LSWR	Renamed 'Ewell West' 09/07/1923. Goods yard closed 01/05/1961
Ewell		G *04/04/1859*	*01/05/1961*		
EWER STREET DEPOT (LOCOMOTIVES)	39 / 1D & 72 / 6B	*??/??/1901*	*??/??/1961*	SECR	Adjacent to Southwark Depot (goods). No engine shed provided, but turntable, coaling stage, water tower present
					Closed 1961, in advance of 18/06/1962 introduction of full electric timetable
EXPRESS DAIRY (MORDEN)	52 / 6B	*??/??/1954*	*30/12/1978*	PRIV	Milk bottling plant

F

NAME: (Previous names indented below)	Page / grid:		Date opened:	Date closed:	Opening company:	NOTES:
Factory Junctions	39 / 4A & 82		01/07/1863	N/A	LCDR	
FAIRFIELD YARD	66 / 2D		*01/09/1890*	*??/02/1933*	LBSCR	Permanent Way yard on truncated Central Croydon branch
FAIRLOP	17 / 4B	P	01/05/1903	N/A	GER	Fairlop Loop closed to LNER passenger services 30/11/1947 to allow electrification and transfer to LTE Central Line. First served by LTE Central Line Trains 31/05/1948. Goods yard closed 24/03/1958.
		G	*01/05/1903*	*24/03/1958*		
Falcon Junction	38 / 6D		02/03/1863	N/A	LBSCR / WLER	
FALCON LANE GOODS	38 / 5D		*01/06/1869*	*03/06/1968*	LNWR	
FALCONWOOD	42 / 5A		01/01/1936	N/A	SR	
FARNINGHAM HOME FOR LITTLE BOYS	58 / 5C		11/10/1870	c.1939	LCDR	Unadvertised station, served home for destitute boys, opened 15/06/1867 (station first use 11/10/1870) Home closed 1961, but station had been demolished in 1939 although date of last use unknown
FARNINGHAM ROAD	58 / 5B	P	03/12/1860	N/A	LCDR	Opened as 'Farningham', suffix '& Sutton-at-Hone' added 01/04/1861, dropped 01/08/1861, renamed 'Farningham Road' 1869, became 'Farningham & Sutton-at-Hone' again 1872, renamed 'Farningham Road' again 05/05/1975 Goods yard closed May 1968, siding served adjacent British Steel works until 1980
Farningham & Sutton-at-Hone		G	*03/12/1860*	*??/05/1968*		
Farningham						
Farningham & Sutton-at-Hone						
Farningham						
FARRINGDON	26 / 5C & 32 / 2C		23/12/1865	N/A	MET	Replaced original Farringdon Street station. City Widened Lines platforms added 01/03/1866 (now 'Thameslink'). Suffix '& High Holborn' replaced 'Street' 26/01/1922, dropped 21/04/1936. NR platforms extended to 12 cars and new entrance hall opened 12/12/2011. Platforms for 'Crossrail 1' expected to open 2018 (linking to Barbican station)
Farringdon & High Holborn						
Farringdon Street						
FARRINGDON GOODS	26 / 5C & 32 / 2B		*01/11/1909*	*01/07/1936*	MET	Also referred to as 'Vine Street' Goods
Farringdon Junction	32 / 3C		01/01/1866	20/03/2009	LCDR / MET	Junction eliminated 24/03/1969 (date of closure, last train 23/03/1969 but junction not disconnected until 03/05/1971) Reinstated 16/05/1988 (introduction of 'Thameslink'), service Farringdon - Moorgate withdrawn 20/03/2009
FARRINGDON STREET	26 / 6C & 32 / 3C		10/01/1863	01/03/1866	MET	Original City terminus of Metropolitan Railway, partially abandoned when new station opened 23/12/1865 but not closed to passengers until 'Widened Lines' platforms opened at new station 01/03/1866. Became GNR goods station
FARRINGDON STREET GOODS	26 / 6C & 32 / 3C		*02/11/1874*	*16/01/1956*	GNR	On site of original Metropolitan Railway passenger terminus
Fawkham Junction	59 / 5A		10/05/1886	N/A	LCDR	Originally junction for Gravesend West Branch, disused 24/03/1968 - 1972 and 1976 - 28/09/2003
FELTHAM	49 / 1B	P	22/08/1848	N/A	LSWR	Goods yard closed 09/09/1968
		G	*22/08/1848*	*09/09/1968*		
Feltham Junction	35 / 6D		01/02/1850	N/A	LSWR	
FELTHAM LOCO SHED	35 / 6D		*??/??/1922*	*09/07/1967*	LSWR	Steam shed closed 09/07/1967. Diesel shed built on site of coal stacking ground, closed 06/01/1969
FELTHAM MARSHALLING YARD	35 / 6C		*1921-1922*	*06/01/1969*	LSWR	Opened in stages 1921-1922.
FENCHURCH STREET	27 / 6A & 74 / 2B		29/07/1841	N/A	LBLR	Advertised opening 02/08/1841, but services actually commenced 29/07/1841. Redeveloped into current layout April 1935
FERME PARK DOWN SIDINGS	14 / 5C		*??/01/1888*	N/A	GNR	Former Ferme Park goods yard, opened ??/01/1888 and effectively closed by 1973
Ferme Park Flyover	14 / 6C		*pre-1895*	N/A	GNR	Appeared between 1876 and 1895 OS, originally 'Harringay Engine Viaduct', and double track (now single)
FIELDWAY	67 / 4D		10/05/2000	N/A	CTL	
FINCHLEY CENTRAL	13 / 4B	P	22/08/1867	N/A	GNR	Opened as 'Finchley & Hendon', '& Hendon' suffix dropped 01/02/1872, 'Church End' suffix added 01/02/1894 Renamed 'Finchley Central' 01/04/1940, first served by and transferred to LPTB Northern Line 14/04/1940, closed to LNER passenger services on same date. Goods yard closed 01/10/1962
Finchley (Church End)		G	*22/08/1867*	*01/10/1962*		
Finchley						
Finchley & Hendon						
Finchley Central Junction	13 / 3B		01/04/1872	N/A	GNR	Divergence of High Barnet Branch from original Edgware Line (now Mill Hill East Branch)
FINCHLEY ROAD (MID)	25 / 3C		13/07/1868	11/07/1927	MID	Renamed 01/09/1868. Re-sited 03/02/1884
Finchley Road & St John's Wood						
FINCHLEY ROAD (MET)	25 / 3C	P	30/06/1879	N/A	MET	Suffix 'South Hampstead' 11/09/1885 - c.1914. Served by Bakerloo Line 20/11/1939 - 01/05/1979, Jubilee Line replacing Bakerloo Line after 01/05/1979. Goods yard opened 01/01/1894, closed 01/08/1941
Finchley Road (South Hampstead)		G	*01/01/1894*	*01/08/1941*		
Finchley Road						
FINCHLEY ROAD & FROGNAL	25 / 2C	P	02/01/1860	N/A	HJR	Renamed 01/10/1880. Goods yard open c.1870 - 02/01/1967. Closed 29/10/1995 - 29/09/1996
Finchley Road St John's Wood		G	*c.1870*	*02/01/1967*		
FINSBURY PARK	26 / 1C & 81	P	01/07/1861	N/A	GNR	Renamed 15/11/1869, also referred to as 'Seven Sisters Road, Holloway' before re-naming GNCR opened 14/02/1904, closed 04/10/1964. GNPBR opened 15/12/1906, southbound tunnel diverted through abandoned northbound GNCR tunnel 03/10/1965. LTB Victoria Line opened 01/09/1968 using former southbound GNCR & GNPBR platforms. Goods yard opened 1865, closed 01/04/1968.
Seven Sisters Road		G	*??/??/1865*	*01/04/1968*		
FINSBURY PARK DIESEL DEPOT	26 / 2C		*??/??/1960*	*??/10/1983*	BR	On site of Clarence Yard. First purpose-built diesel Traction Maintenance Depot in UK, downgraded ??/06/1981
Finsbury Park North Junctions	26 / 1C & 81		22/08/1867	N/A	GNR	Originally junction between GNR main line and branch to Edgware, now a series of crossovers
Finsbury Park South Junctions	26 / 1C & 81		14/12/1874	N/A	GNR	Junction of Great Northern main Line with routes ex-Canonbury & Moorgate
FIRESTONE TYRES (BRENTFORD)	36 / 3C		*??/??/1928*	*31/05/1964*	PRIV	
FORD FREIGHTLINER TERMINAL (DAGENHAM)	30 / 5B		*c.1967*	N/A	PRIV	
FORD MOTOR WORKS (DAGENHAM)	30 / 6A		*??/10/1932*	N/A	PRIV	Production commenced October 1932, continues to manufacture diesel engines
FOREIGN CATTLE MARKET	40 / 3C & 79		*15/12/1900*	*??/??/1914*	PRIV	Accessed via tramway along Grove Street. Market purchased by War Office 1914 and became an army depot remaining in use until at least WW2, Ordnance Survey maps depict tramway in situ up until 1960's
FOREST GATE	28 / 3B		??/??/1840	N/A	ECR	Exact opening date unknown. Closed 01/06/1843 - 31/05/1846. Goods yard east of station (see separate entry)
FOREST GATE GOODS	28 / 2C		*c.1890's*	*07/12/1970*	GER	Site closer to Manor Park station than Forest Gate, adjacent to LTSR route to Barking. Although Borley states Forest Gate opened to 'all' traffic 1840 (i.e. including goods), the yard does not appear on OS maps before 1895, so may have been opened at approximately same time as GER quadrupling work (c.1894)
Forest Gate Junction	28 / 2C		13/04/1854	N/A	ECR / LTSR	
FOREST HILL	54 / 1B	P	05/06/1839	N/A	LCRR	Named 'Dartmouth Arms' until 03/07/1845, when renamed 'Forest Hill'. Suffix 'for Lordship Lane' in use c.1877 to c.1943. Goods yard closed 04/05/1964. Island platform serving the middle 'fast' roads was present, partially staggered to the south of the 'slow' side platforms, but since demolished. Present on 1970 OS, but had been removed by 1983
Forest Hill for Lordship Lane		G	*05/06/1839*	*04/05/1964*		
Forest Hill						
Dartmouth Arms						
Fork Junction	28 / 3A & 77		15/08/1854	01/06/1969	ECR	
Fulham Bridge	38 / 5A		03/06/1899	N/A	LSWR	Built by LSWR but only ever used by District Railway trains. Purchased by LUL 01/04/1994
FULHAM BROADWAY	38 / 3B & 84		01/03/1880	N/A	MDR	Renamed 01/03/1952. Rebuilt 1905 & 2003 (latter rebuilding almost entirely covered over)
Walham Green						
FULWELL	50 / 2B		01/11/1864	N/A	TVR	Suffix '(New Hampton)' added 1874, changed to '& Hampton Hill' 1887, dropped 01/06/1913
Fulwell & Hampton Hill						
Fulwell (New Hampton)						
Fulwell						
Fulwell Junction	50 / 2B		01/07/1894	N/A	LSWR	Junction at west end of Shepperton Spur (Fulwell Curve)
Fulwell Tunnel	50 / 2B		01/11/1864	N/A	TVR	

G

NAME	Page / grid		Date opened	Date closed	Opening company	NOTES
GALLIONS	42 / 1A & 62 / 3D	P	late 1880	09/09/1940	LSKD	Initially 'Central' (opened 03/08/1880) was branch terminus per Quick, Connor and Jackson ('for first few weeks' in latter), so precise date of services to Gallions commencing unknown, had appeared in Bradshaw by November 1880 Gallions branch single until 14/11/1881. Re-sited east 12/12/1886, then again 1924/5 (per Quick). Operated by GER after 1896, ownership later transferred to PLA. Branch closed from 09/09/1940 due to 'Black Saturday' air raid 07/09/1940 (no Sunday service after 27/06/1915). Listed as 'Royal Albert Dock, Gallions' in Borley Branch continued to be used to access coal wharf at Gallions (Cory Brothers) until 17/04/1966
		G	*late 1880*	*17/04/1966*		
GALLIONS REACH	42 / 1A & 62 / 4D		28/03/1994	N/A	DLR	
GANTS HILL	17 / 6A		14/12/1947	N/A	LPTB (CEN)	
GARSTON	2 / 1D		07/02/1966	N/A	BR	
Gas Factory Junction	27 / 5D & 22		26/09/1850	N/A	LBLR / NLR	Junction with curve to Bow (NLR) established 26/09/1850, eliminated 29/12/1967. Junction with LTSR added 31/03/1858 (only extant junction). Junction with access to Bow Road Goods added 1885, eliminated 07/12/1964
Bow Common Junction						
Gasworks Tunnels	26 / 4B & 75 / 76		14/10/1852	N/A	GNR	Tunnels under Regent's Canal approaching King's Cross. Middle bore first, East bore added 1878, West bore 1892 East bore abandoned Spring 1977
George IV Tunnel	41 / 2D		30/07/2011	N/A	SER	
GEORGE STREET	66 / 2C		10/05/2000	N/A	CTL	
GIBBS CEMENT WORKS (WEST THURROCK)	45 / 4A		*c.1880*	*c.1965*	PRIV	Formerly Thames Cement works. Not on 1873 OS map, but present in 1897. Removed between 1961 and 1966
GIDEA PARK	18 / 5D	P	01/12/1910	N/A	GER	Opened as 'Squirrels Heath & Gidea Park', renamed 'Gidea Park & Squirrels Heath' 01/12/1913, '& Squirrels Heath' suffix dropped 20/02/1969. Goods yard in use 06/02/1911 - 07/12/1970 (sited to east of station, page 19 / 5A)
Gidea Park & Squirrels Heath		G	*06/02/1911*	*07/12/1970*		
Squirrels Heath & Gidea Park						
GIDEA PARK CARRIAGE SIDINGS	19 / 5A		*c.1930*	N/A	LNER	
Gidea Park Country End Junction	19 / 5A		01/01/1934	N/A	LNER	Dates from Romford to Brentwood quadrupling
Gifford Street Portals	76		14/11/2007	N/A	LCOR	
GIPSY HILL	53 / 3D	P	01/12/1856	N/A	WELCPR	Sometimes referred to as 'Gypsy Hill' in early years. Suffix 'for Upper Norwood' in use c.1911 - c.1955 Goods yard closed 07/12/1968
Gipsy Hill for Upper Norwood		G	*01/12/1856*	*07/12/1968*		
Gypsy Hill						
GLOBE ROAD & DEVONSHIRE STREET	27 / 5B		01/07/1884	22/05/1916	GER	

NAME: (Previous names indented below)	Page / grid:		Date opened:	Date closed:	Opening company:	NOTES:
GLOBE WORKS	45 / 4D		*c.1870's*	*??/??/1940*	PRIV	Chalk pit and depot, established in 1870's, railway system not used after 1940
GLOUCESTER ROAD	38 / 2C & 84 & 45		01/10/1868	N/A	MET	Initially terminus of MET extension from Praed Street Junction, extended east to Westminster (Bridge) 24/12/1868 MDR platforms opened 12/04/1869 (initially terminus, extended east 01/08/1870). UERL (GNPBR) platforms opened 15/12/1906 as 'Gloucester Road', this name applying to entire station from 1907. Platforms re-arranged 28/07/1957 such that former MET platforms both became eastbound, and former MDR both became westbound. Middle eastbound track removed 01/03/1970 and eastbound former platform 2 (now 3) widened into vacated space and former platform 1 abandoned. Piccadilly Line platforms closed 30/08/1987 - 21/05/1989 (lift replacement works)
Brompton (Gloucester Road)						
Gloucester Road Junction	66 / 1D		c.1865	N/A	LBSCR	Originally junction at north end of 'New Croydon Line', now junction at south end of Selhurst Spur
GOLDERS GREEN	13 / 6B		22/06/1907	N/A	UERL (CCEHR)	Northern terminus of CCEHR from opening to 19/11/1923
GOLDERS GREEN DEPOT	13 / 6B		22/06/1907	N/A	UERL (CCEHR)	Northern Line depot
GOLDHAWK ROAD	37 / 1D & 83		01/04/1914	N/A	MET / GWR	Replaced first Shepherd's Bush MET / GWR station to North
GOODGE STREET	26 / 5B		22/06/1907	N/A	UERL (CCEHR)	Renamed 09/03/1908
Tottenham Court Road						
GOODMANS YARD GOODS	27 / 6A & 74 / 2B		*01/02/1861*	*01/04/1951*	LBLR	Sometimes referred to as 'Minories Goods'
GOODMAYES	29 / 1C	P	08/02/1901	N/A	GER	Goods yard opened 03/06/1901, closed 31/07/1962
		G	*03/06/1901*	*31/07/1962*		
GOODMAYES MARSHALLING YARD	29 / 1C		*??/??/1899*	*31/07/1962*	GER	Enlarged 1911
Goods & Mineral Junction	75		14/10/1852	05/03/1973	GNR	Divergence of route into King's Cross terminus from original route to Maiden Lane station / King's Cross Goods
GORDON HILL	6 / 3D		04/04/1910	N/A	GNR	
GORESBROOK	29 / 5D		TBA	N/A	DLR	Gallions Reach to Dagenham Dock was proposed to open c.2017, but funding removed November 2008
GOSPEL OAK	26 / 2A & 9	P	02/01/1860	N/A	HJR	Renamed 01/02/1867. Platform for THJR opened 04/06/1888, closed to regular traffic 06/09/1926, some excursion traffic remained until ??/08/1939 and platform subsequently demolished. Platform re-opened 05/01/1981 when Barking trains diverted from Kentish Town. Goods yard in use 1862 - 07/08/1972. Became temporary terminus of Richmond trains 20/02/2010 - 01/06/2010 due to LOROL upgrade works.
Kentish Town		G	*??/??/1862*	*07/08/1972*		
Gospel Oak Junction	26 / 2A & 9		30/01/1916	N/A	HJR / THJR	Junction established 30/01/1916, eliminated 03/09/1922. Re-established 11/03/1940
GRAHAME-WHITE AVIATION CO. WORKS	12 / 4B		*15/06/1918*	*28/01/1921*	PRIV	Dates of first & last trains on branch unknown, dates quoted are for the opening / closing of Hendon Factory signalbox, which controlled the junction between the branch and Midland main line. Branch lifted c.1930, but engine shed in Montrose Park and tunnel under Northern Line still remain.
Graham Road Curve	27 / 3B	P	30/06/1986	28/09/1992	BR	Opened for diverted trains ex-Watford Junction upon closure of Broad Street station. Passenger services withdrawn 28/09/1992, but curve retained for empty stock workings
		G	*30/06/1986*	N/A		
GRAHAM ROAD GOODS	27 / 3B		*??/05/1894*	*04/10/1965*	GER	
GRANGE HILL	17 / 2B	P	01/05/1903	N/A	GER	Suffix 'for Chigwell Row' added July 1912, probably used until closure by LNER. Fairlop Loop closed to LNER passenger services 30/11/1947 to allow electrification and transfer to LTE Central Line, re-opening 21/11/1948. Goods yard closed 04/10/1965.
Grange Hill for Chigwell Row		G	*01/05/1903*	*04/10/1965*		
Grange Hill						
Grange Hill Tunnel	17 / 2B		20/04/1903	N/A	GER	
GRANGE PARK	6 / 5D		04/04/1910	N/A	GNR	
GRAVEL HILL	67 / 4C		10/05/2000	N/A	CTL	
GRAVESEND (GRR)	60 / 1B	P	10/02/1845	30/07/1849	GRR	Terminus of Gravesend & Rochester Railway, situated on south side of Thames & Medway canal basin Closed 13/12/1846 - 23/08/1847 by SER due to line improvement works. Closed for good 30/07/1849, replaced by Gravesend (SER) station on their North Kent line, opened the same day
		G	*10/02/1845*	*30/07/1849*		
GRAVESEND (SER)	60 / 1A	P	30/07/1849	N/A	SER	Replaced Gravesend (GRR) station. Carried suffix 'Central' 01/06/1899 - 14/06/1965. Goods yard closed 03/12/1961 Originally laid out with two platform roads either side of a pair of central reversing sidings (one west-facing, one east facing) altered to two 'through' roads c.1899. Bay was present on up side (abolished by 14/03/1971 resignalling?)
Gravesend Central		G	*30/07/1849*	*03/12/1961*		
Gravesend						
GRAVESEND WEST	60 / 1A	P	10/05/1886	03/08/1953	LCDR	Suffix 'West Street' added 01/06/1899, 'Street' dropped 26/09/1949. Closed to passengers with entire branch 03/08/1953, goods withdrawn and branch abandoned 24/03/1968
Gravesend West Street		G	*10/05/1886*	*24/03/1968*		
Gravesend						
GRAYS	45 / 4C	P	13/04/1854	N/A	LTSR	Sometimes referred to as 'Grays Thurrock' in early years. Bay on down side opened 05/11/1900 Closure date of goods yard unknown. Not noted in Borley which suggests it was open in some capacity into the 1980's, goods shed still depicted on 1974-7 OS, but removed by 1984-7
		G	*13/04/1854*	?		
GRAYS CEMENT WORKS	45 / 4B		*c.1880*	*??/??/1920*	PRIV	Not on 1873 OS map, but present in 1897. Closed 1920 (Middleton Press 'Tilbury Loop')
Grays East Junction	45 / 4C		c.1960	N/A	BR	Junction providing access to Tilbury Docks via Seabrook Sidings, replaced former Tilbury North Junction
GREAT PORTLAND STREET	26 / 5A		10/01/1863	N/A	MET	Opened as 'Portland Road', renamed 'Great Portland Street' 01/03/1917, '& Regent's Park' suffix added 1923, dropped 1933
Great Portland Street & Regent's Park						
Great Portland Street						
Portland Road						
GREEN PARK	39 / 1A		15/12/1906	N/A	UERL (GNPBR)	Renamed 18/09/1933. Victoria Line platforms opened 07/03/1969, Jubilee Line 01/05/1979
Dover Street						
GREENFORD (GWR)	23 / 3B	P	01/10/1904	17/06/1963	GWR	Platforms on loops off GWR Birmingham Main line, closed 17/06/1963. Goods yard closed 23/05/1980, subsequently becoming a cement depot
		G	*01/10/1904*	*23/05/1980*		
GREENFORD (LPTB)	23 / 3B		30/06/1947	N/A	LPTB (CEN)	Terminus of Central Line extension from North Acton from opening until 21/11/1948, incorporating central bay for BR Greenford Loop trains (first served 21/11/1948)
Greenford Bay Junction	23 / 3B		21/11/1948	N/A	BR	Greenford Loop passenger services diverted into bay platform in LTE station 21/11/1948
Greenford East Curve	23 / 4B	P	15/06/1903	10/10/1905	GWR	Initially used by temporary goods (03/06/1903) and passenger (15/06/1903) services serving the Park Royal Royal Agricultural showground, disused 04/07/1903 (passenger) 10/08/1903 (goods) - 01/05/1904. Regular passenger services ceased 10/10/1905, singled ??/06/1970
		G	*03/06/1903*	N/A		
Greenford East Junction	23 / 4C		01/10/1904	N/A	GWR	
GREENFORD S & T	23 / 3B		*??/??/1989*	N/A	BR	Sidings formerly served Rockware Glass works
Greenford South Junction	23 / 4B		01/10/1904	N/A	GWR	
Greenford West Curve	23 / 4B	P	01/10/1904	N/A	GWR	Passenger service north of Greenford Bay Junction ceased 21/11/1948. Partially singled 29/05/1990
		G	*01/10/1904*	N/A		
Greenford West Junction	23 / 3B		01/10/1904	N/A	GWR	
GREENHITHE FOR BLUEWATER	44 / 6D		30/07/1849	N/A	SER	Renamed c.1999 (Bluewater shopping centre opened 16/03/1999). Rebuilt 14/03/2008
Greenhithe						
Greenhithe Tunnel	45 / 6A		30/07/1849	N/A	SER	
GREENWICH	40 / 4D		24/12/1838	N/A	LGR	Originally temporary station to west of current, sometimes referred to as 'Church Row', replaced by current station to east 12/04/1840, which originally had two central engine release roads. Terminus until 01/02/1878, when extension to Maze Hill opened (former engine release roads retained as two through roads until first half of 20th century, when removed). DLR platforms opened 20/11/1999, space created using former through roads' track beds to realign 'up' main line road northwards and reposition platform
GREENWICH PARK	40 / 4D		01/10/1888	01/01/1917	LCDR	Renamed 01/07/1900. Passenger service withdrawn Nunhead to Greenwich Park 01/01/1917
Greenwich						
Grosvenor Bridge	39 / 3A & 82		01/10/1860	N/A	VSPR	
GROSVENOR ROAD	39 / 3A		01/11/1867	01/10/1911	LCDR / LBSCR	Open from January 1867 as ticket platforms, full opening 01/11/1867. LBSCR platforms closed before LCDR, on 01/04/1907. LBSCR platforms sometimes referred to as 'Grosvenor Road & Battersea Pier'
Grove Junction (LSWR)	37 / 2D		01/06/1870	01/01/1911	LSWR	Junction at south end of link between MET / GWR Hammersmith & City Rwy. and LSWR Kensington & Richmond Rwy.
Grove Junction (MET / GWR)	37 / 2D		01/06/1870	01/01/1911	LSWR	Junction at north end of link between MET / GWR Hammersmith & City Rwy. and LSWR Kensington & Richmond Rwy. Junction severed November 1914, track lifted along link May 1916
GROVE PARK	55 / 2B	P	01/11/1871	N/A	SER	Became a junction station with opening of Bromley (North) branch 01/01/1878, at which point the station was two through platforms with an up side bay. Rebuilt with three island platforms (six faces) for quadrupling of main line (complete 18/06/1905). Goods yard on up side (closed 04/12/1961), carriage sidings on down (closed 06/11/1976)
		G	*01/11/1871*	*04/12/1961*		
GROVE PARK CARRIAGE SERVICE SHED	55 / 2B		*??/??/1959*	N/A	BR	Commissioned coinciding with Kent Coast electrification scheme
GROVE PARK DOWN (BRAMDEAN) SIDINGS	55 / 1B		*c.1900*	N/A	SECR	EMU stabling sidings (x 8) and unelectrified freight sidings (x 5). On site of SECR Hither Green marshalling yard, established c.1900
Grove Park Junction	55 / 2B		01/01/1878	N/A	SER	
GROVE PARK UP (ST MILDRED'S) SIDINGS	55 / 2A		*c.1900*	N/A	SECR	EMU stabling sidings. On site of SECR Hither Green marshalling yard, established c.1900
Grove Tunnels	39 / 4D		01/08/1865	N/A	LBSCR	North bore opened 01/08/1865, south bore 13/08/1866
Guildford Line Junction	73 / 5C		04/07/1849	N/A	SER	
GUINNESS (PARK ROYAL)	24 / 4A		*??/??/1936*	*06/07/1995*	PRIV	Brewery, production started 1936 and ended Summer 2005. Last rail consignment left 06/07/1995
GUNNERSBURY	37 / 2B & 51 / 2A		01/01/1869	N/A	LSWR	Renamed 01/11/1871. First served District & Metropolitan Railways 01/06/1877 & 01/10/1877 respectively. Last served Metropolitan Railway 01/01/1907. Last served LSWR 05/06/1916. Originally had 5 platforms, 3 of which were abandoned in 1930. Remodelled 1932 by SR.
Brentford Road						
Gunnersbury Junction	37 / 2B & 51 / 2A		01/01/1869	N/A	LSWR	Renamed 24/07/1932 when 'West' junction eliminated
Gunnersbury East Junction						
Gunnersbury West Junction	37 / 2B & 51 / 3A		01/01/1869	24/07/1932	LSWR	Chiswick Curve last use 24/07/1932
GWR CREOSOTING WORKS (HAYES)	35 / 1C		*06/06/1877*	*??/??/1965*	GWR	GWR works for creosoting wooden sleepers, creosote being a by-product from Southall Gas works

H

NAME: (Previous names indented below)	Page / grid:	Date opened:	Date closed:	Opening company:	NOTES:
HACKBRIDGE	65 / 2D	P 01/10/1868	N/A	LBSCR	Goods yard closed 04/01/1965
		G *01/10/1868*	*04/01/1965*		
HACKNEY CENTRAL	27 / 3B	P 26/09/1850	N/A	EWIDBJR	First station opened to east of current site 26/09/1850 as 'Hackney', with goods yard opening 20/10/1850.
Hackney		G *20/10/1850*	*04/10/1965*		Re-sited west 01/12/1870, train service suspended 15/05/1944 (enemy action) but remained open to sell tickets,
					full closure 23/04/1945. Goods yard closed 04/10/1965. Re-opened to passengers 12/05/1980 as 'Hackney Central'
					Closed 20/02/2010 - 01/06/2010 (LOROL upgrade works)
HACKNEY DOWNS	27 / 3B	27/05/1872	N/A	GER	Suffix 'Junction' usually added until 1897/8. Rebuilt with 2 central through roads 01/06/1876, further rebuilt with 4
Hackney Downs Junction					platforms 1894. Interchange walkway to Hackney (NLR) in use 01/12/1885 - 15/05/1944
Hackney Downs North Junction	27 / 2B	01/07/1872	N/A	GER	
Hackney Downs South Junction	27 / 3B	01/06/1876	N/A	GER	Date given is that of quadrupling through Hackney Downs station
Hackney Downs Tunnel	27 / 2B	01/07/1872	N/A	GER	
HACKNEY WICK	27 / 3D	12/05/1980	N/A	BR	Closed 20/02/2010 - 01/06/2010 (LOROL upgrade works)
HACKNEY WICK GOODS	27 / 3C	*25/03/1877*	*06/11/1967*	GNR	Closed ??/06/1877 - 01/03/1878
HADLEY WOOD	5 / 3C	P 01/05/1885	01/03/1950	GNR	Goods yard opened at some point in 1884 as 'Beech Hill Park', passenger station opened 01/05/1885. Goods yard
Beech Hill Park (goods yard only)		G *??/??/1884*	*01/03/1950*		closed 01/03/1950. East Coast main line quadrupling through Hadley Wood Station / tunnels completed 03/05/1959
Hadley Wood North Tunnels	5 / 2C	07/08/1850	N/A	GNR	Original bore is today's 'Up' tunnel, 'Down' bore added 03/05/1959
Hadley Wood South Tunnels	5 / 3C	07/08/1850	N/A	GNR	Original bore is today's 'Up' tunnel, 'Down' bore added 03/05/1959
HAGGERSTON (NLR)	27 / 4A	02/09/1867	06/05/1940	NLR	Closed 06/05/1940, replaced 70 years later by Haggerston (TFL) slightly to the north
HAGGERSTON (TFL)	27 / 4A	27/04/2010	N/A	TFL (LOROL)	Built by TFL for LOROL services
HAINAULT	17 / 3B	P 01/05/1903	N/A	GER	Closed to passengers & goods 01/10/1908, re-opened to passengers 03/03/1930 (goods yard remained closed)
		G 01/05/1903	*01/10/1908*		Fairlop Loop closed to LNER passenger services 30/11/1947 to allow electrification and transfer to LTE Central Line.
					First served by LT Central Line Trains 31/05/1948 (terminus until 21/11/1948)
HAINAULT DEPOT	17 / 3B	*14/12/1947*	N/A	LPTB (CEN)	Ostensibly complete by 1939, used ??/06/1943 - ??/01/1945 for temporary wartime use (rolling stock assembly for
					US Army Transportation Corps). Central Line depot since 14/12/1947 (partial opening), 31/05/1948 (full opening)
Halfpence Lane Tunnel	60 / 5D	28/09/2003	N/A	LCOR	
Hall Farm Curve	15 / 6B	P 26/04/1870	04/10/1914	GER	Part of original GER branch from Lea Valley Line to Shern Hall Street Walthamstow. Passenger service withdrawn
		G *26/04/1870*	*06/11/1967*		04/10/1914, closed to freight and abandoned 06/11/1967
Hall Farm North Junction	15 / 6B	01/08/1872	06/11/1967	GER	Junction between original Shern Hall Street Walthamstow branch and 01/08/1872 line to Hackney Downs,
					eliminated when Hall Farm Curve abandoned 06/11/1967
Hall Farm South Junction	15 / 6B	01/08/1885	11/06/1960	GER	Junction at north end of Coppermill Curve (refer to Coppermill Curve notes)
HAMMERSMITH (MDR)	38 / 2A & 72	09/09/1874	N/A	MDR	MDR terminus 09/09/1874 - 01/06/1877. GNPBR terminus opened to north 15/12/1906, entire station rebuilt with
					Piccadilly Line platforms between District Line platforms for Piccadilly Line westward extension 04/07/1932
HAMMERSMITH (MET / GWR)	38 / 2A & 72	P 13/06/1864	N/A	MET / GWR	Relocated slightly south 01/12/1868. Goods yard closed 01/02/1960
		G *13/06/1864*	*01/02/1960*		
HAMMERSMITH & CHISWICK	37 / 2C & 51 / 2D	P 08/04/1858	01/01/1917	NSWJR	Opened to goods traffic 01/05/1857, passenger traffic 08/04/1858. '& Chiswick' suffix added 01/07/1880
Hammersmith		G *01/05/1857*	*03/05/1965*		Passenger traffic withdrawn 01/01/1917, goods remaining until 03/05/1965, branch formally abandoned 01/01/1966
HAMMERSMITH DEPOT	38 / 2A	*05/11/1906*	N/A	GWR	Hammersmith & City Line depot, built by GWR but used exclusively for Metropolitan Railway electric trains
HAMMERSMITH (GROVE ROAD)	37 / 2D & 72	01/01/1869	05/06/1916	LSWR	Served by GWR 01/06/1870 - 01/11/1870, MET 01/10/1877 - 01/01/1911. Addison Road to Studland Road Junction
					closed 05/06/1916
HAMPSTEAD	25 / 2C	22/06/1907	N/A	UERL (CCEHR)	Was named 'Heath Street' up until point of opening, when renamed 'Hampstead'. Former name still appears
					on tiles at platform level
HAMPSTEAD HEATH	25 / 2D	P 02/01/1860	N/A	HJR	Closed 04/12/1984 - 15/04/1985 (cutting wall collapse) & 29/10/1995 - 29/09/1996 (engineering works)
		G *01/03/1863*	*30/09/1972*		Goods yard opened 01/03/1863, closed 30/09/1972
Hampstead Heath Tunnel	25 / 2D	02/01/1860	N/A	HJR	Closed 29/10/1995 - 29/09/1996 (engineering works)
HAMPSTEAD ROAD	26 / 3A & 58	09/06/1851	05/05/1855	EWIDBJR	Replaced by new station of same name to west (opened on same date), later to become Primrose Hill
Hampstead Tunnel	25 / 3C	15/03/1899	N/A	GCR	
HAMPTON	49 / 4D	P 01/11/1864	N/A	TVR	Originally passing point on single line until 17/07/1878 doubling. Goods yard initially on 'down' side only, additional
		G *01/11/1864*	*03/05/1965*		sidings on 'up' side added 1899. Closed 03/05/1965
HAMPTON COURT	50 / 5B	P 01/02/1849	N/A	LSWR	Suffix '& East Moulsey' added 1869, became 'for East Moulsey' 1897/8, spelling changed to 'for East Molesey'
Hampton Court for East & West Molesey		G *01/02/1849*	*03/05/1965*		1903/4 (suffix also '& East Molesey' at this time). Suffix then changed to 'for East & West Molesey' at some point
Hampton Court for East Molesey					until 1955, when it was dropped and the station became simply 'Hampton Court' again.
Hampton Court for East Moulsey					Goods yard closed 03/05/1965
Hampton Court & East Moulsey					
Hampton Court					
HAMPTON COURT GAS WORKS	50 / 4C	*c.1895*	*??/??/1961*	PRIV	Hampton Court Gas Co. Works founded in mid 19th century, but no rail connection apparent on OS before 1896
Hampton Court Junction	63 / 1C	01/02/1849	N/A	LSWR	Line to Guildford added 02/02/1885. Remodelled with an 'up' diveunder on Guildford line 1908, further 'down'
					flyover to eliminate 'flat' junction for Hampton Court branch added 04/07/1915
HAMPTON WATERWORKS	49 / 3B	*??/??/1897*	*??/07/1964*	PRIV	Waterworks at riverside site established c.1855, receiving coal by river. In 1897 a pumping station was built at
					Kempton Park, with a standard gauge rail connection. In 1915 a 2-foot narrow gauge railway system approx. 5km
					in length was constructed connecting the three pumping station complexes and riverside wharves. The narrow
					gauge system was dismantled in 1947 due to a switch from coal to oil, with the standard gauge sidings ceasing
					to be used after July 1964
HAMPTON WICK	50 / 4D	01/07/1863	N/A	LSWR	
HANGER LANE	24 / 4A	30/07/1947	N/A	LPTB (CEN)	
Hanger Lane Junction	24 / 6A	23/06/1903	N/A	MDR	Divergence of MDR South Harrow branch from original line to Ealing Broadway
HANSON AGGREGATES (DAGENHAM DOCK)	30 / 6A	?	N/A	PRIV	
HANSON AGGREGATES (WEST DRAYTON)	34 / 1D	?	N/A	PRIV	
HANWELL	23 / 6B	01/12/1838	N/A	GWR	Served by District Railway trains 01/03/1883 - 01/10/1885. Suffix '& Elthorne' 01/04/1896 - 06/05/1974
Hanwell & Elthorne					Southern entrance and platform 1 demolished 1977
Hanwell					
HANWELL BRIDGE SIDINGS	36 / 1A	?	N/A	GWR	Currently used by DBS
Hanwell Junction	23 / 6B	03/06/1903	N/A	GWR	Converted to 'single lead' junction 1974
HAREFIELD ROAD	9 / 6C	N/A	N/A	LTE (CEN)	Station to have been built on aborted Central Line extension to Denham, adjacent to former South Harefield Halt
HARLESDEN	24 / 4C & 68 / 6D	15/06/1912	N/A	LNWR	Adjacent to site of LBIR 'Willesden' station open 1842 - 01/09/1866. Served by Bakerloo Line trains since 16/04/1917
HARLESDEN FOR WEST WILLESDEN & STONEBRIDGE PARK	24 / 3C	P 03/08/1875	01/10/1902	MID	Opened as 'Harrow Road for Stonebridge Park & West Willesden', 'Harlesden' substituted for 'West Willesden'
Stonebridge Park for West Willesden & Harlesden		G *03/08/1875*	*06/07/1964*		??/02/1876. Renamed 'Harrow Road' 01/05/1878, suffix 'for Stonebridge & Harlesden' added 01/11/1880.
Harrow Road for Stonebridge & Harlesden					Renamed 'Stonebridge Park for West Willesden & Harlesden' 01/07/1884. Closed to passengers 02/07/1888,
Harrow Road					re-opened 01/03/1893. Re-named 'Harlesden for West Willesden & Stonebridge Park' 01/02/1901.
Harrow Road for Stonebridge Park & Harlesden					Closed to passengers for good 01/10/1902, goods 06/07/1964
Harrow Road for Stonebridge Park & West Willesden					
Harlesden Junction	24 / 4C & 86	02/01/1860	N/A	LNWR / HJR	
HAROLD WOOD	19 / 4B	P 01/02/1868	N/A	GER	Was named 'Heril Wood' until point of opening. Rebuilt due to quadrupling 01/01/1934, platforms were staggered
		G *01/02/1868*	*04/10/1965*		previously ('up' west of 'down'). Goods yard closed 04/10/1965
HARRINGAY	14 / 6C	P 01/05/1885	N/A	GNR	Suffix 'West' in use 18/06/1951 - 27/05/1971. Goods yard closed 01/01/1968
Harringay West		G *01/05/1885*	*01/01/1968*		
Harringay					
Harringay Curve	14 / 6C	P N/A	N/A	GNR / THJR	Harringay Curve possibly laid April 1864 (junction recorded as having been established, but eliminated 5 months
		G ??/04/1864	N/A		later, according to GNR records) then lifted by 1881 perhaps without being used. As the THJR did not open
					until 21/07/1868, if it were used, it could have been in connection with the THJR's construction. Laid again
					15/05/1916 then lifted ??/04/1920, again possibly without having been used. Laid for a third time 08/01/1940
HARRINGAY GREEN LANES	14 / 6D	P 01/06/1880	N/A	THJR	Opened as 'Green Lanes' 01/06/1880, Goods yard probably opened 1882. 'Harringay Park' prefix added
Harringay East		G *c.1882*	*03/02/1964*		30/08/1884. 'Green Lanes' suffix dropped 09/06/1951, renamed 'Harringay Stadium' 27/10/1958. Goods yard
Harringay Stadium					closed 03/02/1964. Renamed 'Harringay East' 14/05/1990, then 'Harringay Green Lanes' 08/07/1991
Harringay Park					
Harringay Park, Green Lanes					
Green Lanes					
Harringay Junction	14 / 6C	??/04/1864	N/A	GNR / THJR	See notes re: Harringay Curve (junction at north end of curve)
Harringay Park Junction	14 / 6C	21/07/1868	N/A	THJR	See notes re: Harringay Curve (junction at south end of curve)
HARRINGTON ROAD	54 / 5B	23/05/2000	N/A	CTL	
HARROW LANE SIDINGS	31 / 4B	*??/??/1866*	*30/08/1981*	NLR	Scrap metal from Harrow Lane represented the last traffic on the Victoria Park - Poplar route
Harrow North Junction	11 / 6B	04/07/1904	N/A	MET	Divergence of Uxbridge Branch
HARROW-ON-THE-HILL	11 / 6B	P 02/08/1880	N/A	MET	Country terminus of Metropolitan Railway 02/08/1880 - 02/05/1885. Renamed 01/06/1894.
Harrow		G *02/08/1880*	*03/04/1967*		Served by GCR since 15/03/1899. Goods yard closed 03/04/1967
HARROW & WEALDSTONE	11 / 4B	P 20/07/1837	N/A	LBIR	Renamed 01/05/1897. First served by Bakerloo Line trains 16/04/1917, service withdrawn after 24/09/1982,
Harrow		G *20/07/1837*	*03/04/1967*		Reinstated 04/06/1984 as terminus. Goods yard closed 03/04/1967

NAME: (Previous names indented below)	Page / grid:		Date opened:	Date closed:	Opening company:	NOTES:
HATCH END	11 / 3A		08/08/1842	N/A	LBIR	Suffix '& Hatch End' added 01/02/1897. Renamed 'Hatch End (for Pinner)' 01/02/1920, suffix dropped 11/06/1956
Hatch End (For Pinner)						Served by London Underground Bakerloo Line trains 16/05/1917 - 24/09/1982. Platforms 3-6 abandoned 07/01/1963
Pinner & Hatch End						Goods yard to the south, adjacent to future Headstone Lane station (see entry below)
Pinner						
HATCH END GOODS	11 / 3A		*08/08/1842*	*14/11/1966*	LBIR	Adjacent to Headstone Lane station
HATTON CROSS	35 / 5B		19/07/1975	N/A	LTE (PIC)	Terminus 19/07/1975 - 16/12/1977 (empty trains ex-Hounslow West commenced reversing here from 14/07/1975)
HAVERSTOCK HILL	25 / 2D		13/07/1868	01/01/1916	MID	Platforms repositioned from original (now 'fast') to new (now 'slow') lines when opened 03/02/1884
Hawkswood Junctions	55 / 5D & 56 / 5A		??/??/1992	N/A	BR	Physical junctions formed 1992 when Tonbridge Slow Loop doubled, leading to short section of bidirectional track
HAYDON SQUARE GOODS	27 / 6A & 74 / 1B		*??/02/1853*	*02/07/1962*	LNWR	Temporary opening February 1853, full opening 12/03/1853
Haydon Square Junction	74 / 2C		*??/02/1853*	*02/07/1962*	LNWR / LBLR	
HAYDONS ROAD	52 / 3C	P	01/10/1868	N/A	LBSCR / LSWR	Renamed 01/10/1889. Closed to passengers 01/01/1917 - 27/08/1923. Goods yard closed 05/12/1966
Haydens Lane		G	*01/10/1868*	*05/12/1966*		
HAYES	68 / 2B	P	29/05/1882	N/A	SER	Initially single platform (current platform 2). Station rebuilt 1933, turntable removed at this time and built over
		G	*29/05/1882*	*19/04/1965*		Goods yard closed 19/04/1965, but sidings retained until January 1971 for engineering purposes
HAYES & HARLINGTON	35 / 1D	P	01/05/1864	N/A	GWR	Served by District Railway trains 01/03/1883 - 01/10/1885. Renamed 22/11/1897. Goods yard closed 02/01/1967
Hayes		G	*01/05/1864*	*02/01/1967*		
HEADSTONE LANE	11 / 3A		10/02/1913	N/A	LNWR	Served by London Underground Bakerloo Line trains 16/05/1917 - 24/09/1982. Hatch End goods yard adjacent
Heathrow Airport Junction	35 / 1A		19/01/1998	N/A	RT	To be remodelled for commencement of 'Crossrail' services 2018
HEATHROW EXPRESS / CONNECT DEPOT	24 / 5C & 86		*19/01/1998*	N/A	BAA	
HEATHROW JUNCTION	34 / 1D		19/01/1998	25/05/1998	BAA	Temporary terminus due to delayed opening of HEX tunnel (collapse during construction 21/10/1994)
						Closed 31/01/1998 - 03/02/1998 (operational problems), closed for good 25/05/1998 when HEX opened fully
HEATHROW TERMINALS 1, 2 & 3	34 / 4D		16/12/1977	N/A	LTE (PIC)	Terminus 16/12/1977 - 12/04/1986. Suffix 'Terminals 1, 2 & 3' added 03/09/1983, 'Central' dropped 12/04/1986
Heathrow Central Terminals 1, 2 & 3						Heathrow Express platforms opened 25/05/1998
Heathrow Central						
HEATHROW TERMINAL 4	34 / 5D		12/04/1986	N/A	LUL (PIC)	LUL platform closed 21/10/1994 - 04/12/1994, then again 06/01/2005 - 17/09/2006 (Terminal 5 Extension)
						Heathrow Express platforms opened 25/05/1998.
HEATHROW TERMINAL 5	34 / 4B		27/03/2008	N/A	BAA	Entire station owned & operated by BAA. Platforms for 'Airtrack' built but project cancelled 11/04/2011
Heathrow Tunnel Junction	34 / 1D		25/05/1998	N/A	RT / BAA	Crossover at mouth of tunnel to Heathrow Airport, current BAA / NR boundary
HENDON	12 / 5D	P	13/07/1868	N/A	MID	Goods yard opened 09/03/1868, passenger station 13/07/1868. Goods yard closed 01/01/1968
		G	*09/03/1868*	*01/01/1968*		
HENDON CENTRAL	12 / 5D		19/11/1923	N/A	UERL (CCEHR)	Terminus of extension from Golders Green 19/11/1923 - 18/08/1924
HENDON FACTORY PLATFORM	12 / 4D		19/05/1918	??/??/1919	PRIV	Station to cater for workers of the Grahame-White aircraft factory. Possibly never used
HENDON RAILTRANSFER STATION	25 / 1A		*c.1979*	N/A	PRIV	Originally GLC facility (30 year lease signed March 1979), subsequently operated by Shanks & McEwan Ltd
Brent Waste Terminal						until expiry of lease. Now operated by Waste Recycling Group, proposed to be moved (Brent Cross development)
HERNE HILL	39 / 6C	P	25/08/1862	N/A	LCDR	Terminus of line to Elephant & Castle until 01/07/1863. Goods yard closed 01/08/1966
		G	*25/08/1862*	*01/08/1966*		
Herne Hill North Junction	39 / 6C		25/08/1862	N/A	LCDR	
Herne Hill South Junction	39 / 6C		01/01/1869	N/A	LCDR	
HERNE HILL SORTING SIDINGS	39 / 5C		*c.1860s*	*01/08/1966*	LCDR	Did not open with line in 1862, but sidings had appeared by 1870
HERON QUAYS	40 / 1D		31/08/1987	N/A	DLR	Closed 09/02/1996 - 22/04/1996 (IRA bomb) and 01/10/2001 - 18/12/2002 (reconstruction)
HERSHAM	62 / 2D		28/09/1936	N/A	SR	
HIGH BARNET	5 / 4B	P	01/04/1872	N/A	GNR	First served by and transferred to LPTB Northern Line 14/04/1940, closed to LNER passenger services on same date.
		G	*01/04/1872*	*01/10/1962*		Goods yard closed 01/10/1962
HIGH BARNET SIDINGS	5 / 4B		*01/04/1872*	N/A	GNR	Originally GNR carriage sidings, became stabling sidings for Northern Line
High Level (or Tottenham South) Curve	26 / 2A & 9	P	01/07/1870	19/01/1964	MID	Connection between THJR and MID goods lines. First passenger use 01/07/1870, closed 19/01/1964
		G	*03/01/1870*	*19/01/1964*		
High Meads Curve	27 / 3D & 77 / 78	P	N/A	N/A	GER	No regular passenger service
		G	*??/??/1881*	N/A		
High Meads Junction	27 / 3D & 77 / 78		??/07/1891	N/A	GER	Junction at north end of Lea & High Meads Curves
High Meads Loop	27 / 3D & 77 / 78	P	N/A	N/A	GER	No regular passenger service. Northern portion under covered way (Stratford City development)
		G	*??/??/1881*	N/A		
HIGH STREET KENSINGTON	38 / 1B & 84	P	01/10/1868	N/A	MET	Metropolitan District Railway platforms opened 03/07/1871. Renamed gradually by 1880. Adjacent goods yard
Kensington (High Street)		G	*04/03/1878*	*25/11/1963*	MID	opened by Midland Railway 04/03/1878, closed 25/11/1963. Terminus 23/07/2011 - 23/08/2011 (engineering work)
HIGHAMS PARK	16 / 3A	P	17/11/1873	N/A	GER	Renamed 'Highams Park (Hale End)' 10/10/1894, then became '& Hale End' 01/05/1899. Suffix dropped 20/02/1969.
Highams Park & Hale End		G	*17/11/1873*	*04/10/1965*		Goods yard closed 04/10/1965
Highams Park (Hale End)						
Hale End						
HIGHBURY & ISLINGTON	26 / 3C	P	26/09/1850	N/A	EWIDBJR	Opened as 'Islington', renamed 'Highbury or Islington' 01/06/1864, then 'Highbury & Islington' 01/07/1872
Highbury (GNCR)		G	*20/10/1851*	*04/08/1969*		GNCR station (separate from NLR premises) opened 28/06/1904 as 'Highbury', '& Islington' added 20/07/1922.
Highbury or Islington (NLR)						LTB Victoria Line platforms opened 01/09/1968, with the southbound using the former northbound GNCR platform,
Islington (EWIDBJR)						and a new northbound GNCR platform built alongside the northbound Victoria Line. Interchange provided with BR
						at this time and original GNCR entrance closed. GNCR platforms closed by LTE 05/10/1975, reopened by BR
						16/08/1976. Goods yard opened for coal only 20/10/1851, transferred to LNWR and opened to general goods traffic
						22/12/1872, closed 04/08/1969. LOROL platforms closed 20/02/2010 - 01/06/2010, upon re-opening formerly
						abandoned northern platforms used (now numbered 7 & 8), with southern 1 & 2 re-opening 06/01/2011 as terminus
Highbury Vale Junction	26 / 2C & 81		??/??/1988	N/A	BR	Junction formed when line through Canonbury Tunnel singled due to 1988 electrification works
HIGHBURY VALE GOODS	26 / 2C & 81		*??/??/1876*	*05/04/1971*	GNR	
HIGHGATE (GNR)	14 / 6A		22/08/1867	05/07/1954	GNR	Nominally opened by Edgware, Highgate & London Railway, which was absorbed by GNR a month before opening
						Original layout of central siding and side platforms replaced by island platform c.1883
						Closed when Alexandra Palace to Finsbury Park service withdrawn 05/07/1954. Had been intended
						for electrification and transfer to LPTB Northern Line, but works abandoned post-WW2
HIGHGATE (LPTB)	14 / 6A		19/01/1941	N/A	LPTB (NOR)	Line through station opened 03/07/1939, but station itself did not open until 19/01/1941
Highgate East Tunnel	14 / 6A		22/08/1867	05/10/1970	GNR	Last passenger use 05/07/1954, remained in use for Northern Line Stock transfer until 05/10/1970
HIGHGATE ROAD HIGH LEVEL	26 / 2A & 9		21/07/1868	01/03/1918	THJR	Closed 31/01/1870 - 01/10/1870. Carried suffix 'for Parliament Hill' ??/11/1894 - 01/07/1903, after which suffix
Highgate Road for Parliament Hill						'High Level' added to distinguish from Low Level station. Most use ceased 01/10/1915, although some MID trains
Highgate Road						started from here until complete closure 01/03/1918
Highgate Road Junction	26 / 2A & 9		03/01/1870	19/01/1964	THJR / MID	Junction at north end of High Level Curve, although route toward Gospel Oak saw no traffic before 04/06/1888
HIGHGATE ROAD LOW LEVEL	26 / 2A & 9		17/12/1900	01/03/1918	MID	
Highgate West Tunnel	14 / 6A		22/08/1867	05/10/1970	GNR	Last passenger use 05/07/1954, remained in use for Northern Line Stock transfer until 05/10/1970
HIGHGATE WOOD DEPOT	13 / 5D		*01/10/1962*	N/A	LTE (NOR)	On site of GNR Wellington Sidings, nominal opening date is that of withdrawal of BR usage of sidings, as Northern
						Line trains had stabled there since 1940. Remodelled 1969-1970, closed 25/03/1984 - 23/01/1989
HILLINGDON	21 / 2D	P	10/12/1923	N/A	MET	Served by District Line from opening until 23/10/1933, Piccadilly Line thereafter. 'Swakeleys' suffix added
Hillingdon (Swakeleys)		G	*10/12/1923*	*10/08/1964*		??/04/1934, gradually dropped. Goods yard closed 10/08/1964. Re-sited west 28/06/1992 (road scheme)
Hillingdon						
HINCHLEY WOOD	63 / 2B		20/10/1930	N/A	SR	
HITHER GREEN	41 / 6A		01/06/1895	N/A	SER	Rebuilt for St Johns to Elmstead Woods quadrupling (completed 18/06/1905) with six platforms. Dartford Line
						platform roads had a central through road between them, removed 1937
HITHER GREEN DEPOT	41 / 6A		*10/09/1933*	N/A	SR	Opened by SR 10/09/1933 as a traction maintenance depot with 6-road engine shed. BR Engineering depot
						established on part of site 1991. Half of original shed demolished 1993 (reduced from 6 roads to 3).
						TMD transferred to EWS (now DBS) and engineering depot transferred to Balfour Beatty 24/02/1996
Hither Green Junction	41 / 6A		01/09/1866	N/A	SER	
HOGSMILL CORN MILLS	64 / 4C		*c.1890*	*??/??/1955*	PRIV	Siding serving corn mills on Hogsmill River
HOLBORN	26 / 6B		15/12/1906	N/A	UERL (GNPBR)	Suffix 'Kingsway' added 22/05/1933, then Central Line platforms opened and 25/09/1933, suffix gradually dropped
Holborn (Kingsway)						Platform for Aldwych service in use 30/11/1907 - 21/09/1940, then 01/07/1946 - 30/09/1994
Holborn						
HOLBORN VIADUCT	26 / 6C & 32 / 4C		02/03/1874	29/01/1990	LCDR	Suffix 'High Level' 01/05/1912 - 01/06/1916. Some platforms closed and track removed 1967
Holborn Viaduct (High Level)						
Holborn Viaduct						
HOLBORN VIADUCT (LOW LEVEL)	26 / 6C & 32 / 4C		01/08/1874	01/06/1916	LCDR	Renamed 01/05/1912
Snow Hill						
HOLLAND PARK	38 / 1B		30/07/1900	N/A	CLR	
HOLLOWAY & CALEDONIAN ROAD	26 / 2C		??/??/1852	01/10/1915	GNR	Originally open for alighting 'up' passengers only, opened fully 01/08/1856. Renamed 06/05/1901
Holloway						
HOLLOWAY CATTLE	26 / 2C		*??/??/1854*	*c.1930's*	GNR	Platforms later used by Holloway Motorail Terminal
HOLLOWAY MOTORAIL TERMINAL	26 / 2C		*30/05/1960*	*15/09/1968*	BR	Used platforms of former Holloway Cattle Station (see above), road access from Caledonian Road
Holloway North Junctions	26 / 2C & 81		14/12/1874	N/A	GNR	
HOLLOWAY ROAD	26 / 2C		15/12/1906	N/A	UERL (GNPBR)	
Holloway South Junctions	26 / 2C		c.1877	N/A	GNR	Junction initially formed when Up Goods viaduct north of Copenhagen tunnels opened 1877

NAME: (Previous names indented below)	Page / grid:		Date opened:	Date closed:	Opening company:	NOTES:
HOMERTON	27 / 3C		01/10/1868	N/A	NLR	Train service suspended 15/05/1944 (enemy action), station fully closed 23/04/1945, subsequently demolished Station rebuilt and re-opened 13/05/1985 on same site as original (coinciding with electrification of route) Closed 20/02/2010 - 01/06/2010 (LOROL upgrade works)
HONOR OAK	40 / 6B	P	01/12/1865	20/09/1954	LCDR	Closed 01/01/1917 - 01/03/1919 and 22/05/1944 - 04/03/1946. Nunhead to Crystal Palace (High Level) closed to all
	54 / 1B	G	01/12/1865	20/09/1954		traffic 20/09/1954 (goods yard depicted on page 54 / 1B)
HONOR OAK PARK	40 / 6B		01/04/1886	N/A	LBSCR	
Hoo Junction	60 / 3C		01/04/1882	N/A	SER / HHR	Junction between SER and HHR branch to Sharnal Street
HOO JUNCTION SIDINGS	60 / 3C		20/02/1926	N/A	SR	Laid out as a marshalling yard by SR, opening 20/02/1926, although some sidings were present on site before this
Hoppity Tunnel	71 / 4D		01/07/1900	N/A	SECR	
HORNCHURCH	31 / 2A	P	01/05/1885	N/A	LTSR	Served by District Railway trains 02/06/1902 - 01/10/1905. Reintroduced 12/09/1932 when route quadrupled,
		G	01/05/1885	??/??/1981		District Line trains utilising the new 'slow' platforms. British Rail services withdrawn by 15/06/1962 and 'fast' platforms abandoned. Ownership of 'Slow' platforms transferred to LTB 01/01/1969. Goods yard closed 1981
HORNSEY	14 / 5C	P	07/08/1850	N/A	GNR	Goods yard enlarged 01/05/1885, closed 07/04/1975
		G	07/08/1850	07/04/1975		
HORNSEY ROAD	26 / 1B		01/01/1872	03/05/1943	THJR	Suffix 'for Hornsey Rise' added in MID timetable 01/02/1880 - 01/07/1903
HORNSEY STEAM SHED	14 / 5C		??/11/1899	??/07/1961	GNR	Shed remains as a store building within Hornsey TMD
HORNSEY TMD (Traction Maintenance Depot)	14 / 5C		16/08/1976	N/A	BR	Built for electrification of King's Cross suburban routes, first electric service Drayton Park-Old Street 16/08/1976 followed by remainder of suburban lines 08/11/1976. On site of Ferme Park 'Up' Yard and Hornsey steam shed
HORNSEY UP CARRIAGE SIDINGS	14 / 4C		?	N/A	GNR	Roads 1-3 in use, roads 4-14 disused. To become new 'Thameslink' Depot c.2018
HORSLEY	69 / 5A	P	02/02/1885	N/A	LSWR	Originally listed in Bradshaw as 'Horsley & Ockham', then became 'Horsley & Ockham & Ripley', sometimes 'for'
Horsley & Ockham & Ripley		G	02/02/1885	c.1965		substituted for '&'. Settled on 'Horsley' 1955
Horsley & Ockham						
Hotel Curve	26 / 4B & 75	P	01/10/1863	08/11/1976	GNR	Curve in 'down' direction connecting MET with GNR, originally to 10/01/1863 MET lines but later to 'Widened Lines'.
		G	01/10/1863	08/11/1976		Carried goods traffic 20/02/1866 - 24/03/1969. Rebuilt with an easier radius 1892, closed when Moorgate trains diverted via GNCR 08/11/1976
HOUNSLOW	36 / 5A	P	01/02/1850	N/A	LSWR	Suffix '& Whitton' 1852 - 06/07/1930 (date that Whitton station opened). Original goods yard closed 06/05/1968
Hounslow & Whitton		G	01/02/1850	06/05/1968		Second goods yard north of the original (also on 'up' side) opened 1931, closed 06/02/1967
Hounslow						
HOUNSLOW CENTRAL	36 / 4A		01/04/1886	N/A	MDR	Originally single platform, line doubled 01/11/1912 (station rebuilding completed 19/10/1912). Renamed 01/12/1925
Heston-Hounslow						First served by Piccadilly Line 13/03/1933. District Line service ceased 10/10/1964
HOUNSLOW EAST	36 / 4A		02/05/1909	N/A	MDR	Opened to replace original Hounslow Town terminal station (closed on same day). Renamed 01/12/1925
Hounslow Town						First served by Piccadilly Line 13/03/1933. District Line service ceased 10/10/1964
Hounslow Junction	35 / 6D		01/01/1883	N/A	LSWR	Junction at north end of Hounslow Spur
Hounslow Spur	35 / 6D	P	01/01/1883	N/A	LSWR	Service reduced significantly May 1987 ('Roundabout' service around Hounslow Loop ceased)
		G	01/01/1883	N/A		
HOUNSLOW TOWN	36 / 4A		01/05/1883	02/05/1909	MDR	Original country terminus of MDR branch from Mill Hill Park (Acton Town). Arranged for through running for never- realised extension to junctions with LSWR on Hounslow Loop and at Strawberry Hill. Suffix 'Town' added 1884.
Hounslow						Closed 01/04/1886 - 01/03/1903, then for good 02/05/1909
HOUNSLOW WEST	35 / 4D		21/07/1884	N/A	MDR	Opened by District Railway, renamed 'Hounslow West' 01/12/1925. First served Piccadilly Line 13/03/1933,
Hounslow Barracks						District Line service ceased 10/10/1964. Closed 12/07/1975 and replaced by new station at lower level to north which opened 14/07/1975, terminus until 19/05/1975 when Hatton Cross extension opened (between 14/07/1975 and 19/07/1975 trains detrained at Hounslow West and ran empty to Hatton Cross to reverse)
HOWARD TENENS DISTRIBUTION CENTRE	29 / 4C		?	N/A	PRIV	Logistics, formerly 'Stora'
HOXTON	27 / 4A		27/04/2010	N/A	TFL (LOROL)	Built by TFL for LOROL services
HST STABLING & MAINTENANCE SHED (OLD OAK COMMON)	24 / 5C & 86		??/09/1976	N/A	BR	Formerly GWR carriage shed, stabling for First GreatWestern stock. To close and relocate to North Pole Depot
HYDE PARK CORNER	39 / 1A		15/12/1906	N/A	UERL (GNPBR)	

I

ICKENHAM	22 / 1A		25/09/1905	N/A	MET	Served by District Line 01/03/1910 - 23/10/1933, Piccadilly Line thereafter
ILFORD	29 / 2A	P	20/06/1839	N/A	ECR	Goods yard to east of station, closed to general goods traffic 06/05/1968 but milk dock remained open until c.1980
		G	20/06/1839	06/05/1968		
ILFORD DEPOT	29 / 1A		c.1900	N/A	GER	First carriage sidings on site c.1900, car sheds added for EMUs March 1949, 'New Shed' opened 1959
Ilford Carriage Sidings Junction	29 / 1B		20/04/1903	30/11/1947	GER	West-facing junction between GER main line and Fairlop Loop
Ilford Depot Country End Junction	29 / 1B		20/04/1903	19/03/1906	GER	Junction at south end of Seven Kings curve
Seven Kings West Junction						
Ilford Depot London End Junction	29 / 2A		??/??1949	N/A	BR	
IMPERIAL PAPER MILLS (GRAVESEND)	60 / 1A		c.1912	c.1968	PRIV	Mills founded 1912, closed 1981. Connected to Gravesend West branch, so external traffic must have ceased by 24/03/1968, although OS maps depict internal railway network in situ until closure of mills
IMPERIAL WHARF	38 / 4C		27/09/2009	N/A	NR (LOROL)	
International Junction	39 / 2C		14/11/1994	14/11/2007	RT	Divergence of lines into platforms 20-24. Disused since 2007, track in situ for future use
Intersection Tunnel	24 / 3A & 68 / 2A		15/06/1912	N/A	LNWR	
ISLAND GARDENS	40 / 3D		31/08/1987	N/A	DLR	One terminus of original DLR system. First station partially built on MER North Greenwich branch viaduct, two platforms present but platform one seldom used after train sets lengthened to two units. Closed on the night of 09/02/1996 by IRA bomb at South Quay, did not re-open until 15/04/1996. Closed 11/01/1999 due to works on the Lewisham extension, new subterranean station opened with extension 20/11/1999, original abandoned
ISLEWORTH	36 / 4B		01/02/1850	N/A	LSWR	Replaced Smallberry Green to east (closed same day). Named 'Spring Grove & Isleworth' 01/10/1855 - ??/08/1911
Spring Grove & Isleworth						(Borley). Quick refers to station opening as 'Isleworth', having '& Spring Grove' suffix added 1854/5, name then
Isleworth						reversed 1874/5 (Spring Grove & Isleworth), reversed back 1895/6, then 'Isleworth for Spring Grove' 1912/3, before becoming 'Isleworth' again 1955.
IVER	34 / 1A	P	01/12/1924	N/A	GWR	Goods yard closed 06/01/1964, sidings remained on site until c.1989
		G	01/12/1924	06/01/1964		

J

JOHNSONS PORTLAND CEMENT WORKS	44 / 6D		??/??/1877	c.1970	PRIV	
JUNCTION ROAD	26 / 2A & 9		01/01/1872	03/05/1943	THJR	Suffix 'for Tufnell Park' dropped 01/07/1903. Has been proposed to be re-opened as 'Tufnell Park'
Junction Road for Tufnell Park						
Junction Road Junction	26 / 2A & 9		02/04/1883	N/A	THJR / MID	Junction between THJR and MID line to Carlton Road Junction

K

KEMPTON PARK	49 / 3B		18/07/1878	N/A	LSWR	At first platform on 'down' side only, 'up' platform added 1879. Initially members only, opened to public 1890 Bay platform on 'up' side removed 1964. Race Days only until 06/03/2006, when full passenger service commenced (unadvertised service started from 05/03/2006)
KENLEY	73 / 1C	P	05/08/1856	N/A	CR	Renamed December 1856. Goods yard closed 03/04/1961
Coulsdon		G	05/08/1856	03/04/1961		
KENNINGTON	39 / 3C		18/12/1890	N/A	CSLR	Sometimes had suffix 'New Street' added 1890-1894. Closed 01/06/1923 - 06/07/1925 (tunnel widening) Charing Cross Branch platforms opened 13/09/1926
KENSAL GREEN	25 / 4A		01/10/1916	N/A	LNWR / UERL	Served by Bakerloo Line from opening
KENSAL GREEN & HARLESDEN	24 / 4D & 86		01/11/1861	01/07/1873	HJR	Platforms were staggered on either side of present Wrottesley Road bridge (down on west, up on east) Replaced by Kensal Green (later Kensal Rise) station to east, opened on same date as closure
Kensal Green Junctions	24 / 4D & 86		02/01/1860	N/A	HJR	
Kensal Green Tunnels	24 / 4D & 86		20/07/1837	N/A	LBIR	Quadrupled by LNWR 1879. DC lines tunnels (2 single track bores) added 10/05/1915
KENSAL RISE	25 / 4A		01/07/1873	N/A	LNWR	Renamed 24/05/1890. Closed 29/10/1995 - 29/09/1996 (engineering works)
Kensal Green						
KENSINGTON & CHELSEA DISTRICT SCHOOL	65 / 6A		??/??/1880	c.1930	PRIV	School near Banstead for poor children of Kensington & Chelsea, served by siding from Epsom Downs branch Established 1880, siding apparent on 1913 OS but had been removed by 1934-5

NAME: (Previous names indented below)	Page / grid:	Date opened:	Date closed:	Opening company:	NOTES:
KENSINGTON (OLYMPIA)	38 / 2A & 84	27/05/1844	N/A	WLR	Opened by WLR as passenger terminus, but passenger services withdrawn and station closed 01/12/1844. Note that prior to the WLR opening, a platform was built on Kensington Canal basin itself, but this was never served by trains Re-opened by WLR slightly to north 02/06/1862, again as terminus (extended to Clapham Junction 02/03/1863) First served MET 01/07/1864, renamed 'Kensington (Addison Road)' 01/10/1868. LNWR trains to Earl's Court started 01/02/1872. Station closed to all services 21/10/1940 (enemy action). Re-opened after WW2 for workers' shuttle service to Clapham Junction (in operation by summer 1946), also to exhibition traffic via District Line starting 19/12/1940, on which date station renamed Kensington (Olympia). District Line bay platform and segregated track towards Earl's Court opened 03/03/1958. Mainline platforms regularly served 01/04/1963 - 15/06/1965 (diversions due to WCML electrification), then again 15/10/1967 - 20/12/1967 (diversions due to Paddington rebuilding) Workers' shuttle to Clapham Junction advertised after 16/05/1983, regular District Line service started 07/04/1986 Mainline station fully re-opened 12/05/1986 (long distance trains), local service Clapham Junction to Willesden Junction restored 31/05/1994. Regular weekday District Line service withdrawn 12/12/2011 (weekend and exhibition traffic remain)
Kensington (Addison Road)					
Kensington					
KENSINGTON OLYMPIA MOTORAIL TERMINAL	38 / 2A & 84	24/05/1966	late 1982	BR	Service withdrawn at end of Summer timetable 1982
KENSINGTON SIDINGS	38 / 5C	*02/03/1863*	N/A	WLER	
KENT HOUSE	54 / 4B	01/10/1884	N/A	LCDR	Line through station quadrupled 10/05/1886
KENT PORTLAND CEMENT WORKS	44 / 6D	*??/??/1922*	*c.1970*	PRIV	
KENTISH TOWN	26 / 2A & 9	13/07/1868	N/A	MID	UERL (CCEHR) station opened 22/06/1907
KENTISH TOWN ENGINE SHEDS	26 / 2A & 9	*08/09/1867*	*??/??/1963*	MID	No.2 and No.3 sheds added 1899
Kentish Town Junction	26 / 2A & 9	03/01/1870	19/01/1964	MID	Junction at south end of High Level Curve to Highgate Road Junction
KENTISH TOWN WEST	26 / 3A	01/04/1867	N/A	HJR	Suffix 'West' added 02/06/1924. Closed 18/04/1971 - 05/10/1981 (arson), again 29/10/1995 - 29/09/1996 (engineering works), and again 20/02/2010 - 01/06/2010 (LOROL upgrade works)
Kentish Town					
KENTON	11 / 5D	P 15/06/1912	N/A	LNWR	Goods yard opened 13/03/1911, passenger station opened later; 15/06/1912. Goods yard closed 03/05/1965 Suffix 'for Northwick Park' in use 01/10/1927 - 07/05/1973. Served by London Underground Bakerloo Line trains since 16/04/1917, but no service 27/09/1982 (last train 24/09/1982) - 04/06/1984
Kenton (for Northwick Park)		G *13/03/1911*	*03/05/1965*		
Kenton					
KEW	37 / 2A & 19	P 01/08/1853	01/02/1862	NSWJR	Initially terminus, through services onto Hounslow Loop commenced 01/06/1854. Passenger service effectively ceased when NSWJR trains to Richmond diverted via Kew and Barnes Curves 01/02/1862, but a once weekly service between Windsor and the Metropolitan Cattle Market at Caledonian Road continued to call until October 1866 Coal yard south of down platform opened July 1856, later incorporated into Kew Bridge North Goods
		G *??/07/1856*	?		
KEW BRIDGE	37 / 2A & 19	P 22/08/1849	N/A	LSWR	Platforms on Kew Curve opened 01/02/1862 (initially had separate NSWJR entrance, which closed 01/07/1918), closed 12/09/1940. Entire station re-named 'Kew Bridge' December 1868. Adjacent goods yard re-named 'Kew Bridge South' 1948 (as distinct from the former MID yard in the Kew Bridge triangle, which became 'North', and the 1929 SR 'New' yard adjacent to Old Kew Junction), goods yard closed 03/04/1967. Per Borley goods facilities opened with passenger station, but none evident on OS before 1895 when a single siding had appeared behind down platform
Kew		G *c.1890*	*03/04/1967*		
KEW BRIDGE NEW GOODS	37 / 2A & 19	*??/??/1929*	*??/??/1977*	SR	Expanded 1930
KEW BRIDGE NORTH GOODS	37 / 2A & 19	*??/??/1863*	?	NSWJR	NSWJR, later MID, goods yard situated in Kew Bridge triangle. Named 'Kew Bridge North' 1948. Closure date not known, possibly c.1980's (still extant in Borley). Note 1863 opening date is sourced from Borley; no evidence is seen of yard until 1895 OS (not present on 1870 1:1,056 or 1882-94 1:2,500 surveys)
Kew Curve (LSWR)	37 / 2A & 19	P 01/02/1862	12/09/1940	LSWR	Regular passenger service (Kew Bridge to Willesden Junction) withdrawn 12/09/1940
		G *01/02/1862*	N/A		
Kew Curve (LNWR)	24 / 5C & 86	P 20/07/1885	N/A	LNWR	Link built to connect NSWJR and HJR, allowing closure of original HJR high level route / platforms to passengers
		G *20/07/1885*	N/A		
Kew East Junction	37 / 2A & 19	01/02/1862	N/A	NSWJR / LSWR	Junction at north end of Kew Curve
KEW GARDENS	37 / 4A	01/01/1869	N/A	LSWR	Served by GWR 01/06/1870 - 01/11/1870, first served MDR 01/06/1877, served by MET 01/10/1877 - 01/01/1911 Sidings and Bay platform in use until 04/07/1931, crossover north of platforms until 31/01/1954
Kew Railway Bridge	37 / 3A	01/01/1869	N/A	LSWR	Also known as Strand-on-the Green bridge
KIDBROOKE	41 / 5C	P 01/05/1895	N/A	BHR	Goods yard a single siding on 'down' side, west of station. In 1917 a large military depot was established to the south of the station, remaining in situ until at least the early 1960's (subsequently redeveloped as the Ferrier Estate) Goods yard closed 07/10/1968
		G *01/05/1895*	*07/10/1968*	BHR	
Kidbrooke Tunnel	41 / 5B	01/05/1895	N/A	BHR	
KILBURN	25 / 3B	24/11/1879	N/A	MET	First served by Bakerloo Line 20/11/1939, last served Metropolitan Line 07/12/1940. Suffix '& Brondesbury' until 25/09/1950. Transferred from Bakerloo Line to Jubilee Line 01/05/1979
Kilburn & Brondesbury					
KILBURN HIGH ROAD	25 / 4B	P c.1851/1852	N/A	LNWR	Opening date unknown, late 1851 or early 1852. Renamed 'Kilburn & Maida Vale' 01/06/1879. Closed 01/01/1917, re-opened 10/07/1922, then renamed 'Kilburn High Road' 01/08/1923. Closed 17/09/2004 - 22/08/2005 (fire) Goods yard opened with passenger station, closed 05/11/1962
Kilburn & Maida Vale		G *c.1851/1852*	*05/11/1962*		
Kilburn					
KILBURN PARK	25 / 4B	31/01/1915	N/A	UERL (BAK)	Terminus from opening until 11/02/1915
KING GEORGE V	41 / 1D & 62 / 5C	02/12/2005	N/A	DLR	Terminus until 10/01/2009 extension to Woolwich Arsenal
KING HENRY'S DRIVE	67 / 5D	10/05/2000	N/A	CTL	
KING WILLIAM STREET	26 / 6D & 72 / 4C	18/12/1890	25/02/1900	CSLR	Original terminus of CSLR from Stockwell. Abandoned when line extended from Borough to Moorgate
KING'S CROSS	26 / 4B & 75 / 76	14/10/1852	N/A	GNR	Replaced original terminus to north (see Maiden Lane GNR). 'Suburban' portion of station to west of main station was separate from opening on 18/12/1874 until incorporated into main station 05/03/1977. Platform 16 of the Suburban station on gradient ascending from the 'Hotel Curve' in use 01/02/1878 - 08/11/1976
KING'S CROSS FUNERAL STATION	75	10/07/1861	03/04/1863	GNR	Funeral traffic only, last recorded departure 03/04/1863
KING'S CROSS GOODS	26 / 4B & 75	*18/11/1850*	*05/03/1973*	GNR	Amalgamation of various facilities, including Potato market, Granary, Eastern & Western Coal drops, and MID goods shed
King's Cross Junction	75	01/10/1863	08/11/1976	GNR / MET	
King's Cross Loop	76	P N/A	N/A	UERL	Connection between Northern and Piccadilly Lines for stock transfer / engineering use. No passenger service ever provided
		G *27/03/1927*	N/A		
KING'S CROSS ST PANCRAS	26 / 5B & 75 / 76	15/12/1906	N/A	UERL (GNPBR)	UERL GNPBR (Piccadilly Line) Platforms opened 15/12/1906 as 'King's Cross', 'for St Pancras' added 1927, became 'King's Cross St Pancras' 1933. CSLR (Northern Line) Platforms opened 12/05/1907 as 'King's Cross for St Pancras', became 'King's Cross St Pancras' 1933, closed 09/08/1922 - 20/04/1924 (tunnel widening), 19/11/1987 - 05/03/1989 (fire) and 16/10/1995 - 17/06/1996 (escalator works). Relocated Metropolitan Line platforms opened 14/03/1941 (see entry for 'King's Cross Thameslink'), initially had a central 'bay' platform that was subsequently lifted late 1940's and later filled in. Victoria Line platforms opened 01/12/1968
King's Cross for St Pancras					
King's Cross					
KING'S CROSS THAMESLINK	26 / 4C & 75	10/01/1863	09/12/2007	MET	Original MET station at King's Cross, platforms on 'Widened Lines' added 17/02/1868. '& St Pancras' after 1925, '&' dropped 1933. Original MET platforms replaced by current station to the west 14/03/1941 (last train 09/03/1941), but platforms on 'Widened Lines' remained open after this date. BR trains ceased to call 03/10/1977 (down) and 14/05/1979 (up), with the station closed from this date. Platforms on 'Widened Lines' re-opened 11/07/1983 as 'King's Cross Midland', also referred to as 'King's Cross Midland City'. Renamed 'King's Cross Thameslink' 16/05/1988, closed again 09/12/2007 (last train 08/12/2007), replaced by platforms under St Pancras International
King's Cross Midland City					
King's Cross Midland					
King's Cross St Pancras					
King's Cross & St Pancras					
King's Cross					
KING'S CROSS 'TOP SHED'	26 / 4B	*??/??/1851*	*17/06/1963*	GNR	One of three engine sheds at King's Cross, the others being the Midland roundhouse (opened February 1859) and the 'Main Line Running shed' (opened 1862)
King's Cross Tunnel	75 / 76	13/07/1868	N/A	MID	Connection between MID and MET 'Widened Lines', currently used by 'Thameslink' services
KING'S CROSS YORK ROAD	26 / 4B & 75	01/01/1866	05/03/1977	GNR	Up (Southbound) only, at north end of York Road Curve toward the Metropolitan Railway. Rebuilt slightly to east 04/03/1878 (due to new bore of Gasworks Tunnel opening). Closed 08/11/1976 when Moorgate trains diverted along GNCR at Finsbury Park, but briefly re-opened 31/01/1977 - 05/03/1977 for use of terminating trains
KINGSBURY	12 / 5B	10/12/1932	N/A	MET	Opened by Metropolitan Railway. Transferred to Bakerloo Line 20/11/1939, Jubilee Line 01/05/1979
KINGSLAND GOODS	27 / 3A & 6	*20/10/1851*	*07/08/1972*	EWIDBJR	
Kingsley Road Junction	36 / 4A	13/06/1905	02/05/1909	MDR	Junction at north end of curve linking Hounslow Town and Heston-Hounslow
KINGSTON (1st)	51 / 6A	21/05/1838	??/??/1845	LSWR	Situated east of King Charles Road. Replaced by Kingston (2nd station, later Surbiton) to west in 1845
KINGSTON (2nd)	50 / 4D	P 01/07/1863	N/A	LSWR	Opened as terminus of branch from Twickenham (Low level station). High level platforms opened on extension to New Malden 01/01/1869, although low level platforms remained open. Station rebuilt 1935 with a new bay platform at the high level, allowing the original low level platforms to close (track retained for a period as carriage sidings). Engine shed became goods shed 1898, goods yard closed 05/09/1966
		G *01/07/1863*	*05/09/1966*		
Kingston Bridge	50 / 4D	01/07/1863	N/A	LSWR	
KINGSWOOD	72 / 4A	P 02/11/1897	N/A	CVR	02/11/1897 is given as opening date for Chipstead Valley Railway (Purley to Kingswood) in Borley, but it also states regular passenger service 'probably' commenced 09/11/1897, Quick states first train 09/11/1897, so 02/11/1897 may have been official / ceremonial opening. Country end terminus until 01/07/1900 SECR extension to Tadworth Goods yard closed 07/05/1962. Suffix dropped 01/12/1968
Kingswood & Burgh Heath		G *02/11/1897*	*07/05/1962*		
Kingswood Tunnel	72 / 4A	01/07/1900	N/A	SECR	
KNIGHT'S HILL GOODS	53 / 1D	*16/05/1892*	*07/10/1968*	LNWR	
Knight's Hill Tunnel	53 / 1C	01/10/1868	N/A	LBSCR	
KNIGHTSBRIDGE	38 / 1D	15/12/1906	N/A	UERL (GNPBR)	Reconstructed, with new Sloane Street entrance, 18/02/1934
KUEHNE + NAGEL LOGISTICS (DAGENHAM DOCK)	30 / 5A	?	N/A	PRIV	Replaced 'Hays Distribution'

L

NAME: (Previous names indented below)	Page / grid:		Date opened:	Date closed:	Opening company:	NOTES:
LADBROKE GROVE	25 / 6A		13/06/1864	N/A	MET / GWR	Opened as 'Notting Hill', sometimes had '(Ladbroke Road)' suffix added 1869 - 1880. '& Ladbroke Grove' suffix
Ladbroke Grove (North Kensington)						added 1880, renamed 'Ladbroke Grove (North Kensington)' 01/06/1919, suffix dropped 1938
Notting Hill & Ladbroke Grove						
Notting Hill (Ladbroke Road)						
Notting Hill						
LADYWELL	40 / 6D		01/01/1857	N/A	MKR	Built by the Mid Kent Railway, but operated by SER from opening. 'Lady Well' used at times as late as 1960
Lady Well						
Ladywell Junction	40 / 6D		01/09/1866	N/A	SER	Junction at south end of Ladywell Loop
Ladywell Loop	40 / 5D	P	01/09/1866	N/A	SER	
		G	01/09/1866	N/A		
LAFARGE AGGREGATES (WEST DRAYTON)	21 / 6B		post-1999	N/A	PRIV	On site of former coal yard
LAMBETH NORTH	39 / 2C		10/03/1906	N/A	UERL (BSWR)	Opened as 'Kennington Road', renamed 'Westminster Bridge Road' 05/08/1906, renamed 'Lambeth (North)'
Lambeth (North)						15/04/1917, renamed 'Lambeth North' c.1928. Closed 10/11/1996 - 14/07/1997 (Bakerloo Line tunnel strengthening)
Westminster Bridge Road						
Kennington Road						
Lampton Junction	36 / 4A		21/07/1884	02/05/1909	MDR	Junction between original MDR Hounslow Town route and subsequent Hounslow Barracks extension
LANCASTER GATE	25 / 5C		30/07/1900	N/A	CLR	Closed 02/07/2006 - 13/11/2006 (lift works)
LANGDON PARK	27 / 6D		10/12/2007	N/A	DLR	Slightly to south of site of South Bromley station (NLR)
LANGLEY	33 / 1C	P	01/12/1845	N/A	GWR	Served by MDR trains 01/03/1883 - 01/10/1885. Suffix 'Marsh' dropped 1849. Goods yard closed 06/01/1964
Langley Marsh		G	01/12/1845	06/01/1964		
LANGLEY OIL TERMINAL	33 / 1C		15/06/1969	c.2000	PRIV	Operated by Total, lease expired December 2002 but usage ceased c.2000, purchased by EWS but now abandoned
Latchmere Curve	38 / 5D	P	02/03/1863	N/A	WLER	Singled at time of electrification July 1993, restored to double track 26/04/2011
		G	02/03/1863	N/A		
Latchmere No.1 Junction	38 / 4D		02/03/1863	N/A	WLER	
Latchmere No.2 Junction	38 / 4D		02/03/1863	N/A	WLER	
Latchmere No.3 Junction	38 / 4D		06/07/1865	N/A	WLER	Junction eliminated 21/01/1936 - 17/08/1994
LATIMER ROAD	25 / 6A & 83		16/12/1868	N/A	MET / GWR	Closed 17/01/2011 - 24/04/2011 (platform lengthening)
Latimer Road Junction	25 / 6A & 83		01/07/1864	01/03/1954	MET / GWR	Originally 'Kensington Junction' before Latimer Road station was opened
Kensington Junction						
LCC CENTRAL TRAM REPAIR WORKS	41 / 3B		??/??/1909	05/07/1952	LCC	
LEA BRIDGE	27 / 1C	P	15/09/1840	08/07/1985	NER	Suffix 'Road' dropped 1841. Goods yard closed 07/12/1970. Closed with Tottenham Hale to North Woolwich service
Lea Bridge Road		G	15/09/1840	07/12/1970		
Lea Bridge Junction	27 / 1C		26/04/1870	06/11/1967	GER	Southern junction of Hall Farm Curve
Lea Curve	27 / 3D & 77 / 78	P	N/A	N/A	GER	No regular passenger service
		G	??/07/1891	N/A		
Lea Junction	27 / 3D & 77 / 78		??/07/1891	N/A	GER	Junction at south end of Lea Curve
LEATHERHEAD (LBSCR)	70 / 3C	P	04/03/1867	N/A	LBSCR	Replaced joint station to north. Combined with former LSWR station by SR 10/07/1927
		G	04/03/1867	c.1965		
LEATHERHEAD (LBSCR & LSWR)	70 / 3C	P	01/02/1859	04/03/1867	LBSCR / LSWR	First station in Leatherhead, at country end of LBSCR / LSWR joint line. Replaced by separate LBSCR and LSWR
		G	01/02/1859	04/03/1867		termini on same day as closure 04/03/1867
LEATHERHEAD (LSWR)	70 / 3C	P	04/03/1867	10/07/1927	LSWR	Replaced joint station to north. Closed when new connection made between former LSWR and LBSCR by SR
		G	04/03/1867	c.1965		10/07/1927. Track through station remained in situ until at least 1970's (rolling stock storage), with northern
						portion of former LSWR route remaining in situ until c.1985
Leatherhead Joint Line Junction	70 / 3C		04/03/1867	10/07/1927	LBSCR / LSWR	Junction between branches to separate LBSCR / LSWR termini. LSWR ceased to be through route 10/02/1927,
						but sidings on former route diverged at this location until c.1985
Leatherhead Junction	70 / 4C		10/07/1927	N/A	SR	Connection installed between former LSWR and LBSCR by SR, allowing LSWR station at Leatherhead to close
LEATHERHEAD NORTH	70 / 2C		N/A	N/A	SR	One of two intermediate stations on Chessington South to Leatherhead route, works abandoned at outset of WW2
LEBANON ROAD	66 / 2D		10/05/2000	N/A	CTL	
LEE	41 / 6B	P	01/09/1866	N/A	SER	Goods yard closed 07/10/1968
		G	01/09/1866	07/10/1968	SER	
Lee Loop Junction	41 / 6A		c.1900	N/A	SECR (?)	Junction at north end of Lee Spur
Lee Spur	41 / 6A	P	N/A	N/A	N/A	Opened c.1900, coinciding approximately with opening of Hither Green marshalling yards
		G	c.1900	N/A	SECR (?)	
Lee Spur Junction	55 / 1A		c.1900	N/A	SECR (?)	Junction at south end of Lee Spur
LEICESTER SQUARE	26 / 6B		15/12/1906	N/A	UERL (GNPBR)	(UERL) CCEHR platforms opened 22/06/1907
Leigham Court Tunnel	53 / 2B		01/12/1856	N/A	WELCPR	
Leigham Junction	53 / 2C		01/08/1871	N/A	LBSCR	
Leigham Spur	53 / 2C	P	01/08/1871	N/A	LBSCR	
		G	01/08/1871	N/A		
Leigham Tunnel	53 / 2B		01/10/1868	N/A	LBSCR	
LEMAN STREET	27 / 6A & 74 / 2C		01/06/1877	07/07/1941	LBLR	Originally built 1872 but Board of Trade refused to sanction opening, so reconstructed and opened 01/06/1877
						Closed 22/05/1916 - 01/07/1919
Leman Street Junction	74 / 2C		17/06/1864	01/09/1966	LBLR / GER	Divergence of East Smithfield / London Docks branch from LBLR line
LEWISHAM	40 / 5D	P	30/07/1849	N/A	SER	Suffix 'Junction' 01/01/1857 - 07/07/1929. Goods yard to east of station on Blackheath line, closed 06/05/1963
Lewisham Junction		G	30/07/1849	06/05/1963		DLR platforms opened 20/11/1999
Lewisham						
Lewisham Crossover Junctions	40 / 5D		01/01/1857	N/A	MKR / SER	Originally simple junction between SER and MKR routes, developed into crossovers following 30/06/1929
Lewisham Junction						opening of SR connection from former LCDR Greenwich Park branch to Lewisham
LEWISHAM ROAD	40 / 5D		18/09/1871	01/01/1917	LCDR	Passenger service withdrawn Nunhead to Greenwich Park 01/01/1917
Lewisham Vale Junction	40 / 5D		29/03/1976	N/A	BR	Junction at south end of Tanners Hill Flydown
LEY STREET YARD SIDINGS	29 / 1A		c.1900	N/A	GER	Part of Ilford Depot complex
LEYTON	28 / 2A	P	22/08/1856	N/A	ECR	Prefix 'Low' dropped 27/11/1867. First served by LPTB Central Line trains 05/05/1947, first trains in the morning
Low Leyton		G	22/08/1856	06/05/1968		remained British Rail services until 01/06/1970 (last train 31/05/1970). Goods yard (P27 / 2D) closed 06/05/1968
Leyton Junction	28 / 2A		05/05/1947	03/05/1971	LPTB / LNER	Junction of ECR Loughton Branch and LPTB Central Line ex-Stratford. Closed 03/05/1971, dismantled 29/10/1972
LEYTON MIDLAND ROAD	27 / 1D	P	09/07/1894	N/A	TFGR	Renamed 01/05/1949. Goods yard (P28 / 1A) open 01/09/1894 - 06/05/1968
Leyton		G	01/09/1894	06/05/1968		
LEYTONSTONE	28 / 1A	P	22/08/1856	N/A	ECR	Original layout with 'down' platform south of 'up' and a small goods yard on 'up' side. 'Down' platform relocated north
		G	22/08/1856	02/09/1955		1891 and new goods yard opened partially on site of original 'down' platform. First served by LPTB Central Line
						trains 05/05/1947 (terminus until 14/12/1947). Goods yard closed 02/09/1955. First trains in morning remained
						British Rail services until 01/06/1970 (last train 31/06/1970)
LEYTONSTONE HIGH ROAD	28 / 1A	P	09/07/1894	N/A	TFGR	Renamed 01/05/1949. Goods yard opened 01/09/1894, closed 06/05/1968
Leytonstone		G	01/09/1894	06/05/1968		
Leytonstone Junction	28 / 1B		14/12/1947	N/A	LPTB / LNER	Divergence of 1947 route to Newbury Park from Epping Line
LILLIE BRIDGE DEPOT	38 / 3B & 84		Mid-1872	N/A	MDR	Originally built by MDR to house their first fleet of locos / coaches (delivered mid-1871), depot complete by mid-1872.
						Became UERL GNPBR (Piccadilly Line) depot between 15/12/1906 - 04/07/1932. Subsequently used for engineering
						purposes, but again became a District Line stabling point after 11/12/2010 due to S7 Stock upgrade works
LIMEHOUSE (1st)	27 / 6C		06/07/1840	04/05/1926	LBLR	Passenger service to Blackwall and North Greenwich withdrawn 04/05/1926
LIMEHOUSE (2nd)	27 / 6C		03/08/1840	N/A	LBLR	Opened as 'Stepney', renamed 'Stepney East' 01/07/1923, platforms to/from Blackwall closed 04/05/1926.
Stepney East						Renamed 'Limehouse' 11/05/1987. Former Blackwall platforms re-opened by DLR 31/08/1987
Stepney						RT platforms closed 22/07/1994 - 12/09/1994 (engineering works)
Limehouse Curve	27 / 6C	P	01/09/1880	01/03/1881	LBLR	Saw passenger use 01/09/1880 - 01/03/1881, not officially closed until 10/05/1963
		G	05/04/1880	05/11/1962		
Limehouse Junction	27 / 6C		05/04/1880	05/11/1962	LBLR	Junction at south end of Limehouse Curve
Linford Street Junction	39 / 4A & 82		17/08/1994	N/A	RT	Date quoted is start of trial Eurostar service, advertised service commenced 14/11/1994. Disused since 14/11/2007
						(diversion of Eurostar to St Pancras), but chord still in situ and traversed by test trains
LION CEMENT WORKS (WEST THURROCK)	45 / 4B		c.1880	??/??/1976	PRIV	Originally Wouldham works. Not on 1873 OS map, but had appeared by 1897. Closed 1976.
Lismore Circus Tunnel	9		09/09/1867	N/A	MID	
LITTLE ILFORD DEPOT	28 / 3D		20/08/1905	01/12/1959	UERL (MDR)	District Railway depot. Closed when Upminster Depot opened, replaced by East Ham BR Depot on same site
LIVERPOOL STREET	26 / 6D & 85		02/02/1874	N/A	GER	First served by Metropolitan Railway 01/02/1875 (direct into GER station, platforms 1 & 2). Separate MET platforms
Bishopsgate (Metropolitan Railway only)						opened as 'Bishopsgate' 12/07/1875, renamed 18/11/1876 (became 'Liverpool Street' 01/11/1909).
						CLR platforms opened 28/07/1912 (terminus until 04/12/1946). Platforms for 'Crossrail 1' expected to open 2018
Liverpool Street Junction	85		12/07/1875	??/??/1907	MET / GER	Junction between MET and connection to GER at Liverpool Street platforms 1 & 2. Last through train 1904, junction
						severed 1907
LLOYD PARK	67 / 3A		10/05/2000	N/A	CTL	

NAME: (Previous names indented below)	Page / grid:		Date opened:	Date closed:	Opening company:	NOTES:
LONDON BRIDGE Tooley Street London	39 / 1D & 72 / 6C		14/12/1836	N/A	LGR	Replaced Bermondsey Street temporary terminus to east. Separate terminus opened by LCRR to north of LGR one 05/06/1839. Initially referred to as simply 'London', or also as 'Tooley Street', in timetables before 1844 Station rebuilt as joint terminus July 1844 (opened while incomplete), and rearranged with LGR / SER trains using the northern (ex LCRR) portion and LCRR / LBRR the southern (ex LGR) portion to eliminate conflicting train movements at Corbett's Lane Junction. Joint station divided into SER and LBSCR portions 02/08/1850 (during this rebuilding period, temporary stations were provided), enlarged 1854. Original LCRR station demolished 1863 to make way for line to Charing Cross (through platforms opened 11/01/1864). Goods traffic handled between 1864 - 1901 (transferred to Ewer Street). Station combined by SR 1928, rebuilt 1971 - 1977, again 2010 - 2018 CSLR Platforms opened 25/02/1900 (closed 16/07/1922 - 23/02/1925 and 02/07/1999 - 05/09/1999 [tunnel works]) Jubilee Line platforms opened 07/10/1999
LONDON CITY AIRPORT	41 / 1D & 62 / 5C		02/12/2005	N/A	DLR	
LONDON FIELDS	27 / 3B		27/05/1872	N/A	GER	Closed 22/05/1916 - 01/07/1919 and 13/11/1981 - 29/09/1986* (fire) *per Quick, Connor states 25/09/1986
LONDON ROAD DEPOT	39 / 2C		*10/03/1906*	N/A	UERL (BSWR)	Bakerloo Line depot
LONG GROVE HOSPITAL	64 / 4A		*20/05/1905*	*??/??/1950*	PRIV	Horton Estate Light Railway opened to supply building materials, later fuel, to hospitals
LONGFIELD Longfield for Fawkham and Hartley Longfield Fawkham for Hartley and Longfield Fawkham Fawkham Road	59 / 6A	P G	12/06/1872 *12/06/1872*	N/A *??/05/1962*	LCDR	Opened as 'Fawkham Road', 'Road' dropped by 1875. Became 'Fawkham for Hartley and Longfield' 1895/6 Renamed 'Longfield for Fawkham and Hartley' 12/06/1961, then 'Longfield' 1968/72. Single carriage siding present on 'up' side, two-road goods yard on 'down', all closed May 1962 (eleven months after June 1961 re-naming per kentrail.org.uk)
LONGFIELD HALT	59 / 5A		01/07/1913	03/08/1953	SECR	Opened by SECR on existing LCDR Gravesend West branch, closed with entire branch 03/08/1953
Longhedge Junctions	39 / 4A & 82		02/03/1863	N/A	WLER / LBSCR	
LORD'S St John's Wood St John's Wood Road	25 / 5D		13/04/1868	20/11/1939	MET	Opened as 'St John's Wood Road', 'Road' suffix dropped 01/04/1925, renamed 'Lord's' 11/06/1939, closed 20/11/1939 and replaced by St John's Wood Station (Bakerloo Line) to north
LORDSHIP LANE	54 / 1A		01/09/1865	20/09/1954	LCDR	Closed 01/01/1917 - 01/03/1919 and 22/05/1944 - 04/03/1946. Closed for good 20/09/1954
LOUGHBOROUGH JUNCTION Loughborough Road	39 / 5C		??/10/1864	N/A	LCDR	First platforms opened on Brixton Spur October 1864 as 'Loughborough Road'. Platforms on lines to Herne Hill and Cambria Spur added 01/12/1872 and station renamed 'Loughborough Junction'. Line to Herne Hill originally quadruple track, one 'up' track removed to make room for island platform while two 'down' roads retained. Post-1925 middle 'down' road removed, side 'down' platform closed, and island platform widened into space vacated by middle 'down' road. Brixton Spur platforms closed 03/04/1916, Cambria Spur platforms closed 12/07/1925 **The above dates are per Borley and Quick, Mitchell & Smith in 'Holborn Viaduct to Lewisham' state that the Brixton Spur platforms were named 'Brixton Junction' upon opening, and the platforms on the Herne Hill route and Cambria Spur opened 01/07/1872 as 'Loughborough Road', before the entire station complex was renamed as 'Loughborough Junction' 01/12/1872*
Loughborough Junction	39 / 5C		01/05/1863	N/A	LCDR	Junctions at north end of Brixton and Cambria Spurs (latter added 01/07/1872)
LOUGHTON (ECR)	8 / 5D	P G	22/08/1856 *22/08/1856*	24/04/1865 *18/04/1966*	ECR	Original terminus of ECR branch from Stratford, sited just south of the High Road. Closed to passengers when line extended to Ongar 24/04/1865. Line lifted beyond a relocated goods station c.1866, second goods yard remaining open until 18/04/1966
LOUGHTON (GER)	8 / 6D		24/04/1865	N/A	GER	Station built to replace original ECR terminus on extension to Ongar, re-sited to east 28/04/1940 by LNER in readiness for LTE services. Majority of passenger services transferred to LTE 21/11/1948 when LTE service commenced (terminus until 25/09/1949), but first trains in the morning remained British Rail services until 01/06/1970
Loughton Junction	27 / 2D		22/08/1856	03/05/1971	ECR	Divergence of ECR Loughton Branch from NER Lea Valley Line. Closed 03/05/1971, dismantled 29/10/1972
LOUGHTON SIDINGS	8 / 6D		*21/11/1948*	N/A	LTE (CEN)	Stabling Sidings for Central Line
Low Level Curve	26 / 2A & 9	P G	17/12/1900 *17/12/1900*	05/01/1981 *05/01/1981*	MID	Curve between THJR and MID 'slow' passenger lines at Kentish Town, abandoned when Barking trains diverted from Kentish Town to Gospel Oak
LOW STREET	46 / 4C	P G	??/07/1861 *??/07/1861*	05/06/1967 *28/09/1964*	LTSR	Exact opening date unknown; first appeared in Bradshaw July 1861. Goods yard closed 28/09/1964, passenger station followed 05/06/1967
LOWER EDMONTON (LOW LEVEL) Edmonton (Low Level) Edmonton	15 / 1B	P G	01/03/1849 *01/03/1849*	11/09/1939 *07/12/1964*	ECR	Opened as 'Edmonton' on original ECR Enfield Branch from Angel Road. 'Low Level' suffix added 22/07/1872 with opening of 'High Level' station. Renamed 'Lower Edmonton (Low Level)' 01/07/1883. Became passenger terminus 01/08/1872 when High Level platforms commenced Enfield (Town) service, closed to passengers 11/09/1939, goods yard closed 07/12/1964 along with entire Angel Road to Lower Edmonton Junction route
Lower Edmonton Junction	15 / 1B		01/08/1872	07/12/1964	GER	Angel Road Junction to Lower Edmonton Junction closed to goods 07/12/1964
LOWER SYDENHAM	54 / 3C	P G	01/01/1857 *c.1857*	N/A *20/06/1966*	MKR	Station re-sited south 1906 (no more precise date known). Goods yard opened 'probably' 1857 per Borley, but is not apparent on 1863 OS map, and cannot be discerned before 1895 survey. Originally short siding north of 'down' platform, much extended through site of original 'down' platform after 1906. Yard closed 20/06/1966
LOWER SYDENHAM GASWORKS	54 / 2C		*??/??/1878*	*22/04/1969*	PRIV	Works established 1854, rail connected since 1878. Closed 22/04/1969, rail connection severed 1971
Lucas Street Tunnels	40 / 4C		30/07/1849	N/A	SER	
LUDGATE HILL	26 / 6C & 32 / 5B		21/12/1864	02/03/1929	LCDR	Terminus until extension to Farringdon opened 01/01/1866. Two island platforms until 1910, when eastern island removed and western island widened
Ludgate Hill Junction	32 / 4B		02/03/1874	29/01/1990	LCDR	Divergence of Holborn Viaduct Branch
Ludgate Junction	38 / 5D		02/03/1863	N/A	LSWR / WLER	
LYONS WORKS (GREENFORD)	23 / 3B		*??/??/1920*	*??/??/1970*	PRIV	

M

MAIDA VALE	25 / 5C		06/06/1915	N/A	UERL (BSWR)	
MAIDEN LANE (GNR)	26 / 4B & 75		07/08/1850	14/10/1852	GNR	London terminus of GNR until King's Cross opened. Also referred to as 'King's Cross'. Trainshed roof retained after closure to passengers as Potato market
MAIDEN LANE (NLR)	26 / 3B & 75		01/07/1887	01/01/1917	NLR	Platforms only ever provided on unelectrified northern 'No.1' NLR lines (original southern lines were 'No.2')
Maiden Lane Curve	75	P G	10/01/1863 *10/01/1863*	10/01/1863 *10/01/1863*	GNR	West-facing curve between MET and GNR York Road Curve. Crossed Hotel Curve on level. Possibly never used
Maiden Lane Junction	75		24/06/1867	??/05/1968	NLR	Junction accessing Maiden Lane goods (later York Way Freightliner terminal)
MAIDEN LANE GOODS	26 / 3B & 75		*24/06/1867*	*??/??/1965*	NLR	Initially cattle only, general goods from 07/01/1868. Site subsequently occupied by York Way Freightliner terminal
MALDEN MANOR	64 / 1C		29/05/1938	N/A	SR	
MANOR HOUSE	14 / 6D		19/09/1932	N/A	UERL (GNPBR)	
MANOR PARK Manor Park & Little Ilford Manor Park for Little Ilford	28 / 2C	P G	06/01/1873 *??/??/1882*	N/A *01/01/1968*	GER	Suffixes 'for Little Ilford' or '& Little Ilford' sometimes used 1895 - 1940. Goods yard opened 1882, closed 01/01/1968
MANOR ROAD GOODS	27 / 1A		*??/12/1872*	*07/12/1964*	GER	
MANOR SIDINGS	44 / 4D		*c.1960's*	N/A	BR	Disused
MANOR WAY Manor Road	42 / 1A & 62 / 3D		??/07/1881	09/09/1940	LSKD	Opened July 1881 as 'Manor Road', renamed 'Manor Way' June 1882. Initially single track, doubled 01/04/1882 Original station west of road bridge demolished and replaced by new station east of bridge c.1887. Operated by GER after 1896, ownership later transferred to PLA. Branch closed from 09/09/1940 due to 'Black Saturday' air raid 07/09/1940 (no trains on Sundays since 27/06/1915). Listed as 'Royal Albert Dock, Manor Way' in Borley
MANSION HOUSE	26 / 6D & 32 / 5D		03/07/1871	N/A	MDR	Terminus of District Railway until 06/10/1884. Closed 29/10/1989 - 11/02/1991 (rebuilding works)
MARBLE ARCH	25 / 6D		30/07/1900	N/A	CLR	
MARLBOROUGH ROAD	25 / 4C		13/04/1868	20/11/1939	MET	Replaced by St John's Wood station (Bakerloo Line) to south
MARYLAND Maryland Point	28 / 3A		06/01/1873	N/A	GER	Renamed 28/10/1940
Maryland East Crossovers	28 / 3A		?	N/A	BR	
MARYLEBONE Great Central (UERL only)	25 / 5D		15/03/1899	N/A	GCR	Terminus of Great Central Railway. UERL BSWR platforms opened as 'Great Central' 27/03/1907, were terminus until 15/06/1907, renamed to 'Marylebone' 15/04/1917 ('Great Central' tiling remains at platform level) NR station closed 15/08/2011 - 22/08/2011 (engineering work at Neasden South Junction)
MARYLEBONE GOODS & COAL	25 / 5C		*11/04/1899*	*28/03/1966*	GCR	Coal & minerals traffic commenced 11/04/1899, general goods commenced 27/04/1899
MAYER-PARRY SCRAP (WILLESDEN)	24 / 5D & 86		*c.1960's*	N/A	PRIV	Car-crushing plant. Opened in 1960's on site of former LNWR electric carriage sidings
MAZE HILL Maze Hill (for National Maritime Museum) Maze Hill & East Greenwich Maze Hill & Greenwich Park Maze Hill & East Greenwich Greenwich (Maze Hill)	41 / 3A		01/01/1873	N/A	SER	Opened as terminus of short branch from Charlton 01/01/1873 as 'Greenwich (Maze Hill)'. Through line to original Greenwich station opened and station renamed 'Maze Hill & East Greenwich' 01/02/1878. Became 'Maze Hill & Greenwich Park' 01/07/1878, reverted to 'Maze Hill & East Greenwich' (or 'Maze Hill [East Greenwich]') 01/01/1899 Suffix dropped and became 'Maze Hill' ??/04/1937 (Borley), although alternative suffix 'for National Maritime Museum' referred to in Quick, with this being dropped in 1955. Two 'down' roads flanked an island platform, with 5 carriage sidings on the 'down' side and 6 on the 'up' (including a 2-road carriage shed). Carriage sidings were never electrified and had ceased to be used by North Kent Line full electrification (1962). Signal box abolished 29/11/1969
Maze Hill Tunnel	41 / 3A		01/02/1878	N/A	SER	
MCVITIE & PRICE'S SIDING	24 / 4B		*??/??/1902*	?	PRIV	Later United Biscuits

NAME: (Previous names indented below)	Page / grid:	Date opened:	Date closed:	Opening company:	NOTES:
MERSTHAM	73 / 3D	P early 1842	N/A	LBRR	Quick states opened with line 12/07/1841, but LBRR Board minute of 01/07/1841 refers to tender for construction being delayed, and a further minute from 16/12/1841 refers to permission being granted for construction spoil to be deposited on adjacent land owned by The Countess of Warwick. An SER board minute from 30/05/1842 refers to consideration of 'pulling down' or 'shutting up' Merstham, so it appears to have opened by this date. Closed by SER 02/10/1843, re-opened 04/10/1844 pending completion of new (current) station to north, re-sited c.1845
		G early 1842	c.1965		
Merstham Tunnel	73 / 5A	12/07/1841	N/A	LBRR	
MERTON ABBEY	52 / 4C	P 01/10/1868	03/03/1929	LBSCR / LSWR	Closed to passengers 01/01/1917 - 27/08/1923, then again for good 03/03/1929 (passenger service Tooting Junction to Merton Park withdrawn). Goods yard remained open until 01/05/1972 (Borley), although the closure date of line from Merton Park to Merton Abbey is given as 05/05/1975 in Borley, so private goods traffic may have remained until latter date, or this may merely be the date of official closure of the route by BR
		G 01/10/1868	01/05/1972		
MERTON PARK	52 / 4B	01/10/1868	N/A	LBSCR / LSWR	Opened by LBSCR & LSWR on their joint loop line from Streatham to Wimbledon as 'Lower Merton', initially platforms on this route only (none on WCRR route), single platform on WCRR route added 01/11/1870. Renamed 'Merton Park' 01/09/1887. Platforms on route to Tooting Junction closed 01/01/1917 - 27/08/1923, then again for good 03/03/1929 Platform on Wimbledon to Croydon route sometimes had 'Halt' added on timetables / tickets 1918 - 1923/4 Closed 02/06/1997 (last train 31/05/1997, no Sunday service), re-opened by Croydon Tramlink 30/05/2000
Lower Merton					
Merton Park Junction	52 / 4B	01/10/1868	05/05/1975	LBSCR / LSWR	
Metropolitan Junctions	39 / 1D & 72 / 6C	01/09/1866	N/A	SER	Junction with curve to Blackfriars opened 01/06/1878. Curve to Cannon Street proposed to be abandoned due to Thameslink-related remodelling of Metropolitan Junction
Mickleham Tunnel	70 / 6C	11/03/1867	N/A	LBSCR	
MIDDLE SIDINGS (SHENFIELD)	20 / 5B	01/01/1934	N/A	LNER	
MIDDLESEX OIL & CHEMICAL WORKS	21 / 6C	c.1964	??/??/1976	PRIV	Last section of GWR Uxbridge (Vine Street) Branch to close
MILDMAY PARK	26 / 3D	01/01/1880	01/10/1934	NLR	
MILE END (ECR)	27 / 5B	c.1841	24/05/1872	ECR	Replaced Devonshire Street, Mile End station to east, later replaced by Bethnal Green Junction station to West
MILE END (MDR)	27 / 5C	02/06/1902	N/A	MDR / LTSR	Served by Metropolitan Line since 30/03/1936 ('Hammersmith & City Line' since 30/07/1990). LPTB Central Line platforms opened 04/12/1946
MILE END GOODS	27 / 5C	??/??/1850	06/11/1967	ECR	Opened as 'Devonshire Street Goods', prefix 'Mile End &' added 01/09/1922, suffix '& Devonshire Street' dropped 01/01/1939
Mile End & Devonshire Street Goods					
Devonshire Street Goods					
MILEAGE YARD	25 / 6B & 67 / 5A	c.1850's	17/07/1967	GWR	Yard was in situ by 1863, originally referred to as 'Crimea Yard' which may suggest opening date between October 1853 and February 1856 (Crimean War). Closed 17/07/1967.
Crimea Yard					
MILL HILL BROADWAY	12 / 2C	P 13/07/1868	N/A	MID	Goods yard opened first; 09/03/1868, passenger station opened 13/07/1868. Suffix 'Broadway' added 25/09/1950, although goods yard was renamed previously (01/07/1950). Goods yard closed 03/08/1964
Mill Hill		G 09/03/1868	03/08/1964		
MILL HILL EAST	13 / 3A	P 22/08/1867	N/A	GNR	Opened as 'Mill Hill', suffix 'for Mill Hill Barracks' added 17/04/1916, renamed 'Mill Hill East for Mill Hill Barracks' 01/02/1928. Closed by LNER 11/09/1939 to allow transfer to LPTB, doubling, and electrification (reopened by LPTB 18/05/1941 as terminus), but electrification only reached Mill Hill East and second track to Mill Hill (The Hale) dismantled without being used. Goods yard closed 01/10/1962.
Mill Hill East for Mill Hill Barracks		G 22/08/1867	01/10/1962		
Mill Hill for Mill Hill Barracks					
Mill Hill					
MILL HILL (THE HALE)	12 / 2C	P 11/06/1906	11/09/1939	GNR	Goods yard opened 18/07/1910. Originally opened as 'The Hale Halt', renamed 'Mill Hill (The Hale)' 01/03/1928 Closed to passengers 11/09/1939 to enable doubling and electrification of Finchley Central to Edgware prior to transfer to LPTB Northern Line. Works abandoned and station did not re-open. Goods yard closed 29/02/1964
The Hale Halt		G 18/07/1910	29/02/1964		
MILLWALL DOCKS	40 / 2D	18/12/1871	04/05/1926	MER	Terminus until 29/07/1872, before this date a temporary station served by horse-drawn trains, after this date reconstructed as a permanent station south of Glengall Road. Often also referred to as 'Millwall Dock' Passenger service to Blackwall and North Greenwich withdrawn 04/05/1926. Crossharbour DLR on same site.
MILLWALL GOODS	40 / 2D	18/12/1871	01/06/1925	MER	Goods station closed 01/06/1925, but goods trains continued to serve the adjacent dock
MILLWALL JUNCTION	40 / 1D & 31 / 4B	P 18/12/1871	04/05/1926	LBLR / MER	Opening coincided with that of Millwall Extension Railway to Millwall Docks. Rebuilt & resited 1888, two platform faces on Blackwall route, one on route to North Greenwich. Passenger services withdrawn from both 04/05/1926
		G 18/12/1871	14/11/1927	LBLR	
MILTON RANGE HALT	60 / 2D	01/07/1906	17/07/1932	SECR	Removed from timetables 17/07/1932, only served 'as required' for adjacent rifle ranges thereafter. Rebuilt in concrete 1954 (previously wood), continued to be served until at least 1956, local services ceased on route 04/12/1961, even then station did not 'officially' close and platforms remained standing until 2008 (up) / 2009 (down)
MILTON ROAD HALT	60 / 1B	01/07/1906	01/05/1915	SECR	Closed as a WW1 economy, did not re-open
MINORIES	27 / 6A & 74 / 2B	06/07/1840	24/10/1853	LBLR	Original LBLR London terminus. Replaced by Fenchurch Street, although both open until 15/02/1849 (Minories closed) then again 09/09/1849 - 24/10/1853 (Minories re-opened, then closed again for good)
Minories Junction	27 / 6A & 74 / 1B	06/10/1884	N/A	MDR / MET	
MITCHAM	52 / 6D	P 22/10/1855	N/A	WCRR	Station opened by WCRR as only intermediate station between Wimbledon and Croydon, 2 platforms from outset (passing loop on single line), following a landslip in 1971 'up' (northern) abandoned. Goods yard closed 01/05/1967, passenger station closed 02/06/1997 (last train 31/05/1997, no Sunday service), re-opened on a new site slightly to east by Croydon Tramlink 30/05/2000
		G 22/10/1855	01/05/1967		
MITCHAM EASTFIELDS	52 / 5D	02/06/2008	N/A	NR	Opened during afternoon of 02/06/2008, platforms staggered either side of level crossing
MITCHAM JUNCTION	52 / 6D	01/10/1868	N/A	LBSCR	Station opened with Streatham - Sutton line (no station on WCRR line prior to this). Separate Croydon Tramlink platforms opened 30/05/2000 following withdrawal of Wimbledon - West Croydon NR trains 02/06/1997
Mitre Bridge Curve	24 / 5D & 86	P 02/09/1867	N/A	LNWR	Loop built to connect WLR with HJR
		G 02/09/1867	N/A		
MITRE BRIDGE EXCHANGE PLATFORMS	24 / 5D & 86	27/05/1844	01/12/1844	GWR / WLR	Exchange platforms built for traffic between WLR / GWR, abandoned when WLR passenger services ceased Location of GWR platforms uncertain, WLR and GWR crossed each other on the level at this location until 1860
MITRE BRIDGE GOODS	24 / 5D & 86	c.1870	c.1965	LNWR	Sidings had appeared by 1870 OS and been removed by 1975, dates not listed in Borley
Mitre Bridge Junction	24 / 5D & 86	02/09/1867	N/A	LNWR	
MONUMENT	26 / 6D & 72 / 4C	06/10/1884	N/A	MDR / MET	Opened as 'Eastcheap', renamed 'The Monument' 01/11/1884, 'The' prefix gradually dropped
The Monument					
Eastcheap					
MOOR PARK	10 / 1A	P 09/05/1910	N/A	MET / GCR	Opened as 'Sandy Lodge', 'Moor Park' prefix after 18/10/1923, 'Sandy Lodge' suffix dropped 25/09/1950 Goods yard closed ??/06/1938. Rebuilt with two new island platforms for quadrupling 23/04/1961
Moor Park & Sandy Lodge		G 09/05/1910	??/06/1938		
Sandy Lodge					
MOORGATE	26 / 6D	23/12/1865	N/A	MET	City Widened Lines platforms opened 01/07/1866, closed 22/03/2009, CSLR platforms opened 25/02/1900. GNCR (later Northern Line, then British Rail) platforms opened 14/02/1904. Station renamed 24/10/1924
Moorgate Street					
MORDEN	52 / 5B	13/09/1926	N/A	UERL (NOR)	Southern terminus of LU Northern Line
MORDEN DEPOT	52 / 6B	13/09/1926	N/A	UERL (NOR)	
MORDEN ROAD	52 / 4B	??/03/1857	N/A	WCRR	Did not open with WCRR, first appeared in timetables March 1857 as 'Morden'. Removed from timetables October & November 1918, upon re-appearing in December 1918, became 'Morden Halt'. Further renamed 'Morden Road Halt' 02/07/1951. 'Halt' dropped 1968. Closed 02/06/1997 (last train 31/05/1997, no Sunday service), re-opened by Croydon Tramlink 30/05/2000. In its mainline guise, was always a single platform on north side of single track
Morden Road Halt					
Morden Halt					
Morden					
MORDEN SOUTH	52 / 6B	05/01/1930	N/A	SR	
MORNINGTON CRESCENT	26 / 4A	22/06/1907	N/A	UERL (CCEHR)	Closed 23/10/1992 - 27/04/1998 for lift replacement works
Mortimer Street Junction	26 / 2A & 9	17/12/1900	05/01/1981	MID	Junction at north end of Low Level Curve, abandoned after diversion of Barking Trains to Gospel Oak
MORTLAKE	37 / 5B	27/07/1846	N/A	LSWR	Carried '& East Sheen' suffix 01/04/1886 - 30/01/1916
Mortlake & East Sheen					
Mortlake					
Mortlake Junction	37 / 5C	01/02/1862	01/01/1869	LSWR	Junction at south end of Barnes Curve. Barnes Curve disused since 01/01/1869 but not dismantled until 1881
MOTSPUR PARK	51 / 6D	12/07/1925	N/A	SR	
Motspur Park Junction	64 / 1D	29/05/1938	N/A	SR	
MOTTINGHAM	55 / 1D	P 01/09/1866	N/A	SER	Opened as 'Eltham', suffix '& Mottingham' added 01/01/1892. '&' became 'for' 1914, reverted to '&' 1922. 'Eltham' dropped and station became 'Mottingham' 26/09/1927. Six carriage sidings were laid west of the station c.1900, all but one were decommissioned along with the goods yard 07/10/1968. The remaining siding was usually left 'clipped' out of use and eventually lifted
Eltham & Mottingham		G 01/09/1866	07/10/1968		
Eltham for Mottingham					
Eltham & Mottingham					
Eltham					
Mount Street Tunnel	41 / 2C	30/07/1849	N/A	SER	
Mountnessing Junction	20 / 4C	01/01/1934	N/A	LNER	Dive-under for Southend Victoria Branch built by LNER 01/01/1934
MUDCHUTE	40 / 2D	31/08/1987	N/A	DLR	Closed on the night of 09/02/1996 by IRA bomb at South Quay, did not re-open until 15/04/1996. Closed 11/01/1999 due to works on the Lewisham extension, new station at a lower level opened with the extension 20/11/1999
MUSEUM DEPOT	37 / 1A	??/10/1999	N/A	LUL	Opened on part of Ealing Common Depot site (and accessible by rail from there) to house LT Museum exhibits
MUSWELL HILL	14 / 4A	P 24/05/1873	05/07/1954	GNR	Nominally opened by Edgware, Highgate & London Railway, which was absorbed by GNR a month before opening Closed to passengers 01/08/1873 - 01/05/1875 and again 29/10/1951 - 07/01/1952 along with entire branch. Had been intended for electrification and transfer to LT Northern Line, but works abandoned post-WW2. Finally closed to passengers when Alexandra Palace to Finsbury Park service permanently withdrawn 05/07/1954. Goods yard remained in use until 14/06/1956 after which time branch abandoned beyond Cranley Gardens
		G 24/05/1873	14/06/1956		

N

NAME: (Previous names indented below)	Page / grid:		Date opened:	Date closed:	Opening company:	NOTES:
Navarino Road Junction	27 / 3A		30/06/1986	N/A	BR	Junction at north end of Graham Road Curve
NEASDEN	24 / 2C	P	02/08/1880	N/A	MET	Opened as 'Kingsbury & Neasden', renamed 'Neasden & Kingsbury' 01/01/1910, suffix dropped 01/01/1932
Neasden & Kingsbury		G	01/01/1894	??/04/1958		Goods yard opened 01/01/1894, closed April 1958. Served by Bakerloo Line 20/11/1939 - 01/05/1979, Jubilee
Kingsbury & Neasden						Line thereafter. Last served regularly by Metropolitan Line 07/12/1940.
NEASDEN COAL	24 / 2C		25/07/1898	04/03/1968	GCR	
Neasden Curve	24 / 2C	P	N/A	N/A	GCR	Curve only regularly used for freight services, originally double track but subsequently singled
		G	01/08/1899	N/A		
NEASDEN DEPOT	24 / 2C		??/??/1882	N/A	MET	Originally Metropolitan Railway Works & Power Station. Substantially rebuilt in 1930s.
						Stabled Bakerloo Line Trains 20/11/1939 - 01/05/1979, Jubilee Line trains thereafter
NEASDEN ENGINE SHED	24 / 3C		15/03/1899	18/06/1961	GCR	
NEASDEN FREIGHT TERMINAL	24 / 2B		05/04/2002	24/03/2007	PRIV	Tibbett & Britten, terminal for imported mineral water. Dates quoted are for beginning of / break in lease of building
						Sidings remain in situ and connected to main line, but obstructed
Neasden Junction	24 / 2C		01/08/1899	N/A	GCR	Junction at southern end of Neasden Curve
Neasden North Junction	24 / 2B		28/04/1923	18/05/1968	LNER	Junctions between Wembley Stadium Loop and former GCR main line
NEASDEN POWER STATION	24 / 1B		??/12/1904	21/07/1968	MET	Metropolitan Railway Power Station, came online December 1904, electric services commenced 01/01/1905
Neasden South Junction	24 / 2C		20/11/1905	N/A	GCR	Junction between GCR lines to Aylesbury and 1905 High Wycombe route (first passenger use 01/03/1906)
						Extensively remodelled 15/08/2011 - 22/08/2011
NEASDEN SOUTH SIDINGS	24 / 2B		?	N/A	GCR	
NECROPOLIS	39 / 2C		13/11/1854	11/05/1941	LSWR	Station for funeral traffic to Brookwood Cemetery. Resited south 16/02/1902 (Waterloo station expansion)
						Last recorded funeral departure 11/04/1941. Partially destroyed by air raid night of 16-17/04/1941, officially
						declared closed 11/05/1941.
NEW ADDINGTON	67 / 5D		10/05/2000	N/A	CTL	
NEW BARNET	5 / 5D	P	07/08/1850	N/A	GNR	Prefix 'New' added 01/05/1884. Goods yard closed 22/08/1966
Barnet		G	07/08/1850	22/08/1966		
NEW BECKENHAM	54 / 4C		01/04/1864	N/A	MKR	Opening coincided with MKR route from here to Addiscombe. Original site south of current station and junction, it is
						thought that there were four platform faces serving the Addiscombe and Beckenham Junction routes. Replaced by
						current 2-platform station to north c.1868 (Borley) / 1866-8 (Quick) / 1866 (Mitchell & Smith). Jackson provides the
						most detail; with the original station closing 'autumn 1866' and the replacement opening 'from October 1866, if not
						a little earlier'. There was a central through road in use 1904 - 1926" to facilitate joining / dividing of trains
						*Jackson states track removed 1926, Mitchell & Smith states road eliminated 1929
New Beckenham Junction	54 / 4C		01/04/1864	N/A	MKR	
NEW CROSS (SER)	40 / 4C & 79 / 80		??/10/1850	N/A	SER	Precise opening date unknown, October 1850. SER began running own trains over ELR 01/04/1880, separate bay
						platform for ELR added on 'down' side 01/10/1884. Served by MDR 01/10/1884 - 06/10/1884 only. Served by MET
						06/10/1884 - 03/12/1906, then again 31/03/1913 onwards, gaining separate 'East London Line' identity during 1980's
						No LUL service 25/03/1995 - 25/03/1998 (engineering work), withdrawn for good 23/12/2007. Former LUL bay
						re-opened by TfL (LOROL) 27/04/2010
NEW CROSS (ELR)	40 / 4C & 79		07/12/1869	01/09/1886	ELR	Original ELR southern terminus. Closed 01/11/1876 - 01/10/1884, MDR service commenced 06/10/1884,
						station closed entirely 01/09/1886 and all services diverted to adjacent New Cross (Gate). Sometimes
						differentiated from New Cross (Gate) by use of 'Low Level' suffix. At times ELR used both this and New Cross
						(Gate) station for terminating services
NEW CROSS DEPOT	40 / 3C & 79		31/03/1913	23/12/2007	MET	Carriage shed built for ELR electrification, MET EMU stabling. Closed with ELL prior to transfer to TfL (LOROL)
NEW CROSS GATE	40 / 4C & 79 / 80		05/06/1839	N/A	LCRR	Served by ELR 01/11/1876 - 01/10/1884. Served by MDR 01/09/1886 - 01/08/1905. Served by MET 31/03/1913
New Cross						onwards, gaining separate 'East London Line' identity during 1980's. 'Gate' suffix added 09/07/1923.
						No LUL service 25/03/1995 - 25/03/1998 (engineering work), withdrawn for good 23/12/2007.
						Served by TfL (LOROL) services since 27/04/2010 (terminus until 23/05/2010)
NEW CROSS GATE DEPOT	40 / 3C & 80		27/04/2010	N/A	TFL (LOROL)	LOROL depot opened coinciding with re-opening / transfer of ELL 27/04/2010, replaced former New Cross Depot
New Cross Gate Down Junction	40 / 4C & 79 / 80		01/11/1876	N/A	NR	Re-established 23/05/20120 due to LOROL extension to West Croydon / Crystal Palace. Connection between ELR
						and LBSCR first formed 01/11/1876 to north of New Cross (Gate) station, junction for 'down' trains relocated
						to present site in late 19th century. Direct connection between LTE and BR removed 17/09/1972. Indirect
						connection between LTE and BR carriage / permanent way sidings removed 12/01/1975. Access to sidings
						remained from south until their abandonment c.1990, current junction established on same site
New Cross Gate Up Junction	40 / 4C & 79 / 80		23/05/2010	N/A	NR	Junction eliminated after 27/04/1966, re-established 23/05/2010 for new flyover (LOROL)
NEW CROSS GOODS	40 / 4C & 79		05/06/1839	06/11/1967	LCRR	Goods yard opened with New Cross (Gate) passenger station, expanded over the years and became GER owned,
						occupying site of New Cross (ELR) station and area to immediate east. Closed 06/11/1967, carriage sidings then
						occupying part of site until c.1990
NEW CROSS LOCO WORKS & ENGINE SHEDS	40 / 4C & 79		05/06/1839	14/06/1947	LCRR	LCRR's original loco works / shed, first shed being an octagonal 'roundhouse'. Loco works subsequently transferred
						to Brighton by LBSCR. Additional engine sheds added ('Middle' and 'New'), as well as carriage works and sidings
						Depot officially closed 14/06/1947, but locos continued to stable until 1951. Sheds demolished 1957, replaced
						by carriage sidings which remained until c.1990 when removed for supermarket development (opened 1996)
New Croydon Line	66 / 1D		c.1865	??/10/1983	LBSCR	in situ by 1870 OS, eliminated during 1983 remodelling of Gloucester Road Triangle
NEW ELTHAM	56 / 2A	P	01/04/1878	N/A	SER	Opened as 'Pope Street', prefix 'New Eltham &' added 01/01/1886, suffix 'Pope Street' dropped 26/09/1927
New Eltham & Pope Street		G	01/04/1878	13/05/1963		Goods yard closed 13/05/1963 (Borley), Jackson states November 1965
Pope Street						
New Guildford Line Junction	63 / 1B		02/02/1885	N/A	LSWR	
New Kew Junction	37 / 3A & 19		01/02/1862	N/A	LSWR	Junction at south end of Kew Curve. 'Up' road extended 220 metres west 1932
NEW MALDEN	51 / 5C		??/12/1846	N/A	LSWR	Opened as 'Malden', exact opening date uncertain, first in timetable December 1846. Renamed 'New Malden &
Malden						Coombe' May 1859, then 'Coombe & Malden' March 1862, 'Malden for Coombe' November 1912, 'Malden' 1955, then
Malden for Coombe						finally 'New Malden' 16/09/1957. Goods yard was remote from station (see separate entry)
Coombe & Malden						
New Malden & Coombe						
Malden						
NEW MALDEN GOODS	51 / 5B		c.1869	03/08/1964	LSWR	Borley states goods opened with passenger station, but no facilities are evident on contemporary OS maps
						Remote from passenger station, accessed from Kingston Loop, which precludes an opening date before 01/01/1869
						Single siding evident on 1868 OS (Kingston loop depicted although not opened until 01/01/1869). Closed 03/08/1964
New Malden Junction	51 / 5C		??/??/1883	N/A	LSWR	Junction between LSWR main line and Kingston Loop. No physical connection until 1883
NEW SOUTHGATE	14 / 2A	P	07/08/1850	N/A	GNR	Opened as 'Colney Hatch & Southgate', reversed to 'Southgate & Colney Hatch' 01/02/1855. Prefix 'New' added
New Southgate & Friern Barnet		G	07/08/1850	07/12/1970		01/10/1876, became 'New Southgate for Colney Hatch' 01/03/1883. Platforms originally staggered with 'up' south
New Southgate for Colney Hatch						of 'down', rearranged April 1890. Renamed 'New Southgate & Friern Barnet' 01/05/1923, suffix dropped 18/03/1971.
New Southgate & Colney Hatch						Closed 25/12/1976 - 14/02/1977 (fire), goods yard closed 07/12/1970.
Southgate & Colney Hatch						
Colney Hatch & Southgate						
NEW WANDSWORTH	38 / 6C	P	29/03/1858	01/11/1869	WELCPR	Passenger station closed 01/11/1869, goods yard 07/10/1968
		G	29/03/1858	07/10/1968		
NEWBURY PARK	17 / 6B	P	01/05/1903	N/A	GER	LNER Fairlop Loop closed to passengers 30/11/1947 to allow electrification and transfer to Central Line.
		G	01/05/1903	04/10/1965		Station re-opened by LPTB Central Line as terminus from Leytonstone 14/12/1947 (until Hainault extension opened
						31/05/1948). Goods yard closed 04/10/1965
Newbury Park Junction	29 / 1B		20/04/1903	30/11/1947	GER	Junction at north end of Newbury Park Junction to Ilford Carriage Sidings Junction curve
NEWBURY PARK SIDINGS	17 / 6B		14/12/1947	?	GER	Opened for Central Line extension from Leytonstone, but lightly used after Hainault Depot's full opening 31/05/1948
NEWINGTON VESTRY DEPOT	39 / 3D		?	?	LCDR	
NINE ELMS	39 / 3B & 57	P	21/05/1838	11/07/1848	LSWR	LSWR London terminus until Waterloo opened. Remained in use for goods traffic until 29/07/1968 ('North' goods)
		G	21/05/1838	29/07/1968		
NINE ELMS DEPOT	39 / 4A & 57		??/??/1885	??/??/1967	LSWR	Locomotive sheds
Nine Elms Junction	39 / 3A & 82		17/08/1994	N/A	RT	Date quoted is start of trial Eurostar service, advertised service commenced 14/11/1994. Little used since 14/11/2007
						(diversion of Eurostar to St Pancras), but chord still in situ and traversed by test trains
NINE ELMS ROYAL STATION	39 / 3B & 57		??/??/1854	??/??/1876	LSWR	Station provided for exclusive use of Queen Victoria
NINE ELMS SOUTH	39 / 3B		??/??/2020	N/A	LUL (NOR)	Intermediate station on proposed Northern Line extension from Kennington to Battersea
NINE ELMS SOUTH GOODS (formerly locomotive works)	39 / 4B & 57		??/??/1843	29/07/1968	LSWR	Opened as LSWR's loco works, which transferred to Eastleigh in 1909. Site then became 'South' goods yard
NINE ELMS, SOUTH LAMBETH GOODS	39 / 4A & 82		??/??/1911	??/??/1980	GWR	Renamed 29/07/1968
South Lambeth Goods						
NOEL PARK & WOOD GREEN	14 / 4C	P	01/01/1878	07/01/1963	GER	Initially terminus of branch from Seven Sisters, until Palace Gates extension opened 07/10/1878
Green Lanes & Noel Park		G	01/01/1878	07/12/1964		Opened as 'Green Lanes', Suffix '& Noel Park' added 01/05/1884, renamed 'Noel Park & Wood Green' 01/01/1902
Green Lanes						Station and entire Palace Gates Branch closed to passengers 07/01/1963, goods yard closed 07/12/1964

NAME: (Previous names indented below)	Page / grid:		Date opened:	Date closed:	Opening company:	NOTES:
NORBITON	51 / 4A	P	01/01/1869	N/A	LSWR	Various suffixes used from opening; 'and Kingston Hill' initially, dropped 1890. 'for Kingston Hill and Richmond Park' 1894, 'for Kingston Hill' 1914, dropped again and became 'Norbiton' 1955. Goods yard closed 03/05/1965
Norbiton for Kingston Hill		G	*01/01/1869*	*03/05/1965*		
Norbiton for Kingston Hill and Richmond Park						
Norbiton						
Norbiton and Kingston Hill						
NORBURY	53 / 4B		01/01/1878	N/A	LBSCR	
NORTH ACTON	24 / 5C & 86		05/11/1923	N/A	UERL / GWR	Platforms built on GWR Birmingham main line and electrified lines used by UERL Central Line. Central pair of GWR goods lines did not have platform faces provided. GWR Birmingham main line platforms closed 30/06/1947, after this date station served by Central Line only. Central pair of goods-only lines abandoned 09/03/1964, the 'down' line subsequently being re-used as the LU Central Line Eastbound road, allowing the original eastbound to become a central reversible road after 22/03/1993
NORTH ACTON HALT	24 / 5B		01/05/1904	01/02/1913	GWR	
North Acton Junction (1)	24 / 5B		30/06/1947	N/A	LPTB (CEN)	Junction between Central Line and extension to Greenford (later West Ruislip)
North Acton Junction (2)	24 / 5B		16/04/1917	09/03/1964	GWR	Junction between GWR Birmingham Main Line and route ex-Viaduct Junction
NORTH DULWICH	39 / 6D		01/10/1868	N/A	LBSCR	
NORTH EALING	24 / 6A		23/06/1903	N/A	MDR	First served Piccadilly Line 04/07/1932, last served District Line 22/10/1933
NORTH END (or BULL & BUSH)	25 / 1C		N/A	N/A	UERL (CCEHR)	Platforms built but station buildings and platform access never completed. Access stairway sunk c.1950's
NORTH GREENWICH (LUL)	41 / 1A		14/05/1999	N/A	LUL (JUB)	Three platform faces from outset, layout to facilitate possible future branch towards Royal Docks
NORTH GREENWICH (MER)	40 / 3D		29/07/1872	04/05/1926	MER	Suffix '(Cubitt Town)' or '& Cubitt Town' sometimes used. Services to North Greenwich and Blackwall ceased 04/05/1926, subsequent DLR station at Island Gardens slightly to north (north side of Manchester Road)
NORTH HARROW	11 / 5A		22/03/1915	N/A	MET / GCR	
North Junction (Mitcham)	52 / 6D		01/10/1868	02/06/1997	LBSCR	Junction eliminated when Wimbledon to West Croydon line closed 02/06/1997 prior to conversion to Tramlink
North Kent East Junction	40 / 3C & 79 / 80		30/07/1849	N/A	LGR / SER	
North Kent Line Connection	45 / 6B		14/11/2007	N/A	LCOR / NR	Junction between HS1 and North Kent Line
North London Incline (GNR)	75 / 76	P	N/A	N/A	GNR	No regular passenger service. Originally double track. Re-aligned during HS1 works to a more southerly route
		G	*??/??/1853*	N/A		
North London Incline (MID)	75	P	N/A	N/A	MID	No regular passenger service
		G	*??/??/1867*	*31/12/1975*		
North London Incline Junction	75		??/??/1867	31/12/1975	MID	
NORTH MIDDLESEX GASWORKS	13 / 3A		*??/??/1869*	*01/10/1962*	PRIV	Jackson gives dates as 1886-1956 (Borley dates quoted)
NORTH POLE DEPOT	24 / 5D & 86		*11/11/1992*	*14/11/2007*	ES	Official opening 11/11/1992 although revenue earning Eurostar operations did not begin until 14/11/1994. Closed when Temple Mills Depot opened 14/11/2007. Mothballed for future use by First GreatWestern
North Pole Junction	24 / 5D & 86		??/10/1860	N/A	WLR / GWR	Formerly provided connection to GWR Main Line, now only North Pole Depot (currently disused)
NORTH SHED (QUEENS PARK)	25 / 4A		*11/02/1915*	N/A	UERL (BAK)	Stabling Shed for Bakerloo Line
NORTH SHEEN	37 / 5A		06/07/1930	N/A	SR	
NORTH WEALD	8 / 1C	P	24/04/1865	N/A	GER	Epping to Ongar transferred to LTE 25/09/1949, Electrified 18/11/1957. Between these dates passenger services provided by BR (steam). Line closed by LUL 30/09/1994, re-opened by Epping-Ongar Railway between Ongar and North Weald 10/10/2004, closed 31/12/2007 for engineering works, re-opened 25/05/2012. Goods yard closed 06/01/1964
		G	*24/04/1865*	*06/01/1964*		
NORTH WEMBLEY	23 / 1D	P	15/06/1912	N/A	LNWR	Referred to as 'East Lane' before opening. Goods yard opened before passenger station 31/10/1910, passenger station opened 15/06/1912, goods yard closed 05/05/1965. Served by Bakerloo Line since 16/04/1917, but no service 27/09/1982 (last train 24/09/1982) - 04/06/1984
		G	*31/10/1910*	*05/07/1965*		
NORTH WOOLWICH	41 / 2D & 62 / 4D	P	14/06/1847	10/12/2006	ECR	Closed 08/09/1940 - 01/01/1941 (air raid damage), 29/05/1994 - 29/10/1995 (Jubilee Line extension works), then permanently 10/12/2006 (closure of North Woolwich branch for partial conversion to DLR). Formerly three platform faces with a central run-around siding and turntable. Reduced to one platform after 25/08/1969 singling east of Custom House, platform then switched from 'down' to 'up' side with 1979 rebuilding. Goods yard closed 07/12/1970
		G	*14/06/1847*	*07/12/1970*		
NORTHFIELDS	36 / 1D		16/04/1908	N/A	UERL (MDR)	Opened as 'Northfield (Ealing)', renamed 'Northfields & Little Ealing' 11/12/1911. Relocated east and renamed 'Northfields' 18/12/1932 due to opening of Northfields Depot. First served by Piccadilly Line 09/01/1933 (terminus) District Line service ceased 10/10/1964
Northfields & Little Ealing						
Northfield (Ealing)						
NORTHFIELDS DEPOT	36 / 2C		*??/??/1932*	N/A	UERL (MDR)	Opened first half of 1932 (before July). Used by Piccadilly Line since 09/01/1933. Ceased to be regularly used by District Line Trains from 10/10/1964.
NORTHFLEET	59 / 1C	P	01/11/1849	N/A	SER	According to Quick does not appear to have opened with line (30/07/1849), first recorded in timetable alteration 01/11/1849 (kentrail.org.uk states opened with line 30/07/1849). Goods yard closed 09/09/1968
		G	*01/11/1849*	*09/09/1968*		
NORTHFLEET CEMENT WORKS	59 / 1C		*14/12/1970*	*13/03/1993*	PRIV	APCM (later Blue Circle), rail consignments 14/12/1970 - 13/03/1993, Crossrail logistics centre now on site
NORTHFLEET CROSSRAIL LOGISTICS CENTRE	59 / 1C		*27/04/2012*	N/A	PRIV	Crossrail spoil terminal (from Royal Oak portal), re-connected to mainline 10-11/09/2011, first test train 27/04/2012
NORTHFLEET HOPE CONTAINER TERMINAL	45 / 6C		*??/??/1978*	N/A	BR	
NORTHFLEET PAPER MILLS	45 / 6B		*c.1886*	*c.1970*	PRIV	Mills erected 1884-1886, appear to have retained rail connection into 1970's
NORTHOLT (GWR)	23 / 3A	P	01/05/1907	21/11/1948	GWR	Suffix 'Halt' until 23/09/1929. Closed to passengers 21/11/1948 (replaced by LTE station), goods 01/09/1952 Suffix 'for West End Halt' referred to in Dewick, but no reference in Borley or Quick
Northolt Halt		G	*01/05/1907*	*01/09/1952*		
NORTHOLT (LTE)	23 / 3A		21/11/1948	N/A	LTE (CEN)	Replaced BR (former GWR) station closed on same day
Northolt Junction	22 / 2C		02/04/1906	N/A	GCR / GWR	New 'down fast' road commissioned alongside original 'up' 30/08/2011
NORTHOLT PARK	23 / 2A		19/07/1926	N/A	LNER	Opened as 'South Harrow & Roxeth', renamed 'Northolt Park for Northolt Village' 13/05/1929 suffix 'for Northolt Village' dropped 13/06/1955
Northolt Park for Northolt Village						
South Harrow & Roxeth						
Northolt Park Junction	22 / 2D		30/08/2011	N/A	NR	Junction between original 'down' line (now slow) and new down fast (parallel to 'up'), commissioned 30/08/2011
NORTHUMBERLAND PARK	15 / 3B		01/04/1842	N/A	NER	Opening date given as 01/04/1842 in Borley, April / October 1841 in Quick. Probably closed for a period late 1842 / early 1843. Opened as 'Marsh Lane', renamed 'Park' 01/06/1852, 'Northumberland Park' 01/07/1923
Park						
Marsh Lane						
NORTHUMBERLAND PARK DEPOT	15 / 4B		01/09/1968	N/A	LTB (VIC)	Sole Depot for Victoria Line. Formerly BR sidings on part of site, laid c.1900's
NORTHWICK PARK	11 / 6C		28/06/1923	N/A	MET	Suffix '& Kenton' dropped 15/03/1937
Northwick Park & Kenton						
NORTHWOOD	10 / 3B	P	01/09/1887	N/A	MET	Goods yard closed 14/11/1966
		G	*01/09/1887*	*14/11/1966*		
NORTHWOOD HILLS	10 / 4B		13/11/1933	N/A	MET / GCR	
Norwood Fork Junction	54 / 6A		01/12/1862	N/A	LBSCR	
NORWOOD JUNCTION	54 / 6A	P	05/06/1839	N/A	LCRR	Opened with line as 'Jolly Sailor', renamed 'Norwood' October 1846. Re-sited south 01/06/1859 and 'Junction' suffix added. Further suffix '& South Norwood for Woodside' added 01/10/1910, dropped 13/06/1955 Date of goods yard closure unknown, not stated in Borley
Norwood Junction & South Norwood for Woodside		G	*05/06/1839*	?		
Norwood Junction						
Norwood						
Jolly Sailor						
NORWOOD JUNCTION LOCO SHED	54 / 5A		*??/??/1935*	*??/01/1964*	SR	
Norwood North Junctions	54 / 5A		01/10/1857	N/A	WELCPR / LBSCR	
Norwood Spur	54 / 5A	P	18/06/1862	01/01/1917	LBSCR	Passenger services ceased 01/01/1917. Singled 1928. All use ended 30/10/1966, but not dismantled until 1972
		G	*18/06/1862*	*30/10/1966*		
NOTTING HILL GATE	38 / 1B		01/10/1868	N/A	MET	CLR station opened 30/07/1900 (no interchange provided). Served by District Line since 01/11/1926 Interchange facilities between Central and Circle / District Lines completed 31/07/1960 Circle / District lines platforms closed 23/07/2011 - 23/08/2011 (engineering work)
NUNHEAD	40 / 5B	P	18/09/1871	N/A	LCDR	Opened as junction station for Blackheath Hill branch, original advertised opening date 01/09/1871, hence Borley gives this as opening date. Quick states that station opening coincided with the delayed opening of the branch, on 18/09/1871. Originally three through tracks / five platform faces with reversing siding to west of station. Relocated West 03/05/1925 by SR, as a new single island platform on the site of former reversing siding Goods yard closed 02/04/1962
		G	*18/09/1871*	*02/04/1962*		
Nunhead Junction	40 / 5B		18/09/1871	N/A	LCDR	Crystal Palace (High Level) branch junction eliminated 20/09/1954
O						
OAKLEIGH PARK	5 / 6D		01/12/1873	N/A	GNR	
OAKWOOD	8 / 5B		13/03/1933	N/A	UERL (GNPBR)	Opened as 'Enfield West', 'Oakwood' suffix added 03/05/1934, renamed 'Oakwood' 01/09/1946
Enfield West (Oakwood)						
Enfield West						
OCKENDON	32 / 5A	P	01/07/1892	N/A	LTSR	Goods yard closed 06/05/1968. Passing loop out of use 24/12/1977 - November 1978 (signal box fire)
		G	*01/07/1892*	*06/05/1968*		
OLD FORD	27 / 4C	P	01/07/1867	N/A	NLR	Goods yard opened 1868, transferred to LNWR 01/11/1870. Passenger service Dalston Junction to Poplar withdrawn 15/05/1944, 'officially' closed 23/04/1945. Goods yard closed 06/11/1967
		G	*??/??/1868*	*06/11/1967*		
OLD KENT ROAD & HATCHAM	40 / 4B & 79		13/08/1866	01/01/1917	LBSCR	Renamed 01/02/1870
Old Kent Road						
Old Kent Road Junction	40 / 4B & 79 / 80		13/03/1871	N/A	LBSCR / ELR	Junction formed 13/03/1871, ELR route abandoned 30/06/1911, Old Kent Road Spur abandoned 02/11/1964 and junction eliminated. Re-established 24/06/2012 (date of line being energised to allow testing to begin)
Old Kent Road Spur	40 / 3B & 79	P	N/A	N/A	LBSCR	Opened at some point in 1871, never saw regular passenger traffic (if any). Although engineered for double track, continuous double track never appears to have been present. Closed 02/11/1964
		G	*??/??/1871*	*02/11/1964*		

NAME: (Previous names indented below)	Page / grid:		Date opened:	Date closed:	Opening company:	NOTES:
Old Kew Junction	37 / 2A & 19		15/02/1853	N/A	NSWJR / LSWR	Remodelled ??/11/1981 to a single-lead junction
OLD OAK COMMON DIESEL DEPOT	24 / 5D & 86		*c.1964*	*??/04/2009*	BR	Established on site of former steam shed. Closed April 2009 to allow future use of site as 'Crossrail' depot
Old Oak Common East Junction	24 / 5D & 86		*??/11/1912*	N/A	GWR	
Old Oak Common Flyover	24 / 5D & 86		*??/11/1912*	N/A	GWR	Built for light engine / empty carriage access to Old Oak Common Depot, singled 04/09/1967
OLD OAK COMMON STEAM SHED	24 / 5C & 86		*17/03/1906*	*??/03/1964*	GWR	After shed's demolition one turntable retained as part of diesel depot
OLD OAK COMMON SIDINGS	86		*c.1880*	N/A	GWR	First sidings appeared on site c.1880 (between 1871 and 1896 OS), initially named 'West London Sidings' adjacent to GWR main line
Old Oak Common West Junction	24 / 5C & 86		03/06/1903	N/A	GWR	
Old Oak Junction	24 / 5C & 86		20/07/1885	??/??/1977	NSWJR / LNWR	Junction abolished 1977 (effectively moved south to Acton Wells Junctions)
OLD OAK LANE HALT	24 / 5C & 86		01/10/1906	30/06/1947	GWR	Closed 01/02/1915 - 29/03/1920. 'Bay' platform on down side in use 20/06/1932 - 02/06/1940
OLD OAK SIDINGS	24 / 4C & 86		*c.1890*	N/A	NSWJR	Sidings had appeared on site by 1893 OS
OLD STREET	26 / 5D		17/11/1901	N/A	CSLR	GNCR (later Metropolitan Railway, then Northern Line, then British Rail) platforms opened 14/02/1904 CSLR platforms closed 09/08/1922 - 20/04/1924. GNCR platforms became southern terminus 06/09/1975, closed 04/10/1975, re-opened by British Rail 16/08/1976 (terminus until 08/11/1976)
ONGAR	8 / 1D	P	24/04/1865	N/A	GER	Epping to Ongar transferred to LTE 25/09/1949, Electrified 18/11/1957. Between these dates passenger services provided by BR (steam). Line closed by LUL 30/09/1994, re-opened by Epping-Ongar Railway between Ongar and North Weald 10/10/2004, closed 31/12/2007 for engineering works, re-opened 25/05/2012. Goods yard closed 18/04/1966
		G	*24/04/1865*	*18/04/1966*		
ORIENT WAY SIDINGS	27 / 1C		*30/05/2008*	N/A	NR	On site of Stratford Traction Maintenance Depot. Replaced Thornton Fields Sidings. First test train 19/05/2008, was to open 29/05/2008, but no trains stabled until 30/05/2008
ORPINGTON	56 / 4C	P	02/03/1868	N/A	SER	Initially two platform faces on double track, although Borley states goods facilities opened with passenger station, kentrail.org.uk website states goods facilities not provided until c.1890, corroborated by contemporary OS maps Extensively remodelled 1904 for quadrupling; engine shed and four carriage sidings provided on 'down' side and passenger facilities expanded to four through platforms and London-facing bays on the 'up' and 'down' sides At time of electrification (c.1925), 'down' carriage sidings covered by shed and engine shed abandoned (becoming permanent way depot). Goods yard closed 07/10/1968, site then occupied by 'up' carriage sidings Additional 'down' bay platforms 7 and 8 opened and 'down' carriage shed demolished 1992, 'up' carriage sidings lifted weekend of 13-14/03/1993
		G	*c.1890*	*07/10/1968*		
Orpington North Junction	56 / 3C		06/06/1904	N/A	SECR	Junction formed through Chislehurst to Orpington quadrupling
Orpington South Junction	56 / 4C		06/06/1904	N/A	SECR	Junction formed through Chislehurst to Orpington quadrupling
OSTERLEY	36 / 3B		01/05/1883	N/A	MDR	First served by Piccadilly Line 13/03/1933. Re-sited west and renamed 'Osterley' 25/03/1934
Osterley & Spring Grove						District Line service ceased 10/10/1964
OVAL	39 / 3C		18/12/1890	N/A	CSLR	Opened as 'The Oval', prefix dropped c.1894. Also known as 'Kennington Oval' between 1890-1894
The Oval						Closed 29/11/1923 - 01/12/1924 (tunnel widening)
OXFORD CIRCUS	26 / 6A		30/07/1900	N/A	CLR	UERL (BSWR) station opened 10/03/1906 (combined with original CLR station 16/08/1925), further new concourse opened c.1967 / 1968 in anticipation of Victoria Line opening. Victoria Line platforms opened 07/03/1969
OXSHOTT	63 / 6A	P	02/02/1885	N/A	LSWR	Variously '- & Fair Mile', '- & Fairmile', '- for Fair Mile' and 'for Fairmile' until becoming 'Oxshott' 13/06/1955
Oxshott & Fair Mile		G	*02/02/1885*	*c.1965*		
OXSHOTT BRICK WORKS	62 / 6D		*c.1885*	*??/??/1958*	PRIV	Works established 1866 but could not have been rail served before 02/02/1885 opening of adjacent line Sidings present on 1895 OS, the previous 1884 OS pre-dated line opening. Production ceased 1958
Oxted Tunnel	74 / 6C		10/03/1884	N/A	SER / LBSCR	

P

NAME: (Previous names indented below)	Page / grid:		Date opened:	Date closed:	Opening company:	NOTES:
PADDINGTON (GWR 1st)	25 / 6C & 67 / 5C	P	04/06/1838	29/05/1854	GWR	Original GWR terminus. Replaced by Paddington (2nd) 29/05/1854 (passengers), closed to goods traffic 29/12/1975
		G	*04/06/1838*	*29/12/1975*		
PADDINGTON (GWR 2nd)	25 / 6C & 67 / 6C		16/01/1854	N/A	GWR	Replaced 1st station (passengers only), opened to departures 16/01/1854, arrivals 29/05/1854
PADDINGTON (MET 1st)	25 / 6C & 67 / 5C		10/01/1863	N/A	MET / GWR	Suffix 'Bishop's Road' dropped, station designated 'Paddington Suburban', and rebuilt as 4 through roads / 2 island platforms 10/091933. 2 middle roads became terminal 1966. Northernmost platforms 15 & 16 became LTB only and southernmost platforms 13 & 14 became BR only, and terminal, 12/11/1967. Connections between LTB and BR removed and subsequently connecting footway built between platform 12 and 13 across old trackbed
Paddington (Bishop's Road)						
PADDINGTON (MET 2nd)	25 / 6C & 67 / 6C		01/10/1868	N/A	MET	Platforms on District / Circle Lines, subway to GWR station built 22/10/1887. UERL BSWR platforms added 01/12/1913 (terminus until 31/01/1915). Suffix 'Praed Street' dropped 11/07/1948 (never applied to Bakerloo Line). Circle / District lines platforms closed 23/07/2011 - 23/08/2011 (engineering work)
Paddington (Praed Street)						
PADDINGTON NEW YARD	25 / 5B & 67 / 4A		*13/04/1908*	*29/12/1972*	GWR	Goods yard opened on site of former engine shed (open 02/03/1852 - 18/03/1906). Replaced by stone terminal 1975
PALACE GATES WOOD GREEN	14 / 4C	P	07/10/1878	07/01/1963	GER	Entire Palace Gates Branch closed to passengers 07/01/1963. Goods yard opened 14/10/1878, closed 05/10/1964
		G	*14/10/1878*	*05/10/1964*		
PALACE GATES COAL CONCENTRATION DEPOT	14 / 4C		*??/07/1958*	*??/??/1984*	PRIV	Charringtons Ltd.
PALACE OF ENGINEERING	24 / 2B		*23/04/1924*	*03/12/1962*	PRIV	Originally rail-served exhibition hall, later goods station
PALMERS GREEN	14 / 2C	P	01/04/1871	N/A	GNR	Suffix added 01/10/1876, dropped 18/03/1971. Goods yard closed 01/10/1962
Palmers Green & Southgate		G	*01/04/1871*	*01/10/1962*		
Palmer's Green						
Park Junction	13 / 5D		24/05/1873	18/05/1957	GNR	Junction between Alexandra Palace Branch and original line to Edgware. Goods traffic ceased to Cranley Gardens 18/05/1957, after which time junction eliminated
PARK ROYAL (GWR)	24 / 5B		15/06/1903	27/09/1937	GWR	Opened to special traffic 25/05/1903, public traffic commenced 15/06/1903. Closed 05/07/1903 - 01/05/1904 then again 01/02/1915 - 29/03/1920. Large goods yard to north (see separate entry below)
PARK ROYAL (UERL)	24 / 5A		06/07/1931	N/A	UERL (DIS)	Replaced original station to north. Served by Piccadilly Line since 04/07/1932, last served District Line 22/10/1933. Suffix 'Hanger Hill' in use 01/03/1936 - 1947
Park Royal (Hanger Hill)						
Park Royal						
PARK ROYAL GOODS	24 / 5B		*03/06/1903*	*??/??/1982*	GWR	
PARK ROYAL & TWYFORD ABBEY	24 / 4A		23/06/1903	06/07/1931	MDR	Suffix '& Twyford Abbey' added 01/05/1904. Replaced by current Park Royal station to south
Park Royal						
PARK ROYAL WEST HALT	24 / 5A		20/06/1932	15/06/1947	GWR	
Park Street Tunnels	26 / 4A		20/07/1837	N/A	LBIR	
Parks Bridge Junction	40 / 5D		01/09/1866	N/A	SER	Junction at north end of Ladywell Loop
PARSONS GREEN	38 / 4B		01/03/1880	N/A	MDR	
PARSONS GREEN SIDINGS	38 / 4B		*01/03/1880*	N/A	MDR	District Line stabling sidings
Paxton Tunnel	54 / 3A		01/08/1865	20/09/1954	LCDR	Nunhead to Crystal Palace (High Level) closed 20/09/1954 (Passengers and Goods)
PECKHAM COAL	40 / 4A		*23/03/1891*	*??/08/1961*	LNWR / MID	High and low level sidings connected by a wagon hoist. Traffic ceased in 1958, officially closed August 1961
PECKHAM RYE	40 / 4A		01/12/1865	N/A	LBSCR	Entire station built by LBSCR, but LCDR-served platforms (to / from Crystal Palace H.L.) opened first 01/12/1865 LBSCR-served platforms (to / from London Bridge) opened 13/08/1866, originally 3 platforms (two up, one down), additional 'up main' platform and track removed 1933, new island platform constructed in vacant space and original side 'up local' and 'down' platforms abandoned 1961
PECKHAM RYE DEPOT	40 / 5A		*01/02/1909*	*c.1961*	LBSCR	Originally built to accommodate stock for LBSCR South London Line overhead electrification. Site previously occupied by berthing sidings for East London Railway trains. Overhaul work transferred to Selhurst 31/12/1958, Lighter repairs continued for a further two years
Peckham Rye Junction	40 / 5A		01/10/1868	N/A	LBSCR	
PENGE	54 / 4C		03/05/1858	c.1860	WELCPR	Probably opened with WELCPR Bromley Junction to Shortlands line 03/05/1858. Closure date unknown, 'by end of 1860' per Quick, c.1861 per Cobb. Also referred to as 'Beckenham Road', Tramlink station of that name on site today
PENGE EAST	54 / 3B	P	01/07/1863	N/A	LCDR	Opened as 'Penge', but listed as 'Penge Lane' in Bradshaw 1864-79 (Borley), Quick states 1864-9 & 1867
Penge Lane		G	*01/07/1863*	*07/11/1966*		Renamed 'Penge East' 09/07/1923. Goods yard closed 07/11/1966
Penge						
Penge Junction	54 / 4C		01/07/1863	N/A	LCDR / WELCPR	
Penge Tunnel	54 / 3A		01/07/1863	N/A	LCDR	
PENGE WEST	54 / 4B	P	05/06/1839	N/A	LCRR	Opened as 'Penge' with line 05/06/1839, closed c.1841 (Borley), or 'probably by mid-1840' (Quick).
Penge Bridges		G	*01/07/1863*	*04/05/1964*		Re-opened 01/07/1863, listed as 'Penge Bridges' in Bradshaw 1864 - 1879. Suffix 'West' added 09/07/1923
Penge						Goods yard closed 04/05/1964
Pepper Hill Tunnel	59 / 3C		14/11/2007	N/A	LCOR	
PERIVALE (GWR)	23 / 4C		01/05/1904	15/06/1947	GWR	Closed 01/021915 - 29/03/1920 and again for good 15/06/1947 (replaced by Perivale [LPTB] to the east)
Perivale Halt						Carried 'Halt' suffix until 1927
PERIVALE (LPTB)	23 / 4C		30/06/1947	N/A	LPTB (CEN)	
Perry Street Fork Junction	43 / 5C		01/05/1895	N/A	BHR	Junction at south end of Erith Loop
PETTS WOOD	56 / 6A	P	09/07/1928	N/A	SR	Goods yard closed 07/10/1968
		G	*09/07/1928*	*07/10/1968*		
Petts Wood Junctions	56 / 6A		08/09/1902	N/A	SECR	Junctions at southern ends of Tonbridge Loops, originally 'Orpington Junction', renamed 'Petts Wood' upon opening of latter station (09/07/1928). 'Slow' junction made 08/09/1902, 'Fast' 14/09/1902
Orpington Junction						
Petts Wood South Junction	56 / 2B		?	N/A	BR?	
PHIPPS BRIDGE	52 / 5C		30/05/2000	N/A	CTL	
PICCADILLY CIRCUS	26 / 6A		10/03/1906	N/A	UERL (BSWR)	UERL (GNPBR) platforms opened 15/12/1906, extensively rebuilt 10/12/1928 (original buildings closed 21/07/1929)

NAME: (Previous names indented below)	Page / grid:		Date opened:	Date closed:	Opening company:	NOTES:
PIMLICO (LTE)	39 / 3B		14/09/1972	N/A	LTE (VIC)	
PIMLICO (WELCPR)	39 / 3A & 82		29/03/1858	01/10/1860	WELCPR	Original terminus of WELCPR (later LBSCR). Closed when VSPR route to Victoria station opened
PINNER	10 / 4D	P	25/05/1885	N/A	MET	Country terminus of Metropolitan Railway until 01/09/1887. Goods yard closed 03/04/1967
		G	25/05/1885	03/04/1967		
PLAISTOW	28 / 4B	P	31/03/1858	N/A	LTSR	First served by District Railway 02/06/1902, line quadrupled 1905, District trains then using 'slow' platforms to north
		G	31/03/1858	01/05/1953		Served by Metropolitan Line since 30/03/1936 ('Hammersmith & City Line' since 30/07/1990)
						Main line services non-stopped since 15/06/1962, and 'Fast' platforms abandoned. Goods yard closed 01/05/1953
PLAISTOW MOTIVE POWER DEPOT (MPD)	28 / 5B		30/09/1911	??/06/1962	LTSR	Steam shed replacing original 1899 shed adjacent to Plaistow Works, closed when steam traction withdrawn
PLAISTOW WORKS	28 / 4B		??/??/1880	??/??/1932	LTSR	LTSR locomotive works, ceased servicing locos 1925, remained as servicing point for wagons until 1932
PLAISTOW & WEST HAM GOODS	28 / 6A		01/10/1906	06/08/1984	GER	Connection to main line taken out of use 13/06/1984, 'official' closure 06/08/1984. Date of last train unknown
PLASSER WORKS (WEST EALING)	23 / 6C		??/??/1969	N/A	PRIV	Assembly of railway equipment, manufacture since 1977. Formerly GWR signal engineers works (c.1900's)
PLUMSTEAD	42 / 2B	P	16/07/1859	N/A	SER	Goods yard closed by BR 04/12/1967. Re-opened 08/12/1971, mainly for paper traffic. Connection in situ and yard
		G	16/07/1859	04/12/1967	SER	is 'not in regular use', but will be lifted in connection with 'Crossrail' works. Date of last use unknown
Plumstead Portal	42 / 2B		??/??/2018	N/A	NR (XRAIL)	
Point Pleasant Junction	38 / 5B		01/07/1889	N/A	LSWR	'Up' line abandoned 04/04/1987, bridge demolished 1990 (unsafe). 'Down' line bi-directional since 11/02/1991
PONDERS END	7 / 5C	P	15/09/1840	N/A	NER	Goods yard closed 02/11/1964
		G	15/09/1840	02/11/1964		
PONTOON DOCK	41 / 1C & 62 / 5B		02/12/2005	N/A	DLR	
POPLAR (LBLR)	41 / 1A & 31 / 4C		06/07/1840	04/05/1926	LBLR	Passenger service to Blackwall withdrawn 04/05/1926
POPLAR (EWIDBJR - Did Not Open)	40 / 1D & 31 / 4B		N/A	N/A	EWIDBJR	Platforms constructed 1851 but station did not open
POPLAR (NLR)	27 / 6D & 31 / 4B		01/08/1866	15/05/1944	NLR	Station initially carried suffix '(East India Road)' to distinguish from the first, unopened, EWIDBJR station to the south.
Poplar (East India Road)						Operated as terminus for service ex-Broad Street except between 01/09/1870 - 01/07/1890 when some trains
						continued to Blackwall. Passenger service Dalston Junction to Poplar withdrawn 15/05/1944, 'official' closure did not
						occur until 23/04/1945. Present-day DLR 'All Saints' station built on same site
POPLAR (DLR)	40 / 1D & 31 / 6B		31/08/1987	N/A	DLR	Reconstructed with four platforms 28/03/1994 (Beckton extension)
POPLAR DEPOT	40 / 1D & 31 / 6B		31/08/1987	N/A	DLR	Original DLR Depot
POPLAR DOCK GOODS (GNR)	40 / 1D & 31 / 5C		01/09/1878	??/??/1968	GNR	
POPLAR DOCK GOODS (GWR)	40 / 1D & 31 / 4C		01/04/1878	??/??/1940	GWR	
POPLAR DOCK GOODS (MID)	41 / 1A & 31 / 5C		01/12/1882	04/05/1956	MID	Suffix 'Riverside' added by BR January 1951
Portobello Junction	25 / 5B		16/01/1854	N/A	GWR	Originally divergence of routes into original and current Paddington termini
Potters Bar Tunnels	5 / 1C		01/08/1850	N/A	GNR	Original bore is today's 'Up' tunnel, 'Down' bore added 03/05/1959
Pouparts Junction	38 / 4D & 82		01/12/1867	N/A	LBSCR	Junction between original WELCPR route to Pimlico and subsequent route to Victoria
POYLE ESTATE HALT	34 / 4A		04/01/1954	29/03/1965	BR	
POYLE FOR STANWELL MOOR HALT	34 / 5A		01/06/1927	29/03/1965	GWR	Renamed 26/09/1927
Stanwell Moor & Poyle Halt						
Praed Street Junction	25 / 6C		01/10/1868	N/A	MET	No service towards High Street Kensington 23/07/2011 - 23/08/2011 (engineering works)
PRESTON ROAD	12 / 6A		21/05/1908	N/A	MET	Opened with 'for Uxendon and Kenton' suffix, 'and Kenton' dropped 01/07/1923, 'for Uxendon' dropped c.1924
Preston Road for Uxendon						Southbound / Up platform re-sited north 22/11/1931, Northbound / Down re-sited north 03/01/1932
Preston Road for Uxendon and Kenton						
PRIMROSE HILL	25 / 3D & 58		05/05/1855	23/09/1992	NLR	Replaced 'Hampstead Road' station to east. Renamed 'Chalk Farm' 1862. Closed 01/01/1917 - 10/07/1922.
Chalk Farm						Renamed 'Primrose Hill' 1950. Due to close when Watford Junction to Liverpool Street service withdrawn, but trains
Hampstead Road						ceased calling prematurely due to flooding (last eastbound 18/09/1992, last westbound 22/09/1992)
Primrose Hill Junction	58		10/07/1922	N/A	LNWR	
Primrose Hill Tunnels	25 / 3D & 58		20/07/1837	N/A	LBIR	2nd tunnel added 02/06/1879, 3rd tunnel added 10/07/1922
PRINCE REGENT	41 / 1C & 62 / 5B		28/03/1994	N/A	DLR	
PRINCESS ROYAL DISTRIBUTION CENTRE	24 / 3B & 68 / 3D		??/??/1996	N/A	PRIV	Royal Mail depot
PUDDING MILL LANE	27 / 4D		15/01/1996	N/A	DLR	Planned opening 02/01/1996, but delayed. To be re-sited south in connection with 'Crossrail 1' works 2013
PURFLEET	44 / 3B	P	13/04/1854	N/A	LTSR	Goods yard closed 02/11/1964 (although adjacent oil terminal remained open significantly longer)
		G	13/04/1854	02/11/1964		
PURFLEET FOSTER YEOMAN STONE TERMINAL	44 / 4C		?	N/A	PRIV	Deep Water Wharf
PURFLEET RIFLE RANGE HALT	44 / 2B		??/10/1921	31/05/1941	LTSR	Opened to public October 1921, but had been served as required since July 1910 for military traffic
PURFLEET THAMES TERMINAL	44 / 4C		c.1960's	N/A	PRIV	Deep Water Wharf (containers)
PURLEY	66 / 5C	P	12/07/1841	N/A	LBRR	Opened as 'Godstone Road', closed to passengers 01/10/1847 - 05/08/1856. Re-opened 05/08/1856 as 'Godstone
Caterham Junction		G	12/07/1841	06/01/1969		Road, Caterham Junction'. Renamed 'Caterham Junction' October 1856, then 'Purley' 01/10/1888
Godstone Road, Caterham Junction						Goods yard closed 06/01/1969, aggregates terminal established on part of site (Day & Sons)
Godstone Road						
Purley Chipstead Line Junction	66 / 6C		21/11/1897	N/A	SER	
Purley North Junction	66 / 5C		?	N/A	LBSCR	
PURLEY OAKS	66 / 5D		05/11/1899	N/A	LBSCR	
Purley South Junction	66 / 5C		05/08/1856	N/A	CR / LBSCR	
PUTNEY	38 / 5A		27/07/1846	N/A	LSWR	Expanded to four platforms 1886 (quadrupling)
PUTNEY BRIDGE	38 / 5A		01/03/1880	N/A	MDR	Opened as 'Putney Bridge & Fulham' as terminus of MDR extension from West Brompton.
Putney Bridge & Hurlingham						Extension to Wimbledon opened 03/06/1889 by LSWR, although no LSWR trains used route. Suffix '& Fulham'
Putney Bridge & Fulham						replaced by '& Hurlingham' 01/09/1902, station re-arranged 1910. Suffix '& Hurlingham' dropped 1932.

Q

NAME: (Previous names indented below)	Page / grid:		Date opened:	Date closed:	Opening company:	NOTES:
QUAKER OATS (SOUTHALL)	36 / 1A		?	?	PRIV	
Quarry Tunnel	73 / 5A		05/11/1899	N/A	LBSCR	
QUEENS PARK	25 / 4B	P	02/06/1879	N/A	LNWR	Served by Bakerloo Line since 11/02/1915 (terminus until 10/05/1915). LNWR mainline platforms closed 01/01/1917
Queens Park (West Kilburn)		G	02/06/1879	06/07/1964		but retained for occasional use. Suffix 'West Kilburn' by dropped 1954 (never applied to Bakerloo Line). Goods yard
						(to west of station between DC lines and LNWR main lines) opened with passenger station, closed 06/07/1964
QUEEN'S ROAD	27 / 2B		N/A	N/A	GER	Platforms built 1875 but station did not open, formally abandoned 1895. Also referred to as 'Queen's Down Road'
						and 'Down Road, Clapton'. Platforms demolished c.1965
QUEENS ROAD GOODS	15 / 6D		01/09/1894	06/05/1968	MID	Opened as 'Boundary Road Goods', but renamed 'Queen's Road Goods' late in 1894
Boundary Road Goods						
QUEENS ROAD PECKHAM	40 / 4B		13/08/1866	N/A	LBSCR	Renamed 01/12/1866. Opened with 3 platform faces / tracks, middle track / platform taken out of use 1933
Peckham						Rebuilt with island platform on vacant space 1977, side platforms demolished
QUEENSTOWN ROAD BATTERSEA	39 / 4A & 82		01/11/1877	N/A	LSWR	Renamed 12/05/1980
Queens Road Battersea						
QUEENSBURY	12 / 4A		16/12/1934	N/A	LPTB (MET)	Opened by LPTB Metropolitan Line. Transferred to Bakerloo Line 20/11/1939, Jubilee Line 01/05/1979
QUEENSWAY	25 / 5C		30/07/1900	N/A	CLR	Renamed 01/09/1946. Closed 07/05/2005 - 14/06/2006 for lift replacement
Queens Road						

R

NAME: (Previous names indented below)	Page / grid:		Date opened:	Date closed:	Opening company:	NOTES:
RADLETT	3 / 1C	P	13/07/1868	N/A	MID	Goods yard opened before passenger station (date unknown), and was initially named 'Aldenham'
		G	c.1867	25/03/1968		prior to passenger opening. Goods yard closed 25/03/1968
Radlett Junction	3 / 2D		?	N/A	?	
RAINHAM	30 / 6C	P	13/04/1854	N/A	LTSR	Station re-sited south 1962, new platforms on original goods yard site. Replacement goods yard closed 04/10/1965
		G	13/04/1854	04/10/1965		
RANELAGH BRIDGE DEPOT	25 / 6C & 67 / 5B		??/??/1907	??/??/1980	GWR	Depot for stabling locomotives, converted from steam to diesel April 1964
RAVENSBOURNE	55 / 4A	P	01/07/1892	N/A	LCDR	Goods yard closed 04/09/1961
		G	01/07/1892	04/09/1961		
RAVENSCOURT PARK	37 / 2D		01/04/1873	N/A	LSWR	Opened by LSWR. First served MDR 01/06/1877. Served by MET 01/10/1877 - 01/01/1911 (MET / GWR joint after
Shaftesbury Road						01/01/1894). Renamed 01/03/1888. Rebuilt from 2 side platforms to 2 island platforms when route quadrupled
						03/12/1911 (LSWR northern island, MDR southern island). LSWR service ceased and northern island abandoned
						05/06/1916. Eastbound District Line started using north face of north island from 05/06/1932. Piccadilly Line started
						running non-stop through middle platforms 04/07/1932.
Ray Street Gridiron	32 / 2B		17/02/1868	N/A	MET	Widened Lines dive-under, replaced by a concrete raft 1960
RAYNERS LANE	10 / 6D	P	26/05/1906	N/A	MET	Served by District Line Trains 01/03/1910 - 23/10/1933, Piccadilly Line thereafter. 'Halt' suffix dropped 1934/5
Rayners Lane Halt		G	26/05/1906	10/08/1964		Goods yard closed 10/08/1964
Rayners Lane Junction	11 / 6A		01/03/1910	N/A	MET / MDR	Rayners Lane to South Harrow built by Metropolitan Railway 1904, but no regular trains until MDR in 01/03/1910
						MET operated a dump in the angle of the junction for ash from Neasden power station and other waste 1912 - 1955

NAME: (Previous names indented below)	Page / grid:		Date opened:	Date closed:	Opening company:	NOTES:
RAYNES PARK	51 / 4D	P	30/10/1871	N/A	LSWR	From the 04/04/1859 opening of the LSWR Epsom route there was a junction at this location with no station
		G	c.1900	04/12/1967		(initially 'Wimbledon Junction'). Subsequent to station opening 30/10/1871, new 'up' platforms constructed due to
						diveunder for up Epsom line (opened 16/03/1884). Date of goods yard opening uncertain: Borley states open with
						passenger station, but no yard is apparent on 1897-8 OS (had appeared on 1913 OS). Yard closed 04/12/1967, but
						sidings retained for use as a permanent way depot until late 1983
Raynes Park Junction	51 / 4D		04/04/1859	N/A	LSWR	Junction between LSWR main line and Epsom line. Initially named 'Wimbledon Junction'
Wimbledon Junction						
Reading Lane Junction	27 / 3B		30/06/1986	N/A	BR	Junction at south end of Graham Road Curve
RECTORY ROAD	27 / 2A		27/05/1872	N/A	GER	Closed 09/12/1972 - 17/01/1973 (fire)
REDBRIDGE	16 / 6D		14/12/1947	N/A	LPTB (CEN)	
REDHILL	73 / 5C		29/01/1844	N/A	SER	First served by SER trains 29/01/1844 as 'Reigate', allowing original SER Reigate station south of the SER / LBRR
Red Hill Junction						junction to close. Building from original station moved to this location during February 1844, fully opened 05/03/1844
Reigate						LBRR trains began calling here 15/04/1844, allowing their original station to south to close. Rebuilt 1858 and
						renamed 'Red Hill Junction'. Became 'Redhill' 07/07/1929 (before this date variously 'Red Hill' / 'Redhill' / 'Reigate'
						with 'Junction' sometimes added per Quick). Separate goods yards associated with original LBRR and SER stations
						(see entries for 'Reigate'), supplemented by larger yard in vee between Tonbridge and Brighton Lines, appeared on
						OS between 1896 and 1913 surveys so presumably opened c. time of Quarry Line opening 1899
Redhill Tunnel	73 / 5C		05/11/1899	N/A	LBSCR	
REEDHAM	66 / 6B		01/03/1911	N/A	SECR	Closed 01/01/1917 - 01/01/1919. 'Halt' dropped 05/07/1936
Reedham Halt						
REEDHAM SIDINGS	73 / 1B		c.1899	N/A	LBSCR	Appear to have been laid c. time of Quarry Line opening
REEVES CORNER	66 / 2C		10/05/2000	N/A	CTL	
Regent's Canal Junction	76		14/11/2007	N/A	LCOR / NR	
REGENT'S PARK	26 / 5A		10/03/1906	N/A	UERL (BSWR)	Closed 10/07/2006 - 13/06/2007 (lift replacement)
REIGATE (LBRR)	73 / 6C	P	12/07/1841	15/04/1844	LBRR	First station in Reigate area, opened with LBRR route Croydon Junction to Haywards Heath, situated on Hooley Lane
Red Hill		G	12/07/1841	c.1965		Closed when LBRR trains began serving present-day Redhill station north of junction with SER 15/04/1844
Red-Hill & Reigate Road						Opened as 'Red-Hill & Reigate Road', before being shortened to 'Red Hill', named 'Reigate' at point of closure
						Goods yard depicted on OS until 1963-8, unknown when public goods traffic ceased
REIGATE (SER)	73 / 6C	P	26/05/1842	29/01/1844	SER	Second station in Reigate area, situated immediately south of SER / LBRR junction. Closed when SER trains first
		G	26/05/1842	c.1965		began to serve present-day Redhill station, allowing first station building to be dismantled and rebuilt at new site
						Goods yard depicted on OS until 1935 (shed demolished by 1963-8), unknown when public goods traffic ceased
REMENHAM SIDING	33 / 5B		c.1920's	c.1930's	PRIV	Served a gravel pit. Does not appear on OS maps before 1926 or after 1938
Renwick Road Junction	29 / 5D		14/11/2007	N/A	LCOR / NR	
RICHMOND	36 / 5D	P	27/07/1846	N/A	LSWR	Opened as country terminus of branch from Battersea Junction (east of current Clapham Junction station), goods
		G	27/07/1846	06/05/1968		facilities assumed to have opened at same time as passenger station. Original terminus given over wholly to goods
						traffic and new through platforms built to north on extension to Datchet 22/08/1848. New 5-platform terminus
						opened to north of 22/08/1848 station 01/01/1869 to coincide with opening of line from Kensington (Addison Road).
						First served MDR 01/06/1877, then MET 01/10/1877. MET service ceased from 01/01/1907. Original 1846 terminus
						closed to goods traffic 1936 and demolished, new goods station opening north-east of 1869 passenger station
						November 1936. 1848 and 1869 portions of station rebuilt and combined 01/08/1937. November 1936 goods
						station (on page 37 / 5A) closed 06/05/1968. Centre road between platforms 3 and 4 taken out of use 1970
Richmond Bridge	36 / 5D		22/08/1848	N/A	LSWR	
RICHMOND GASWORKS	37 / 5A		??/??/1882	??/??/1933	PRIV	
Richmond Junction (Kensington)	38 / 1A & 83		01/01/1869	05/06/1916	LSWR / WLR	Junction between WLR and LSWR Richmond branch
Richmond Junction (Richmond)	37 / 5A		01/01/1869	28/12/1972	LSWR	Direct connection between lines ex-Kew Gardens and ex-North Sheen eliminated 28/12/1972, but indirect link
						via Richmond station platform 3 established 1985 for stock transfer between North London Line and Selhurst Depot
RICKMANSWORTH	1 / 6C	P	01/09/1887	N/A	MET	Country terminus of MET until 08/07/1889. Goods yard closed 14/11/1966
		G	01/09/1887	14/11/1966		
RICKMANSWORTH (CHURCH STREET)	1 / 6C	P	01/10/1862	03/03/1952	WRR	Branch from Watford Junction; closed to passengers 03/03/1952, goods 02/01/1967
Rickmansworth		G	01/10/1862	02/01/1967		Suffix 'Church Street' in use from 25/09/1950 until closure
RICKMANSWORTH NORTH SIDINGS	1 / 5C		c.1890	N/A	MET	Stabling Sidings for Metropolitan Line, first siding on site by 1896 OS
RICKMANSWORTH SOUTH SIDINGS	1 / 5C		c.1960	N/A	LTE (MET) ?	Not present on 1938 OS, but had appeared by 1961/2 (possibly commissioned for 1960 Amersham electrification?)
RIDDLESDOWN	66 / 6D		05/06/1927	N/A	SR	
Riddlesdown Tunnel	66 / 6D		10/03/1884	N/A	LBSCR / SER	
RIPPLE LANE FREIGHTLINER TERMINAL	29 / 5D		??/??/1972	N/A	BR	Partially on site of Ripple Lane 'Hump' marshalling yard (closed 1968)
RIPPLE LANE YARD	29 / 5D		c.1940	N/A	LMS	Opened c.1940, main line tracks diverted around site 27/05/1960, reconstructed as 'Hump' marshalling yard 1961,
						closed 1968 and replaced by Freightliner Terminal (opened 1972)
RODING VALLEY	16 / 2C		03/02/1936	N/A	LNER	Fairlop (later Hainault) Loop closed by LNER 30/11/1947 to allow electrification and transfer to LTE Central Line
						Station re-opened 21/11/1948 by LTE following electrification
Rolt Street Junction	40 / 3C & 79 / 80		01/04/1880	N/A	ELR	SER service to Liverpool Street via ELR commenced 01/04/1880. Rolt Street Junction to New Cross (SER) became
						bi-directional (former 'down' only spur) 01/10/1884 when ELR bay platform opened at New Cross. 'Up' spur
						remained in use for goods / through traffic until 16/04/1966. After this date junction was point where double track
						ex-Canal Junction became single bi-directional track to New Cross
ROMFORD	18 / 6C	P	20/06/1839	N/A	ECR	Carried the suffix 'for Hornchurch, Upminster & Corbet's Tey' according to Dewick, but no other reference found
		G	20/06/1839	?		Platform for Upminster originally a separate LTSR station, opening 07/06/1893, combined 01/04/1934.
						Goods yard remains partially in use as engineers depot, date of closure to general goods traffic unknown
ROMFORD FACTORY	19 / 5A		??/??/1843	?	ECR	ECR's locomotive works until 1847 (when relocated to Stratford) then wagon cover factory after 1854
Romford Junction	18 / 6C		07/06/1893	N/A	LTSR / GER	Removed 1930's, reinstated 21/07/1940
ROSHERVILLE HALT	60 / 1A		10/05/1886	16/07/1933	LCDR	Suffix 'Halt' added 17/06/1928
Rosherville						
ROTHERHITHE	40 / 1B		07/12/1869	N/A	ELR	First served MET & MDR 01/10/1884, last served MDR 01/08/1905, no service MET 03/12/1906 - 31/03/1913.
						Separate 'East London Line' identity introduced during 1980's. Closed 25/03/1995 - 25/03/1998 & 23/12/2007 -
						27/04/2010 (engineering work), upon latter re-opening became TfL (LOROL) station
ROYAL ALBERT	41 / 1C & 62 / 5B		28/03/1994	N/A	DLR	
ROYAL ARMY SERVICE CORPS DEPOT (FELTHAM)	49 / 1B		c.1930	??/??/1958	PRIV	Not present on 1920 OS, but had appeared by 1932. Branch partly tramway, passing west side of 'The Green'
						and along Browells Lane. Not used after 1958
ROYAL ARSENAL RAILWAY (WOOLWICH)	42 / 2C		??/??/1859	??/??/1967	SER	
ROYAL BETHLEM HOSPITAL	67 / 1C		??/??/1928	??/??/1930	PRIV	3/4 Mile siding from Eden Park in use during construction of the Hospital, abandoned when construction completed
Royal Curve	33 / 1C	P	N/A	N/A	GWR	Not used for regular passenger traffic; Royal and excursion trains only
		G	08/10/1849	26/07/1970		
ROYAL DOCKYARD (WOOLWICH)	41 / 2D		c.1880	c.1962	PRIV	Branch to dockyard not apparent on 1873 OS, but had appeared by 1896, so approximate 1880 opening assumed.
						Was still in use 11/07/1961 (Middleton Press album 'Charing Cross to Dartford'), but was abandoned by 1962 and the
						tunnel under Woolwich Church Street blocked
ROYAL MINT STREET GOODS	74 / 2B		01/08/1858	01/04/1951	LBLR	Tower Gateway DLR station occupies much of site
Royal Mint Street Junction	27 / 6A & 74 / 2C		29/07/1991	N/A	DLR	Divergence of DLR Bank extension from original route to Tower Gateway
ROYAL OAK	25 / 6C & 67 / 5B		30/10/1871	N/A	MET / GWR	Last GWR service called 01/10/1934. Ownership transferred to LTE 01/01/1970
ROYAL SHOWGROUND	24 / 4B		23/06/1903	27/06/1903	LNWR	Only open for duration of Royal Agricultural Society show 1903
ROYAL VICTORIA	41 / 1B & 62 / 5A		28/03/1994	N/A	DLR	
RUGBY ROAD	37 / 1C		08/04/1909	01/01/1917	NSWJR	
RUISLIP	10 / 6B	P	04/07/1904	N/A	MET	Served by District Line Trains 01/03/1910 - 23/10/1933, Piccadilly Line thereafter. Goods yard closed 10/08/1964
		G	04/07/1904	10/08/1964		
RUISLIP DEPOT	22 / 1B		21/11/1948	N/A	LTE (CEN)	Depot for Central Line and Transplant (Engineering)
RUISLIP GARDENS	22 / 1B		09/07/1934	N/A	GWR / LNER	Platforms on 'slow' GWR / LNER lines only (South Ruislip to West Ruislip formerly quadruple). LTE Central Line
						platforms added 21/11/1948, BR platforms closed 21/07/1959.
RUISLIP MANOR	10 / 6B		05/08/1912	N/A	MET	Served by District Line trains from opening to 23/10/1933, Piccadilly Line thereafter. Closed 12/02/1917 - 01/04/1919
Ruislip Manor Halt						Suffix 'Halt' until 1934/5
RUSHETT	63 / 5D		N/A	N/A	SR	One of two intermediate stations on Chessington South to Leatherhead route, works abandoned at outset of WW2
RUSSELL SQUARE	26 / 5B		15/12/1906	N/A	UERL (GNPBR)	

S

NAME: (Previous names indented below)	Page / grid:		Date opened:	Date closed:	Opening company:	NOTES:
ST ANN'S ROAD	14 / 6D		02/10/1882	09/08/1942	THJR	
ST HELIER	52 / 6B	P	05/01/1930	N/A	SR	Goods yard closed 06/05/1963
		G	*05/01/1930*	*06/05/1963*		
ST HELIER ESTATE RAILWAY	65 / 1C		*??/??/1928*	*??/??/1936*	LCC	Railway system built by the LCC to convey building materials to the then under construction St Helier Estate
St James Road Junction	66 / 1D		22/05/1865	??/10/1983	LBSCR	Junction at southern end of West Croydon Spur
ST JAMES'S PARK	39 / 1B		24/12/1868	N/A	MDR	Also spelt 'St James' Park'. Rebuilt 1927 - 1929 (construction of 55 Broadway above)
ST JAMES STREET WALTHAMSTOW	15 / 5C		26/04/1870	N/A	GER	Originally single platform on 'up' side, Shern Hall Street to Clapton Junction doubled 1873 and 'down' platform built
ST JOHNS	40 / 4D		01/06/1873	N/A	SER	Originally had three island platforms with six faces onto five tracks, southernmost island abandoned 1926, then middle ('fast') island demolished 1973 and 'fast' roads straightened. Now only 'slow' island remains, with two faces
ST JOHN'S WOOD	25 / 4C		20/11/1939	N/A	LPTB (BAK)	Replaced Marlborough Road Station to north. Named 'Acacia Road' until opening. Opened by Bakerloo Line, transferred to Jubilee Line 01/05/1979
St John's Wood Tunnel	25 / 4C		15/03/1899	N/A	GCR	
ST MARGARETS	36 / 6C		02/10/1876	N/A	LSWR	Additional 'up' platform added 26/11/1899
ST MARY CRAY	56 / 6C	P	03/12/1860	N/A	LCDR	Rebuilt with four platforms due to quadrupling 31/05/1959. Goods yard closed 07/10/1968
		G	*03/12/1860*	*07/10/1968*		
St Mary Cray Junctions	56 / 5A & 6A		19/06/1904	N/A	SECR	Junctions at southern end of Chatham Loops
ST MARY'S (WHITECHAPEL ROAD)	27 / 6B & 85		03/03/1884	01/05/1938	SER	First served by SER trains ex-ELR (terminus), withdrawn 01/10/1884. MDR / MET joint line to Whitechapel did not open until 06/10/1884. Renamed 26/01/1923. Closed due to Aldgate East being relocated eastwards
St Mary's						
St Mary's Curve	27 / 6B & 85	P	03/03/1884	06/10/1941	MDR / MET	Built as part of MDR / MET Whitechapel extension, but first used by SER between 03/03/1884 - 01/10/1884.
		G	*03/03/1884*	*23/12/2007*		MET use commenced 01/10/1884, MDR 06/10/1884. Closed to passenger services 01/08/1905 (MDR) and 06/10/1941 (MET), retained for stock transfer thereafter until 23/12/2007 when ELL closed for extension
St Mary's Junction	27 / 6B & 85		01/10/1884	23/12/2007	MDR / MET	Junction at north end of St Mary's Curve, MDR service to Whitechapel commenced 06/10/1884 although empty stock workings to Whitechapel commenced 5 days before with the MET service to New Cross
ST PANCRAS INTERNATIONAL	26 / 4B & 75 / 76		01/10/1868	N/A	MID	Extensively rebuilt for Eurostar services; last Midland mainline train left trainshed 09/04/2004, temporary station to northeast opened 12/04/2004. Main trainshed reopened for international trains and suffix 'International' added 14/11/2007. Platforms below original station opened for 'Thameslink' 09/12/2007 (see 'King's Cross Thameslink')
St Pancras						
ST PANCRAS GOODS	26 / 4B & 75 / 76		*??/07/1862*	*29/04/1968*	MID	Initial access via GNR, then also NLR (GNR connection subsequently severed) full opening 09/09/1867
St Pancras Junction (MID)	75		*??/??/1867*	*31/12/1975*	MID / NLR	
St Pancras Junction (GNR)	75		*??/??/1853*	*14/11/2007*	GNR / NLR	
ST PAUL'S	26 / 6D		30/07/1900	N/A	CLR	Renamed 01/02/1937
Post Office						
St Paul's Bridge	32 / 6C		10/05/1886	N/A	LCDR	Built alongside original Blackfriars Bridge
St Paul's Road Junction	26 / 3B & 75 / 76		13/07/1868	N/A	MID	Junction providing access to St Pancras Goods (MID route to MET 'Widened Lines' opened 13/07/1868) Access to St Pancras goods removed 29/04/1968, Churchyard sidings remain as truncated route
ST QUINTIN PARK & WORMWOOD SCRUBS	24 / 5D & 86		01/08/1871	03/10/1940	LNWR / GWR	Opened as 'Wormwood Scrubs', renamed 'St Quintin Park & Wormwood Scrubs' 01/08/1892. 'Scrubs' sometimes spelt 'Scrubbs' in both titles. Platforms relocated north 01/11/1893. Destroyed by fire 03/10/1940 and ceased to be served by trains, not officially closed until 01/12/1940
Wormwood Scrubs						
Salmons Lane Junction	27 / 6C		05/04/1880	05/11/1962	LBLR	Junction at north end of Limehouse Curve
SANDERSTEAD	66 / 4D	P	10/03/1884	N/A	LBSCR / SER	Goods yard closed 20/03/1961
		G	*10/03/1884*	*20/03/1961*		
SANDILANDS	67 / 2A		10/05/2000	N/A	CTL	
Sandilands Tunnels	67 / 2A		10/08/1885	N/A	LBSCR / SER	Line through tunnel closed by BR 16/05/1983, re-opened by CTL 10/05/2000
SEABROOK SIDINGS	45 / 4C		*??/??/1884*	N/A	PRIV	Sidings initially provided access to Seabrookes Brewery (see below). Now provide access to Tilbury Docks following abolition of Tilbury North Junction c.1960
SEABROOKES BREWERY	45 / 4C		*??/??/1884*	*??/??/1940*	PRIV	Brewery established 1799, acquired siding 1884. Sold to Charringtons 1929, siding lifted 1940
SELHURST	53 / 6D		01/05/1865	N/A	LBSCR	
SELHURST DEPOT	53 / 6D		*??/??/1911*	N/A	LBSCR	Sidings first laid on site c.1890 (not on 1879-1887 OS but had appeared by 1896). Became a depot 1911
Selhurst Junctions	53 / 6D		01/12/1862	N/A	LBSCR	
SELSDON	66 / 3D	P	10/08/1885	16/05/1983	LBSCR / SER	For first month 'Selsdon Road Junction', then 'Selsdon Road'. Woodside platforms closed 01/01/1917 - 01/05/1919
Selsdon Road		G	*10/08/1885*	*07/10/1968*		Renamed 'Selsdon' 30/09/1935. Oxted Line platforms closed 14/06/1959, Woodside platforms 16/05/1983
Selsdon Road Junction						Goods yard closed 07/10/1968, but oil depot established on site (latterly Cory), remaining open until March 1993
Selsdon Road Junction	66 / 4D		10/03/1884	??/03/1993	LBSCR / SER	Last traffic to Selsdon oil depot March 1993, but junction remains in situ
SEVEN KINGS	29 / 1B		01/03/1899	N/A	GER	
Seven Kings Curve	29 / 1B	P	N/A	N/A	GER	Never used for regular passenger traffic, route obliterated by Ilford Depot 'New Shed' 1959
		G	*20/04/1903*	*19/03/1956*		
SEVEN SISTERS	15 / 5A		22/07/1872	N/A	GER	Platforms for Palace Gates Branch open 01/01/1878 - 07/01/1963. Victoria Line station opened 01/09/1968 Borley refers to goods yard opening c.1878 (no closure date quoted), may refer to cold store to north on up side
Seven Sisters Chord	15 / 5A	P	01/01/1880	N/A	GER	Opened to goods 1879, passengers 01/01/1880. Closed to passengers 07/01/1963, singled ??/05/1977
		G	*??/??/1879*	N/A		Electrified and re-opened to passengers 1989
Seven Sisters Junction	15 / 5A		*??/??/1879*	N/A	GER	Junction at north end of Seven Sisters Chord (see notes above)
Seven Sisters South Junction						
Seven Sisters North Junction	15 / 5A		01/01/1878	07/02/1965	GER	Junction of Palace Gates branch
Shacklegate Junction	50 / 2B		01/07/1894	N/A	LSWR	Junction at east end of Shepperton Spur (Fulwell Curve)
SHADWELL	27 / 6B		01/10/1840	N/A	LBLR	LBLR station opened 01/10/1840 as 'Shadwell', suffix '& St George's East' added 01/07/1900. Closed 22/05/1916 - 05/05/1919, and again 07/07/1941. Rebuilt as an island platform and re-opened by DLR 31/08/1987 as 'Shadwell'.
Shadwell & St George's East (LBLR)						ELR station opened 10/04/1876 as 'Shadwell', first served MET & MDR 01/10/1884. Suffix '& St George-in-the-East'
Shadwell & St George-in-the-East (ELR)						added 01/07/1900, last served MDR 01/08/1905, suffix dropped 1918. No service MET 03/12/1906 - 31/03/1913.
Shadwell						ELL platforms closed 25/03/1995 - 25/03/1998 & 23/12/2007 - 27/04/2010 (engineering work)
Sheet Factory Junction	28 / 4A & 77		29/04/1846	12/03/1973	ECTJR	Junction at south end of Stratford Eastern Curve
Sheepcote Lane Curve	38 / 4D	P	06/07/1865	*25/05/2004*	WLER	Opened 06/07/1865 (all traffic), passenger services ceased 13/03/1912, goods 21/01/1936, track lifted 1937.
		G	*06/07/1865*	*14/11/2007*		Re-laid for Eurostar access to North Pole Depot (commissioned in advance of 17/08/1994 commencement of 'demonstration' service), Eurostar connecting service to Cardiff commenced 24/10/1994, regular passenger services ceased with effect from 25/05/2004 (last train 21/05/2004), shadowed by token bus service until 'official' closure 14/12/2004 (last bus 07/12/2004). Curve effectively redundant since 14/11/2007 opening of St Pancras International and closure of North Pole Depot, but remains in situ
SHENFIELD	20 / 5B	P	29/03/1843	N/A	ECR	Opened as 'Shenfield', but closed to passengers ??/03/1850 due to lack of patronage. Re-opened by GER
Shenfield & Hutton		G	*29/03/1843*	*04/05/1964*		01/01/1887 as 'Shenfield & Hutton Junction', with the suffix 'Junction' being dropped later that year.
Shenfield & Hutton Junction						Rebuilt 01/01/1934 due to quadrupling work. Goods yard closed 04/05/1964. Suffix '& Hutton' dropped 20/02/1969.
Shenfield						
Shenfield Country End Junction	20 / 4C		01/01/1934	N/A	LNER	
Shenfield London End Junction	20 / 1C		01/01/1934	N/A	LNER	
Shenfield Southend Line Junction	20 / 5C		01/10/1889	N/A	GER	
SHEPHERD'S BUSH (CLR)	38 / 1A & 83		30/07/1900	N/A	CLR	Terminus of Central London Railway until 14/05/1908. Sometimes had suffix 'Green' added Closed 01/02/2008 - 05/10/2008 (reconstruction)
SHEPHERD'S BUSH (MET / GWR) (1st)	37 / 1D & 83		13/06/1864	01/04/1914	MET / GWR	Replaced by Shepherd's Bush (now Shepherd's Bush Market) to north and Goldhawk Road to south
SHEPHERD'S BUSH (MET / GWR) (2nd)	38 / 1A & 83		01/07/1864	01/11/1869	MET / GWR	Existence of this station is unclear: appeared on contemporary maps. Presumably opened 01/07/1864 on spur between MET / GWR Hammersmith & City Railway and WLR (no platforms apparent on WLR). If opened, was soon replaced by Uxbridge Road Station to south of junction between spur and WLR 01/11/1869
SHEPHERD'S BUSH (LSWR)	38 / 1A & 83		01/05/1874	05/06/1916	LSWR	Addison Road to Studland Road Junction abandoned 05/06/1916
SHEPHERD'S BUSH (WLR)	38 / 1A & 83		27/05/1844	N/A	WLR	Inaugural WLR passenger service withdrawn 01/12/1844 and station closed, when services to Kensington recommenced 02/06/1862, station did not re-open but was subsequently replaced by Uxbridge Road to south 01/11/1869 (later closing 21/10/1940). New NR (LOROL) station named Shepherd's Bush built on original 1844 station site, opening 28/09/2008. Present 'down' platform occupies approximate site of 27/05/1844 platform Present 'up' platform partially built upon site of southern end of MET / GWR spur to Latimer Road
SHEPHERD'S BUSH MARKET	37 / 1D & 83		01/04/1914	N/A	MET / GWR	Replaced Shepherd's Bush (MET / GWR) (1st) to south. Renamed 12/10/2008
Shepherd's Bush						
Shepherd's Lane Junction	39 / 5B		01/05/1867	N/A	LCDR	Junction between 25/08/1862 LCDR Herne Hill to Stewarts Lane route and high level line to East Brixton, but no physical connection between the two routes installed until late 1970's / early 1980's Victoria resignalling
SHEPPERTON	48 / 6D	P	01/11/1864	N/A	TVR	Suffix 'for Halliford' sometimes used 1914 - 1955. 'Up' platform road designated a siding after 05/02/1915 and all
Shepperton for Halliford		G	*01/11/1864*	*01/08/1960*		passenger traffic reversed via 'down' platform. Turntable removed August 1942, goods yard closed 01/08/1960 (Borley), Jackson states 07/10/1960
Shepperton Spur	50 / 2B	P	01/07/1894	N/A	LSWR	Curve opened 01/07/1894, but possibly saw no regular traffic until 01/02/1895 (Borley). Utilised for race specials to
Fulwell Curve		G	*01/07/1894*	N/A		Kempton Park from opening (as well as goods), but no ordinary passenger services used curve before 01/06/1901
SHERN HALL STREET, WALTHAMSTOW	15 / 5D		26/04/1870	17/11/1873	GER	Terminus of single track branch from Lea Bridge Junction, replaced by Wood Street when line extended to Chingford
SHERWOOD HOSPITAL & POWER STATION	64 / 5A		*??/??/1918*	*??/??/1950*	PRIV	Horton Estate Light Railway opened to supply building materials, later fuel, to hospitals
SHOREDITCH (NLR)	27 / 5A & 85		01/11/1865	04/10/1940	NLR	Closed by enemy action, booking office remained open until 17/11/1941

NAME: (Previous names indented below)	Page / grid		Date opened:	Date closed:	Opening company:	NOTES:
SHOREDITCH (ELR)	27 / 5A & 85		10/04/1876	11/06/2006	ELR	Became northern passenger terminus of ELR upon electrification 31/03/1913 (through goods traffic remained). 'Down' platform abandoned 1928 and all services reversed off 'up'. Through goods traffic, connection to GER main line, and down through road abandoned 17/04/1966. Closed 25/03/1995 - 27/09/1998 (engineering works). Closed for good 11/06/2006 (last train 09/06/2006) to allow East London Line Extension works to commence
SHOREDITCH (DUNLOE STREET) GOODS DEPOT	27 / 4A		??/03/1893	03/06/1968	LNWR	
SHOREDITCH HIGH STREET	27 / 5A & 85		27/04/2010	N/A	TFL (LOROL)	On site of northern portion of Bishopsgate Goods yard (formerly Bishopsgate High Level station)
SHORTLANDS	55 / 5A		03/05/1858	N/A	WELCPR	Opened as 'Bromley' at terminus of WELCPR extension from Bromley Junction. Renamed 'Shortlands' 01/07/1858, line then extended to Southborough Road (now Bickley) four days later 05/07/1858
Bromley						
Shortlands Junction	55 / 5A		01/07/1892	N/A	LCDR	Remodelled 1958-9 then again as a 'flying' junction June 2003
SIDCUP	56 / 2C	P	01/09/1866	N/A	SER	Opened with line 01/09/1866 according to Borley, Quick & Jackson, but kentrail.org.uk website states station did not
		G	01/09/1866	15/08/1966		open until the following month (i.e. October 1866). Goods yard closed 15/08/1966, partially replaced by new siding 1967 to facilitate reversal of trains. According to Quick carried suffix 'for Halfway Street' in Bradshaw 1867 - 1893
Silk Stream Junction	12 / 4D		14/09/1890	N/A	MID	Junction between Midland Main Line and freight flyover
Silo Curve	76	P	N/A	N/A	LCOR / NR	No regular passenger service
		G	14/11/2007	N/A		
Silo Curve Junction	76		14/11/2007	N/A	LCOR / NR	
SILVER STREET	15 / 2A		22/07/1872	N/A	GER	Suffix 'for Upper Edmonton' in use c.1883 - 1933
Silver Street for Upper Edmonton						
Silver Street						
SILVERTOWN	41 / 1C & 62 / 4B	P	19/06/1863	10/12/2006	ECR	Closed 08/09/1940 - 01/01/1941 (air raid damage), 29/05/1994 - 29/10/1995 (Jubilee Line extension works), then
Silvertown & London City Airport		G	19/06/1863	early 1993		permanently 10/12/2006 (closure of North Woolwich branch for partial conversion to DLR). Former 'up' platform closed 25/08/1969 when passenger route singled (former 'up' line became bidirectional goods line, taken out of use 29/03/1993). Goods yard to west of station accessed via Silvertown Tramway, scrap metal traffic remained until early 1993 (formally abandoned 29/03/1993). '& London City Airport' suffix added 04/10/1987, removed 24/09/2000
Silvertown						Line through station site to re-open 2018 (Crossrail 1 Abbey Wood branch), but station not planned to re-open
Silvertown Tramway	41 / 1B & 62 / 4B	P	14/06/1847	26/11/1855	ECR	Part of original ECR extension from Thames Wharf to North Woolwich. After opening of diversionary route via
Woolwich Abandoned Line		G	14/06/1847	29/03/1993		Custom House 26/11/1855, line became goods only but remained a through route. Swing Bridge across entrance to Royal Victoria Dock removed c.1950 and line became accessible from Silvertown end only. Last goods movement took place in early 1993 and line abandoned 29/03/1993. Route now partially followed by DLR Woolwich Arsenal line Officially became 'Woolwich Abandoned Line' in 1855, but more commonly referred to as 'Silvertown Tramway'
Silwood Junction	40 / 2B & 79 / 80		13/03/1871	N/A	ELR	Junction established 13/03/1871, further junction for 'up' road to New Cross Gate added 01/07/1876. Old Kent Road route
Deptford Road Junction						closed 30/06/1911, lifted 1913. Junction eliminated 01/11/1964 with 'up' road to New Cross. Gate closing. Remodelled to a 'flying' layout and re-established 24/06/2012 as 'Silwood Junction' (date line energised to allow testing to begin)
SINGLEWELL MAINTENANCE DEPOT	60 / 4B		??/04/2007	N/A	LCOR	
SLADE GREEN	43 / 5C		01/07/1900	N/A	SECR	Renamed 01/08/1953
Slades Green						
SLADE GREEN DEPOT	43 / 5D		27/10/1899	N/A	SECR	Current EMU berthing shed is original 27/10/1899 steam shed (extended June 1954). Maintenance shed added 1925, demolished and completely rebuilt on same site 08/04/1991
Slade Green Junction	43 / 5C		01/05/1895	N/A	BHR / SER	Junction at north end of Erith Loop
SLOANE SQUARE	38 / 2D		24/12/1868	N/A	MDR	
SLOUGH	33 / 1C	P	01/06/1840	N/A	GWR	Trains began calling at Slough 01/05/1839, although objections from Eton College initially prevented the
		G	01/06/1840	27/07/1975		construction of a station. Station opened 01/06/1840, initially with a single platform to the south of the main line. Served by MDR trains 01/03/1883 - 01/10/1885. Station rebuilt and relocated west 08/09/1884. Goods yard closed 27/07/1975.
Slough West Junction	33 / 1C		08/10/1849	N/A	GWR	Originally junction at northern end of Royal Curve (closed 26/07/1970), today a set of junctions between the 'fast' and 'slow' roads west of Slough
SMALLBERRY GREEN	36 / 4C		22/08/1849	01/02/1850	LSWR	Temporary country terminus of LSWR Hounslow Loop until 01/12/1850 completion, situated at Wood Lane level
Hounslow						crossing. Officially named 'Hounslow' (timetable, and almost certainly tickets and station nameboards), but was so remote from Hounslow that the name 'Smallberry Green' was commonly used. Replaced by Isleworth to west
Smithfield Curve	32 / 3C	P	01/09/1871	01/04/1916	LCDR	
		G	01/09/1871	01/04/1916		
SMITHFIELD GOODS	26 / 6C & 32 / 3C		03/05/1869	30/07/1962	GWR	
Smithfield Sidings	32 / 3C		c.1885	N/A	LCDR	Laid originally c.1885 (portion of Smithfield market above built 1886-8). Abandoned with rest of Snow Hill Tunnel but 2 sidings (originally 4) re-laid as part of 'Thameslink' project. Used by services terminating at City Thameslink
Smithfield Tunnel	32 / 3C		01/07/1866	22/03/2009	MET	Farringdon to Moorgate (NR) closed 22/03/2009 due to platform lengthening at Farringdon
SNARESBROOK	16 / 5B	P	22/08/1856	N/A	ECR	Opened as 'Snaresbrook', suffix '& Wanstead' added ??/11/1898, became 'for Wanstead' 1929, dropped 14/12/1947
Snaresbrook for Wanstead		G	22/08/1856	01/08/1949		Bay platform on 'down' side added 1893. Majority of passenger services transferred to LPTB 14/12/1947.
Snaresbrook & Wanstead						Goods yard closed 01/08/1949. Bay platform on down side abandoned 1950. First trains in the morning remained
Snaresbrook						British Rail services until 01/06/1970 (last train 31/05/1970)
Snow Hill Junction	32 / 3C		01/09/1871	01/04/1916	LCDR	Junction at southern end of Smithfield Curve
Snow Hill Tunnel	32 / 3C		01/01/1866	N/A	LCDR	Line closed through tunnel 24/03/1969 - 16/05/1988
SOMERS TOWN GOODS	26 / 4B & 75		01/11/1887	23/04/1968	MID	Renamed 01/08/1892. British Library now occupies site
St Pancras New Goods						
SOUTH ACTON	37 / 2B & 51 / 1B		01/01/1880	N/A	NSWJR	UERL (MDR) platform opened 13/06/1905, closed 02/03/1959 (last train 28/02/1959). Bay platform on 'down' side for Hammersmith & Chiswick Branch
South Acton Junction	37 / 2B & 51 / 1B		01/01/1869	N/A	NSWJR / LSWR	
SOUTH BERMONDSEY	40 / 3B & 79 / 80		13/08/1866	N/A	LBSCR	Renamed 01/12/1869. Closed 01/01/1917 -01/05/1919. Relocated south by SR 17/06/1928
Rotherhithe						
South Bermondsey Junction	40 / 3B & 79 / 80		01/01/1871	N/A	LBSCR	Spur to Bricklayers Arms Junction opened 01/01/1871
SOUTH BROMLEY	27 / 6D		01/09/1884	15/05/1944	NLR	Passenger service Dalston Junction to Poplar withdrawn 15/05/1944, 'official' closure 23/04/1945
SOUTH CROYDON	66 / 3D		01/09/1865	N/A	LBSCR	
South Croydon Junction	66 / 3D		10/03/1884	N/A	LBSCR / SER	
SOUTH DOCK	40 / 1D		18/12/1871	04/05/1926	MER	Island platform between single passenger line and passing loop. Due to locomotives not being permitted to work
South West India Dock						through West India Docks initially, trains were horse-hauled through station until August 1880. Traction was
South Dock						switched to steam at boundary of Millwall Dock co until this date for final stretch to North Greenwich. Sometimes known as 'South West India Dock' 1881 - 1895. Passenger service withdrawn 04/05/1926
SOUTH EALING	36 / 1D		01/05/1883	N/A	MDR	First served by Piccadilly Line 09/01/1933. District Line ceased from 10/10/1964. Rebuilt with 4 platforms 1932
SOUTH GREENFORD	23 / 4B		20/09/1926	N/A	GWR	Suffix 'Halt' dropped 05/05/1969. 'Up' platform removed early 1990's due to embankment instability,
South Greenford Halt						not reinstated until 26/10/1999
SOUTH HAMPSTEAD	25 / 3C		02/06/1879	N/A	LNWR	Closed 01/01/1917, re-opened and renamed 10/07/1922
Loudoun Road						
SOUTH HAREFIELD HALT	9 / 6C	P	24/09/1928	01/10/1931	GCR / GWR	Renamed 29/05/1929. Goods yard opened 27/06/1929. Closed to passengers and general goods 01/10/1931.
Harefield Halt		G	27/06/1929	01/01/1953		Goods siding served Peerless wire fence co. between 1933 and 01/01/1953
SOUTH HARROW	23 / 1B		28/06/1903	N/A	MDR	Terminus 28/06/1903 - 01/03/1910. First served Piccadilly Line 04/07/1932. Last served District Line 23/10/1933. Re-sited to north 05/07/1935
SOUTH HARROW GASWORKS	23 / 1B		??/??/1910	04/04/1954	PRIV	
SOUTH HARROW SIDINGS	23 / 1B		28/06/1903	N/A	MDR	Stabling sidings (formerly depot) for Piccadilly Line (previously District Railway)
South Harrow Tunnel	23 / 2B		02/04/1906	N/A	GCR	
South Junction (Mitcham)	52 / 6D		01/10/1868	02/06/1997	LBSCR	Junction eliminated when Wimbledon to West Croydon line closed 02/06/1997 prior to conversion to Tramlink
SOUTH KENSINGTON	38 / 2C & 45		24/12/1868	N/A	MET	Opened by MET as part of 24/12/1868 MET / MDR extension to Westminster (Bridge) - boundary between two companies was east of station (South Kensington East Junction). MDR opened own platforms to south of MET 10/07/1871. UERL (GNPBR) platforms opened 08/01/1907. Middle bay road removed & filled in 28/07/1957, tracks reconfigured at same time such that former MET = eastbound and former MDR = westbound. Northernmost platform road (eastbound Circle) removed 08/01/1967, southernmost (westbound District) removed 30/03/1969, station reconstruction completed 21/10/1973
South Kensington East Junction	38 / 2D & 45		10/07/1871	28/07/1957	MDR / MET	Initially site of 'end on' junction between MET and MDR, became traditional junction when MDR opened its own lines through South Kensington 10/07/1871. Junction eliminated when tracks reconfigured 28/07/1957
SOUTH KENTISH TOWN	26 / 3A		22/06/1907	05/06/1924	UERL (CCEHR)	
SOUTH KENTON	23 / 1D		03/07/1933	N/A	LMS	Served by Bakerloo Line since opening, except 27/09/1982 (last served 24/09/1982) - 04/06/1984
SOUTH MERTON	52 / 5B		07/07/1929	N/A	SR	Temporary country terminus of Wimbledon - Sutton line until full opening 05/01/1930
SOUTH METROPOLITAN GAS COMPANY			?	?	PRIV	
SOUTH QUAY	40 / 1D		31/08/1987	N/A	DLR	Closed 09/02/1996 - 15/04/1996 (IRA bomb adjacent to station). Closed again 23/10/2009, re-opening 125m east 26/10/2009 to facilitate longer platforms (original site constrained by adjacent curves)
SOUTH RUISLIP	22 / 2C	P	01/05/1908	N/A	GCR / GWR	Opened as 'Northolt Junction'. Renamed 'South Ruislip & Northolt Junction' 12/09/1932. Suffix dropped 30/06/1947.
South Ruislip & Northolt Junction		G	01/05/1908	27/01/1964		First served by Central Line Trains 21/11/1948. Good facilities closed 27/01/1964, although milk traffic remained
Northolt Junction						until 1972. Up slow track removed and up platform widened to abut former up fast track 1973
SOUTH SHED (QUEENS PARK)	25 / 4B		11/02/1915	N/A	UERL (BAK)	Stabling Shed for Bakerloo Line
SOUTH TOTTENHAM	15 / 6A	P	01/05/1871	N/A	THJR	Goods yard opened by MID on same date as passenger station. Suffix '& Stamford Hill' dropped 01/07/1903
South Tottenham & Stamford Hill		G	01/05/1871	04/07/1966	MID	Goods yard closed 04/07/1966 (usually referred to as 'Tottenham Goods')
South Tottenham East Junction	15 / 5A		09/07/1894	N/A	TFGR / THJR	Junction between THJR and TFGR

NAME: (Previous names indented below)	Page / grid:	Date opened:	Date closed:	Opening company:	NOTES:
South Tottenham West Junction	15 / 5A	??/??/1879	N/A	GER	Junction between THJR and Seven Sisters Chord (refer to notes for latter).
SOUTH WEST SIDINGS	24 / 5C & 86	*c.1870*	N/A	NSWJR	Sidings had appeared on site by 1871 OS
SOUTH WIMBLEDON	52 / 4B	13/09/1926	N/A	UERL (NOR)	(Merton) suffix added c.1928, but gradually dropped. Still appears on some station signage at platform level
South Wimbledon (Merton)					
South Wimbledon					
SOUTH WOODFORD	16 / 4B	P 22/08/1856	N/A	ECR	Opened as 'George Lane', Renamed 'South Woodford (George Lane)' 05/07/1937. Ownership and majority of
South Woodford (George Lane)		G *22/08/1856*	*06/01/1964*		passenger services transferred to LPTB 14/12/1947, when 'George Lane' suffix dropped.
George Lane					Goods yard closed 06/01/1964. First Trains in the morning remained British Rail services until 01/06/1970.
SOUTHFLEET	59 / 3C	P 10/05/1886	03/08/1953	LCDR	Opened as an island platform with Gravesend West branch. Closed to passengers 03/08/1953, goods 11/06/1962
		G *10/05/1886*	*11/06/1962*		Line through station site closed 24/03/1968, but was re-opened due to establishment of APCM (later Blue Circle)
					coal terminal on station site 1972, which remained in operation until 1976
Southfleet Junction	59 / 3D	14/11/2007	N/A	LCOR	Route to Fawkham Junction rarely used after 14/11/2007
SOUTHALL	35 / 1D	P 01/05/1839	N/A	GWR	Sometimes had suffix 'Brentford Junction' added. Served by District Railway 01/03/1883 - 01/10/1885
		G *01/05/1839*	*02/01/1967*		Goods yard closed 02/01/1967
SOUTHALL EAST SIDINGS	36 / 1A	*??/07/1859*	N/A	GWR	First engine shed on site ??/07/1859 (single road). Rebuilt 1884 & 1954, steam allocation withdrawn 31/12/1965.
					Became DMU depot 03/01/1966, until November 1986. Taken over by GWR Preservation Group 1988 (became
					'Southall Railway Centre'), further taken over by Flying Scotsman Railways July 1997
SOUTHALL GAS WORKS	35 / 1C	*??/??/1869*	*??/??/1961*	PRIV	Opened by Brentford Gas Company
Southall West Junction	35 / 1D	18/07/1859	N/A	GWR	Junction between GWR main line and Brentford Branch. Direct access from branch to main line restored March 1995
					(shunt move via Down yard had been necessary previously)
SOUTHBURY	7 / 5B	P 01/10/1891	N/A	GER	Opened as 'Churchbury', closed to passengers 01/10/1909 - 01/03/1915 then again 01/07/1919.
Churchbury		G *01/10/1891*	*07/12/1970*		Re-opened as 'Southbury' 21/11/1960, goods yard closed 07/12/1970.
SOUTHFIELDS	52 / 1A	03/06/1889	N/A	LSWR	Putney Bridge to Wimbledon built by LSWR, initially operated by MDR only, LSWR services commenced 01/07/1889
					Last regular main line passenger service withdrawn 05/05/1941, although services called on occasions until 1969
					Station ownership transferred to LUL 01/04/1994 along with entire Putney Bridge to Wimbledon route
SOUTHGATE	6 / 6B	13/03/1933	N/A	UERL (GNPBR)	
SOUTHWARK	39 / 1C	20/11/1999	N/A	LUL (JUB)	
SOUTHWARK DEPOT (GOODS)	39 / 1D & 72 / 6B	*??/??/1901*	*03/10/1960*	SECR	Provided goods facilities transferred from London bridge, adjacent to Ewer Street locomotive depot. General goods
					ceased 03/10/1960, parcels 1969. Became EMU stabling sidings after 1969, decommissioned May 1983
SOUTHWARK PARK	40 / 2B & 79	01/10/1902	15/03/1915	SECR	
SPA ROAD, BERMONDSEY	40 / 2A	08/02/1836	15/03/1915	LGR	Temporary London terminus of LGR until 10/10/1836 extension to Bermondsey Street. Closed 14/12/1836 (Quick),
Spa Road & Bermondsey					'end of 1838' (Mitchell & Smith) or 'probably' February 1843 (Borley). Re-opened as permanent structure 'probably'
					30/10/1842 (Quick - also Mitchell & Smith), or 'probably' February 1843 (Borley). Resited east 01/09/1872.
					Usually 'Spa Road & Bermondsey' until 1877, after 1877 usually 'Spa Road, Bermondsey'. Closed to passengers
					15/03/1915, but used by railwaymen until 21/09/1925
SPENCER ROAD HALT	66 / 3D	01/09/1906	15/03/1915	LBSCR / SER	
SPITALFIELDS GOODS	27 / 5B & 85	*c.1840*	*06/11/1967*	ECR	Brick Lane Goods (opened ECR c.1840) amalgamated with Whitechapel Coal (opened GER 01/11/1866) 01/01/1881
Whitechapel Coal					to form Spitalfields Goods. Closed 06/11/1967
Brick Lane Goods					
Springhead Junctions	59 / 1C	13/12/2009	N/A	NR	Regular services from Faversham to St Pancras commenced 13/12/2009
Spur Junction	54 / 5A	18/06/1862	30/10/1966	LBSCR	Junction at north end of Norwood Spur
STAINES	48 / 2A	P 22/08/1848	N/A	LSWR	Opened as 'Staines', suffix 'Old' added 1885, changed to 'Junction' 1889, suffix dropped 1920/1. Suffix 'Central'
Staines Central		G *22/08/1848*	*??/??/1973*		added 26/09/1949, dropped 18/04/1966. Two goods yards (west and east) had ceased to be used by 1973
Staines Junction					
Staines Old					
Staines					
Staines Bridge	48 / 2A	04/06/1856	N/A	LSWR	
STAINES CARRIAGE SIDINGS	48 / 2B	*??/??/1974*	N/A	LSWR	
Staines Curve	48 / 2A	P N/A	N/A	LSWR	No regular passenger service
		G *07/04/1877*	*18/03/1965*		
Staines East Junction	48 / 2A	04/06/1856	N/A	LSWR	
STAINES HIGH STREET	48 / 2A	01/07/1884	30/01/1916	LSWR	
Staines High Street Junction	48 / 2A	07/04/1877	18/03/1965	LSWR	Junction at north end of Staines Curve
STAINES LINOLEUM WORKS	48 / 2A	*??/??/1887*	*??/??/1957*	PRIV	Extensive internal network of narrow gauge lines as well as standard gauge lines connected to GWR and LSWR
Staines Moor Junction	47 / 1D	23/06/1940	16/12/1947	SR	Curve between GWR and SR established as a diversionary route during WW2, little used
STAINES WEST	48 / 2A	P 02/11/1885	29/03/1965	GWR	Suffix 'West' added 26/09/1949. Passenger service West Drayton to Staines West withdrawn 29/03/1965, but
Staines		G *02/11/1885*	*02/11/1953*		traffic to Staines West oil terminal remained. Goods yard closed 02/11/1953, but re-opened as oil terminal 24/06/1964
Staines West Junction (1st)	48 / 2A	07/04/1877	18/03/1965	LSWR	Junction at south end of Staines Curve
Staines West Junction (2nd)	47 / 1D	24/01/1981	24/06/1991	BR	Established for access to Staines West oil terminal after M25 severed GWR route to West Drayton
					First train special passenger service 24/01/1981, last use 24/06/1991. Still in situ but disused
STAINES WEST OIL TERMINAL (SHELL / BP)	48 / 2A	*24/06/1964*	*24/06/1991*	PRIV	On site of former Staines West goods yard (closed 02/11/1953). Accessed by GWR Staines West branch from
					West Drayton until 16/01/1981. New connection to LSWR Windsor branch commissioned 24/01/1981, when a
					special passenger train became last train to traverse length of GWR Staines West branch. Oil trains ran via
					LSWR route after this date, and GWR branch subsequently severed by M25 motorway south of Colnbrook
STAMFORD BROOK	37 / 2C & 51 / 2D	01/02/1912	N/A	UERL (MDR)	Island platform built only for District Line (LSWR trains non-stopped). Due to forthcoming Piccadilly Line extension,
					eastbound District Line diverted via former 'up' LSWR road so new platform opened on that line 05/06/1932
STAMFORD HILL	15 / 6A	22/07/1872	N/A	GER	
STANMORE	11 / 2D	P 10/12/1932	N/A	MET	Opened by Metropolitan Railway. Transferred to Bakerloo Line 20/11/1939, Jubilee Line 01/05/1979
		G *10/12/1932*	*31/03/1936*		Goods yard closed 31/03/1936 (Now stabling sidings). Third platform opened 26/06/2011
STANMORE VILLAGE	11 / 2D	P 18/12/1890	15/09/1952	LNWR	'Village' suffix added 25/09/1950. Stanmore Village to Belmont closed to passengers 15/09/1952,
Stanmore		G *18/12/1890*	*06/07/1964*		goods 06/07/1964.
Stanmore Branch Junction	11 / 4C	18/12/1890	05/10/1964	LNWR	Southern quarter mile of branch retained as head shunt for Harrow & Wealdstone goods until 03/04/1967
Star Bridge	73 / 3A	05/11/1899	N/A	LBSCR	Point where LBSCR 'Quarry Line' crosses original LBRR
STAR LANE	28 / 6A	31/08/2011	N/A	DLR	
STEPNEY GREEN	27 / 5B	23/06/1902	N/A	MDR / LTSR	Served by Metropolitan Line since 30/03/1936 ('Hammersmith & City Line' since 30/07/1990)
Stepney East Junction	27 / 6C	02/04/1849	??/??/1951	LBLR	Junction points removed 1951, although original LBLR route along north side of Limehouse Basin remained
Stepney Junction					accessible from east end (Limehouse Junction) as a siding until 1962
STEWARTS LANE (LCDR)	39 / 4A & 82	01/05/1863	01/01/1867	LCDR	
STEWARTS LANE (WELCPR)	39 / 4A & 82	29/03/1858	01/12/1858	WELCPR	Opened by WELCPR, but operated by LBSCR from outset
STEWARTS LANE DEPOT	39 / 4A & 82	*??/02/1862*	N/A	LCDR	Land purchased by LCDR 1861. Roundhouse opened February 1862, erecting shop in operation 1869 - 1904
Longhedge Locomotive Works					(work then transferred to Ashford, Kent). Renamed 'Stewarts Lane' after 1933-4 rebuilding. Steam ceased 1963
STEWARTS LANE GOODS	39 / 4A & 82	*15/01/1862*	*02/11/1970*	LCDR	
Stewarts Lane Junction	39 / 4A & 82	25/08/1862	N/A	LCDR	
STEWARTS LANE STONE TERMINAL	82	?	N/A	PRIV	
STOKE NEWINGTON	27 / 1A	27/05/1872	N/A	GER	Terminus from opening until 22/07/1872. Goods yard to north of Stoke Newington Tunnel (see 'Manor Road Goods')
Stoke Newington Tunnel	27 / 1A	22/07/1872	N/A	GER	
STOAT'S NEST	73 / 1B	12/07/1841	01/12/1856	LBRR	Opened with LBRR Croydon Junction to Haywards Heath route as request stop, permanent premises opened 1842
Stoat's Nest Junction	73 / 1B	05/11/1899	N/A	LBSCR / SER	Junction former by opening of LBSCR 'Quarry Line'
STOAT'S NEST QUARRY	73 / 2B	*pre-1868*	*c.1970*	PRIV	Quarry began to be worked c.1805, rail connection depicted on 1868 OS, last shown 1965-7, absent 1975
Stockley Park Flyover	34 / 1D	19/01/1998	N/A	RT	Flyover carrying 'up' line ex-BAA Heathrow Airport branch
STOCKWELL	39 / 4B	18/12/1890	N/A	CSLR	Terminus of CSLR 18/12/1890 - 03/061900. Line closed for tunnel widening 28/11/1923, station re-opened to south
					01/12/1924. Victoria Line platforms opened 23/07/1971
STOCKWELL DEPOT	39 / 4B	*18/12/1890*	*29/11/1923*	CSLR	Original CSLR Depot, accessed by a steep incline (cable haulage), later replaced by hydraulic lift (one car capacity)
					Closed with rest of CSLR 29/11/1923 for tunnel widening works, remained closed when CSLR re-opened 1924
					due to access having become available to Golders Green Depot via 20/04/1924 Euston to Camden Town link
STONE CROSSING	44 / 6D	02/11/1908	N/A	SECR	Suffix 'Halt' dropped 05/05/1969
Stone Crossing Halt					
STONEBRIDGE PARK	24 / 3B & 68 / 6B	15/06/1912	N/A	LNWR	Served by Bakerloo Line Trains since 01/08/1917. Terminus of Bakerloo Line services 24/09/1982 - 04/06/1984
					Goods station site remote (to north west), see separate entry below
STONEBRIDGE PARK DEPOT	24 / 3A & 68 / 3B	*09/04/1979*	N/A	LTE (BAK)	Bakerloo Line Depot, on site of former LNWR power station
STONEBRIDGE PARK GOODS	24 / 3A & 68 / 4B	*19/08/1912*	*??/06/1951*	LNWR	Heavy Repair shop later built on same site
STONEBRIDGE PARK POWER STATION	24 / 3A & 68 / 3B	*24/02/1916*	*30/07/1967*	LNWR	LNWR power station, Stonebridge Park Depot later built on same site
STONELEIGH	64 / 3C	17/07/1932	N/A	SR	
STRATFORD	28 / 3A & 77 / 78	P 20/06/1839	N/A	ECR	NER platforms opened 22/11/1841 (initially separate station, combined with ECR station 01/04/1847). 'Low Level'
Stratford (West Ham)		G *20/06/1839*	?		ECR platforms opened 16/10/1854. Sometimes had suffix '(West Ham)' appended 1898 - 1923. LPTB Central Line
Stratford					platforms opened 04/12/1946 (terminus until 05/05/1947). First DLR platform 4 opened 31/08/1987 (until then never
					utilised BR bay platform), closed and replaced by platforms 4a & 4b 18/06/2007 & 09/12/2007. LUL Jubilee Line
					platforms opened 14/05/1999. 'Low Level' NR platforms closed and replaced by new platforms 1 & 2 14/04/2009
					before being converted for DLR use (opened 31/08/2011 as platforms 16 & 17). Central Line westbound platform
					3a opened 05/09/2010. Goods yard to east of station, date of closure unknown (not stated in Borley)

NAME: (Previous names indented below)	Page / grid:		Date opened:	Date closed:	Opening company:	NOTES:
Stratford Central Junction East	28 / 3A & 77 / 78		15/09/1840	N/A	ECR / NER	
Stratford Central Junction West	28 / 3A & 77 / 78		15/08/1854	N/A	ECR	
Stratford Country End Crossovers	28 / 3A & 78		?	N/A	BR	
Stratford Eastern Curve	28 / 3A & 77	P	N/A	N/A	ECTJR	Never saw regular passenger services
		G	*29/04/1846*	*12/03/1973*		
Stratford Eastern Junction	28 / 3A & 77		29/04/1846	12/03/1973	ECTJR / ECR	Junction at north end of Stratford Eastern Curve
STRATFORD FREIGHTLINER TERMINAL	27 / 3D		*04/07/1967*	*??/??/1998*	BR	
STRATFORD HIGH STREET	28 / 4A & 78		31/08/2011	N/A	DLR	On site of former Stratford Market station
STRATFORD INTERNATIONAL	27 / 3D & 78		30/11/2009	N/A	LCOR	Opened with advent of Southeastern services into St Pancras International. DLR platforms opened 31/08/2011
STRATFORD MARKET	28 / 4A & 77		14/06/1847	06/05/1957	ECR	'Stratford Bridge' until 01/11/1880 when renamed 'Stratford Market'. Relocated slightly to east 1892 (quadrupling).
Stratford Market (West Ham)						Carried suffix '(West Ham)' 1898 - 1923. Current Stratford High Street DLR station occupies same site
Stratford Market						Large goods yard to south of station (see separate entry below)
Stratford Bridge						
STRATFORD MARKET DEPOT	28 / 4A		*14/05/1999*	N/A	LUL (JUB)	Jubilee Line Depot, on site of former Stratford Market Goods
STRATFORD MARKET GOODS	28 / 4A		*01/10/1879*	*05/11/1984*	GER	Fruit & Vegetable Market, with adjacent goods depot. Sidings retained for engineering use until 1988, then lifted
Stratford Southern Curve	28 / 4A & 77	P	14/06/1847	28/10/1940	ECR	Closed to passenger services 28/10/1940, fell into disuse by early 1980's, junctions eliminated 03/11/1984
		G	*14/06/1847*	*03/11/1984*		
Stratford Southern Junction	28 / 4A & 77		14/06/1847	03/11/1984	ECR	Junction at east end of Stratford Southern Curve
STRATFORD TRACTION MAINTENANCE DEPOT (TMD) (1st)	77		*c.1847*	*??/??/2001*	ECR	ECR locomotive works. Overhaul work continued until 31/03/1991 (closure of diesel repair shop), loco stabling continued
Stratford Works						Relocated to Temple Mills 2001 due to Channel Tunnel Rail Link works at Stratford (see Stratford TMD [2nd])
STRATFORD TRACTION MAINTENANCE DEPOT (TMD) (2nd)	27 / 1C		*??/??/2001*	*??/??/2007*	EWS	Relocated depot closed and replaced by Orient Way Sidings
Stratford Western Junction	28 / 4A & 77		14/06/1847	03/11/1984	ECR	Junction at west end of Stratford Southern Curve
STRAWBERRY HILL	50 / 1B		01/12/1873	N/A	LSWR	
STRAWBERRY HILL DEPOT	50 / 2B		*01/05/1897*	N/A	LSWR	Fulwell Depot opened 01/05/1897 with a six-road engine shed (current 'A' shed). In 1908 the shed was extended by
Fulwell Depot						three roads with the addition of the 'B' shed. The shed roads were electrified 30/01/1916, the steam allocation
						subsequently being transferred to the new Feltham shed in 1923. EMU depot always referred to as 'Strawberry Hill
						Depot'. Site of former coal dump sidings became additional stabling sidings ('Field Sidings') in 1936
Strawberry Hill Junction	50 / 2B		01/11/1864	N/A	LSWR / TVR	Junction between LSWR Kingston Branch (now Loop) and Thames Valley Railway (Shepperton Branch)
Thames Valley Junction						
STREATHAM	53 / 3B	P	01/10/1868	N/A	LBSCR	
		G	*01/10/1868*	*07/10/1968*		
STREATHAM COMMON	53 / 4B	P	01/12/1862	N/A	LBSCR	Suffix 'Greyhound Lane' in use 01/09/1868 - 01/01/1870
Streatham Common (Greyhound Lane)		G	*01/12/1862*	*07/10/1968*		
Streatham Common						
Streatham Common Junction	53 / 3A		01/10/1868	N/A	LBSCR	Spurs at Streatham thought to have opened at same time as Peckham - Sutton line (01/10/1868) (Borley)
STREATHAM HILL	53 / 2B	P	01/12/1856	N/A	WELCPR	Opened as 'Streatham', became either 'Streatham & Brixton Hill' or simply 'Brixton Hill' 01/09/1868, further renamed
Streatham & Brixton Hill		G	*c.1856*	*??/??/1938*		'Streatham Hill' 01/01/1869. There was a coal yard present on 'down' side west of station as early as 1869 OS,
Streatham						possibly opened with passenger station, closed and converted to EMU stabling sidings 1938 (no mention in Borley)
STREATHAM HILL DEPOT	53 / 2B		*c.1890*	N/A	LBSCR	Carriage sidings had appeared by 1895 OS on 'up' side (not present on 1874-5 OS). Shed added in mid-20th century
						(not apparent before 1951-2 OS). Sidings on down side originally coal yard, converted for stabling 1938
Streatham Junction	53 / 3B		01/10/1868	N/A	LBSCR	Spurs at Streatham thought to have opened at same time as Peckham - Sutton line (01/10/1868) (Borley)
Streatham North Junction	53 / 3A		01/10/1868	N/A	LBSCR	Spurs at Streatham thought to have opened at same time as Peckham - Sutton line (01/10/1868) (Borley)
Streatham South Junctions A & B	53 / 3A		01/10/1868	N/A	LBSCR	Spurs at Streatham thought to have opened at same time as Peckham - Sutton line (01/10/1868) (Borley)
Streatham South Junction C	53 / 3A		01/10/1868	N/A	LSWR & LBSCR	Spurs at Streatham thought to have opened at same time as Peckham - Sutton line (01/10/1868) (Borley)
Streatham Tunnel	53 / 2B		01/10/1868	N/A	LBSCR	
STROUD GREEN	14 / 6C		11/04/1881	05/07/1954	GNR	Closed when Alexandra Palace to Finsbury Park service withdrawn 05/07/1954 after a previous closure period
						29/10/1951 - 07/01/1952. Branch had been intended for electrification and transfer to LPTB Northern Line,
						but works abandoned post-WW2
Studland Road Junction	37 / 2D		01/06/1877	03/12/1911	LSWR / MDR	Junction physically eliminated through 03/12/1911 quadrupling between there and Turnham Green
Subway Tunnel	25 / 6B & 67 / 5A		12/05/1878	N/A	MET / GWR	Diveunder provided to eliminate the Hammersmith & City Railway's original level crossing of the GWR main line
SUDBURY & HARROW ROAD	23 / 2C	P	01/03/1906	N/A	GCR	Goods yard closed 03/05/1965. Platforms originally provided on loops off two central 'fast' roads, which were
		G	*01/03/1906*	*03/05/1965*		subsequently removed. Original platforms then abandoned and replaced by 'island' on site of 'fast' roads.
SUDBURY HILL	23 / 2B		28/06/1903	N/A	MDR	Suffix 'for Greenford Green' 1904 - 1938. First served Piccadilly Line 04/07/1932,
Sudbury Hill for Greenford Green						last served District Line 23/10/1933
SUDBURY HILL HARROW	23 / 2B	P	01/03/1906	N/A	GCR	Terminus from opening until 02/04/1906. Renamed 19/07/1926. Goods yard closed 03/05/1965
South Harrow		G	*01/03/1906*	*03/05/1965*		Platforms originally provided on loops off two central 'fast' roads. Loops and platforms later removed with new
						platforms being constructed alongside original 'fast' roads. Closed 22/09/1990 - 07/10/1990
Sudbury Junction	24 / 3B & 68 / 2C		*c.1890*	N/A	LNWR	Willesden Relief lines and diveunder added c.1890
Brent Junction						
SUDBURY TOWN	23 / 3D		28/06/1903	N/A	MDR	Suffix 'for Horsenden' 1904 - 1938. First served Piccadilly Line 04/07/1932, last served District Line 23/10/1933
Sudbury Town for Horsenden						
Sudbury Town						
SUNBURY	49 / 4B	P	01/11/1864	N/A	TVR	Originally passing point on single line until 17/07/1878 doubling. Goods yard closed 01/08/1960 (Borley), Jackson
		G	*01/11/1864*	*01/08/1960*		states 07/10/1960
SUNDRIDGE PARK	55 / 4B		01/01/1878	N/A	SER	Renamed 01/07/1894
Plaistow						
SUNNYMEADS	33 / 4B		10/07/1927	N/A	SR	
SURBITON	50 / 6D	P	??/??/1845	N/A	LSWR	Replaced Kingston (1st) station 1/2 mile to east at some point in 1845. Also initially named 'Kingston', suffix
Surbiton & Kingston		G	*??/??/1845*	*01/11/1971*		'Junction' added December 1852. Renamed 'Surbiton & Kingston' 01/07/1863 (on same day that current 'Kingston'
Kingston Junction						station opened). Renamed 'Surbiton' 01/10/1867. Goods yard closed 01/11/1971
Kingston						
Surrey Canal Junction	40 / 3C & 79 / 80		01/09/1849	N/A	LGR / SER	Junction between Bricklayers Arms Branch and LGR, former disused since 1981, but junction remains in situ
North Kent West Junction						Easternmost portion of Bricklayers Arms Branch to be re-used from 2018 as Bermondsey dive-under
Bricklayer's Arms Junction						leading to junction being re-established in use. Originally 'Bricklayers Arms Jcn', currently 'North Kent West Jcn'
SURREY CANAL ROAD	40 / 3B & 80		TBC	N/A	TFL (LOROL)	Proposed station on LOROL East London Line extension Phase 2. Unlikely to open with line 09/12/2012,
						due to insufficient funds, but foundations for station building / platforms are being constructed
SURREY QUAYS	40 / 2B & 79 / 80		07/12/1869	N/A	ELR	First served MET & MDR 01/10/1884, last served MDR 01/08/1905, no service MET 03/12/1906 - 31/03/1913.
Surrey Docks						Renamed 'Surrey Docks' 17/07/1911, then 'Surrey Quays' 24/10/1989. Closed 25/03/1995 - 25/03/1998
Deptford Road						& 23/12/2007 - 27/04/2010 (engineering work), upon latter re-opening became TFL (LOROL) station
SUTTON	65 / 3B	P	10/05/1847	N/A	LBSCR	Originally two-platform through station, additional platforms on Epsom Downs branch added 22/05/1865
		G	*10/05/1847*	*07/10/1968*		Goods yard closed 07/10/1968
SUTTON COMMON	65 / 2B		05/01/1930	N/A	SR	
Sutton East Junction	65 / 3C		22/05/1865	N/A	LBSCR	Route to Mitcham Junction opened 01/10/1868
Sutton West Junction	65 / 3B		05/01/1930	N/A	SR	
SWANLEY	57 / 6B	P	01/07/1862	N/A	LCDR	Opened by LCDR at divergence of Sevenoaks Railway (nominally independent by operated by LCDR) branch to
Swanley Junction		G	*01/07/1862*	*16/05/1964*		Bat & Ball station from LCDR main line. Four platform faces, opened a month after branch line. Initially 'Sevenoaks
Sevenoaks Junction						Junction', renamed 'Swanley Junction' 01/01/1871, then 'Swanley' 16/04/1939. Rebuilt on a site west of the junction
						with two island platforms 02/07/1939. Goods yard closed 16/05/1964 to public traffic, but two sidings retained as
						part of Westinghouse training compound (sidings currently disused)
Swanley Junction	57 / 6B		02/06/1862	N/A	SOR / LCDR	Initially 'Sevenoaks Junction', presumably renamed in conjunction with Swanley (Junction) station 01/01/1871
Sevenoaks Junction						
SWANSCOMBE	45 / 6B		06/07/1930	N/A	SR	Replaced original Swanscombe Halt 770 metres west 06/07/1930. Suffix 'Halt' dropped 05/05/1969
Swanscombe Halt						
SWANSCOMBE HALT	45 / 6A		02/11/1908	06/07/1930	SECR	Replaced by new halt 770 metres to east (see 'Swanscombe')
SWANSCOMBE PORTLAND CEMENT WORKS	45 / 6B		*??/??/1929*	*??/??/1982*	PRIV	Britain's first cement works, opened 1825 with internal narrow gauge rail network. Connected to North Kent line
						and converted to Standard gauge 1929. Closed when chalk pits exhausted 1982.
SWISS COTTAGE (MET)	25 / 3C		13/04/1868	18/08/1940	MET	Terminus of branch from Baker Street until 30/06/1879
SWISS COTTAGE (LPTB)	25 / 3C		20/11/1939	N/A	LPTB (BAK)	Opened by Bakerloo Line, transferred to Jubilee Line 01/05/1979
SYDENHAM	54 / 3B		05/06/1839	N/A	LCRR	Rebuilt 1853-4 (quadrupling)
Sydenham Down Junction	54 / 3B		10/06/1854	N/A	LBSCR	
SYDENHAM HILL	54 / 2A		01/08/1863	N/A	LCDR	
Sydenham Up Junction	54 / 3B		10/06/1854	N/A	LBSCR	
SYON LANE	36 / 3C		05/07/1931	N/A	SR	

T

NAME: (Previous names indented below)	Page / grid:		Date opened:	Date closed:	Opening company:	NOTES:
TADWORTH	71 / 4D	P	01/07/1900	N/A	SECR	Terminus until extension to Tattenham Corner opened 04/06/1901 (please see Tattenham Corner entry for pre-25/03/1928 service patterns beyond Tadworth). Goods yard closed 07/05/1962. Suffix dropped 01/12/1968
Tadworth & Walton on the Hill		G	*01/07/1900*	*07/05/1962*		
Tanners Hill Flydown	40 / 5D	P	29/03/1976	N/A	BR	Doubled for Thameslink upgrade, works commenced 06/04/2012, completed 06/06/2012
		G	*29/03/1976*	N/A		
Tanners Hill Junction	40 / 5D		29/03/1976	N/A	BR	Junction at north end of Tanners Hill Flydown
TARMAC STONE TERMINAL (HAYES)	35 / 1B		*??/??/1968*	N/A	PRIV	
TARMAC TOPMIX STONE TERMINAL (PADDINGTON)	25 / 5B & 67 / 5A		*??/??/1975*	*??/??/2010*	PRIV	Opened 1975 on site of Paddington New Yard, closed 2010 to allow construction of 'Crossrail 1' To re-open on same site upon completion of Crossrail 1 works c.2018
TARMAC TOPMIX STONE TERMINAL (PARK ROYAL)	24 / 5B		?	N/A	PRIV	
TATTENHAM CORNER	71 / 2D	P	04/06/1901	N/A	SECR	First use for a race meeting 04/06/1901, initially appears to have been race / excursion specials only. All day service commenced June 1902 (Bradshaw), albeit Summer only until end Summer 1914. Army camp use September 1914 to 1919. Race specials recommenced 29/04/1919, full public re-opening 25/03/1928 (electrification). Goods yard closed 02/04/1962. Reduced from original six platforms to three 29/11/1970. Original station building demolished by a train over-running buffers 01/12/1993, replacement opened March 1994
		G	*04/06/1901*	*02/04/1962*		
TAYLOR'S LANE POWER STATION	24 / 3C		*??/??/1903*	*c.1990*	PRIV	Originally built by Willesden Urban District Council. Decommissioned 1972 and replaced by current power station 1979, sidings connected until at least 1990 (Quail), and remain in situ at power station end
TEDDINGTON	50 / 3C	P	01/07/1863	N/A	LSWR	Suffix variously '(Bushey Park)', '& Bushey Park' or 'for Bushey Park' until August 1911 when station became simply 'Teddington' (Borley). Suffix carried until 1955 in Bradshaw (per Quick). 'Bushey' also spelt 'Bushy' at times. Goods yard closed 03/05/1965
Teddington for Bushey Park		G	*01/07/1863*	*03/05/1965*		
Teddington & Bushey Park						
Teddington (Bushey Park)						
TEMPLE	26 / 6C		30/05/1870	N/A	MDR	Prefix 'The' dropped gradually by c.1883
The Temple						
Temple Mills East Junction	28 / 2A & 77 / 78		??/??/1881	N/A	GER	High Meads Loop opened 1881
TEMPLE MILLS EUROSTAR DEPOT	27 / 1D		*07/10/2007*	N/A	LCOR	Partly on site of Temple Mills Marshalling Yard. Formal opening 02/10/2007, came into use 07/10/2007
TEMPLE MILLS LOCO & WAGON WORKS	27 / 2D & 27		*??/??/1850*	*??/??/1963*	ECR	
TEMPLE MILLS YARD	27 / 1D & 27		*??/??/1871*	N/A	GER	First goods sidings opened 1871. Expanded 1877, 1893 & 1930, reconstructed as a 'hump' yard December 1958 No longer used as a Marshalling yard; some engineering use. Much of original site occupied by Eurostar Depot
THAMES AMMUNITION WORKS	44 / 3A		*??/??/1917*	*c.1918*	PRIV	Connected to external rail network during latter stages of WW1 only, via 1 1/2 mile light railway from Slade Green
Thames Bridge (Windsor)	33 / 4B		08/10/1849	N/A	GWR	Track singled 09/09/1963
THAMES DITTON	50 / 6B		??/11/1851	N/A	LSWR	Opened November 1851 (Jackson), Quick states first in timetable December 1851
Thames Tunnel (ELR)	40 / 1B		07/12/1869	N/A	ELR	Opened to pedestrian traffic 25/03/1843, first trains ran through tunnel 07/12/1869
Thames Tunnel (LCOR)	44 / 5D & 45 / 5A		14/11/2007	N/A	LCOR	
THAMES WHARF	41 / 1B & 62 / 4A		*29/04/1846*	*04/10/1965*	ECTJR	Midland Railway goods yard opened 1870 adjacent to existing GER (former ECTJR / ECR)
THAMES WHARF	41 / 1B & 62 / 5A		N/A	N/A	DLR	Proposed station on DLR Woolwich Arsenal line, dependant on adjacent housing development
Thames Wharf Junction	41 / 1B & 62 / 3A		26/11/1855	04/10/1965	ECR	Junction between original line to North Woolwich and 1855 route via Custom House. Eliminated when Thames Wharf Goods closed (original North Woolwich route 'Silvertown Tramway' had been severed by then)
THEOBALDS GROVE	7 / 2A	P	01/10/1891	N/A	GER	Closed 01/10/1909 - 01/03/1915 & 01/07/1919 - 21/11/1960. Goods yard opened 02/04/1900, closed 03/01/1966
		G	*02/04/1900*	*03/01/1966*		
THERAPIA LANE	66 / 1B		30/05/2000	N/A	CTL	
THERAPIA LANE DEPOT	66 / 1B		10/05/2000	N/A	CTL	Sole depot for London Tramlink Croydon (first section opened 10/05/2000), on site of former permanent way sidings
THEYDON BOIS	8 / 3A	P	24/04/1865	N/A	GER	Suffix 'Bois' added 01/12/1865. Goods yard opened 1886. Majority of Passenger services transferred to LTE 25/09/1949, but first trains in the morning remained BR services until 01/06/1970. Goods yard closed 18/04/1966
Theydon		G	*??/??/1886*	*18/04/1966*		
THORNEY MILL SIDINGS	34 / 1B		*11/07/1943*	N/A	GWR	Formerly used for Coal, Oil, Scrap metal and Stone traffic, today only Stone traffic remains.
THORNEY MILL STONE TERMINAL (BARDON)	34 / 1B		*??/??/1986*	N/A	PRIV	Current terminal opened 1986, stone traffic to site had occurred prior to this
THORNTON FIELDS CARRIAGE SIDINGS	27 / 4D & 77		*??/??/1928*	*16/06/2008*	GER	Points 'clipped' out of use and overhead wires de-energised 16/06/2008, 'officially' closed 30/06/2008. Site cleared for 2012 Olympic park. Replaced by Orient Way Sidings (opened 30/05/2008)
THORNTON HEATH	53 / 5C	P	01/12/1862	N/A	LBSCR	Goods yard on 'up' side, coal yard on 'down' side, all closed 07/10/1968
		G	*01/12/1862*	*07/10/1968*		
Three Bridges	36 / 1A		15/07/1859	N/A	GWR	Unusual feature where rail, canal, and road intersect (rail below canal, road above canal). Date stated is that of special passenger train run on Brentford Dock branch, regular goods trains followed three days later
THURROCK CHALK & WHITING Co. WORKS	44 / 3C		?	*c.1980*	PRIV	
TIDAL BASIN	41 / 1B & 62 / 3A		??/02/1858	15/08/1943	ECR	Borley gives name as 'Victoria Docks, Tidal Basin', this name also given in Quick in use 1882-1914 (GER timetables)
TILBURY EAST CONTAINER TERMINAL	45 / 5D		*??/??/1970*	N/A	BR	
Tilbury East Curve	46 / 6A	P	14/08/1854	??/??/1985	LTSR	Opened as part of LTSR extension from Tilbury to Stanford-Le-Hope. Regular passenger trains ceased 1985 when trains from London to / from Southend ceased reversing at Tilbury Riverside
		G	*14/08/1854*	*30/11/1992*		
Tilbury East Junction	46 / 6A		c.1855	30/11/1992	LTSR	Junction at east ends of Tilbury North / East Curves
TILBURY GRAIN TERMINAL	45 / 5C		*??/??/1969*	N/A	BR	
TILBURY INTERNATIONAL RAIL FREIGHT TERMINAL	46 / 6A		*c.2000*	N/A	BR	Opened on site of former carriage sidings subsequent to closure of Tilbury Riverside station
Tilbury Junction	27 / 5D & 22		17/05/1869	13/09/1959	NLR	Junction at north end of curve between NLR at Bow and LTSR at Bromley
TILBURY MARINE	46 / 6A		15/05/1927	01/05/1932	PLA	Platform adjacent to Tidal basin within Tilbury Docks opened by PLA to serve boat trains
TILBURY MOTIVE POWER DEPOT	46 / 6A		*13/04/1854*	*18/06/1962*	LTSR	Original 2 road engine shed adjacent to Tilbury South Junction, replaced by 4 road shed adjacent to Tilbury North Curve 1912 (original had closed 1908). Rebuilt 1956, closed due to LTSR electrification 18/06/1962
Tilbury North Curve	46 / 6A	P	??/??/1985	N/A	LTSR	Opened c.1855. No regular passenger trains until 1985 when London to Southend services ceased reversing at Tilbury Riverside station and began to run direct from Tilbury Town to East Tilbury
		G	*c.1855*	N/A		
Tilbury North Junction	45 / 4D		17/04/1886	c.1960	LTSR	Primary junction giving access to Tilbury Docks (opened 17/04/1886), eliminated during resignalling c.1960 when access provided via Grays East Junction instead
TILBURY POWER STATIONS	46 / 6B		*??/??/1956*	?	PRIV	Tilbury 'A' (oil fired) commissioned 1956, mothballed 1981, demolished 1999. Tilbury 'B' (coal & biomass fired) commissioned 1968, still in operation but rail connection severed (date unknown).
Tilbury Railport Junction	46 / 5A		c.1855	N/A	LTSR	Junction at west end of Tilbury West / North Curves. Eliminated when Tilbury Riverside closed 30/11/1992, but re-established to provide access to Tilbury International Rail Freight Terminal
Tilbury West Junction						
TILBURY RIVERSIDE	46 / 6A	P	13/04/1854	30/11/1992	LTSR	Terminus of original LTSR line from Forest Gate Junction. Branch to Stanford-Le-Hope (and subsequently towards Southend) added 14/08/1854. 'Fort' suffix applied from opening until 1866 (although not always), 'Riverside' suffix added 1935 (in timetable with effect from 06/07/1936). Until 1985 all services reversed at station, after 1985 trains between London and Southend ran direct, with only trains remaining being Upminster via Ockendon service Upminster via Ockendon service truncated at Grays and station closed 30/11/1992. Goods yard closed 06/05/1968 Site partially occupied by Tilbury International Rail Freight Terminal
Tilbury		G	*13/04/1854*	*06/05/1968*		
Tilbury Fort						
Tilbury South Junction	46 / 6A		14/08/1854	30/11/1992	LTSR	Junction at south end of Tilbury West and East curves
TILBURY TOWN	45 / 5D		17/04/1886	N/A	LTSR	Opened to public on same date as adjacent Tilbury Docks (17/04/1886) according to Quick (who also states had been open to dock construction workers from c. May 1884). Borley gives opening date of 15/06/1885. Renamed 'Tilbury Town for Tilbury Docks' 03/08/1934, 'for Tilbury Docks' suffix dropped 1958
Tilbury Town for Tilbury Docks						
Tilbury Docks						
Tilbury West Curve		P	13/04/1854	30/11/1992	LTSR	Part of original LTSR route from Forest Gate to Tilbury (Riverside). After 1985 London to Southend trains ceased reversing via Tilbury Riverside, only Upminster via Ockendon trains remained, these withdrawn 30/11/1992 Curve remains as access to Tilbury International Rail Freight Terminal
		G	*13/04/1854*	N/A		
TOLWORTH	64 / 2A	P	29/05/1938	N/A	SR	Initially temporary terminus, with 'down' platform only in use; extended to Chessington South and 'up' platform opened 28/05/1939. Goods yard expanded 1940, ceased handling general goods traffic 03/05/1965, but dedicated coal terminal had opened 04/01/1965. Aggregates traffic commenced c.1981, then coal traffic ceased c.1989. Aggregates traffic then ceased July 1993 before re-starting c.1998 (Day Group)
		G	*29/05/1938*	N/A		
Tonbridge Fast Loop	55 / 5D & 56 / 6A	P	14/09/1902	N/A	SECR	Referred to as 'Bickley Loop' until 1959. Originally single track, doubled in readiness for Eurostar services 1992
		G	*14/09/1902*	N/A		
Tonbridge Line Junction	73 / 6C		26/05/1842	N/A	SER / LBRR	
Tonbridge Slow Loop	55 / 5D & 56 / 6A	P	08/09/1902	N/A	SECR	Referred to as 'Bickley Loop' until 1959. Originally single track, doubled in readiness for Eurostar services 1992
		G	*08/09/1902*	N/A		
TOOTING	52 / 3D	P	01/10/1868	N/A	LBSCR / LSWR	Opened as a 4-platform station at divergence of LBSCR / LSWR joint loop line from Streatham to Wimbledon Named 'Tooting Junction' initially, original closed and replaced by 2-platform station east of junction 12/08/1894 Closed to passengers 01/01/1917 - 27/08/1923. Suffix 'Junction' dropped 01/03/1938 (physical junction had been severed 10/03/1934), after 10/03/1934 goods yard accessed via Merton Park, closed 05/08/1968
Tooting Junction		G	*01/10/1868*	*05/08/1968*		
TOOTING BEC	52 / 2D		13/09/1926	N/A	UERL (NOR)	Renamed 10/10/1950
Trinity Road (Tooting Bec)						
TOOTING BROADWAY	52 / 3D		13/09/1926	N/A	UERL (NOR)	
Tooting Junction	52 / 3D		01/10/1868	10/03/1934	LBSCR / LSWR	Junction eliminated 10/03/1934 and Tooting (Junction) to Merton Park route became a siding accessed from latter
TOTTENHAM COURT ROAD	26 / 6B		30/07/1900	N/A	CLR	UERL (CCEHR) platforms opened 22/06/1907 as 'Oxford Street', renamed 09/03/1908. Northern Line platforms closed 02/04/2011 - 28/11/2011 (engineering work). Platforms for 'Crossrail 1' expected to open 2018
Oxford Street (CCEHR only)						
TOTTENHAM HALE	15 / 5B	P	15/09/1840	N/A	NER	Opened as 'Tottenham', suffix 'Hale' added ??/06/1875, dropped ??/11/1938, reinstated 1968 LTB Victoria Line station opened 01/09/1968. Goods yard closed 1968
Tottenham		G	*15/09/1840*	*??/??1968*		
Tottenham Hale						
Tottenham						
Tottenham North Curve (MID)	9		*02/04/1883*	N/A	MID	No regular passenger service

NAME: (Previous names indented below)	Page / grid:	Date opened:	Date closed:	Opening company:	NOTES:
Tottenham North Curve (THJR)	15 / 5B	P 21/07/1868	01/11/1925	THJR	Opened with rest of THJR 21/07/1868 (passenger service), no regular freight until 1886. Closed to passengers
		G ??/??/1886	11/06/1961		01/11/1925, closed to freight and abandoned 11/06/1961
Tottenham North Curve Tunnels Nos. 1, 2 & 3	9	02/04/1883	N/A	MID	
Tottenham North Junction	15 / 5B	21/07/1868	11/06/1961	THJR / GER	Northern end of Tottenham North Curve (THJR) (see notes above)
Tottenham South Curve	15 / 5B	P 01/01/1880	N/A	THJR	First trains 1868 (goods), passenger services commenced 01/01/1880, ceased 07/01/1963, reintroduced 1989
		G ??/??/1868	N/A		
Tottenham South Junction	15 / 5B	??/??/1868	N/A	THJR / GER	Junction between Tottenham South Curve and GER (see notes above)
Tottenham West Junction	15 / 5B	??/??/1868	11/06/1961	THJR	Southern end of Tottenham North Curve (THJR) (see notes regarding Tottenham North Curve THJR)
TOTTERIDGE & WHETSTONE	5 / 6C	P 01/04/1872	N/A	GNR	Suffix '& Whetstone' added 01/04/1874. First served by and transferred to LPTB Northern Line 14/04/1940,
Totteridge		G 01/04/1872	01/10/1962		closed to LNER passenger services on same date. Goods yard closed 01/10/1962
TOWER GATEWAY	27 / 6A & 74 / 2B	31/08/1987	N/A	DLR	Closed 30/06/2008 - 02/03/2009 (rebuilding from 2 tracks to 1 track to accommodate longer trains)
TOWER HILL (MDR / MET)	27 / 6A & 74 / 2B	06/10/1884	05/02/1967	MDR / MET	Replaced former 'Tower of London' Station to East. Renamed 'Tower Hill' 01/09/1946, closed and replaced on
Mark Lane	& 72 / 5D				original 'Tower of London' site to east by 'Tower Hill' (MET) 05/02/1967
TOWER HILL (MET)	27 / 6A & 74 / 2B	25/09/1882	N/A	MET	Terminus of MET extension from Aldgate 25/09/1882 - 06/10/1884, replaced by Mark Lane station to west 06/10/1884
Tower of London					when MET / MDR route from Mansion House to Aldgate East opened, although 'Tower of London' did not close until
					13/10/1884. Re-opened as 'Tower Hill' 05/02/1967, replacing 'Tower Hill' (MDR / MET) station (former 'Mark Lane').
TRIANGLE SIDINGS	38 / 2C & 84	c.1915	N/A	UERL (MDR)	Sidings laid between 1914 and 1916 Ordnance surveys. Closed for S Stock upgrade work 11/12/2010, trains
					stabled at Lillie Bridge instead
TRUMPER'S CROSSING HALTE	36 / 1B	01/07/1904	01/02/1926	GWR	Closed 22/03/1915 - 12/04/1920. The full length former name stated is that which appeared on nameboards
Trumper's Crossing (for Osterley Park) Halte					
TUFNELL PARK	26 / 2A & 9	22/06/1907	N/A	UERL (CCEHR)	
TUFNELL PARK GOODS	26 / 1B	15/02/1886	06/05/1968	GER	Goods yard to south of station in triangle beyond Tulse Hill South Junction, closed 07/09/1964. Pair of sidings
TULSE HILL	53 / 1C	P 01/10/1868	N/A	LBSCR	provided on 'down' side. Station had an overall roof spanning its four platforms until c.1900
		G 01/10/1868	07/09/1964		
Tulse Hill North Junction	53 / 1C	01/01/1869	N/A	LBSCR / LCDR	
Tulse Hill South Junction	53 / 2C	01/11/1870	N/A	LBSCR	Junction at north end of Leigham and West Norwood Spurs
TUNNEL CEMENT WORKS (THURROCK)	44 / 4D	?	?	PRIV	
TURKEY STREET	7 / 2B	P 01/10/1891	N/A	GER	Opened 01/10/1891 as 'Forty Hill', closed 01/10/1909 - 01/03/1915 and again 01/07/1919.
Forty Hill		G 01/10/1891	01/06/1966		Reopened 21/11/1960 as 'Turkey Street'. Goods yard closed 01/06/1966
TURNHAM GREEN	37 / 2C & 51 / 2C	01/01/1869	N/A	LSWR	Opened by LSWR. Served by GWR 01/06/1870 - 01/11/1870. First served MDR 01/06/1877. Served by MET
					01/10/1877 - 01/01/1911 (MET / GWR joint after 01/01/1894). Rebuilt from 2 side platforms to 2 island platforms
					when route quadrupled 03/12/1911 (LSWR northern island, MDR southern island). LSWR service ceased and
					northern island abandoned 05/06/1916. Eastbound District Line started using north face of north island from
					05/06/1932. Piccadilly Line started running non-stop through middle platforms 04/07/1932 (but started calling at
					these platforms at extremes of traffic day from 23/06/1963)
Turnham Green Junction	51 / 2C	01/07/1879	N/A	LSWR / MDR	Junction between LSWR route to Richmond and MDR branch to Ealing Broadway
TURNPIKE LANE	14 / 5C	19/09/1932	N/A	UERL (GNPBR)	
TWICKENHAM	36 / 6C	P 22/08/1848	N/A	LSWR	Original station west of London Road. Engine shed added June 1850, rebuilt 01/07/1863, closed 1897
		G 22/08/1848	02/01/1967		Additional 'up' platform added when junction to west of station became 'flying' 1882. New station to east of London
					Road with 2 bay platforms for rugby traffic opened 28/03/1954 (original station closed same day). Goods yard
					closed 02/01/1967.
Twickenham Junction	50 / 1B	01/07/1863	N/A	LSWR	Junction between LSWR Windsor Line and branch to Kingston. Was a 'flat' junction until flyover opened 22/10/1883
TWYFORD ABBEY HALT	24 / 4A	01/05/1904	01/05/1911	GWR	Replaced by Brentham station to west. Slightly east of present Hanger Lane station
TWYFORD ABBEY SIDINGS	24 / 4B	26/03/1903	c.1955	LNWR	Built to serve Royal Agricultural Showground, remained in situ and lifted by 1955

U

NAME: (Previous names indented below)	Page / grid:	Date opened:	Date closed:	Opening company:	NOTES:
Up Empty Carriage Tunnel	26 / 4A & 58	10/07/1922	c.2000	LNWR	Colloquially known as the 'Rat Hole', abandoned circa resignalling in Euston area 1999 - 2000
UP SIDINGS (EUSTON)	26 / 4A	?	N/A	LNWR	
UP CARRIAGE SIDINGS (VICTORIA)	39 / 3A	c.1880's	N/A	LBSCR	Not present on 1875 OS map, but had appeared by 1896
Up Slow Flyover (Wimbledon)	52 / 2B	17/05/1936	N/A	SR	Allowed reconfiguration of LSWR main line between Wimbledon and Clapham Junction
UP YARD (REDHILL)	73 / 5C	post 1849	N/A	SER	Sidings on site on 1871 OS, possibly laid at same time as Guildford Line c.1849
UPMINSTER	31 / 2C	P 01/05/1885	N/A	LTSR	Served by District Railway trains 02/06/1902 - 01/10/1905. Reintroduced 12/09/1932 when route quadrupled, which
		G 01/05/1885	07/12/1964		also resulted in station rebuilding and relocation of original 1885 engine shed (demolished 1931, rebuilt 1935).
					Separate platform for Romford service opened 20/05/1957. Goods yard closed 07/12/1964.
UPMINSTER BRIDGE	31 / 2B	17/12/1934	N/A	LMS	Opened by LMS on the 1932 'slow' lines only, served exclusively by District Line trains from outset
UPMINSTER DEPOT	31 / 1C	01/12/1959	N/A	LTE (DIS)	South of site accommodated 5 stabling sidings for District Line trains since 12/09/1932. Depot construction
					commenced 01/12/1958, completed 29/06/1959, full opening 01/12/1959.
Upminster East Junction	31 / 2C	01/07/1892	N/A	LTSR	Junction between LTSR main line and Ockendon Loop
Upminster West Junction	31 / 2C	07/06/1893	20/05/1957	LTSR	Junction between LTSR main line and Romford Branch, eliminated when LTE and BR segregated at Upminster
UPNEY	29 / 4B	12/09/1932	N/A	LMS	Barking to Upminster quadrupled by the LMS 12/09/1932 and Upney station opened, served by UERL District Line
					from opening. Ownership transferred to LTB 1970
UPPER HALLIFORD	49 / 4A	01/05/1944	N/A	SR	Opened as 'Halliford Halt', prefix 'Upper' added 22/05/1944. 'Halt' dropped 05/05/1969. Initially opened with only
Upper Halliford Halt					a 'down' platform (single line working), 'up' platform opened 06/05/1946
Halliford Halt					
UPPER HOLLOWAY	26 / 1B	P 21/07/1868	N/A	THJR	Closed 31/01/1870 - 01/10/1870. Opened as 'Upper Holloway', suffix 'for St John's Park and Highgate Hill' added
Upper Holloway for St John's Park		G c.1870	06/05/1968		01/03/1871, '- and Highgate Hill' dropped 01/04/1875, then '- for St John's Park' dropped 01/07/1903 (i.e. returned
Upper Holloway for St John's Park and Highgate Hill					to 'Upper Holloway' from this date). Goods yard opened c.1870, closed 06/05/1968
Upper Holloway					
UPPER SYDENHAM	54 / 2A	01/08/1884	20/09/1954	LCDR	Closed 01/01/1917 - 01/03/1919 and 22/05/1944 - 04/03/1946. Closed for good 20/09/1954
UPPER WARLINGHAM	74 / 2A	P 10/03/1884	N/A	LBSCR / SER	Opened as 'Upper Warlingham', '& Whyteleafe' suffix added 01/01/1894, dropped 01/10/1900. 'for Riddlesdown'
Upper Warlingham for Riddlesdown		G 10/03/1884	04/05/1964		suffix added 1912 (LBSCR timetable), until 1926/7. Goods yard closed 04/05/1964
Upper Warlingham					
Upper Warlingham & Whyteleafe					
Upper Warlingham					
UPTON PARK	28 / 4C	17/09/1877	N/A	LTSR	First served by District Railway 02/06/1902, line quadrupled 1905, District trains then using 'slow' platforms to north
					Served by Metropolitan Line since 30/03/1936 ('Hammersmith & City Line' since 30/07/1990)
					Main line services non-stopped since 15/06/1962, and 'Fast' platforms abandoned. Goods yard situated to east of
					passenger station on a short branch line (see separate entry below)
UPTON PARK GOODS	28 / 4C	01/04/1895	??/07/1989	LNWR	Built to serve adjacent British Uralite plc. works, halt opened for workers only early 1901, to public 01/07/1906
URALITE HALT	60 / 1A	01/07/1906	04/12/1961	SECR	
UXBRIDGE (1st)	21 / 2C	P 04/07/1904	04/12/1938	MET	Served by District Line 01/03/1910 - 23/10/1933, Piccadilly Line thereafter until closure. Closed to passengers
		G 04/07/1904	01/05/1939		04/12/1938 and replaced by Uxbridge (2nd) to west, goods yard remained open until 01/05/1939 (became sidings)
UXBRIDGE (2nd)	21 / 3C	04/12/1938	N/A	LPTB (MET / PIC)	Replaced 1st station, closed on same date
UXBRIDGE HIGH STREET	21 / 2B	P 01/05/1907	01/09/1939	GWR	Goods yard open 11/05/1914. No passenger service 01/01/1917 - 03/05/1920, withdrawn for good 01/09/1939
		G 11/05/1914	24/02/1964		although 'official' closure not until 25/09/1939. Goods yard closed 24/02/1964 and most of branch abandoned
UXBRIDGE ROAD	38 / 1A & 83	01/11/1869	21/10/1940	WLR	Replaced Shepherd's Bush (MET / GWR) (2nd) to north, located to south of 1844 WLR Shepherd's Bush station
					Shepherd's Bush (NR) station opened slightly to north of site 28/09/2008
UXBRIDGE ROAD GOODS	38 / 1A & 83	??/??/1844	01/11/1967	WLR	Goods yard to north of Shepherd's Bush (WLR) station, probably not open continuously in early years
Shepherd's Bush Goods					Subsequently re-named after Uxbridge Road passenger station (opened 01/11/1869)
Uxbridge Road Junction	38 / 1A & 83	01/07/1864	01/03/1954	WLR / MET / GWR	Junction at southern end of spur to Latimer Road, 'up' platform of present-day Shepherd's Bush NR station
					occupies site of junction
UXBRIDGE SIDINGS	21 / 3C	??/??/1942	N/A	LPTB (MET)	Metropolitan Line stabling sidings. On site of former Goods yard, closed 01/05/1939 (see Uxbridge [1st])
UXBRIDGE VINE STREET	21 / 3C	P 08/09/1856	N/A	GWR	'Vine Street' suffix added 01/05/1907. Passenger station closed with withdrawal of passenger services on branch
Uxbridge		G 08/09/1856	13/07/1964		10/09/1962, goods yard closed and branch abandoned 13/07/1964

V

NAME: (Previous names indented below)	Page / grid	Date opened:	Date closed:	Opening company	NOTES:
VAN DEN BURGHS & JURGENS (PURFLEET)	44 / 4C	?	N/A	PRIV	Stork margarine manufacturers, disused but still in situ
VAUXHALL	39 / 3B	11/07/1848	N/A	LSWR	Victoria Line station opened 23/07/1971. No dedicated goods yard, but milk traffic was handled on platform 1
Vauxhall Bridge					
Ventnor Road	65 / 4B	03/10/1982	N/A	BR	Point where single track commences on Epsom Downs Branch (singled 03/10/1982)
Viaduct Junction	25 / 6A & 83	16/04/1917	09/03/1964	GWR	Through goods route closed on quoted date, but access to Wood Lane milk depot remained until 1966
VICARAGE ROAD	2 / 5B	??/??/2016	N/A	LUL (MET)	Proposed new station on re-opened Croxley Green branch (funding announcement 14/12/2011, expected opening 2016). Immediately to west of former Watford Stadium station, to replace this and former Watford West stations Also referred to as 'Watford General Hospital'
VICTORIA	39 / 2A	01/10/1860	N/A	VSPR	Opened by Victoria Station & Pimlico Railway, a joint venture between the LBSCR, LCDR, GWR & LNWR LBSCR portion opened first, served by LCDR trains from 03/12/1860. Separate LCDR station opened 25/08/1862 LBSCR and LCDR stations reconstructed 1908 and 1907-9 respectively, entire station combined by SR 1924 and platforms numbered consecutively 21/09/1925. MDR station opened 24/12/1868, connected to mainline termini via a subway 12/08/1878. Victoria Line platforms opened 07/03/1969 (terminus until 23/07/1971)
VICTORIA & ALBERT GOODS	41 / 1C & 62 / 3B	??/??/1902	?	GWR	GWR goods depot accessed via Gallions Branch, opened 1902, closure date unknown
VICTORIA (GROSVENOR) CARRIAGE SHED	39 / 3A	c.1860's	N/A	LCDR	Was in situ by early 1870's
VICTORIA PARK	27 / 3C	14/06/1856	08/11/1943	NLR	Initially opened for a single day 29/05/1856 (celebrations for end of Crimean War), date quoted is date of full opening. Sometimes referred to as 'Victoria Park, Hackney Wick' until c.1859. Resited South 01/03/1866 with four platforms at new site. Stratford-bound 'down' platform little used and removed 1895, with all GER trains reversing via the 'up' platform ex-Stratford. Former GER platform abandoned 01/11/1942 followed by former NLR platforms 08/11/1943
Victoria Park, Hackney Wick					
VICTORIA PARK & BOW	27 / 4D & 22	02/04/1849	06/01/1851	LBLR / ECR	Exchange platforms between ECR and LBLR (Blackwall Extension Railway), opened with latter route from Stepney (East) Junction. LBLR platforms closed 26/09/1850, ECR platforms closed 06/01/1851. Also referred to as 'Old Ford'
Victoria Park Junction	27 / 3C	15/08/1854	03/10/1983	NLR / ECR	Poplar Branch singled 19/08/1979, officially closed 03/10/1983 (little or no traffic subsequent to Harrow Lane Sidings closure 30/08/1981). Junction points eliminated and remainder of branch dismantled 05/05/1984
VICTORIA ROAD GOODS (ROMFORD)	18 / 6D	??/07/1896	04/05/1970	LTSR	
VIRGINIA WATER	47 / 5B	09/07/1856	N/A	LSWR	Suffix 'for Wentworth' January 1929 - 1955
Virginia Water for Wentworth					
Virginia Water					
Virginia Water East Junction	47 / 5B	01/10/1866	??/06/1966	LSWR	Junction at east end of Virginia Water West Curve
Virginia Water Junction	47 / 5B	01/10/1866	N/A	LSWR	
Virginia Water North Junction					
Virginia Water South Junction	47 / 5B	01/10/1866	??/06/1966	LSWR	Junction at west end of Virginia Water West Curve
Virginia Water West Curve	47 / 5B	G 01/10/1866	??/06/1966	LSWR	Opened 1866 as single track (at same time as line to Chertsey, 01/10/1866?). Had been doubled by 1914 per OS Closed June 1966
Voltaire Road Junction	39 / 5A	early 1980's	N/A	BR	Junction installed during Victoria resignalling late 1970's / early 1980's
VOPAK (PURFLEET)	44 / 5D	?	?	PRIV	Formerly Van Ommeren. Petrochemical / liquid gas storage and distribution, still active but rail connection removed

W

NAME:	Page / grid	Date opened:	Date closed:	Opening company	NOTES:
WADDON	66 / 2B	P ??/02/1863 G ??/02/1863	N/A 07/10/1968	LBSCR	Exact opening date unknown, first appeared in timetables February 1863. Goods yard closed 07/10/1968
WADDON MARSH	66 / 2B	06/07/1930	N/A	SR	Opened by SR at time of electrification with an island platform and passing loop on otherwise single passenger line Suffix 'Halt' dropped 05/05/1969. Passing loop decommissioned 13/05/1984. Wimbledon to West Croydon closed by Railtrack 31/05/1997 (date of last train; official date of closure 02/06/1997). Re-opened by Croydon Tramlink on new site to the south 30/05/2000
Waddon Marsh Halt					
WALLINGTON	66 / 3A	P 10/05/1847 G 10/05/1847	N/A 06/05/1963	LBSCR	Renamed 01/09/1868. Goods yard closed 06/05/1963. Reversing siding west of station installed c.1916, present on 1956-7 OS, possibly decommissioned with signal box 26/11/1972. Station extensively rebuilt 13/09/1983
Carshalton					
WALTHAM CROSS	7 / 1C	P 15/09/1840 G 15/09/1840	N/A 04/07/1966	NER	Opened as 'Waltham', suffix 'Cross' added 01/12/1882. Passenger station closed and relocated South 1885 (exact date unknown). Suffix '& Abbey' in use 01/05/1894 - 20/02/1969. Goods yard closed 04/07/1966
Waltham Cross (& Abbey)					
Waltham Cross					
Waltham					
WALTHAMSTOW CENTRAL	15 / 5D	P 26/04/1870 G 26/04/1870	N/A 02/11/1964	GER	Originally single platform on 'up' side, Shern Hall Street to Clapton Junction doubled 1873 and 'down' platform built Opened as 'Hoe Street'; suffix 'Walthamstow' added 1886, although this was often omitted. Goods yard closed 02/11/1964. Renamed 'Walthamstow Central' 06/05/1968. LTB Victoria Line terminus opened 01/09/1968
Hoe Street, Walthamstow					
Hoe Street					
WALTHAMSTOW QUEEN'S ROAD	15 / 5D	09/07/1894	N/A	TFGR	Suffix 'Queen's Road' added 06/05/1968, see 'Queen's Road Goods' entry for goods yard (remote from station)
Walthamstow					
WALTON-ON-THAMES	62 / 2B	P 21/05/1838 G 21/05/1838	N/A c.1965	LSWR	Opened as 'Walton', suffix '& Hersham' added 1849, became 'Walton for Hersham' 1913, then 'Walton-on-Thames' 30/09/1935
Walton for Hersham					
Walton & Hersham					
Walton					
WALWORTH ROAD	39 / 3D	01/05/1863	03/04/1916	LCDR	Renamed January 1865
Camberwell Gate					
WALWORTH ROAD COAL	39 / 2D	16/11/1871	30/04/1973	MID	
WANDLE PARK	66 / 2C	30/05/2000	N/A	CTL	
WANDSWORTH COMMON	52 / 1D	P 01/12/1856 G c.1869	N/A 28/09/1964	WELCPR	Opened as 'Wandsworth', suffix 'Common' added January 1858. WELCPR's temporary London terminus until 29/03/1858 extension to Pimlico (WELCPR), on which date first station closed (replaced at that time by New Wandsworth to north). When New Wandsworth closed 01/11/1869, it was replaced by the second 'Wandsworth Common' slightly to the south of the 01/12/1856 station. Goods yard given as opening c.1869 in Borley (at same time as 2nd passenger station?), closed 28/09/1964
Wandsworth					
WANDSWORTH ROAD	39 / 4A & 82	01/03/1863	N/A	LCDR	LBSCR-served platforms opened by LCDR 01/05/1867, LCDR-served platforms closed 03/04/1916
WANDSWORTH ROAD GOODS	39 / 4A & 82	??/??/1874	30/04/1973	MID	
WANDSWORTH TOWN	38 / 5C	27/07/1846	N/A	LSWR	Line quadrupled 1886. Renamed 07/10/1903
Wandsworth					
WANSTEAD	16 / 6C	14/12/1947	N/A	LPTB (CEN)	
WANSTEAD PARK	28 / 2B	09/07/1894	N/A	TFGR	
WAPPING	40 / 1B	07/12/1869	N/A	ELR	Northern terminus of ELR until 10/04/1876, suffix '& Shadwell' also dropped on same date. First served MET & MDR 01/10/1884, last served MDR 01/08/1905, no service MET 03/12/1906 - 31/03/1913. Separate 'East London Line' identity introduced during 1980's. Closed 25/03/1995 - 25/03/1998 & 23/12/2007 - 27/04/2010 (engineering work), upon latter re-opening became TfL (LOROL) station
Wapping & Shadwell					
WARREN STREET	26 / 5A	22/06/1907	N/A	UERL (CCEHR)	Renamed 07/06/1908. Victoria Line platforms opened 01/12/1968 (terminus until 07/03/1969)
Euston Road					
WARWICK AVENUE	25 / 5C	31/01/1915	N/A	UERL (BSWR)	
WARWICK ROAD GOODS	38 / 2B & 84	27/05/1844	17/07/1967	WLR	Initially southern extremity of WLR (Kensington Canal Basin). In c.1865 basin filled in and site developed as Warwick Road goods yard accessed from south ex-WLER
Kensington Canal Basin					
Warwick Road Junction	38 / 3B & 84	01/02/1872	N/A	MDR	Curve towards Kensington (Addison Road) built 1869-1870, but no regular use until 01/02/1872 Remodelled as a 'flying' junction 1914
WATERLOO	39 / 1C	11/07/1848	N/A	LSWR	LSWR terminus, replacing Nine Elms station. Known alternatively as 'Waterloo Bridge' until 1882. Expanded 03/08/1860 (Windsor or 'North' station), link to SER opened 11/01/1864 (only used July 1865 - December 1867). Expanded again 16/12/1878 ('South' station), further platforms added November 1885, 1909, 06/03/1910. Connection to SER removed 26/03/1911. Designations of 'North', 'Central' and 'South' stations removed and platforms renumbered 01/10/1912. Station rebuilt to pre-Eurostar form, official opening 21/03/1922. WCIR platforms opened 08/08/1898, UERL (BSWR) 10/03/1906, UERL (CCEHR) 13/09/1926, LUL (JUB) 24/09/1999 Waterloo & City Line platforms closed 08/08/1992 - 06/09/1992 & 28/05/1995 - 19/07/1993. Transferred to LUL 01/04/1994. Bakerloo Line platforms closed 10/11/1996 - 14/07/1997. Eurostar services terminated here 14/11/1994 - 14/11/2007 (unadvertised trial services commenced 17/08/1994), dedicated platforms 20-24 currently abandoned, but platform 20 expected to re-open for domestic services 2014
Waterloo Curve	82	P 17/08/1994 G 17/08/1994	14/11/2007 N/A	RT	Date quoted is start of trial Eurostar service, advertised service commenced 14/11/1994. Disused since 14/11/2007 (diversion of Eurostar to St Pancras), but chord still in situ and traversed by test trains / railtours. Briefly blocked late 2011
WATERLOO DEPOT	39 / 1C	08/08/1898	N/A	WCIR	Waterloo & City Line depot
WATERLOO EAST	39 / 1C	01/01/1869	N/A	SER	Replaced Blackfriars (SER) station to the east. Opened as 'Waterloo Junction', connection to Waterloo LSWR opened 11/01/1864, but only used July 1865 - December 1867 (i.e. before station opened), and taken out of use 26/03/1911 Suffix 'Junction' dropped 07/07/1935, renamed 'Waterloo East' 02/05/1977
Waterloo					
Waterloo Junction					
WATFORD	2 / 4B	P 02/11/1925 G 02/11/1925	??/??/2016 14/11/1966	MET / LNER	Not intended to be terminus (see Watford Central below). Goods yard closed 14/11/1966. Proposed to close 2016 when 'Croxley Link' built
WATFORD CENTRAL	2 / 4C	N/A	N/A	MET / LNER	Envisaged as terminus of MET / LNER Watford branch, station building remains ('Moon Under Water' pub)
WATFORD HIGH STREET	2 / 4C	01/10/1862	N/A	WRR	Served by London Underground Bakerloo Line Trains 16/04/1917 - 27/09/1982. To be served by Metropolitan Line from 2016
Watford High Street Junction	5 / 5C	10/02/1913	23/03/1996	LNWR	Last train ran ex-Croxley Green 22/03/1996, but junction not severed until 2005. To be re-established 2016

NAME: (Previous names indented below)	Page / grid:		Date opened:	Date closed:	Opening company:	NOTES:
Watford East Junction	1 / 5D		02/11/1925	N/A	MET / LNER	
WATFORD JUNCTION	2 / 3C	P	20/07/1837	N/A	LBIR	Opened as 'Watford', re-sited south and suffix 'Junction' added 05/05/1858 coinciding with opening of the
Watford		G	*20/07/1837*	*??/??/1965*		St Albans (Abbey) branch. Served by London Underground Bakerloo Line Trains 06/04/1917 - 27/09/1982.
						Former goods yard (closed to public goods traffic 1965) now used as Civil Engineers' sidings. To become terminus
						of LUL Metropolitan Line from 2016 (diversion from Watford station via 'Croxley Link')
WATFORD NORTH	2 / 2C	P	01/10/1910	N/A	LNWR	Renamed 01/03/1927. Goods yard situated to north, opened with passenger station. General goods traffic ceased
Callowland		G	*01/10/1910*	*??/??/1988*		01/04/1970, but remained open for heating oil, later M25 construction materials, finally dog food, until 1988 closure
Watford North Curve	1 / 5D	P	02/11/1925	N/A	MET / LNER	Used by early morning and late night passenger services only. Normal daytime passenger service in operation
		G	*02/11/1925*	N/A		02/11/1925 - 31/12/1933 and 06/10/1941 - 03/01/1960, proposed to be reinstated for an Aylesbury to Watford
						Junction service operated by Chiltern if 'Croxley Link' built.
Watford North Junction (1)	1 / 6D		02/11/1925	N/A	MET / LNER	
Watford North Junction (2)	2 / 3B		??/??/1874	N/A	LNWR	
Watford South Curve	1 / 6D	P	02/11/1925	N/A	MET / LNER	
		G	*02/11/1925*	*N/A*		
Watford South Junction (1)	1 / 6D		02/11/1925	N/A	MET / LNER	
Watford South Junction (2)	2 / 3C		01/10/1862	N/A	WRR / LNWR	
WATFORD STADIUM	2 / 5B		04/12/1982	14/05/1993	BR	Opened using funds from Watford FC. Only served on Match days, last recorded train 14/05/1993
						Not proposed to re-open when 'Croxley Link' built (replaced by Vicarage Road immediately to west)
Watford Tunnels	2 / 1B		20/07/1837	N/A	LBIR	Original tunnel used by 'fast' roads, second bore used by 'slow' roads added by LNWR 1874
WATFORD WEST	2 / 5B		15/06/1912	23/03/1996	LNWR	Last train ran on Croxley Green Branch 22/03/1996, initially closed 'temporarily' for bridge work, replaced by bus
						service which ran until 26/09/2003. Not proposed to re-open when 'Croxley Link' built (replaced by Vicarage Road)
Watford West Junction	2 / 5C		15/06/1912	02/01/1967	LNWR	
WELLESLEY ROAD	66 / 2D		10/05/2000	N/A	CTL	
WELLING	42 / 5C	P	01/05/1895	N/A	BHR	Goods yard closed 03/12/1962
		G	*01/05/1895*	*03/12/1962*		
WELLINGTON SIDINGS	13 / 5D		*??/??/1867*	*01/10/1962*	GNR	Goods sidings in use in 1867, Carriage sheds opened 1881. Latter used by Northern Line Trains after 1940,
						BR use ceased 01/10/1962. Now Highgate Wood Depot (Northern Line)
WELSH HARP	12 / 6D		02/05/1870	01/07/1903	MID	For excursion traffic to Brent Reservoir (Welsh Harp)
WEMBLEY CENTRAL	24 / 2A	P	08/08/1842	N/A	LBIR	Opened as 'Sudbury', '& Wembley' suffix added 01/05/1882. Became 'Wembley for Sudbury' 01/11/1910, renamed
Wembley (for Sudbury)		G	*08/08/1842*	*04/01/1965*		'Wembley Central' 05/07/1948. Served by Bakerloo Line Trains 16/04/1917 - 24/09/1982, 04/06/1984 - present.
Sudbury & Wembley						Goods yard closed 04/01/1965.
Sudbury						
Wembley Central Junction	24 / 3A		15/06/1912	N/A	LNWR	
WEMBLEY DEPOT	24 / 2B		*30/06/2005*	N/A	NR	Chiltern Railways light maintenance depot
WEMBLEY PARK	24 / 1B	P	12/05/1894	N/A	MET	Served by Bakerloo Line Trains 20/11/1939 - 01/05/1979, Jubilee Line thereafter.
		G	*12/05/1894*	*05/07/1965*		Goods yard Transferred to LNER 01/12/1937, closed 05/07/1965
WEMBLEY PARK SIDINGS	24 / 1A		*c.1894*	N/A	MET	First sidings present on 1896 OS, so possibly same vintage as station (12/05/1894). Much expanded with 9-road
						carriage shed between 1920 and 1935 OS, demolished 2005 and replaced by 5 open air sidings
WEMBLEY STADIUM (LNER)	24 / 2B	P	28/04/1923	18/05/1968	LNER	Renamed 'Wembley Stadium' 15/09/1927, name varied before this date. Wembley Stadium Loop last used 18/05/1968,
Wembley Exhibition		G	*??/??/1921*	*03/12/1962*		officially closed 01/09/1969, dismantled 19/10/1969. Goods yard (to south) in use 1921 - 03/12/1962
Exhibition Station, Wembley						
WEMBLEY STADIUM (GCR)	24 / 2A		01/03/1906	N/A	GCR	Opened as 'Wembley Hill', renamed 'Wembley Complex' 08/05/1978, renamed 'Wembley Stadium' 11/05/1987
Wembley Complex						
Wembley Hill						
WEMBLEY YARD	24 / 3A & 68 / 5A		*c.1912*	N/A	LNWR	First sidings appeared on site by 1912, subsequently expanded. New freight distribution centre opened 06/09/1993
Wembley Yard South Junction	68 / 3C & 68 / 3C		c.1912	N/A	LNWR	
WEST ACTON	24 / 6B		05/11/1923	N/A	UERL (CEN)	Line through station opened by GWR 16/04/1917 (goods only) with UERL passenger trains commencing 03/08/1920
						Station built by UERL, opening 05/11/1923
WEST BROMPTON	38 / 3B & 84		01/09/1866	N/A	WLER	MDR platforms opened 12/04/1869 as terminus from Gloucester Road, line extended to Putney Bridge 01/03/1880
						Main line platforms closed 21/10/1940 and subsequently demolished, but rebuilt and re-opened 30/05/1999
WEST BYFLEET	61 / 5A	P	01/12/1887	N/A	LSWR	Opened as 'Byfleet & Woodham', renamed 'Byfleet for Woodham & Pyrford' 1913, then 'West Byfleet' 05/06/1950
Byfleet for Woodham & Pyrford		G	*01/12/1887*	*c.1965*		
Byfleet & Woodham						
WEST CROYDON	66 / 1C		05/06/1839	N/A	LCRR	Country terminus of LCRR until 10/05/1847, original terminus was 'up' bay, current through platforms added on
Croydon						Epsom extension on this date. Gained prefix 'West' 1850 (sometimes reversed to 'Croydon West') per Borley,
						Mitchell & Smith refer to opening as 'Croydon', becoming 'Croydon Town' May 1847, then 'West Croydon' April 1851
						Engine shed closed 1935. No record of goods facilities. Bay platform for Wimbledon services closed 02/06/1997
						Tramlink platform opened 10/05/2000
West Croydon Spur	66 / 1D		22/05/1865	??/10/1983	LBSCR	Opened on same day as Epsom Downs Branch. Closed due to Gloucester Road Triangle remodelling October 1983
WEST DRAYTON	34 / 1C		04/06/1838	N/A	GWR	Served by MDR trains 01/03/1883 - 01/10/1885. Re-sited east 09/08/1884. Suffix '& Yiewsley' added 1895,
West Drayton & Yiewsley						
West Drayton						
WEST DRAYTON COAL	21 / 6B		*18/12/1963*	*07/04/1999*	PRIV	Lafarge stone terminal now on site
WEST DULWICH	53 / 1D		??/10/1863	N/A	LCDR	Opened as 'Dulwich', first in Bradshaw October 1863. 'West' prefix added 20/09/1926
Dulwich						
WEST EALING	23 / 6C	P	01/03/1871	N/A	GWR	Opened as 'Castle Hill', suffix 'Ealing Dean' added ??/06/1875. Served by District Railway 01/03/1883 - 01/10/1885
Castle Hill, Ealing Dean		G	*01/03/1871*	*23/05/1980*		Renamed 'West Ealing' 01/07/1899. 'New' goods yard opened 03/02/1908, 'Old' goods yard closed ??/11/1968
Castle Hill						Platform 1 removed ??/11/1973. Milk dock closed c.1978, 'New' goods yard closed 23.05.1980. Platform 4 (up slow)
						originally east of bridge, re-sited to west 1991.
West Ealing Junction	23 / 6C		03/06/1903	N/A	GWR	
West Ealing West Loop	23 / 6C	P	15/06/1903	10/10/1905	GWR	Initially used by temporary goods (03/06/1903) and passenger (15/06/1903) services serving the Park Royal Royal
Hanwell Loop		G	*03/06/1903*	N/A		Agricultural showground, disused 04/07/1903 (passenger) 10/08/1903 (goods) - 01/05/1904. Regular passenger
						services ceased 10/10/1905. Originally 'Hanwell Loop', became 'West Ealing West Loop' in the 1950's.
						Singled at southern end 1974
WEST END SIDINGS	25 / 3B		*??/??/1868*	*??/??/1968*	MID	
WEST FINCHLEY	13 / 3C		01/03/1933	N/A	LNER	First served by and transferred to LPTB Northern Line 14/04/1940, closed to LNER passenger services on same date
WEST GREEN	14 / 5D	P	01/01/1878	N/A	GER	Station and entire Palace Gates Branch closed to passengers 07/01/1963. Goods yard closed 05/10/1964
		G	*01/01/1878*	*05/10/1964*		
WEST HAM	28 / 5A		01/02/1901	N/A	LTSR	First served by District Railway 02/06/1902, line quadrupled 1905, District trains then using 'slow' platforms to north
West Ham Manor Road						Served by Metropolitan Line since 30/03/1936 ('Hammersmith & City Line' since 30/07/1990). Carried suffix 'Manor
West Ham						Road' between 11/02/1924 - ??/01/1969. 'Fast' platforms abandoned 01/01/1916, taken out of use 1940, demolished
						1956. Low Level (BR) Platforms opened 14/05/1979, closed 29/05/1994 - 29/10/1995, then again 10/12/2006 for
						conversion to DLR, re-opening 31/08/2011. 'Fast' (former LTSR) Platforms re-built and re-opened 30/05/1999.
						Jubilee Line Platforms opened 14/05/1999.
WEST HAM SOUTH GOODS	28 / 6C & 62 / 3B		*c.1892*	*07/12/1964*	GER	
WEST HAMPSTEAD (MET)	25 / 3B		30/06/1879	N/A	MET	Country terminus of Metropolitan Railway until 24/11/1879. Last served Metropolitan Line 07/12/1940.
						Served by Bakerloo Line 20/11/1939 - 01/05/1979, Jubilee thereafter
WEST HAMPSTEAD (LNWR)	25 / 3B		01/03/1888	N/A	LNWR	Renamed 05/05/1975. Closed 29/10/1995 - 29/09/1996 (engineering works)
West End Lane						
WEST HAMPSTEAD THAMESLINK	25 / 3B	P	01/03/1871	N/A	MID	Opened as 'West End (for Kilburn & Hampstead)', suffix dropped 01/07/1903
West Hampstead Midland		G	*01/03/1871*	*03/08/1970*		Renamed 'West End & Brondesbury' 01/04/1904*, then 'West Hampstead' 01/09/1905
West Hampstead						Renamed 'West Hampstead Midland' 25/09/1950, 'Thameslink' substituted for 'Midland' 16/05/1988
West End & Brondesbury*						Goods yard closed 03/08/1970. Rebuilt with a new entrance on Iverson Road, opening 14/12/2011
West End						
West End (For Kilburn & Hampstead)						**Discrepancy between Borley and Quick; Quick states 'West Hampstead & Brondesbury' 01/04/1904 - 01/09/1905*
WEST HARROW	11 / 6A		17/11/1913	N/A	MET	
WEST HORNDON	32 / 1D	P	01/05/1886	N/A	LTSR	Country terminus of LTSR from opening until 01/06/1888. Renamed 01/05/1949. Goods yard closed 07/09/1964.
East Horndon		G	*01/05/1886*	*07/09/1964*		
WEST INDIA DOCKS	40 / 1D & 31 / 4A	P	06/07/1840	04/05/1926	LBLR	Goods yard to north east of passenger station on a lower level, Midland Railway coal yard adjacent
		G	*c.1892*	*06/11/1967*	LBLR	
WEST INDIA QUAY	40 / 1D & 31 / 6A		31/08/1987	N/A	DLR	Closed 14/10/1991 (last train 11/10/1991) - 28/06/1993 due to reconstruction. Eastbound trains ex-Bank ceased
						serving after 24/08/2009 (Delta Junction remodelling)
WEST KENSINGTON	38 / 2B & 84		09/09/1874	N/A	MDR	Renamed 01/03/1877. Adjacent goods yard opened by Midland Railway (see entry below)
North End (Fulham)						
WEST KENSINGTON GOODS & COAL	38 / 3B & 84		*25/03/1878*	*14/07/1965*	MID	
West Kensington East Junction	38 / 2B & 84		09/09/1874	N/A	MDR	Junction between 1872 route to WLER and 1874 extension to Hammersmith
West Kensington West Junction	38 / 2A & 84		25/03/1878	14/07/1965	MDR / MID	Junction allowing access to West Kensington Goods
West London Extension Junction	84		02/03/1863	01/01/1923	WLR / WLER	'End on' junction between WLR and WLER, elimination given here nominally as date of Grouping
WEST LONDON JUNCTION	24 / 4D & 86		27/05/1844	01/12/1844	WLR / LBIR	Exchange platforms built for traffic between WLR / LBIR, abandoned when WLR passenger services ceased
West London Junction (1st)	86		27/05/1844	N/A	WLR / LBIR	

NAME: (Previous names indented below)	Page / grid:		Date opened:	Date closed:	Opening company:	NOTES:
West London Junction (2nd)	24 / 5D & 86		??/10/1860	27/10/1990	GWR	Junction between 'West London Loop' (linking WLR and GWR) and GWR main line
West London Junction (3rd)	38 / 4D		06/07/1865	N/A	WLER / LSWR	Junction eliminated 21/01/1936 - 17/08/1994
West London Loop	86	P	??/10/1860	27/10/1990	GWR	Country-facing connection between GWR and WLR
		G	*??/10/1860*	*27/10/1990*		
WEST LONDON WASTE TRANSFER STATION	22 / 2D		*??/??/1980*	N/A	PRIV	
WEST NORWOOD	53 / 2C		01/12/1856	N/A	WELCPR	Opened as 'Lower Norwood', renamed 01/01/1886
Lower Norwood						
West Norwood Junction	53 / 2C		01/11/1870	N/A	LBSCR	Junction at south end of West Norwood Spur
West Norwood Spur	53 / 2C	P	01/11/1870	N/A	LBSCR	
		G	*01/11/1870*	N/A		
WEST PARK HOSPITAL	64 / 5A		*??/??/1918*	*??/??/1950*	PRIV	Horton Estate Light Railway opened to supply building materials, later fuel, to hospitals
WEST RUISLIP	22 / 1A	P	02/04/1906	N/A	GCR / GWR	Opened as 'Ruislip & Ickenham', renamed 'West Ruislip for Ickenham' 30/06/1947. First served by LTE Central Line 21/11/1948 as terminus, suffix 'for Ickenham' gradually dropped thereafter. Goods yard closed 06/10/1975. Down slow line removed and down platform widened to abut former down fast line ??/05/1990
West Ruislip (For Ickenham)		G	*02/04/1906*	*06/10/1975*		
Ruislip & Ickenham						
WEST SIDINGS (SOUTHALL)	35 / 1D		*c.1860*	N/A	GWR	First sidings on site by late 1860's, expanded to current layout in early 20th Century. Southernmost 3 sidings referred to as 'Down Yard'
WEST SILVERTOWN	41 / 1B & 62 / 5A		02/12/2005	N/A	DLR	
WEST SUTTON	65 / 3B		05/01/1930	N/A	SR	
West Thurrock Junction	45 / 4A		01/07/1892	N/A	LTSR	Third road added between here and Grays for Upminster trains early 1960
WEST THURROCK POWER STATION	45 / 4A		*??/??/1962*	*??/??/1993*	PRIV	
WEST THURROCK SIDINGS	45 / 4A		*c.1940*	N/A	LMS	Not present on 1920 OS map, but had appeared by 1947. Officially 'disused' and still connected, but overgrown
WEST WICKHAM	67 / 1D	P	29/05/1882	N/A	SER	Goods yard closed 02/09/1963
		G	*29/05/1882*	*02/09/1963*		
WEST YARD (RIPPLE LANE)	29 / 5C		*c.1940*	N/A	LMS	See entry for 'Ripple Lane Yard'
WESTBOURNE PARK	25 / 5B & 67 / 5A		01/02/1866	N/A	MET / GWR	Opened as 'Westbourne Park & Kensal Green' (HCR only), re-sited west and suffix dropped 30/10/1871 GWR main line services not thought to call until 01/11/1871. BR platforms closed 16/03/1992, remaining platforms had previously transferred to LTE ownership 01/01/1970
Westbourne Park & Kensal Green						
WESTCOMBE PARK	41 / 3B		01/05/1879	N/A	SER	Opened as 'Coombe Farm Lane', renamed later in 1879
Coombe Farm Lane						
WESTFERRY	40 / 1D		31/08/1987	N/A	DLR	
WESTMINSTER	39 / 1B		24/12/1868	N/A	MDR	Terminus until 30/05/1870. Renamed 1907. Jubilee Line platforms opened and station rebuilt 22/12/1999
Westminster Bridge						
WEYBRIDGE	61 / 3D	P	21/05/1838	N/A	LSWR	Carried suffix 'Junction' 1848 - 1858/9
Weybridge Junction		G	*21/05/1838*	*c.1965*		
Weybridge						
Weybridge Junction	61 / 3D		14/02/1848	N/A	LSWR	Junction between LSWR main line and branch to Chertsey (later Virginia Water)
Wharncliffe Viaduct	23 / 6B		04/06/1838	N/A	GWR	GWR main line crossing of the Brent Valley
Wheeler Street (or Bishopsgate) Junction	27 / 5A & 85		10/04/1876	N/A	GER / ELR	Originally junction between ELR and GER (severed 17/04/1966), crossovers remain on GER main line
Whipps Cross Tunnel	16 / 6B		22/08/1856	N/A	ECR	
WHITE CITY (LPTB)	25 / 6A & 83		23/11/1947	N/A	LPTB (CEN)	Replaced Wood Lane (CLR) Station
WHITE CITY (MET / GWR)	38 / 1A & 83		01/05/1908	25/10/1959	MET	Opened as 'Wood Lane (Exhibition)', closed to regular traffic 01/11/1914, opened on special occasions thereafter including 12/12/1914 - 29/04/1915 (weekday evenings and weekends for servicemen). Renamed 'Wood Lane (White City)' 07/10/1920, renamed 'White City' 23/11/1947, closed for good 25/10/1959. LUL opened new station 12/10/2008 on opposite side of Wood Lane (named 'Wood Lane')
Wood Lane (White City)						
Wood Lane (Exhibition)						
WHITE CITY SIDINGS	38 / 1A & 83		*30/07/1900*	N/A	CLR	Opened as Wood Lane Depot, the CLR's sole depot. Rearranged as White City Depot 1949, further replaced by new facility to west 15/01/2007 which was subsequently rafted over and covered by Westfield shopping centre Referred to as 'White City Sidings' at current location
White City Depot						
Wood Lane Depot						
WHITE HART LANE	15 / 3A	P	22/07/1872	N/A	GER	Goods yard closed to public traffic ??/01/1968, saw some private traffic until 02/07/1977
		G	*22/07/1872*	*02/07/1977*		
WHITECHAPEL	27 / 6B & 85		10/04/1876	N/A	ELR	MDR platforms opened 06/10/1884 (terminus until 02/06/1902). 'Whitechapel (Mile End)' until 13/11/1901, suffix then dropped. MDR platforms served by MET 03/12/1906 - 31/03/1913 then again 30/03/1936 - present ('Hammersmith & City Line' since 30/07/1990). ELR platforms first served by MET 31/03/1913, later became 'East London Line', closed 25/03/1995 - 25/03/1998 and 22/12/2007 - 27/04/2010 (engineering works). LUL platforms reduced from 4 to 2 31/01/2011. Platforms for 'Crossrail 1' proposed to open 2018
Whitechapel (Mile End)						
Whitechapel Junction	27 / 6B & 85		01/10/1884	23/12/2007	SER / ELR	Junction at southern end of St Mary's Curve
WHITECROSS STREET GOODS	32 / 3D		*c.1880*	*pre-1965*	MID	Appeared between 1875 and 1896 OS. Present on 1954 OS, but site cleared for 1965 re-alignment of railway
WHITTON	36 / 6A		06/07/1930	N/A	SR	
Whitton Junction	36 / 6A		01/01/1883	N/A	LSWR	Junction at south end of Hounslow Spur
WHYTELEAFE	73 / 2D	P	01/01/1900	N/A	SECR	
		G	*01/01/1900*	*28/09/1964*		
WHYTELEAFE SOUTH	74 / 3A		05/08/1856	N/A	CR	Opened as 'Warlingham', renamed 'Whyteleafe South' 11/06/1956
Warlingham						
WILLESDEN	24 / 4C & 68 / 6C		early 1841	01/09/1866	LBIR	Exact opening date unknown; thought to be 1841 before 10/06/1841. On Acton Lane Adjacent to current Harlesden station, replaced by Willesden Junction to east 01/09/1866
WILLESDEN BRENT SIDINGS	24 / 4B & 68 / 5C		*c.1890*	N/A	LNWR	First sidings appeared on site c.1890
WILLESDEN EURO TERMINAL	24 / 4C & 86		*??/??/1967*	N/A	BR	On site of Willesden North Carriage Sidings. Container traffic ceased c.2006, only engineering traffic remains
WILLESDEN 'F' SIDINGS	24 / 3B & 68 / 2C		*c.1940*	N/A	LMS	Sidings appeared between the late 1930's and mid-1950's
WILLESDEN GREEN	25 / 3A		24/11/1879	N/A	MET	Country terminus of Metropolitan Railway until 02/08/1880. Suffix '& Cricklewood' 01/06/1894 - 1938. Last served Metropolitan Line 07/12/1940. First served by Bakerloo Line 20/11/1939, transferred to Jubilee Line 01/05/1979. Goods yard remote from station (see separate entry below).
Willesden Green & Cricklewood						
Willesden Green						
WILLESDEN GREEN GOODS	24 / 2D		*??/??/1899*	*03/01/1966*	MET	
Willesden High Level Junction	24 / 5C & 86		20/07/1885	N/A	LNWR	
WILLESDEN JUNCTION	24 / 4D & 86	P	01/09/1866	N/A	LNWR / HJR	Replaced 'Willesden' station to west (closed on same date). Initially platforms on LNWR main line (low level) and original 1860 HJR route (high level). Further high level platforms added 02/09/1867 with opening of LNWR Mitre Bridge Curve linking HJR and WLR. Original high level platforms closed 20/07/1885 with opening of Kew Curve, which allowed all high level passenger traffic to pass through 02/09/1867 platforms, although the original high level line remained in use until 01/05/1892. Third high level platform (no.11) added 1894 for reversing trains ex-WLR. New low level platforms (2 through and 2 'bay') added for DC electric trains 15/06/1912, served by Bakerloo Line trains since 10/05/1915. Platform 11 abandoned 20/10/1940. All low level platforms except the 'DC line' platforms closed 03/12/1962. One of the low level bays taken out of use c.1964. Goods yard north of station off HJR route, after closure to general goods traffic, sidings remained open to serve works (MG gas products) until c.2000
		G	*01/09/1866*	?		
Willesden Junction (Acton Branch)	24 / 4C		21/07/1963	N/A	BR	
WILLESDEN SHED	24 / 4C & 86		*??/??/1873*	*27/09/1965*	LNWR	Upon closure loco allocation transferred to Willesden TMD, Willesden Euro terminal built on site 1967
Willesden Suburban Junction	24 / 4D & 86		15/06/1912	N/A	LNWR	
WILLESDEN TRAINCARE CENTRE	24 / 4D & 86		*c.1965*	N/A	BR	Built to replace Willesden Shed, opened on site of former South Carriage Shed
WILLOW WALK GOODS	40 / 2A & 4		*??/??/1847*	*07/03/1932*	LBSCR	Amalgamated with Bricklayers Arms by SR 07/03/1932, but fabric of depot remained in use until 01/08/1977 closure
WIMBLEDON	52 / 3A	P	21/05/1838	N/A	LSWR	Opened as 'Wimbledon & Merton' south of Wimbledon Bridge. Upon its opening on 22/10/1855, the WCRR had a separate terminus, which was incorporated into main station during 1869 rebuilding. Entire station re-sited to north side of bridge 21/11/1881. Current LUL District Line platforms opened 03/06/1889 as a separate station, referred to as 'Wimbledon North' until amalgamated with rest of station 1929. Suffix '& Merton' dropped 01/06/1909 A platform remained in vicinity of original station, south of the bridge, on the north side of the formation, referred to as 'Volunteer Platform' due to military use pre-WWI. Subsequently became a milk dock in 1926. There were 3 other goods facilities: Wimbledon West yard (see separate entry), a small yard on the east side of the station, and a larger yard adjacent to Wimbledon North station. All public goods traffic ceased 05/01/1970. Former island platforms 9 & 10 used by trains between Tooting and Sutton reduced to a single through platform 9 to allow formation of a terminal bay for Tramlink, opening 30/05/2000
Wimbledon & Merton		G	*c.1838*	*05/01/1970*		
WIMBLEDON BOROUGH COUNCIL SIDING	52 / 2B		*??/??/1898*	*??/??/1965*	PRIV	Power station and refuse destructor
WIMBLEDON CHASE	52 / 4A		07/07/1929	N/A	SR	
Wimbledon East 'A' Junctions	52 / 3B		01/10/1868	N/A	LSWR / LBSCR	
Wimbledon North Junction	52 / 3A		03/06/1889	N/A	LSWR	
WIMBLEDON PARK	52 / 2B		03/06/1889	N/A	LSWR	Putney Bridge to Wimbledon built by LSWR, initially operated by MDR only, LSWR services commenced 01/07/1889 Last regular main line passenger service withdrawn 05/05/1941, although services called on occasions until 1969 Station ownership transferred to LUL 01/04/1994 along with entire Putney Bridge to Wimbledon route
WIMBLEDON PARK SIDINGS	52 / 2B		*c.1910*	N/A	LSWR	Part of Wimbledon Traincare Depot (SWT). Not present on 1899 OS but had appeared by 1913. Shed erected over six roads nearest the mainline c. time of electrification (25/10/1915), current carriage cleaning shed
Wimbledon South 'B' Junction	52 / 3A		22/10/1855	02/06/1997	LSWR / WCRR	Junction eliminated when Wimbledon to West Croydon line closed prior to conversion to Tramlink
WIMBLEDON TRAINCARE DEPOT	52 / 2B		*c.1910*	N/A	LSWR	First carriage sidings appeared c.1910 (see 'Wimbledon Park Sidings'). Site expanded to north with Durnsford Road sidings & power station 1915 (see separate entries)
Wimbledon West 'C' Junctions	52 / 4A		07/07/1929	N/A	SR	

NAME: (Previous names indented below)	Page / grid:		Date opened:	Date closed:	Opening company:	NOTES:
WIMBLEDON WEST YARD	52 / 4A		*c.1880*	*c.2000*	*LSWR*	Sidings on site appeared between 1869-77 and 1895 OS. S&T works and coal yard also on site. Some track remains in situ, but disconnected from running line
WINCHMORE HILL	6 / 6C	P	01/04/1871	N/A	GNR	Goods yard closed 01/10/1962
		G	01/04/1871	01/10/1962		
Windmill Bridge Junctions	66 / 1D		01/12/1862	N/A	LBSCR	
WINDSOR & ETON CENTRAL	33 / 4B	P	08/10/1849	N/A	GWR	Opened as 'Windsor', suffix '& Eton' added 01/06/1904, further suffix 'Central' added 26/09/1949.
Windsor & Eton		G	08/10/1849	06/01/1964		Served by MDR trains 01/03/1883 - 01/10/1885. Goods yard closed 06/01/1964. Platforms 3 & 4 decommissioned
Windsor						17/11/1968, followed by platform 2 05/09/1969. Platform 1 subsequently truncated twice (station rebuilding)
WINDSOR & ETON RIVERSIDE	33 / 4C	P	01/12/1849	N/A	LSWR	Original station temporary, permanent station opened 01/05/1851. Opened as 'Windsor', suffix '& Eton' added
Windsor & Eton		G	01/12/1849	05/04/1965		10/12/1903, further suffix 'Riverside' added 26/09/1949. Engine shed probably opened with station and remained in
Windsor						use for a while after electrification (1930). Goods yard closed 05/04/1965.
Windsor Branch Junction	33 / 1C		08/10/1849	N/A	GWR	
Slough East Junction						
WOLDINGHAM	74 / 4B	P	01/07/1885	N/A	LBSCR / SER	Renamed 01/01/1894. Goods yard closed 04/05/1959
Marden Park		G	01/07/1885	04/05/1959		
WOOD GREEN	14 / 4C		19/09/1932	N/A	UERL (GNPBR)	
Wood Green North Junction	14 / 4B		01/04/1871	N/A	GNR	Divergence of GNR Enfield Branch (now Hertford Loop) from main Line
Wood Green Tunnels	14 / 3B		07/08/1850	N/A	GNR	
WOOD LANE (CLR)	38 / 1A & 83		14/05/1908	23/11/1947	CLR	Terminus of CLR until 03/08/1920 (on terminal loop). After 03/08/1920 through platforms to Ealing Broadway open resulting in triangular formation. Replaced by White City (LPTB) to north 23/11/1947
WOOD LANE (LUL)	25 / 6A & 83		12/10/2008	N/A	LUL (HCL)	
Wood Lane Junction	24 / 6D		03/08/1920	19/06/1938	GWR	Junction eliminated when parallel freight lines opened to North Acton 19/06/1938
WOOD LANE MILK DEPOT	83		*?*	*??/??/1966*	*PRIV*	
WOOD STREET	16 / 5A	P	17/11/1873	N/A	GER	Goods yard in use 20/04/1893 - 06/05/1968. Also referred to as 'Walthamstow Wood Street'. Became 'Wood Street'
Wood Street, Walthamstow		G	20/04/1893	06/05/1968		18/03/1971. Loco shed and carriage sidings opened ??/03/1897. Loco shed closed 1960 and Carriage Sidings abandoned 1986
WOODFORD	16 / 3C	P	22/08/1856	N/A	ECR	Platforms originally 'staggered' (up south of down). Majority of passenger services transferred to LPTB 14/12/1947,
		G	22/08/1856	18/04/1966		terminus for Central Line from that date until 21/11/1948. Goods yard closed 18/04/1966.
						First trains in the morning remained British Rail services until 01/06/1970 (last train 31/05/1970)
Woodford Junction	16 / 2C		20/04/1903	N/A	GER	Divergence of Fairlop Loop (= Hainault Loop) from Epping Line
WOODFORD SIDINGS	16 / 3C		*c.1910*	*N/A*	*GER*	Central Line stabling sidings, laid by the GER by 1920 (appear on 1920 Ordnance Survey map, but not on 1898)
WOODGRANGE PARK	28 / 3C	P	09/07/1894	N/A	LTSR	Goods yard opened 01/01/1895, closed 07/12/1964
		G	01/01/1895	07/12/1964		
Woodgrange Park Junction	28 / 3C		09/07/1894	N/A	LTSR / TFGR	
WOODMANSTERNE	72 / 1D		17/07/1932	N/A	SR	
WOODSIDE	67 / 1A	P	??/07/1871	N/A	LBSCR / SER	Exact opening date unknown, first appeared in Bradshaw July 1871. Carried suffix '& South Norwood' 01/10/1908 -
Woodside & South Norwood		G	??/07/1871	30/09/1963		02/10/1944. Goods yard closed 30/09/1963. Closed by RT 02/06/1997 (last train 31/05/1997, no Sunday service),
Woodside						re-opened by Croydon Tramlink 23/05/2000
Woodside Junction	67 / 1A		10/08/1885	16/05/1983	LBSCR / SER	
WOODSIDE PARK	13 / 2C	P	01/04/1872	N/A	GNR	Opened as 'Torrington Park', suffix 'Woodside' added 01/05/1872. Renamed 'Woodside Park' 01/05/1882.
Woodside Park for North Finchley		G	01/04/1872	01/10/1962		Suffix 'for North Finchley' added 01/02/1894, dropped by 1927. First served by and transferred to LPTB Northern Line
Woodside Park						14/04/1940, closed to LNER passenger services on same date. Goods yard closed 01/10/1962
Torrington Park, Woodside						
Torrington Park						
WOODSTOCK ROAD	37 / 1C & 51 / 1D		08/04/1909	01/01/1917	NSWJR	
WOOLWICH	42 / 2A		??/??/2018	N/A	NR (XRAIL)	Proposed station on Crossrail 1 Abbey Wood branch
WOOLWICH ARSENAL	42 / 2A	P	01/11/1849	N/A	SER	Goods yard closed 17/05/1965. DLR platforms opened 10/01/2009 (official opening 12/01/2009)
		G	01/11/1849	17/05/1965	SER	
WOOLWICH DOCKYARD	41 / 2D		30/07/1849	N/A	SER	Initially simply 'Woolwich', suffix 'Dockyard' added when Woolwich Arsenal station opened 01/11/1849
Woolwich						
WORCESTER PARK	64 / 1C	P	04/04/1859	N/A	LSWR	Renamed February 1862. Goods yard closed 06/05/1963
Old Malden & Worcester Park		G	04/04/1859	06/05/1963		
WORCESTER PARK BRICKWORKS	64 / 2C		*??/??/1898*	*c.1950s*	*PRIV*	
WRAYSBURY	33 / 6C	P	22/08/1848	N/A	LSWR	Village name formerly spelt 'Wyrardisbury', but station always appears to have used modern spelling
		G	22/08/1848	??/??/1962		Station re-sited south 01/04/1861. Goods yard closed 1962

Y

NAME	Page / grid		Date opened	Date closed	Opening company	NOTES
YEOVENEY	33 / 6D		01/03/1892	14/05/1962	GWR	Opened as 'Runemede Range', suffix dropped 09/07/1934. Renamed 'Yeoveney' 04/11/1935. Suffix 'Halt' sometimes
Runemede						appended to all three names. Request stop in daylight hours only, closed prior to withdrawal of passenger services
Runemede Range						from branch. Mitchell & Smith ('Branch Lines of West London') give opening date of c.01/04/1887
YORK ROAD	26 / 4B & 75		15/12/1906	17/09/1932	UERL (GNPBR)	
York Road Curve	75		01/10/1863	08/11/1976	GNR	Curve in 'up' direction connecting GNR with MET, originally to 10/01/1863 MET lines but later to 'Widened Lines'.
						Carried goods traffic 20/02/1866 - 24/03/1969. Closed when Moorgate trains diverted via GNCR 08/11/1976
YORK WAY FREIGHTLINER TERMINAL	26 / 3B		*15/11/1965*	*??/05/1968*	*BR*	On site for former Maiden Lane goods yard
York Way North Junction	76		14/11/2007	N/A	LCOR / NR	
York Way South Junction	76		14/11/2007	N/A	LCOR / NR	

References

It would be impossible to list every single reference source here, as they run into many hundreds in several formats. I have selected those upon which I have relied the most heavily and those whose accuracy I have the most confidence in.

Chronology of London Railways
H.V. Borley
Railway & Canal Historical Society 1982
ISBN 978-0-901461-33-9

Passenger Railway Stations in Great Britain – A Chronology
Michael Quick
Railway & Canal Historical Society 2009
ISBN 978-0-901461-57-5

London's Local Railways
Alan A. Jackson
Capital Transport 1999
ISBN 978-1-85414-209-2

The Railways of Great Britain – A Historical Atlas (Second Edition)
Colonel Michael H. Cobb
Ian Allan 2006
ISBN 978-0-7110-3236-1

Railway Track Diagrams – Quail Track Diagrams

2 – Eastern	Third Edition	TRACKmaps 2006	ISBN 978-0-9549866-2-9
3 – Western	Fifth Edition	TRACKmaps 2010	ISBN 978-0-9549866-6-7
4 – Midlands & North West	Second Edition	TRACKmaps 2005	ISBN 978-0-9549866-0-5
5 – Southern & TfL	Third Edition	TRACKmaps 2008	ISBN 978-0-9549866-4-3

Capital Transport Illustrated Histories

The Jubilee Line – Mike Horne 2000   ISBN 978-1-85414-220-7
The Bakerloo Line – Mike Horne 2001   ISBN 978-1-85414-248-1
The Metropolitan Line – Mike Horne 2003   ISBN 978-1-85414-275-7
The First Tube: The Story of the Northern Line – Mike Horne & Bob Bayman 1990   ISBN 978-1-85414-128-6
The Circle Line – Desmond F. Croome 2003   ISBN 978-1-85414-267-2
The Piccadilly Line – Desmond F. Croome 1998   ISBN 978-1-85414-192-7
The Central Line – J Graeme Bruce & Desmond F. Croome 2006   ISBN 978-1-85414-297-9
Going Green: The Story of the District Line – Piers Connor 1994   ISBN 978-1-85414-162-0

Middleton Press Albums (unfortunately too many of these invaluable titles to list individual publication years and ISBN numbers)
Vic Mitchell and Keith Smith
Harrow to Watford, Marylebone to Rickmansworth, Paddington to Princes Risborough, Paddington to Ealing, Ealing to Slough, Willesden Junction to Richmond, Charing Cross to Dartford, Branch Lines of West London, West London Line, Victoria to Bromley South, East London Line, North London Line, South London Line, London Bridge to East Croydon, Waterloo to Windsor, Clapham Junction to Beckenham Junction, Lines around Wimbledon, Kingston and Hounslow Loops, London Bridge to Addiscombe, Mitcham Junction Lines, West Croydon to Epsom, Victoria to East Croydon, Holborn Viaduct to Lewisham (in association with Leslie & Philip Davis), Crystal palace (High level) and Catford Loop (in association with Leslie & Philip Davis)

J.E. Connor
Branch Lines around North Woolwich, Finsbury Park to Alexandra Palace, Branch Line to Ongar, Fenchurch Street to Barking, Branch Lines of East London, Liverpool Street to Ilford, St Pancras to Barking, Liverpool Street to Chingford

Dr Edwin Course	Barking to Southend, Tilbury Loop
Charlie and Jim Connor	King's Cross to Potters Bar
Geoff Goslin and J.E. Connor	St Pancras to St Albans
Dave Brennand	Ilford to Shenfield
Keith Scholey	Euston to Harrow & Wealdstone

The London Railway Record (Multiple editions) – Connor & Butler Ltd

Websites

Clive's Underground Line Guides (CULG)	http://www.davros.org/rail/culg/
Disused Stations – Closed railway stations in the UK	http://www.disused-stations.org.uk/sites.shtml
Kentrail.org.uk	http://www.kentrail.org.uk/index.htm
The Signal Box: Track layout diagrams	http://www.signalbox.org/diagrams.php
locosheds.co.uk	http://www.locosheds.co.uk/index.php
London Reconnections	http://www.londonreconnections.com/
old-maps.co.uk	http://www.old-maps.co.uk/index.html
Google Maps	http://maps.google.co.uk